TRIUMPH

For Andrew, who stopped his share.

*Goaltender for Winnipeg's
Victoria Hockey Club of 1899*

A BREED APART

AN ILLUSTRATED
HISTORY OF GOALTENDING

DOUGLAS HUNTER

TRIUMPH
BOOKS
CHICAGO

TRIUMPH
Distributed in the United States by Triumph Books
644 South Clark Street
Chicago, Illinois 60605
(312) 939-3330

A VIKING BOOK
Published by the Penguin Group
Penguin Books Canada Ltd, 10 Alcorn Avenue, Toronto, Ontario, Canada M4V 3B2
Penguin Books Ltd, 27 Wrights Lane, London W8 5TZ, England
Viking Penguin, a division of Penguin Books USA Inc., 375 Hudson Street, New York,
New York 10014, U.S.A.
Penguin Books Australia Ltd, Ringwood, Victoria, Australia
Penguin Books (NZ) Ltd, 182–190 Wairau Road, Auckland 10, New Zealand

Penguin Books Ltd, Registered Offices: Harmondsworth, Middlesex, England

First published 1995
10 9 8 7 6 5 4 3 2 1

Printed and bound in Italy on acid neutral paper

ACKNOWLEDGEMENTS

This book would not exist had a lightbulb not appeared over the head of Wayne Epp, who thought it was time somebody took a good hard look at those folks behind the mask. Penguin Books Canada executive assistant Jane Cain then brought Wayne's suggestion into the publisher's editorial circle, whereupon it was flung in my direction. My thanks to both Wayne and Jane for a concept I took to with great delight.

This is the fourth book that I have written, but the first that I have also designed and illustrated. Going solo on an illustrated book can feel like starring in some cliched B-movie in which a neophyte ends up flying a 747. Keeping the machine in the air isn't the tricky part; it's *landing.* In this situation you need lots of trained professionals on the ground to talk you in, telling you what a fine job you're doing while judiciously spraying the runway with fire-retardant foam and calling in every emergency response vehicle from miles around. I'm relieved to say that the fact you are reading these words is proof I did not buzz the control-tower upside-down, at least not more than once. Profuse thanks are extended to the publishing professionals at and associated with Penguin who took turns at the mike and brought me and this project back to earth, safe and sound, if a little twitchy. They are publisher Cynthia Good, my editor, Meg Masters, freelance copy editor Jem Bates, art director Martin Gould, production director Dianne Craig and production editor Lori Ledingham. Publicity manager and confirmed hockey connoisseur Scott Sellers also weighed in with his ideas on who should be in this volume, and at times I actually listened. To all of the above, and to the rest of the Penguin staffers (Jackie, Louise, Sharon, Barb) who kept me running nearly on time and at top speed, my gratitude. My thanks also to a friend and publishing professional, Robin Brass, for his voluminous advice and occasional use of his studio.

The meat and potatoes of this book were made possible by the cooperation of two key groups: the archivists at the Hockey Hall of Fame, and the goaltenders who were so generous with their time. Craig Campbell, Jeff Davis and Phil Pritchard at the hall were full of advice and assistance. Craig (who is known to stop pucks just because he likes to) bore the brunt of my demands on their time and patience, and did a terrific job of digging up photographs that have never before been published.

For a bunch of people who are supposed to be a breed apart, the members of the goaltending fraternity were quick to welcome into their midst a total stranger. Gerry McNeil, Johnny Bower, Glenn Hall, Dave Dryden, Frank Brimsek, Emile Francis, Ed Giacomin and Chuck Rayner made it possible for me to appreciate their profession in a way I never could have from films, photographs, yellowing clippings and volumes of anecdotes and statistics alone. They learned from the greats before them, were greats themselves, and in some cases they went on to coach a new generation of greats. Collectively they provided a wonderful perspective on what has changed, and what has not, in the business of stopping pucks, and on what it has meant to be a goaltender. I must also thank several shooters—Dave Keon, Ted Kennedy and Don Rope—for their valued input.

Finally, a word of appreciation to my wife and children, for putting up for so long with a dad who seemed to spend most of his waking hours transfixed before a computer monitor in the basement, and for peeling my fingers off the joystick when everything had stopped moving.

Douglas Hunter

CONTENTS

Above: Hockey team of Gleichen, Alberta, 1920/21

For a guide to the career chart format used in this book, see pages 16–17.

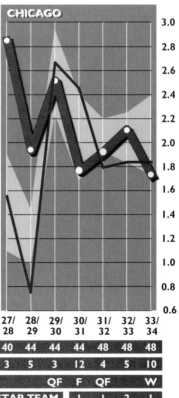

CHICAGO

	27/28	28/29	29/30	30/31	31/32	32/33	33/34
GAMES	40	44	44	44	48	48	48
SHUTOUTS	3	5	3	12	4	5	10
STANLEY CUP			QF	F	QF		W
ALL-STAR TEAM			I		I	2	I

WHAT'S IT *all about,* ALFIE?

WHO HONOURS THE GOALTENDER MOST? OTHER GOALTENDERS, MAINLY. EVER SINCE SOMEONE FIRST STOPPED A PUCK, THEY HAVE TRULY BEEN A BREED APART

N o other athlete quite measures up to hockey's goaltender. People who seek out parallels, even goaltenders themselves, tend to turn to baseball. Sometimes they select the pitcher, because, like the goaltender, his role is so distinct from that of his teammates, and because the game's outcome rides so much on his singular performance. And, like a goaltender, he can be unceremoniously yanked from the game when things aren't going well. Others cite the catcher, because of the similarity of his equipment, and of his duty to stop a hard projectile. But Eddie Giacomin, who played catcher in the off-season while starring in goal for the New York Rangers, stresses that at least the catcher knows what's coming at him, because he gives the pitcher the signal for a particular pitch.

"A baseball catcher's job is the closest thing to it," Gerry Cheevers has observed. "I mean, he alone dons the tools of ignorance and crouches behind the plate like an orangutan. But even the catcher goes up to hit like the rest of the ballplayers. So we goaltenders, alone and unloved, tend to be very proud bastards."

There really is no one else like them. Hockey's goaltenders are a breed apart, and always have been.

No role in team sport has such violence associated with it. Injury, now much less a part of goaltending with advances in equipment, is an essential part of its lore, and is still implicit, even though the goaltenders themselves have tended to downplay the risk. Terry Sawchuk, for one, insisted that defencemen bore the brunt of the game's abuse. Yet the goaltender alone dresses for the worst. He is sheathed in more paraphernalia than a medieval knight, deliberately placing himself in the path of a chunk of vulcanized rubber hurtling at more than 100 miles per hour. Sticks whack him. Skates threaten to slice him open. Opposing players bowl him right over, jab at his underbelly as he smothers a loose puck.

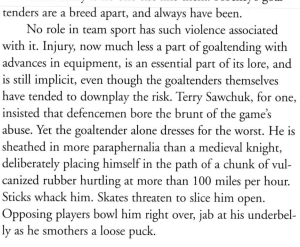

THE NEW YORK RANGERS SCORE ON MONTREAL'S BILL DURNAN, WHO HAS LOST HIS STICK, IN 1949. DURNAN WON SIX VEZINAS IN SEVEN SEASONS, BUT THE PRESSURES OF PERFORMANCE CONSUMED HIM. WHEN THE RANGERS RACED TO A 3–0 SERIES LEAD AGAINST MONTREAL IN THE 1950 SEMIFINAL, DURNAN QUIT, UNABLE TO FACE ANOTHER SHOT.

Few people remember particular saves by a goaltender. Rather, they remember the goals that got by them. Scarcely a spring goes by when someone in the thrall of the latest playoffs doesn't remind former Montreal goaltender Gerry McNeil of the overtime goal by Bill Barilko that won the Maple Leafs the 1950/51 Stanley Cup. And they remember the violence. The most gripping images of the goaltender are of Georges Vezina leaving the ice of the Montreal Forum for the last time in 1925, coughing up blood as tuberculosis advanced to claim him. They include Jacques Plante in 1959 leaving the ice bloodied for the umpteenth time, and returning wearing the first functional face mask. And even after the mask had become part of the game, the stitches painted onto Gerry Cheevers' mask reminded fans of the implicit hazards of the profession.

Other injuries can't be fixed with casts or stitches. Coaches humiliate you by pulling you out of the game in front of a crowd of thousands, thereby blaming you alone for a bad night by the team. You are praised routinely as the most important player on a team, but routinely overlooked when it comes to handing out major trophies or the fattest contracts.

Who honours the goaltender most? Other goaltenders, mainly. The National Hockey League's Hart Memorial Trophy, awarded to the player judged most valuable to his team, has been awarded to a goaltender only four times since its creation in 1923, and not once since 1962. The Hart voting has seen great names like Sawchuk, Bower, Hall, Giacomin, Esposito, Dryden, Cheevers and Parent, to name but a few, skate by, and has passed over every one of them. Of more than fifty numbers retired by NHL teams, only four were worn by goaltenders, and all were retired after expansion came to the league in 1967.

There is still a sense of fraternity among them. The rest of the game understands that there cannot be a game without them, but historically has shown reluctance to make their duties physically and mentally tolerable. Yet there has never been a shortage of young men—and women—determined to join this peculiar fraternity. "It's amazing the number of goaltenders that came up who were that good," says Chuck Rayner of his glory days after the Second World War, when there was no mask, the slapshot was a newly arrived terror, the crease was at its smallest size in history, and the stresses of the game were driving one star netminder after another into early retirement, only to be replaced by fresh cannon fodder of equal or greater talent.

There is a fable-like quality common to many great careers. The young hopefuls arrive as raw, eager rookies, sometimes in their teens, to replace a beloved star, sometimes drinking from the Stanley Cup in their very first tour of duty. And in time, perhaps in only a few seasons, the team's management decides that the once-sparkling rookie has given them all they can wring from him, and

they sell him or trade him. And lo and behold, another raw, eager rookie is ready to take his place on the ice and taste the champagne, just as he once did. The king is dead; long live the king.

The cycle rolls on, each generation experiencing a different game from the one they inherited. It has always changed, and continues to change. The goaltenders themselves sometimes fail to appreciate how much it has changed, to realize, irrespective of the fact that there are still six players on each team, two nets, one puck and a sheet of ice 200 feet long and 85 feet wide, that every era has made its own particular demands on the goaltender. For the first few decades of the sport, until 1917, a goaltender wasn't allowed to drop to the ice. For decades more, he was permitted to catch the puck, but not to hold it, or to smother it. It wasn't until the Second World War that goaltenders began wearing a proper catching glove, a fact that astonishes goaltenders who know stealing a goal in the palm of their hand, to be one of the position's most basic, elegant attractions. And until the mid-1960s, professional goaltenders overwhelmingly carried their teams singlehanded. Nobody would take their place in mid-game, except in the case of the most serious injury, and even then, goaltenders like Roy Worters remained in the net when they should have been on their way to the hospital for surgery.

Their lives were defined so much by their equipment—the lack of it or the quality of it—that it is equipment the retired ones cite overwhelmingly when they explain how and why their position has changed. They pay the compliments they feel the new breed deserve, but they also voice their concerns over what has happened to the craft they helped shape. They wish they could do it all over with the equipment now used. They try not to give weight to numbers of any kind, be it a goals-against average or a won-lost record or a save percentage. Goaltenders knew when they played a good game, whether they won 1–0 in double overtime or lost 9–0, and they still know that. Back in 1899, Quebec goaltender Frank Stocking stated: "It is a mistake for a goal minder to imagine that he is not doing his duty because three or four or more points have been scored against him, because the fault may, and very often does, rest upon the poor assistance he receives from his defence and forwards." Goaltenders are still nodding enthusiastically at those words.

They knew what it took to play the position well, but they had to listen to coaches and managers who thought they knew better. When they tried to tell a coach that someone had scored with a drop shot, they had to listen to that coach telling them there was no such thing. When they tried to tell an equipment manufacturer that the padding was wrong, and couldn't make them understand, they had to put up with what they were given or make the gear themselves. When a league's finer minds decided to change rules that directly affected the

goaltender, there was almost certainly no goaltender in the room. They took what the game fired at them, and did their best to turn it away.

They made for some of the game's best analytic minds. Emile Francis shone behind the bench and in management; Bill Durnan, Turk Broda, Clint Benedict and Gerry Cheevers, to name only a few, tried coaching, and Ken Dryden described on paper the position, and the game itself, the way it had never been described. They were able to do so because they played a role that allowed for contemplation, for seeing the entire game in motion before them and around them. They rested at the very heart of what it means to win and lose.

No other player feels the responsibility of success and failure as they do, and they can be hurt by it in ways more painful than the way a puck can hurt. They are measured by relative failure, which can make it difficult to find comfort in success when the team as a whole does not succeed. If three goals get by him and his team only produces two in response, then he has failed, even if he has not. In a nominally team sport, he stands truly apart, almost solitarily accountable, all too easy to damn when praise, in fact, is called for. And because there is such a separateness to his role, he can allow that separateness to make a team's failure his own. And if he takes the opposite tack, and turns failure back upon the team, then he is an arrogant loner and an eccentric and not a "team" player.

It is difficult to appreciate, when the team is passing around the plate of bitter pills, that the goaltender has the most difficulty choking one down, because once he has swallowed one he might as well swallow all of them. Once a goaltender concedes that the score should not have been 3–2 for the other side, then the rest of the team is off the hook. Rather than thinking that they—all twenty of them—should have come up with one more goal to tie it, they may conclude that they in fact produced all the points necessary. It was their own goaltender, one man, who gave away the goal they could not produce. After all, if it is true that a goaltender is singlehandedly capable of winning a game, then surely he is singlehandedly capable of losing one. A goaltender who believes the former is predisposed to believe the latter. He is hardwired to be both hero and goat.

Any exploration of goaltending's history is plagued by an unanswerable question: who was the greatest? The goaltenders themselves do their best to answer this, and never by suggesting themselves. But too many of the greats are no longer alive to speak for their era, and there are too many distinct eras to the game. You can compare the greats from one era or another, but you cannot measure them qualitatively against one another. You can only understand what made them special at the time they played the game.

In the modern era—that is, from the time the two-line offside was introduced in 1943 (and the slapshot soon thereafter) until the present day—three names consistently surface when excellence is the subject. They are all from the Original Six days, which ended with the NHL's expansion in 1967/68 to twelve teams: Terry Sawchuk, Jacques Plante and Glenn Hall. They are important because they had long careers at the peak of their profession, and they made contributions to the game that are still evident. You could pick Hall above all others if only because, in an evolutionary sense, he falls into a logical chain of excellence. It begins with Tiny Thompson in Boston in the 1930s, moves to Chuck Rayner in New York in the 1940s and early 1950s, is taken up by Hall in the mid-1950s and carried forward into the early 1970s, and is assumed by Tony Esposito and Ken Dryden in the 1970s. Every goaltender today who plays the ubiquitous inverted-V style owes Hall and his "butterfly" style a debt.

But in mulling over the identity of the signature goaltender, this writer cannot help thinking of a virtual unknown, a hapless minor-leaguer named Alfie Moore who was pulled off a bar stool and pressed into service as the starting goaltender for the Chicago Blackhawks in the opening game of the 1937/38 Stanley Cup. The Blackhawks starter Mike Karakas was unable to play because of a broken toe, and Moore was the best the Blackhawks could do in very convoluted circumstances (see Chapter 3). When he took to the ice of Maple Leaf Gardens that night to face down the season's champions from Toronto, he was unloved by all. The Blackhawks didn't want him, and the Leafs and their home crowd wanted him shelled without mercy. But after scoring on Moore on their first shot, the Leafs could not get another by him for the rest of the night, while Chicago put three behind Toronto's Turk Broda.

Moore was the consummate goaltender—truly alone, truly apart and truly triumphant. He lived the dream that all goaltenders dream: to show all comers and all doubters what he was made of, to snatch up the glory from the attacking player, juggle it in his glove and toss it into the corner. A rare few players on the ice, players like Orr and the Rocket and Gretzky and Lemieux, have known what it is like to be someone upon whose performance an entire game can hinge. Every goaltender in every game ever played has known that same feeling. It is the most exhilarating, intoxicating and, sometimes, destructive burden in sport.

Alfie Moore never played another game as important as the opening match of the 1937/38 Stanley Cup, but he skated off the ice of Maple Leaf Gardens with the most important prize of his profession: the respect of the man in the net at the other end of the rink. "We threw everything at him but the house," Turk Broda declared.

When you think of the greats, and what makes for great goaltending, spare a moment's consideration for Alfie. ❍

ACCOLADES

In addition to their "own" trophies, the Vezina and the Jennings, NHL goaltenders are as eligible as any other player for a wide variety of awards. But as the record book shows, goaltenders are more likely to be honoured by some prizes than by others. They are regularly feted in voting for the Conn Smythe and the Calder, yet rarely win the top-player awards, the Hart and the Pearson. And goaltenders have been shut out entirely in voting for the Lady Byng, which recognizes sportsmanship and gentlemanly conduct.

HART MEMORIAL TROPHY

Awarded to the player voted "most valuable to his team" by hockey writers and broadcasters. Since its dedication in 1923, it has been won by only four goaltenders, the last, Jacques Plante, in 1961/62.

CONN SMYTHE TROPHY

Awarded to the most valuable player in the Stanley Cup playoffs in a vote by the league board of governors. The playoffs are when the best goaltenders shine, and in twenty-nine seasons the trophy has been awarded to ten netminders—including three (Roger Crozier, Glenn Hall and Ron Hextall) on the losing team.

CALDER MEMORIAL TROPHY

Awarded to the player voted the most outstanding rookie by hockey writers and broadcasters. The league's top rookie has been named since 1932/33; the actual trophy was introduced in 1937/38. It has consistently recognized the efforts of rookie goaltenders, who have won it (or been runner-up) in seventeen of sixty-three seasons.

BILL MASTERTON TROPHY

Awarded by the Professional Hockey Writers Association to "the NHL player who exemplifies the qualities of perseverance, sportsmanship and dedication to hockey." Glenn "Chico" Resch is the only goaltender to have received it.

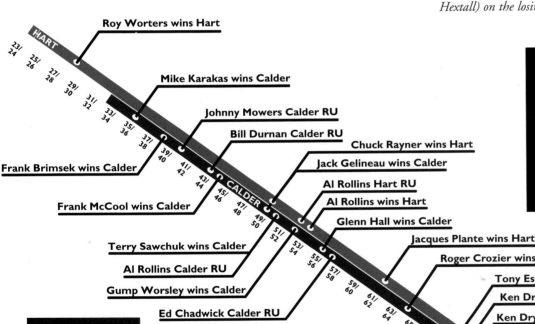

LESTER B. PEARSON TROPHY

Awarded by the NHL Players' Association to the league's outstanding player. Mike Liut has been the lone goaltending recipient.

Roy Worters wins Hart

Mike Karakas wins Calder

Johnny Mowers Calder RU

Bill Durnan Calder RU

Chuck Rayner wins Hart

Jack Gelineau wins Calder

Frank Brimsek wins Calder

Al Rollins Hart RU

Al Rollins wins Hart

Glenn Hall wins Calder

Frank McCool wins Calder

Jacques Plante wins Hart

Roger Crozier wins Calder

Tony Esposito wins Calder

Terry Sawchuk wins Calder

Al Rollins Calder RU

Ken Dryden wins Conn Smythe

Gump Worsley wins Calder

Ken Dryden wins Calder

Rogatien Vachon Hart RU

Ed Chadwick Calder RU

Glenn Resch Calder RU

Roger Crozier wins Conn Smythe

Glenn Hall wins Conn Smythe

Tom Barrasso wins Calder

Bernie Parent wins Conn Smythe

Ed Belfour wins Calder

Dominik Hasek Hart RU

Mike Liut wins Pearson

Martin Brodeur wins Calder

Glenn Resch wins Masterton

Billy Smith wins Conn Smythe

Patrick Roy wins Conn Smythe

Ron Hextall wins Conn Smythe, Calder RU

Bill Ranford wins Conn Smythe

Patrick Roy wins Conn Smythe

THE GREATS

A compilation of Vezina winners and other star goaltenders over the history of the National Hockey League

Player careers are shown with a red bar, with Vezina awards in gold and Jennings awards in green. If the player won both the Vezina and the Jennings in the same season, a green circle with a gold center is employed. Vezina awards are keyed to the vertical white "season" lines. Careers may include partial seasons and seasons in the World Hockey Association. Dashed red lines indicate periods of absence from the NHL or minimal appearances, WHA years excepted. **H** denotes induction in Hockey Hall of Fame.

The Vezina Trophy was first awarded by the NHL in 1926/27. Prior to that season, this chart shows the league-leading goals-against average as posted by a particular goaltender. From 1926/27 to 1963/64, the Vezina was awarded to the goaltender playing the most games on the team with the leading GA. Beginning in 1964/65, the Vezina was shared by all the active goaltenders on the team posting the leading GA. Where a single goaltender was the recipient, this chart shows his personal GA. Where the Vezina was shared, the team GA is used.

Since 1981/82, the Vezina has been awarded to an individual goaltender on the basis of a vote by hockey writers and broadcasters. In 1981/82, a new trophy, the William M. Jennings Award, was introduced to recognize goaltending excellence according to the old Vezina criterion. The "Jennings" average is plotted in green, and winners are indicated in the career bars with a green dot.

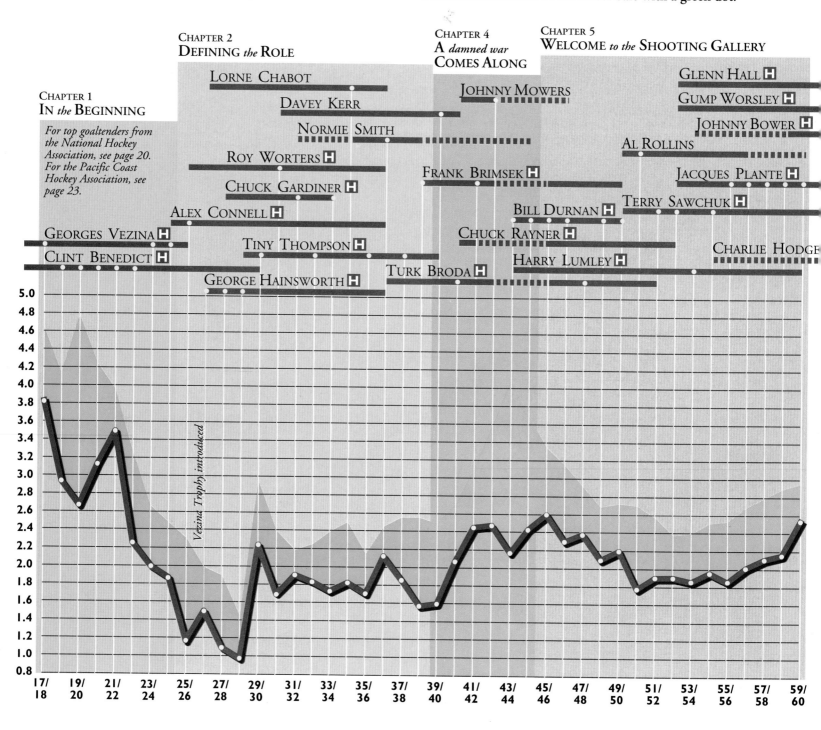

For top goaltenders in
the WHA, see page 139

CHAPTER 10
MODERN *Times*

Eras are colour-
coded according
to chapters in
the book.

Vezina and Jennings
averages are plotted
against the NHL's
overall GA average
(LGA), shown in blue.

CHAPTER 7
The MORE *the* MERRIER

CHAPTER 10
MODERN *Times*

BRIAN HAYWARD

DARREN JENSEN

RICK WAMSLEY

ROLAND MELANSON

AL JENSEN

REGGIE LEMELIN

PAT RIGGIN

CHAPTER 5
WELCOME *to the* SHOOTING GALLERY

TONY ESPOSITO H

BERNIE PARENT H

GARY SMITH

GILLES VILLEMURE

ED GIACOMIN H

ROGATIEN VACHON

BOB FROESE

GRANT FUHR

ANDY MOOG

PETE PEETERS

TOM BARRASSO

GLENN HALL H

GUMP WORSLEY H

JOHNNY BOWER H

AL ROLLINS

JACQUES PLANTE H

TERRY SAWCHUK H

GERRY CHEEVERS H

CHARLIE HODGE

HARRY LUMLEY H

BILLY SMITH H

DENIS HERRON

ROGER CROZIER

KEN DRYDEN H

CHICO RESCH

DENIS DEJORDY

DON EDWARDS

BOB SAUVE

MICHEL LAROCQUE

RICHARD SEVIGNY

JOHN VANBIESBROUCK

PELLE LINDBERGH

DOMINIK HASEK

ED BELFOUR

RON HEXTALL

PATRICK ROY

| 5.0 |
| 4.8 |
| 4.6 |
| 4.4 |
| 4.2 |
| 4.0 |
| 3.8 |
| 3.6 |
| 3.4 |
| 3.2 |
| 3.0 |
| 2.8 |
| 2.6 |
| 2.4 |
| 2.2 |
| 2.0 |
| 1.8 |
| 1.6 |
| 1.4 |
| 1.2 |
| 1.0 |
| 0.8 |

53/54 55/56 57/58 59/60 61/62 63/64 65/66 67/68 69/70 71/72 73/74 75/76 77/78 79/80 81/82 83/84 85/86 87/88 89/90 91/92 93/94

PLAYING *by* *the* NUMBERS

WHAT, IF ANYTHING, CAN A GOALTENDER'S GOALS-AGAINST AVERAGE TELL US ABOUT THE QUALITY OF THE PLAYER?

How do you measure success by addressing failure? This has been the longstanding difficulty in qualifying empirically the performances of goaltenders. For much of hockey's history, the standard measure has been the player's average goals-against per game (GA), following the logic that the fewer pucks that get by a goaltender, the better he is at his job. Until 1981/82, the Vezina Trophy for the league's top goaltender was awarded to the one(s) on the team allowing the fewest total goals over the season, and there have been times when the Vezina's recipient has been decided by only one goal—such as in its inaugural season, 1926/27, when the Canadiens' George Hainsworth edged out the Maroons' Clint Benedict, and in the early 1950s, when Terry Sawchuk of the Red Wings twice fell short by the narrowest margin. But in 1981/82, the National Hockey League decided that raw numbers weren't telling the full story of goaltending excellence, and put the Vezina to a vote among sports writers and broadcasters. The Jennings Award was introduced to recognize goaltending excellence along the old GA criteria.

If the award system had not changed, Grant Fuhr probably never would have won a Vezina. He earned it in 1987/88, despite what on paper might have seemed a mediocre season. His GA was 3.43, not much better than the league's goals-against average (LGA) of 3.7. In fact, no fewer than twelve regular NHL goaltenders posted better GAs than him that season, and eight teams recorded fewer total goals-against than his team, the Edmonton Oilers. As a raw number, Fuhr was on par with Rick Wamsley, who recorded the same GA as Fuhr while playing for St. Louis and Calgary that season.

But the media types who voted for Fuhr were responding to qualities that the simplistic GA could not convey. At a time when the practice of having two goaltenders share a team's netminding workload was well established, Oilers coach and general manager Glen Sather went with Fuhr for a record seventy-five of eighty regular-season games. The Oilers were a free-wheeling offensive machine, recording the second-highest number of goals in the league that season through the efforts of players like Gretzky, Kurri and Messier,

and sometimes Fuhr was left to his own devices in keeping the score in Edmonton's favour. He recorded his lowest GA since his rookie season of 1981/82, and managed to amass his most shutouts to date, four. Once the regular season was over, Fuhr backstopped the Oilers all the way through the playoffs to his, and the Oilers', fourth Stanley Cup. In the process he also made it onto the first All Star team. No other goaltender in the eyes of the media had gotten the job done the way Fuhr had that season.

From 1926/27 to 1963/64, only the goaltender who had played the most games for a team with the lowest GA was awarded the Vezina. That changed in 1964/65, when Sawchuk insisted on sharing it with Bower. Had the pre-1964/65 system been followed in 1987/88, the Vezina would have been won by Patrick Roy instead of Fuhr. Had the system used from 1964/65 to 1980/81 been followed, Roy would have shared the Vezina with Brian Hayward, who played the bulk of the remaining Canadiens games. (Instead they won the Jennings.)

In recent years, GA has been seen as, at best, a thumbnail sketch of a goaltender's skill. More often today statisticians turn to a goaltender's save percentage. Rather than focusing on how many pucks get by a goaltender, the save percentage illuminates how many he manages to stop. GA has long been recognized as, in part, a team statistic. A team that stresses defence, and that allows the opposition few scoring opportunities, is going to have goaltenders whose GAs look very handsome indeed. If a game ends in a 3–3 tie, the goaltender who faced forty shots that night did at least as good a job as his counterpart who faced only twenty. Both had a 3.00 average on the night, but the former's save percentage was .925, while the latter's was .850. But not even goaltenders are happy with this statistical approach. Greats like Glenn Hall will insist that it's not the number of shots you face, but the quality. Twenty accurate ones are a lot tougher to deal with than forty routine ones, as North American goaltenders facing the great Soviet teams of the 1970s will attest. And if he gets too few shots in a game, a goaltender can lose his sharpness and be more vulnerable than one being shelled.

This book employs GA figures in its history of the game and its players because they are historically consistent and are still employed, despite the advent of the save-percentage figure. But it also strives to place the GA in perspective. It isn't appropriate or fair to compare GAs of goaltenders from different eras, as LGA in the NHL has fluctuated wildly over its eight-decade history. (See the chart "The Greats" on pages 14 and 15 for an historical overview of the changes in LGA and league-leading GAs in the National Hockey League. LGA trends for the original National Hockey Association appear on page 20, for the Pacific Coast Hockey Association and associated western leagues on page 23, and for the World Hockey Association on page 139.)

That is why, in the statistical presentations in this book, goaltender performances have been placed in their historical context. Individual GAs are plotted against a goaltending "sweet spot" of better than average performances, its upper range set by LGA, its lower range by the league-leading GA, the historic standard for Vezina awards. In this way the reader can gain a sense of how big an edge a team enjoyed over its opponents through the skills of its goaltender. And to give greater perspective, the average scoring output of the goaltender's team is also shown. Was he playing for a high-scoring team—one that favoured offence over defence, or was so powerful that few scoring chances got through to the goaltender? Or was he playing on a team with low scoring production—one that was either defensive-minded or just not very good? And how were all three of these trends changing over the career of the player?

Consider just two Vezina winners from the past and how different their circumstances were. Chuck Gardiner won a Vezina with the Chicago Blackhawks in 1931/32. Jacques Plante won one with the Montreal Canadiens in 1958/59. Gardiner won his with a GA of 1.92; at the time, LGA was 2.2. This means Gardiner gave the Blackhawks a netminding advantage of less than three-tenths of a goal per game over the league average—one of the lowest in the history of Vezina winners, and an indication of netminding parity at the time. But Chicago didn't do much with the advantage Gardiner gave them. The Blackhawks only averaged 1.79 goals per game in 1931/32, leaving themselves with a scoring deficit. Not surprisingly, the Blackhawks had a losing record that season.

Jacques Plante won the Vezina in 1958/59 with a GA of 2.16, not as good as Gardiner's 1.92 of 1931/32. But did that make Gardiner's effort the superior one? When Plante won the Vezina, LGA was 2.90—he was more than seven-tenths of a goal better (on paper) than whoever was at the other end of the rink on a given night. In producing its fourth successive Stanley Cup–winning season, the team pumped out a commanding 3.69 goals per game, producing a net scoring advantage of +1.53. The Blackhawks of 1931/32, on the other hand, had a scoring deficit of -0.13.

But as Plante's career illustrates, with goaltending statistics, location, as in real estate, is everything. Traded to the lowly Rangers in 1963, his GA leapt nearly a full goal. After playing for two seasons for a team that scored fewer goals than he allowed, Plante quit.

Plante and Gardiner were two skilled goaltenders separated by more than a quarter-century who turned in Vezina performances within very different contexts. In Montreal, Plante didn't have to toil behind a team that didn't do much scoring. Gardiner never had to face something called a slapshot, the rules in his era forbade

NUMBERS TELL THE STORY

A quick study of the career statistics of the Chicago Blackhawks' Chuck Gardiner provides a guided tour of the chart format used throughout this book.

In five of seven NHL seasons, Gardiner posted a GA (red line) within the league's goals-against "sweet spot" (blue background). The upper range of the sweet spot is defined by the league goals-against average (LGA), the lower range by the league-leading GA that season.

From 1926/27 to 1963/64, the Vezina was awarded to the goaltender who played the majority of games on the team with the lowest GA. This means that an individual's Vezina-winning GA could be lower than the team GA that brought him the trophy. In 1950/51, for example, Toronto's GA was 1.97, while the GA of its Vezina-winning goaltender, Al Rollins, was 1.77. Where the Vezina has been awarded to a single goaltender, his personal GA has been used to determine the league-leading GA. Where the GA has been shared by two goaltenders, their team GA has been used.

Gardiner's team, the Blackhawks, was often weak in scoring (goals-per-game production, in maroon). Even so, Gardiner produced Vezina-winning seasons in 1931/32 and 1933/34 (yellow dot). Below the graph, Gardiner's games played, shutout record, his team's playoff record and his All Star team appearances are listed ("1" for first team, "2" for second team). The NHL convened an All Star team for the first time in 1930/31.

Playoff formats have varied greatly in the NHL. Prior to the 1926/27 season,

CHICAGO							
	27/28	28/29	29/30	30/31	31/32	32/33	33/34
GAMES	40	44	44	44	48	48	48
SHUTOUTS	3	5	3	12	4	5	10
STANLEY CUP				QF	F	QF	W
ALL-STAR TEAM					1	2	1

when the Stanley Cup was not the exclusive property of the NHL, playoff records are only shown for Cup finals. Otherwise, playoff records for the team on which a goaltender played that season are coded as follows: Blank—missed playoffs; QF—appeared in quarterfinal; PR—appeared in preliminary round; CC—appeared in conference championship; SF—appeared in semifinal; DSF—appeared in division semifinal; DF—appeared in division final; F—appeared in Stanley Cup final; W—won Stanley Cup.

screening the goaltender, and with no icing rule his defence could quickly nullify an offensive press by dumping the puck in the other end. On the other hand, Gardiner was not allowed to hold the puck to get a faceoff when the heat was turned up. And until Plante, there was no such thing as a true face mask.

And context, ultimately, is what this book is about: not simply statistics, or the greatness conferred by them, but the very different circumstances in which goaltenders have played in hockey history. ○

CHAPTER 1

c. 1875–1924/25

IN *the* BEGINNING

NO PADS, NO SPECIAL GLOVES OR STICKS, NO HOLDING THE PUCK, AND NO FALLING DOWN: GOALTENDING IN HOCKEY'S INFANCY WAS "DIFFICULT" AND "THANKLESS"

THE MONTREAL CANADIENS PRACTISE AT AN OUTDOOR RINK IN VERDUN, QUEBEC, IN A STILL TAKEN FROM A FILM MADE IN JANUARY 1924. THE GOALTENDER AT THE FAR END OF THE RINK IS GEORGES VEZINA; THIS IS THE ONLY KNOWN IMAGE OF VEZINA IN A GAME SITUATION. THE IDENTITY OF THE GOALTENDER IN THE FOREGROUND IS NOT KNOWN. HE IS WEARING CRICKET-STYLE LEG PADS WITH HEAVY FELT BACKING, WHICH ARE ABOUT TO BE MADE OBSOLETE BY EMIL "POP" KENESKY'S LEATHER PADS.

Hockey is not a timeless game. Its origins are obscure and endlessly debated, and its most fundamental rules were revised ceaselessly, even decades into its existence as a popular professional sport. Baseball as played in the 1920s was much the same as it is today, but a hockey fan transported back into a rinkside seat before the Depression would find the game decidedly odd. Even into the Second World War, there was much to hockey that would cause the time-travelling fan to scratch his head. Since the beginning, though, there have been undisputable constants: hockey is a team sport, it is played on ice by people wearing skates, it involves a projectile and sticks, and there are goals at either end of the rink. And there has always been a player standing in front of the goal, defending it at all costs.

Various North American centres, principally Montreal, Kingston and Halifax, lay claim to the game's invention. What is indisputable is that in 1886, the regulations employed in eastern Canada were codified as the fourteen-point "Montreal Rules," set down by delegates from Montreal, Ottawa, Quebec City, Toronto and Kingston at the Montreal Winter Carnival. It was in many aspects a winterized form of lacrosse. Like lacrosse, it was an "onside" game, with no forward passing. It used seven players a side in a similar configuration—the defensive "point" and "cover point" positions were straight out of lacrosse. And so were the goals: two posts six feet apart and six feet high, topped with flags. The goal height would soon be reduced to four feet, where it has remained. The regulations regarding goaltending were strict, and would survive, word for word, right through the First World War: "The goalkeeper must not during play, lie, kneel, or sit upon the ice, but must maintain a standing position." He was allowed no equipment other than a stick, and his stick was no different from that of any other player.

Hockey was also popular in the northeastern U.S.,

A BREED APART

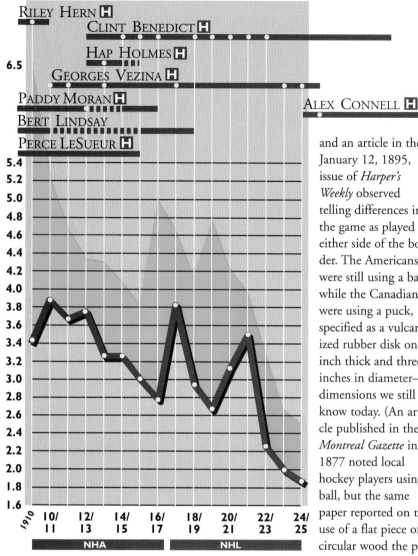

RILEY HERN H

CLINT BENEDICT H

HAP HOLMES H

GEORGES VEZINA H

PADDY MORAN H

BERT LINDSAY

PERCE LESUEUR H

ALEX CONNELL H

6.5

5.4
5.2
5.0
4.8
4.6
4.4
4.2
4.0
3.8
3.6
3.4
3.2
3.0
2.8
2.6
2.4
2.2
2.0
1.8
1.6

1910 | 10/11 | 12/13 | 14/15 | 16/17 | 18/19 | 20/21 | 22/23 | 24/25

NHA   NHL

A GOALTENDER AT MONTREAL'S VICTORIA SKATING RINK, CIRCA 1893, PLAYS WITH THE MINIMAL EQUIPMENT TYPICAL OF THE EARLY GAME. HE GUARDS A GOAL FORMED BY POSTS TOPPED BY FLAGS, AN ARRANGEMENT BORROWED FROM LACROSSE.

and an article in the January 12, 1895, issue of *Harper's Weekly* observed telling differences in the game as played on either side of the border. The Americans were still using a ball, while the Canadians were using a puck, specified as a vulcanized rubber disk one inch thick and three inches in diameter— dimensions we still know today. (An article published in the *Montreal Gazette* in 1877 noted local hockey players using a ball, but the same paper reported on the use of a flat piece of circular wood the previous year.) The *Harper's* writer noted that offside rules in Canada were strictly observed, "which obviates any necessity of the three-foot goal line." This suggests the Americans were using a privileged zone in which defending players could receive forward passes from their goaltender. Such a three-foot zone showed up in the Ontario Hockey Association rules in 1905 and was moved steadily outward to thirty feet. Allowing the goaltender alone to make forward passes, though permitted in the Pacific Coast Hockey Association, didn't come to the National Hockey League until 1921/22.

The *Harper's* article also makes clear that the Americans were the first to use a goal with a crossbar, since it noted that the Canadian goals are "four, not three feet high, and have no bar—an obvious advantage for the goal-keeper." Although nets may have been used by OHA teams earlier than the *Harper's* article, the device is known to have been introduced in Montreal in the winter of 1899 by the *Montreal Herald's* sporting editor, Bill Hewitt, father of broadcaster Foster Hewitt. He got the idea from a friend travelling in Australia, who probably saw them being used in field hockey. The

Canadian Amateur Hockey League, with teams in Ottawa, Montreal and Quebec City, adopted a net in late 1899, when Frank Stocking and Arthur Scott of the Quebec Hockey Club presented a small model for approval by the CAHL at its annual meeting in Montreal on December 9. Stocking was the goaltender for the Quebec team from 1893 to 1901, and the net was needed to cut down on disputed goals. On December 30, Stocking and Scott's simple net was used in an exhibition game. It consisted of two wooden posts six feet apart and four feet high, with no connecting crossbar. There was no "lid" to catch rising shots that might pass between the posts but sail above the net. The net was approved for league use, and in short order the wooden uprights were replaced with uncapped steel ones. These hollow posts, it is said, were used as spittoons by the tobacco-chewing goaltenders of the era, their less accurate lobs staining the ice around them.

Despite the prohibition on special equipment in the 1886 rules, those players seconded to guard the goal were not going to put up with the resultant physical abuse for very long. The practice of wearing special leg pads appears to have arisen early, in Winnipeg, far from the rule sticklers back east. An 1891 photograph of a hockey team believed to be at the Winnipeg Military School shows a sensible goaltender wearing cricket pads. In the east, the earliest known use of cricket pads by goaltenders is 1895, when Fred Chittick of the CAHL Ottawa team wore them. They were popularized in 1896, when George "Whitey" Merritt of the Winnipeg Victorias became the first goaltender to wear them in a Stanley Cup game. On February 14, 1896, he used them to shut out the Montreal Victorias, 2–0. They created a sensation, and were soon being worn by goaltenders everywhere.

Frank Stocking would recall that, in addition to these shin pads, goaltending equipment in these years consisted of a fur cap stuffed down the front of one's

A BREED APART

THE FIRST KNOWN USE OF LEG PADS BY A GOALTENDER IS DOCUMENTED IN THIS 1891 PHOTO, THOUGHT TO HAVE BEEN TAKEN AT THE WINNIPEG MILITARY SCHOOL. THE WHITE CRICKET-STYLE PADS CAN BE SEEN CLEARLY.

pants, a pair of ordinary leather gloves and a stick similar to that of a defenceman. Goaltenders and defencemen used a stick with a wider than normal blade, achieved by attaching a strip of wood to the top of a regular blade with nails or wire. The sticks were otherwise of one piece, and very tough. Two-piece sticks, with a separate blade slotted and glued into the shaft, didn't appear until 1928 when hardwood became scarce.

The playing stick used by "skaters" in the late nineteenth century was fundamentally recognizable: the blade could be no wider than three inches (a maximum the game still employs) and no longer than thirteen inches. Before the First World War, goaltenders began using a "built-up" stick, which carried the three-inch width of the blade a foot or more up the front of the shaft. In 1911, Spalding was selling an "autograph" model endorsed by Riley Hern, goaltender of the Stanley Cup–winning Montreal Wanderers of 1907, 1908 and 1910.

The dimensions for the rinks of the modern North American game—200 feet by 85 feet—were established by the ice surface at Montreal's Victoria Skating Rink, home ice to the Montreal Amateur Athletic Association, which had been playing hockey there since the 1870s. (Tom Patton, the Montreal AAA goaltender, is thought to have brought hockey to Toronto in 1887; the Ontario Hockey

Association was formed in 1890.) But not every neighbourhood had a sheet of ice this size. The Ontario Hockey Association Rules of 1896 gave no suggested rink dimensions, but the Amateur Hockey Association of Canada in 1896 and the Amateur Hockey League of New York were specific: 112 feet by 58 feet. In its infancy, hockey was often played on curling rinks, a sport gaining popularity at the same time as hockey. Using the 112 by 58 prescription, a hockey rink could be created by limiting play to four or five curling sheets. The Amateur Hockey Association of Canada called for the goal line to be placed "at least five feet" from the end of the ice surface; rules of American amateurs called for at least ten feet, and not more than fifteen, a prescription more attuned than the Canadian one to the ten-foot gap the future National Hockey League would adopt.

In the seven-man game played before the First World War (which lasted until the 1922/23 season in the Pacific Coast league), the rulemakers were unanimous on the role of the goaltender. The regulations of the Amateur Hockey League of New York, the Amateur Hockey Association of Canada and the Ontario Hockey Association were virtually identical. As the OHA directed in 1896, "The goalkeeper must not during play, lie, sit, or kneel upon the ice; he may, when in goal, stop the puck with his hands, but shall not throw or hold it. He may wear pads, but must not wear a garment such as would give him undue assistance in keeping goal." These specifications held for another quarter-century—the 1920 amateur rules repeated the wording verbatim, although for some reason the NHL's forerunner, the National Hockey Association, formed in 1909, omitted the word "lie" from its rulebook, as evidenced by the surviving 1916/17 edition.

The regulations created a stand-up game with only minimal protection for the goaltender, who had to guard the same goal area—twenty-four square feet—as his modern counterpart. By 1916, the National Hockey Association allowed goaltenders a maximum stick width of 3.5 inches, thereby permitting the essential "paddle" shaft and large blade we know today. Regulations still limit the goaltender's stick width to 3.5 inches.

The goaltender's gloves underwent glacial changes. Because he was so limited in how he could handle the puck, there was little call for specialization beyond extra protection. The turn-of-the-century rules allowed any player to stop the puck with the skate "or any part of

Continued on page 25

AT 200 FEET BY 85 FEET, THE "IDEAL" SIZE OF PROFESSIONAL HOCKEY RINKS WOULD DWARF THE EARLY AMATEUR GAME'S PRESCRIBED RINK (SHOWN IN LIGHT BLUE), 112 FEET BY 58 FEET. IN THIS LAYOUT FROM 1918/19, THE NHL'S SECOND SEASON OF OPERATION, GOAL LINES ARE SET TEN FEET FROM THE END OF THE RINK, WHICH WOULD REMAIN STANDARD FOR THE GAME UNTIL 1990/91, WHEN ANOTHER FOOT WAS ADDED. IN 1918/19, THE NHL BORROWED BLUELINES FROM THE PCHA, CREATING A CENTRE-ICE NEUTRAL ZONE IN WHICH FORWARD PASSING WAS PERMITTED. IN THEIR ORIGINAL POSITION (DOTTED BLUE LINES), THEY WERE SET TWENTY FEET TO EITHER SIDE OF CENTRE ICE. THE PCHA POSITIONED THEM SIXTY-SEVEN FEET FROM THE END OF THE RINK TO CREATE THREE EQUAL PLAYING ZONES (SOLID BLUE LINES).

IN THE BEGINNING

Go West, Young Men

Some of the game's greatest goaltenders were stars not of the NHL, but of the PCHA

It wasn't until the mid-1920s that the NHL emerged as the dominant brand of the professional game. The league did not become the sole proprietor of the Stanley Cup until 1927; for more than a decade, beginning in 1915, the trophy demanded an end-of-season match between the champion club of two leagues: the NHL (its predecessor, the NHA) in the east, and the Pacific Coast Hockey Association in the west, with the short-lived Western Canada Hockey League also becoming involved in Stanley Cup play in the early 1920s. During those years, some of the very best goaltenders in the game were associated with professional hockey in western Canada, sometimes exclusively.

Three of them, Hap Holmes, Hugh Lehman and George Hainsworth, have been inducted into the Hockey Hall of Fame.

The Pacific Coast league was the brainchild of Frank and Lester Patrick, both born in the east, both of whom played defence. In 1909, the brothers were working for their father's lumber business in British Columbia when they surrendered to a hail of contract offers from the fledgling National Hockey Association and signed on with the Renfrew Creamery Kings. The payroll of the team was so outlandishly high—twenty-six-year-old Lester got $3,000, twenty-four-year-old Frank $2,000, for the twelve-game season, making them better paid on a per-game basis than the best American baseball play-

HUGH LEHMAN WAS A PERENNIAL ALL STAR, PLAYING IN EVERY ONE OF THE PCHA'S FIFTEEN SEASONS.

ers—that the team immediately became known as the Millionaires.

These shocking sums were being spent by Renfrew backer Amby O'Brien in a quixotic pursuit of the Stanley Cup. Like many sports entrepreneurs who would follow him, O'Brien discovered that money wouldn't necessarily buy him success—Renfrew finished third in the NHA for two seasons running, then folded.

By then, the Patrick brothers were back in B.C., joining forces with their father to launch a professional league of their own. Selling the lumber business, they built Canada's first artificial-ice arenas, in Vancouver and Victoria, added a third franchise venue, New Westminster, and in 1911 were up and running as the PCHA.

They had learned an important lesson from their experience with Renfrew: top hockey talent like themselves put fans in the seats, and damn the expense. The Patricks, star players themselves, launched a bidding war with their former employers in the NHA, luring away some major talents. Among them from the Renfrew line-up were Cyclone Taylor and goaltender Bert Lindsay, father of future NHL scoring star Ted Lindsay.

Lindsay and Lester Patrick had worked together as hired guns with the Edmonton Eskimos of 1908, who lost a Stanley Cup match to the Montreal Maroons. Bert Lindsay played four seasons with the Victoria Aristocrats, where Lester Patrick was team manager and captain while playing the defensive "point" position of the old seven-man game.

Lindsay was thirty-one when he finished up with the PCHA in 1915. In his second season he posted the league's lowest GA and was named to its All Star team, but he never did get to play in a Stanley Cup final against the easterners while with the Pacific Coast league. Cup competition wasn't yet open to PCHA teams when Lindsay and the Aristocrats went east to meet the Quebec Bulldogs, who had just won the cup, in 1913. The western team proved its worth by beating the Bulldogs 2–1 in a best-of-three exhibition series. The following season the Aristocrats were back east for a supposedly official cup series against the Toronto Blueshirts, Amby O'Brien's follow-up to the Renfrew team. But Lindsay didn't make the trip, and the Aristocrats lost a bitterly fought series, which, in any case, turned out to be unofficial because the Millionaires hadn't taken care of their paperwork in filing their challenge.

The NHA and the PCHA, however, had come to an agreement with the trustees of Lord Stanley's cup to have its possession decided every year by a series between the champions of the two leagues, with the location of the series alternating between coasts and individual games alternating between the rules of the two leagues. (Among other differences, the PCHA stuck to the old seven-man game.) In 1915, the cup match came west. Frank Patrick's

Vancouver Millionaires were ready for the Ottawa Senators with Cyclone Taylor still in the lineup and a sharp easterner, Hugh Lehman, between the posts.

Lehman was from Bert Lindsay's old stamping ground of Pembroke, Ontario. The record books list his year of birth as 1895, but this would have made him a ten-year-old when he began playing on professional and semi-professional teams in Sault Ste. Marie, Kitchener and Pembroke in 1905. A more likely year of birth is 1885. Lehman headed west for the debut of the PCHA. "Old Eagle Eyes" played twenty-three years of hockey, twenty-one of them professionally, and was on the ice for every single PCHA season. For the first three seasons he played for the New Westminster Royals; in his first season he posted the best GA; in his third, he was named to the All Star team. For 1914/15 he switched to Frank Patrick's Vancouver Millionaires.

Patrick himself played infrequently that year but was on the ice when Lehman and the Millionaires, in the first cup final on the coast, demolished the visiting Senators with scores of 6–2, 8–3 and 12–3. The Senators' young netminder Clint Benedict, a future star of the NHL, was humiliated by the drubbing. The quality of play in the PCHA could not be doubted.

Lehman played in five more Stanley Cups with Vancouver, four in a row from 1921 to 1924, but never won another. He was still one of the dominant goal-tenders, vying for the league's top-goaltender honours with another eastern import, Harry "Hap" Holmes.

Born in Aurora, Ontario, Holmes joined the Toronto Blueshirts in 1912/13, and was with the team when they defeated Lester Patrick's Aristocrats in the 1914 Stanley Cup. When the Patricks decided to set up a new PCHA team in Seattle called the Metropolitans for 1915/16, they raided the Blueshirts payroll, hiring away Holmes, among others.

Holmes and the Metropolitans made it to the cup final the next season, meeting the Montreal Canadiens at home in Seattle. Seattle won the best-of-five decisively in four games, with Holmes outduelling Georges Vezina. The next season, 1917/18, Holmes won another Stanley Cup—this time as the goaltender of the Toronto Arenas in a one-season return to his old league, which had just been reincarnated as the NHL.

Holmes made it into his third straight Stanley Cup final in 1918/19, this time as a Metropolitan again, and again playing at home against Montreal. His netminding opponent was—again—Vezina, and the two men were a ready-made contrast for sportswriters. Holmes, who was never seen to crack a smile, was called "nerveless"; Vezina was "high strung"—a curious description of a man who was known as the Chicoutimi Cucumber for his trade-mark coolness. If he was uncharacteristically rattled in this series, he had good reason: in the first game, playing

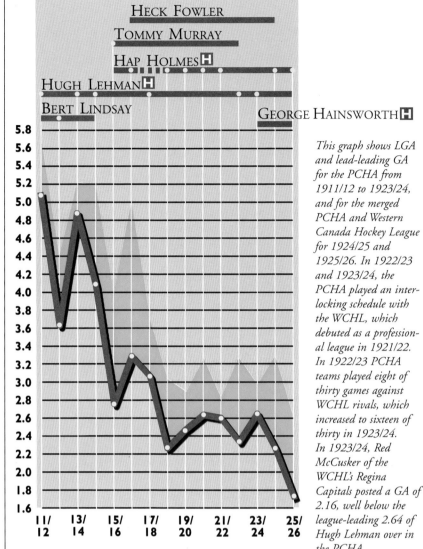

This graph shows LGA and lead-leading GA for the PCHA from 1911/12 to 1923/24, and for the merged PCHA and Western Canada Hockey League for 1924/25 and 1925/26. In 1922/23 and 1923/24, the PCHA played an inter-locking schedule with the WCHL, which debuted as a profession-al league in 1921/22. In 1922/23 PCHA teams played eight of thirty games against WCHL rivals, which increased to sixteen of thirty in 1923/24. In 1923/24, Red McCusker of the WCHL's Regina Capitals posted a GA of 2.16, well below the league-leading 2.64 of Hugh Lehman over in the PCHA.

under PCHA rules, Vezina was shelled 7–0. Seattle was leading the series 2–1 when an epic battle of defensive hockey erupted in game four. Played under six-man eastern rules, the two teams, with Holmes and Vezina the focus of attention, hammered away at each other like two ironclads, unable to make a dent. After eighty minutes of hockey, the two exhausted teams were still scoreless, and the match was declared a

HAP HOLMES OUTDUELLED SUCH NHA/NHL STARS AS CLINT BENEDICT AND GEORGES VEZINA IN STANLEY CUP MATCHES. HE ENDED HIS CAREER WITH THE NHL'S NEW DETROIT FRANCHISE.

draw. Montreal tied the series at two wins apiece, but then North America's influenza epidemic struck the team rosters; Canadiens defenceman Joe Hall went to hospital and died there. The series was cancelled, and for the first and only time in Stanley Cup history, there was a year without a winner.

Holmes played in three more Stanley Cup finals, winning once, as a Victoria Cougar (as the Maroons were renamed in 1921) in 1925 over the Canadiens, a match that produced another showdown between Holmes and Vezina, who was playing his last season before tuberculosis claimed him. By then the PCHA was struggling. A new rival arose in 1921 in the form of the Western Canada Hockey League, with teams in Edmonton, Calgary, Regina and Saskatoon. In 1922/23, the PCHA followed the example of the NHL and WCHL by dropping the rover and playing the six-man game so that it could play an interlocking schedule with the WCHL. In 1924/25, the two western leagues merged under the WCHL name. In its final season, 1925/26, it was known as the Western Hockey League.

Hap Holmes played on regardless of league transmogrifications. In a press description of a heroic Holmes effort against the Saskatoon Sheiks in 1925, he is a thirty-six-year-old warrior in "white pads, battered skates [and a] dinky skull cap" and covered, suggests the writer, with "horseshoes, four-leaf clovers and rabbit's feet."

In the last gasp of the PCHA/WCHL/WHL, Holmes and the Victoria Cougars lost the Stanley Cup in four games to the Montreal Maroons. Every win for Montreal was a shutout by Clint Benedict, with whom Holmes had tangled in the cup final of 1920, a series that had also gone Benedict's way as he played net for Ottawa. Benedict was the only goaltender to post a better lifetime GA than Holmes's (at 2.90) during Holmes's PCHA reign. Holmes had the best GA in the western league in seven of ten seasons. Yet he was regularly consigned to honourable mention at awards time, being named a second-team All Star seven times and a first-team All Star only once. Lehman earned ten first-team All Star placings. And as professional hockey in western Canada entered its final years, it provided the debut for a latecomer to the professional goaltending ranks:

George Hainsworth (see page 42).

When the WHL folded after the 1925/26 season, player contracts were sold to the NHL, which used them mainly to fill the rosters of its expansion clubs in New York, Detroit and Chicago. Hugh Lehman's contract was bought by Chicago, and he played forty-four games for them in their opening season. They finished third in the five-team American division, but also allowed more goals than any other team in the league. Lehman played four more games the following season, and was 1–2–1 when he replaced Barney Stanley (who had played with the Stanley Cup–winning Vancouver Millionaires of 1915) as coach at mid-season. In his first game behind the bench, Chicago lost 10–0 to Montreal. The Blackhawks won only seven games the entire season, and Lehman never coached another NHL game.

Hap Holmes played two seasons for Detroit. Despite being on an expansion team, Holmes posted reasonable GAs of 2.33 and 1.80, and in his second season recorded an impressive eleven shutouts in forty-four games. Holmes was thirty-nine at the end of the 1927/28 season, when his ambitions turned to ownership. He set up a franchise for the new International League in Cleveland, called the Falcons, but as the Depression set in Holmes could not hang on and Al Sutphin took over the ownership. When the American League was formed in 1936 from the remnants of the International League, Sutphin was in charge and the team became the Barons, but Holmes was at least still on the payroll. He died in 1940 while on vacation in Florida; the Barons ran a tribute to Holmes in its program for years. In 1947, Sutphin put up a trophy in Holmes's name to honour the American League's top goaltender, which is still being given out today.

Norman "Heck" Fowler, who was born in Saskatoon, spent eight seasons in the western professional game and made two All Star teams, but he was quick to light, attracting two fighting suspensions in 1921/22. He also liked to watch things light, and legend has it that his reputation as a fire nut cost him his job. In 1923/24, Fowler and the rest of Lester Patrick's Victoria Cougars were coming out of their Regina hotel to play a game when a fire truck went by. Fowler jumped on the back to see the blaze and the game had to be delayed until he was retrieved. An exasperated Patrick sold his contract to the Bruins, with whom he played seven games in 1924/25 before appearing in another eight back in the western league for Edmonton.

As for Bert Lindsay, he returned east after the 1914/15 season and played for the Montreal Wanderers and the Toronto Arenas of the newly formed NHL in 1917/18 and 1918/19. At the end of the Second World War, Lindsay tried to sell the NHL on a goal net with flexible safety posts. The league declined. ❍

Continued from page 21

the body," but the OHA rules restricted stopping the puck with the hand to the goaltender alone. (This was known as "knocking on.") As with their first specialized sticks, goaltenders tended to use whatever the defencemen used. Gloves with extra padding in the thumb and back of the hand were available by 1915. The trapper-style catching glove and stick-side blocker were a long, long way in the future, and so, of course, was the mask.

I n a game without slapshots and without players dressed like gladiators, the goaltender's role in hindsight might seem genteel, played as the game so often was by the refined, casual-looking Ivy Leaguers and gentlemen athletes who populated team photographs at the turn of the century. But accounts of the day leave no doubt that, even in the game's infancy, the goaltender's role was demanding. "[A] clever goal-tend intercepts many a try-for-goal, though at the cost of as many bruises where his body has met the flying puck," assured the 1898 *Ice Hockey and Ice Polo Guide*.[1] "He very rarely leaves his station between the goal-posts, and then only after signalling the point to fall back into his position, the goal-tend having left same in order to return a long 'lift' [a rink-long clearing shot in the days

---

[1]Ice polo, as played by the New England Skating Association at the turn of the century, employed a sheet of ice 150 feet long, with five players aside, sticks four feet long, and essentially followed the rules of polo, without the horses. The game was also popular in the Canadian Maritimes, but hockey overtook the sport in both locales.

before the icing rule] which has dropped back of and near the posts, the opposing forwards, of course, being at some distance down the rink.

"Through the agility of a clever goal-tend the score of a match is often kept down to a small number of goals, as he kills many tries which would score but for his good work. The rules forbid him to lie, sit or kneel upon the ice, and compel him to maintain a standing position. When a scrimmage occurs near his goal, his is the most difficult, and usually the most thankless, work of any man on the team. Though he may frequently gain a momentary possession of the puck, he seldom has room or time to pass it far down the rink or even directly to one of his own side. His play then is to shoot it off to one side of the rink, either to the right or left of the goal, thus preventing another try-for-goal until the puck is worked back again into a favorable position..."

Then, as today, goaltending was physically and mentally trying, and no team could hope for any success without a good "goal-tend" between its posts. The style of play of the early game—not falling down, not wandering from the net—would persist for decades as the model of the proper way to play the position, even after the rules that ordered him to stay on his feet were elimi-

S. MATSUMIYA, GOALTENDER FOR VANCOUVER'S ASAHI ATHLETIC CLUB TEAM OF 1919/20, WEARS STANDARD CRICKET-STYLE LEG PADS AND NOVEL THREE-DIGIT GLOVES.

nated. Ironically, in this most emphatic stay-at-home era of the profession, in 1905 and 1906 goals were actually scored by a goaltender named Brophy in CAHL games, one of them against Paddy Moran of the Quebec Bulldogs. And the fact that Riley Hern had played forward as well as goal suggests that these prototypic goaltenders were not as fixed in their assignments as the record might suggest. On balance, though, it was not a position given to roaming. It was not uncommon for goaltenders to play in a pair of boots rather than skates. Georges Vezina, who joined the Canadiens in 1910 at age twenty-three, didn't even learn to skate until he was eighteen.

There has never been an easy time to be a goaltender. The absence of a slapshot would have been of little comfort to the goaltenders who faced, with the most minimal protection, wicked, rising wrist shots and, worst of all, backhands fired (usually with little accuracy) from close in that were powerful and often inadvertently at head level. And a goaltender

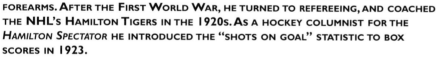

A MEMBER OF THE 1909 AND 1911 STANLEY CUP TEAMS, PERCE LESUEUR (SHOWN HERE ON AN IMPERIAL TOBACCO TRADING CARD OF 1910/11) WAS A NOTEWORTHY INVENTOR AS WELL AS A GREAT GOALTENDER.

IN 1912, HE DEVISED THE FIRST GOAL NET THAT COULD TRAP RISING SHOTS (SHOWN BELOW LEFT, AS PICTURED IN THE 1929 CAHA RULEBOOK). BEFORE THEN, NETS WERE OPEN AT THE TOP, AS IN THE CASE OF THE MODEL ADVERTISED BY SPALDING IN 1908 (BELOW RIGHT). HE ALSO CREATED A SPECIAL GAUNTLET GLOVE FOR GOALTENDERS, WHICH PROVIDED MORE PROTECTION TO THE FOREARMS. AFTER THE FIRST WORLD WAR, HE TURNED TO REFEREEING, AND COACHED THE NHL'S HAMILTON TIGERS IN THE 1920S. AS A HOCKEY COLUMNIST FOR THE HAMILTON SPECTATOR HE INTRODUCED THE "SHOTS ON GOAL" STATISTIC TO BOX SCORES IN 1923.

HIS STICK (BOTTOM), AN EARLY "BUILT-UP" MODEL, WAS USED FROM 1905 TO 1910. HE INSCRIBED IT WITH ALL HIS MAJOR WINS, AS WELL AS THE LATIN PHRASE FOR "THE HAND THAT TURNS AWAY THE BLOW."

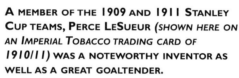

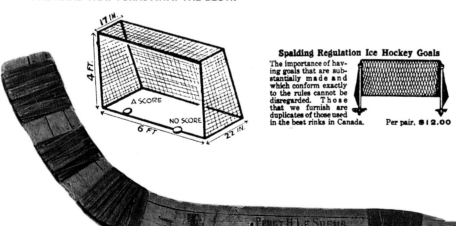

Spalding Regulation Ice Hockey Goals

The importance of having goals that are substantially made and which conform exactly to the rules cannot be disregarded. Those that we furnish are duplicates of those used in the best rinks in Canada.

Per pair, $12.00

could not get himself or his team out of trouble by grabbing or falling on the puck and securing a faceoff. As the 1909 American Amateur Hockey League Rules prescribed, "The player in the goal position may catch the puck, but if he does he must at once drop the puck to the ice at his own feet." The requirement that the goaltender immediately drop any puck he caught would be part of the game well into the 1930s. And a goaltender in the NHA who dropped to the ice was penalized with a fine.

The National Hockey Association, with teams in Quebec, Montreal and Ottawa, came up with an historic innovation for its 1911/12 season: a six-skater lineup. William Northey, secretary of the Montreal Arena Co., was credited with suggesting it, undoubtedly inspired by the money that would be saved on players, as the NHA was engaged in a salary war with the Pacific Coast Hockey Association (see "Go West, Young Men," page 22). The NHA dropped the rover from the forward ranks, and the defensive unit remained at three. In the seven-man game, the defence corps lined up lacrosse-style from the goal forward—the goaltender first, then the point (slightly off centre), then the cover-point. In the new, six-man game, and with the arrival of the blueline, which the easterners also adopted (from the PCHA in 1918/19), the defending players assumed the present configuration, with a goaltender and two defencemen, arranged left and right.

The NHA added another game innovation in its 1912/13 season: the modern goal net. Perce LeSueur, or Peerless Percy, a goaltender with the Ottawa Senators, was assigned by his league to design a standard net that would reduce controversies over whether or not the puck actually passed between the posts. LeSueur's was the first to use the crossbar and a webbed top to trap rising shots. LeSueur's rectangular net, maintaining the standard six foot by four foot opening, was seventeen inches deep at the top and twenty-two inches at the bottom. The net was used by the NHA and its successor, the NHL, until 1927, and it would remain a standard net in the CAHA rulebook right to the Second World War. In 1913/14, the NHA painted a goal line on the ice between the posts for the first time. The rink-wide goal line would not appear until the dawn of the Second World War, as the game had no icing rule.

The NHA was transformed into the NHL when team owners in Montreal, Ottawa and Quebec could no longer get along with their Toronto franchisee, Eddie Livingstone. (Toronto had joined the league as the Blueshirts in 1912/13.) They left

Livingstone alone in the NHA, which promptly ceased to exist, and started afresh as the NHL in 1917/18 with their existing teams and a new Toronto squad, the Arenas. It was a hectic debut, with the Quebec Bulldogs deciding to sit out the season and the Montreal Wanderers withdrawing from competition after six games when Montreal Arena, home ice to both the Canadiens and the Wanderers, burned down. Only three teams—the Canadiens, the Ottawa Senators and the Toronto Arenas—completed a twenty-two-game schedule.

The league had decided to carry on under the NHA regulations, with one significant change: goaltenders were now allowed to fall to the ice to stop a shot. The amateur game did not take readily to this revolution. The 1920 amateur rules still insisted on the ban on lying, kneeling or sitting.

It was clear to the organizers of the professional game that the goaltenders were in need of a playing edge. Although the 1898 *Ice Hockey and Ice Polo Guide* had praised the ability of the "goal-tend" to keep scoring low, the game as played by the pros was a high-scoring one. In the NHA, LGA had declined steadily, from 6.46 in 1910 to 3.83 in 1915/16. But in 1916/17, it shot up more than a goal, to 4.99. Out west in the PCHA, there was a similar jump, and LGA was almost identical to the NHA's. Even with permission to flop to the ice, goaltenders in the infant NHL had GAs that were higher than at any other point in league history. LGA in 1917/18 was 4.65; the best GA in the league was 3.82, posted by Georges Vezina of the Canadiens.

For more than a decade, the league struggled to bring more balance to the offensive and defensive games, shifting it steadily away from the traditional onside game to one in which forward passing became increasingly tolerated, but with quick strikes reined in through the use of distinct playing zones. For its second season, 1918/19, the NHL introduced bluelines. Positioned twenty feet on either side of centre ice, these created a neutral zone in which forward passing (and kicking the puck) was allowed, as in the larger neutral zone of the PCHA, which consumed one-third of the ice surface. Forward passing was still banned in the defensive zones, but for the 1921/22 season goaltenders alone were allowed to pass the puck forward to their own blueline, a derivation of the OHA and PCHA rules.

The changes in passing rules, and the new ability of the goaltender to launch counterattacks with forward breakout passes, had immediate impact on goals-against figures. LGA tumbled to 3.25 in 1922/23, and kept on falling. In 1923/24, it was down to 2.66, and Clint Benedict of the Ottawa Senators registered the lowest GA to date, 2.25.

About this time, the goaltenders received a significant new weapon that helped push down their individual GAs and overall LGA: substantial leg pads. Emil "Pop" Kenesky of Hamilton, Ontario, is generally credited with their invention. Tradition has it he was watching a local Catholic league match and noticed how pucks were glancing off the curved surface of the goaltender's cricket-style pads and into the net. Kenesky modified an existing pad, increasing the padding and in the process widening it to twelve inches. The new pads caught on in the local league and in 1924 attracted the interest of Percy Thompson, coach of the Hamilton Tigers, who asked Kenesky to repair the pads of Jake Forbes. An eight-game losing streak ended the first time Forbes wore them, and Kenesky was off and running in a new career as he fielded orders from top goaltenders everywhere.

Kenesky may not have been the first man to make the big leather pads. Alex Connell of the Ottawa Senators was the first goaltender to have a set of Kenesky pads made from scratch, but Tiny Thompson, who became a star goaltender with the Bruins, was playing Senior hockey in Minnesota when he had his first pair made in 1924. Thompson never said where he got his (which he wore for his entire career), but it's doubtful he went all the way to Hamilton for them, and photos of Connell's and Thompson's pads reveal distinctive constructions. Still, if Kenesky didn't invent them outright, he perfected them, and remained the pad-maker of choice for goaltending's elite right through the 1970s.

From the goaltender's perspective, the league's rule-makers had a Midas touch—whatever changes they made to the game, their jobs became easier, if the downward spiral of LGA is any indication. Overwhelmingly, the next two decades would be devoted to finding a balance between offence and defence in the league's rules. In the process, the goaltender's duties would undergo their own evolution, rapidly closing in on a role the game today would recognize. ○

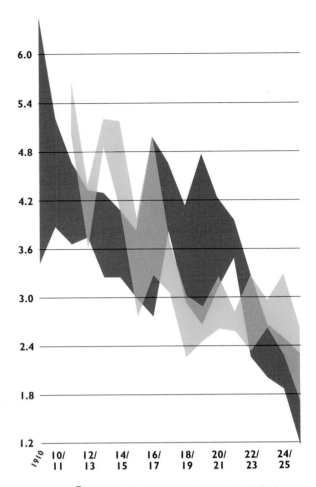

PLOTTED AGAINST EACH OTHER ARE THE GOALTENDING "SWEET SPOTS" OF THE NHA/NHL (IN RED) AND OF THE PCHA (IN BLUE). FOR ITS LAST TWO SEASONS, THE PCHA MERGED WITH THE WESTERN CANADA HOCKEY LEAGUE. THE UPPER RANGE OF EACH SWEET SPOT IS THE LEAGUE GOALS-AGAINST AVERAGE (LGA); THE LOWER RANGE IS THE BEST INDIVIDUAL GA IN THE LEAGUE THAT SEASON. IN ITS FIRST YEARS, THE PCHA PLAYED A MUCH HIGHER SCORING GAME, BUT FROM 1918/19 TO 1921/22, THE PCHA'S RANGE DROPPED SIGNIFICANTLY BELOW THAT OF THE NHL. THE RANGE IN THE WESTERN LEAGUE REMAINED RELATIVELY STABLE FOR THE REST OF ITS HISTORY, WHILE NHL GA PLUNGED WITH THE REFORMS IN OFFSIDE AND PASSING RULES. BUT THERE WAS LITTLE TO CHOOSE BETWEEN THE BEST GOALTENDERS OF THE TWO LEAGUES.

ice. He finished the game and only then went to hospital; he couldn't eat solid food for two weeks. A hand fracture kept him out of the line-up for two games. He played in a cast, with his stick and glove taped to his arm. His only extended spell out of the game came when Ching Johnson fell on him and hurt his knee, causing him to miss six weeks of play.

Worters had taken his game south in 1924 with Lionel Conacher to play for the Pittsburgh Yellow Jackets, a nominally amateur outfit. When the Yellow Jackets joined the NHL in 1925 (and became the Pirates), Worters hit the big leagues, but he was still fre-quenting the shady margin of organized sport, in which he had been tainted in Timmins. The Pirates were run by a former world lightweight boxing champion named Benny Leonard. "Being a fighter," Conn Smythe said in his memoirs, "he thought all sports were crooked." Leonard would talk to Smythe about "my turn" to win. He once cut off a ten-minute overtime in a home game against Smythe's Leafs at thirty seconds, to preserve a tie. "Well, timekeepers sometimes could be influenced in those days," Smythe explained.

Worters played for them for three years, and the Pirates had reasonable seasons—Worters left them just as they started to become truly awful. In his first season,

Worters was part of a record-setting goaltending nightmare. In a game between his Pirates and the New York Americans, 141 shots were fired, 73 of them on Worters. Amazingly, the final score was only 3–1 for the Americans.

In 1928/29, Worters followed Conacher to the charismatic Americans, a tough-luck outfit owned by the notorious bootlegger Bill Dwyer. When the Pirates hit hard times and moved to Philadelphia in 1930, play-ing as the Quakers for one season before folding, Dwyer stepped in at mid-season and essentially took over the team. By then Dwyer had acquired Worters by offering Leonard an estimated $20,000 plus the Americans' reserve goaltender.

At his very first Americans practice, Worters was cut behind the left ear by a Babe Dye shot. Later that season, playing the Leafs in Toronto, left-winger Danny Cox caught him square in the mouth. The puck knocked out two teeth, broke off two more, and cut him for two stitches on the outside and three on the inside of his upper lip.

Worters' attitude to injuries was nothing if not philosophical. "People have the wrong idea about injuries you get in hockey," he once said. "A fellow gets hit in the mouth or on the forehead or over the eye, and it bleeds a lot, and everybody says: 'Ooh! Looka the blood! And he's staying there, too. What a game guy he is!' Why shouldn't he stay in there? It doesn't hurt to bleed, and the chances are the injury looks much worse than it is. A cut around the head—unless it's right in the eye, so that the sight is blurred—shouldn't bother anybody. The injuries that stop you are on the arms or legs, so that you can't move around. Then if you don't get out you're crazy, because you're only handicapping your team."

In Pittsburgh the word "wizardry" was applied to his work; they called him "the Phantom" in New York because of the magic of his performances. The Americans had a good season in 1928/29, finishing second to Montreal in the inappropriately named Canadian division, but were eliminated by the Rangers in the playoffs. Still, Worters' performance was so impressive that season that he became the first goaltender to earn the Hart Trophy, awarded to the player judged most valuable to his team. In securing a shutout against the Bruins, for example, Worters had turned away seventy-two shots.

He spent part of the following season with the Canadiens, then returned to the Americans for the rest of his career. In 1930/31, Worters won the Vezina with a GA of 1.68, nearly six-tenths of a goal below the GA Tiny Thompson posted in winning the Vezina the previous season. With that achievement on his résumé, Worters went to Dwyer and demanded a three-year contract for $8,500 a year, and he wanted it in U.S. funds. The salary was an extraordinary sum, and the U.S. funds made it even more extraordinary, as the Canadian dollar, badly devalued in the Depression, was converting at rates upwards of forty-eight per cent. Dwyer gave Worters what he asked; it was said that Dwyer was always amused by the performances his pint-sized goaltender turned in.

With that contract, Worters committed himself to a career backstopping a sad-sack franchise, as the Americans slipped into the league cellar during the Depression years. In most seasons, Worters' GA was worse than the LGA, but he was viewed as the classic Great Goaltender on a Bad Team. He was named to the second All Star team, behind Chicago's Chuck Gardiner, in 1931/32 and 1933/34. His childhood friend Charlie Conacher called him the best goaltender he ever shot a puck at. His teammate and roommate Red Dutton would recall Worters "using the backs of his hands to divert pucks to the corners, so you very seldom scored on a rebound on Roy. His hands took terrible punishment and I marvel at the little guy and the way he had splints put on his fingers before a game."

The Americans returned to the playoffs after a six-season absence in 1935/36, to be eliminated by Toronto in the semifinal. It was something of a swan song for both Worters and Dwyer: Worters would never have another playoff game, and the Depression had left Dwyer so impoverished that the league had to take over the team. Dutton stopped playing to become coach and general manager, and from 1943 to 1945 served as the league's interim president.

In 1936/37, with two games left in the season, Dutton made an appalling discovery: that Worters "had a hernia and that it was a bad one, and that he had played five previous games with this hernia and had told no one about it. He pleaded with me to allow him to play as there were only two games to go. He wanted to finish his season as he said it was going to be his last."

He did play the games, and the season was his last. Worters retired with happy consequences. He went into the hotel business, buying a spot with a tavern in Toronto's Italian neighbourhood. A good second baseman with some of the leading amateur teams around Toronto when he was a kid (he had even played football, despite his size), Worters became a devotee of the professional Maple Leafs ball club, and liked to talk baseball strategy with whoever was the team manager. He sold his hotel in 1949 and prepared himself for early retirement, but went back into the business in the 1950s when he teamed up with Charlie Conacher to build the Skyline Hotel near Malton Airport, and then the Conroy (an amalgam of their names) on Dufferin Street. Conacher would quip that he hadn't seen his business partner in two years—Worters was too busy playing the stock market. Worters had just retired for the third time in 1957 when throat cancer claimed him. He was elected to the Hockey Hall of Fame in 1969. ○

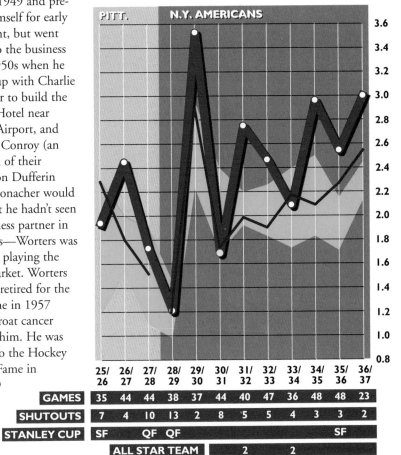

	25/ 26	26/ 27	27/ 28	28/ 29	29/ 30	30/ 31	31/ 32	32/ 33	33/ 34	34/ 35	35/ 36	36/ 37
GAMES	35	44	44	38	37	44	40	47	36	48	48	23
SHUTOUTS	7	4	10	13	2	8	5	5	4	3	3	2
STANLEY CUP	SF		QF	QF								SF
ALL STAR TEAM							2		2			

Worters spent part of the 1929/30 season with the Montreal Canadiens.

TINY THOMPSON BATTLED HIS NERVES AND THE

TINY,
PERFECT

LEAGUE TO WIN AN UNPRECEDENTED FOUR VEZINAS

Boston Garden

OFFICIAL PROGRAM 35¢

Sport News
BOSTON BRUINS HOCKEY

"TINY" THOMPSON
1927-28 - 1935-36
ALL TIME BRUINS
ALL STARS SERIES

C ECIL "TINY" THOMPSON WAS NOT TINY. ROY "SHRIMP" WORTERS, WHO WAS THE GREATEST GOALTENDER IN THE GAME, AS FAR AS

THOMPSON WAS FETED IN THIS OFFICIAL BOSTON GARDEN PROGRAM, SHORTLY BEFORE THE BRUINS SOLD HIM TO DETROIT. THE ILLUSTRATION IS BASED ON THE PHOTOGRAPH ON THE PRECEDING PAGE, TAKEN AFTER THE BRUINS WON THE 1928/29 STANLEY CUP WITH THE ROOKIE NETMINDER.

Thompson was concerned—now there was a goaltender who lived up to his billing. But Thompson, who stood five-foot-ten, managed to do what neither Worters nor any other goaltender before them had done: he won four Vezinas. It wasn't until Bill Durnan came along that his performance was surpassed.

Thompson was like Durnan—like a lot of goaltenders—in that the game was a battle of nerves for him. He would begin the season around 170 pounds, and when it was over (forty-four games later at the beginning of his career, forty-eight at the end) he had shed ten of them. Some of them went to sweat, but it was said that some of them went to anxiety. At the end of the day, goaltending to Thompson could be classified as a business of relative failure: the less you failed, the better you were. And when you failed, somebody wrote it down as a statistic. Watching the 1970 Stanley Cup, he noted, "The pressure in cases like these has to be on the goalie—if he misses, the error is in the book, a goal against. When the shooter blows one, it is forgotten."

The 1970 final was of particular interest to him. Chicago was playing Boston, and as Chicago's chief scout, Thompson had a professional involvement. But the series also pitted brother against brother—Tony Esposito in goal for Chicago, Phil Esposito at centre for Boston. There was a lot of back and forth in career lines in that series. Phil had played for Chicago for four seasons before being dealt to Boston; Tiny Thompson had spent most of his career in Boston, before becoming a Chicago scout at the beginning of the Second World War. Then there was Tiny's older brother, Paul, who'd spent eight of his thirteen NHL seasons in Chicago. That was where the 1970 series became personal for Thompson, because he, too, had played against his brother when the cup was at stake. In his very first season in the league, Tiny had faced down Paul in the final, when Paul was playing left wing for the Rangers. Tiny had come out ahead in that encounter. In 1970, it would be the sniping brother's turn.

Paul Thompson was never a sniper the way Phil Esposito would be, but for six straight seasons as a Blackhawk in the 1930s he led the team in scoring. And in 1935/36, the brothers made it onto the All Star team

together—Tiny on the first team, Paul on the second. The only other brothers to have been picked together were Lionel and Charlie Conacher, in 1933/34. But it would happen again with those Espositos—in 1969/70, 1971/72, 1972/73 and 1973/74.

The Thompsons came out of Alberta, and though Paul's NHL career started sooner, in 1926/27, Tiny was the older brother, by eighteen months. They were precocious kids. Tiny was playing Junior hockey with the Calgary Monarchs in 1919/20, when he was only fourteen, and over three seasons played for three different Alberta Junior clubs, the last of them in Bellevue, a southern mining town. In 1922, at seventeen, he began a two-season stint with the Bellevue Bulldogs, a Senior club.

In 1924, Tiny was playing Senior hockey for the Duluth Hornets of the Minnesota Central League. Amateur hockey was only nominally amateur: he was almost certainly getting paid to play. Thus, when he was traded to another Senior club, the Minneapolis Millers, in 1925, it was probably a moot point that he became a professional in 1926, playing for the above-board professional Millers' team in the American Hockey Association.

In 1924, Tiny got his first set of leather leg pads. In later years he never said who made them. He got them just as Pop Kenesky of Hamilton, Ontario, was starting to make them for the elite ranks, and while it's possible he ordered a set from Kenesky, it's more probable he had them made right in Duluth. He would remember them as enormous, fourteen inches wide, and it was said that to close the gap between his legs Thompson would have to overlap the pads. As the maximum pad width was cut to twelve, and then ten inches, Thompson took the pads to a harnessmaker to have them recut. Remarkably, these were the only pads he wore in his entire career.

In 1928, the Boston Bruins came calling. It was a young franchise beginning its fifth season; after a horrible debut in which the team won only six games, the Bruins had steadily improved. They'd finished first in the league's American division in 1927/28, but had been eliminated in the semifinal. The Bruins bought the contracts of two Minneapolis players: Thompson, and Ralph "Cooney" Weiland, a small, agile centre who turned twenty-four that autumn. Tiny Thompson was twenty-three. When they got to camp, Weiland was teamed up with Dit Clapper and Dutch Gainor, and the Bruins had the Dynamite line. Hal Winkler, an old pro from the western league, was the Bruins starting goaltender. He'd played for Edmonton and Calgary from 1922 to 1926, and when the western league folded he landed with the Rangers, who then dealt him to Boston. He was about to start his third NHL season, and he was thirty-six years old. The Bruins' new coach, Cy Denneny, decided to start Thompson in the opener against the Pittsburgh Pirates, and after that never bothered to switch back to Winkler, who didn't play another NHL game.

It was an oddball year in the league. The ongoing efforts to increase offence backfired spectacularly with the zone passing reforms, which still didn't allow players to pass the puck across any blueline. LGA sank to its historic low of 1.45, and in Montreal George Hainsworth posted his record GA of 0.98. In New York, Roy Worters of the Americans picked up thirteen shutouts in thirty-eight games, posted a GA of 1.21 and won the Hart Trophy, becoming the first goaltender to be named the league's most valuable player. Thompson certainly did all right. He recorded twelve shutouts and a GA of 1.18, and played superbly when it mattered most. In the best-of-three playoff semifinal and final, Thompson logged three shutouts in five games. In the semifinal, he outduelled Hainsworth, and in the final, John Roach played well, but not well enough, for the Rangers as Boston won the cup in two straight games. Thompson's playoff GA was 0.60.

I t was a brilliant start to what would be a brilliant career, but for Boston there would not be another Stanley Cup for more than a decade, even though a superb Bruins team emerged from the blue-line offside reform of 1929/30 that ushered in a new era of offence. That season, the Bruins won thirty-eight of forty-four games, Cooney Weiland won the scoring title and Thompson won the Vezina, but the team could not win the Stanley Cup as Hainsworth's Canadiens swept them two straight. Thompson would later say that he had great respect for the veteran Hainsworth (he turned thirty-five after that cup series), even though he didn't see him in his prime. If Thompson didn't think the 1930 Stanley Cup was Hainsworth at his best, then he must have thought that Hainsworth had once been a superhuman goaltender.

"He worries a lot," one contemporary writer said of Thompson. He worried so much in 1931/32 that he was unable to play four games. The Bruins started a fellow Albertan, Percy Jackson, in his stead, and Jackson performed respectably in his first NHL games, recording a 2.07 average. Tiny became "frantic" at the idea he was washed up. His wife was so distraught that she left Boston, staying home in Calgary during all succeeding seasons. But Thompson did come back, and the following season, 1932/33, won his second Vezina.

In April 1933, Thompson played what he would describe as both his hardest and his best game. It was game five in the semifinal series with the Maple Leafs, which the Leafs led two games to one. Lorne Chabot was in goal for Toronto, and through all of regulation time he and Thompson kept the game scoreless. The game went into overtime, and appeared destined to stay there. At about one o'clock in the morning, there was even talk of deciding the game with a coin toss. They kept on playing, and a Maple Leaf substitute player named Ken Doraty took to the ice. Doraty was never more than a fringe player, but he showed a flair for playoff hockey, registering seven goals and two assists in the fifteen post-season games in which he appeared. Doraty came into the game with fresh legs, skated around Boston's exhausted defensive great Eddie Shore, and after 104 minutes and 46 seconds of overtime, put the puck past Thompson. An estimated 200 shots had been stopped by both goaltenders in what became known as the Doraty Derby. Three seasons later, Chabot, now with the Maroons, staged another shutout marathon, this time with Normie Smith of Detroit, in the opening game of the Stanley Cup. When Mud Bruneteau finally scored on Chabot, 176 minutes and 30 seconds of overtime had been played. It remains the longest game on record, the Thompson–Chabot duel the second longest.

The only truly poor season Thompson and the Bruins had was 1933/34, when Thompson, for the one time in his Boston career, allowed more goals than the team scored; it was also the second and last time that his GA was above LGA while in Boston, the first time having been in his nerve-wracked 1931/32 season. When the Senators had returned to competition after a one-year Depression hiatus in 1932/33, they hired Cy Denneny, who had coached the Bruins to their 1928/29 Stanley Cup. Denneny bought the Bruins' captain, Cooney Weiland, and his linemate, Dutch Gainor. At first Boston shrugged off the loss, winning their division that season. But the team went into the cellar in 1933/34, winning only eighteen of forty-eight games.

The next season the Bruins were right back on top of their division.

It was the season that the NHL introduced the penalty shot, an innovation of the defunct western league. Alex Connell of the Montreal Maroons was the first goaltender to be beaten by one, and when Thompson's career was over he would be proud of the fact that no one had beaten him on a penalty shot, ever.

Despite the ups and downs of the Bruins, Thompson was consistently on top of the goaltending game. After making the second All Star team in 1930/31 (the first season in which the league had an All Star team), he returned to the second team in 1934/35 and made the first team in 1935/36 and 1937/38. Thompson won his third Vezina in 1935/36, and became the first goaltender to register an assist when he fed a pass to defenceman Babe Siebert and Siebert scored. Thompson's fourth Vezina came in 1937/38, the season the Bruins unveiled the "Kraut" line of Milt Schmidt, Woody Dumart and Bobby Bauer. Boston was a great team through these latter years, finishing first or second in their division, but the Bruins could not convert their sterling regular seasons into a Stanley Cup.

Like Davey Kerr of the Rangers, Thompson subscribed to the theory that using your eyes too much was bad for them, so he didn't do much reading. "The only thing a goaltender has," he would explain, "is his eyes." At the beginning of the 1938/39 season, Thompson, citing an eye ailment, sat out two games. In his stead Boston played a twenty-three-year-old prospect from its American league affiliate, the Providence Reds. The previous season, Frank Brimsek had recorded a GA of 1.79 in Providence, an AHL record that still stands. When Thompson was ready to play again Brimsek was sent back to Providence, but Bruins GM Art Ross saw the future with 20/20 clarity. Tiny was the reigning Vezina-winner and first-team All Star, but he was also thirty-three. On November 28, Ross cut a deal with Detroit's Jack Adams, selling Thompson for $15,000, a good Depression-era price for a top goaltender. After playing nine games of the new season with Providence, Brimsek became a Bruin.

Thompson had long been a fan favourite in Boston, but Brimsek quickly made the customers forgive Ross, and forget Thompson, by recording six shutouts in his first eight games. That spring, the Bruins with Brimsek finally won the Stanley Cup that had been eluding them all through the 1930s. Detroit finished fifth of seven teams, scoring twenty-one fewer goals than Thompson allowed, and were eliminated in the semifinal.

In 1938/39, Paul Thompson played his last NHL game and took over as coach of the Blackhawks. Tiny played one more season before hanging up his own skates and joining his brother in Chicago, where he became the team's chief scout. In 1944, Tiny appeared in a game for the RCAF Mustangs. When the game was over, he threw away the pads he'd had for twenty years.

Tiny Thompson was elected to the Hockey Hall of Fame in 1959. He died in Calgary in 1981. ○

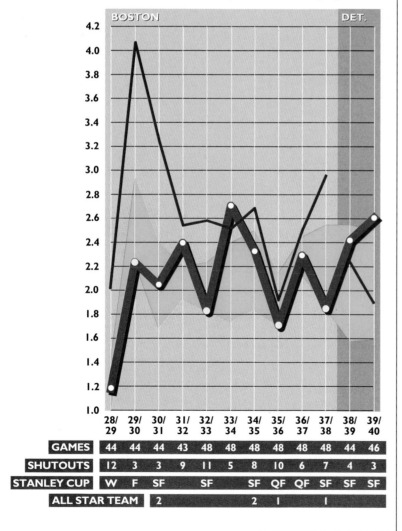

	28/29	29/30	30/31	31/32	32/33	33/34	34/35	35/36	36/37	37/38	38/39	39/40
GAMES	44	44	44	43	48	48	48	48	48	48	44	46
SHUTOUTS	12	3	3	9	11	5	8	10	6	7	4	3
STANLEY CUP	W	F	SF		SF		SF	QF	QF	SF	SF	SF
ALL STAR TEAM		2					2	1		1		

TOOLS *of the* TRADE

Equipment from the interwar years

Above: skates worn by Roy Worters, who starred with the Pittsburgh Pirates and the New York Americans, 1925/26 to 1936/37.

Above right: gloves worn by Lorne Chabot, who played from 1926/27 to 1936/37 with the New York Rangers, Toronto, the Montreal Canadiens, the Montreal Maroons, Chicago and the New York Americans. The gauntlets, made of fibreboard about one-eighth of an inch thick, originally may have been covered with leather. It's also possible these gloves were worn inside a pair of defenceman's gloves. The gloves are thickly padded and of soft leather.

Right: leather leg pad worn by John Ross Roach, who played for Toronto, the New York Rangers and Detroit from 1921/22 to 1934/35.

Below: stick used by Georges Vezina at the end of his career with the Montreal Canadiens (1910 to 1925/26). The original tape is missing, revealing the stick's construction: a regular stick with wood strips added to increase its width on the blade and shaft to 3.5 inches.

CHAPTER 3

"*Hey,* ABBOTT!"

WHEN GOALTENDERS WENT DOWN, THE STRANGEST REPLACEMENTS WOULD STEP IN. THESE WERE MOMENTS OF UNPREDICTABLE HEROISM

An oddity of professional goaltending for decades was that, while it may have been the most specialized, the most dangerous and perhaps the most demanding position on the ice, if not in all team sports, it also was, at times, played by men who were less than prepared for the task at hand. In addition to the sometimes doubtful talents pressed into service during wartime, there were the hapless individuals who came to play for a game or less simply because nobody else was available. No one ever hears of an untried amateur being directed to the mound to pitch in the opening game of a World Series, or pushed onto the playing field to quarterback a Super Bowl team. Yet it seemed that hockey was a rodeo at which at any moment some poor soul could be hauled out of the stands and thrust onto the back of a furious bull.

The reason was parsimony. Owners of professional teams did their utmost to keep costs down, and one of the easiest ways was by maintaining a minimum player lineup. In the professional game's earliest days, teams sometimes used more than one goaltender, as the Ottawa Senators did just before the First World War in employing both Clint Benedict and Perce LeSueur. But cutting costs soon put an end to that. During the 1920s, NHL teams routinely hit the road with only ten men; in 1928/29, league rules called upon teams to dress at least eight but no more than twelve players, exclusive of goaltenders. And when it came to goaltenders, the professionals thought one was just fine. The 1929 Canadian Amateur Hockey Association rulebook, in contrast, stated that each team was allowed ten players for a match, two of whom must be goaltenders.

It wasn't until the 1965/66 NHL season that league rules made it mandatory for teams to have two fully suited, ready-to-play goaltenders at every game. In 1950/51, the league called upon the home team to have an emergency goaltender in attendance, in full equipment, at every game, to be used by either team in the event of illness or injury. This was often a young amateur from the home team's farm system, installed (not quite dressed to play) in the press box. The Detroit Red Wings would offer up assistant trainer Lefty Wilson, who would turn in dogged, creditable performances against his own team,

THE MOST FAMOUS GOALTENDING SUBSTITUTION IN HOCKEY HISTORY WAS MADE BY LESTER PATRICK, WHO AT AGE FORTY-FIVE CAME OUT FROM BEHIND THE NEW YORK RANGERS BENCH IN THE 1927/28 STANLEY CUP TO REPLACE AN INJURED LORNE CHABOT—AND WIN THE GAME.

much to their disgust. But before 1950/51, injured goaltenders had to be replaced by whatever warm body was available, and only with the approval of the opposing team.

There were many occasions on which an injured goaltender wasn't replaced at all; he played on, knowing there was no one adequate to fill his skates. In the third game of the 1929/30 Stanley Cup final, Detroit goaltender Wilf Cude was accidentally struck in the face by the stick of Blackhawks right-winger Rosie Couture when he dropped to block a shot near the end of the second period. The blow knocked him unconscious, but he returned from the dressing room ten minutes after being carted off the ice. His face was bloody and his right eye was nearly closed up, but he finished the game and preserved the Red Wings' 5–2 lead.

The policy of substitutions produced some of the game's most absurd, and most dramatic, moments. The first person listed in the alphabetical directory of NHL goaltenders is George Abbott, who played one game for Boston in 1943/44. Boston was in Toronto for a road game and, in the revolving-door goaltending mess in which the Bruins found themselves after Frank Brimsek entered the Coast Guard, they had no starter when Brimsek understudy Bert Gardiner came down with the flu. The Maple Leafs helpfully came up with Abbott, who happened to be an ordained minister and who suited up in the Bruins dressing room in an advanced state of terror. Bruins captain Dit Clapper, moving to ease the nerves of the reverend (who was busy putting his skates on the wrong feet), declared, "Don't worry, Abbott. We'll get the bastards. Those sons of bitches won't beat us." The Bruins lost, 7–3. Hence, Abbott's lifetime NHL GA of 7.00.

The playoffs saw some remarkable substitutions. In 1938, Chicago's Mike Karakas broke a toe in the final game of the semifinal and was lost for the first few games of the final against the Maple Leafs. Chicago coach Bill Stewart and general manager Bill Tobin wanted to replace him with the Rangers' sensational Davey Kerr, but the Leafs were having none of that. On game day the Leafs' assistant GM, Frank Selke, told the Blackhawks that Alfie Moore would be a suitable choice. A Toronto resident, Moore had played eighteen games for the New York Americans in 1936/37, and in the past season had been in goal for the Pittsburgh Hornets, the Leafs' American League farm club.

According to Blackhawks tradition, Chicago left-winger John Gottselig was dispatched to fetch Moore. He headed for Moore's house, where he found Moore's wife, but not Moore. She told him to check a local bar. Moore wasn't there, either, but at that bar Gottselig was directed to yet another bar, where Moore was ensconced, quaffing beer. Whether or not Moore was soused is a matter of debate. When he saw Gottselig walk in, he reputedly asked him if he had a spare ticket for the big game. Gottselig, of course, had the perfect viewing spot for Moore: the Blackhawks net.

Foster Hewitt would recall that a "messenger" was sent out to find Moore, while Stewart and Tobin continued to argue back at the Gardens with Leaf GM Conn Smythe and Selke for the right to use Kerr. It's been said that the Blackhawks were put in this goaltending bind because there was no time to bring in their practice goaltender, Paul Goodman, who was under contract with Chicago but playing in Wichita, Kansas. But it seems that the Blackhawks were trying to pull a fast one, and had intended all along to use Kerr in the final. After all, Karakas's injury had come in the preceding series, not the night before, and in the last Stanley Cup, when starter Normie Smith was injured in the first game, the Red Wings showed up for the second game with a minor-league backup, Earl Robertson, as his replacement. (As with so

THE INJURY OF CHICAGO GOALTENDER MIKE KARAKAS (BELOW) SHORTLY BEFORE THE 1938 STANLEY CUP TOOK MINOR-LEAGUER ALFIE MOORE (RIGHT) OFF A TORONTO BARSTOOL AND DEPOSITED HIM IN THE BLACKHAWKS NET FOR THE OPENING GAME AT MAPLE LEAF GARDENS.

many untested goaltenders, Robertson proved equal to his assignment: the Red Wings won, 4–2, and went on to win the cup.)

The Blackhawks were very much the underdogs, having finished the regular season in third place in the four-team American division, with only fourteen wins in forty-eight games, while the Leafs had finished atop the Canadian division with ten more wins. Chicago had produced the least number of goals, 97, while Toronto had produced the most, 151, and Chicago had allowed 139 goals compared to Toronto's 127. Without Karakas, the Blackhawks would need brilliant goaltending to keep the Toronto offence down to a dull roar and allow their own lukewarm firepower to make a game of it. Kerr seemed to be more of a ringer than an emergency fill-in.

With less than an hour to go before the opening faceoff, the management of the two teams were still bickering over who would appear in the Chicago net. Right by the press box, Stewart accused Selke of stiffing him with a half-drunk substitute and of lying about Moore's quality. Conn Smythe boiled over. A veteran of the First World War, Smythe had personally dispatched a German soldier with his service revolver, and was not a man to inflame. By way of defending the honour of his old friend Selke, Smythe lunged at Stewart. It took several men to pull them apart.

According to Hewitt, the Blackhawks were openly cool to Moore when he, and not Kerr, entered their dressing room to suit up. Contentedly seated on a bar stool hours earlier, he had been transformed into an unwelcome palooka in the most important match in hockey. As far as the Blackhawks were concerned, clever Conn Smythe had managed to roll a hand grenade right into their lineup. Thus, when Moore took to the ice, he stood alone against everyone in Maple Leaf Gardens— against his own teammates, against the hometown fans, against the opposing Leafs and against the Leaf brass, who had made him a minor leaguer in favour of Turk Broda.

The first Leaf shot beat Moore, but then he buckled down, or sobered up, and shut down the Leafs. The Blackhawks rose to the occasion of his unexpected performance and put three unanswered goals behind Broda. A delighted Tobin asked Moore how much the win was worth. Moore asked for $150. Tobin gave him $300.

For the next game, Smythe declared Moore ineligible to play, and league president Frank Calder ordered Chicago to use Goodman. He had never played an NHL game, and the Leafs swamped the Blackhawks, 5–1. Chicago brought back Karakas and fitted his skate with a steel guard to protect his broken toe. Chicago won the cup by sweeping the next three games. When the victory was celebrated back in Chicago, the team brought in Moore and presented him with an engraved gold watch.

Moore's performance in the 1938 Stanley Cup tends to be cast as a lone moment of glory for an embittered minor pro, but he proved to be a very good goaltender in the American League. The season that followed his

Stanley Cup heroics, Moore made the second All Star team with the Hershey Bears. He made brief returns to the NHL: two games with the Americans in 1938/39, and one game with Detroit in 1939/40. Perhaps, as some were wont to suggest, he was one of those very good goaltenders who got stuck toiling for subpar teams. As for poor Goodman, he played quite well for Chicago in fifty-two games over the next two seasons, logging six shutouts and recording a GA of 2.17. Karakas ended up playing in the American League with Providence, making the first All Star team in 1940/41 and the second team in 1942/43 before returning in 1943/44 to the Blackhawks for three more seasons. He joined his fellow Minnesotan Frank Brimsek in the U.S. Hockey Hall of Fame.

No goaltending substitution is more famous than that of forty-five-year-old Lester Patrick, who came from behind the bench to play goal for his New York Rangers in the 1928 Stanley Cup. The Rangers were playing the Montreal Maroons in the best-of-five series and were already down a game when their star netminder, Lorne Chabot, was knocked unconscious by a Nels Stewart backhand early in the second period of the second game. The game was in Montreal—the entire series was in Montreal, because the Barnum & Bailey Circus was occupying Madison Square Garden—and Patrick, the Rangers coach, attempted to bring the Ottawa Senators' great goaltender, Alex Connell, down from the stands to plug the gap. Maroons general manager Eddie Gerard refused to agree to the Connell substitution. Patrick had ten minutes to come up with a replacement. His centre, Frank Boucher, nominated Patrick himself.

When Boucher was starring in the old Pacific Coast league with Frank Patrick's Vancouver Maroons, he had played against Lester Patrick. He may have been forty-five during this Stanley Cup final, but two seasons earlier, Lester had played twenty-three games, virtually a full season, on defence for his Victoria Cougars. And when the short-tempered Cougars goaltender Heck Fowler received two fighting suspensions in 1921/22, Patrick had taken his place in the net. At Boucher's urging, Patrick donned Chabot's equipment. Patrick was six-foot-one and lanky, with a shock of white hair. Facing the Rangers at the other end of the rink was Clint Benedict, perhaps the greatest goaltender of the era.

Patrick made for a stunning, unthinkable sight, and his players protected him ferociously, forcing the Maroons whenever possible to shoot from far out or from bad angles. A rinkside cheering section of league managers—Conn Smythe from Toronto, Leo Dandurand of the Canadiens, and Jack Adams of Detroit—shouted encouragement to Patrick and instructions to both Patrick and his players. The game remained scoreless through to the end of the period, and thirty seconds into the third, Rangers captain Bill Cook gave his team the lead. But with only minutes to play, Stewart, who had already KO'ed Chabot, beat Patrick with a rebound and tied

the game. After seven minutes of overtime, Boucher ended Patrick's forty-six-minute nightmare by scoring on Benedict and tying the series. For the rest of the series, New York brought in Joe Miller, who had played twenty-eight games for the New York Americans that season, and the Rangers won the cup.

Patrick, needless to say, never played goal again. He lives on in the record book with a sparkling 1.30 GA as a result of that single, harrowing game. Miller moved on to the dreadful Pittsburgh Pirates (and its last-season incarnation, the Philadelphia Quakers) for three seasons. The series loss was Benedict's last Stanley Cup appearance. Two seasons later, the facial injuries he suffered when hit by a Howie Morenz blast forced him out of the NHL. And after being struck by Nels Stewart's backhand, Chabot never again played for New York. The next season, Patrick dealt the goaltender whose injury had forced him to tend net to the Maple Leafs. ○

| *"HEY, ABBOTT!"*

CHAPTER 4

1939/40–1944/45

A *damned* <u>war</u> COMES ALONG

WHEN THE WORLD WENT TO WAR, GOALTENDING WENT WITH IT. AND WHEN THE STARS RETURNED, THEY RETURNED TO A GAME THAT WAS ALMOST UNRECOGNIZABLE

The Second World War played havoc with professional hockey, as it did with so many aspects of North American life. For six seasons, the NHL struggled to ice a quality product—even to ice a product at all. Goaltending suffered greatly, and the game suffered because of it.

LGA in the NHL had run around a steady 2.5 from 1933/34 to 1938/39, but as soon as hostilities erupted, it soared: to 2.7 in 1940/41, 3.1 in 1941/42, 3.6 in 1942/43 and a peak of 4.08 in 1943/44. But why LGA climbed so rapidly cannot be answered simplistically. True, the bulk of the game's great goaltending stars did join the military, but they didn't do so until well into the war. When the Bruins set two records that still stand for shots on goal—most in a single game (eighty-three) and most in one period (thirty-three)—on March 4, 1941, against Chicago, they still only won the game 3–2. Paradoxically, it wasn't until Frank Brimsek, Turk Broda, Johnny Mowers, Sugar Jim Henry and Chuck Rayner were all out of the league, in 1943/44, that LGA began its decline to normal levels. There was more at work than diluted rosters: the game was undergoing important changes, not only in who was playing it but in how it was played.

At the beginning of the war, the NHL was packed with extraordinary goaltending talent, led by Brimsek in Boston. He won two Vezinas and two Stanley Cups in the years leading into war, and made eight straight All Star appearances in the seasons he wasn't in the military. Three other goaltenders won the Vezina between 1939/40 and 1942/43: Walter "Turk" Broda in Toronto, who had come into the league in 1936/37, the veteran Davey Kerr of the Rangers and Johnny Mowers, who was twenty-four when he took over the Red Wings' goal from Normie Smith in 1940/41.

Kerr was one of the greatest goaltenders of the

TURK BRODA (*FAR RIGHT*), **STAR GOAL-TENDER OF THE TORONTO MAPLE LEAFS, WEARS A DIFFERENT KIND OF UNIFORM CIRCA 1943. BRODA SPENT THE WAR PLAYING SOFTBALL AND HOCKEY OVERSEAS ON CANADIAN ARMY TEAMS. HIS CONTROVERSIAL ENLISTMENT IGNITED A NATIONAL DEBATE OVER THE PREFERENTIAL TREATMENT GIVEN PROFESSIONAL ATHLETES BY THE MILITARY.**

A BREED APART

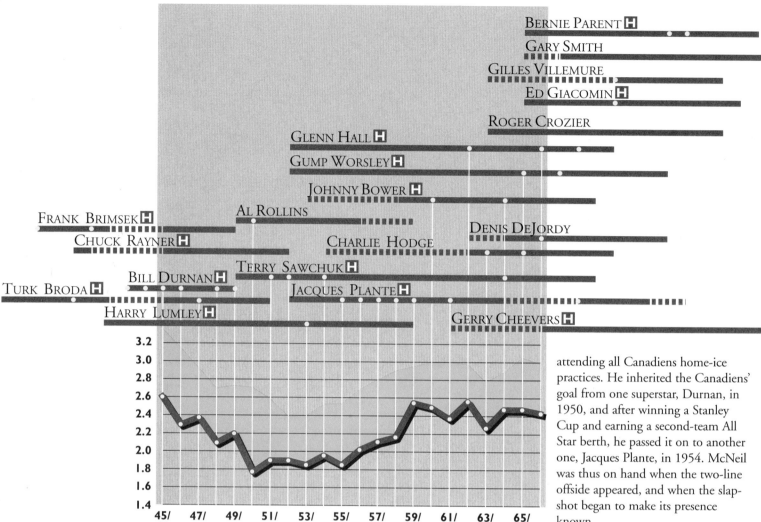

at the game he had re-engineered with the two-line off-side and suspected it had all turned out worse for the men in the nets. "Goaltenders were being subjected to a much more difficult assignment than they'd ever known before," he would reflect. "Power plays, deflected shots, and pileups in front of them that blocked their vision were presenting them with tensions and obstacles and injuries almost unknown five years earlier." After a game in Montreal in January 1949 in which his goaltender, Chuck Rayner, had been subjected to wave after wave of bleu, blanc et rouge piling up in his crease, an exasperated Boucher told the press he wanted to see the crease depth extended from three to four feet. It wasn't until 1951/52 that Boucher got his way. A foot was added to both crease dimensions, increasing the rectangle to four feet by eight feet. By then, the imperative to give the goaltender more turf had been made more emphatic by the arrival of a terrible new offensive weapon in the NHL: the slapshot.

Gerry McNeil was a goaltending bridge between the war years and the glory days of the Original Six. His first training camp as a Canadien had come as a seventeen-year-old in 1943, and for the next seven seasons he was Durnan's understudy, playing for the Montreal Royals of the Quebec Senior league and attending all Canadiens home-ice practices. He inherited the Canadiens' goal from one superstar, Durnan, in 1950, and after winning a Stanley Cup and earning a second-team All Star berth, he passed it on to another one, Jacques Plante, in 1954. McNeil was thus on hand when the two-line offside appeared, and when the slapshot began to make its presence known.

Credit for inventing the slapshot has long been given to Bernie "Boom Boom" Geoffrion, who played his first games as a Canadien in 1950/51. He was almost certainly the first to use it consistently and well in the postwar NHL, but there was nothing new about the shot itself. It had been around in one form or another since the 1930s. The reason it wasn't used much before Geoffrion, says Frank Brimsek, is that it was so inaccurate. "Bun Cook had the best I'd ever seen," says Brimsek, who retired at the end of the 1949/50 season, before Geoffrion arrived in the league. Cook played in the NHL from 1926/27 to 1936/37, every season but the last as a New York Ranger; Cook then coached Brimsek in Providence in the American League. "He was the only guy with a slapshot who knew where it was going," maintains Brimsek. "He knew *exactly* where it was going." The shot Brimsek feared was not the slapshot, but the drop shot of Rangers star Bryan Hextall. Brimsek swears Hextall's shot could drop four feet on the way to the net. If you set up to take it on the chest, you had to make sure you kept your pads together as it could wind up shooting between your ankles.

McNeil saw plenty of the slapshot as it took firmer hold after the war. Unlike other goaltenders who faced Geoffrion's blast every fifth game, McNeil confronted it day in, day out, in practice. But he was never that impressed with the slapshot as an offensive weapon. McNeil frankly saw the shot as little more than showboating, a crowd pleaser. "A chap would wind up at the blueline, and if you played the angles, you didn't care where the hell it went. It was going to hit you, or hit the glass. But the people loved it because it hit the glass with a bang. I didn't think much of it for scoring."

Besides, the slapshot made for sloppy hockey. It wasn't a finesse tool, like the clever passing and needle-threading wrist shots that made the goaltender of McNeil's era stick close to the net and play his angles carefully. The slapshot seemed to be fired with no particular part of the net in mind, or propelled wildly into a screen of bodies in the slot in the hope that it would bounce somehow past the goaltender—off a stick, a leg, anything. (While attacking players had always taken up station on the goaltender's doorstep, the physical "slot" didn't arrive until 1942, when the introduction of faceoff circles created a discernible territory defined by the crease on one end and the inner arcs of the two circles to either side.)

Glenn Hall, who played his first NHL games in 1952/53, saw the slapshot's effectiveness not in its accuracy (of which it had very little) but in its ability to intimidate the goaltender. It was fast, it could hurt, it increased the shooter's range and so could arrive through a screen of bodies, and, most unnervingly, it could be tipped and rise unnoticed into the goaltender's face.

Even when the slapshot was a well-established part of the game, its potency in the hands of an NHL star could be a terrifying revelation to a young goaltender entering the professional ranks. "You've no idea how hard National Leaguers can shoot that puck until you've been hit a few times. It comes as a great shock," Gerry Cheevers recalled in 1971. "My first professional camp was with Toronto in 1961. The first time Frank Mahovlich hit my shoulder

with a shot, I staggered back and my shoulders banged into the crossbar. It was as much from the surprise as the force of the shot. I just hadn't expected a puck could feel like that. It was as though somebody had wound up ten feet in front of me and thrown a rock as big as an orange."

(Bower says Mahovlich's slapshot was particularly dangerous because it was a rising one.)

When Glenn Hall reaches for words with which to pay tribute to Dave Dryden, who served as his backup in Chicago in the 1960s, his choice is telling: "He could hold the crouch." Goaltending was a profession of technique, true, but it was also, and perhaps ultimately, one of nerves. In Hall's succinct compliment, holding the crouch implies doing what every nerve fibre in your body was screaming at you not to do when someone like Bobby Hull wound up. Your instinct was to flinch, to come out of your stance and draw yourself taller, to raise your catching glove out of its low position to protect your face, which had no mask to preserve it. The impulse was stronger when the shot was screened. You had no idea where it was going to come from unless you got down in your crouch, covered the net, did your job and actively looked for the approaching shot. Your job was to get in the puck's way, and it didn't matter that the puck, in this new era of the slapshot, could do devastating harm, even when you did see it coming.

The slapshot did not purge the game of the traditional wrist shot—far from it. In the hands of skilled players, the wrist shot was still an effective tool, assuredly the most effective scoring tool. "The Rocket had the most accurate shot," says Bower. "He had a wrist shot he could put anywhere, and it was never the same place." But with the arrival of the slapshot, the goaltender had no choice but to move out from the crease, to take the net away from a distant shooter coming in on the

Continued on page 91

SKATES WORN BY JOHNNY BOWER OF THE TORONTO MAPLE LEAFS

A REALLY BIG DEAL

**AL ROLLINS AND HARRY LUMLEY
WERE THE FOCAL POINTS OF ONE OF
THE GAME'S BLOCKBUSTER TRADES**

AFTER WINNING A
STANLEY CUP AND A
VEZINA IN TORONTO,
AL ROLLINS (*BELOW*)
WAS TRADED TO
CHICAGO, WHERE HE
WON THE HART
TROPHY. THE TRADE
BROUGHT HARRY
LUMLEY (*OPPOSITE*)
TO THE LEAFS, WITH
WHOM HE WON A
VEZINA.

They were born a month apart in 1926, though miles apart—Harry Lumley in Owen Sound, Ontario, Al Rollins in Vanguard, Saskatchewan. It would take twenty-six years for their lives to complete their unusual collision course, when two talented goaltenders who fell under the sway of Maple Leafs magnate Conn Smythe figured in one of the game's biggest trades.

Harry Lumley had broken into the NHL as a seventeen-year-old Junior player with the Barrie Colts, when Detroit acquired his rights from New York and put him on the ice in a three-game tryout in 1943/44 before assigning him to the Indianapolis Capitols of the American League. These were the war years, when goaltending talent was hard to come by, and Lumley turned out to be a stellar replacement for Johnny Mowers, who was in the Canadian air force. Lumley played another twenty-one games in Indianapolis in 1944/45 before moving up to the Red Wings for good. He held the Maple Leafs to nine goals and shut them out twice in

the seven-game defensive gridlock that was the 1944/1945 Stanley Cup. The Leafs won that series, but Lumley won Conn Smythe's admiration. In 1947/48, Lumley was back again facing Toronto, this time on the receiving end of a four-game Stanley Cup sweep by the Leafs.

After the Red Wings and Lumley finally won the Stanley Cup in their third consecutive attempt in 1949/50, Detroit seized upon another new netminding star, Terry Sawchuk, and dealt Lumley to Chicago. The Blackhawks were a defensive sieve; in Lumley's first season with them, they allowed twice as many goals as the regular-season champions, Lumley's old Red Wings.

Meanwhile, Al Rollins was making his way into the NHL. His unlikely break came when Baz Bastien, the heir apparent to Turk Broda, lost an eye to an errant shot at the first day of the Leaf training camp in September 1949. Broda played another full season in the Leaf net, relieved for two games by Rollins, who was called up from Kansas City in the U.S. League, a minor pro loop a notch below the American League. In 1950/51, Rollins played forty of seventy games (Broda took the rest), recorded a paltry 1.77 goals-against average and won the Vezina as the Leafs won the Stanley Cup. The next season he played every single game for the Leafs, posted a very respectable 2.22 goals-against average and finished second to Terry Sawchuk in the Vezina race. But it wasn't enough. The Leafs thought they could do better.

The Toronto fans and media had never forgotten Lumley's performances in the 1944/45, 1947/48 and 1948/49 Stanley Cups. Even with the struggling Blackhawks, Lumley continued to impress. "When he was with Chicago, he played awfully, awfully well," says Ted Kennedy, the Leaf captain at the time. "Chicago was strong offensively, but not defensively. Any time Chicago beat us, it was because of Lumley. The Toronto press were lobbying the Leafs to get him."

As it happened, Blackhawks GM Bill Tobin had long hankered after some of the talent in the Leafs superlative defensive corps. Back when Bastien was injured, Tobin, up at the Blackhawks training camp in North Bay, was willing to give up a goaltender if Toronto were willing to send him in return a proven defenceman, either Jimmy Thomson or Gus Mortson. Smythe turned him down—at the time, Tobin didn't have a goaltender of Lumley's calibre to deal. But just before training camp in 1952, the Leafs and the Blackhawks were ready to do business. Lumley came to Toronto. In return, Toronto sent Chicago an astonishing package: their Vezina-winner, Rollins, their star centre, Cal Gardner, a minor-league prospect, Ray Hannigan, and the defensive standout Tobin had long coveted, Gus Mortson, who became the Blackhawks captain.

Although neither team built a Stanley Cup winner out of the trade, Rollins and Lumley continued to star. Lumley stayed in Toronto for four seasons, winning the

Continued from page 89

wing or standing back at the blueline. He had to find some compromise between moving out far enough to cut down the angle, but not so far that the speeding puck, reaching him quicker than if he had stayed back in the crease, cut down his available reaction time. A puck clocked at 100 miles an hour is travelling 147 feet a second. That means it moves from the shooter back at the point to the goal line sixty feet away in 0.41 seconds. If the goaltender moves out ten feet, the puck reaches him in 0.34 seconds. And once out of the crease, he was vulnerable to being caught out of position by a feigned shot that became a cross-ice pass, by a long rebound or by a shot that missed the net entirely and ricocheted off the boards or the glass to an open man.

He was leaving the crease not only to take away the net from the distant shooter, but to play the puck, feeding breakout passes, moving behind the net, as Plante showed, to intercept dump-in shots wrapping around the back boards. Now that the goaltender was in the territory of the skaters, he had to skate like never before, to cover as much ice as possible. But those goaltenders who did wander, who knew they had to wander to play the puck as a third defenceman, often had to overcome the prejudices of management. "Staying in the net has always been a team philosophy instead of an individual philosophy," says Glenn Hall. "I was told: Don't stop a puck that's going to miss the net. You might deflect it in. Well, if you're that bad, you shouldn't be playing. The goalkeeper's idea of how the position should be played often varied quite a bit with management's idea." Gump Worsley has observed: "Coaches tell you never to kick at the puck with your skates because you might kick it backwards into the net. What do they know?"

The advent of the slapshot was a watershed in the goaltender's profession. It added a recklessness and degree of violence hitherto unseen. It set off an arms race between the attacking player and the goaltender that escalates still. The slapshot came to dominate the game, the sticks grew curves, the shots became ever harder and (in the hands of some practitioners) more accurate. The tactics of offence and defence adjusted markedly to accommodate it. And goaltenders made their own changes—in equipment, in playing style.

For the most part, goaltending was still a standup job. This was partly a matter of survival. With no mask, and slapshots, sticks and skates flying, you wanted to keep your head above the fray. "If we went down," says Johnny Bower, "we got up real quick." The rare netminders who did drop to the ice as a matter of course, like Gump Worsley or Jack Gelineau, were known as "flip-flops." When they were on the ice, they were said to be taking a swim in a frozen pond.

Stylistic variations did emerge. Terry Sawchuk would sink into a "gorilla crouch," doubled over so that his face seemed scarcely to clear his knees, hands at the ready. Glenn Hall introduced the butterfly style: knock-kneed, feet wide apart to cover the corners of the goal, hands and

Vezina in 1953/54 with a GA of 1.86 and making the first All Star team in 1953/54 and 1954/55. The Leafs then signed a promising goaltending rookie, Ed Chadwick, who became the runner-up in Calder voting in 1957; Lumley dropped out of the NHL and reappeared in Boston in 1957/58. He spent three seasons with the Bruins, who lost the Stanley Cup final to Montreal in 1957/58, before retiring in 1959/60. Rollins endured five trying seasons in Chicago with a GA routinely over 3.00. Although he was never named to an All Star team, in 1953/54 Rollins became only the third goaltender to win the league's coveted Hart Trophy, having already been a runner-up to Gordie Howe in Hart voting in 1952/53. In 1957, Glenn Hall arrived in Chicago from Detroit, replacing Rollins as an NHL starter. He was playing in Winnipeg when he resurfaced for nine games with the Rangers in 1959/60. Rollins then went into coaching and management in minor pro hockey in the western U.S., and also coached in the WHA.

Harry Lumley was elected to the Hockey Hall of Fame in 1980. Despite having won the Hart, a Stanley Cup and a Vezina, Al Rollins has still not been elected to the Hall. ○

stick at the ready to cover the new scoring spot, the "five hole" between his legs. The changes came as the goaltenders responded to the realities of the new offensive game, and as they brought to bear new weapons of their own.

The equipment with which goaltenders had first greeted the new game wasn't up to the job. "You're wearing up to forty pounds of padding as you stand there in front of a cage that is four feet high and six feet wide, and you're expected to be as agile as a ballet dancer," Worsley has noted.

The goaltenders took it upon themselves, often with considerable frustration, to get the manufacturers to make equipment that actually worked. "The only difference between a monkey and a goalkeeper is a goalkeeper has one arm turned forwards," says Hall, referring to the arm that holds the stick. "That's where I wanted the padding, and I couldn't get it across to the people that I was no longer a monkey. I was totally out of the tree and I wanted one arm turned."

Gloves experienced a rapid evolution, initiated by the goaltenders themselves as they strove to come up with an equaliser for the new offensive style (see pages 96–97). But there was still much work to be done. Johnny Bower wore a three-finger catching glove made by Pop Kenesky that "weighed ten pounds. If I couldn't catch the puck, I knocked it down with it."

The pads pioneered by Pop Kenesky underwent very few changes. Harry Lumley introduced the use of a "scoop," a crease or pocket at the shins which made pucks drop to the ice rather than rebounding. Turk Broda had the padding extend along either side of the skate to improve blocking around the blades. But that, fundamentally, was it. They were still made of horsehide, felt and rubberised canvas, with kapok for stuffing in the front and deer hair on the sides.

The canvas might have been rubberised, but that didn't mean the pads stayed dry. They were notorious for gaining weight as a game progressed, soaking up so much water that they felt like two sacks of wet cement on the legs. "I can close my eyes and think of how heavy they were in the third period," says Hall. "*Heavy*," McNeil recalls. "It was unbelievable. The felt got wet and stayed wet for a long time, and just about doubled the weight of the pads. I would love to start over and try the new equipment." Brimsek notes that sweat would also weigh down the equipment and the wool jerseys, although he personally wasn't bothered that much by the weight. For Bower, the weight was noticeable, and he would try to prevent the pads from soaking up water by treating them with dubbin (waterproof grease) and wrapping his legs in dubbin-treated tape. Wet ice was even more treacherous to the goaltender in that he had difficulty controlling his slide when he went down. Rinks with soft ice, like Madison Square Garden and Boston Garden, were the toughest for netminders to play in because of the sloppy conditions.

Although players like Tiny Thompson had owned their own equipment back in the 1920s and 1930s, by the war years equipment generally was the property of the team. A good set of Kenesky pads, conscientiously waterproofed and regularly repaired, could last four seasons, and teams hated coughing up for a new set. "You had such difficulty getting new pads," says Hall. "They never wanted to trade a goalkeeper with new pads. They wanted to trade him with old pads. So you would say to the trainer: Is there a trade coming? How come I can't get new pads?"

No one wore them into a game fresh out of Kenesky's shop. Brimsek says he liked to wear a pair for at least two weeks in practice. Glenn Hall and Johnny Bower practised with a new pair for three to four months before they were ready to take them into a game. "You might get a new pair prior to playoffs, but they weren't good," says Hall. "You didn't have them broken in. Now you can take them right off the rack, put them on and have no problem. After having a new pair in the playoffs, you'd go to training camp, and you'd have a pretty good pair, but you'd get them soaking wet and they would deteriorate like you wouldn't believe."

The goaltenders were, as always, a fraternity. Some, like Brimsek, never felt anything less than a full member of their team; others, like McNeil, were conscious of the separateness of their role. "That was one of the things told to me by management when I first came up," says McNeil. "You're by yourself. Don't take sides with defencemen. Just stay out of it. You couldn't sit down with someone playing the same position and talk something over. There was no one else around." But as a group, their ties cut across team barriers. They were virtually self-taught. Some coach or manager always had a particular theory about how the position should or should not be played, but for the most part they developed their skills on their own, which gave them distinctive styles, probably more distinctive than at any future point in the game. Brimsek blames today's similarity on the media. Back then, "you learned it yourself. Today they watch television and they copy that. In my day there was no television, and that was good. You learned to play a style that was best for you."

They learned by watching the goaltender at the other end of the rink. "If you didn't watch the opposing goalkeeper, you weren't paying attention," says Hall. It was by studying Jack Gelineau in his brief Boston career, says Hall, that he really appreciated the blocking possibilities of the stick-side glove. When Johnny Bower was playing for the Cleveland Barons in the American League, the team's general manager, Jim Hendy, sent him to Detroit to watch the young Terry Sawchuk play. Bower took notes on Sawchuk's style, and reviewed them with Hendy back in Cleveland. "I had a three-quarters crouch then," says Bower. The field trip to watch Sawchuk led him to adopt a more compressed crouch. And when Bower came up to the New York Rangers for the 1953/54 season, the man he was replacing, Chuck Rayner, told him his stick work was poor. Rayner gave him some tips on the poke check, and Bower became

one of the best at it, knocking away the puck as well as taking out the feet of the player without incurring a penalty. Rayner also passed along one of his ruses for beating the three-second rule for goaltenders getting rid of a caught puck: buy time by juggling it in your glove in such a way that you don't appear to have gained control of it. Emile Francis was a young hopeful in the Rangers net when Frank Brimsek, playing for the Bruins, took time after a game to dispense some advice. Like a lot of hockey players of the era, Francis was keen on baseball in the off-season, playing shortstop. Brimsek told Francis he was playing goal too aggressively, coming out too quickly, just like a shortstop going after a grounder, then having to back up. Brimsek advised him to hold back before committing himself as a shooter approached. And Francis made a huge contribution to goaltenders everywhere when he introduced the baseball-style catching glove (see page 96).

For many goaltenders, the changes the game underwent from the middle of the Second World War forward were too much to bear. It was bad enough that offence had become so aggressive, that the slapshot had arrived and that they wore no mask. What made it literally unbearable for some was the length of the season.

In the professional game's early years, two dozen games would constitute a season. The NHL season had jumped from twenty-four to forty-four games between 1923/24 and 1926/27, but even with that increase, goaltenders managed to have long careers right through the 1930s. Until midway through the Second World War, the league played a forty-eight-game schedule. In 1942/43, with the reduction of the league from seven to six teams after the New York Americans folded, the schedule underwent a nominal increase, to fifty games.

Continued on page 98

UNMASKED: WHEN GERRY CHEEVERS ARRIVED IN THE NHL IN THE MID-1960S, HE PLAYED BAREFACED, BUT NOT FOR VERY LONG. HIS MASK, COVERED IN STITCHES, BECAME A PERSONAL TRADEMARK AND A SYMBOL OF THE MOST DANGEROUS JOB IN TEAM SPORTS.

| *WELCOME TO THE SHOOTING GALLERY*

JOHNNY BOWER

AFTER THIRTEEN YEARS AS A MINOR-LEAGUE PHENOMENON, THE MAN WHO WOULD WIN FOUR STANLEY CUPS AND TWO VEZINAS FINALLY GOT OFF THE BUS IN TORONTO

He spent, in his own words, "thirteen years riding the bus." Indeed, John William Bower had an entire career in the American Hockey League, from 1945/46 to 1957/58, before he at last found stardom in the NHL with the Toronto Maple Leafs. He'd been one of the brightest lights of the AHL for, it seemed, forever. It had also seemed that the six-team NHL loop, with only one goaltender per team, was never going to find room for him.

He got his first chance to show he belonged in the big league in 1953/54 when called up by the Rangers; by then he had toiled for eight seasons with the Cleveland Barons of the AHL. He had a solid season in New York, playing all seventy games and recording five shutouts and a 2.60 GA for a team that won only twenty-nine games. The Rangers mystified him by shipping him back to Cleveland and reverting to Gump Worsley, who had been the Calder winner with New York in 1952/53 but had been sent back to the minors after recording a GA of 3.06 with two shutouts in fifty games. Bower was retrieved by New York for seven games over the next three seasons, but nothing came of it. He

appeared in danger of having his career unfold like that of his AHL contemporary Gil Mayer, who in six seasons was named a league All Star five times and its outstanding goaltender four times, but could not break into the NHL. Bower settled back into the routine of the bus, sure he was going to make it someday.

He finally got there in the fall of 1958, when Punch Imlach, newly hired as the coach and general manager of the struggling Toronto Maple Leafs, drafted him. Bower was the top goaltender in the AHL at the time. In 1957/58, he won the league's most valuable player award for the third straight season. It was also the third straight season he had been the league's first-team All Star goaltender, an honour he held five times. The season also brought him his second straight—and third career—top-goaltender award. And he had just turned in an outstanding performance for Cleveland in the playoffs against Imlach's Springfield Indians. About to turn thirty-four, Johnny Bower was finally getting a real shot at the NHL.

He didn't squander the opportunity, although he was at first reluctant to take it, having become so established in Cleveland. With the rejuvenated Leafs he played for eleven more seasons, won the Vezina twice and the Stanley Cup four times.

The long and tortuous road to glory for Bower had begun in the northern Saskatchewan town of Prince Albert, where he was born in 1924 (despite persistent rumours that he is a lot older than the record books say, Bower insists on that birthdate). There wasn't a lot of money around when he was growing up in the Depression. The favourite source of cheap hockey pucks for Bower and his chums was the horses that came into town on weekends. When the horse droppings froze solid, they made perfect pucks. "You didn't want to get hit in the mouth with one," he remembers.

Bower went into the army during the Second World War, and while overseas looked into playing goal for a military team, but the teams were so loaded with professional talent like the Leafs' Turk Broda that he wasn't judged good enough. Bower had entered the Canadian army in 1940 as an underage sixteen-year-old. When he came out of the service in 1944, he was twenty, and still eligible to play a year of Junior hockey. But he didn't have a birth certificate to prove it, and while Bower did play another Junior season, it served as the source of the rumour mill about his true age—some people weren't prepared to believe that he could have spent four years in the military and still be eligible for Junior play. In 1945, he joined Cleveland of the AHL.

As a Maple Leaf, Bower was instrumental in the Stanley Cup victories of the 1960s, yet his résumé is surprisingly thin on official accolades. He was named to only one NHL All Star team. He only won his second Vezina because fellow Toronto netminder Terry Sawchuk insisted on

	N.Y. RANGERS		IN AHL		TORONTO											
	53/54	54/55	55/56	56/57	57/58	58/59	59/60	60/61	61/62	62/63	63/64	64/65	65/66	66/67	67/68	68/69
GAMES	70	5		2		39	66	58	59	42	51	34	35	24	43	20
SHUTOUTS	5	0		0		3	5	2	2	1	5	3	3	2	4	2
STANLEY CUP				SF		F	F	SF	W	W	W	SF	SF	W		QF
ALL STAR TEAM									I							

Bower played one game for Toronto in 1969/70.

sharing the trophy and prize money with him. The trophy's rules at the time specified that the prize go to the goaltender who had played the most games on the team with the lowest GA, and Sawchuk had played thirty-six games to Bower's thirty-four. The league relented, and from then on the Vezina was shared by the regular goaltenders on the team with the lowest GA. The performance of Bower and Sawchuk also encouraged the league to make it mandatory for teams to have two dressed-to-play goaltenders on hand for every game, beginning in 1965/66.

Yet by rights there should have been more awards for Bower. In three other seasons he posted a personal GA better than the team GAs that won other players the coveted Vezina, but Bower had nothing to show for it. Bower was an affable old pro, a standup goaltender whose reflexes defied his age, whose importance to the success of the Leafs failed to register with the media types who overlooked him in All Star voting.

By 1968/69, time was catching up with him. At forty-four, his play still sparkled, but his eyesight was weakening, and to preserve it he reluctantly decided to

don a mask. He never really got used to the device—like other goaltenders, he found it restricted his vision, and he tended to lose sight of the puck when it was down around his feet. When a long shot beat him, Bower protested to an angry Imlach that he had been screened. Imlach played him the game film: "There wasn't anybody within twenty feet of me."

The decision to hang up the pads was simplified by the firing of Punch Imlach at the end of the 1968/69 season after the Leafs were blown out of the quarterfinal in four straight games (and a combined score of 17–0) by the Bruins. Within minutes of the Imlach sacking, Bower publicly announced his retirement. He was one of a handful of players in a team otherwise united in their loathing of Imlach who had always respected the boss without ever kowtowing to him.

He played one game in 1969/70, then moved into scouting with the Leafs, and later served as a goaltending coach. In 1976, he was elected to the Hockey Hall of Fame. He still runs a goaltending school, and on November 8, 1994, Johnny Bower says he really did celebrate his seventieth birthday. ○

JOHNNY BOWER HAD A FULL CAREER WITH THE CLEVELAND BARONS IN THE AMERICAN LEAGUE BEFORE MOVING UP TO THE NHL WITH THE TORONTO MAPLE LEAFS.

Hands _of_ Time

LIKE MANY GOALTENDERS, TURK BRODA OF THE MAPLE LEAFS WAS KEEN ON BASEBALL, PLAYING SOFTBALL AS A CATCHER IN THE OFF-SEASON

GLOVE WITH REINFORCED FINGERTIPS WORN BY BILL TOBIN, EDMONTON ESKIMOS, C. 1925

Considering how many goaltenders were enthusiastic baseball players, it took a remarkably long time for the fraternity to add a proper catching glove to its tool kit. Catching gloves right into the Second World War were little more than heavy-duty defenceman's gloves. Players like Frank Brimsek can recall wearing a kid leather glove inside their regular glove to take some of the sting out of nabbing a puck virtually barehanded. By the end of the war, gloves with rudimentary cages were appearing, but it took the initiative of a teenage goaltender who also happened to be a hardball shortstop to make the great leap forward.

Emile Francis, who went on to become coach and general manager of the New York Rangers, was playing Junior hockey for the Moose Jaw Canucks at the start of the Second World War. He took a Roger McGuinn model three-finger first baseman's glove made by Rawlings to a shoemaker and had him sew on a regular hockey glove gauntlet. He used the glove without incident in Junior hockey, and it caused no fuss when he was called up by the Chicago Blackhawks in 1946/47 and played his first NHL game, against Boston. The second game, a Thursday-night match in Detroit, was another matter. The Red Wings coach and general manager, Jack Adams, spied the glove on Francis during the pregame warmup, and summoned referee King Clancy to the Detroit bench. "Adams is pointing at me. I'm looking at my pads, looking around, trying to figure out what's wrong. Finally King Clancy skates over and says, 'Let me see that glove you've got there.' I took it off and showed it to him. He says, 'You can't used that. It's illegal. It's too big.' I said, 'Who says so?' He says, 'Jack Adams.' I told him, 'I tell you what, King. If I can't use this glove, you've got no game tonight.' Those days a team only had one goalkeeper." Clancy agreed to allow him to wear it, but on the condition that Francis showed the glove to league president Clarence Campbell that Saturday at the NHL head office in Montreal, when the Blackhawks would be in town playing the Canadiens. Campbell gave Francis's glove his blessing, and goaltending

THREE-FINGER KENESKY MODEL

TRAPPER WORN BY MANNY LEGACÉ, GOALTENDER FOR CANADA'S 1993 WORLD JUNIOR CHAMPIONS

TRAPPER WITH EARLY "CHEATER" EXTENSION ON THUMB, WORN BY PELLE LINDBERGH, PHILADELPHIA FLYERS, 1985/86

acquired an entirely new dimension of play.

"I should have patented it," Francis laments. He didn't, and his three-finger prototype became a production standard.

In time, the catching glove came to resemble less a first baseman's glove than a catcher's mitt. The trapper-style glove had more padding and, most important, more area overall. There was (and is) nothing in the NHL rulebook about precise dimensions of the catching glove, only a proviso—added at the time of Francis's innovation—that the cage could be no larger than the span between thumb and forefinger. Through this loophole Mike Palmateer, who tended net for Toronto and Washington from 1976/77 to 1983/84, was able to introduce the "cheater," an extension of the outside edge of the thumb that increased the glove's overall area. Combined with the slablike pad along the wrist, the cheater has made the modern catching glove as much a blocker as a device with which to snag the puck.

The stick-side glove underwent a parallel evolution. Before the Second World War, goaltenders either wore heavy-duty defenceman's gloves, or added protection to the glove with a felt sheath. Extra padding began to appear—Frank Brimsek used a wrap with bamboo ribbing. Mitts began to appear that had heavy padding built into them, and, gradually, a slablike rectangular blocker became standard by the end of the Original Six era. The Cooper "waffle board" became a virtual standard. Today's blockers have lost the waffle look and are more flexible, with the top portion angled outward to help direct rebounds. ○

FELT WRAP WORN ON STICK GLOVE BY DAVEY KERR, c. 1940

PADDED STICK-HAND MITT WORN BY GERRY COLEMAN, A MONTREAL JUNIOR CANADIEN GOALTENDER IN THE 1940s

COOPER "WAFFLE-BOARD" BLOCKER WORN BY ED GIACOMIN, 1977/78

EMILE FRANCIS, WHO INVENTED THE BASEBALL-STYLE CATCHING GLOVE WHILE PLAYING JUNIOR HOCKEY IN THE 1940s, HAS PADDING APPLIED TO THE BACK OF HIS STICK GLOVE AS A CHICAGO BLACKHAWK, c. 1947

BLOCKER WORN BY MANNY LEGACÉ, GOALTENDER FOR CANADA'S 1993 JUNIOR WORLD CHAMPIONS

Continued from page 93

In 1946/47, with the league stabilised in its Original Six configuration, the schedule was expanded to sixty games. Then Leaf GM Conn Smythe called for an increase to seventy games, and he wanted roster sizes increased from seventeen to eighteen skaters so he could carry six dressed-to-play defencemen, rather than the normal five. Smythe got his way on the number of games, but not on the number of players. The teams would have to get by with seventeen skaters, exclusive of goaltenders. And when it came to goaltenders, owners still generally thought one per team was just fine.

The league began to churn through goaltending talent at an alarming rate. The first casualty was Bill Durnan, whose career ended in the middle of the 1950 playoffs when he could not bring himself to return to the ice. Gerry McNeil, who replaced him, could endure the game for only four seasons.

With the careers of veterans ending during and after the war years, and because, during the war years, teams were running through goaltenders like so much Kleenex, genuine goaltending talent, particularly new blood, was never more valued. Bill Durnan was runner-up for the top rookie award, the Calder, in 1943/44, and Frank McCool won it in 1944/45. From 1949/50 to 1956/57, the Calder was practically a goaltending trophy. In 1949/50, Jack Gelineau won it; in 1950/51, Terry Sawchuk won it and Al Rollins was runner-up. Gump Worsley won it in 1952/53. Glenn Hall took it in 1955/56, and Ed Chadwick was runner-up in 1956/57. Goaltenders also figured in the Hart, which went to the player judged most valuable to his team. In 1949/50, Chuck Rayner became the first goaltender to win the Hart since Roy Worters in 1928/29; Al Rollins took the honour in 1953/54, and in 1961/62, Jacques Plante would become the last one to win it to date.

The talent that wasn't replaced quickly, that managed to stick with the job and make a full career of it, often paid a price. Terry Sawchuk aged rapidly under the stress of the postwar game and was considered washed up after five seasons. Harry Lumley became a different person when a game was imminent. "When he came into the dressing room at 6:30 or 7:00 prior to the game," Leaf captain Ted Kennedy recalls, "he went into a complete shell. No one spoke to him. He was psyching himself up for the game, I guess, but you never kidded with him. That was Lum. But after the game, he was completely relaxed, the life of the party." Gump Worsley impressed everyone with his seemingly happy-go-lucky nature, but was driven into temporary retirement in November 1968 by a nervous breakdown. Jack Gelineau inherited the Bruins goal from the beloved Brimsek, but he didn't last even as long as McNeil, playing only two full NHL seasons before deciding that his future lay in the insurance business.

By the mid-1950s, the goaltending profession fell into its old pattern of established practitioners enjoying long careers. Despite Frank Boucher's concerns about the unprecedented pressures on the goaltender, the game weeded through a formidable talent pool and came up with a handful of players who could perform with consistent skill and who were determined, for better or for worse, to stick with the job. It had always been a profession whose members seemed to get better with age, once they had overcome the initial terrors of the big-league game. Experience improved them, much as it did defencemen. (In 1971, Gerry Cheevers recounted how Bernie Geoffrion, who had become a scout, hailed Cheevers and his netminding partner, Eddie Johnston, as they left a St. Louis hotel. "You're in great shape, Eddie," Geoffrion said. "You're only thirty now. You've hardly started.") There were a lot of tricks of the trade to master, and defencemen and goaltenders didn't have the pressures of high-speed play that put a premium on fresh young legs. Forwards might get better with age too, but there was a point at which experience could not compensate for tiring bodies and a weaker shot. With goaltenders, as long as they could maintain their reflexes, their eyesight and their nerves, their careers could stretch into the double digits in seasons. Jacques Plante, Gump Worsley, Johnny Bower, Terry Sawchuk, Glenn Hall and Charlie Hodge all had long careers in the Original Six that extended into the NHL's expansion era.

That the top goaltenders managed to hang in so long is a tribute to their fortitude, for when the curved stick showed up, the goaltender's lot became even more hellish, if that were possible. Although Andy Bathgate of the Rangers experimented with the novelty in the late 1950s, the true development took place in Chicago, beginning in 1961. Stan Mikita and Bobby Hull experimented with different ways to bend the blade and arrived at a compromise in shape that would allow them still to stickhandle and give and receive passes while gaining the shooting benefits of the blade. The curve of the blade turned the slapshot into an entirely new and terrible creature. To borrow from baseball, what had been a fastball became an even faster fastball that behaved like a knuckleball. But Ed Giacomin, who was a baseball catcher in the off-season, makes an important distinction between the goaltender facing a curved-stick slapshot and a catcher facing a knuckleball. The catcher signals the pitcher, and knows exactly what is coming his way.

In the Bryan Hextall days, players created their drop shots with straight blades by "cutting" the puck—striking on an angle to induce spin. The curved blade added much more spin to the puck, and on the way to the net it danced and dipped and behaved in entirely unpredictable ways. The shooter didn't know where it was going any more than the goaltender did. It was the ultimate siege weapon, and it elevated the shooter's art of intimidating the goaltender to its apex. Sticks reached such monstrous curves that in 1968/69 the curve limit was set at 1.5 inches, but even that proved excessive. In 1969/70, the curve was limited to an inch, and in 1970/71 it was reduced again to half an inch. Gerry Cheevers would remark on how frightening Bobby Hull's

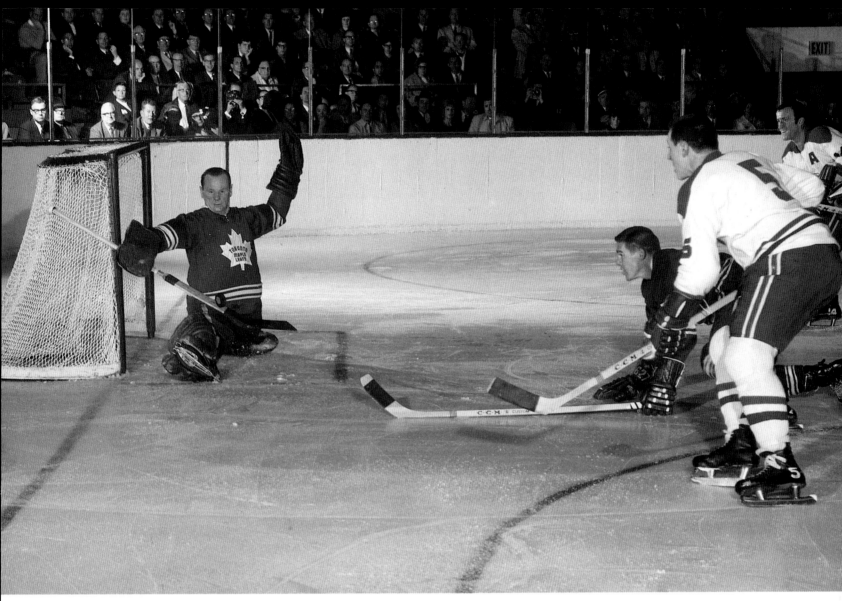

shot was, but said that his brother Dennis's was even worse: the younger Hull, he was convinced, had absolutely no idea where his slapshot was going. Goaltenders were working in a shooting gallery, and the shooters were wielding bazookas with wonky sights. Every now and then, a player managed to rifle a shot past the goaltender from centre ice.

The new ability of shooters to make the puck drop or dance with a slapshot propelled by a curved stick was not something management was necessarily quick to grasp. Johnny Bower was once beaten by a Geoffrion blast from just inside the Leaf blueline. Bower was sure the shot was going to go over the crossbar, but when he stuck out his glove to catch it, it shot between his legs. "That puck dropped three feet. I looked over to the bench, and Punch pulled his hat down over his face. All I could see was his nose. I thought, 'Oh boy, I'm in trouble.' " When he tried to explain to Imlach that the puck had dropped, Imlach wasn't having any part of it. "Pucks don't drop!" he told Bower.

T he debut of the mask in 1959 gave netminders like Jacques Plante, who introduced it, the will to continue playing in this era of terrible new offensive weapons. The innovation didn't exactly sweep the league. A mask was considered all right for practices,

but not for games. Although Terry Sawchuk donned the device during the Original Six era, veterans like Johnny Bower and Glenn Hall only wore one at the very end of their careers, in the expansion era. It took hold most firmly among the young prospects still making their way toward the professional ranks. Even then, some of them had to be convinced the hard way of the mask's appropriateness in the evolving world of slapshots and curved sticks. Gerry Cheevers would become famous in Boston for his face mask adorned with stitches, which became a visceral public image of the carnage the mask prevented. But when Cheevers came up to the professional game in 1961, like the majority of goaltenders he was still playing barefaced. In his first exhibition game with the Leafs, Leo Boivin of Boston hit him above the eye with a shot that dazed him and required stitches. He had never been cut in his amateur days. Cheevers carried on barefaced, but was finally convinced of the need for the mask while playing for the Leafs' American League farm team, the Rochester Americans. In a January 1965 game, Cheevers was nailed by a shot from Red Berenson of the Springfield Indians. It wasn't a slapshot but a backhand; it knocked out three upper and three lower teeth and cut him for thirty-five stitches. "It was a mess," he would write. "I was spitting blood and teeth as they led me to

Continued on page 102

JOHNNY BOWER SHUTS THE DOOR ON THE MONTREAL CANADIENS. HE WAS A CLASSIC STANDUP GOALTENDER. "IF WE WENT DOWN," HE SAYS, "WE GOT UP REAL QUICK."

GUMP WORSLEY

BEST REMEMBERED AS A STANLEY CUP STANDOUT WITH THE CANADIENS, HE FIRST HAD TO SERVE ELEVEN SEASONS IN THE "JAILHOUSE" OF NEW YORK

Lorne "Gump" Worsley had an evocative way of describing his job: when he was in the crease, he was "in the barrel." He made the ride over the NHL's Niagara Falls 932 times, and despite a few crash landings and some scary leaks, after twenty-one seasons he was able to walk away with his body and mind intact.

Worsley was the hard-living product of a dirt-poor Depression childhood. He dabbled in juvenile delinquency in Montreal's working-class north end neighbourhood of Point St. Charles, and quit school to go to work at fourteen. He picked up the nickname "Gump" as a kid, his flat-top brushcut reminding a friend of the cartoon character Andy Gump.

He didn't start playing goal until his final year of Juvenile eligibility, when a coach told him he was too small to play any other position. Despite being a native Montrealer, he was no fan of the Canadiens. His parents were from Scotland, and his dad had followed the old Maroons, the city's anglo team. Although he saw Bill Durnan play at the Forum, his netminding idols were Frank Brimsek of the Bruins and Davey Kerr, the old Rangers star.

The family was so poor—Worsley's father was out of work for five years during the 1930s—that he had to borrow goalie equipment from the Montreal Boys Association when he tried out for the Quebec Junior A's Verdun Cyclones. When he made the team, he was the only English-speaking kid in the lineup, and the experience taught him French in a hurry.

Verdun was a newly minted farm team of the New York Rangers, which made it Worsley's destiny to play for the star-crossed Rangers teams of the 1950s, which were nothing like the ones Kerr had starred on. At five-seven, Worsley was shaped like the barrel in which he imagined himself riding. He covered the net in an acrobatic style, standing out in an era in which the standup style was de rigueur.

Despite being cast against type, he made steady progress in the Rangers system, but in 1953 he suffered the first of several professional indignities. In 1952, Worsley had been brought up from the Saskatoon Quakers of the minor pro Pacific Coast league to replace the veteran Chuck Rayner. While his GA in his debut season was a mediocre 3.06, this was New York he was toiling for, and he earned the league's Calder Trophy. Worsley was astonished when Rangers GM Frank Boucher decided to send him to the Vancouver Canucks of the Western Hockey League instead of playing him in New York the very next season. Boucher had decided to try instead a new signing from the American League, Johnny Bower. Boucher's latest find had an even better season on paper than Worsley's, with a GA of 2.60. But then it was Bower's turn to be baffled as he was shipped back to the American League and Worsley was retrieved from Vancouver for 1954/55.

This time Worsley was able to stick with the starting job, but it wasn't necessarily a change for the better. The team as a whole struggled under the erratic leadership of coach Phil Watson, and the strain of losing season after season got to Worsley. After 1958, Worsley has recalled, "The next three years were pure misery for me—the darkest of my career. I was doing a lot of drinking then, using the bottle to chase all those bad games and bad goals."

Publicly, Worsley came across as an impish, happy-go-lucky sort; privately, the game weighed on him as heavily as it did any goaltender. "I suffered fits of depression after many losses. I found it hard to sleep. I'd toss and turn in bed, get up and have a smoke, pace the floor, and then climb back into bed. Instead of counting sheep, I'd

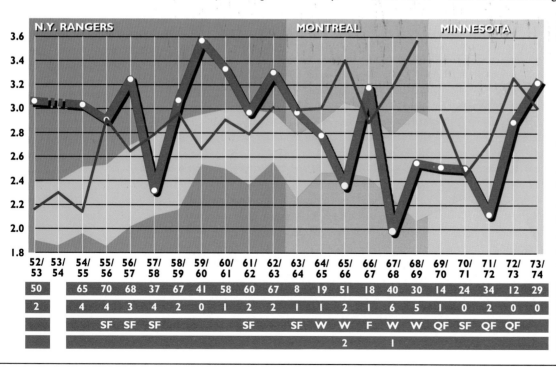

	52/53	53/54	54/55	55/56	56/57	57/58	58/59	59/60	60/61	61/62	62/63	63/64	64/65	65/66	66/67	67/68	68/69	69/70	70/71	71/72	72/73	73/74
GAMES	50		65	70	68	37	67	41	58	60	67	8	19	51	18	40	30	14	24	34	12	29
SHUTOUTS	2		4	4	3	4	2	0	1	2	2	1	1	2	6	5	1	0	2	0	0
STANLEY CUP			SF	SF	SF				SF		SF		W	W	F	W	W	QF	SF	QF	QF	
ALL STAR TEAM														2	1							

find myself seeing the pucks that beat me or almost tore my head off."

Worsley suffered facial cuts requiring more than 200 stitches during his career, but when Jacques Plante introduced the mask to the league in 1959, Worsley was one of the fraternity's diehard critics of the new device. When anyone asked him why he didn't wear a mask, his standard reply was: "My face is a mask."

His life and career were delivered a badly needed reprieve on June 4, 1963, a date Worsley would refer to as "the day I got out of the Rangers jailhouse." Worsley was part of a seven-player deal between the Rangers and the Canadiens that saw a stunned Jacques Plante go to New York and an ecstatic Worsley return to his home town.

The trade, initially at least, didn't work out well for either goaltender. Plante boasted about winning yet another Vezina, but found out how hard it is to keep a GA below 3.00 when playing for the Rangers. After a season and a half, New York sent him to Baltimore of the American League, thereby provoking his retirement. As for Worsley, a hamstring injury at the start of the 1963/64 season sent him to the Quebec Aces of the American League for what was supposed to be a recuperative stint. It turned into a season and a half in the minors as Plante's former backup, Charlie Hodge, took the starting job and won a Vezina.

Worsley finally got a taste of hockey glory in the 1964/65 Stanley Cup. After playing only nineteen games for the Canadiens that season, he was expected to carry Montreal through the playoffs. A torn thigh muscle put him out of action for three games of the final against Chicago. Coach Toe Blake then dumbfounded the recuperating Worsley by tapping him, rather than Hodge, for a ride in the barrel in game seven. Worsley shut out the Blackhawks 4–0 and learned, at last, what it was to be a champion.

He repeated the experience in 1965/66 and in 1967/68, winning the Vezina in both seasons—the first time with Hodge, the second time with Rogie Vachon. He also made the All Star team in both seasons. But Worsley also had the dubious privilege of being the winning goaltender in two Stanley Cups in which the losing goaltender won the Conn Smythe. Detroit's Roger Crozier won it in 1965/66, Glenn Hall of St. Louis in 1967/68. Worsley was annoyed on both occasions. In the 1965/66 playoffs, Worsley would recall, "I'd played all ten playoff games and had allowed only twenty goals. Roger had given up twenty-six in twelve games and

wound up on the losing team." In the 1967/68 playoffs, Worsley couldn't help but note that his GA was 1.88, while Hall's was 2.43.

The November following the Stanley Cup victory over St. Louis, Worsley suffered a nervous breakdown. Expansion in 1967 now meant lots of time in airplanes, of which Worsley was petrified, and the cumulative seasons of stress were provoking hallucinations. It all caught up with him on a flight from Montreal to Los Angeles. When the Canadiens' flight stopped over in Chicago, Worsley got off, announced his retirement, got on a train and returned to Montreal. For the next month, he visited a psychiatrist every day to conquer his anxieties and control his fear of flying. When Montreal tried to demote him to its new Montreal Voyageurs American League farm team the next season, Worsley quit.

He was then drafted by the Minnesota North Stars, and made a four-season comeback, teamed with the lanky Cesare Maniago in a pairing known as "Mutt and Jeff." In his final season, 1973/74, Worsley gave in to the arguments of his wife and donned a mask. The final goal scored on him, number 2,624, was from the stick of Philadelphia enforcer Dave Schultz. Worsley noted that Schultz was born in 1949, the year he had played his first professional game. He was forty-four when he climbed out of the barrel for the last time. His election to the Hockey Hall of Fame came in 1980. Today, the Gumper lives in Montreal. ○

WORSLEY KEEPS HIS EYE ON THE JOB DURING HIS YEARS IN THE NEW YORK RANGERS "JAILHOUSE."

Continued from page 99

the infirmary. I can still see a couple of those teeth landing in my glove." Cheevers embarked on two seasons of
experimenting to come up with a mask he could live
with.

A BURNT-OUT CASE:
TERRY SAWCHUK'S
CAREER WAS ALL TOO
TYPICAL IN THE GOAL-
TENDING TRADE IN THE
EARLY 1950s. AFTER
FIVE SUPERB SEASONS,
HE WAS CONSIDERED
WASHED UP.

Contriving a suitable mask was partly a matter of
overcoming the visibility limitations that had foiled
Clint Benedict back in 1930. Like many experienced
goaltenders donning a mask for the first time, Cheevers
found it restricted his vision when he looked down at his
feet. He finally found one he liked through Bruins alum-
nus Woody Dumart, who had a sporting goods store in
Boston. A former plumber named Ernie Higgins had
come into the store one day to show Dumart a mask
he'd made for his son. Dumart put Higgins in touch
with Cheevers; for $125 Cheevers had a mask he liked
and Higgins had a newfound career supplying other
NHL goaltenders, like Eddie Johnston, Les Binkley, Al
Smith and Doug Favell. Cheevers' experience was typi-

cal. For years masks were custom made by garage-based
entrepreneurs or even goaltenders themselves, rather than
mass-produced.

But the advent of the mask also required a change
in the goaltenders' mentality. In 1964, Clint Benedict
rejected the idea that machismo had held off the perfec-
tion of the mask. "We took such a beating anyway that
nobody would have thought it sissified," he said. "No, it
was a case of not developing one that was practical." But
Cheevers saw hockey culture as definitely playing a role
in the mask's slow acceptance. By the fall of 1967, when
he first wore a model he could live with at the Bruins'
training camp, "most of the stigma attached to mask-
wearing had disappeared. And there was a stigma—or, at
least, there had been." As Ed Giacomin recalls, wearing a
mask could get you labelled "chicken." When someone
asked Plante if wearing a mask made him a coward, he
shot back: Does jumping out of an airplane without a
parachute make you brave?

A BREED APART | 102

League managers and owners were slow to recognize that employing more than one steady goaltender would be a sensible solution to the game's rising number of burnouts. And goaltenders in general helped the old system persist by demanding to play every game possible—partly out of pride, partly out of not wanting to have to compete for their job with an equal on the roster. For nearly two decades after the war, teams were content to stick with a single starter, and if he could no longer cut it, there was always some other young hopeful willing to give it a go. Frank Boucher had tried to buck that trend in New York, using both Chuck Rayner and Sugar Jim Henry after the war, but in the end the accountants deemed it too expensive and Henry was traded to Chicago. The stability in goaltending ranks that took hold in the mid-1950s seemed to obviate, for a time, any need to provide relief. And the arrival of the mask, which gave some of the position's great stars the nerve to stay at the job, cut down further on turnover.

It wasn't until the early 1960s that the NHL again began to see tag-team goaltending lineups in the manner of Rayner and Henry. In Toronto, Don Simmons, who had been acquired from Boston, came to share a significant part of the netminding workload with Johnny Bower, playing twenty-eight games in 1962/63 and twenty-one in 1963/64, and making valued contributions to the Stanley Cup wins in both seasons.

The most famous, and most influential, tag-team approach arose in Toronto in 1964, when Maple Leafs GM and coach Punch Imlach acquired Terry Sawchuk from Detroit to share the net with Bower. The NHL wanted teams to have two dressed-to-play goaltenders on hand for the 1964/65 playoffs, but they could still use only one during the season. Imlach was a genius at getting extra miles out of veteran players. Bower had been playing professionally since 1945, Sawchuk since 1947, and Imlach figured they could both produce excellent performances if only the NHL played a thirty-five-game season. To achieve the same end, Imlach split the goaltending assignment between them, and Toronto had the lowest GA in the league that year.

Imlach didn't have a schedule for who was playing when. He based his decision on who would start the game on how the goaltenders performed in the pregame warmup. "I needed about thirty to forty shots to get warmed up," says Bower. "With Terry, about ten seemed to be enough. He was ready." Notes Dave Keon, who began his fifth season with the Leafs when Sawchuk came aboard, "With Terry, the fewer shots in warmup the better. John wanted as close to game conditions as possible." It worked out that in 1964/65 Sawchuk played thirty-six games, Bower thirty-four.

When the league tried to give Sawchuk the 1964/65 Vezina, since he had played two more games for Toronto than Bower, he refused it. It had been Bower's shutout performance in the final game of the season that allowed the Leafs to permit two fewer goals-against than Detroit rookie Roger Crozier, who played every game for the Red Wings. Sawchuk wanted

Bower's name on the trophy, too, and the prize money split between them. (Bower also had the lower GA of the pair, 2.38 to Sawchuk's 2.56.) The league acquiesced, and not only changed the rules of the Vezina, but recognized the wisdom in Imlach's strategy, regardless of the age of the players, and made it mandatory the following season for teams to dress two goaltenders for each regular-season game.

The two-dressed-to-play rule helped ease in a new generation of netminders just as the league prepared itself for expansion. Gerry Cheevers, Ed Giacomin and Bernie Parent, among others, made their first appearances in the waning years of the Original Six, so that when the league doubled in size in 1967, and kept on growing, they had the experience of the league at its most intensely competitive. During the 1960s, the difference between Vezina-winning GAs and the LGA was routinely three-tenths of a goal or less, and stayed that way until 1969/70, when the diluted talent of the expansion years began driving a statistical wedge between the very best goaltending and LGA.

In 1964/65, a new prize was added to the league's silverware collection: the Conn Smythe Trophy, awarded to the most valuable player in the Stanley Cup playoffs in the opinion of the league board of governors. Remarkably, in only its second season, the Smythe was awarded to Roger Crozier, whose Red Wings had lost the series 4–2 to Montreal. Two seasons later, in 1967/68, the board of governors again awarded the trophy to a member of the losing team, and again, the recipient was a goaltender, Glenn Hall of the new expansion club, the St. Louis Blues. Goaltenders have long figured prominently in the trophy's history. Of the thirty recipients to date, ten have been in the net.

For many observers, the glory years of the Original Six era also came to represent the glory of the goaltending trade. The netminders faced the fully developed slapshot, propelled by an alarmingly curved stick. Few wore a face mask, and the equipment, despite having evolved considerably, was still cumbersome; leg pads were two inches narrower then and the catching glove didn't cover nearly the area of open net it does today. The four-by-eight crease was much smaller than the six-foot-radius semicircle introduced to the NHL in 1987/88, and the safety of the goaltender did not have the priority it enjoys in today's game. The three goaltenders most commonly cited as the greatest ever—Glenn Hall, Jacques Plante and Terry Sawchuk—were synonymous with the era. But if goaltending's glory years are behind it, Hall, now the goaltending coach of the Calgary Flames, is not one to say so. "The position," he says, "has never been played better." ○

THE MASSIVELY CURVED STICK OF THE 1960s (THIS ONE WIELDED BY CURVE INNOVATOR STAN MIKITA) MADE THE GOALTENDER'S JOB EVEN MORE HELLISH, IF THAT WERE POSSIBLE. THIS SCYTHE TURNED THE SLAPSHOT INTO A FASTBALL THAT BEHAVED LIKE A KNUCKLEBALL.

WELCOME TO THE SHOOTING GALLERY

KING OF PAIN

TERRY SAWCHUK EXEMPLIFIED THE DARKER ELEMENTS THAT MAKE FOR GREAT GOALTENDING

WHEN GOALTENDERS ARE ASKED TO NAME THE GREATEST PLAYER AT THEIR POSITION, EVER, THEIR OPINIONS ARE INEVITABLY SHAPED BY THE PARTICULAR ERAS IN WHICH THEY PLAYED. TERRY

Sawchuk is one exception who manages to rise above all eras. On January 28, 1952, Frank Boucher, who had played against the likes of Georges Vezina and gone on to coach and manage in the era of Frank Brimsek, Bill Durnan and Chuck Rayner, dispensed with all equivocation. "Terry Sawchuk is the greatest goalie in the history of league hockey," he pronounced.

On paper, Sawchuk's career was not distinguished with quite the same superlatives as his fellow Original Sixers Jacques Plante and Glenn Hall. In his first five full NHL seasons, during which Boucher made his pronouncement, he was sensational, earning an All Star berth in every one of them. He was the first goaltender since Brimsek both to win the Calder and to land on the first All Star team in his rookie season. He also won three Vezinas in five seasons, being edged out by a single goal in the other two. But the last fifteen seasons of his career were a constant struggle to reaffirm his greatness. In the end, he died tragically, broken by life and by the game, a sobering example of the burden an overwhelming talent can place on a player's shoulders, and also of the darker elements that can make for great goaltending.

Born in 1929 in Winnipeg, Sawchuk was raised in the north end neighbourhood of Morse Place, excelling on both the rink and the ball diamond. He was such a good baseball player that he would attract tryout offers from the St. Louis Cardinals and the Pittsburgh Pirates. One of his opponents in minor league hockey in Winnipeg was Don Rope, who went on to play hockey for Canada in two Olympics.

"When Terry's team was well ahead in the second period," says Rope, "he'd take his goal pads off, leave on his goal skates and play defence. That amazed me, that he could play with those skates on."

His talent was apparent so early that

he scarcely had a chance to have an amateur career. Professional hockey was desperate for new recruits at the end of the Second World War, and Sawchuk was swept up in one of the successive waves of Canadian teenagers who turned professional at the time. Detroit already had its eye on him when he was twelve. At fifteen he was playing Junior hockey for the Winnipeg Rangers. His professional rights were secured by Detroit, and he was transferred to Galt in the Junior A OHA. Detroit then moved him to the Windsor Junior Spitfires, but the season had just begun when the Red Wings signed the seventeen-year-old to a professional contract and shipped him to Omaha of the U.S. League, a midwestern loop, in 1947.

After winning rookie of the year honours in the U.S. League, he moved up a notch to the Indianapolis Capitals of the American League, where he won his second straight rookie of the year award in 1948/49. "Sawchuk displayed remarkable fortitude during the late stages of the season, playing his position although suffering painful injuries, which only forced him to miss one game," noted the league's 1949/50 statistical "red book" of his rookie-season performance. In Omaha, he had nearly had his career ended by a three-stitch cut to his eye. There would be no shortage of injuries over the remainder of his career. A bad fracture in his right arm, suffered as a kid playing football, necessitated three operations and caused the arm to heal two inches shorter than the left one, and his elbow would be a ceaseless source of bone chips—about sixty in all (some twenty of which Sawchuk collected in a jar and displayed on his mantel).

Sawchuk would experience a punctured lung in a car accident in 1954, torn tendons in his hand, an emergency appendectomy, ruptured spinal discs and a wide assortment of facial cuts. In 1966, *Life* magazine published a photo of Sawchuk with his face a mass of scars, most of them convincingly added by a makeup artist to illustrate what Sawchuk would look like if he hadn't followed Jacques Plante's lead and started to wear a mask. But Sawchuk's scars ran much deeper than those an artist could apply. He was plagued by injuries, but also defined by them. Privately, some goaltenders feel that pain was not simply a consequence of the job for Sawchuk, but actually *was* the job. He felt it, and in some terrible symbiosis, embraced it in a way that no goaltender had since Roy Worters. The essential darkness of his career was foreshadowed by the death from heart failure of his seventeen-year-old brother Mike when Terry was just ten. Sawchuk inherited his goaltending equipment, and so set forth on his career in a dead man's armour.

He was called up for seven games by Detroit in 1949/50, when Harry Lumley sprained his ankle. The Red Wings won the Stanley Cup on their third successive attempt that spring with Lumley, but Sawchuk was so startling a young talent that Detroit general manager Jack Adams dealt away Lumley to Chicago while he was still hot to make room for Sawchuk. A few months shy of his twenty-first birthday, Sawchuk had a starting job in the NHL.

In his third professional league, Sawchuk won yet another rookie of the year trophy, led the league with eleven shutouts, produced a GA of 1.99, one goal shy of the Vezina, and made the first All Star team. The next season, Sawchuk played a central role as Detroit capped its fourth straight regular-season title by sweeping Montreal in four games in the cup final. The Red Wings didn't lose one playoff game, and in his eight appearances, Sawchuk allowed only five goals. His 1.90 GA for the season brought him the Vezina and a return to the first All Star team.

In 1951/52, "Boom Boom" Geoffrion was rookie of the year as he brought the slapshot into the postwar game. Sawchuk's unorthodox style—the "gorilla crouch" that saw him compress his body so that his face was well down below the crossbar—allowed him to keep his eye on incoming pucks, but in the new era of the slapshot and aggressive screening of the goaltender, the technique took extraordinary nerve.

Detroit won yet another season title in 1952/53; Sawchuk, with his 1.90 GA, picked up another Vezina and still another first-team All Star appearance. But in only his third season, the game was taking its toll. A big man, he had ballooned to nearly 230 pounds in Omaha, and at training camp in 1951/52 weighed in at 220. He'd gotten down to 195 that season, and in 1952/53 he resolved to lose weight again. He shed it at an alarming rate, dropping below 170. Gaunt and temperamental, Sawchuk

made the second All Star team, missed the Vezina by one goal again and saw the team through to another Stanley Cup victory.

In 1954/55, Sawchuk made another second-team appearance, earned his third Vezina and helped Detroit win another Stanley Cup in a seven-game final against Montreal. But the greatest goaltender ever was coming apart. After surrendering eight goals to the Bruins in February 1955, the worst performance of his career, the Red Wings gave him a holiday to pull himself together. While Sawchuk was recuperating, Detroit brought in prospect Glenn Hall. Hall was so good that Detroit viewed Sawchuk as another Lumley: still a hot property who should be traded to make way for fresh talent. The Bruins, in the market for a goaltender, negotiated with Detroit for one, thinking the tight-lipped Adams was prepared to deal Hall. They were amazed when it turned out to be Sawchuk, who was part of a record nine-player swap between the two clubs.

It was a professional and personal catastrophe for Sawchuk. The Bruins were entering some lean seasons, winning only twenty-three of seventy games in 1954/55 and 1955/56. In 1955/56, Sawchuk's first season in Boston, the Bruins missed the playoffs and for the second straight season didn't put a single player in the top-ten scorers' list. Things actually went well for Sawchuk in 1955/56, as he played sixty-eight games and recorded a reasonable GA of 2.66, with nine shutouts, but it was his first full NHL season in which his GA wasn't below 2.00.

In his second Boston season, Sawchuk tired visibly. In December, he was diagnosed with mononucleosis and hospitalised for two weeks. When it came time to return to play, he couldn't find his form and withdrew into a shell, saying he was quitting the game. His own physician declared he was "on the verge of a complete nervous breakdown." Boston GM Milt Schmidt suspended him

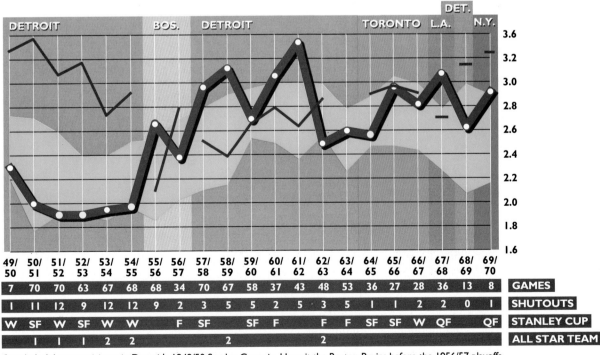

	49/50	50/51	51/52	52/53	53/54	54/55	55/56	56/57	57/58	58/59	59/60	60/61	61/62	62/63	63/64	64/65	65/66	66/67	67/68	68/69	69/70	
GAMES	7	70	70	63	67	68	68	34	70	67	58	37	43	48	53	36	27	28	36	13	8	
SHUTOUTS	1	11	12	9	12	12	9	2	3	5	5	2	5	3	5	1	1	2	2	0	1	
STANLEY CUP	W	SF	W	SF	W	W		F	SF		SF	F		F	F	SF	SF	W	QF		QF	
ALL STAR TEAM		1	1	1	2	2			2						2							

Sawchuk did not participate in Detroit's 1949/50 Stanley Cup win. He quit the Boston Bruins before the 1956/57 playoffs.

could be close to his wife and children again. He got his way. Detroit sold Hall to Chicago and brought Sawchuk home. In 1959, Sawchuk became an American citizen.

Sawchuk never completely recovered from his purgatory in Boston. He always seemed frailer than he had before mononucleosis had sidelined him; he was certainly leaner, and his accumulating injuries did not help. Nor would he ever again post the kind of save statistics that had distinguished his first five seasons in Detroit. As well, the Red Wings he returned to were not the Red Wings of the early 1950s. In his first season back, Detroit finished third overall and were swept by Montreal in the semifinal. The team finished last in 1958/59, missed the playoffs again in 1961/62 and finished fourth in the intervening seasons. Gone were the days when Sawchuk could record a season GA below 2.00. For two seasons in fact, it rose above 3.00.

But Sawchuk was not finished. He was still capable of a game-saving performance, and his decision to follow Jacques Plante's lead and begin wearing a mask in games (he'd been wearing one in practice for several seasons) in 1962/63 gave him renewed confidence. The Red Wings made it to the Stanley Cup finals in 1962/63 and 1963/64; his 1962/63 season was as good as any he had experienced in nearly a decade as he made the second All Star team.

In December 1963, Sawchuk followed up an early-season slump with a bout of back trouble. The Red Wings tried out a new goaltender, Roger Crozier, for fifteen games, and while his GA was 3.40, compared to the 2.60 of Sawchuk, the twenty-two-year-old Crozier was the franchise's future. At the end of the season, Detroit elected to leave the thirty-five-year-old Sawchuk off its protected list. Punch Imlach snapped him up and made him a Maple Leaf.

Imlach already had one veteran goaltender, Johnny Bower, on the roster, and even though the league did not require teams to employ two goaltenders in the regular

DOWN BUT NOT OUT: TERRY SAWCHUK DISPLAYS A TRADEMARK FEARLESSNESS IN THE DETROIT GOAL.

indefinitely after he failed to show up for a practice, but showed sympathy by allowing that Sawchuk's mental health problems, if legitimate, would give him an out.

Sawchuk fled back to the Detroit suburb of Union Lake, where his American wife, Patricia, and children lived. He was so upset by his treatment in the Boston press that he threatened to file lawsuits. Patricia also filed for divorce. Sawchuk was able to patch up the marriage, and asked that he be traded back to Detroit so that he season, Imlach had found success using Don Simmons to relieve Bower for fifty-eight games over the previous three seasons. With the thirty-five-year-old Sawchuk and the forty-year-old Bower, Imlach now had two star veterans who could relieve each other. They ended up splitting the season almost exactly down the middle, and together they won the Vezina.

Sawchuk and Bower were very different goaltenders. Sawchuk was a bigger, rangier man. Bower was a practice goaltender—he worked hard when a game wasn't on the line, which is what Punch Imlach liked to see in any player. Sawchuk wanted nothing to do with the puck when the shooting didn't count. A dozen shots would constitute a pregame warmup for him. His mechanics were always fundamentally there. What mattered was whether or not Sawchuk, on that night against that team, was prepared to make the sacrifices one of his great performances demanded. Sawchuk had been hurt badly time and again, and seemed to understand that pain, or the willingness to experience pain, was an inextricable part of his game. He didn't need someone shooting at him to figure out if he could stop a game full of pucks. He just had to decide he was prepared to stop the ones ahead of him that night in any way possible. His donning of the mask, long before contemporaries like Bower, Worsley and Hall joined him in following Plante's lead, was his one significant concession to his own well-being.

In 1966/67, Sawchuk was at the heart of the Leafs' return to Stanley Cup glory. The team, overwhelmingly staffed by veterans, finished third overall, with nine fewer wins and sixty fewer total goals than the Blackhawks, who set a league scoring record. But in their semifinal series, the big guns of Chicago, with their menacing slapshots propelled by sticks curved like scythes, could not put enough pucks past Bower and Sawchuk, whose finest moment came in game five, with the series tied two-up. Bower played the first period, but Sawchuk took over in the second. Despite firing forty-nine shots at him over the final two periods, the Blackhawks could not score on him and lost 4–2.

"I'd never had any trouble scoring against Sawchuk, ever, while he was with Detroit," Bobby Hull recalled for writer D'Arcy Jenish. "We started the period on a power play and I drilled a shot that hit him in the shoulder, and he lay on the ice for about fifteen minutes. He got up and he was as loose as a goose. I had eleven shots on him and couldn't put a pea past him. I broke the handle of his stick twice. He was laying prone on the ice, and I fired one upstairs. He threw his leg up, and I stuck the puck right on the end of his skate. He just played fantastic." The win broke the back of the Blackhawks, and Toronto went on to meet Montreal in the final.

Sawchuk started the opening game and bore the brunt of a 6–0 loss. Imlach switched to Bower, who helped them take the series lead. When Bower strained a muscle warming up for game four, Sawchuk stepped in, and surrendered another six goals as Montreal tied the series. But Imlach stuck with Sawchuk, and gave him the assignment for game five in Montreal. It was the right decision: Toronto won 4–1, and returned home to win the last Stanley Cup of the Original Six era with Sawchuk backstopping a 3–1 win. Sawchuk had just won his first Stanley Cup in twelve seasons. In voting for the Conn Smythe Trophy, awarded to the most valuable player of the playoffs, he was edged out by Dave Keon, but Leaf management awarded him its J.P. Bickell Trophy as the team's top player. In the dressing room after the victory, he announced that he didn't care if he never played another game. "I'm going to leave it in good style," he decided.

The Leafs had been able to win because Sawchuk, particularly against Chicago, had been willing to go out and inflict on himself whatever harm was necessary. His capacity for the physical abuse that came with the position seemed infinite, but it wasn't. He might not have cared to play another game after the 1966/67 Stanley Cup, but he tried to, and there was no glory in it.

His life rapidly unravelled. In the expansion draft he was picked up by Los Angeles, whose coach, Red Kelly, had been on the ice with Sawchuk the previous spring in the Leaf cup victory. In a game against the Blackhawks in the dreaded Chicago Stadium, a shot by Pit Martin hit him in the mask so hard that both of his eyes closed up with the swelling. His old team, Detroit, retrieved him for 1968/69, but he only saw action in thirteen games.

When the pain was no longer delivered by the game, it was as if Sawchuk had to inflict the pain upon himself. The Rangers signed him on for 1969/70, but by then Sawchuk was battling the bottle and was deeply despondent, separated from his wife, cut off from his seven children. At the end of the season, in which he played only eight games, he brought the roof down on himself. Sawchuk had been sharing a rented house on Long Island with teammate Ron Stewart, and they fell into an argument about money owed on the rent and Sawchuk's lack of enthusiasm for cleaning the place up before they vacated it. Sawchuk attacked Stewart, at first outside a neighbourhood bar, again on the lawn of the house. In the confused scuffle, Sawchuk injured himself falling on either Stewart's knee or a barbecue. He was rushed to hospital, where his gall bladder was removed, but a lacerated liver meant two more trips into the operating room. After a month in hospital, Sawchuk died. A formal investigation was held into Stewart's role, but Sawchuk had completely exonerated him while in hospital, blaming himself entirely.

He was forty years old and had played 63,496 minutes of regular-season and playoff hockey in the NHL and allowed 2,668 goals. He had played in eleven All Star games, second only to Glenn Hall's thirteen appearances. He had 103 shutouts, nine more than George Hainsworth. He had appeared in the most regular-season games of any goaltender—971, 65 more than Glenn Hall. And he had 435 wins. Jacques Plante would fall short of tying his mark by one win.

Sawchuk had the swiftest election to the Hockey Hall of Fame of any player. He was enshrined the year after his death. ○

"Mr. Goalie"

Glenn Hall: the goaltender who "does it all"

PERHAPS NO GOALTENDER HAS HAD SO LASTING AN EFFECT ON HIS PROFESSION AS GLENN HALL. WHEN YOU WATCH ALMOST ANY STAR GOALTENDER TODAY, BE HE ED

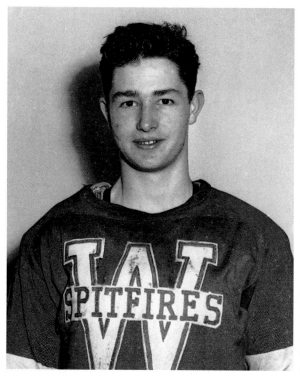

HALL CAME OUT OF HUMBOLDT, SASKATCHEWAN, TO PLAY FOR THE WINDSOR SPITFIRES, THE RED WINGS' JUNIOR AFFILIATE ACROSS THE DETROIT RIVER.

Belfour or Felix Potvin, you are watching someone whose technical skills descend in a straight line from Hall's revolutionary butterfly style. If their puck-handling, particularly with their stick, is noteworthy, there, too, they owe a debt to Hall. And if they show daring in their peregrinations from the crease, and skill in their skating, Hall is in them there, too. Most important, if they approach their profession methodically, with the most careful preparation, they should know that Hall was there before them, as prepared as anyone for the job at hand.

Hall did not have an exclusive claim to goaltending's fundamentals, but he embodied all of them in a way that few practitioners ever have. His monicker "Mr. Goalie" was entirely deserved. Glenn Hall was everything a great goaltender was supposed to be.

His greatness was impressively consistent. He won the Calder and made the second All Star team when he played his first full NHL season in 1955/56; thirteen seasons later, in 1968/69, he won his third Vezina and made the first All Star team, his eleventh such appearance. And in his final season, 1970/71, he was still at the top of the class, capable, if he had been so inclined, to go right on playing and winning.

Born in Humboldt, Saskatchewan, in 1931, Hall came from a corner of Canada that produced a bumper crop of hockey players in general and goaltenders in particular. The province had produced Johnny Bower in 1924, Emile Francis and Al Rollins in 1926, and Chuck Rayner in 1920. It was Rayner who made a lasting impression upon him when Hall visited the goaltending camp Rayner and his business and netminding partner, Jim Henry, ran out of their fishing camp, Hockey Haven, on Lake of the Woods in northwestern Ontario

in the late 1940s. Today Hall ranks Rayner second to Terry Sawchuk in all-time goaltending talent. Hall was playing Junior hockey in Windsor, Ontario, at the time, and made the trip to Hockey Haven in the company of another young goalkeeper, Bill Tibbs. "The goalkeepers were more of a fraternity then," Hall says. "We drove up, and they were just really, really nice to us."

There was less emphasis in that encounter with Rayner and Henry on particular tricks of the trade than on a general approach to the profession. Rayner was famous with the Rangers for his aggressive approach to the game, which was anchored in his skating and stick skills. These would become fundamental skills for Hall as well. "If you can't skate, you're not going to be a very good goalkeeper," he maintains. "If you can skate, you can adapt to the conditions thrown at you." And as the slapshot came to the fore, skating skill became an essential part of the goaltender's ability to adjust his style to the radically altered offensive strategies and the pressures they placed on him. Puck-handling with the stick also became critical. "I remember how strong Charlie Rayner was with the stick. I didn't really learn to use the stick until I was thirty years old, partly because I wasn't strong enough.

"When I'm talking to young players," Hall adds, "the first things I stress are skating and effort. In the old days, the expression was: Don't think, because you'll weaken the club. Do everything that's automatic. It's about preparation, getting the mind set properly. I don't particularly care for kids coming to the rink and saying, 'I hope I play well.' They should be saying, 'I *should* play well. I've practised well, I know the opposition, I'm in good shape, I've looked after myself, I've eaten properly.' It's no guarantee that you *will* play well, but at least you're prepared."

"Glenn took the job really seriously," says Dave Dryden, who was Hall's backup in Chicago in the 1960s before Dryden became a regular starter with the expansion Buffalo Sabres. "Some of the ways goaltenders took it seriously destroyed them. Glenn's way was to be well rested and prepared and to look after himself."

Hall began his professional career in 1951 with the American League's Indianapolis Capitals, a troubled outfit embarking on its final season. He then moved for three seasons to the Edmonton Flyers of the Western Hockey League, a very good tier-two loop that emerged after the Second World War. The team boasted an exceptionally talented lineup of future NHL stars, including Hall, Johnny Bucyk, Vic Stasiuk and Norm Ullman. He saw minimal action with the NHL team that owned his rights, the Red Wings, coming up for six games in 1952/53 and two games in 1954/55. In those years, Detroit had Sawchuk, who had also played Junior hockey briefly in Windsor. But Detroit was burning out Sawchuk, who had entered the NHL in 1949, and traded him to Boston in 1955 in a four-for-five swap that helped overhaul the lineup that had just won Detroit the Stanley Cup. Sawchuk was the cornerstone of the deal, having just won his third Vezina in four seasons. With Sawchuk out of the way, Hall came up to the big league.

He had a superb rookie season in 1955/56, winning the Calder and making the second All Star team as he played all seventy games for Detroit and recorded twelve shutouts and a GA of 2.11. Detroit made it to the cup final again, but the Canadiens, with the new Vezina winner, Jacques Plante, in net, took the series in five games. Montreal would win five straight cups, and Plante five straight Vezinas.

Hall took his place in the elite ranks of goaltending as the slapshot was completely overhauling traditional notions about offence, and with it defence. "The game changed," says Hall. "You were looking at more screens, and then I got into the butterfly kind of by accident."

The butterfly style, pioneered by Hall while in Detroit, did not immediately supplant more traditional goaltending techniques, but it took hold with the next generation of players, in particular Tony Esposito, and is the essential inspiration for the inverted-V style and outright butterfly of today's goaltenders. It was widely disparaged because it broke—or seemed to break—two sacred tenets of goaltending: you stayed on your feet, and your kept your legs together. But notwithstanding the rules on how goaltenders were supposed to play, the fact was that so-called standup goaltenders often found themselves on the ice, as any survey of game photos will reveal. And they often had their legs apart. With the butterfly, the lanky Hall, who was six feet tall and weighed about 160 pounds, had his feet widely spaced, but his knees close together with the pads backstopping the stick.

"People talk about the drop shot going between the legs," says Hall. "Well, any shot is capable of going between the legs. You had to play with your legs a little wider to pick up post shots. When you were playing with your legs wider apart, you were vulnerable to the 'five hole.' I found that with the legs open I

wasn't strong enough to stop the puck with the stick. If I did the butterfly, I could get the stick back to the pads." That, and his hands, took care of the five hole. And when he dropped to the ice, Hall kept his knees together and splayed his legs to either side, creating a leather wall ten inches high across the goal.

But it was still seen as falling to the ice, which grated on purists. "A lot of people call it going down, but it's not," he insists. "Your body is still erect." It's hard to argue with Hall. When traditional standup goaltenders went down, they tended to look completely helpless—lying on their stomachs, their sides, their backs, limbs flailing. Hall was still upright from the knees up, on the job, able to get back to his feet again quickly.

Hall lasted only two seasons in Detroit, despite being an All Star in both seasons. When an effort to form a league players' association was crushed in 1957, most vigorously by Jack Adams in Detroit, several organizers were banished to the Chicago Blackhawks, among them Ted Lindsay and Hall of the Red Wings in a six-player deal. In getting rid of Hall, Adams brought Sawchuk back from Boston. But Dryden suspected that the butterfly style, as much as any labour organizing, was behind Hall's trade. "I always thought that Glenn must have had some real run-ins in Detroit with the way he played. He had just started to use the butterfly style, and I had the feeling, from the way we talked, that Detroit management didn't think that was the way you played the game. But it's the enduring style. Glenn was right on so many blessed things. He was the best that I ever saw play. There's no question. He always seemed kind of tragic because he didn't get the recognition he should have had."

He came to play in one of hockey's truly unique environments: the cramped confines of Chicago

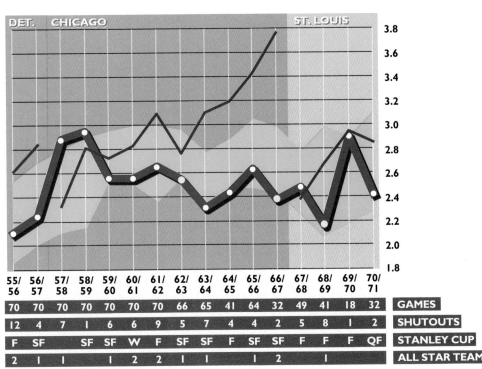

	55/ 56	56/ 57	57/ 58	58/ 59	59/ 60	60/ 61	61/ 62	62/ 63	63/ 64	64/ 65	65/ 66	66/ 67	67/ 68	68/ 69	69/ 70	70/ 71	
GAMES	70	70	70	70	70	70	70	66	65	41	64	32	49	41	18	32	GAMES
SHUTOUTS	12	4	7	1	6	6	9	5	7	4	4	2	5	8	1	2	SHUTOUTS
STANLEY CUP	F	SF		SF	SF	W	F	SF	SF	F	SF	SF	F	F	F	QF	STANLEY CUP
ALL STAR TEAM	2	1	1		1	2	2	1	1		1	2		1			ALL STAR TEAM

Hall played six games (with one shutout) for Detroit in 1952/53, and two games for Detroit in 1954/55.

The neck was an area even the best masks left vulnerable. One solution arrived at was a hinged guard that swung forward so that the goaltender could tilt his head down without the bottom of the mask hitting his chest. Billy Smith wore this one with the New York Islanders in 1976/77.

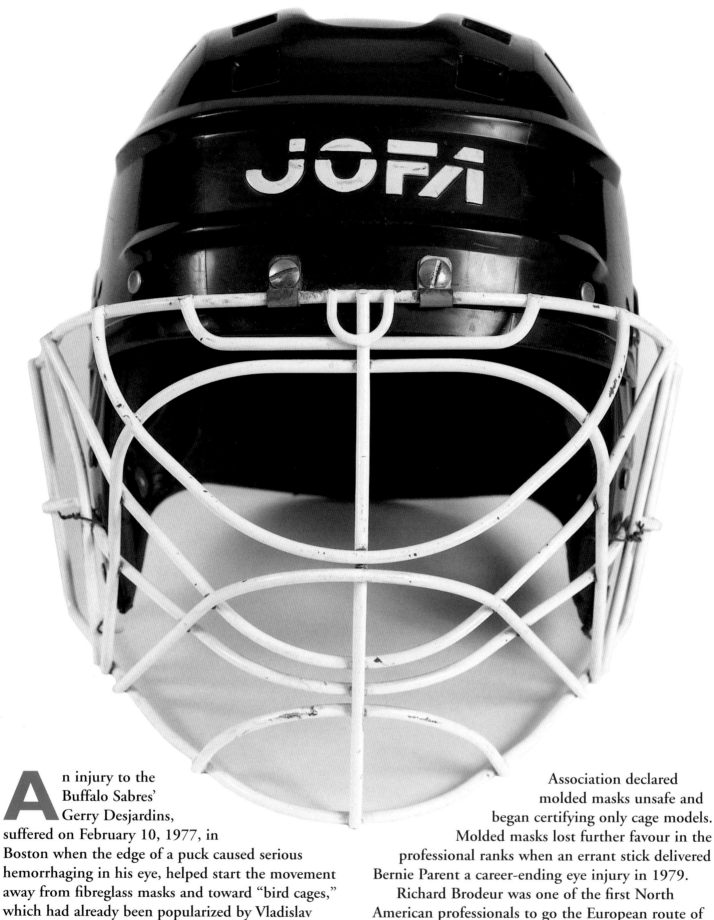

An injury to the Buffalo Sabres' Gerry Desjardins, suffered on February 10, 1977, in Boston when the edge of a puck caused serious hemorrhaging in his eye, helped start the movement away from fibreglass masks and toward "bird cages," which had already been popularized by Vladislav Tretiak in the 1972 Canada–Russia series.

In October 1978, the Canadian Standards Association declared molded masks unsafe and began certifying only cage models. Molded masks lost further favour in the professional ranks when an errant stick delivered Bernie Parent a career-ending eye injury in 1979.

Richard Brodeur was one of the first North American professionals to go the European route of wearing a cage/helmet, donning this model by Sweden's Jofa.

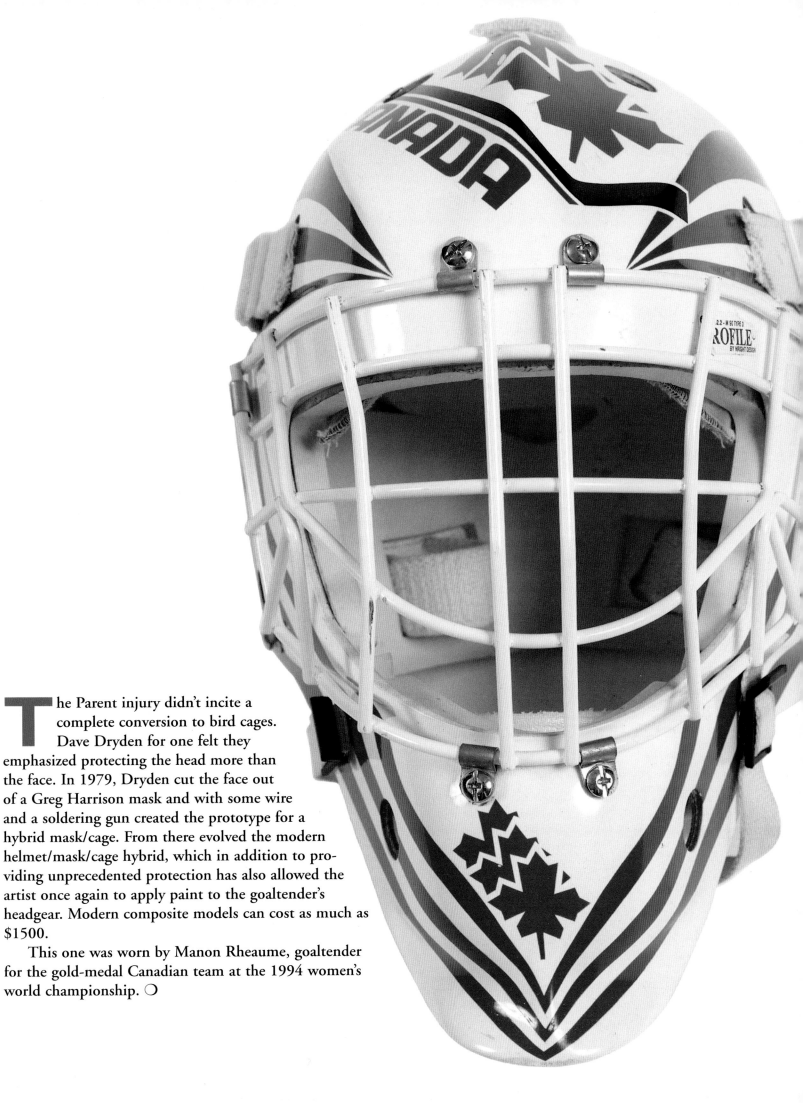

The Parent injury didn't incite a complete conversion to bird cages. Dave Dryden for one felt they emphasized protecting the head more than the face. In 1979, Dryden cut the face out of a Greg Harrison mask and with some wire and a soldering gun created the prototype for a hybrid mask/cage. From there evolved the modern helmet/mask/cage hybrid, which in addition to providing unprecedented protection has also allowed the artist once again to apply paint to the goaltender's headgear. Modern composite models can cost as much as $1500.

This one was worn by Manon Rheaume, goaltender for the gold-medal Canadian team at the 1994 women's world championship. ○

CHAPTER 7

1967/68–1980/81

The MORE *the* MERRIER

IN TEN YEARS, BIG-LEAGUE HOCKEY WENT FROM EMPLOYING SIX TO MORE THAN SIXTY FULL-TIME GOALTENDERS. BUT THERE WAS NO SECURITY IN NUMBERS

DAVE DRYDEN OF THE BUFFALO SABRES COUNTERS A BREAKAWAY BY THE VANCOUVER CANUCKS WITH A POKE CHECK. BOTH TEAMS JOINED THE NHL IN 1970. DRYDEN BECAME PART OF ANOTHER GREAT EXPANSION IN PROFESSIONAL HOCKEY WHEN HE CROSSED OVER TO THE WORLD HOCKEY ASSOCIATION IN 1974.

For two decades following the Second World War, goaltending was a profession with limited employment opportunities. The National Hockey League emerged from the war as a six-team loop; a territorial agreement with the American Hockey League limited its expansion opportunities in the east, and team owners were not interested in taking their product west of Lake Michigan. The AHL, for its part, had shrunk from a high of eleven teams to six teams after the war. This meant that there were only a dozen "elite" professional clubs offering jobs to goaltenders, and each club had only one such job to offer.

When the NHL introduced its "two dressed to play" goaltender rule in 1965/66, goaltending employment in the premium league immediately doubled. It doubled again in 1967/68, when the league at last expanded, to twelve teams, with new franchises in Minnesota, Philadelphia, Oakland, Los Angeles, St. Louis and Pittsburgh. Two more franchises, in Buffalo and Vancouver, arrived in 1970/71.

In 1972/73, the job market for goaltending, and for players in general, exploded with the debut of the new twelve-team World Hockey Association. By mid-decade, the WHA had fourteen teams, the NHL eighteen, and each team needed at least two goaltenders. Where there had been only six starting goaltending jobs in the NHL in the early 1960s, by the mid-1970s there were sixty-four in the NHL and the WHA. (In the meantime, the AHL had been transformed into a development league for the NHL.)

While this exponential increase in professional teams meant that goaltenders of average professional skill could now have something approaching a career, expansion brought other consequences. In the 1960s, the six-team NHL had enjoyed the greatest parity of its history. Vezina-winning GAs, as we have seen, routinely bettered LGA by three-tenths of a goal or less. While you couldn't win without great goaltending, there was no excuse for a team not

A BREED APART   134

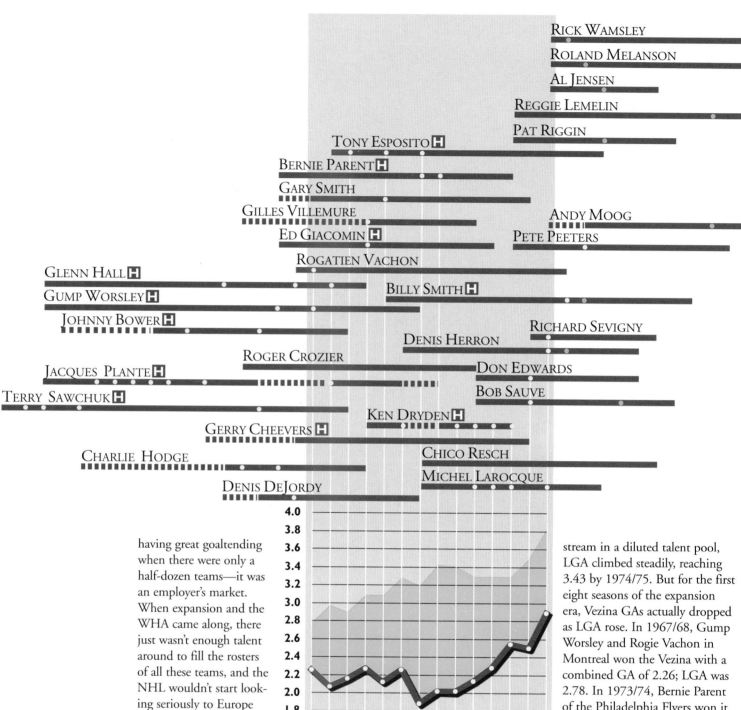

RICK WAMSLEY
ROLAND MELANSON
AL JENSEN
REGGIE LEMELIN
PAT RIGGIN
TONY ESPOSITO H
BERNIE PARENT H
GARY SMITH
GILLES VILLEMURE
ANDY MOOG
ED GIACOMIN H
PETE PEETERS
ROGATIEN VACHON
GLENN HALL H
GUMP WORSLEY H
BILLY SMITH H
JOHNNY BOWER H
RICHARD SEVIGNY
DENIS HERRON
ROGER CROZIER
JACQUES PLANTE H
DON EDWARDS
TERRY SAWCHUK H
BOB SAUVE
KEN DRYDEN H
GERRY CHEEVERS H
CHARLIE HODGE
CHICO RESCH
MICHEL LAROCQUE
DENIS DEJORDY

4.0 3.8 3.6 3.4 3.2 3.0 2.8 2.6 2.4 2.2 2.0 1.8

67/ 68   69/ 70   71/ 72   73/ 74   75/ 76   77/ 78   79/ 80

ROGATIEN VACHON'S PERFORMANCE IN THE 1976 CANADA CUP WAS ONE OF THE OUTSTANDING GOALTENDING EFFORTS OF THE DECADE. HE SURRENDERED ONLY SIX GOALS IN THE SIX-GAME ROUND-ROBIN.

having great goaltending when there were only a half-dozen teams—it was an employer's market. When expansion and the WHA came along, there just wasn't enough talent around to fill the rosters of all these teams, and the NHL wouldn't start looking seriously to Europe for fresh faces until the early 1980s.

The results, from the goaltending perspective, were threefold. Some teams tried to get by with a revolving door of mediocre netminders. Some very good netminders ended up playing for indifferent teams whose rosters were stocked with raw amateur recruits, journeymen of middling talent and over-the-hill vets, none of whom would have been on the ice back in the glory days of the Original Six. And those teams that were very good, and had very good goaltending, stood head and shoulders above the rest of the league. Some of the greatest spreads between Vezina-winning GAs and LGA were recorded in the 1970s.

As the decade progressed and more teams came on stream in a diluted talent pool, LGA climbed steadily, reaching 3.43 by 1974/75. But for the first eight seasons of the expansion era, Vezina GAs actually dropped as LGA rose. In 1967/68, Gump Worsley and Rogie Vachon in Montreal won the Vezina with a combined GA of 2.26; LGA was 2.78. In 1973/74, Bernie Parent of the Philadelphia Flyers won it with a GA of 1.89 (he shared it with Tony Esposito of Chicago, whose GA was 2.04). Parent's GA was the lowest in Vezina history since Jacques Plante's 1.86 of 1955/56. When Plante won it, LGA was 2.53; when Parent won it, LGA was 3.2. A huge gap had arisen between the very best and middle-of-the-road in goals-against statistics.

The early expansion years were littered with blowout games and absurdly powerful individual clubs from the Original Six who beat up most mercilessly on the expansion teams. The Buffalo Sabres were only a few months into their first season when they

Continued on page 142

ANOTHER game in TOWN

WHEN WHA DOLLARS LURED AWAY PLAYERS FROM NHL PAYROLLS, GOALTENDERS WERE AT THE FRONT OF THE LINE

For seven seasons in the 1970s, the upstart World Hockey Association provided hockey fans in North America with an alternative to the NHL. The league has mainly been credited with setting off a massive escalation in player salaries, but the WHA deserves more credit than it normally gets for bringing European talent and their style of play to this side of the Atlantic. In addition to Swedish scoring stars like Anders Hedberg and Ulf Nilsson (imported by the Winnipeg Jets of the WHA, swiped away by the New York Rangers of the NHL), the WHA also introduced from Finland goaltender Rainer (Markus) Mattsson, who played with the Quebec Nordiques and the Winnipeg Jets for the last two seasons of the WHA. When the Jets joined Quebec, the Edmonton Oilers and the Hartford Whalers in moving into the NHL after the WHA folded in 1979, Mattsson made the transition as well, and played four seasons in the NHL in Winnipeg, Minnesota and Los Angeles. Mattsson was in his final NHL season, in Los Angeles in 1983/84, when he snapped Wayne Gretzky's record-setting point-scoring streak after fifty-one games.

The WHA got its start signing journeymen NHLers and just enough big stars to make the new league a serious contender for the public's affections. Bobby Hull's defection from the Chicago Blackhawks to the Winnipeg Jets was the most famous, but for its first season of operation the WHA also scored big by landing Boston goaltender Gerry Cheevers for its Cleveland Barons franchise. Cheevers had won the Stanley Cup the preceding spring; when he reported to Cleveland, he did not simply take the money and run. He stuck with Cleveland for two and a half seasons before the Barons' financial problems and a dispute with its management sent him back to the Bruins.

The WHA had less success with

Bernie Parent, who only stayed one season with the Philadelphia Blazers before money matters made him switch to the Philadelphia Flyers of the NHL, with whom he promptly won two straight Stanley Cups, Vezinas and Conn Smythe trophies.

In all, forty-four goaltenders who played in the NHL also played in the WHA. Many of them, like Parent and Cheevers, tried out the new league for a season or two before returning to the old league. Gerry Desjardins had been around the NHL for six seasons when he crossed over to the Baltimore Blades, a one-season phenomenon, in 1974/75. When Baltimore folded, Desjardins returned to the NHL to play for Buffalo. After Desjardins arrived in Buffalo, Gary Bromley left, spending two seasons in the WHA, with Calgary in 1976/77 and Winnipeg in 1977/78, before returning to the NHL to play for Vancouver.

The WHA allowed some aging veterans and second-stringers from way back to enjoy something of a return to the limelight. At age forty-five, Jacques Plante came out of retirement to play thirty-one games for Edmonton in 1974/75. Two aging backup goaltenders, Marcel Paille and Robert Perrault, also secured some ice time. Paille, who had been a substitute goaltender for the Rangers from 1957/58 to 1964/65, was forty when he relieved Parent for fifteen games with the Blazers in 1972/73. Perrault had played thirty-one games with Montreal,

GERRY CHEEVERS WAS ONE OF THE WHA'S FIRST STAR SIGNINGS, JOINING THE CLEVELAND BARONS IN THE LEAGUE'S OPENING SEASON AFTER WINNING THE STANLEY CUP WITH BOSTON.

Detroit and Boston between 1955/56 and 1962/63; he was forty-one when he played one game for the L.A. Sharks in 1972/73. Jack McCartan, goaltender for the 1960 U.S. Olympic champions, resurfaced as a Minnesota Fighting Saint in 1972.

In its efforts to attract fans, the WHA resorted at times to gimmickry. A coloured puck was tried, and for a spell the league allowed a goal scored in the final two minutes of play to count as two goals. The WHA was overall a higher-scoring league than the NHL, and its best team GAs were generally as high as the NHL's LGA, partly because the WHA used overtime for regular-season games. Goaltenders were solid rather than spectacular, and a few made homes for themselves in the WHA. Les Binkley had played five seasons for the Pittsburgh Penguins when he switched to the new league in its inaugural season, playing a total of four seasons, mainly in relief, for Ottawa and then Toronto. Joe Daley, who had played in Pittsburgh, Buffalo and Detroit, switched to the Winnipeg Jets and was in the net for Winnipeg for every one of its WHA seasons. Dave Dryden left Buffalo to play with the Chicago Cougars (he had been Glenn Hall's backup with the Blackhawks in the 1960s) in 1974/75. He then spent four more seasons in the WHA with the Edmonton Oilers while his brother Ken was starring in the NHL with Montreal. Gary Kurt, who had played for the California Seals, switched to the WHA in its first season and stayed there for five seasons.

Don McLeod had played eighteen games as a back-up in Detroit and Philadelphia when he joined the new league, and spent six full seasons with it. Wayne Rutledge had been a regular in the net for the L.A. Kings for three seasons when he joined the Houston Aeros, and was a stalwart goaltender there for six seasons. Ernie "Suitcase" Wakely had been around the NHL since 1962 when he joined the Jets for their first season, and played on five different teams in the WHA right through to its last season. Al Smith was a backup in Toronto from 1965/66 to 1968/69 before he landed a starting position in Pittsburgh and then Detroit from 1969/70 to 1971/72. He, too, jumped to the new league, playing for New England for three seasons. Then it was back to the NHL and Buffalo for a backup job for two seasons before returning to the starting job in New England. When New England joined the NHL (as Hartford) in 1979/80, Smith came along, and then played one more season in Colorado. Andy Brown had been a backup in Detroit and Pittsburgh from 1971/72 to 1973/74 when he joined the Indianapolis Racers (where Wayne Gretzky made his professional debut) for three seasons.

As the seasons passed, the WHA was able to get to goaltenders before they had played their first NHL game. Jean-Louis Levasseur, for example, was around the WHA for four seasons, but saw most of his ice time with Minnesota, New England and Edmonton in 1976/77 and 1977/78. After the league died, he appeared in one NHL game, with Minnesota in 1979/80.

Some future goaltending stars and regular starters in the NHL broke into the professional ranks in the WHA. Mike Liut was drafted fifty-sixth overall by the St. Louis Blues in 1976, but after playing another season of collegiate hockey at Bowling Green he chose to join the WHA's Cincinnati Stingers in 1977/78, and played there for two seasons. When the WHA folded, he signed with the Blues, and became one of the league's premier netminders. In 1980/81, Liut won the Lester Pearson award as the league's most valuable player, as selected by the players' association.

Pat Riggin played in Birmingham in the WHA's final season, then came over to the NHL for nine solid seasons, the best of them with the Washington Capitals in the mid-1980s. In 1983/84, Riggin and Al Jensen shared the Jennings.

Ed Mio played in Indianapolis and Edmonton for the last two WHA seasons. Moving over to the NHL, he spent seven seasons with Edmonton, the Rangers and Detroit. Ron Grahame was one of the best goaltenders the WHA ever had, and he spent four seasons with the champion Houston Aeros before coming over to the NHL for four seasons in Boston, Los Angeles and Quebec. Michel Dion played more than four seasons in Indianapolis and Cincinnati; when the WHA folded he was good enough to play six seasons in the NHL in Quebec, Winnipeg and Pittsburgh. Finally, Richard Brodeur carved out a solid career in both leagues. He starred with the Quebec Nordiques for the entire life of the WHA. Nine quality seasons in the NHL, most of them with Vancouver, followed. ○

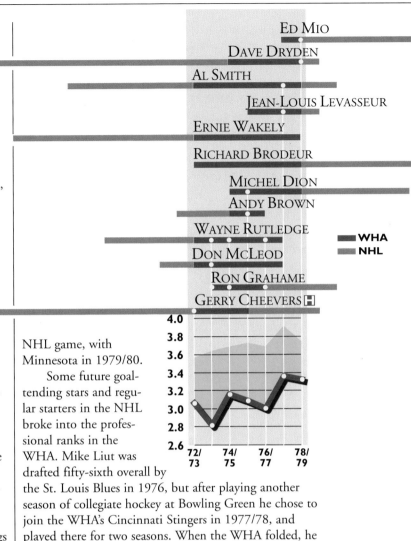

ROGATIEN VACHON

POISED TO INHERIT THE CANADIENS GOAL FROM GUMP WORSLEY, "ROGIE" INSTEAD BECAME THE TOAST OF L.A.

Just before the start of the Stanley Cup final of 1966/67, Leaf coach and general manager Punch Imlach let fly with a classic put-down of a player. Sizing up the not very big and not very well known Montreal Canadiens goaltender, twenty-one-year-old Rogatien Vachon, Imlach quipped, "Do they think they can win from us with a Junior B goalie in the net?"

As it turned out, Montreal couldn't. An aging Leaf team won the cup in six games. But in the process, Rogie Vachon made it known that he was anything but Junior B quality. At five-foot-seven, one of the smallest men ever to play the position professionally, he was to be a giant in the game.

Imlach's jab was a half-truth. Vachon indeed had only progressed as far as Junior B as a teenager. One of eight kids born to a dairy farmer in Palmarolle, about fifty miles from Noranda-Rouyn in Quebec's northern mining country, he had come south to try out for the Junior A Canadiens, only to be sent east to the townships south of Quebec City to play for the Thetford Mines Junior B outfit.

But after this stint, he rose rapidly through the hockey hierarchy. Turning pro, he was moved by Montreal to the Quebec Aces of the American League for ten games in 1966, then to Houston of the Central League for 1966/67. When Houston starter Gerry Desjardins injured his knee, Vachon got the chance to shine, putting in thirty-four impressive games. The Canadiens brought him up for nineteen games in 1966/67 to spell Gump Worsley, and from then on he was an NHL fixture.

Thwarted by Imlach's aging Leafs in 1966/67, he won his first Stanley Cup in 1967/68. That season, he and Worsley shared the Vezina with a combined 2.26 GA, the best performance the trophy had inspired since Jacques Plante in 1958/59. In the 1968/69 playoffs he took over from Worsley when the veteran dislocated his finger, and completely shut down the emerging Bruins, recording a playoff GA of 1.42 as Montreal won another cup. When a nervous breakdown ended Worsley's Montreal career the following autumn, Vachon inherited the Canadiens net. But when Boston won its first Stanley Cup since forever that spring, Vachon's Montreal career began to unravel.

He blew hot and cold the following season, 1970/71, and as the playoffs approached the Canadiens unveiled a secret weapon. Ken Dryden, nine inches taller than Vachon, beat back the big Bruins shooters in Montreal's famous quarterfinal victory, then won the Conn Smythe as Montreal regained the cup.

Vachon watched from the bench for the entire playoffs as Dryden dazzled. Both the Canadiens and Vachon could see where the team's netminding future lay. After playing in only one period of one game—and letting in four goals—in the new season, Vachon went to general manager Sam Pollock that November and asked to be traded. In two days, he was on his way to L.A.

A trade to an inept expansion club was often hockey's death march to Bataan, but for Vachon it was a career-making move. He married his Montreal girlfriend, grew his hair long, sprouted a Fu Manchu moustache, and became the most beloved hockey figure in the history of the Kings, more beloved than even their latter-day saviour, Wayne Gretzky. He was named the Kings' most valuable player in 1973, 1974, 1975 and 1977, and was adored as much for his on-ice performances as for his charitable work away from the rink. His physical and emotional character was tailor-made for a warm California reception. Back in Montreal, his loss was mourned widely and unrelentingly. The Canadiens had the brilliant, lanky, cerebral Dryden, but a big part of the fans' hearts was still with the gnome-like Quebecer who had been poised to inherit Worsley's crease.

He defied the game's tradition of smaller goaltenders being the most acrobatic: he stayed on his feet and made up for his size by playing his angles carefully. Largely on the strength of his performances, the Kings became a much better team.

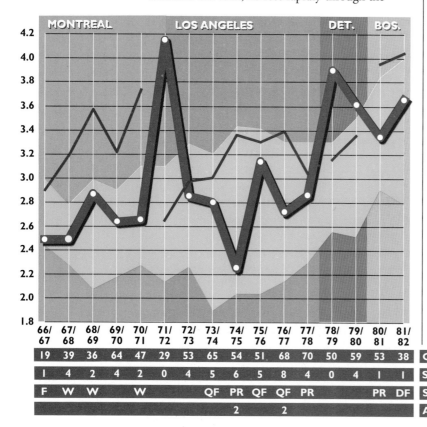

	66/67	67/68	68/69	69/70	70/71	71/72	72/73	73/74	74/75	75/76	76/77	77/78	78/79	79/80	80/81	81/82	
	19	39	36	64	47	29	53	65	54	51	68	70	50	59	53	38	GAMES
	1	4	2	4	2	0	4	5	6	5	8	4	0	4	1	1	SHUTOUTS
	F	W	W		W			QF	PR	QF	QF	PR			PR	DF	STANLEY CUP
									2			2					ALL STAR TEAM

The Kings were out of the playoffs from 1969/70 to 1972/73, made it as far as the quarterfinal in 1973/74, then turned it all around in one magnificent season.

Vachon launched the 1974/75 season by recording a GA of 1.41 in the first seventeen games; it was the best start since 1957/58, when Jacques Plante had managed a GA of 1.33 in his first fifteen games. The Kings won nine more games and amassed twenty-seven more points than in the previous season, and finished only eight points behind the league leaders. Vachon was touted as a Hart contender. Had he won it, he would have been the first goaltender since Plante to do so. But L.A. bowed out of the playoffs in the preliminary round and Bobby Clarke, who led the Flyers to their second straight Stanley Cup, edged Vachon in Hart voting. *Hockey News,* however, named Vachon the league's player of the year.

Jovial and big-hearted, in competition he was a focused terror. "Ounce for ounce, Rogie has to be one of the fiercest competitors in sport," said L.A. defenceman Terry Harper, who had followed Vachon to the coast from the Canadiens in 1972. "He gets mad when you beat him, in a scrimmage or a shooting session." Vachon explained: "When you lose, you want to die."

L.A. never did make it to a Stanley Cup final with Vachon. He made his most lasting mark in the international forum. In the 1976 Canada Cup, neither Bernie Parent nor Ken Dryden was available to play for Team Canada, and Vachon was one of several bright though less lauded netminders, including Glenn "Chico" Resch and Gerry Cheevers, who stepped into the void. They all understood that whoever started the tournament and stayed hot would play every game, and it happened that it was Vachon who caught fire, turning in one of goaltending's greatest performances. In the first six games of the tournament, he allowed only six goals; when it was over, and Team Canada had defeated Czechoslovakia in two straight games in the best-of-three final, Vachon was named the team's most valuable player. But the tournament's MVP award went to Bobby Orr, a sentimental favourite whose knee problems had kept him out of the 1972 Canada–Russia series. Vachon was vocally miffed. "I have to be honest," he said. "I thought I deserved the big award. Everyone said I would get it and I was disappointed when I did not."

After two more seasons in L.A., Vachon became a free agent, and surprised the sport by opting to go to Detroit, lured by a five-year, $1.9 million contract. He had two catastrophic seasons, and would come to blame himself for most of his woes. An arbitrator had ordered Detroit to give up Dale McCourt to L.A. as compensation, but McCourt balked, gaining a restraining order that allowed him to nix the move. Detroit fans were soured by the kerfuffle, and Vachon didn't help matters by playing poorly. For two seasons, his GA reached previously uncharted personal heights. Detroit marched him to doctors, suspecting he had double vision. By the end of the 1979/80 season, Detroit had him on waivers, his contract available to any other NHL team for just $3,500. Everyone passed, but then Boston took a chance on him—Gerry Cheevers had just retired from playing and was now coach—and traded away their very capable veteran netminder, Gilles Gilbert, to get him. Gilbert didn't fare any better in Detroit than Vachon had: his GA jumped by more than a goal and went over the 4.00 plateau. In Boston Vachon posted better than average GAs for two seasons before deciding to retire.

Vachon was sending out résumés in 1984, looking for work as a goaltending or assistant coach, when he received an extraordinary offer from his old team, the Kings: how would he like to be general manager? He took over that autumn, and in January 1985 his welcome back was pressed home by the retirement of his number. He retired in 1991/92, but then came back as assistant to the club president. When president Bruce McNall was indicted on fraud charges, Rogie put up the bail money. ○

A BIG-HEARTED MAN AWAY FROM THE RINK, IN HIS CREASE VACHON WAS A FOCUSED TERROR: "WHEN YOU LOSE, YOU WANT TO DIE." IN 1975, HE JUST MISSED BECOMING THE FIRST GOALTENDER SINCE JACQUES PLANTE TO WIN THE HART TROPHY.

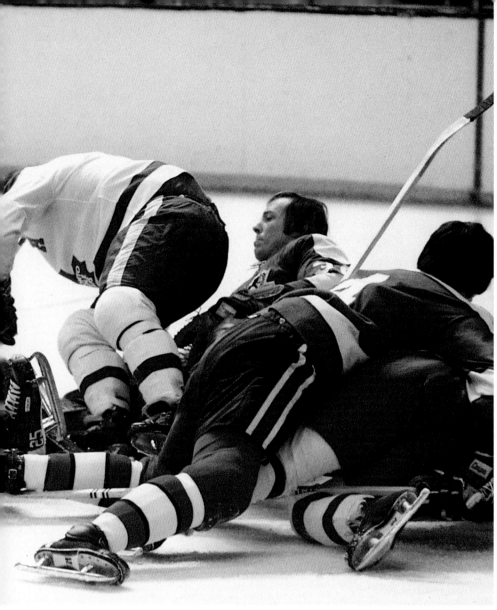

with Montreal in 1980/81. In 1981/82, the New York Islanders won their third straight Stanley Cup that season, but they would have to win their fourth straight before goaltender Billy Smith was awarded the Conn Smythe, bringing to an end the long drought for goaltenders. During these years, goaltenders were also overlooked entirely in Calder voting. Ken Dryden won it in 1971/72, but no goaltending rookie would again be honoured until Buffalo's Tom Barrasso in 1983/84.

In the gold rush of professional hockey in the 1970s, goaltenders for the most part got left behind. The game celebrated its scoring stars as never before; the arrival of the fifty-goal men, and the bidding wars for their services between the NHL and WHA, created great divides between the top-dollar superstars and the journeymen. More often than not, the goaltenders, regardless of their skill levels, were lumped in with the journeymen. Despite the long-held maxim of hockey that a club couldn't win without goaltending, the goaltenders weren't attracting the sterling salaries being tossed in the direction of the big points-producers. Only in the last few years have goaltenders been able to secure salaries in line with their marquee status in the game. Ed Giacomin, looking for any way to get ahead, struck a deal with Champion spark plugs to carry an advertisement for them ("Spark with Eddie") right on his mask. Needless to say, the league vetoed the initiative.

It was an era when goaltenders attracted more abuse than admiration. The expansion years helped resuscitate the "great goaltender on a bad team" label, which hadn't been used much in the Original Six days (netminders like Gump Worsley and Chuck Rayner, who suffered with the Rangers of the 1950s and early 1960s excepted). Gilles Meloche was typical, spending all sixteen seasons of his NHL career with expansion clubs. He toiled thanklessly for the woeful Oakland Seals and their temporary incarnation, the Cleveland Barons. For his first three seasons as a Seal, he averaged more than four goals per game. He enjoyed a few seasons of success with Minnesota, but then ended his career on the pitiful Penguins. He played in 788 NHL games and won 270.

The greatest abuse a goaltender came to suffer in the expansion years came not at the hands of the opposition, but at the hands of his own team, in particular his coach and general manager. The "two dressed to play" rule of 1965/66 may have allowed goaltenders to play less than a full season, and so preserve their skills and sanity as the schedule moved toward eighty games and beyond, but it also laid the foundation for some new twists that undermined the goaltender's self-respect.

Before 1965/66, the goaltender's confidence was not to be messed with by his team. His play was not criticised by his teammates, and if he had an off night, then it was a given that the whole team had an off night. On psychologically healthy teams, an 8–0 blowout was something suffered by the team, not by the man between the posts alone. If a goaltender began to lose his edge, he could be replaced, but certainly never in mid-game. That

THE LAST OF THE BAREFACED WARRIORS: ANDY BROWN WAS STILL PLAYING WITHOUT A MASK WITH THE PITTSBURGH PENGUINS (HERE IN THEIR ORIGINAL BLUE UNIFORMS) IN 1974.

Continued from page 136

were pelted by seventy-two shots at Boston Garden on December 10, 1970, and lost 8–2. The Bruins, with scoring stars like Phil Esposito, Bobby Orr, Ken Hodge and Johnny Bucyk, amassed 399 goals that season, 108 more than Montreal, the next-best offensive unit. They were the first team to have three forty-goal scorers (and two fifty-goal scorers), and with Eddie Johnston and Gerry Cheevers sharing the net, they were shoo-ins for a Stanley Cup. But when they met Montreal in the quarterfinal, they were stopped cold by Ken Dryden, who had only played six games for Montreal that season. The expansion years may have provided whipping boys for the best clubs, but they had not changed the paramount importance of goaltending in the playoffs. Dryden won the Conn Smythe as Montreal captured the cup, and Bernie Parent won it with Philadelphia in 1973/74 and 1974/75.

After 1974/75, the NHL governors seemed to forget about goaltenders for the next seven seasons of Smythe awards. Coincidentally, LGA continued to climb, reaching a record 4.0 in 1981/82, and Vezina GAs climbed with it. Even so, Ken Dryden, who won five Vezinas (the last three with Michel Larocque), was never far from his career GA of 2.24. League-leading GAs reached 2.90

was as unthinkable as it was impossible, since no one else qualified was on hand to take his place. Normally it took a serious injury to remove a goaltender from the ice.

Punch Imlach, the Leaf coach and general manager who had paved the way for the two-goaltender rule by employing both Johnny Bower and Terry Sawchuk, did switch from one to the other during a game, but only between periods. The one and only time Bower was pulled right off the ice was in 1968/69, the last season of his career, when St. Louis scored on him three times in the first period and Imlach decided to play Bruce Gamble in his stead. It was a home game for the Leafs, and when Bower was summoned to the bench, the fans didn't quite know what to make of it. They responded by giving Bower an ovation.

The two-goaltender rule had made it possible to "pull the goalie"—yank him right out of the net during a stoppage in play and send in a replacement. (Some coaches experimented with using the second goaltender like a relief pitcher in baseball, sending him in to "close" a game.) Other players had this happen to them all the time. If they weren't playing well, they came off on a routine line change, rode the bench or saw minimal ice time. But nobody got removed from the ice quite like a

goaltender. It was a new, and supremely humiliating, experience in effect to be told by your coach, in front of all of your teammates, the opposing players and the crowd in the arena, that you were playing so badly that someone else was getting a turn. It was hard enough to summon the nerve just to play the position. Now the goaltender took up his station in the crease knowing that he could have his ego crushed in full public view if the martinet behind the bench felt the last goal had been on the soft side.

Not every coach was wont to pull the goaltender, but it came to happen enough that "Pull the goalie!" became a common refrain by frustrated home-ice fans. With another dressed-to-play goaltender handy on the bench, the goaltender on the ice could now serve as a scapegoat for whatever was going wrong in the game. A bad goal that was really the fault of the defencemen could get the crowd on the goaltender's back. Being stuck with the goat's role was particularly infuriating to goaltenders who still considered hockey a team sport, and who thought that the lack of backchecking by the big-salary forwards deserved at least some of the blame for the numbers on the score clock.

Continued on page 146

143 | *THE MORE THE MERRIER*

GERRY CHEEVERS

THE GUY WHO NEVER WON A VEZINA OR MADE AN NHL ALL STAR TEAM WAS THE BEST TRETIAK HAS EVER SEEN

When it came to applying math to goaltending, the most important function to Gerry Cheevers was not division, but subtraction. "I don't care that much about my average," he wrote in 1971. "My philosophy's always been that the other team can fill the net on me as long as we get one more goal."

Cheevers' average wasn't ever shabby, but it wasn't ever good enough to earn him a Vezina based on the old standard of team GA. Other measurements could be applied to his game: he set a record for the longest undefeated streak for a goaltender—thirty-two games (twenty-four wins, eight ties) in 1971/72; and for the most consecutive playoff wins—ten, in 1969/1970. And his career win percentage of .676 was bested only by Ken Dryden's .758.

Incredibly, Cheevers never won any kind of award, major or minor, while in the NHL. His career got off to too tentative a start to attract a Calder. In his Stanley Cup victories with Boston, he was overshadowed by the likes of Phil Esposito and Bobby Orr, which ruled out a

CHEEVERS WAS THE MAN IN THE FRIGHT-NIGHT MASK, GUARDING THE BRUINS GOAL THROUGH A COMBINATION OF INSTINCT AND ACROBATICS. FEW GOALTENDERS HAVE BEEN MORE EXCITING TO WATCH.

Conn Smythe. And he never made it onto an NHL All Star team. Cheevers' greatness wasn't etched in any piece of silver but the Stanley Cup. Yet teammates and opponents knew his worth. Vladislav Tretiak has called him the greatest goaltender he has ever seen.

With the exception of a two-and-a-half-season side-trip into the World Hockey Association, Cheevers spent his major-league professional career with the NHL's Bruins, and will always be remembered as the guy in the scarred mask with the great Boston teams of the early expansion years.

Growing up in St. Catharines, Ontario, "Cheesie" was scouted for the Leafs by his own dad, a star lacrosse player and minor hockey coach. The elder Cheevers engineered a scholarship for his son with the Leafs' Junior affiliate, the St. Michael's College Majors, and he was the goaltender on the last great St. Mike's team of 1960/61, which won the Memorial Cup.

As the property of the Leafs, Cheevers butted his head against a glass ceiling placed over his career by the existence of Johnny Bower and then Terry Sawchuk on the Leaf roster. Toronto tried him for two games in 1961/62, in which he gave up seven goals, and shipped him hither and yon—to Sault Ste. Marie and Sudbury in the Eastern Canadian Professional League, to the Rochester Americans in the American League. While with Rochester, he made the first All Star team of 1964/65 as the Americans won the league championship. But in the NHL intraleague draft that summer, the Leafs left Cheevers unprotected in favour of Bower and Sawchuk.

It was, in fact, the second straight season Cheevers had been left unprotected, and this time there was a taker. Boston signed him, paid the Leafs the requisite $30,000 fee, and shipped him to the Oklahoma City Blazers of the Central League. Joe Crozier, coach of the Rochester Americans, sensed that a big one had got away. "Cheevers is the most exciting goalie you'll ever see," he reportedly told the Bruins. "He'll have your fans on the edge of their seats all night."

He came up to Boston for seven games in 1965/66 and allowed thirty-four goals, but three of his games were shutouts. Harry Sinden was Oklahoma's player-coach, and when he was hired as the Bruins' coach the following season, he brought along Cheevers, who had been named the league's outstanding goaltender.

Cheevers' style was aggressive and instinctive. The only goaltender to accumulate more penalties than him during his time in the NHL was Billy Smith of the New York Islanders. Counting his WHA minutes, he became the all-time leader, with 304. Known for his enthusiasm in clearing his crease with his stick, he offered in 1970, "I'm not dirty, just aggressive," and added, "Fighter pilots have machine guns. I have only my mask and stick."

Cheevers was always good for a quote, which made him popular with scribes. But he never grandstanded, being known above all as a team player and, ultimately, a clutch player. "He's the kind of guy you can count on to make the big saves that turn games around," Sinden said in 1970. "He'll let the odd softie in but he gets the big ones. You prefer that to having a guy who gets all the softies and misses the big ones."

Two of his greatest assets were his skating and stick-handling. He was the equivalent of a third defenceman, and his puck-handling had undoubtedly been helped by his lacrosse play, which he had given up in the 1960s for fear of an injury that would hamper his hockey career. At St. Mike's he had even played on left wing for a dozen games when the Leafs brought in prospect Dave Dryden to give him some Junior A exposure. It was the one and only time in his career that he had a breakaway on Roger Crozier. Crozier stopped him, and so did every other goaltender he skated in on.

The Bruins won two Stanley Cups with Cheevers in the early 1970s, and then lost him to the rogue WHA. He was the first big signing for the league after Bobby Hull, becoming a Cleveland Crusader with a seven-year, $1.4 million contract the autumn that followed Boston's 1971/72 Stanley Cup win.

At first everything seemed swell with Cheevers and the new league. He was its top goaltender in 1972/73, and in 1975 was named Cleveland's player-coach. In 1974, the WHA All Stars played the Soviet national team in an eight-game series. The pros lost, but with dignity, and Cheevers was critical to their respectable showing.

But the WHA experience soured for Cheevers. The Cleveland franchise began to run dry on funds. Pay cheques were bouncing; Cheevers was privately lending teammates money to tide them over. Then team manager Jack Vivian suspended Cheevers and fined him $1,000 in the middle of the 1975/76 season after a 4–2 loss to Indianapolis, saying "We haven't been getting $200,000 worth of goaltending out of him." Cheevers, incensed, said that Vivian had "accused me of not trying and not caring." He was released from his WHA contract and returned to Boston. In his first game back as a Bruin, he shut out Detroit 7–0.

Cheevers was part of the Team Canada training camp in 1976 that ultimately resulted in Rogie Vachon playing all the team's games. Watching Cheevers perform at camp, fellow netminder Glenn Resch paid tribute. "Gerry brings a lot of class to the position of goaltending. Everyone thinks of the goalie as the flake and the guy who is a bit weird. He defies all that. He doesn't have the best technique in certain instances but he's an intelligent guy, a thinking goalie. He reacts to situations better than others. He doesn't lose his angles and has excellent anticipation."

Harry Sinden summed him up more succinctly in 1969: "Gerry would throw his head in the way of the puck in order to stop a shot."

The Bruins he returned to were not the flashy squad of the early 1970s. These were the dedicated grinders of

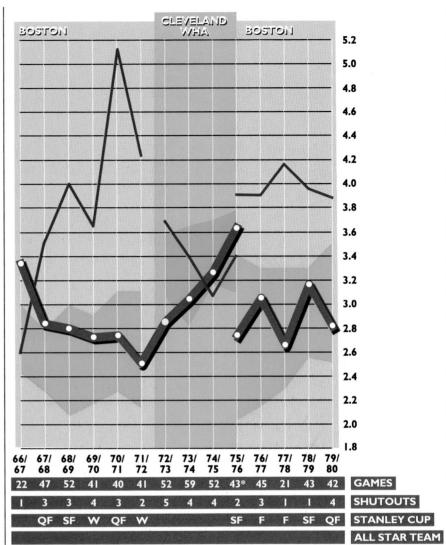

	66/67	67/68	68/69	69/70	70/71	71/72	72/73	73/74	74/75	75/76	76/77	77/78	78/79	79/80	
GAMES	22	47	52	41	40	41	52	59	52	43*	45	21	43	42	
SHUTOUTS	1	3	3	4	3	2	5	4	2	3	1	1	4		
STANLEY CUP	QF	SF	W	QF	W					SF	F	F	SF	QF	
ALL STAR TEAM															

Cheevers played two games for Toronto in 1961/62 and seven games for Boston in 1965/66.
*Cheevers played twenty-eight games (with one shutout) for Cleveland and fifteen games (with one shutout) for Boston in 1975/76.

coach Don Cherry, with Sinden as general manager, who couldn't quite win a Stanley Cup in two tries against the Canadiens. In 1978, in a Stanley Cup game against Montreal in the Forum, Cheevers turned in a performance that elicited every manner of sportswriting superlative, despite his being on the losing team.

Cheevers was plagued by knee problems through much of his career, and at the end of the 1979/80 season he could not continue. He had long had an interest in horse racing—Bobby Orr had been an investor with him in the Four-Thirty stable, named after their sweater numbers—but Cheevers had scarcely time to call himself retired from hockey before Sinden signed him right back on as the Bruins coach. He lasted four and a half seasons, with Boston finishing first or second in their division in the first four, before Sinden fired him in the middle of the 1984/85 season as the team struggled. He was inducted into the Hall of Fame before the year was out. His signature mask took up a place of honour on his living-room coffee table. ○

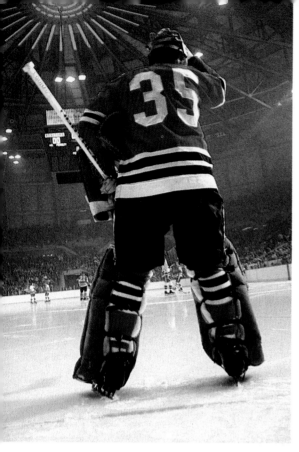

I N ONE CONSPICUOUS HONOUR, **NHL** GOALTENDERS LAG FAR BEHIND THEIR TEAMMATES. OF MORE THAN FIFTY NUMBERS THAT HAVE BEEN RETIRED BY LEAGUE TEAMS, ONLY FOUR HAVE BEEN WORN BY A MAN IN THE NET.

IT MAY HAVE BEEN THE CASE THAT TEAMS WERE ONCE RELUCTANT TO TAKE GOALTENDING NUMBERS OUT OF CIRCULATION, AS TRADITIONALLY THEY HAVE ONLY WORN EITHER THE FIRST NUMBER OR ONE OF THE LAST. WHATEVER THE REASON, STARS LIKE BILL DURNAN AND TERRY SAWCHUK NEVER HAD THEIR NUMBERS HOISTED INTO AN ARENA'S RAFTERS THE WAY MAURICE RICHARD OR GORDIE HOWE HAVE. EVERY GOALTENDING NUMBER RETIREMENT CAME AFTER THE LEAGUE EXPANSION OF 1967.

HERE ARE THE LUCKY FEW:

35 TONY ESPOSITO, CHICAGO BLACKHAWKS
30 ROGATIEN VACHON, LOS ANGELES KINGS
1 ED GIACOMIN, NEW YORK RANGERS
1 BERNIE PARENT, PHILADELPHIA FLYERS

IN ADDITION TO THESE, IN 1995 THE TORONTO MAPLE LEAFS PAID SPECIAL TRIBUTE TO THE "1" WORN BY JOHNNY BOWER AND TURK BRODA WITH A COMMEMORATIVE BANNER, FOLLOWING RECENT CLUB POLICY TO HONOUR RATHER THAN RETIRE NUMBERS.

Continued from page 143

A whole new territory of mind games opened up. The idea that the team stood behind its goaltender was challenged. If the goaltender was having a bad second period, or perhaps a game or two, the team was supposed to bolster his confidence, get him back in the groove. But with another NHL-quality goaltender in the roster, reassurance was no longer so readily offered. Perhaps the team didn't feel like getting behind this goaltender any more. Perhaps they felt that a change would be good, and if a coach sensed that his team thought this way, he might change goaltenders, whether in the middle of the game or in the middle of a road trip, just to give them the psychological boost they craved. A hot goaltender could lift the team as a whole to a higher plane of performance. But just as easily, a struggling goaltender could drag them down. With two goaltenders on hand, it was far easier for the coach to cut loose a goaltender, however unfair this might be, to get his team back afloat.

Two-goaltender lineups have very rarely featured two players of equal or near-equal ability. The trend has long been to have a "starter" and a backup who plays when the starter is injured or needs a rest. Emile Francis, the former goaltender who coached and managed the Rangers in the 1960s and 1970s, firmly believes that a team has to have one main goaltender. Francis's Vezina-winning pairing of Gilles Villemure and Ed Giacomin worked, Giacomin feels, because Villemure was not hankering to play half the games. He was happy providing backup services, which left him time to indulge his passion for horse racing. (In the off-season, Villemure was a first-rate trotter driver.)

In rare instances, teams have used two goaltenders as alternating equals, as in the case of Boston's Gerry Cheevers and Eddie Johnston in the early 1970s, and Chuck Rayner and Jim Henry, the pioneering tag-team of the Rangers, in the late 1940s. Both pairings worked because the players got along and didn't feel particularly threatened that the other guy was going to take his job away. A

Machiavellian coach or general manager could use this fear to wring a more concerted effort out of a goaltender—or think they could, when in fact all they were doing was destroying the player's self-esteem. While having two first-class goaltenders in the roster can push each of them to a higher level of play as they try to beat each other to the starting job, often the two (or even three) goaltender lineup has led to conflict between the goaltenders, or at least between the goaltender riding the bench and management. Someone ends up getting the bulk of the work, and even with two relative equals, a team will almost always go exclusively with whoever is judged "hot" once the playoffs start. In the 1980s, Andy Moog endured the frustrating experience of playing half or more of the Edmonton Oilers' regular-season games, only to have Grant Fuhr draw the starting assignment in the playoffs. After the 1986/87 season, Moog left the Oilers to play with Canada's Olympic team, then resumed his NHL career as the main goaltender for the Bruins.

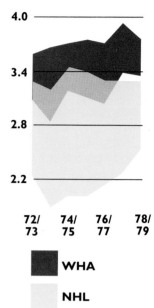

IN THE 1970s, GOALTENDING IN THE **NHL** WAS MARKED BY AN ENORMOUS SPREAD BETWEEN **LGA** AND VEZINA-WINNING PERFORMANCES, WHILE THE DIFFERENCE BETWEEN THE BEST GOALTENDING PERFORMANCES AND THE AVERAGE ONES WAS MUCH TIGHTER IN THE RIVAL **WHA**. THE BEST **GA** IN THE **WHA** WAS OFTEN AS HIGH AS, OR HIGHER THAN, THE **LGA** OF THE **NHL**, UNDOUBTEDLY BECAUSE THE **WHA** EMPLOYED OVERTIME IN REGULAR-SEASON GAMES.

I t was during the 1970s that goaltenders forged new personae for themselves. The arrival in force of the mask in the 1960s had robbed them of their identities. Their faces obscured, they lost the presence they had enjoyed with spectators in the game's barefaced days. One could not imagine a modern goaltender, sealed up inside his headgear, jabbering away at the opponents and teammates the way Chuck Gardiner had in Chicago in the 1930s.

Mind you, it added an aura of mystery to their personalities. At the end of a game, it became a treat for spectators to watch the goaltender lift away his mask, like a fencer, to reveal what sort of man lurked beneath all that equipment. If he won, he was pleased, his hair dripping with sweat, his animated features the antithesis of his mask's android stolidity. If he lost, he might not remove the mask at all, storming off the ice toward the dressing room with his inner self still firmly encased.

Gerry Cheevers was the first goaltender to exploit the expressive possibilities of the inexpressive mask. During a practice in 1967/68, the first season of the expansion era, Cheevers was hit on his new mask by a shot from Fred Stanfield. As a joke, the nick in the mask was painted in as stitches to represented the injury that might have been. By 1971, Cheevers had added 110 stitches to three different masks. The macabre visage turned the goaltending trade into a funhouse nightmare; it was entirely appropriate that when the *Friday the 13th* film series was launched, its principal nemesis, the psychopathic Jason, sported a goaltender's mask. The anonymity of the mask gave the chainsaw-wielding maniac the depth of character required.

As other players started to decorate their masks, they tended to stick to the safety of team logos. Cheevers' buddy Doug Favell added whimsy to the process by spray-painting his mask orange in honour of Halloween (that funhouse nightmare again). Masks became more adventurous, more stylised, more...outspoken. The most repressed players in the rink, restricted to one corner of the ice, buried under increasingly complex equipment, assaulted by 100-m.p.h. pieces of rubber, jerked from their creases by capricious coaches, began shouting back, not with their voices, but with their faces. They became a combination of samurai warrior, Kabuki actor, comic book superhero and professional wrestling weirdo. When confirmed eccentric Gilles Gratton had a startling lion's face painted on his mask (in honour of his astrological sign, Leo), the art of the mask reached its nadir, and so did the ability of the goaltender to transform himself into something other than the nerve-racked loner the public expected him to be. The goaltender became the most fascinating character in the game, if not in professional sport. He became the only professional athlete with an alter ego.

Vladislav Tretiak was puzzled by the North American game as he found it in the 1970s. He derided the style of some NHL players, who seemed to eschew the nifty playmaking of his comrades in favour of pure firepower. Opponents seemed to want to shoot the puck right through him rather than outsmart him. But he admired the goaltenders. "What first impressed me about Canadian goalkeepers was their amazing ability to come out of the net while under attack in order to cut down the angles," he has written.

Professional hockey in the late 1970s reached simultaneous highs and lows—there were more teams than ever before, and great concerns about the overall quality of play in the light of humiliations suffered at the hands of touring Soviet hockey teams, which culminated in the 8–1 defeat of Team Canada in the deciding game of the 1981 Canada Cup. Throughout it, the quality of goaltending was never questioned. And despite the tremendous expansion in total teams, the profession was almost completely dominated when it came time for accolades by Montreal's Ken Dryden. As the Canadiens won four straight Stanley Cups, Dryden won four straight Vezinas and was voted to the first All Star team four straight times. Others vied for attention—Don Edwards and Bob Sauve in Buffalo, Glenn "Chico" Resch and Billy Smith with the New York Islanders, Rogie Vachon in Los Angeles, Gerry Cheevers in Boston, Bernie Parent in Philadelphia, Eddie Giacomin in New York. When Dryden retired at the end of the 1978/79 season, a changing of the guard was again under way in the netminding ranks. Bernie Parent was forced to retire that season because of an eye injury. Eddie Giacomin had played his last nine games in 1977/78, and Gerry Cheevers, who had somehow had one of the NHL's great careers without ever winning a Vezina or landing on an All Star team, hung in for one more season following Dryden's retirement.

Dryden's retirement left a vacuum; he had been one of those goaltenders, like Benedict, Vezina, Brimsek, Durnan, Sawchuk, Plante and Hall, who were recognized as players whose greatness transcended their particular era. But even in Dryden's years, the game had come to take for granted the greatness of goaltending in a way it never had before. Goaltenders were there to stop pucks, and if the pucks didn't get stopped, you pulled them off the ice and sent in another one. It had become a shooter's game: they won the Harts and the Conn Smythes. Defencemen wanted to be Bobby Orr, and the discipline of allowing as a team a minimum of goals became a rare pursuit. When Dryden retired, LGA was at 3.30. Already nudging upward in the 1970s, it increased rapidly in his absence, and as four surviving teams of the great WHA experiment were folded into the NHL, it reached 4.0 in 1981/82. The four-goal barrier hadn't been broken since the free-for-all wartime season of 1943/44. Tony Esposito, who had recorded a 1.76 GA in 1971/72, saw his GA reach 4.52 in 1981/82. It would take another decade for the NHL to move away from the high-scoring game. Changes in basic game philosophy would help make it happen, but ultimately it was up to the goaltenders. And ten years after Dryden retired, the position had undergone a revolution in equipment and technique the likes of which had not been seen since the catching glove and the slapshot had transformed the goaltender's role in the first seasons of the Original Six. ○

IN JANUARY 1975, KIM CROUCH, AN EIGHTEEN-YEAR-OLD GOALTENDER FOR THE MARKHAM WAXERS OF THE ONTARIO JUNIOR A, WAS WEARING THE MASK AT TOP WHEN A SKATE SLICED A SIX-INCH CUT IN HIS NECK, SEVERING HIS JUGULAR VEIN. KIM NEARLY BLED TO DEATH ON THE ICE; THE WOUND TOOK FORTY STITCHES TO CLOSE. KIM'S BRUSH WITH DEATH INSPIRED HIS FATHER ED, THE FIRE CHIEF OF WHITBY, ONTARIO, TO INVENT THE CROUCH COLLAR. INSIDE IS BALLISTIC NYLON, THE MATERIAL BUTCHERS USE TO PROTECT THEMSELVES. THE FIRST MODEL (MIDDLE) WAS PATENTED IN CANADA IN 1976. A REVISED MODEL (BOTTOM) RECEIVED A U.S. PATENT IN 1987.

BERNIE PARENT

THE SECOND COMING OF JACQUES PLANTE WAS THE GOALTENDER TO BEAT IN THE MID-SEVENTIES

The first time Bernie Parent ever played goal, he was scored on twenty times. His older brother was coaching a Pee Wee team in Long Pointe, a town outside of Montreal, in 1956, and the regular goaltender couldn't play. Eleven-year-old Bernie was pressed into service, and suffered a drubbing that only made him determined to learn how to stop pucks. He practised for a month, got another chance and won 5–3. He was almost twenty years away from winning two Stanley Cups, two Vezinas and two Conn Smythes, but he was on his way.

For two seasons in the mid-1970s, Bernie Parent was the biggest name in goaltending, at least in the NHL. As the last line of defence for the Philadelphia Flyers, he helped give the Broadstreet Bullies legitimacy as a champion hockey club. It may have been chock full of grinders and brawlers, but the first expansion club to win a Stanley Cup also had the second coming of Jacques Plante. Neither of the Flyers' back-to-back cup wins, the first against Boston, the second against Buffalo, would have been possible without Parent.

He came out of Junior hockey as championship material. Starting out with Rosemount of the Quebec Junior league in 1962/63, he moved over to the Niagara Falls Flyers of the OHA for two seasons. He was named the Ontario Junior A's top goaltender in both seasons. Paired with Doug Favell, a buddy of Gerry Cheevers' from St. Catharines (their dads played lacrosse together), he was a member of the Memorial Cup–winning Flyers team of 1965.

Signed by the Bruins, Parent was sent to Oklahoma City of the Central League for the 1965/66 and 1966/67 seasons. At the time the Bruins had a surfeit of goaltending prospects, including Cheevers, and had been confident enough to deal away the rights to Ken Dryden in 1964. Parent played fifty-seven games up in Boston over those two seasons, backing up Eddie Johnston, but he did not impress, and his $7,500 salary flew through his fingers. When expansion came in 1967, the Flyers claimed him in the draft, and picked Favell as well.

Parent logged three and a half solid seasons in Philadelphia before being dealt to Toronto on January 31, 1971, in a multi-player deal that included Maple Leaf netminder Bruce Gamble. Gamble lasted only another year before heart problems forced him from the game. For Parent, the trade was an unexpected trip to finishing school. Waiting for him in Toronto was that wily sage of the nets, Jacques Plante, in the twilight of his career but still capable of making the second All Star team that season. Looking at Parent in 1971, Cheevers noted, "He's probably got more natural ability than any goaltender in this league. I don't know too much about his desire, though... He's not the most enthusiastic goaler I can think of."

Parent had grown up watching Plante on "Hockey Night in Canada." Now taken under his hero's wing, Parent was turned into a Plante "carbon copy" (in Gump Worsley's words), right down to the way he threw his arms up in a V-for-victory after a win. Physically, they weren't much alike—Parent was a bit on the chunky side. As Cheevers put it, "He's sort of a fat Jacques Plante." In one important respect, their styles were far apart. Parent never developed Plante's nerve in roaming from the net. "It's like a kid who goes into the woods with his father," Parent explained. "As long as I'm close to the net, I figure I'm all right."

Plante trained him so well in Toronto that in 1972 the Flyers gave up a first-round draft choice and Favell to retrieve Parent, who was packaged with a second-round Toronto pick. But then the WHA came calling. The Flyers never got a

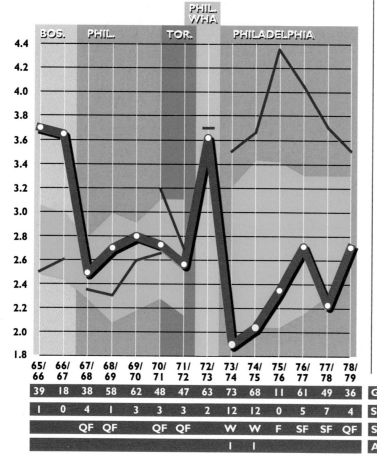

A STANLEY CUP–WINNING PARENT SKATE, AUTOGRAPHED BY THE FLYERS

	BOS.		PHIL.				TOR.	PHIL. WHA	PHILADELPHIA				
	65/66	66/67	67/68	68/69	69/70	70/71	71/72	72/73	73/74	74/75	75/76	76/77	77/78	78/79
GAMES	39	18	38	58	62	48	47	63	73	68	11	61	49	36
SHUTOUTS	1	0	4	1	3	3	2	12	12	0		5	7	4
STANLEY CUP			QF	QF		QF	QF		W	W	F	SF	SF	QF
ALL STAR TEAM									1	1				

chance to put Parent back on the ice. The Miami Screaming Eagles of the new league signed him with a five-year, $750,000 deal that included a new boat, house and car every year. In his final season in Toronto, Parent had been making $40,000. When the Miami team failed to materialize for the first WHA season, 1972/73, Parent's contract was picked up by the league's Philadelphia Blazers club.

It was an unhappy experience. He broke his toe at the start of the season, played in front of crowds of 2,000, and allowed a goal a game more than he had in Toronto. When he refused to play after an overtime loss in the first game of the playoffs against the Cleveland Barons, who had Cheevers, teammates accused him of walking out on them; the Blazers, sans Parent, were swept four straight. But Parent said money was the issue: he had discovered that $400,000 of his salary package, which was supposed to be in escrow, wasn't. His WHA rights were transferred to the New York Golden Blades, which had no bearing on Parent's plans. He was going across town to the Flyers.

"I used to watch poor Bernie in a WHA game," said Fred Shero, the Flyers' coach. "And, hell, he had to stop forty-five shots a game. Rather than hurting him, the WHA made him a better goalie. He'd never seen so many shots in an NHL game."

In his first game back in the NHL, Parent let in seven goals in twelve minutes, and Shero pulled him. Opening-night jitters dispensed with, he grew his trademark moustache and turned into a brick wall, winning the Vezina with a GA of 1.89, leading the league with twelve shutouts and anchoring the Flyers' Stanley Cup win that spring with a 2.02 average and two shutouts in seventeen games.

"When Parent is out there," said Shero, "we know we can win games we have no business winning."

His pregame regimen was uncomplicated: half a dozen beers and eight hours of sleep. In 1974/75, he won another Vezina, another Stanley Cup and another Conn Smythe. "Bernie makes you feel like you can walk on water," said Flyers captain Bobby Clarke. In this fifteen-game playoff campaign, Parent's GA was 1.89, with four shutouts. No goaltender had a better GA or more

shutouts in the 1973/74 or 1974/75 playoffs.

A neck injury in 1975/76 reduced his season to eleven games; Wayne Stephenson played net for the Flyers as Montreal defeated them in the final to begin a four-cup winning streak. The injury also denied him the chance to play in the 1976 Canada Cup.

He always feared a serious injury, hoping to enjoy the kind of endless career Plante had, and he was fortunate that, apart from his neck problems, the game had been kind to him. But on February 17, 1979, in a home game against the Rangers, a stick to the eye ended his professional career at 671 regular-season games, with a lifetime NHL GA of 2.55.

"I feel bad about the whole thing," he said at the end of the season, when doctors told him there was no way he could return to play, "but all good things must come to an end sometime. I've got many pleasant memories, especially those two Stanley Cups." A religious man, Parent could be found giving motivational talks at schools and churches when he wasn't off bow hunting or deep-sea fishing. He stayed in the Flyers organization as a goaltending coach. The team retired his number, and in 1984 he was inducted into the Hockey Hall of Fame. ○

PARENT SCRAMBLES AGAINST HIS FORMER TEAM, THE TORONTO MAPLE LEAFS, WHERE FOR ONE AND A HALF SEASONS JACQUES PLANTE TAUGHT HIM EVERYTHING HE KNEW.

ED GIACOMIN

IN AN ARENA NOTORIOUS FOR TURNING ON ITS STARS, "FAST EDDIE" WAS ALWAYS A FAVOURITE OF RANGERS FANS

GIACOMIN TRIED TO CARRY A "SPARK WITH EDDIE" ADVERTISEMENT ON HIS MASK AT THE END OF HIS CAREER. THE LEAGUE WOULDN'T ALLOW IT, BUT THE SPARKING MOTIF HE'D HAD PREPARED SURVIVED IN HIS FINAL MASK, WORN AS A DETROIT RED WING.

Frank Boucher's description of Chuck Rayner as "brilliantly aggressive" could be applied with equal confidence to Eddie Giacomin, who took charge of the New York Rangers goal more than a decade after Rayner's performances had earned him the Hart Trophy. But if there was an essential similarity in the attitude Rayner and Giacomin brought to the assignment of playing goal for New York, it was a quirk of history rather than a case of emulation on Giacomin's part. "Fast Eddie" Giacomin never saw Rayner play, and growing up in Sudbury, Ontario, his goaltending hero was Turk Broda, because Toronto was the team young boys like Giacomin followed devotedly on "Hockey Night in Canada."

Giacomin's success required enormous persistence. At fifteen he was cut at a tryout for the Hamilton Red Wings, Detroit's Junior affiliate; at eighteen, he was sent home from a Detroit tryout. A kitchen stove explosion severely burned his legs and feet and nearly claimed his ability to skate. After playing two seasons of industrial-league back in Sudbury, he got a break through his brother Rollie, five years older than him and an accomplished goaltender in his own right, who provided crucial

tutorials to the young Eddie. Rollie had been invited to play for the Washington Presidents of the minor pro Eastern Hockey League, but couldn't go, and sent Eddie in his place. The younger Giacomin played so well that he was invited to the training camp of the American League's Providence Reds.

In refining his game, Giacomin took inspiration from the butterfly style of Glenn Hall and the wandering tendencies of Jacques Plante. He made his NHL debut in 1965/66 after five seasons in Providence. The Reds, which had no parent NHL club, were a struggling outfit, and Giacomin never did win the Holmes, the AHL's version of the Vezina. Nor did he ever make an AHL All Star team. But Rangers coach and GM Emile Francis, a former goaltender himself, knew talent when he saw it, and cut a deal for Giacomin. Much was made of Giacomin's arrival in New York, as Francis dealt away four players to the Reds to get him.

Giacomin had a disappointing rookie season: in thirty-six games his GA of 3.66 was more than half a goal above LGA. "I was so excited," says Giacomin. "I was twenty-six and I didn't think I was ever going to make it to the NHL. I forgot that I was there to stop pucks."

Fortunately for Giacomin and the Rangers, Francis gave him another chance, and made him the team's regular starter for 1966/67. Giacomin responded magnificently. In only his second season in the big league, he was named to his first professional All Star team—and onto the first team, no less, ahead of Glenn Hall. For five straight seasons, Giacomin was either a first or second team appointee. His GA dropped to 2.61 in his second season, and just kept getting better. By 1970/71, it was down to 2.16, and with his backup Gilles Villemure, Giacomin won the Vezina with a combined GA of 2.27.

The Rangers of Emile Francis and Eddie Giacomin were a true sporting dynasty. After the team had missed the playoffs in Giacomin's debut season, the Rangers were part of the "second season" for the next nine years. The peak of his career in New York came in 1971/72, when the Rangers reached the Stanley Cup final for the first time since Rayner and company in 1949/50. Like the Rangers more than thirty seasons before them, Giacomin's Rangers lost, this time to Boston.

"It was Eddie's ambition to score a goal," says Francis. Giacomin came awfully close twice on empty nets. In a game against the Maple Leafs, he nearly did it on a fluke clearing shot, flipping the puck off the glass and down the ice. The puck ran out of steam in the Toronto crease. Against the Canadiens in Montreal,

	65/66	66/67	67/68	68/69	69/70	70/71	71/72	72/73	73/74	74/75	75/76	76/77	77/78
GAMES	36	68	66	70	70	45	44	43	56	37	33	33	9
SHUTOUTS	0	9	8	7	6	8	1	4	5	1	2	3	0
STANLEY CUP		SF	QF	QF	QF	SF	F	SF	SF	PR			QF
ALL STAR TEAM		1	2	2	2	1							

Gump Worsley had just been pulled for an extra skater when Giacomin made a deliberate bid for a goal, taking aim at the empty Montreal net. He was so sure it was going in that he was celebrating his achievement when the puck glanced off the outside of the post.

Giacomin came perilously close to becoming the first goaltender ever to be scored on by another goaltender, when he came up against the ambitions of Gary "Suitcase" Smith. Smith would share the Vezina with Tony Esposito in Chicago in 1971/72, but from 1967/68 to 1970/71 Smith was toiling for the Oakland Seals. (He was called "Suitcase" because he played on eight different teams in his fifteen-season career.) During a near-fateful game between the Seals and the Rangers, Smith took it upon himself to get the Seals on the scoreboard, and took off for the Rangers end, crossing centre ice. "Rod Seiling was the last man back," Giacomin remembers. If Smith had managed to beat Seiling, there would have been a truly spectacular breakaway. The rules were later changed to forbid the goaltender from crossing centre ice. Giacomin has no idea why. "The goaltenders never make the rules," he says. "They're always changing the rules to make it worse for the goaltenders."

Growing up in Sudbury, Giacomin played a lot of three-on-three pick-up hockey, in which the goaltender often played as a forward as well, and this helped make Giacomin a particularly strong skater. He made for a dashing, handsome figure in the New York goal, with carefully groomed hair and an unmarked face. In his entire career, he was cut for about a dozen stitches, and only took to wearing a mask later in his career because of increasing concerns about eye injuries.

Giacomin's final seasons were marked by significant changes in professional hockey. The explosion of professional clubs through the arrival of the WHA and expansion in the NHL had made for a very different game on the ice. "There was more open ice," he says: a less disciplined style created more three-on-one rushes and breakaways, which helped boost LGA in the latter half of the 1970s. And he found the air travel wearying. That, more than anything, was the reason you needed a backup goaltender, says Giacomin. When he started out in the league, there was a seventy-game schedule; in four seasons from 1966/67 to 1969/70 he played all but six games, and from 1966/67 to 1968/69 led the league in victories. But once teams started having to roam all over the continent, those seventy games, which increased to eighty by 1974/75, became a lot harder to play. "The time changes really got to you. You needed somebody else to take your place."

In 1975/76, John Ferguson replaced Emile Francis as the Rangers' general manager. Giacomin was thirty-six and, in Ferguson's book, yesterday's man. In November 1975, to the dismay of intensely loyal New York fans, Ferguson sold Giacomin to Detroit. When he made his first visit back to Madison Square Garden as a Red Wing, the ovation was deafening, and Detroit won 6–4. It was one of the few high points for Giacomin that season. The Red Wings logged their sixth spring without a playoff appearance, but the Rangers didn't make the playoffs, either. The Red Wings missed the playoffs again in 1976/77, and after playing only nine games in 1977/78, Giacomin retired.

The Rangers became one of only four NHL teams to retire a goaltender's number when they put aside his "1" for good. After a spell in the restaurant business in Michigan, Giacomin returned to New York to serve as a goaltending coach from 1986 to 1989 under GM Phil Esposito, who as a Bruin had taken the Stanley Cup away from him in 1972. He was elected to the Hockey Hall of Fame in 1987. Fast Eddie now lives in Florida. ○

GIACOMIN HAD A PONDEROUS RISE TO STARDOM, WHICH INCLUDED FIVE ANONYMOUS SEASONS IN THE AMERICAN LEAGUE. WHEN HE WAS ELECTED TO THE NHL'S FIRST ALL STAR TEAM IN HIS SECOND SEASON, IT WAS THE FIRST ALL STAR TEAM HE'D EVER MADE.

CHAPTER 8

INTERNATIONALE

GOALTENDING STARS OF THE INTERNATIONAL AMATEUR GAME

The Czechoslovakian national team of the 1970s, which won world titles in 1972, 1976 and 1977, featured outstanding goaltending by Jiri Holecek *(spread)* and Vladimir Dzurilla *(inset)*. Dzurilla was a star of the 1976 Canada Cup, delivering Team Canada its only loss of the tournament, a 1–0 shutout.

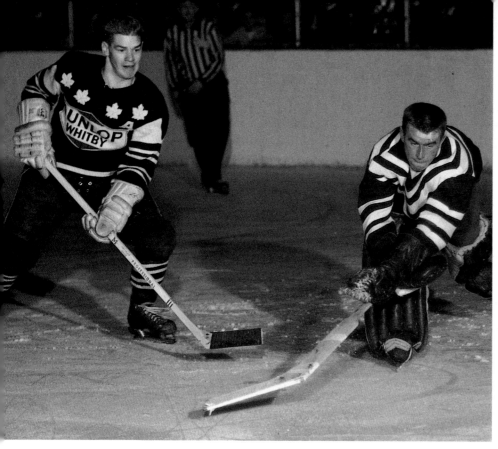

When Vladislav Tretiak showed up in Montreal in September 1972 to face the cream of Canadian professionals, Canadian strategists thought he was the least of their worries. After all, the word on Tretiak (on Soviet goaltenders in general) was that they were the weak spot in the Russian ice machine. Back in 1957, for example, a team of Soviet selects played the Whitby Dunlops at Maple Leaf Gardens with a netminder named Erkin *(above left)*, and lost 7–2. Tretiak, of course, proved himself to be any-

thing but a weak spot. And he was no fluke. The Russians had won big games before with great goaltending. Their goaltender when they won their first world championship, in 1954, was Nikolai Puchkov *(above right, with trophy)*, whose talent rivalled Tretiak's. A soccer player, he didn't even begin playing hockey until age twenty, four years before winning the world title. Puchkov stunned the Canadians by delivering them a 7–2 loss in the gold-medal game, and he went on to anchor a long string of Soviet international victories.

Every twenty years, the United States hosts a winter Olympics and stages a miracle on ice with some clutch goaltending. Jack McCartan did it in Squaw Valley in 1960 *(left)*, making thirty-nine saves in a 2–1 semifinal win over Canada on the way to a gold medal. In 1980 in Lake Placid, Jim Craig held off the Russians in a 4-3 semifinal victory that allowed the Americans to go on to win gold. Neither McCartan nor Craig were able to repeat their amateur successes in the professional arena. McCartan had an eight-game stint with the Rangers after the Olympics, then came back with the WHA's Minnesota Fighting Saints in 1972. Craig played twenty-three games with the Bruins after the Olympics, and three games with the Minnesota North Stars in 1983/84.

omen have been playing hockey just about as long as men, but it has taken high-profile victories by the Canadian women's team at the world championships to reaffirm the legitimacy of women's hockey. The team's goaltender Manon Rheaume *(left, at the 1994 worlds)* has been pursuing doggedly a professional career in a game otherwise dominated by men.

Goaltenders didn't get much better than Joe Sullivan, who decided professional hockey was no way to make a living. Sullivan was the netminder for the University of Toronto team that won the first Memorial Cup, the Canadian Junior hockey championship, in 1919. As a member of the superb University of Toronto Varsity Grads, which was managed by future Maple Leaf impresario Conn Smythe, Sullivan wore the maple leaf at the 1928 Olympics *(right and below)*. He was never scored on in the entire tournament as Canada struck gold. Returning home, he debated turning pro with Smythe's newly acquired Maple Leafs, but resolved that a career in medicine was the more prudent course. Sullivan became a leading surgeon specializing in hearing problems. Active in the Progressive Conservative party, he was appointed to the Canadian Senate in 1957. ○

CHAPTER 9

TROIKA

IN THE 1970S, THE DOMINANT NAMES IN GOALTENDING WERE TRETIAK, DRYDEN AND ESPOSITO

OPPOSITE: TONY ESPOSITO CAME OUT OF OBSCURITY TO WIN THE CALDER AND THE VEZINA WITH A RECORD FIFTEEN SHUTOUTS IN 1969/70. HE REGULARLY PLAYED THE BULK OF THE BLACKHAWKS SEASON UNTIL HIS RETIREMENT IN 1984.

BELOW: A PROGRAM FROM THE 1972 CANADA–RUSSIA SERIES, SAVED BY A CANADIAN FAN WHO MADE THE TRIP TO MOSCOW.

Three goaltenders provided the dominant images of their profession in the 1970s. Others shared the limelight—Gerry Cheevers for one, Bernie Parent for another. But in Ken Dryden, Tony Esposito and Vladislav Tretiak the public found a troika of netminding stars. Their paths crossed and recrossed in some of the most exciting hockey ever played. Though they all burst upon the scene within a two-season span, there was a considerable spread in their ages: Esposito was born in 1943, Dryden in 1947, Tretiak in 1952. They were similar if only because they were so different from everyone else: each came from a background very different from the kind that customarily led to netminding excellence.

Ken Dryden is remembered, above all, for The Stance: hands atop his stick, chin atop his hands, one knee flexed, more contemplative of the spectacle of the game than the spectators on the other side of the boards. Goaltending, ultimately, is a reactive discipline, and it has been Ken Dryden's metier to react as arrestingly on the ice as off. For most of his little more than eight seasons in the NHL, he was the game's dominant goaltender. But in a discipline of outsiders, he was an outsider even among them.

He was so different as a character that the fact he was one of the best ever to wear a set of pads became almost secondary to his mystique. He is not usually cited as one of the all-time goaltending greats. Dryden himself, in his book, *The Game*, declared, "For me, the greatest goalies must always be Hall, Sawchuk, Plante and Bower." But greatness in the net certainly was the foundation of everything else that Dryden was and became.

Ken was overnight famous, his ambitions played out under a harsh public glare. He amazed and confounded observers by making a law degree as important a goal as winning Stanley Cups. His older brother Dave, also a professional goaltender, was methodically and successfully pursuing similar dreams of forging a professional life away from the rink. But Dave was able to do this beyond the limelight that held Ken. For the younger Dryden, any ambition to satisfy his personal goals had to defy notions of his obligations, real and imagined, to his country and to the greatest hockey team in the world.

Tony Esposito also had an older hockey brother, the celebrated Phil. The Espositos were much closer in age than the Drydens—Tony and Phil were separated by fourteen months, Ken and Dave by six years. But with the Espositos there was a sense of "younger" and "older" as strong as with the Drydens. Both Dave and Phil served as mentors and role models to their siblings.

And both sets of brothers had fathers in the construction industry. Patrick Esposito worked for Algoma Contracting in Sault Ste. Marie, Ontario; Murray Dryden sold bricks and building materials. Their parents were also, to varying measure, hockey parents. Murray Dryden paved the backyard of the family home in the Toronto suburb of Islington with red asphalt, turning it into a year-round road hockey arena. Windows were boarded over and barred to prevent breakage; some days Margaret Dryden felt as if she was living in prison. Patrick Esposito was absolutely devoted to minor hockey, making sure Algoma Contracting sponsored the teams his sons played on, and when he decided the Soo needed a Junior A hockey club, he pooled his resources and with several partners founded the Greyhounds.

Dryden played Junior B in Toronto, and was good enough to be selected in the NHL's draft of unsigned amateurs in June 1964, not yet seventeen. Dryden was picked third by Boston, fourteenth overall. Boston thereupon committed one of the greatest recruiting errors of that decade, rivalled only by the Toronto Maple Leafs' failure to secure the rights to Brad Park in 1966, when Park was playing right in the Toronto feeder system. (For that matter, Toronto had also overlooked Ken Dryden, even though he, too, was in their territory—they had even once held the contract of brother Dave.) Right after the draft, Boston traded its rights to Ken Dryden and Alex Campbell to Montreal in exchange for the rights to Guy Allen and Paul Reid. Of the four, only Dryden ever played professionally.

At the age Dryden was drafted, Tony Esposito wasn't close to sure he was going to play professional hockey. He grew up in the shadow of his supremely talented older brother, and the fact that he had to wear glasses when he played (with a cage protector) hampered his game. His parents invested money in contact lenses when he was about sixteen, a considerable investment then, and that probably saved his career. Even then, he showed much more promise as a football halfback than as a hockey player. He hung in as a Juvenile player until his final year of eligibility, at eighteen, and then dropped out of hockey in favour of football. He probably would never have played Junior A if his dad hadn't organized the Greyhounds and the team hadn't badgered him into joining.

His Junior career was brief, lasting only the 1962/63 season. At nineteen, he got a hockey scholarship to Michigan Tech, arranged for him by a Soo sporting goods dealer, Al Bumbacco. In three seasons between 1964 and 1967, he played in fifty-one games with a 2.60 average. Whatever equivocation he had shown about the game back in the Soo, at Michigan Tech he was a standout. Twice named an All American, in 1965 he led Tech to the

Continued from page 175

Or is he? Skill, as we have seen, is a difficult thing to assess using a measuring stick of raw numbers. If the goaltenders aren't better, they are assuredly different, and the game around them is different. The goaltender has never been more respected. Leaving aside the permissiveness in equipment, significant changes in the playing rules have also served to increase the goaltender's comfort zone. In 1987/88, the league introduced a dual crease—adding a six-foot semicircular crease as it prepared to phase out the old four-by-eight rectangle. In 1991/92, the rectangle disappeared, and penalties were conferred on attacking players infringing on the crease or making unnecessary contact with the goaltender. A goal would also be disallowed if an attacking player was standing on or inside the crease line, or had his stick inside it. At the same time, however, the NHL goaltender's job has been made more of a challenge in the NHL by the addition in 1990/91 of an extra foot of space between the back of the net and the end boards. With more room for attacking players to direct scoring chances from behind the net, it should be no surprise that goaltenders like Arturs Irbe and Dominik Hasek, at ease on the international amateur game's larger ice surface, have done so well in the NHL.

Not all goaltenders are cheering the general progress from which the latest members of the fraternity benefit. Frank Brimsek and Gerry McNeil watch modern goaltenders ply their trade and blanche at what they see. For one thing, they wander too much. "I don't like it now," Brimsek declares. "They have no business roaming. They get caught so badly, it's pathetic. They'd be wise to fine the guy $500 for every goal that got by. In my day, you could hit a goaltender. Once he left the crease, he was another player. You can't do that now.

"You just worried about the angles," adds Brimsek. "But I didn't come out like they do today. You'd lose the direction of the net. You wouldn't know where it is."

"There was a lot more passing then than now," says McNeil. "It's more bashing now. They come in and have to wind up and shoot. It used to have a little more finesse. If you went down, the guy would go to the other side of you."

Maybe, McNeil concedes, goaltenders today have adopted a style they have to play. For it is a different game entirely from the one he knew.

Three of the great stars of the Original Six and the expansion years, Glenn Hall, Johnny Bower and Eddie Giacomin, have gone on to coach the new generation. Glenn Hall is the goaltending coach for the Calgary Flames, Johnny Bower still runs his hockey camp, and Eddie Giacomin was the New York Rangers' goaltending coach under general manager Phil Esposito from

Continued on page 188

GERRY CHEEVERS SWORE A GOALTENDER WOULD HAVE BEEN KILLED IF THE MASK HADN'T BEEN INVENTED. IN THE 1993 NHL PLAYOFFS, THE VALUE OF THE MODERN GOALTENDER'S HELMET WAS REAFFIRMED WHEN A SLAPSHOT BY LEAF CAPTAIN WENDEL CLARK HIT ST. LOUIS GOALTENDER CURTIS JOSEPH WITH SUCH FORCE THAT HIS HELMET (*ABOVE*) WAS TORN OFF. JOSEPH IS ALIVE AND WELL AND PLAYING GOAL.

BILLY SMITH

"BATTLIN' BILLY" WAS THE ULTIMATE MONEY GOALIE AS THE ISLANDERS WON FOUR STANLEY CUPS

Some goaltenders are remembered for their unique style. Billy Smith is one of them, but it's not for the way he stopped pucks. It's for the way he sent people to the infirmary with his stick. Battlin' Billy was more tenacious in clearing his crease than Gerry Cheevers, and slightly less manic about it than Ron Hextall. He was a self-proclaimed goaltending goon, an agitator who stirred up trouble when the rest of his team didn't, and he thought they should. All hacking and slashing aside, though, Smith was one of goaltending's true greats, his career stretching from 1971 to 1989, with all but five games played as a New York Islander. In only two seasons was his GA lower than LGA—his first and his last, and in those seasons his team's scoring dipped below LGA as well.

NEW YORK ISLANDERS

	72/73	73/74	74/75	75/76	76/77	77/78	78/79	79/80	80/81	81/82	82/83	83/84	84/85	85/86	86/87	87/88	88/89	
GAMES	37	46	58	39	36	38	40	38	41	46	41	42	37	41	40	38	17	
SHUTOUTS	0	0	3	3	2	2	1	2	2	0	1	2	0	1	1	2	0	
STANLEY CUP			SF	SF	SF	QF	SF	W	W	W	W	F	DF	DSF	DF	DSF		
ALL STAR TEAM										1								

Smith played five games for Los Angeles in 1971/72 with a 4.60 GA.

Like Jacques Plante, Smith was an iconoclast who went his own way. He warmed slowly to strangers, and told Islanders coach Al Arbour what he was and wasn't prepared to do. He was prepared to win games, big ones and small ones. He skipped team meetings. He avoided practices and training camp, arguing that he was only asking for an injury. But he wasn't lazy. Smith was a devoted tennis player, and believed that the game helped a goaltender with his footwork. He also swore by the ability of video games to hone hand–eye co-ordination. He played them at home with his kids; more seriously, he worked out on a machine developed by an ophthalmologist, Dr. Leon Revien, designed to "strengthen vision and reflexes." Old-time netminders like Davey Kerr, who avoided movies and wore sunglasses when he read to preserve his eyesight, would have been appalled by the sight of Smith parked in front of Dr. Revien's device, trying to stop a dot shooting across the screen at 250 miles an hour, or trying to identify fourteen digits flashed on the screen for 1/100th of a second. As odd as the training method was when Smith became an advocate in the early eighties, such tools are now a standard part of off-ice preparation for goaltenders.

Smith didn't keep a book on shooters like other goaltenders, because he said the best opponents changed their tactics. He paid attention to his GA, but if a game was going well he wasn't adverse to trying something unorthodox, since he didn't believe practice was the place to learn anything. Like Plante before him, he was able to go his own way because he won games. There was no way to argue with the fact that Smith knew what he was doing.

Smith grew up in the eastern Ontario town of Perth and played his Junior hockey in nearby Smith Falls and Cornwall. Drafted by the L.A. Kings in 1970, he was assigned to Springfield in the American league for two seasons, and won the league championship in 1970/71. He saw action in five games with L.A. in 1971/72, but when the Kings acquired Rogie Vachon from Montreal in November 1971, he was made expendable. The New York Islanders, a new franchise joining the league in 1972, picked him in the expansion draft. Ten years later, Smith would be the only original Islander left on the team.

That was no big surprise: the original team was pretty awful, winning only ten of seventy-eight games in its first season, thirteen in its second. Al Arbour was hired as coach for the second season, and with GM Bill Torrey he began to build a contender. Glenn "Chico" Resch, four years older than Smith, was made a tag-team netminding partner in 1974. They were an odd couple: Resch was far more gregarious, always ready to talk to the press. "Chico, he'd talk to the wall if it would listen," Smith reflected in 1979. Smith, on the other hand, mistrusted the press, at least early in his career, annoyed by misquotes. But they meshed well, playing tennis together and respecting each other's desire to play as many games as possible.

Resch attracted the most attention. For five straight seasons his GA was below 2.50 and he made the second All Star team in 1975/76 and 1978/79. Smith's one note of glory came in 1979, when the Colorado Rockies pulled their goaltender in favour of an extra attacker and accidentally put the puck in their own net with an errant pass. Because Smith was the last Islander to touch the puck, he was credited with the goal, a first for an NHL goaltender.

As the Islanders turned into a Stanley Cup contender, Smith began to attract attention too. Notwithstanding a very good GA, Smith was making headlines as a hatchet man. "I don't bother people unless they're bothering me," he said in 1982. "I just try to give myself a little working room. But if a guy bothers me, then I retaliate." It was a standard explanation by stick-wielding goaltenders (Davey Kerr would have agreed with him at least on this), but Smith also had a pugnacious streak to which he freely owned up. In the playoffs of 1977/78 and 1978/79, the Islanders had appeared ready to challenge Montreal's grip on the Stanley Cup, but never got the chance, bowing out to Toronto and the Rangers before they could reach the final. Smith, for one, felt the team had let itself be pushed around. He was determined to start pushing back.

Almost overnight, Smith was heralded as the game's greatest goaltender. Ken Dryden and Gerry Cheevers retired; Bernie Parent was forced out by an eye injury. The Islanders won the Stanley Cup in 1979/80, then Resch moved on to the expansion Colorado Rockies. And there was Smith, winning Stanley Cups—four in a row. He won the Vezina in 1981/82, the first season in which the trophy was put to a vote rather than being awarded to the goaltenders on the team with the lowest GA, now the domain of the Jennings. For good measure, Smith and his new partner, Rollie Melanson, won the Jennings in 1982/83. He was named to his first (and last) NHL All Star team in 1981/82. In1983/84, when the Islanders' cup streak ended with a final-series loss to Edmonton, Smith broke Ken Dryden's record of eighty playoff wins.

"He may be the all-time money player," Torrey said in May 1983 after cup number four was in the bag and Smith had won the Conn Smythe. Indeed, money was a critical bottom line to him. He didn't believe in shaking hands with opponents after a playoff series loss because congratulations seemed a bit hypocritical when the other guy was picking up the bonus money.

His most lasting contribution to the game may have come through the injuries he inflicted on opponents. In the 1981/82 playoffs, Vancouver's Tiger Williams expressed the desire to "punch Smith in the esophagus so he has to eat out of a blender for six months." His slash of Glenn Anderson in the 1982/83 Stanley Cup brought calls from the Oilers for his suspension. In 1985, he broke the cheek and jaw of Blackhawk Curt Fraser, incurring a six-game suspension. "If they change the rules and make the crease bigger," he said at the time of the Fraser injury, "it would stop all this cheap stuff. I've been recommending that for ten years and it's like talking to a wall."

In 1987, the league finally listened, and introduced the six-foot semicircular crease. Smith enjoyed two seasons of NHL hockey with it before retiring at thirty-nine and becoming a goaltending coach. In 1993, Smith became the first goaltender who had his big wins in the 1980s to be inducted into the Hall of Fame. ○

LAST MAN BACK: SMITH WAS THE ONLY ORIGINAL ISLANDER LEFT WHEN THE TEAM WAS WINNING STANLEY CUPS, TEN YEARS AFTER IT ENTERED THE LEAGUE.

ED BELFOUR

INSPIRED BY ESPOSITO, TUTORED BY TRETIAK, HE HAS SHOT FROM OBSCURITY INTO GOALTENDING'S ELITE RANKS

Until Tom Barrasso came along in 1983, goaltenders flew in the face of accepted hockey recruiting wisdom. Taking them in the first round of the amateur draft was a waste of a pick because goaltenders rarely showed their true potential when they were still young amateurs. It was almost unheard of for a young amateur to come into the NHL and immediately cause a sensation. Those who did—Tony Esposito and Ken Dryden were two—had had some grooming in the American collegiate and minor pro system, and were at least true to form in not having been top draft picks.

When Barrasso was picked by Buffalo in the first round, and came into the NHL right out of a Boston high school at age eighteen to win the Calder and the Vezina, traditional wisdom was stood on its head. Three years later, Ron Hextall crashed into the league after a short minor pro stint and won just about all the goaltending marbles. In 1990, it was Ed Belfour's turn.

Belfour did not burst into the NHL with quite the suddenness of Barrasso, but it was an impressive arrival nonetheless. It was the standard "out of nowhere" tale, Ed Belfour's nowhere being Carman, Manitoba, population 3,500. "In grade three, I drew a couple pictures of Tony Esposito and I won first prize in an art show," he would relate; naturally, he developed an Esposito butterfly style.

The professional hockey world paid him scant attention. At twenty-one, he came to the University of North Dakota on a hockey scholarship. As with Esposito and Dryden (and Jon Casey, his predecessor at North Dakota), the U.S. collegiate system fed him into the NHL pipeline. North Dakota won the national title in Belfour's first season, 1986/87, as Belfour compiled a 29–4 record, with a GA of 2.43. His performance got him on the western collegiate first All Star team, but in the amateur draft that summer, every NHL club passed on him. In September, though, Chicago—Espo's team—signed him as a free agent.

Belfour was assigned to Saginaw of the International League, where he was named rookie of the year and a first-team All Star in 1987/88. His next season was split between Saginaw and the Blackhawks; in his twenty-three appearances for Chicago,

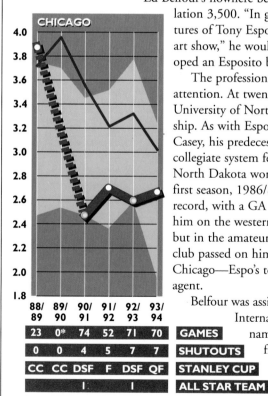

CHICAGO

	88/89	89/90	90/91	91/92	92/93	93/94	
	23	0*	74	52	71	70	**GAMES**
	0	0	4	5	7	7	**SHUTOUTS**
	CC	CC	DSF	F	DSF	QF	**STANLEY CUP**
				I		I	**ALL STAR TEAM**

*Belfour played nine games for Chicago in the 1989/90 playoffs, with a 2.49 GA.

his 3.87 average indicated a need for more minor-league seasoning. Chicago acquired Greg Millen from the Nordiques; with no ice time available, Belfour chose to make a detour into the Canadian Olympic team program. At the end of the season, though, the Blackhawks brought him up for the playoffs. They got as far as the conference championship, and Belfour's 4–2 record, with appearances in a total of nine games, produced a 2.49 average. For 1990/91, the starter's job was his.

A storybook season unfolded, abetted by the collapse of the Soviet Union, which permitted Vladislav Tretiak to venture overseas as a goaltending coach for the first time in 1990. Chicago hired him, and Belfour became his star pupil. Belfour led the league in games played (seventy-four), in wins (forty-three), in GA (2.47) and in save percentage (.910). Named to the first All Star team, he walked away from the league's annual awards presentation with just about everything there was for a goaltender to win: the Vezina, the Jennings and the Calder.

One cloud cast a shadow over his marvellous rookie season. The Blackhawks had been blown out of the playoffs by the upstart Minnesota North Stars; Belfour went 2–4 with a 4.07 GA. For many pundits, the true measure of a goaltender's greatness is not GA or save percentage, but whether or not he can deliver a championship. Having won every goaltending honour in his first full tour of duty in the NHL, Belfour now faced the task of proving himself as a netminder who can get the Stanley Cup into the Windy City, which had fallen short in every season since 1960/61.

He has at least shown himself to be the real thing, not a one-season wonder who fades quickly after a spectacularly showy debut. In his second season he became the third-highest-paid goaltender in the league at $925,000, behind Toronto's newly acquired Grant Fuhr ($1.6 million) and Montreal's Patrick Roy ($1.2 million). His second tour didn't bring any silverware, though he did lead the league with five shutouts and his playoff performance was solid: a league-leading 2.47 GA with twelve wins in eighteen starts. In their drive to a Stanley Cup appearance, the Blackhawks won a record eleven straight games. But then, so did the Pittsburgh Penguins, and when Chicago and Pittsburgh met in the final, it was no contest. The more experienced Tom Barrasso was exceptional as Belfour and the Blackhawks went down four straight.

In 1992/93, Belfour was back collecting prizes, winning the Vezina and the Jennings as well as making the first All Star team. But after another fine season, the Blackhawks made an early exit from the playoffs. That June, trade rumours swirled around Belfour. He was now twenty-eight; perhaps it was time the Blackhawks cashed him in with a lucrative trade. The team had been keeping another promising netminder, Jimmy Waite, in the wings since drafting him eighth overall in 1987. Chicago had already parted with Dominik Hasek

in August 1992, trading him to Buffalo. The Blackhawks had picked up the Czech star as a draft afterthought in 1983, taking him 199th in the fourth round. He was spectacular in the 1991 Canada Cup, and with the crumbling of the Eastern bloc, was ready to come to the professional game. Hasek would have an outstanding season in 1993/94, winning the Jennings and the Vezina and finishing runner-up in Hart voting.

Chicago general manager Bob Pulford chose to stick with Belfour, and Waite went to the new San Jose Sharks. The Blackhawks finished fifth of six in the Western Conference's very competitive central division and made a quick exit from the playoffs. It was a season when Belfour lived up to the temperamental reputation he'd had since his North Dakota days. In December 1993, Belfour's relatives had come out to see him play the Winnipeg Jets, but when he let in two goals on the first four shots, coach Darryl Sutter pulled him. Belfour boiled over at the humiliation, throwing his stick at the bench and delivering Sutter a public tongue-lashing. He also led the league in shutouts for the third straight season, and when no individual honours came his way, he made his displeasure known. Fan voting chose two other goaltenders from the central division, Curtis Joseph of St. Louis and Felix Potvin of Toronto, as starters in the All Star game. "They get a lot more coverage than I do," he complained. "Toronto's a big-time hockey market. I get tired of hearing all the time that Joseph stops the most shots. Anyone can stop shots from the red line." ○

AS A KID, BELFOUR WON AN ART CONTEST DRAWING PICTURES OF TONY ESPOSITO. HE NOW PLAYS FOR ESPOSITO'S OLD TEAM, WINNING GAMES WITH ESPOSITO'S STYLE.

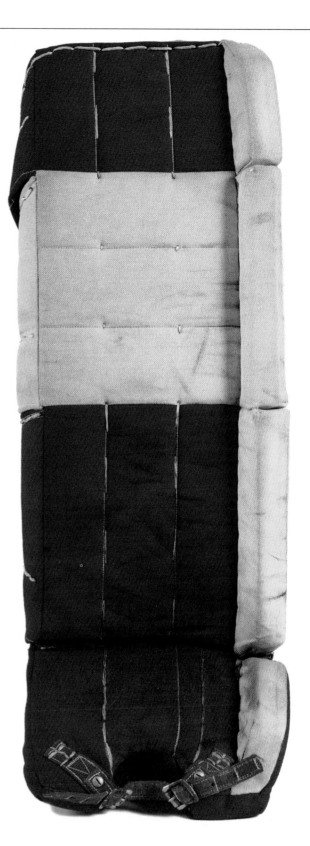

Early in the 1986/87 season, Calgary Flames goaltender Reggie Lemelin tried out this prototype set of synthetic leg pads made by inventor Jim Lowson. They were undersize, even by the old ten-inch width standard, and in the spring Lemelin got a new pair. The synthetic pads were one-third the weight of conventional ones. Lemelin found they took the strain off his back, and they helped revitalize his career.

Synthetic leg pads are now a standard part of the goaltender's inventory, but the look and feel of leather has not vanished. Modern pads with leather exteriors take advantage of new construction techniques and materials to solve the problems of deterioration and weight gain associated with their spongelike predecessors. This set was worn by Corey Hirsch, goaltender for Canada's silver medal team at the 1994 Olympics.

FELIX POTVIN

AFTER A FOUR-GAME TRYOUT IN 1991/92, THE CAT CAME BACK TO THE LEAF GOAL, A YEAR AHEAD OF SCHEDULE

The annual universal draft is a place old hockey hands are constantly telling young hopefuls to avoid. Don't go and sit in the arena, waiting for your name to be selected by one of the NHL teams. Stay home and wait for the news by telephone, if and when it comes. Because when you aren't selected, the sense of rejection, of failure, is excruciating.

Felix Potvin made the mistake of attending the 1989 draft at Minnesota's Met Center. He was told that if he was going to be picked, it would come in the first three rounds. When selections moved on to round four, and no one had chosen him, the eighteen-year-old goaltender for the Chicoutimi Sagueneens was left alone and in tears in the stands.

It was the only hiccup in Felix Potvin's rise to NHL stardom. He has come to take his place in goaltending's top ranks by following a steady, logical progression. In a profession in which the best consistently show up from the most unexpected avenues, Felix the Cat has come into the big city right down Main Street, in plain view the whole way.

Like Ron Hextall, he has hockey in his blood. His father, Pierre, was a centre in the Quebec Senior league who chose firefighting over the opportunity to turn pro in the Bruins system. Felix started out playing as a forward in the east end Montreal neighbourhood of Anjou, but the equipment the goaltenders got to wear intrigued him. As an Atom, he was enrolled in a goaltending school by his parents, and that fixed his future. Though he grew up in greater Montreal, he was not a Canadiens fan. He followed the Nordiques, and as a role model looked to the Islanders' Billy Smith.

After his rejection in the 1989 draft, Potvin went back to the Sagueneens and the Quebec Junior league and fine-tuned his game. His GA in the offence-minded Quebec league dropped from 4.66 to 3.99. And in the summer of 1990, the Toronto Maple Leafs spoke for him in the second round of the draft, taking him thirty-first overall. He returned to the Sagueneens for one more season, a superb one. His GA fell to 2.70 as he was named the top Junior goalie in Quebec and in Canada and placed on the first All Star team of the Quebec league and the Memorial Cup national Junior tournament. In 1991, he was the number two goaltender on the Canadian World Junior championship team.

For 1991/92, Toronto assigned him to their American League farm club, the St.

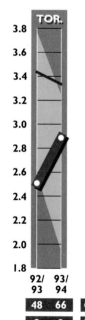

TOR.		
92/93	93/94	
48	66	GAMES
2	3	SHUTOUTS
CC	CC	STANLEY CUP
		ALL STAR TEAM

Potvin played four games for Toronto in 1991/92, with a 2.29 GA.

John's Maple Leafs. Toronto's development program had provided frustratingly few genuine talents over the years—trades were usually used to bring in new faces—so the Leafs were determined to bring Potvin along carefully, giving him two years in the American League before making an NHL starter out of him. As Potvin went to Newfoundland, the Leafs cut a deal with Edmonton for Grant Fuhr. The celebrated veteran could give the team solid netminding during the seasons Potvin's skills were maturing.

He took to the American League readily. In December 1991, St. John's coach Marc Crawford promised the media: "When Felix Potvin arrives in the NHL, it will be for good." He came up to the Leafs for four games, and while he was tagged for two losses and a tie, his GA was 2.29. Back in the American League, Potvin won its rookie of the year and top goaltender award and made the first All Star team.

At the start of the 1992/93 season, he was only twenty-one, but by his age Tom Barrasso had already been in the NHL three seasons. Although slated to spend another season in St. John's, injuries to both Fuhr and his backup, Rick Wamsley, meant he got the call-up. In nine games, he won six, tied one and lost two, with a 2.65 GA, the third best in the league. The trade rumours—which Leaf general manager Cliff Fletcher dismissed—began to swirl around Fuhr. And when Potvin hit a pre-Christmas slump, a disappointed young prospect was sent back to the minors as Fuhr took over again.

In the new year, though, another Fuhr injury brought Potvin back. That January, Potvin won seven of nine starts and attracted a player-of-the-week accolade from the league. Coach Pat Burns moved quickly to reconfigure his netminding lineup. An expansion draft was coming that summer, for the Anaheim Mighty Ducks and the Florida Panthers, and the Leafs were in danger of losing either Potvin or Fuhr. Burns named Potvin the Leafs' starting goaltender, a half-season ahead of schedule, and on February 2 Fletcher dealt Fuhr to Buffalo.

Potvin was named the league's rookie of the month for February, and became a strong candidate for the Calder, although ultimately the scoring binge of Teemu Selanne (who by the time he arrived in the NHL had spent four years in Finland's professional league) would land the rookie trophy for the Winnipeg right-winger. His season GA of 2.50 was the best individual GA in the league, and his 2.84 GA for twenty-one playoff games was outstanding, as the Leafs endured three series that went the full seven games, with Potvin playing in every one of them. And he was only making $145,000.

That summer, his agent, the former Canadiens enforcer Gilles Lupien, made an astounding contract demand: the Leafs were going to pay Potvin $2 million, or he wasn't going to play. Sixteen NHL goaltenders were making more than $1 million a season. Fletcher, who initially offered $300,000 in return, was outraged—he wasn't disposed to paying one of the highest goaltending salaries in the league to someone coming off a rookie season, and wasn't moved by the new deal Montreal struck with Patrick Roy that September, which would pay him a minimum of $16 million over four years. An angry Fletcher explored the possibility of trading Potvin to the Nordiques, who were thrilled at the prospect. Potvin was a bit taken aback by all the brinkmanship—he took a less strident public stand than his agent, saying he only wanted the going rate, which wasn't necessarily $2 million. The quiet young man didn't seem to have an ounce of egotism in his soul, which saved him from becoming an outcast with Toronto fans.

Potvin and the Leafs finally settled at $1.2 million, and the season started in fine style. The Leafs set a league record by amassing ten consecutive wins from the start of the season, and Potvin was named the league's player of the month for October as he won nine of those games, with a 2.20 GA and a save percentage of .934.

Then came the mid-season slump. If Potvin has shown a weak spot, it is his streakiness. He is not—yet—a Ken Dryden who might lose the odd game, but almost never two in a row. Having already been voted by fans the starting goaltender for the Western Conference in the All Star game, Potvin's play hit the skids. He was pulled three times in seven games in favour of Damian Rhodes, who had played with Potvin in St. John's. Burns then sat him out for a spell and he regained his form, but at the beginning of the playoffs it happened again. When the Leafs met the unheralded San Jose Sharks in the opening round, Potvin was initially swamped by soft goals. Leading 3–1 in one game, the Leafs fell behind as San

Jose scored four times on eight shots; in the third period, the Sharks scored three more on five shots. Potvin snapped out of his struggle with the shrinking puck and finished his eighteen-game playoff tour with a 2.46 GA.

He had showed himself to be a genuine major-league goaltender in his second season, but could not yet claim a place in the exclusive ranks of the elite reserved for Roy and Belfour and a handful of others. It was noted that fifteen other goaltenders who had played at least twenty-five games in 1993/94 had a better GA, and he was ninth overall on save percentage. As he himself said in September 1994, "I think there are a lot of ways I can improve." ○

POTVIN IS A MODERN GOALTENDING RARITY, A TALENT CAREFULLY GROOMED BY AN NHL CLUB RATHER THAN ONE BURSTING ONTO THE SCENE FROM VIRTUAL OBSCURITY.

TAKE YOUR PICK

SINCE THE UNIVERSAL AMATEUR DRAFT WAS INTRODUCED BY THE NHL IN 1969, NO GOALTENDER HAS EVER BEEN PICKED FIRST OVERALL. BLAME THE RAY MARTINIUK SYNDROME: THE MONTREAL CANADIENS USED A FIRST-ROUND DRAFT PICK TO TAKE THE FLIN FLON JUNIOR FIFTH OVERALL IN 1970, THE SECOND UNIVERSAL AMATEUR DRAFT HELD BY THE LEAGUE, AND HE NEVER MADE IT TO THE PROS. TEAMS WERE THEREAFTER LEERY OF COMMITTING THEIR FIRST PICK TO THE UNPREDICTABLE TALENTS OF YOUNG NETMINDERS. EVEN SO, SEVEN NHL GOALTENDERS—TOM BARRASSO (ABOVE), MICHEL LAROCQUE, GRANT FUHR, JIMMY WAITE, JIM RUTHERFORD, BOB SAUVE AND MARTIN BRODEUR—HAVE BEEN SELECTED IN THE FIRST ROUND.

A NUMBER OF TOP GOALTENDERS WERE NEVER PICKED, INSTEAD BEING SIGNED AS FREE AGENTS AFTER MAKING THEIR MARK IN THE U.S. COLLEGE SYSTEM. THEY INCLUDE ED BELFOUR AND JON CASEY (BOTH UNIVERSITY OF NORTH DAKOTA), BRIAN HAYWARD (CORNELL), GLENN HEALY (WESTERN MICHIGAN), CURTIS JOSEPH (WISCONSIN) AND BOB MASON (MINNESOTA-DULUTH; U.S. OLYMPIC TEAM).

Pick	Player
5th	Tom Barrasso, Buffalo, 1983
6th	Michel Larocque, Montreal, 1972
8th	Grant Fuhr, Edmonton, 1981 Jimmy Waite, Chicago, 1987
10th	Jim Rutherford, Detroit, 1969
17th	Bob Sauve, Buffalo, 1975
20th	Martin Brodeur, New Jersey, 1990
23rd	Craig Billington, New Jersey, 1984
24th	Sean Burke, New Jersey, 1985
28th	Mike Richter, New York Rangers, 1985 Curt Ridley, Boston, 1971
31st	Al Jensen, Detroit, 1978 Felix Potvin, Toronto, 1990
33rd	Pat Riggin, Atlanta, 1979
35th	Pelle Lindbergh, Philadelphia, 1979
37th	Don Beaupre, Minnesota, 1980
38th	Kelly Hrudey, New York Islanders, 1980
45th	Ken Wregget, Toronto, 1982
51st	Patrick Roy, Montreal, 1984
52nd	Bill Ranford, Boston, 1985
56th	Mike Liut, St. Louis, 1976 Mike Vernon, Calgary, 1981
58th	Rick Wamsley, Montreal, 1979
59th	Rollie Melanson, New York Islanders, 1979
64th	Tim Chevaldae, Detroit, 1986
72nd	John Vanbiesbrouck, New York Rangers, 198
107th	Kirk McLean, New Jersey, 1984
119th	Ron Hextall, Philadelphia, 1982
125th	Reggie Lemelin, Philadelphia, 1974
132nd	Andy Moog, Edmonton, 1980
138th	Vladislav Tretiak, Montreal, 1983
196th	Arturs Irbe, Minnesota, 1989
199th	Dominik Hasek, Chicago, 1983

Continued from page 179

1986 to 1989. They praise the new breed, above all for their reflexes, but they also express concerns about the way the position has come to be played. It used to be thought that the risk of serious injury hampered the effectiveness of the goaltender. Now, some of those goaltenders who once feared for their lives fear that goaltenders who no longer fear for their lives aren't as sharp or as attentive as they should be. Giacomin sees a strict positional game as devoted to angles as it ever was. The goaltender places himself in the predetermined place to cover off the net for a particular shooter, but now there is an important difference. With all the equipment a goaltender wears today, once in position he just has to hope the puck hits him, whether he sees it coming or not. If it hits him in the middle of the forehead, it's not fun, but he won't necessarily be going to the hospital. Back in the bad old days of goaltending, the netminder had to track the puck relentlessly, never losing sight of it. If he did, and he didn't know when or where it was coming from, it could take out all his teeth. Modern equipment has saved incalculable amounts of dental work, but at the same time Bower feels it has cost some goaltenders their powers of concentration. Being indestructible has made them to some degree inattentive. "They don't follow the puck as much, with so much equipment on," he says. "When we didn't have the equipment, we were more cautious."

Dave Dryden sees a subtle but important change in the way goaltenders are playing high shots. In his day, when a shot came in at shoulder level, the goaltender threw up his shoulder and arm to block it, and instinctively leaned his head away from the shoulder that would take the shot. Today, he sees goaltenders leaning their helmeted heads *into* the shot, using the head as one more part of the body to stop the puck.

The strict positional game has undoubtedly been given more emphasis by the fact that, in today's NHL, it's all but impossible for a goaltender truly to know the moves of every shooter, the way goaltenders in the Original Six days did. Back then, a grand total of about seventy forwards were dressed to play in the league. Now there are more than three hundred. Some teams

A BREED APART | 188

meet each other only a few times each season, and because goaltenders rarely play most of a season, they gain even less exposure to all the shooters. What's more, many big guns, such as Sergei Federov, Pavel Bure, Jeremy Roenick and Mark Recchi, have completed (as of the end of 1993/94) only about four seasons or less in the NHL. Facing them down are a new crop of goaltending stars who are also new faces in the league. It's a big change from the 1960s, when a goaltender like Johnny Bower, who had been playing professionally since 1949, was confronting the likes of Jean Beliveau, who had been playing professionally since 1950.

The size of the league, and the relative infrequency of play between particular teams, has placed a heightened emphasis on a goaltender's ability to perform in the playoffs. Thirty years ago, a playoff series was an extension of regular-season rivalries. When the Leafs played the Canadiens, they knew exactly who they were facing, and the goaltenders knew exactly whose scoring efforts they were trying to stymie. Today, goaltenders in playoff series find themselves playing opponents they scarcely know. Those who succeed manage to rise to the pressure of a series while proving a quick study of vaguely understood opponents. Today's playoff hockey may be the most demanding a goaltender has ever confronted.

It is less an art now than a science. Historically, goaltenders have broken every golden rule coaches have tried to impose on them. If they weren't supposed to wander, they wandered. If they were supposed play barefaced, they wore a mask. If the equipment they were given wasn't good enough, they made their own or told the manufacturer exactly what to make. They were individuals in every sense, alone in their role on the team, often as distinct in style from each other as a moat is from a brick wall. They came upon the best way to play the position largely on their own, watching other, more experienced goaltenders for clues to self-improvement. Sometimes they weren't technically perfect, but they made up for it in intelligence and tenacity. Now there are manuals, and video replays, and hand-eye co-ordination testing, and one-on-one coaching. A goaltender must be trained the way a fighter pilot is trained, and there is definitely a right way and a wrong way to fly this aircraft today.

Glenn Hall echoes the general concerns about the trade. He agrees that goaltending has become dominated by one particular style, an inverted-V modification of his original butterfly stance. "What bothers me is that they accept not seeing the puck," he says. "They accept the screen, which is unacceptable to accept."

Goaltending as exemplified by the professional North American game has undergone changes that are inextricably linked to the changes in the game as a whole. A much more diverse talent pool has emerged. Goaltenders are still coming out of the prairies and other far-flung quarters of the Canadian hinterland, but they are also coming out of Europe in record numbers as the NHL has filled its rosters with ever-more players from Scandinavia and eastern Europe. From 1969 to 1973, NHL teams chose one European in its annual draft. From 1974 to 1979, forty-six were selected. From 1980 to 1989, there were 457. Goaltenders drafted these days don't just come from places like Saskatoon. They come from Czech addresses like Pardubice (Dominik Hasek), Hradec Kralove (Robert Horyna) and Kladno (Milan Hnilicka). They also hail from Schaffhausen in Switzerland (Pauli Jaks); from Helsinki (Markus Ketterer, Timo Lehkonen, Sakari Lindfors), Uusikaupunki (Kari Takko) and Savonlinna (Jarmo Myllys) in Finland; from Dabrowa Bialostocka in Poland (Peter Sidorkiewicz); from Riga in Latvia (Arturs Irbe); and from Stockholm (Tommy Soderstrom, Pelle Lindbergh). The modern game has also seen the deepest American netminding talent since Mike Karakas and Frank Brimsek came from Minnesota to the NHL in the 1930s. Jon Casey, Bob Mason and Damian Rhodes are three recent Minnesota products. And three of the most accomplished goaltenders of the past decade are also Americans: Tom Barrasso was born in Boston, John Vanbiesbrouck in Detroit, Mike Richter in Philadelphia.

There is a sense that today's players are less recognizable as individuals, as true personalities, with all the marvellous quirks that go along with the territory (although this probably applies to all professional athletes, and not just to goaltenders). It is impossible to scan the ranks of modern goaltenders and pick out the equivalent of a Gump Worsley, a Gerry Cheevers, a Chuck Gardiner, a Jacques Plante. Who are they, besides superlative technicians? They have never been more anonymous. When goaltenders played barefaced, their individuality was obvious. The arrival of the mask at first obscured it, but then artistic impulses allowed the creation of colourfully painted alter egos. Today, the cage-style helmets have robbed them to some degree of this individuality. The face is dimly seen through wire, the paint restricted to the surrounding fibreglass. The helmets are colourful, but they are no longer masks in the traditional theatrical sense. The players have been swallowed up by their equipment.

And yet they are still unquestionably some of the game's great stars. They are what sets the sport apart from football and baseball and basketball. When the Stanley Cup is on the line, they are on their goal line. When New York met Vancouver in the 1993/94 final, one of the best in recent memory, the performances of Mike Richter for New York and Kirk McLean for Vancouver were front and centre. And as Vancouver pelted Richter with shots in the final moments of the final game, striving in vain to tie the score, Richter was the focus of all attention, on the ice, in the stands, on millions of televisions. He was doing what the goaltender has always done: making the difference between winning and losing. ○

HE *Shoots,*
HE *Scores!*

RON HEXTALL WAS NOT
THE FIRST GOALTENDER TO
HAVE AMBITIONS OF PUTTING

a puck in the opposing team's net. Eddie Giacomin had pursued the dream over a career stretching from 1965 to 1978, and came as close as hitting the post. Technically, the first goal had already been scored by an NHL goaltender when Ron Hextall came to the league in 1986. It belonged to Billy Smith, but it was really an artifice of scorekeeping. In a game on November 28, 1979, between Smith's New York Islanders and the Colorado Rockies, the trailing Rockies had pulled the goaltender in favour of an extra attacker. An errant Colorado pass in the Islanders' end went the length of the ice and into the Colorado net. Because Smith had been the last Islander to touch the puck, the goal was his.

But this wasn't the kind of goal that Giacomin had been trying to score. An audacious goaltender could try the most direct route, as Gary Smith did while in Oakland when he took off with the puck at Giacomin and got as far as centre ice before the last Ranger back prevented a breakaway. But the accepted way for the goaltender to score, if he ever were to, would be to wait for the other team to pull its goaltender, corral the puck and then fire it some 180 feet down the ice, hoping to hit the six-foot-wide net. In some seventy years of NHL hockey, no goaltender had ever managed this ice carnival feat.

Hextall was not going to wait passively for the opportunity. When he reached the NHL he made up to 300 rink-length shots in a day to hone his aim. He used a stick with a curved blade to give his shot more power. In practice, he could hit the far net five times out of ten. He was going to succeed. This was, after all, a Hextall.

Growing up on a farm near Brandon, Manitoba, Ron Hextall was blessed by some of the greatest hockey genes in the country. His grandfather Bryan had starred with the New York Rangers in the

1930s and 1940s, and had scored the winning goal in the 1939/40 Stanley Cup. His drop shot had been a goaltending terror. Ron's father, Bryan Jr., had also played for the Rangers—briefly, in 1962/63—before logging seven seasons from 1969 to 1976 mainly with Pittsburgh. And his uncle Dennis had played twelve seasons from 1968 to 1980, the first with the Rangers, the rest with Los Angeles, California, Minnesota, Detroit and Washington.

All of the preceding Hextalls had been forwards, and of modest dimensions—Bryan Sr. five-foot-ten, Bryan Jr. and Dennis five-foot-eleven. Ron towered at six-foot-three, and around age eight he decided he was going to be a goaltender.

Being a large man, and growing up in the glory days of Ken Dryden, he took the Canadiens netminder as a role model. He played three seasons on a nondescript Brandon Wheat Kings Junior team; his GA was as high as 5.77, but Ron proved himself to be a tenacious team player. In the league final one season, Hextall cut a cast off his broken ankle to play against Regina, losing in overtime.

He was not the hottest prospect around. Philadelphia drafted him 119th overall in the summer of 1982, after his first Brandon season. When he finished with the Wheat Kings in 1984, the Flyers sent him at first to Kalamazoo of the International League, and after nineteen games moved him up a notch to the Hershey Bears of the American League. Hershey is a Pennsylvania town not far from Philly, which made it easy for Flyers goaltending coach and netminding legend Bernie Parent to drop in on Hextall's games and practices and give him pointers. He was the first goaltending coach Hextall had ever had.

"His greatest strength is here," Parent would say, tapping his head. "He can allow a bad goal or have a bad period and put it out of his mind. He's on an even keel. A goalie has to be like that or he won't last."

Hextall didn't win the American League's top goaltender award, but in 1985/86 he won the rookie award, played more games than any other goaltender, led the league with five shutouts and was named to its first All Star team. The Flyers brought him into the 1986 training camp, and the rangy twenty-two-year-old was up against stiff competition for a job. The death of its star goaltender, Pelle Lindbergh, in an alcohol-related car accident in 1985, had left the club reeling, but Bob Froese and Darren Jensen had stepped into the gap and played well enough to win the Jennings in 1985/86. Hextall was so good in training camp and in exhibition games that Jensen's NHL career was effectively ended; Froese was traded to the Rangers to make way for the rookie.

Hextall was a classic overnight goaltending success. He came into the league that autumn and not only made a place for himself in the elite ranks, but showed an entirely new way for the position to be played.

Other goaltenders had been called "third defencemen" in their time for the way they handled the puck in

their own end. With Hextall, opposing players and coaches were ready to move him up onto a forward line. In Hextall's first month in the NHL, Leaf coach John Brophy said: "He shoots the puck so well he could play point on the power play." Other goaltenders, like Tom Barrasso, were very capable stickhandlers. Hextall took the goaltender's art of puck control to a new level. He wandered far and wide from the net to snare loose pucks, delivering pinpoint breakout passes that erased the effectiveness of dump-and-chase hockey; he was so effective that he could catch forecheckers badly out of position when one of his passes launched a Philadelphia counterattack. He came out of the minors to assume one of the most important roles on the Flyers team, serving as both a defensive and an offensive threat, as well as the emotional core to the team. He fused the size and quickness of Dryden, exceeded the puck-handling skills of Rayner, Hall, Plante and Giacomin (while wearing the cumbersome gloves of the modern game) and wrapped it all in a team-based perspective that was worthy of Cheevers.

His brilliance in his rookie season was such that, when it came time for the Edmonton Oilers to defend their Stanley Cup against the Flyers that spring, the main subject was Hextall. "We have to do anything possible to keep the puck away from Hextall," said Wayne Gretzky. "He's so good with the puck he's an added offensive threat. I've never seen anyone handle the puck like this kid." If you didn't know better, you would have thought Gretzky was talking about an opposing centre.

The Oilers' goaltender, Grant Fuhr, suggested Edmonton "bump him a bit. He's hot-headed. You can make him lose his concentration if he loses his temper."

There was that about him. Hextall had a very short fuse attached to a highly combustible stick hand. When he wasn't using his stick to let fly breakout passes, he was chopping and hacking at opposing players who wandered into his crease. Since the crease was introduced in 1934, the game's history has been peppered with goaltenders—Davey Kerr among the earliest, Gerry Cheevers and Billy Smith among the most recent—who vigorously defended their allotted territory. But no one has ever defended his domain with quite the menace of Hextall. His rookie season was the last before the NHL introduced the expanded semicircular crease, five seasons before the league would toughen up its interference rules with regard to goaltenders. "Running" the goaltender was part of the game, and Hextall was giving no quarter. In that first season, he logged 104 penalty minutes, a record for a goaltender, which meant that fifty-two of the power plays he faced were of his own making.

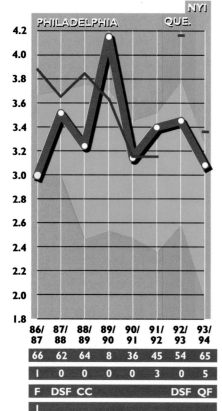

	86/87	87/88	88/89	89/90	90/91	91/92	92/93	93/94	
	66	62	64	8	36	45	54	65	GAMES
	1	0	0	0	0	3	0	5	SHUTOUTS
	F	DSF	CC				DSF	QF	STANLEY CUP
	1								ALL STAR TEAM

And even when he was within the rulebook's bounds, he was hyper-aggressive. In their Wales Conference series against Montreal, the defending Stanley Cup champions, Hextall's pregame warmup included clanging his stick resoundingly on both posts and charging the Montreal bench to whack the boards with his stick.

Against Edmonton in the final, Hextall laid out Kent Nilsson with a wicked slash to the back of his legs. There were long and loud calls for Hextall's suspension, and the league finally assessed an eight-game one—which would begin the next season, after the playoffs were through.

Edmonton built a 3–1 series lead, then watched Philadelphia fight back to force a deciding seventh game. The Oilers prevailed with a 3–1 win, but Hextall's performance (the Nilsson slash delicately overlooked) had been so fundamental to the Flyers' performance that he was given the Conn Smythe award as the series' MVP. More awards followed. He outpolled Mike Liut of Hartford 65–60 to win the Vezina, and just missed the Calder as Luc Robitaille of the Kings edged him 208–190.

With an eight-game suspension awaiting him at the start of the new season, Hextall's bad-boy reputation moved up a notch with an embarrassing incident at the August training camp for Team Canada, preparing for the Canada Cup in September. In a goalmouth scramble, Hextall caught left-winger Sylvain Turgeon with his stick, breaking his arm. Hextall swore it was an accident, but he received a stiff lecture from Team Canada coach Mike Keenan, who was his coach in Philadelphia.

Keenan was concerned enough about Hextall's temper that he had brought in Dr. Carl Botterill, a psychologist with the University of Manitoba, to work with Hextall to control his impulses. The new, larger crease, rather than giving him more security, gave him even more area of the ice in which to feel free to discipline opposing players. Notwithstanding Dr. Botterill's counselling, in his second tour of duty Hextall began collecting even more penalty minutes than he had in his rookie season.

H e had been waiting for the right situation to try the shot: a pulled goaltender, a loose puck and at least a two-goal lead. He didn't want to jeopardise the team's lead by risking an icing call and a faceoff back in their own end if the margin was only a goal. In Philadelphia's Spectrum on December 8, 1987, the Boston Bruins provided the proper alignment of variables. At 18:11 of the third period, down 4–2, Bruins coach Terry O'Reilly pulled Reggie Lemelin in favour of an extra attacker. When the Bruins dumped the puck in the Flyers' end, Hextall considered trying the shot, then decided it was too risky. But on the next dump-in, he was ready. Bruins defenceman Gord Kluzak fired the puck wide of the net. Hextall moved out, laying his stick on the ice to prevent the puck from reaching the boards. With a powerful flick of his curved blade, he sent the puck spinning above everybody's head, not touching down until it was just outside the Bruins blueline. It slammed into the Boston net inside the right post. The Flyers bench emptied. The Spectrum erupted. Ron Hextall now had as many goals as shutouts in the NHL.

The Flyers were eliminated from Stanley Cup contention in the division semifinal in the spring of 1988, an exit that also brought about the firing of Mike Keenan, who moved on to Chicago. Hextall logged another season as the Flyers' main goaltender, and in the 1988/89 playoffs repeated his 1987 scoring miracle. On April 11, the Washington Capitals became the second team to make the mistake of pulling the goaltender when they were down by two goals and Ron Hextall was on the ice. In three tries to score a goal in the NHL, Hextall had succeeded twice. And he now had more goals than shutouts in the NHL.

He was now immortal, but he was about to become truly notorious. In the Conference Championship series against Montreal, Canadiens defenceman (and Norris winner) Chris Chelios caught Flyer Brian Propp with an elbow that knocked him unconscious but did not produce a penalty. Hextall, above all other Flyers, did not forget the incident. In the dying moments of game six, with the Flyers' elimination assured, Hextall dashed out some forty feet from his net and swung his stick at Chelios's head. Chelios saw him at the last moment, ducked and felt only the wrath of Hextall's blocker.

To many observers, Hextall was now at worst a maniac, at best an impetuous team player who didn't understand what was and was not appropriate in the name of honour. Was the near-decapitation of Chelios the act of someone Bernie Parent thought was on "an even keel"? Hextall's wife Diane, a former fifth-ranked Canadian figure skater, emphasised the essentially gentle nature of her husband. He doted on his family. He was not a guy who tore up bars. Writing in the Toronto *Sun* in February 1990, Bob Olver argued, "The team is an extension of his family. He'll react to protect a teammate with the same ferocity with which he would protect his wife, his children, his parents."

But in the fall of 1989, the team—at least the management—was no longer as close as family for Hextall. Unhappy with the multi-year contract he had signed at the end of his rookie season, he stayed put in Brandon, working out with his old Junior team for six weeks before at last reporting. The Flyers, who had Pete Peeters (the Vezina winner with Boston in 1982/83) and Ken Wregget(a fellow Brandon native), seemed to have plenty of goaltending talent on hand. Plagued by injuries, Hextall only played eight games that season.

His days as the Flyers' dominant goaltender were over. Coach Paul Holmgren, impressed with the Rangers' success with the tag-team of Mike Richter and John Vanbiesbrouck, opted for a similar strategy in Philadelphia, and Hextall divvied up the 1990/91 season with Peeters and Wregget. In exhibition play at the start of the 1991/92 season, Hextall's slash of Detroit Jim Cummins earned him a six-game suspension.

For the third straight season, Philadelphia missed the playoffs. That summer, the NHL turned into a bidding free-for-all as the Quebec Nordiques put their intransigent draftee Eric Lindros on the open market. Hextall was one of six players and two first draft choices Philadelphia traded to Quebec to get Lindros. Hextall played well for the high-scoring Nordiques, but after only one season he was on the move again. The league was holding an expansion draft to fill the rosters of the Anaheim Mighty Ducks and the Florida Panthers, and teams could lose a maximum of two players—one forward and one defencemen or goaltender. Teams deep in goaltending talent wanted to get the best price on the open market, rather than settle for expansion compensation. New York decided to move John Vanbiesbrouck; Toronto offloaded Grant Fuhr. Knowing Hextall would be vulnerable to the draft, the Nordiques traded him to the Islanders, pairing him with their 1993 first-round draft pick to get Mark Fitzpatrick and the Islanders' first-round 1993 draft pick .

He had a difficult season, culminating in a horrible playoff. On their way to their 1994 Stanley Cup victory, the Rangers knocked off Hextall and the Islanders in four straight in the preliminary round. Hextall was up for grabs again, and this time it was the Flyers who did the grabbing. Eight years after stunning the league with his rookie performance, Ron Hextall was starting all over in the city of brotherly love. ○

AFTER SIX SEASONS IN PHILADELPHIA, HEXTALL WAS SHIPPED TO QUEBEC IN THE BLOCKBUSTER ERIC LINDROS TRADE OF 1992. THE NORDIQUES THEN TRADED HIM TO THE ISLANDERS RATHER THAN RISK LOSING HIM IN THE 1993 EXPANSION DRAFT. ONE SEASON LATER, HIS CAREER CAME FULL CIRCLE AS THE FLYERS REACQUIRED HIM FOR 1994/95.

HE SHOOTS, HE SCORES!

COLD FURY

AN UNWAVERING

PRESENCE IN

FOUR STANLEY

CUP VICTORIES,

GRANT FUHR

NEARLY

SUCCUMBED TO

PRESSURES

OF LIFE AWAY FROM THE RINK

"Grant never gets excited," said Grant Fuhr's teammate Wayne Gretzky in April 1985, as the Edmonton Oilers marched toward their second Stanley Cup.

THE EDMONTON OILERS GAMBLED IN THE 1981 DRAFT, USING THEIR FIRST-ROUND PICK TO SECURE FUHR. THE PROMISING YOUNG ALBERTAN WAS WELCOMED TO THE TEAM AT THE DRAFT BY WAYNE GRETZKY.

"He never gets mad. He never gets happy. His attitude to anything is just, 'Oh well.' He's like a relief pitcher. Nothing gets him down. Nothing gets him up. He's a hard guy to describe."

By then Gretzky had been a teammate of Grant Fuhr's for four seasons, and it seems in retrospect that he, like many people, scarcely knew who Fuhr was. He was, it is now apparent, rock-steady on the ice, but off the ice a shy young man who for a half-dozen years turned to drugs and alcohol rather than confronting his problems. When he was "outed" as a cocaine user by his ex-wife Corrine at the start of the 1990/91 season, one of the greatest goaltending careers was almost irreparably derailed. That he has been able to recover from this scandal, and the humiliation and suspension that went with it, is a tribute to his quiet determination and the faith others have placed in it.

In his greatest years, he was the security blanket of a young, creative offensive machine, the Edmonton Oilers. Fuhr was often left on his own, as Gerry Cheevers had been by the Bruins of the early 1970s, to keep the score in Edmonton's favour. His GA, as with Cheevers', was irrelevant when it came to assessing his skill. And like Cheevers, the normal accolades regularly passed him by. Cheevers never made an NHL All Star team, while Fuhr, after being named to the second team in his rookie season, had to wait until he and the Oilers were on their way to winning their fourth Stanley Cup before he was named to an All Star team again.

He was raised in Spruce Grove, Alberta, twenty miles west of Edmonton, by white parents who adopted him when he was thirteen days old. When he arrived in the NHL, writers felt duty-bound to acknowledge his race, but he refused to make an issue of being black. "My colour doesn't matter much, does it?" he proposed to a scribe in January 1982, and that was pretty well the end of that subject.

He was fortunate to have been raised in a town only five miles from Stony Plain, where goaltending great Glenn Hall has his farm; as a result, Fuhr had Hall as a coach while in Pee Wee, and he came to play with a trademark Hall butterfly style. He was so good so young that in 1979, at seventeen, he was on his way to Victoria, B.C., to play for the Cougars in the Western Hockey League Junior A. He had also been sought out by the Calgary Wranglers, but Fuhr picked Victoria "because I'd never been there before and the weather was better than Calgary's."

In two seasons in Victoria, Fuhr racked up victories. He won thirty of forty-three games with a GA of 3.14 in 1979/80, forty-eight of fifty-nine games with a league-leading GA of 2.78 in 1980/81, and was a first-team All Star in the western league in both seasons. The Cougars won their league title in 1980/81, and the only knock anyone could come up with against Fuhr was that he was fairly ordinary in the playoffs, with a GA of 3.00. In his first season, scouts called him the best Junior prospect since Bernie Parent.

He would always be a three-goal-a-game goaltender, often higher, not often lower. He has never challenged the two-goal GA the way other greats have, and this has been mainly because of the kind of teams he has played on. Fuhr has always excelled as the last line of defence in the wide-open game.

The professional club most interested in him was his hometown team, the Edmonton Oilers. Their veteran netminder from the club's WHA days, Dave Dryden, had retired early in the 1979/80 season, moving into the assistant coach's job. Dryden set out to find his own replacement. "I spent two to three weeks scouting Juniors, scouting Fuhr and Moog. I really liked Moog." The Oilers took Andy Moog deep in the 1980 draft, 132nd overall. Like Fuhr, he was a product of the Western Junior A, and he played seven regular-season and nine playoff games for the Oilers in 1980/81, with another twenty-nine for Billings in the Central League.

While Moog showed well in the Oilers' playoff games, he had just turned twenty-one and the Oilers decided he needed more seasoning in Billings. To cover all their goaltending bases, Oilers scout Barry Fraser wanted to use Edmonton's 1981 first-round pick to get Fuhr. Coach and general manager Glen Sather agreed. "It was a big decision to take a goaltender in the first round," said Sather in 1982, "especially after the way Andy Moog played in the playoffs. But we discussed every angle and I always remember what Emile Francis told me years ago—that you can't have enough defence. Well, we figured we can't have enough good goaltenders."

Fuhr came into the Oilers' starting lineup that first season, and played wonderfully, losing only five of forty-eight games, but he was overlooked entirely in Calder voting, despite making the second All Star team. "He's a little like Tony Esposito," said Eddie Johnston, the former Bruins goaltender, who was coaching Pittsburgh that season. "He gets down like Tony O, but he covers a fair amount of the net. He also shuts you off very quick. I had heard he was going to be one helluva goaltender and he certainly has shown me that." Oilers assistant coach Billy Harris (Dave Dryden had moved on to coach Peterborough of the OHA Junior A), who played right wing for Toronto from 1955 to 1965, noted: "The only rookie goalie I've seen with as much poise, and as cool as this kid is, was Johnny Bower. But Johnny was in his thirties when he was a rookie and had been a pro a dozen years."

The Oilers went from fifteenth to second place in the league standings in one season, but in the first round of the playoffs were upset by Los Angeles, the last team to qualify for the post-season. The next season hit Fuhr with the traditional sophomore goaltending jinx. By January, Edmonton fans were booing him as his GA hit 4.28, and he was demoted to the Moncton Alpines of the American League for ten games. Ed Chadwick, Edmonton's goaltending coach, who had played for Toronto in the late 1950s and had groomed Chico Resch for the New York Islanders down in the Central League in the early 1970s, was assigned the task of smoothing out Fuhr's wrinkles. Andy Moog became the main Oilers netminder, carrying them to their first Stanley Cup appearance, against the reigning Islanders. The Islanders had struggled to sixth overall in the standings, but jelled in the playoffs as Billy Smith held the Oilers to only six goals in a four-game sweep and won the Conn Smythe.

In 1983/84, Fuhr was back, and in form, and Moog moved onto the Oilers back burner as the team started winning Stanley Cups. Moog would play half the regular season, sometimes filling in for Fuhr when injuries waylaid him, but when the playoffs rolled around, Moog would go back on the bench. In four seasons from 1983/84 to 1986/87, Moog appeared in only eleven playoff games.

In 1986/87, Fuhr appeared poised to win the Conn Smythe as the Oilers led the Philadelphia Flyers three games to one in the Stanley Cup final. But when Ron Hextall's goaltending got the Flyers back in the series,

forcing a deciding seventh game that Edmonton won, the Smythe went to Hextall.

The next season, 1987/88, Fuhr recorded his signature performance. Back in 1971, Gerry Cheevers had declared that "nobody can play seventy games plus nowadays. Nobody." Bernie Parent proved him wrong, logging seventy-three with Philadelphia in 1973/74. In 1987/88, Fuhr broke Parent's record, playing seventy-five regular-season games (leading the league with forty wins), as a frustrated Andy Moog quit the Oilers to play for the Canadian national and Olympic teams. Fuhr at last won the Vezina and made it onto the first All Star team; while he was touted for the Hart, it went to Mario Lemieux. In the playoffs, Fuhr won sixteen of nineteen games as the Oilers took their fourth Stanley Cup in five seasons.

The brutal pace of that season's games was an anomaly for Fuhr. He generally played about forty to forty-five games, his ice time cut down in part by injuries that constantly nagged him. A bad knee kept him out of the 1984 Canada Cup; he separated his shoulder in February

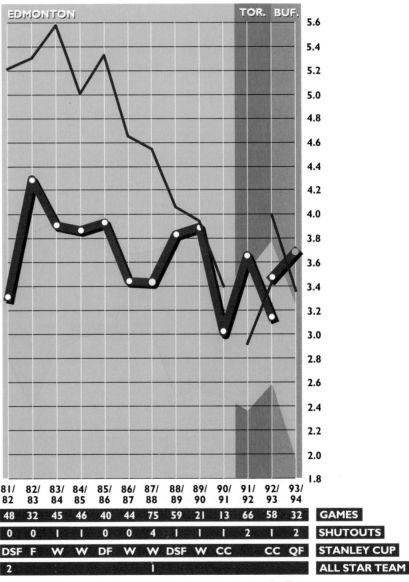

	81/82	82/83	83/84	84/85	85/86	86/87	87/88	88/89	89/90	90/91	91/92	92/93	93/94	
	48	32	45	46	40	44	75	59	21	13	66	58	32	**GAMES**
	0	0	1	1	0	0	4	1	1	1	2	1	2	**SHUTOUTS**
	DSF	F	W	W	DF	W	W	DSF	W	CC		CC	QF	**STANLEY CUP**
	2						1							**ALL STAR TEAM**

In 1992/93, Fuhr played twenty-nine games, with one shutout, for Toronto, and twenty-nine games for Buffalo.

1985 when he fell on his stick.

But he never made an issue of his injuries, or the bruises he nursed, or the way his teammates did or did not support him. "Nothing ever seems to bother Grant," Gretzky said in the 1984/85 playoffs, "or if it does he's able to keep it disguised. He never gets excited when things are going good or down in the dumps when they're bad. He just stays on a steady, even keel. No matter how many mistakes are made in front of him or how badly guys goof up on a play, he never blames anyone else for a goal against him."

After the glorious 1987/88 campaign, Fuhr's starting job could not have seemed more secure. On March 8, 1988, the Oilers traded away the frustrated, absent Moog to Boston for Bill Ranford. (In Boston, Moog shared the Jennings with Reggie Lemelin in 1989/90, and could boast the highest percentage of winning career games of any active goaltender.) Ranford filled in for six games for Fuhr at the end of the season, resting up the starter for the playoff drive. Ranford appeared destined to be another Moog, a talented understudy for the ever-reliable Fuhr.

But the Oilers were, in retrospect, the most insecure club in hockey even as they won their fourth cup. That August, club owner Peter Pocklington began cashing in his assets, dealing Wayne Gretzky, Mike Krushelnyski and Marty McSorley to Los Angeles. Fuhr had an uncharacteristically sub-par season in 1988/89, and

Ranford stepped in for twenty-nine games. Fuhr took over in the playoffs again, and the first round paired Gretzky's Kings against his old teammates. The Oilers built a 3–1 series lead, only to have the Kings, with Kelly Hrudey holding its shooters to six goals, come back to take the series.

Fuhr appeared to lose control of his life in the summer of 1989. He filed his retirement papers that June, and talked about selling cars for a living. His agent, Rich Winter, suspected drug use, despite his many denials, and made him take a test. When it came out positive, Fuhr agreed to enter the Straight Center in St. Petersburg, Florida, in August. Gretzky had come close to the essence of Fuhr in these years when he noted in 1985 the possibility that Fuhr might be disguising his feelings. Since about 1983, Fuhr had been

seeking relief from the pressures of the game, and the pressures he placed on himself, in alcohol and then drugs. Although he would never specifically refer to cocaine (simply referring to a "substance"), and he would refute any suggestion that he had suffered from an addiction, as a self-described introvert he had taken to drugs to feel part of the "in crowd" (as he put it), and to avoid dealing with problems. A quality essential to his career as a superb goaltender—keeping his emotions in check—nearly ruined him. "I basically self-destructed," he said in January 1991.

His drug use came close to being exposed when *Sports Illustrated* ran a story in 1986 alleging cocaine use by several unnamed Oilers. Fuhr was confronted by Sather at this time about his use, as well as by the RCMP, and vigorously denied it. Sather himself then blasted the magazine for printing allegations the Oilers said were without foundation.

Despite the ongoing personal problems, Fuhr was ceaselessly feted as the most level-headed, unflappable of people. "Pressure has little effect on Fuhr," assured the Toronto *Sun* in February 1988, the month Fuhr signed a new eight-year deal worth $400,000 a season. "He doesn't get uptight about a lot of things," Sather said at the time. "He's very relaxed emotionally and he's a confident, level-headed guy. He's got the right attitude to play goal."

Fuhr himself contributed to the image of nonchalance. "Life is too short to get tense about anything," he offered in the spring of 1985. His lightning-fast hands were compared with those of Philadelphia netminder Pelle Lindbergh, a portentous choice, as Lindbergh was killed in the fall of 1985 driving his sports car at high speed under the influence of alcohol.

When he came out of the Straight Center in August 1989, Fuhr moved through a flurry of changes. He separated from Corrine, dropped both his retirement plans and Winter as his agent, and signed a new deal with Sather. But he was no longer the Oilers' starting goaltender. Ranford played fifty-six regular-season games and all twenty-two playoff games in 1989/90, winning the Conn Smythe that eluded Fuhr as the Oilers brought the Stanley Cup back to Edmonton.

Fuhr's personal problems might never have come to public light had Corrine not decided to tell all to the *Edmonton Journal* in September 1990, one week after Fuhr had remarried. Her story included the nightmare of drug dealers coming to the house during the 1983/84 playoffs, threatening to "kneecap" Fuhr if he didn't come up with drug debts. Fuhr was furious, and saw it as nothing more than spite on Corrine's part, despite her avowal that it was a move to make him confront his problems. Fuhr said he'd been clean since his visit to the Straight Center in August 1989, and that the exposé had proved especially hurtful to the eldest of his and Corrine's two daughters. Agreeing to be interviewed by the *Journal*, he explained, "I was trying to get my life straightened out. I wasn't happy."

Corrine's revelations and Fuhr's acknowledgment that he had been treated for substance abuse landed a hot potato in the lap of NHL president John Ziegler. The league had adopted a "zero tolerance" policy on drug use: if you were revealed to have used drugs, you were gone. Although Fuhr insisted the drug years were behind him, and that he was continuing to receive counselling to keep himself straight, the league's strict policy led Ziegler to banish Fuhr from the game for one year.

As much as the game had been a source of pressure, to Fuhr it was also his sanctuary, and he was not going to give it up easily. "Once I'm on the ice, I'm in my own little world and I enjoy it," he said in 1990. "I have fun when I'm on the ice and nobody can take it away from me."

Much outrage ensued. The Oilers were accused of having turned a blind eye to Fuhr's problems. Corrine insisted she had taken her concerns directly to Sather during her marriage to Fuhr, but that nothing had come of it. The league was berated for a draconian policy that would effectively punish any player who admitted to a drug problem and turned to his team for help. Rather than keeping drug users out of the league, it kept them secretly bottled up within it, with no way to get help without destroying their careers at the same time. Smarting under the attacks, the league commuted Fuhr's ban to sixty games. In February 1991, Fuhr returned to the ice to shut out the New Jersey Devils.

Fuhr appeared in twenty-one games in the last few months of the season, then played the majority of the playoff games, seventeen in all, as the Oilers struggled past Calgary and Los Angeles before bowing to the late-surging Minnesota North Stars.

While Sather had gone back to Fuhr as his starting goaltender after his suspension was over, the Oilers decided that henceforth Ranford was to be their starter. In September 1991, the Oilers traded Fuhr, along with Glenn Anderson and Craig Berube, to the Toronto Maple Leafs. "I think he's got a great psyche for a goalie," said Toronto coach Tom Watt. "He never gets excited about anything. You can drop a bomb beside him and he might turn his head." The Leafs made him the league's highest-paid goaltender with a $1.6 million salary, $350,000 ahead of Patrick Roy. It was a resounding expression of confidence in Fuhr as a franchise player. Whatever his problems might have been in the past, they were not now a part of his game or his life.

His new career in Toronto started shakily. He was injured, and not playing well, and when an unspecified family crisis arose in the first month of the season, Fuhr disappeared while the team was in Winnipeg. The incident blew over, but by December dissatisfied Leaf fans were booing him at home, which outraged him. As the

Leafs found their form in the second half of the season, though, Fuhr was a key ingredient in the turnaround.

He might have lasted longer in Toronto had injuries not continuously sidelined him. While Fuhr was sitting out two such spells in 1991/92, Felix Potvin came up from the minors and proved he was ready for the NHL slightly ahead of schedule. Not wanting to lose Fuhr in the expansion draft that summer, in February 1992 the Leafs shipped him to Buffalo in a trade that bagged them three players in return, including Dave Andreychuk.

Fuhr was a solid performer in Buffalo, though the Sabres' goal became primarily the domain of Dominik Hasek, a veteran of the Czech national team who won the Vezina and shared the Jennings with Fuhr in 1993/94 and was a runner-up for the Hart. Hasek's GA was by far the more impressive of the Jennings pair: 1.95 compared to Fuhr's 3.68. Hasek appeared in all of the Sabres' 1993/94 playoff games, and the following summer was rewarded with a three-year $8-million contract. When Fuhr showed up for the lockout-shortened 1994/95 season, he was wearing generic white pads...a colour that could be worn while playing for any team. Fuhr was now thirty-three; Hasek was about to turn thirty. Though Hasek was no fresh-scrubbed rookie, Fuhr well understood who had the upper hand in securing the starting job. He began the season fully prepared for the trade he was sure would come. In February, it came. Wayne Gretzy's Kings got him. ○

AS THE GREAT OILERS TEAM OF THE 1980S WAS BROKEN UP BY OWNER PETER POCKLINGTON, FUHR CAME EAST TO PLAY FOR THE MAPLE LEAFS. WHEN FELIX POTVIN DEMONSTRATED MAJOR-LEAGUE TALENT AHEAD OF SCHEDULE, THE LEAFS DEALT FUHR TO BUFFALO.

KING OF THE HILL

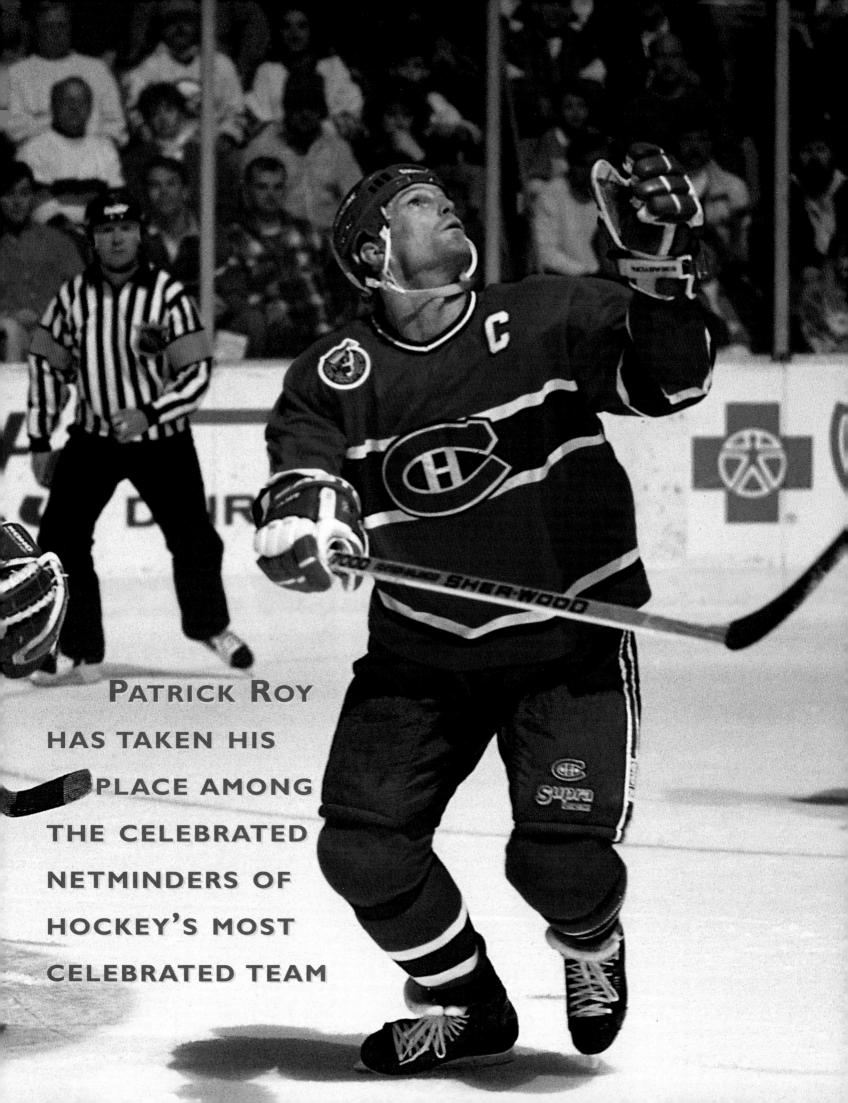

PATRICK ROY
HAS TAKEN HIS
PLACE AMONG
THE CELEBRATED
NETMINDERS OF
HOCKEY'S MOST
CELEBRATED TEAM

Preface

Five years ago, a book like this would have been nearly impossible to prepare; five years from now, it may be easy. At present, we're somewhere in the middle: It wasn't easy, but I hope you'll agree it was worthwhile.

Libraries have increasing opportunities to make their online catalogs work and look the way they would like (and that will serve their patrons). Libraries can certainly benefit from a range of examples to see what's possible and how it seems to work. From a user's perspective, the online catalog is the set of available screen displays: that's where the user and the system connect.

The best way to show catalog screens is to capture the screens as they appear in operating online catalogs. Five years ago, that wasn't feasible. The only way to capture screens was by photographing them; the results would have been difficult and expensive to publish. Until recent years, most screen simulations were typeset and failed to provide accurate screen images for a variety of reasons.

I've been a desktop publisher for several years now, producing four books, a number of newsletters, and other publications. Some of those publications have included screen images actually taken from operating applications using screen-capture programs. Since most current online catalogs either use per-sonal computers as terminals or can be used from personal computers, I realized that the combination of screen-capture software and desktop publishing might make a publication like this one feasible.

I have the fortune to be in a neutral position at the moment. I don't work for a catalog vendor (and never have); I don't serve as a consultant to libraries and have only once, briefly, consulted for an online catalog vendor (Dynix); I don't work in a library that uses a specific online catalog. I'm also not an information researcher. In short, I don't come to the evaluation of an online catalog with a particular set of biases.[1]

When I first considered this project, it seemed like an opportunity to update my 1987 book *Patron Access: Issues for Online Catalogs* (G. K. Hall) and add a substantial appendix showing a few screens from each of perhaps two dozen catalogs. After verifying that, as far as I could determine, no other writer or institution had current plans to gather together a substantial set of screen images from many different catalogs, I prepared a proposal for G. K. Hall. As that proposal was refined and accepted, the expectation was that the book would be traditional size (6 by 9 inches), start with 150 to 200 pages of my text, and include 250 to 300 pages of contributions, with 400 or

---

1 That's probably too strong a statement, but my biases don't rule out consideration of any reasonably contemporary catalog design.

500 screens from perhaps two dozen contributors.

Charles W. Bailey, Jr., at the University of Houston, founded and (until recently) moderated PACS-L, the Public-Access Computer Systems list server that, as of late 1991, links more than 3,000 librarians and other interested parties. A call on PACS-L for volunteers yielded more than twenty responses representing several locally developed catalogs and users of various commercial systems. I prepared a list of 42 vendors offering online catalogs (including CD-ROM catalogs); letters went out to all vendors except for the few that I had already identified contributors for. Several vendors responded; many did not. A second mailing brought a few more responses. Fully half of the supposed vendors, including a few that regularly advertise in the library literature, never responded in any way.

In all, 42 contributors were identified, representing 40 different systems and two very different versions of each of two particular systems. Thirteen of these were library-developed systems; the rest were commercial systems, including some based on CD-ROMs and others running entirely on personal computers. I could establish no basis for rejecting any of the contributions; the nature of the book changed as a result. G. K. Hall agreed to a larger page size and more pages. I gave up any attempt to update the relatively comprehensive *Patron Access*, choosing instead to provide a series of informal essays on catalog-design issues and to recognize that about three-quarters of the book would be examples of catalogs.

For various reasons, ten contributions did not arrive. People change jobs; priorities change; crises arise. My thanks to those who let me know that they couldn't make it and why; I remain curious as to a few cases in which repeated letters yielded no response, including one contribution from a vendor.

As you can see from the Contents, the balance of systems shifted as a result of drop-outs. Seven locally developed systems are represented, as are 25 commercial systems. Systems range from the very small (catalogs running on a single PC or Macintosh) to the very large (e.g., NOTIS and the MELVYL system). Two CD-ROM products are included and more than one system uses windows and graphic user-interface techniques. I'm delighted to say that contributions came from school libraries, technical libraries, law libraries, and public libraries as well as the academic libraries that sometimes dominate online catalog research and publishing.

The path from idea to the printed page is never easy, but it was more difficult than usual on this occasion. I had a surprising amount of trouble dealing with the variety of screen-capture programs and hardware platforms, the decisions made during screen capture, and the variety of understandings as to what was needed. Somehow, most of it worked out. There were times—as I was trying to find a workable graphics conversion routine or appropriate reproduction scale for certain screens—when I began to question my sanity in taking on this project. That question has no easy answer, but the remarkable variety of interesting contributions that emerged did keep me going.

What This Book Is Not

This book is *not* a replacement for any of the major online catalog books of the last decade. Charles R. Hildreth's *Online Public Access Catalogs: The User Interface* (Dublin, Ohio: OCLC, 1982, now apparently out of print) continues to be worthwhile reading, and will always be a landmark in the field. Joseph R. Matthews's *Public Access to Online Catalogs* (second edition, New York: Neal-Schuman, 1985) offers good advice and a look at many earlier systems, a few of which also appear in this book (although usually in somewhat different form). Although Matthews was not able to provide realistic screen images for most catalogs, his book nonetheless offered an enormous range of insights into how catalogs actually work. There are others in the field that I've failed to mention; my apologies.

This book also does not replace my own earlier works in the field, *Patron Access: Issues for Online Catalogs* (Boston: G. K. Hall, 1987) and (with Lennie Stovel and Kathleen Bales) *Bibliographic Displays in the Online Catalog* (White Plains, N.Y.: Knowledge Industry Publications, 1986; available through G. K. Hall). Part I of this new book does update some aspects of *Patron Access* but focuses more on new aspects of catalogs; the earlier work also goes into greater detail than space allows this time.

Most importantly, this book is not a set of pat answers or a prescription for The Perfect Catalog. The more I learn about online catalogs, how they are used and what designs have been tried, the more I understand that I'll never have the answers—and that there is no such thing as The Perfect Catalog.

I believe that most systems represented in this book are much better than most systems in Joe Matthews's 1985 book—just as those systems represented improvements over the systems mentioned in Hildreth's book and studied in the early 1980s. Should a new edition of this book appear in a few years, some of the systems will show significant improvements over what's here—but there will still be a number of different approaches to the online catalog, many of them equally valid for their intended audience.

Acknowledgments

The people who made this book possible are listed in the Contents and profiled at the end of the book. My deepest thanks to all of them.

Charles W. Bailey, Jr., deserves more than my thanks for founding PACS-L and moderating that remarkable ongoing electronic discussion. I have gained much from the contributions of dozens of people on PACS-L. Some of those insights are credited in the book, but in most cases I can only say that many of you have enriched my understanding and caused me to reconsider aspects of online catalogs.

Thanks also to Michele Dalehite and Linda Miller, who, as organizers of the 1991 LITA Screen Design Preconference, invited me to provide the keynote address. That presentation is, in a way, an early and even terser version of much of Part I.

Linda Ann Driver, library director at the College of Notre Dame in Belmont, CA, offered many useful ideas and put up with my trials and tribulations during this project. She's also my wife, which probably explains the latter.

Steve Cisler of Apple Computer made it possible for me to include screens captured on Apple Macintosh computers, in those cases where contributors did not have access to Macs equipped with SuperDrives, by copying the files over to MS-DOS diskettes.

Joan Aliprand and Lennie Stovel reviewed the manuscript before submission to G. K. Hall, working on an unusually tight schedule. My thanks to them for their acute observations. Naturally, errors and omissions are mine, and everything in Part I should be taken as my opinion. Many names in Part II are trademarks of various firms; they are noted as such only in those cases where the firms (or the users) informed me.

THE ONLINE CATALOG BOOK
Essays and Examples

1

Introduction

What would your online catalog look like if you could start over? In other words, how would you design an online catalog if you could start from scratch?

That's a reasonable question at this point, because you may be able to do just that in the near future, or something very much like it. Where it counts—at the user interface—libraries of all sizes and varieties can expect to have more flexibility in the future, more freedom to put together fresh designs. That doesn't mean that public and academic libraries will be "rolling their own" complete systems, as some universities have done in the past. It does mean that future commercial systems should offer design possibilities far beyond what's been available in the past.

We're not quite there yet, at least not in most libraries—and most libraries won't be there for a few years to come. Meanwhile, we are gaining more flexibility, and a few libraries are moving forward with completely new designs. Computers continue to provide more power for less money; higher-quality displays continue to get cheaper; and the models are now in place to make a crucial leap forward in user interface flexibility.[1]

As libraries and vendors gain more flexibility in catalog design, as catalogs extend beyond traditional bibliographic information to new areas of secondary and primary information, and as we try to make effective use of increasing computer power (and increasing comfort with computers), we need to consider the issues involved in catalog design. As we try to prepare the most pleasing user interfaces, we need to see how various possibilities work.

That's the basis for this book: to discuss current issues in catalog design and to offer existing catalogs as sources of ideas for new and revised catalogs. This book doesn't replace the classic works on online catalogs, and I expect to see many good articles and books in the future that will help move us forward by providing theoretical and research-based recommendations for future designs.

No Single Solution

We all had the same card catalogs for decades; why shouldn't we all have the same online catalogs for the future—preferably the best possible online catalog?

---

1 These three paragraphs served as the introduction to "Starting Over: Current Issues in Online Catalog User Interface Design," my keynote address for the LITA Screen Design Preconference held June 27, 1991, in New Orleans, Louisiana.

If I believed that there was such a thing as "the best possible online catalog," either as an economically feasible possibility or even as a plausible theory, this book would not appear. Instead, I would defer to the researchers, theorists and standards-makers who could prepare The Ideal Catalog and bring it to fruition.

Fortunately, there's no such thing. No single catalog design is, or can be, the best for all users in all libraries at all times. The concept of an ideal design for a specific library may not even make any sense. Ideal for what purposes? For which users?

In truth, card catalogs have never been quite as uniform as people seem to recall. Some libraries had dictionary catalogs; some had two-way divided catalogs; some had four-way divided catalogs. RLG and OCLC, for example, have each offered millions of variations in how information appears on cards (and in what information appears) to meet the needs of user libraries. And neither one ever did print certain headings in different colors—one of those niceties many libraries wanted, though you would be hard-pressed to find a patron who understood the significance of the colors.

It's only natural to idealize the card catalog as we struggle with its replacement, making of it some unified, universally understood system it really never was. Every patron knows how to open a drawer—but did every patron, using a new library, know whether the drawer he or she was opening was in the right section of the catalog, or understand the library filing rules?

Few Easy Answers

There are those who will tell you they have easy answers for many (or perhaps all) of the issues and questions raised in this book. They may be right. I'm neither a consultant (at least

to libraries) nor a research scientist, and I don't claim to have superior, all-encompassing knowledge of users and their needs. Who am I to say that nobody else has such knowledge?

Some issues can be settled fairly easily—although the more you learn about users, libraries, and the varieties of existing systems, the more you wonder just how many of those easy solutions are wholly valid. I'll try to identify those cases as I go, and make it clear where I have a strong opinion but have no idea whether that opinion is likely to be correct. The latter cases far outnumber the former. If I had no opinions, I wouldn't be writing this book.

At the very least, some principles of user interface design appear to be well established in a variety of fields, not simply within libraries. It's possible to violate those principles and succeed, but the principles do offer a good basis for building an effective system.

Current and Future Issues

Catalog-design issues involve more libraries, librarians, and vendors than ever before, and the range of issues is growing rather than shrinking. Four major trends, all of them supported by improved and less expensive technology, cause these expansions:

- Powerful microcomputers, cheap CD-ROM mastering, and cheaper magnetic storage make it feasible for tens of thousands of smaller libraries to install full-scale online catalogs.

- Most libraries with online catalogs more than two or three years old are considering replacements or major upgrades, as libraries and vendors recognize that four-year-old systems are rarely competitive in today's market.

- Online catalogs increasingly offer on-site users much more than bibliographic access to the books and nonbooks in a single library, and the expanded services and clientele not only add new issues but can require rethinking old ones.

- Links among catalogs and remote access to multiple catalogs are growing and changing in ways difficult to predict, but that change assumptions about the community of users and the nature of service.

Chapters 2 through 7 deal primarily with existing issues in online catalog design: issues that have been dealt with in systems on the market but not necessarily in any final manner. Chapters 8 through 12 concentrate on the issues that appear most troublesome for the near future—although, to be sure, some libraries have grappled with these issues over the past few years. Chapter 12 specifically deals with the expansion of online catalogs beyond traditional bibliographic information.

Personal Bias

Although it will become clear in the rest of this book, I should mention up front that I'm a traditionalist where "libraries without bookstacks" or "virtual libraries" are concerned. I believe that physical libraries, places with substantial collections of books and other media, will continue to be vital operations for decades to come. That's true both for public libraries, where the library serves many functions in addition to providing access to cultural memory, and for academic libraries in vital institutions. To my mind, a campus without a library is a contradiction in terms.

That doesn't mean I think libraries should not provide remote access to their online catalogs, that they should not provide access to other collections, or that they should not facilitate interlibrary circulation. It also doesn't mean I believe a library is only a place

of books. It does mean that books and other materials continue to be at the heart of a good library—and that a good library is much more than an agency for finding facts. Contemporary and future online catalogs will go "beyond the walls" for libraries, in both directions—but if we expect to maintain a cultural memory, the library itself should remain.

Building on the Past

Just as effective libraries will add electronic resources to print resources, discarding print in some cases where electronic equivalents are clearly superior, effective online catalogs should be based on the lessons of the past as well as the possibilities of the future.

Chapter 5 deals specifically with design principles that have been around for years. Many of these were established through research done in past decades (not usually in the library field). It's easy to ignore the established principles when dealing with new technology, but it's a mistake.

It's also a mistake, at least for the foreseeable future, to ignore the surprisingly sophisticated heritage of library automation over the past three decades. I was originally planning to leave out any discussion of the MARC formats as the basis for any online catalog, assuming that nobody would seriously suggest a current catalog design that did not import, understand, and export true MARC. Fortunately—or, in some ways, unfortunately—I read a library periodical blurb in the summer of 1991 about a wonderful new micro-based system that would offer everything a library could possibly want in an online catalog. It couldn't read MARC records, but it would accept ASCII text. Apparently the message hasn't quite gotten across. Some comments about MARC remain, in chapter 3.

We might not need to worry about the past if libraries had unlimited funds and unlimited time. We don't now, and I see no likelihood of that situation changing. Librarians and vendors must learn from the past and build on it, both in order to improve the future and to make that future possible.

As should be clear, this book doesn't offer radical new strategies to turn a library into the ideal information center. Other writers will offer innovations far beyond the ideas discussed in this book. I hope to provide an informal framework for considering such innovations, many of which will be vitally useful for specialized libraries and, in some cases, beneficial for general libraries. Others would be ruinous if implemented in public or general academic libraries. Fortunately, budgetary realities usually prevent serious consideration of ruinous strategies—but some common sense, combined with a broad picture of current issues, should help to strengthen the case for evolution rather than revolution.

Learning from Others

Part I updates my 1987 book *Patron Access: Issues for Online Catalogs* (while not replacing it). It offers a wide-ranging, informal discussion of issues to be considered in redesigning existing catalogs, extending catalogs, designing and implementing new systems. Most of the ideas in Part I came from extensive reading, discussions, and the electronic discussions on the Public-Access Computer Systems list server, PACS-L@UHUPVM1 on BITNET. I claim credit for the synthesis and actual text but not for all the ideas themselves, many of which came from others.

Part II gives us the chance to learn from others—specifically, to gain ideas for online catalog designs and techniques and to see how design possibilities work out in practice. More than 30 colleagues tell you about their own online catalogs and show a large sampling of actual screens from the catalogs.

I can think of few more valuable ways to improve your own thinking about online catalogs than to listen in on the thinking of others. Ideally, vendors and those planning the actual screen design should travel around the country asking why decisions were made and trying out the catalogs. That's impractical, of course: it would be too expensive and would present too much of a burden to the catalog designers and implementers who were frequently visited.

Some academic librarians currently "visit" remote catalogs over the Internet. But many good catalogs aren't on the Internet— and most librarians, particularly those installing the bulk of today's newer systems, don't have access to the Internet. Most of this book offers a compact, fast, and easy way to do much the same thing.

Every catalog in Part II presents a few good ideas, with almost every catalog showing at least one idea or approach not represented in the others. You will see more than 750 screens, together with 60,000 words of informed commentary. You should find that the work of others will help you to clarify your own thinking and create your own new ideas and approaches.

Further Reading

The essays that make up Part I are not scholarly and do not provide extensive footnotes or suggestions for further reading. Some commentary is based on research (mostly done by others), but much is not. You should read these essays skeptically. They represent my views and my own understanding of the online catalog arena. To paraphrase a noted information researcher, putting something into a book doesn't automatically make it true.

Calling something the results of information research doesn't automatically make it true, either. Without knowing all the background, details, and handling of a given test, you can't be sure the results are meaningful—even if you grant the validity of the statistics themselves, which you shouldn't automatically do. That's particularly true for catalog research, since there are so many variables in online catalog design.

I'm not saying that all catalog research is worthless, but I am saying that a great many assertions supposedly based on research can't be taken at face value. "Proven" is a strong word; there's very little actually proven in the area of online catalogs.

That caution needs to be kept in mind when you read contemporary (or older) works by researchers in the field. Many of the works are well worth reading and can provide useful insights and advice—but read them just as cautiously as you should read the essays in this book.

That said, I will also say that Charles R. Hildreth is always worth reading and that he will guide you to other worthwhile writers and researchers such as Chris Borgman and Karen Markey. I may disagree with much of what they say, and may question some of their assertions, but they write clearly and provide enough background information so that you can draw your own conclusions.

There are many books and articles on online catalogs. A search of the RLIN books database in mid-November 1991, using subjects beginning "Catalogs, on-line" as the search, yields 248 titles and editions, 127 of them published since 1986. Chances are, every one of those has some useful information; almost certainly, none of them has all the answers and none should be read as received truth.

The field will continue to grow and change. Based on my own experience, I would monitor *Information Technology and Libraries*, *Library Hi Tech*, *Public-Access Computer Systems Review* (an electronic journal), and, perhaps to a lesser degree, *RQ* and *Library Resources and Technical Services*. Valuable articles also appear in a number of other journals.

Organization

The Online Catalog Book is really two books in one. Part I is *about* online catalogs. It is a series of essays dealing with contemporary issues in design and implementation. The second part is a series *of* online catalogs—32 examples of existing systems, written by people who know the systems and illustrated with actual screens from the catalogs.

Part I does not provide a recipe for the perfect online catalog; there is no such thing. It will not tell you how to design the best online catalog for your institution; that would be presumptuous for any outsider. Part I won't give you definitive answers. It discusses issues and offers opinions, but very few of those opinions are so solidly based as to be conclusive.

Part II is *not* a market survey of current online catalogs and can't be used as a buying guide. It is far from complete, several of the systems aren't commercially available, and it can't possibly be up to date—even when this book is first published, much less when you're buying a system. In any case, that's not the reason for Part II.

Instead, Part II is a sourcebook of ideas about online catalogs and how they work. You will see a surprising range of command and menu techniques, different ideas as to the best combination of displays, different approaches to online help, different choices of labels and ordering of fields for single-record displays, different approaches to extending the catalog, and, perhaps most important, how all those pieces fit together into complete systems.

Some of the systems in Part II use CD-ROMs to store the catalog. Others are also microcomputer-based, either on PC-DOS or Macintosh equipment. Some systems were developed by single institutions; some represent institutional adaptations or front-ends for other systems; and some represent commercially-available systems. Some of the systems in Part II are marketed to special libraries, some to small libraries, some to school libraries, and some to large academic libraries; others try to cover the field.

A few of the systems in Part II were already on the way out when the contributions were prepared; nonetheless, they offer interesting examples of how online catalogs can work. Many of the commercial systems will have changed between the time of contribution and the time you read this book. And, of course, some of the commercial systems will look quite different in different installations: the library-configurable catalog is nothing new for some vendors.

Part II should offer a wealth of ideas for any catalog designer or implementer. I have found the process of gathering and preparing these chapters quite educational and absolutely fascinating; I trust you'll get most of the same benefit from the results. Don't ask me what my favorite catalog from Part II is: I don't have one, and there are several that I like quite well (and none that can't bear improvement, of course). Don't ask what the "worst" catalog in Part II is: that depends on your tastes, your library and your patrons.

The Catalog Collection

While I would never attempt a true market survey, a different resource is available if your library (or your firm) wants to see even more screens from the systems in Part II, larger examples of some of the screens, and quite possibly some additional or updated systems. The introduction to Part II discusses that resource, *The Catalog Collection*: how you can acquire it and how you can contribute to it.

Part I

Essays on Catalog Design

2

The Library-Defined Catalog

Within the next few years, even the smallest library will have the luxury and burden those university libraries that built their own online catalogs have had for some time. You will be able to make your online catalog serve your library's special needs: you will have a library-defined catalog, even though you purchased it from a vendor.

Naturally, you'll be able to use the vendor's defaults, and some will find those the most sensible options. But you will have increasing flexibility to move beyond those defaults. To do so, you need to think about the options and some of the trade-offs they involve.

Menus and Commands

Most current online catalogs are either menu driven or command driven, but some command-driven systems offer the option of showing choices in such a way that they become essentially menu driven. In future catalogs, you may be able to specify a pure-menu interface, a pure-command interface, a prompted-entry interface, a dual-mode interface where the user selects which mode to use, or a command-menu hybrid. Which should you choose?

The set of choices has changed within the last few years. Totally menu-driven systems, where no text is ever keyed, have almost disappeared from the market, except for one or two older CD-ROM catalogs. The inability to key a search argument even as an entry point to browsing makes such catalogs too restrictive and cumbersome for all but the smallest libraries.

Current trends will make command-menu hybrids more and more attractive over the next few years; chapter 8 discusses some of these trends. Meanwhile, libraries must choose which basic approach to follow.

Each type of user interface has advantages and disadvantages. The opinions in the brief definitions and discussions that follow are my own; examples, as available, can be studied in Part II of this book.

Pure-Menu Interfaces

A pure-menu interface does not accept commands at all. The only keystrokes that cannot be replicated by moving a highlight bar and pressing function keys come when the user actually enters a name, title, subject, or other search argument. Systems that consistently require choices of numbers from lists are pure-menu interfaces, as are any systems in which a text-entry area is visible only after function keys or alternatives have been used to select an action.

Many people assume that pure-menu interfaces are more friendly than other user interfaces and make catalog use easier for first-time and infrequent users. At the very least, a pure-menu system should always offer some idea of what to do next. That considerable advantage may account for the high percentage of pure-menu interfaces among commercial catalogs.

Most older pure-menu interfaces are slower than other interfaces and become cumbersome for complex searches, sometimes ruling out such searches. Such systems typically allow little room to expand the catalog's functionality. One characteristic of most older pure-menu systems (and some prompted systems) is that certain apparently logical actions can't be taken at certain points because they're not on the current menu.

Newer menu systems are more flexible, faster, and less restrictive than older designs, as vendors and libraries take advantage of PC power and new trends in user-interface design.

Examples of pure-menu systems in Part II include the Data Research Information Gateway, MacLAP, IMPACT, INLEX/3000, MARCIVE/PAC, and Winnebago CAT. These are all reasonably modern systems, free of most of the worst limitations of older menu systems.

Pure-Command Interfaces

A pure-command interface has no menus but always offers a command line. It may offer suggestions for actions, but may also provide as little help as a prompt such as >.

For an experienced user, pure-command interfaces almost always offer the fastest possible route to a specific item. Such interfaces tend to require fewer screens to navigate an activity and can usually be expanded with little difficulty and without losing coherence.

On the other hand, pure-command interfaces leave new users completely at a loss and tend to abandon infrequent users at the point at which they've reached their first result. Commands can be cryptic, and it can be surprisingly easy to become frustrated and lost.

Absolutely pure-command systems, with few suggestions for actions, are on the decline. Examples in Part II include InfoTrax and TOMUS. Geac 9000 and *plus* (Purdue) show command systems with extensive suggestions.

Prompted-Entry Interfaces

These systems might also be called "fill-in-the-blanks." While commands are textual and can sometimes be keyed in their entirety, the normal mode of operation is for keyed commands (chosen from menus) to result in full-screen instructions, based on which the user fills in the rest of the command.

Prompted-mode interfaces can offer nearly as much ease of use as pure-menu systems—and can involve the slowness and inflexibility of older menu systems as well. Some prompted-entry interfaces appear to be overlays for systems based on menu techniques, and some such interfaces have some of the limitations typical of older menu systems (e.g., the inability to perform a new search directly from a record display).

The extent of prompting can vary from little more than command-with-suggestions to very nearly pure menu. Examples in Part II include CL-CAT and Dynix.

Dual-Mode Interfaces

Some university-developed and commercial systems offer the choice of two modes—typically a pure-command mode with suggestions or a menu/prompted mode. Such a system can serve both beginning and experienced users—but only if it's easy to switch back and forth between modes, and if the modes relate clearly to one another.

Examples in Part II include Josiah (shown in prompted-entry mode), the MELVYL system (shown in command mode), PHOENIX (shown in command mode) and TECHLIBplus (shown in prompted mode).

Command-Menu Hybrids

Hybrid systems can offer menu-based choices with full use of a command line at any time, or they can work from a command line with pull-down or otherwise accessible menus available at any time. A user can work almost entirely with function keys and menus, but menu choices and function keys always replicate commands that can be used directly.

Chapter 8 discusses two factors that I believe will make hybrid systems more common over the next few years. More catalogs will offer a common command language, one that a significant number of users will already know; and common user interface design principles will make hybrid catalogs more powerful and attractive. In the long run, most libraries will probably find that hybrid systems offer the best balance of accessibility for new users, flexibility for the changing system, and speed and power for experienced users.

Hybrid systems in Part II include some fairly unusual combinations. DOBIS with the Macintosh front end offers a hybrid prompted-entry and icon/menu combination. IO+ offers a complex hybrid that can't be described in a single sentence. LS/2000 offers a fairly terse and unforgiving hybrid, actually closer to a dual-mode system. UTCAT offers a fairly straightforward hybrid, a pure-command system that shows lots of possibilities and offers a menu as needed. Add a command line to the Data Research Information Gateway, or turn the UTCAT suggestions and menus into pull-down choices, and you have hybrid systems for the future.

Choice of Commands, Menus, and Prompts

Even beyond selecting the fundamental approach (which may be inherent in choice of system), a library may have considerable flexibility in choosing the commands to be implemented (or at least their names), the shape of menus, and which prompts and suggestions will appear at which points—or how extensive prompting will be.

Later chapters deal with aspects of these choices, which involve thinking about the user, considering the collection and nature of the library, establishing a coherent interface, planning for the future, and considering overall trends.

Synonyms and Forgiveness

You haven't finished defining menus and commands until you've dealt with synonyms and forgiveness: whether the catalog will accept unambiguous synonyms for commands, and to what extent the catalog will forgive unambiguous user mistakes. Forgiveness may not be a key issue in pure-menu systems (if you can do only what's on the list, you can't do anything "wrong"), but in every system it's important to think about getting from the user's language to the system's language as smoothly as possible.

That's true for menus as well as commands. If the terms on a menu don't make sense to a user—either because the vocabulary is confusing or because different choices aren't really different from the user's perspective—the menu won't accomplish its supposed ease of use.

Acceptance of synonyms is one aspect of forgiveness; this and other aspects are discussed in more detail in chapters 7 and, to some extent, 8 and 10. The basic guidelines in this area would appear to be these:

- If different functions (or indexes, etc.) in the catalog will appear to be the same thing to a typical user, it would be better to make them a single thing.

- If users are likely to use different words for the same function or index, it would be nice to recognize and accept those words.

Indexes

Your library will almost certainly be able to define what indexes your catalog supports, what fields and subfields are supported in each index, and exactly what "support" means. That's one of the most troublesome areas of online catalog design, one of several with no clearly "right" answers. Comments about indexing will appear in several chapters; some introductory notes follow.

Part II of this book shows some aspects of the choices made in some existing systems, but not all of them. You can see the kinds and number of indexes used, but these contributions do not include such details as the fields and subfields represented in each index (details that can run to several pages for a good catalog).

What Kinds of Index?

An index can be one of three flavors:

- Word or keyword indexes treat each word from a field or subfield as a separate indexable point. The title of this book would generate three entries: Online, Catalog and Book. Some word indexes contain positional information—that is, it is possible to ask for "ONLINE appearing within three words of BOOK." That feature, typi-

cal for online-database searching, is unusual for online catalogs and may be more trouble than it's worth for most situations. Typically, a word-index search will automatically apply Boolean ANDs for each word in a search after the first: thus, "find title online catalog" (where "title" is a word index) is equivalent to "find title online and title catalog."

- Heading indexes or "exact" indexes treat the field or subfield as a whole, after applying normalization rules. The title of this book would be a single entry: Online Catalog Book. Every good heading index supports right truncation, either explicitly or implicitly; thus, a formulation such as "find title online catalog*," where "title" is a heading index and * is the truncation symbol, should retrieve this book. Number indexes (call number, ISBN, ISSN, etc.) are usually heading indexes.

- Phrase indexes or string indexes treat each *series* of words within a field or subfield as a separate indexable point, possibly limiting the length of a series to the longest plausible search string (e.g., 48 or 64 characters). The title of this book would generate three phrases: Online catalog book, Catalog book, and Book. A phrase index may be autotruncating; thus "find title online cat," where "title" is a phrase index, would retrieve this book (and many others).

Some systems add personal-name indexes with special normalization rules to deal with variations in name citations, but these three types cover most index possibilities. Relatively few current online catalogs include phrase indexes. Word indexes tend to yield more relevant results, but also more irrelevant results, whereas heading indexes tend to avoid irrelevant results at the expense of some relevant results.

Some catalogs have used nothing but word indexes, sometimes with only two indexes (word and name). Unfortunately, many words occur very frequently and many items have titles consisting entirely of nondistinctive words. A catalog with only word indexes can either add many nondistinctive words to the stoplist (in which case some titles essentially won't be searchable at all) or expect patrons to key in quite a few words (in which case the computer overhead will lead to slow response). While word indexes may serve subject-searching (and inexact-searching) needs well, their exclusive use can place an excessive burden on the known-item searcher.

Exclusive use of heading indexes places a similarly excessive burden on subject searchers and those with human (that is, faulty) memories. In Part II, you'll see several cases in which the contributors search for Norman Mailer's *Of a Fire on the Moon* using the form most likely to be remembered, "Fire on the Moon." With word indexing, throwing away "on the," this yields the desired title and a few others. With phrase indexing, as in DOBIS, it will yield only the desired title. With heading indexes, the result is the one that librarians should dread in an online catalog: "no records found."

Normalization and Non-Roman Information

Naturally, index entries must be normalized—and the same normalization must be applied to searches. That means dropping initial articles for heading searches; developing a consistent set of rules for what constitutes a "word" (how are hyphens handled? slashes?); ignoring upper- and lower-case; and dealing with special characters and diacritics in a coherent manner.ONormalization

While special characters can typically be dealt with through equivalents, the same is not true for materials in non-Roman scripts and may not be true for diacritics. It has been quite conclusively demonstrated that roman-

ized forms of languages such as Chinese and Hebrew do not provide acceptably distinctive retrieval: the romanized forms just aren't clear enough. Those institutions with significant collections of non-Roman materials need to have them properly cataloged in the vernacular, and need to provide appropriate index, retrieval, and display mechanisms for those readers who need access to the materials. That's becoming increasingly feasible, but is still nontrivial.

What Indexes and How Many?

Existing online catalogs may have anywhere from 2 to 32 or more indexes, although most examples seem to either have 5 to 6 or 10 to 15. Although you can't be sure that the examples in Part II show *all* of the indexes actually available on each system, in most cases all of the normally-visible indexes appear.

A case can be made for providing from five to eight indexes, at least if there's a way to make multiple-index Boolean searching (for author and title) easy and clear. My candidates for those indexes would be:

- **Name**, a word-within-field index containing authors, added authors, personal and corporate name, and series entries). Word within field, here and below, means that when more than one word is provided, the words must all appear within the same field.

- **Title**, a word-within-field index containing all title fields and subfields, including series entries. Additionally, **Exact Title (Xtitle)**, a heading index for browsing and for known-item retrieval

- **Subject** (or **Topic** or **About**), a word-within-field index containing all subject fields. Additionally, **Exact Subject (Xsubject)**, a heading index for precise retrieval.

- **Word** or **Keyword**, a word index (quite possibly the default index) providing access to all of the above and, at the library's thoughtful option, otherwise unindexed fields such as notes.

- **Number** or **Code**, a heading index with automatic right truncation providing access to all useful coded values, such as ISBN, ISSN, LCCN, class numbers, CODEN, and local call number.
- **Call Number** or **Shelf**, a heading index with automatic right truncation, providing access only to the local call number.

Filtering should also be possible using a clear function key or prompt, enabling users to limit a given search by language, date range, country or medium (form of material).

A number of existing catalogs use schemes similar to this one, although typically **Number** is split into multiple indexes (unnecessarily, I suspect) and the first two indexes tend not to be word-within-field.[1]

Any good contemporary catalog should support some form of Boolean searching, although this can be difficult to do clearly. Some intriguing ideas for prompting Boolean searches appear in Part II. If a Boolean search technique is sufficiently clear and simple, an author-title index should not be necessary.

I don't believe there's any place in contemporary catalogs for derived-key indexes (e.g., **ONLCATBOO** as a derived title key for this book). The worst such indexes are those that are hidden from the user—that is, the user keys a reasonable search string and the catalog turns it into mush. Derived-key indexes appear to combine the worst features of heading indexes (poor recall) with results that make no coherent sense and can exhibit strikingly poor precision.

What Fields and Subfields?

Once you've selected a set of indexes, you must decide what goes into each index. That's not quite as straightforward as it might seem, although for many libraries the default suggestions of vendors may work quite well.

If your library catalog uses the MARC format as its basis, as every competent online catalog should at this point, you will probably define inclusions at the MARC field and subfield level. To come up with a suitable library definition, you need to understand the format and what it means for your database—but you also need to consider the needs and expectations of the users.

Don't assume that you can go through fields and subfields saying "this field belongs in Index A; this field belongs in Index B." Almost every good indexing scheme will include some fields and subfields in more than one index.

The clearest cases for double-indexing come with fields 600-611, personal and corporate names as subjects. If your name index is called "name" rather than "author," a strong case can be made that *all* personal names should be included in the index. You need to decide whether including items *about* someone in a search for items *by* them is a service or disservice to the user. I would regard it as a service in most collections. (Personal and corporate series entries also belong in this index.) Author portions of author-title added entries belong here as well.

Almost as clear-cut is the case for uniform titles, title portions of author-title added entries, and series entries as part of the title index. In this case, no double indexing is involved.

---

1 I have previously advocated that the first three indexes (Name, Title, and Subject) should be internal-phrase indexes. Thanks to recent discussions and implementation considerations, I now doubt the wisdom of that earlier advocacy. There are no simple solutions.

Tougher questions arise with overall indexes, word indexes, code-number indexes, and catalogs that use a greater variety of indexes. Should your overall index (if you have one) include some or all of the notes fields? Is it possible to parse contents fields so that they can be reflected in name and title indexes, for the many records where this would not be redundant with added-entry indexing? Which coded fields should be searchable?

Filtering

Some catalogs (and probably most of them in the future) will also support filtering techniques, ways for users to limit the scope of their search results. You may need to decide what filters are included and how they are represented. For large libraries and for multi-location catalogs, filtering may be an essential element of successful searching; it can also, unfortunately, eliminate items that might be useful.

One situation seems clear: any catalog that serves an individual library and includes (or offers access to) the holdings of other libraries *must* offer an easy way to limit results to the "home institution"—and a clearly marked indication that more information is available. Most users, most of the time, want something they can obtain on the spot. Forcing them to wade through regional or statewide holdings when they're only interested in something actually on the shelves is not a service. I haven't seen a catalog that allows filtering by circulation status—that is, "only show me material that's on the shelves and that can be checked out"—but it's not a bad idea.

A few of the catalogs in Part II provide clear filtering or limiting methods, not all of them shown in the screens. The most common and sensible limits are by date range, language, media, and library location, as in the Data Research Information Gateway, CL-CAT, Geac 9000, and the MELVYL system. Others, such as The Assistant, offer fewer limiting choices.

Material Formats

One aspect of searching can be dealt with in two different ways, one of which seems decisively better for now and for the future: representation of different material types actually held in the library. Should videos, sound recordings, computer files, maps, scores, and books all be included and intermixed in normal searches (unless the user specifically limits the search), or should they be separate databases, separately searchable? A few years ago, the question might have been more controversial, but at this point, there's no good reason to separate material formats.

The best arguments for integrating all material forms are: (a) that the records are all compatible at this point and will continue to be in the future; (b) that casual searchers will almost certainly find resources they would otherwise have missed. For a dramatic example of the latter, search for items by and about Martin Luther King, Jr., in almost any medium-size or large library. Part II shows some of the results: adding immeasurably to the book resources is the wealth of visual material and some sound recordings the average searcher wouldn't think to look for. If you have the choice, put them all together—but let users who need to limit searches do so. (These users are more likely to be interested only in certain *nonprint* materials: if I'm looking for a performance of *Macbeth*, I'd rather not have to plow through all the printed editions.)

Browse or Result;
Authority File or Titles?

What happens when a user enters a search? To some extent, the answer depends on the system you obtain—but here again, your library will have decisions to make for your next catalog. There have been some fairly radical proposals, such as engaging the user in a dialogue to assure that the catalog fully "understands" the needs of the user (a proposal that would enrage the casual shelf-browser and known-item searcher!), but even within the bounds of reasonable service there are many options.

Single-index non-Boolean searches, the majority of all searches in most catalogs, offer the most alternatives. Take, for example, name searches. A name search could result in

- A name-authority browse (with a high-lighted line either at the name searched, at the first name that begins with the searched name, or with a dummy entry in the alphabetic slot of the nonexistent searched name), preferably showing cross-references, postings, and, by default or through a function key, additional information about the names where available;

- A similar browse, but of the name index it-self—preferably denormalized to upper- and lower-case;

- One of these browses *only* if there are no items for the author as searched, yielding a set of items (or a single-item display) if there are such items;

- A set of name headings based on assumed truncation for the entered name, where the result set might or might not contain cross-references but would not be browsable "before" the entered search or "after" the last entry beginning with the searched portion (in a true phrase index, this may be the most plausible alternative);

- A set of items if there are any, with "No items found" displayed otherwise.

To my mind, those alternatives are listed here in descending order of desirability—although considerable evaluation and testing would be needed before deciding to show additional authority-file information by default! Typically, the choice between the first and second options, which are the ones most likely to satisfy users, depends on whether the catalog actually *has* a proper name authority file.

To find or to browse—that's the basic question here. Some catalogs deal with it by offering both choices, either as separate function keys or menu choices or as separate commands. The problem with that option is that users must recognize the virtues of "browse," even though the natural selection will be "find."

The issues for subject searches are essentially the same as for name searches, with true phrase searching complicating the issue somewhat. Subject searches are much more likely to yield cross-references, however—and not only "see" references (which a number of catalogs deal with) but the more difficult "see also" or "broader term/narrower term" references.

In any case of cross-references, the library or vendor must make a crucial decision: what do you do when the search exactly matches an unused form that has a single "see" reference? If you have opted to show a browse display, the answer is simple: you show the browse, with the form and its reference both highlighted—with postings (number of items) shown for the reference, if possible. If you have opted to go directly to results, one "obvious" but, I would argue, wrong choice is to give them the results for the proper form. Those results should be offered, perhaps, but only with an *extremely* clear indication that the search has been modified, and why. Otherwise, the user loses control.

For "see also" references—and particularly for authors with multiple pseudonyms—the case is even clearer. It is a substantial service to the user to show the references, indicating that there's more related information available. It is a substantial disservice to the user to throw all those items onto the screen. There are certainly some multiple-by-line authors for whom I'd like to know all the forms, and I would look for those books at some point. And there are authers whose other books I really don't care about. For example, if I'm looking for Reverend Dodgson's works on symbolic logic, I'm probably not interested in Lewis Carroll's publications, even if they were by the same person.[2]

There are fewer choices for title searches: they can result either in title-list browses or result sets. Again, I might argue for the former, if only to reduce the number of no-result cases where the user really doesn't know what to do next. A good case can be made, however, that the title browse should only happen when there are no actual matches. That may be inconsistent from a system design viewpoint, but it gets the user to actual record displays in the fastest reasonable manner.

When it comes to multiple-index and Boolean searching, I see little alternative to producing result sets. Boolean summaries (see the UTCAT, INLEX and Geac 9000 systems in Part II) do appear to be nice devices for users, particularly if these summaries appear *only* when there are no results. Every catalog, for every library, should be designed so that a user is left with a "No results" statement, and

no other assistance, only if the user has entered what is clearly an expert-level search (if there is such a thing).

Boolean searching doesn't come naturally to most patrons. Part II shows some possible solutions; these will be discussed further in chapter 7.

Other forms of browsing should also be supported, either as default-finding mode or as options. The most obvious is call number or "shelf" browsing, which may even be treated as a special case for specific results—"Want to see nearby items?"

Related-Record Searching

Every future online catalog should include related-record searching, preferably made no more difficult than moving a highlight bar to a field within a record display and pressing a function key or answering a question. Unlike so many other issues of access, where the needs of the quick-search user must be balanced against those of the extended searcher, this one is straightforward: the *only* negative consequence is that the system needs to be able to process related-record searches.

A related-record search is a search for other items that have the same author, added author, subject, or series statement as the record currently being displayed. The most obvious related-record searches are subject searches based on subject headings within a single-record display. For these, I might go so far as to second Charles Hildreth's suggestion[3] that a message such as "This item and others in the library are about the following subjects:" should appear above the set of subjects, to alert the users that they *can* get other items on the same subject.

2 This discussion, and some related ones elsewhere, assume that a catalog represents consistent cataloging. That's frequently not the case, which raises a complex set of issues not dealt with in this book.

3 In a PACS-L message, probably also in other publications

It doesn't make sense to limit related-record searching to subjects, however. A series search is sensible for a number of purposes, and it's not at all uncommon to wish to search for other items by a particular author (or conductor or orchestra or corporate body). Why should the user need to rekey the entire heading and determine what kind of entry it is, when the computer already has that information?

Some catalogs have offered related-record searching (sometimes under names such as Jump or Bridge) for years, but the feature is still present only in a minority of existing catalogs, apparently a small minority. That's a shame; it should not be true five years from now. While many users will go no further than the single record (and, indeed, may never even display the longer form), many others would explore subjects and other aspects if they understood how to do so. The worst cases, unfortunately all too common, are those catalogs—usually menu-driven—in which the user can't even perform a subject search or author search while still looking at the record (perhaps retrieved by a title search) that includes the wanted heading![4]

Display Options

For some years now, most catalogs have been extensively library-defined in terms of how results appear. Sometimes, you can determine how many different display options appear. More frequently, you can determine what fields and subfields appear in each option; the order in which they appear; whether the longest single-record display resembles a card, offers labeled fields, or takes some other form

entirely; and—for labeled displays—what labels will be used and how they will appear. Future catalogs will almost certainly offer even more flexibility in these areas.

All of these decisions involve trade-offs: between the ability to show all of most records on single screens and the ease of reading and understanding the information; between fast browsing through lengthy result sets, intelligible entries, and open, well-spaced displays; between library tradition and apparent logical grouping; and between staff needs and presumed user needs.

A typical catalog (excluding, for the moment, expanded features) will need at least 3 different displays, and a case can be made for offering 5 different displays.[5] The 3 basic displays are as follows:

- **Multiple-record display** as the end result of any search that yields more than one item (or, in some catalogs, the end result of every successful search). May be one line or several lines per item; can include call number, location, and status for hurried users.

- **Full-record display**, either labeled or cardlike, including call number(s), location(s), and status.

- **MARC display**, showing the "guts" of the record—which need not be on the menu or offered as a normal alternative but should be available for the small percentage of users who can use it (see below, "Staff and Public Modes").

There are two other options, which may or may not be needed or sensible:

- **Brief or medium single-record display**, including copy status, call numbers, and locations but excluding some portion of

---

4 "For related records, try to remember this heading, or write it down. Then, when we let you enter the new search. . . ." Sometimes, user friendly can be distinctly searcher hostile.

5 These numbers do not include alternatives for users whose primary language is not English, discussed in chapter 10.

the bibliographic information. Many catalogs include such a display; they vary widely on what constitutes "brief" or "medium," as can be seen in Part II.

- **Alternative full-record display**, offering a compact unlabeled display (possibly cardlike) for catalogs where the default display is labeled, or vice-versa. Some have suggested that a catalog should include a toggle function key that sets the "current" single-record display to either cardlike or labeled, depending on the user's preference. If the toggle reverts to a default setting on a timeout (the same point at which the catalog reverts to the Welcome screen), this may be a useful suggestion.

The examples in Part II show just how different these displays can be—and there are certainly other very different examples in use. In almost every chapter in Part II, every display alternative available in the system appears, so that you can see how well or badly they work.

Should the full display be labeled? Probably, although there are no clear winners as to the proper labels for certain fields (see below, "Labels and Sequence"). Labels not only identify the portions of a record more clearly, they typically assure that the display will be more open and, as a result, more legible. Labels can be used to group all authors together, eliminating the questionable "main entry" distinction—although, as illustrated in Part II, this can pose other problems.

On the other hand, there is no question that an effective labeled display will take up more lines than a cardlike display offering the same information—and, for the current generation of catalog users, the cardlike display offers a certain familiarity. The first point means that for records that include all bibliographic fields many more records will require more than one screen for a labeled display than for a cardlike display. That's particularly

true if the cardlike display omits spacing between major areas and if the labeled display starts each field on a new line.

The second point may be specious, and raises an important question. First, while catalog cards are indeed "familiar," the general sense of most catalog research is that users (by and large) don't understand all of the information on catalog cards. Below the description, catalog cards serve librarians more than they serve typical users. Second, the familiarity of the catalog card may be a good reason *not* to use it for online catalog displays, since the online catalog *should not* be an electronic card catalog but should be much more flexible and efficient.

While I would probably use a labeled full display when designing an online catalog, I've talked to designers and implementers who, after reading and thinking about the cases for and against labels, deliberately chose to sacrifice a certain measure of obviousness (labeled) for a certain measure of compactness (unlabeled). After all, there are also advantages to seeing the entire record on a single screen.

Unlabeled displays need not be cardlike. Josiah, for example, uses a clear, compact unlabeled display for its "detailed" record that, while clearly based on catalog-card order, is not cardlike in its format. At the other extreme, Winnebago CAT and MacLAP both emulate the card even to the point of multiline call numbers and "holes" at the bottom. I almost get the sense that, on a color monitor, MacLAP might display results of a subject search with the subject heading emblazoned in red at the top of the card.

If your library elects to use multiple-line brief displays or brief or medium displays, one guideline should be obvious (but has not always been followed): a field should carry the same label on every display in which it is labeled. Any other practice invites confusion.

Fields to Display

What fields should appear in each display? Again, existing systems vary considerably on every type of display.

The most controversial area may be the full display. I would argue, fairly strenuously, that every bibliographic field (that is, every textual field within the MARC record, 100 through 840, excluding only fields known not to be intended for display) should appear in a full display—but many libraries elect to leave some fields out.

There can be several reasons for leaving textual fields out of displays, but few of the reasons make sense in a typical library. One reason is to save space, perhaps to assure that subjects will appear on the first screen of a display. A better way to handle that issue is to show subjects before notes (and, quite possibly, before material description or even publisher name and address)—but not to leave out the notes.

I've seen it suggested that added entries serve no purpose in an online catalog because they should also be reflected in the body of the entry. Perhaps, although that's not always a sure thing—but the added entry will reflect the official form of a name, and can (and should) be available for a one-key related-item search. Frankly, if you're going to leave out added entries because they appear in the body of the entry, why not leave out the main entry (other than title) as well? (No, that's not a serious suggestion—although you might consider always *displaying* the title first and grouping all names together.)

The most probable reasoning for leaving some fields out of the displays is based on studies that show that a high percentage of users need only a few elements of a bibliographic record. That's doubtless true—but making that argument the basis for *suppressing* data is equivalent to throwing out books (where space is not a problem) because they appeal only to 5 or 10 percent of the users. Libraries have traditionally attempted to serve *all* their users as well as possible. In the case of an online catalog with a properly maintained MARC database, the information is there: failing to display it seems contrary to the basic principles of library service.

In a great many cases notes *are* important—and your "unimportant" note may be the next patron's vital piece of information. If I'm looking for a recording or performance of a popular piece or play, the cast or performers note may be the most important element on the display. If I'm looking for one or two books on a subject, the bibliography note can be important, as can some other notes. Indeed, I can't think of a single textual field that is not demonstrably of value to a significant percentage of users. You've got the information: you should absolutely, definitely display it.

When it comes to nontextual fields, the case is far less clear. Some users will employ ISBN, ISSN, LCCN, and possibly some other control numbers. Some coded elements (portions of fields 007 and 008, for example) might even be useful, but only if they can be translated into accessible information. There are coded fields in music records that, theoretically, could be enormously helpful for retrieval and for filtering—but the coding is arcane, they haven't been used comprehensively, and few catalogs use them. That may be a pity, but it's the truth. For most catalogs, few coded fields other than control numbers should appear, *except* on the MARC display.

What about language, country, and date? Country and date will usually appear as part of the publication field ("imprint," for those of you who like traditional library jargon). Knowing the language of the work can certainly be helpful when deciding whether to use it, but I wonder if that information isn't sufficiently obvious from the rest of the bibliographic record? My naïve reaction has been that if I can't understand the bibliographic entry, as a user I don't much care what language it's in: I won't be able to read it in any case. That may be too simple—but if you're going to show the language, translate it into a full name, not a three-character code.

Labels and Sequence

What labels should you use and how should you use them? Should you label each field or each type of field? Should each field begin on a new line? What sequence should fields appear in? And, at a higher level, what sequence should records appear in (within a set of results)?

The last question may be the easiest to answer. Every good future catalog should show results in an "obvious" sequence—which normally means that records should be "in order" as they appear on a multiple-result screen. If the multiple-result screen shows author-title first, records should be in order by author and title. If the screen shows title first, they should be in order by title. If you want records to appear in descending order by publication date—a decision that makes perfectly good sense for some science and special libraries but is intellectually questionable for the humanities and most general libraries—the date should appear first. Unsorted result sets should disappear in the next generation of catalogs—and a result set that is in a hidden order is, from the user's perspective, unsorted.

As to the other questions: I know of no single answers and have considerable difficulty suggesting a "best" answer. If I ever design a catalog, I will come up with answers, to be sure—but I might want to reconsider those answers over time. If you're designing *or* im

plementing a catalog, chances are you'll need to make those decisions. Rather than discuss my personal preferences, vague as they may be, it makes more sense to show you some existing decisions. The figures at the end of this chapter, each representing a *partial* screen from one of the systems in Part II (cut off at the right so that six screens could fit on each page while keeping the figures legible), will give you several examples of possible choices for labels and sequence. The decision, as always, must be yours.

Help and Tutorials

Part of the library-defined catalog is library-defined help screens and online tutorials. Some of these will be supplied by vendors, but many will be open to library modification or may be entirely supplied by each library.

Later chapters discuss principles relevant to designing help and online tutorials, in particular chapters 5 through 7.

Staff and Public Modes

Chances are, your next system (and possibly your current system) will allow you to define more than one access mode. There may be good reasons to have somewhat different user interfaces for remote users (over networks or modems) than for local users, particularly as modern user interfaces take advantage of the processing power of PCs in lieu of terminals, but the differences should be kept as small as possible.

Should technical processing or other staff have a catalog mode different from the public's? If so, what should the differences be? The only clear-cut argument for separate modes doesn't relate directly to the online catalog but rather to the linked circulation function: patrons should not have access to information on other patrons (which means, in general, forbidding access to any patron information), and they should not be able to alter information within the system.

But patron information doesn't belong in the online catalog in any case; it belongs in other aspects of the system. More typically, a staff mode will have retrieval capabilities or displays different from the public mode. That distinction seems questionable and, to some extent, self-defeating. Yes, there are a few patrons who will use MARC displays—and who can probably guess the display command if your system is defined coherently (they'll probably try "M" or "MARC" or "tagged"). It's hard to understand why staff should have retrieval capabilities that are *forbidden* to the public—although staff are likely to make better use of the command alternative that should be available on most future catalogs.

Why self-defeating? Because staff members will also be helping users make effective use of the online catalog; in some libraries, almost every staff member (or at least librarian and other professional) will spend some time on the front lines. Staff members can be more helpful if the interface they're used to is the interface they're helping out with. So what if they give away a shortcut? Is there something wrong with patrons becoming experts?

There may be good reasons for separate staff modes, but think about those reasons carefully. With effective interface designs, there is no good reason to deny power to the public—and every reason to support it.

Additional Functionality

If the catalog and the library are successful, the catalog will expand in several ways, all of them defined by the library (with the support of the vendor). You may elect to add electronic mail or electronic reference functions. You may elect to add self-service renewal or other online functions. You will probably add databases, some of them home-grown, some of them licensed.

With luck and good advance planning, you'll be able to add these new functions coherently, maintaining a clear overall design for the catalog. Chapter 6 spends more time on coherent interface design; chapter 12 deals with expanding the catalog.

Conclusion

If you already have an online catalog, chances are your library had quite a lot to do with defining the way it works. When you upgrade or replace your current catalog, your library will probably control even more of its appearance and functionality. Right now, a number of system designs will build a Playing Time index for sound recordings or a Nonspecific Relationship index to field 787 in serials, if some library really wants such indexes. You probably don't want a Playing Time index, and certainly don't want an index to nonspecific relationships. But you have, and will have, enough flexibility so that your catalog really will be *your* catalog. The rest of this book, particularly Part II, and the books and articles that have appeared over the past decade will help inspire you to make that catalog a good one, but only you can determine what that means in your library, at a particular time, for your patrons.

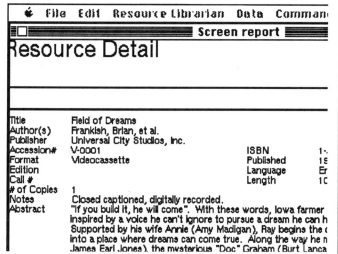

Figure 2.1: Resource Librarian, labeled display

```
FULL RECORD
=========================================================
AUTHOR:          Gershwin, George, 1898-1937.
UNIFORM TITLE:   Rhapsody in blue
TITLE:           Fiedler conducts Gershwin
PUBLISHED:       New York : RCA, 1987.
DESCRIPTION:     1 sound disc : digital, stereo. ; 4 3/4
NOTES:           6519-2-RG RCA Papillon Collection
                 Boston Pops Orchestra; Earl Wild, pian
                 Compact disc.
SUBJECTS:        Orchestral music
                 Concertos (Piano)
                 Piano with orchestra
OTHER AUTHORS:   Wild, Earl.
                 Fiedler, Arthur, 1894-1979.
                 Gershwin, George, 1898-1937. / Concerto
                 major.
                 Gershwin, George, 1898-1937. / An Amer
=========================================================
For next screen, press ENTER
->
Options:  BACk  HELp  EXPlain  NEWs  COMment  KEY
Search commands:  A  AI  T  TI  TK  AT  S  C  IN  CO
```

Figure 2.2: UTCAT, labeled display

```
Your search:   FIND SUBJECT MARTIN LUTHER KING JR
Items found:   22 at PRINCETON LIBRARIES

Item 2.

AUTHOR          Cone, James H.
TITLE           Martin & Malcolm & America : a dream or a n
                Cone.
PUBLICATION     Maryknoll, N.Y. : Orbis Books, c1991.
DESCRIPTION     xv, 358 p., [17] p. of plates : ill. ; 25 c
NOTES           Includes bibliographical references (p. 321
SUBJECTS        1. King, Martin Luther, Jr., 1929-1968- Phi
                Malcolm, 1925-1965- Philosophy. 3. King, M
                1929-1968- Religion. 4. X, Malcolm, 1925-1
                Afro-Americans- Intellectual life. 6.
                Afro-Americans- Religion. 7. Black nationa
                States. 8. United States- Race relations.
OTHER HEADINGS  I. Martin and Malcolm and America.

Press RETURN to see next screen, or type HELP, then press R
->
```

Figure 2.3: TOMUS, labeled display

```
                                                DISPL
Main Title  : The law of real property
Authorship  : by Herbert Thorndike Tiff
Publisher   : Callaghan
City        : Chicago, Ill.,
Date        : 1940
Collation   : xxxvi, 1219 p. 23 cm.
Edition     : New abridged ed
Author      : Tiffany, Herbert Thorndik
              Callaghan and Company
              Zollman, Carl.
Subject     : Real property - United St
Note        : Spine title: Tiffany real
Add. Title  : Tiffany real property.

Location    : Main Library
Call Number : KF 570 .T54 1940
```

Figure 2.4: The Assistant, labeled display

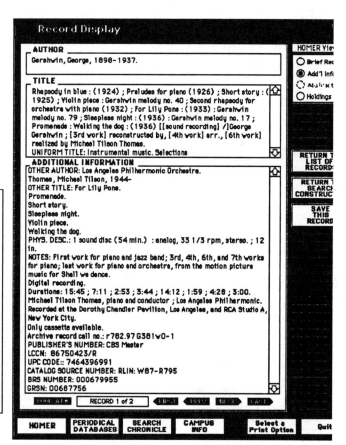

Figure 2.5: USCInfo, labeled display

```
┌─ Title  1  of  1 ──── Title Display ───────
│
│         Title> Managing high-technology companies
│
│
│        Author> Riggs, Henry E.
│
│   Corp Author>
│
│       Call No: HD62.37.R53
│      Subjects> High technology industries -- Managemen
│     Collation> xvii, 333 p. : ill. 25 cm.
│     Publisher> Belmont, Calif. : Lifetime Learning Pub
│       Edition>
│        Series>
│        Medium:
│         Notes> "Lifetime learning series in managing h
└───────────────────────────────────────────
```

Figure 2.6: TECHLIBplus, labeled display

```
Search request: FIND PA KING, MARTIN LUTHER
Search result:  34 records in the TEN-YEAR Catalog databas

Type HELP for other display options.

5. VIDEORECORDING

Title:           King, I have a dream. Oak Forest, IL : MPI
Description:     1 videocassette (VHS) (28 min.) : sd., col.

Stock No.:       MP 1350 MPI Home Video

Notes:           Consists chiefly of the speech of Rev. Mart
                 delivered at the Lincoln Memorial, Washin
                 28, 1963.
                 Title from label on cassette.
                 "MP 1350".

Subjects:        King, Martin Luther, Jr., 1929-1968.
                 Afro-Americans — Civil rights.
                 Baptists — United States — Clergy — Biog
                                     (Record 5 continues
Press RETURN to see the next screen.
TEN->
```

Figure 2.9: MELVYL, labeled display (1)

```
SEARCH  a:king, martin luther<80-85
MONOGRAPH              (Screen 1 of 1)        Rec
OCLC #/2/2076         Purdue #19/594         No1
PERS AUTH: King, Martin Luther.           +───
    TITLE: Strength to love / Martin Luther King, Jr.  | Op
   IMPRINT: Philadelphia : Fortress Press, c1981.       | nr
   DESCRIPT: 155, [4] p. ; 22 cm.                        | pr
                                                         | ns
  DEWEY NUM: 252.06 K585s, 1981                          | ps
   HOLDINGS: HSSE Library                                | mr
             copy 1                                      |sav
                                                         |ext
 TOPIC SUBJ: Afro-American Baptists--Sermons.            | sm
             Sermons, American.                          | q
      LCCN: 80-2374                                      | h
      ISBN: 0800614410 : $4.25                         +───



ENTER OPTION --> █
```

Figure 2.7: plus, labeled display

```
Search request: FIND PA KING, MARTIN LUTHER
Search result:  34 records in the TEN-YEAR Catalog database

Type HELP for other display options.

5. (continued)
                 March on Washington for Jobs and Freedom, 19
                 Historical films.
                 Biographical films.
                 Short films.
                 United States — Race relations.

Other entries: King, Martin Luther, Jr., 1929-1968.
               I have a dream.

Call numbers:  UCI    Main Lib  E185.61 .K52 1986 Lib Media




There are no more records to display. Type PS to see previo
TEN->
```

Figure 2.10: MELVYL, labeled display (2)

```
d14
SET:    2, ITEM:    4 OF    4, RECORD #:  595330
LOCATION: Educ Res Ctr/A.V.
CALL #:   793 BAC
AUTHOR:   Bach, Johann Sebastian, 1685-1750
OTHER:    Magnificat, BWV 243, D major. Latin.
TITLE:    Magnificat {sound recording} / J.S. Bach. —
IMPRINT:  {Amsterdam} : Philips, 1985.
COLLATION: 1 sound disc (42 min.) : digital ; 4 3/4 in.
NOTES:    Philips Digital Classics: 411 458-2.
CONTENTS: Magnificat, BWV 243 (26 min.) — Jauchzet Go
          tate BWV 51 (16 min.).
NOTES:    Emma Kirkby, soprano ; Monteverdi Choir ; En
          ; John Eliot Gardiner, conductor.
SUBJECTS: Magnificat (Music)
SUBJECTS: Cantatas, Sacred
SUBJECTS: Choruses, Sacred (Mixed voices) with orchest
OTHER:    Kirkby, Emma.
OTHER:    Gardiner, John Eliot
───×───1───×───2───×── More - Press CLEAR/PF8 ─×
```

Figure 2.8: PHOENIX, labeled display

```
┌─COMBINED SEARCH:ANY-MARTIN LUTHER KING JR,DATE-1980-1985─
│┌─TITLE:"I have a dream—" the life of Martin Luther King──
││ ┌──────── CATALOG RECORD DISPLAY ───────────
│││
│││         TITLE: "I have a dream—" videorecording : the li
│││                Luther King / [CBS News]
│││ PUBLICATION INFO: New Brunswick, N.J. : Phoenix/BFA Films &
│││ PHYSICAL DESC: 1 videocassette (35 min.) : sd., b&w ; 3/4
│││          NOTE: Originally released in 1968 as motion pict
│││                Film Associates.
│││          NOTE: U-matic 3/4 in. format.
│││          NOTE: Narrator, Paul Richards.
│││  SUMMARY NOTE: Uses actual news film footage in a study o
│││                Martin Luther King and the forces that bro
│││                leadership of his people.
│││       SUBJECT: King, Martin Luther, Jr., 1929-1968.
│││       SUBJECT: Afro-Americans — Biography.
│││       SUBJECT: Afro-American clergy — Biography.
│││       SUBJECT: Afro-Americans — Civil rights.
│││  OTHER AUTHOR: CBS News.
│││  OTHER AUTHOR: Phoenix/BFA Films & Video.
│││
│↑↓-Scroll    PgUp,PgDn-Page   ──Previous record  ←Next
│F1-Help      F6-Save    F7-Print      F9-Back     F10-M
```

Figure 2.11: MARCIVE/PAC, labeled display

PUBLIC CATALOG

```
TL799.M6  M26
    AUTHOR:        Mailer, Norman.
    TITLE:         Of a fire on the moon.
    EDITION:       [1st ed.]
    PUBLISHER:     Boston, Little, Brown [1970]
    PHYSICAL DESC: vii, 472 p. 22 cm.

    SUBJECTS:      Project Apollo (U.S.)
                   Space flight to the moon
                   Astronauts - United States
                   United States - Civilization - 1945-


LOCATION      CALL#/VOL/NO/COPY              STATUS

*RESERVE DESK  TL799.M6 M26 c.1              On Reserv
```

Figure 2.12: LS/2000, labeled display

```
To see more of the catalog entry (if it is on more than one scr
the NEXT key or the PREV key.

AUTHOR       BEATLES
Beatles.         The Beatles [sound recording]              198


CALL NUMBER   CD MR BEAT BEA B-43 v.1        AudioVis  ON
              CD MR BEAT BEA B-43 v.2        AudioVis  ON

AUTHOR        Beatles.
TITLE         The Beatles [sound recording] / The Beatles.
PUBLICATION   [London] : Parlophone, [1987?], p1968.
DESCRIPTION   2 sound discs : digital, stereo. ; 4 3/4 in.   + 2

NOTE          Compact discs.
NOTE          Commonly known as: The white album.
NOTE          Lyrics (22 p. : ill. (some col.)) included.
NOTE          v.1 Back in the U.S.S.R. — Dear Prudence — Gla
              la- di, ob-la-da — Wild honey pie — The contin
              Bungalow Bill — While my guitar gently weeps / H

              CALL     MARC          5   16
              NUMBER   DISPLAY           C
```

Figure 2.13: INLEX, labeled display

```
FORD Online BiblioTech Library System
                              Title Search
Full citation: Book
CID: 23707                    Key: MEGATRENDS 2000: TEN
Call no.:CIR 306.0973 N151

Security class:
Main author:    Naisbitt, John
Title statement: Megatrends 2000: ten new directions for the 1
                Naisbitt and Patricia Aburdene.
Publisher:      Morrow
Place of pub.:  NY
Pagination:     384 p.

Pub. date:      1990               Edition:
ISBN:           0-688-07224-0      OCLC:
Vendor No.:

M. Master Menu        4. prev record      7. change in
2. display pg. 2      5. next record      8. display o
3. display pg. 3      6. short citation   9. index sca
Press <DOWN> arrow to scan forward, <UP> arrow to scan back.
Press <CTRL/Z> once to change start, twice for Catalog Browsing
                          ..
```

Figure 2.14: BiblioTech, labeled display

```
*
*        2 MUSIC (Phonos & scores)
*
*        Type BRIEF to display your result
*
*  CATALOG selected
*  Type command, then press RETURN   (BREAK to restart, enter STOP
: det

**********************************************************

      BY:  Bach, Johann Sebastian, 1685-1750.
           Stader, Maria.
           Topper, Hertha.
           Haefliger, Ernst, 1919
           Fischer-Dieskau, Dietrich, 1925
           Engen, Kieth.
           Richter, Karl, 1926
           Munchener Bach-Chor.
           Munchener Bach-Orchester.
   TITLE:  Mass in B minor, BWV 232
           Masses, BWV 232
TITLE-NOTE: Johann Sebastian Bach.
PUBLISHED: (West) Germany : Archive Production, (1961)
```

Figure 2.15: InfoTrax, labeled display (1)

```
   SUBJECT:  Masses.
   CALL NO:  PHONO G BACH MAS S77
   OCLC NO:  2744680
   MATERIAL: Sound Recording
             Music
*
*  --More--   Press RETURN to continue

DESCRIPTION: 3 sound discs (122 min.) : analog, 33 1/3 rpm, stereo
             in.
      NOTES: Sung in Latin.
             Ed. recorded: Werke, Jg. 6 (Leipzig : Bach-Gesellscha
             1856).
             Program notes in English, German, and French, by Geor
             Dadelsen, and text, with German, English, and Fren
             translations ((16) p. : ill.) and supplementary no
             card) laid in container.
     SERIES: Archive Production, 9th research period: The works o
             Sebastian Bach. Ser. C: Masses and Magnificat
             Archive Production, 9th research period. Ser. C.

BARCODE   COLLECTION DESCRIP.  COPY  STATUS       DUE DATE
--------  ---------- --------  ----  ------------ --------
100263331 PHONO                      AVAILABLE
*
*  ----- Record 1 of 2 -----
```

Figure 2.16: InfoTrax, labeled display (2)

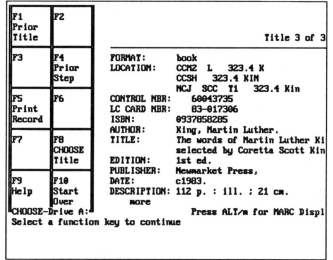

Figure 2.17: IMPACT, labeled display

```
099 TECHNICAL AND AUTOMATED  - IRIS LIBRARY SYSTEM -  L


   AUTHOR King, Martin Luther.
    TITLE King, Malcolm, Baldwin : three interviews / b
          new introduction.
  EDITION 1st Wesleyan paperback ed.
PUBLISHER Middletown, Conn. : Wesleyan University Press
          Distributed by Harper & Row, 1985.
  DESCRIP viii, 65 p. : ports. ; 21 cm.
    NOTES Rev. ed. of: The Negro protest. 1963.
OTHER AUT X, Malcolm, 1925-1965. * Baldwin, James, 1924
          Bancroft, 1914- * Baldwin, James, 1924- Negro
 SUBJECTS Afro-Americans -- Civil rights. * Afro-Americ
          United States -- Race relations.
  LC CARD  83023498
     ISBN 0819560901 (pbk. : alk. paper) :


  BRF - see locations and call numbers   CIT - return
  FOR - see next citation in list        BAC - see pre
  CON - see next screen                  CAT - begin c
  REV - revise current search            CMD - see add
```

Figure 2.18: Geac 9000, labeled display

```
--------------------------------------------------
AUTHOR(s):       Gershwin, George,  1898-1937.
TITLE(s):        Selections
                 Gershwin.  [Sound recording]

                 RCA Victor  TR3-5006.  [1964?]
                 1 reel.  3 3/4 ips.  4-track.  stereo
Contents:        An American in Paris -- I got rhyth
                 in Blue -- Cuban overture -- Conc
                 Earl Wild, piano (in the Rhapsody a
                 Pops Orchestra; Arthur Fiedler, c

OTHER ENTRIES:   Symphonic poems.
                 Musicals Excerpts, Arranged.
                 Piano with orchestra.
                 Concertos (Piano).
Format:          Sound recording
                 Wild, Earl.  prf
                 Fiedler, Arthur,  1894-1979.  cnd
                 Boston Pops Orchestra.  prf
LOCN: HU   AV/C        STATUS: Not checked out --
CALL #: TAPE 230
```

Figure 2.19: CARL, labeled display

```
SEARCH: RHAPSODY IN BLUE
ITEM   9 OF  16

Author: Gershwin, George, 1898-1937.
Uniform Title: Concerto, piano, orchestra, F major; arr
Title: Concerto in F ; Three preludes ; Rhapsody in blue {sound
/ George Gershwin.
Published: {S.l.} : Stradivari, p1988.
Physical Description: 1 sound disc : digital ; 4 3/4 in.
Author Names:   1. Krieger, Norman  2. Castagnetta, Grace, 191
Gershwin, George, 1898-1937. Preludes, piano. 1988.  4. Gers
George, 1898-1937. Rhapsody in blue; arr. 1988.
Subjects:   1. Piano music, Arranged.   2. Piano music.

Location and call number:
1. ORWIG CD   M37.047 C6x 1988

FOR MORE INFORMATION:
   Type another item number OR        D -- Detailed Reco
   Type a letter from the right: >> ▓  M -- Multiple item
   Then press RETURN                  S -- Start a New S

PF1=>Help    PF3=>Search Menu    PF5=>Dir Cmd    PF9=>Options Menu
```

Figure 2.20: Josiah, labeled display

```
                                  [FULL RECORD]
SEARCH TERM(S): (SU=KING AND TITLE=DREAM) AND FOR=MED
REFERENCES FOUND:   1
------------------------------------------------------
LOCATION:    LR & C  2d fl
CALL NO:     128(Vid.C.)
TITLE:       King I have a dream
PUBLISHER:   [s.l.] : MPI Home Video, c1986.
DESCRIPT:    1 videocassette (28 min.) : sd., b&w  with c
             in.
LOCAL NOTE:  $19.95.
NOTE 1:      SUMMARY: Presents the famous speech of Marti
             at the Lincoln Memorial (Wash. D.C.) on Augu
NOTE 2:      VHS Format
SUBJECT 1:   King, Martin Luther, Jr., 1929-1968.
SUBJECT 2:   Afro-Americans--Civil rights--Videocassette.


PRESS YOUR CHOICE: _                   [SEARCH HISTORY] t
[NEXT] Page.                           [COPY] Availabilit

[HELP] for Assistance.                 [START OVER] Compl
```

Figure 2.21: CL-CAT, labeled display

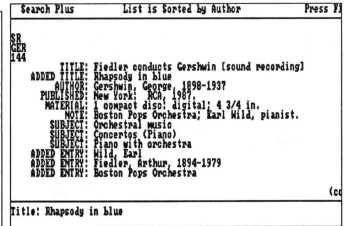

Figure 2.22: Catalog Plus, labeled display

```
□■ ▬▬▬▬▬▬▬▬▬▬▬▬▬▬ DOBIS Online Catalog ▬
  Online catalog
  Combined Boolean Search
  Full information    Document   31327748

  Title:      Martin Luther King Jr. kit : the man, his dr
              for civil rights.
  Publisher:  ABC News Interactive [production company] ;

  Series:     Instant replay of history
  Author(s):  Koppel, Ted. / ABC News Interactive. / Optic
  Subjects:   King, Martin Luther, Jr., 1929-1968. / Civil
              United States. / Afro-American clergy United
              Afro-Americans Biography.

  Contains:   1 videodisc : sd., col. ; 12 in. + 4 computer
  Copies:     Location  Call number                  Stat
  General     wg        HYPER 3 FITC


  Type code (see below), then RETURN
  _
              f forward  c copies    s short

                                                        •

  (HELP) (Begin) (Names) (Titles) (Subj.) (Boo
```

Figure 2.23: DOBIS, labeled display

```
———————— DRA Library — Holdings Display ┐
Find...          Full          Help...        B
╞══════════════ BIBLIOGRAPHIC INFORMATION ══════╡
  Call Num:  VIDEO 1179

     Title:  In remembrance of Martin videorecording / V
 Published:  Dallas, Tex. : Idanha Films ; Alexandria, V
             [distributor], 1986.
    Paging:  1 videocassette (60 min.) : sd., col. ; 1/2

     Notes:  Made in cooperation with Martin Luther King
             Nonviolent Social Change.
   Credits:  Creator and director, Kell Kearns.

Annotation:  Records the tributes to the life and accomp
             Martin Luther King Jr. which took place in
             the first federal holiday honoring Dr. King

  Subjects:  King, Martin Luther, Jr., 1929-1968.
  Subjects:  Afro-Americans—Civil rights—United States
```

Figure 2.24: Data Research, labeled display

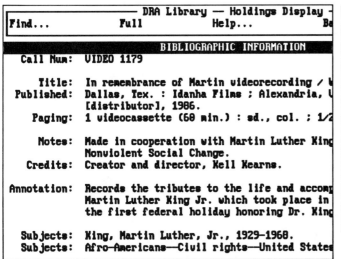

Figure 2.25: Marquis, labeled display

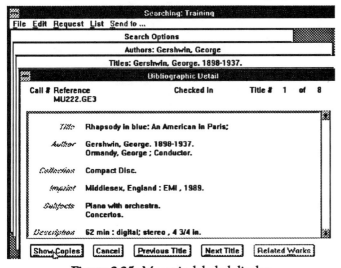

Figure 2.26: Dartmouth, labeled display

```
You searched for the AUTHOR: gershwin george

AUTHOR    Gershwin, George, 1898-1937.
TITLE     Piano music. Selections.
          Rhapsody in blue ; Preludes for piano ; Short story ; Violin
          piece ; Second rhapsody for orchestra with piano ; For Lily
          Pons ; Sleepless night ; Promenade : walking the dog [sound
          recording] / Gershwin.
PUBL INFO New York, N.Y. : CBS Records, p1985.
SUBJECT   Piano with jazz ensemble.
          Piano music.
          Piano with orchestra.
DESCRIPT  1 sound disc : digital ; 4 3/4 in.
SERIES    CBS Records masterworks.
NOTES     First work for piano and jazz band; 3rd, 4th, 6th, and 7th wor

    LOCATION        CALL #                    STATUS
1 > UNLV Nonbook   M22.G47 T46x - Compact Disc  NOT CHCKD OUT

M > MORE BIBLIOGRAPHIC Record    N > NEW Search
R > RETURN to Browsing           A > ANOTHER Search by AUTHOR
F > FORWARD browse               Z > Show Items Nearby on Shelf
B > BACKWARD browse              O > OTHER options
Choose one (M,R,F,B,N,A,Z,S,P,O)
```

Figure 2.27: INNOPAC, labeled display

```
>di 7 1
Screen 001 of 001  Record 0007 of 0007 UML
LOCTN: AGRICULTURE MAIN STACKS HV 696 F6 H8 no.3 c.1-2
AUTHR: Clausen, A. W.
TITLE: Poverty in the developing countries, 1985 : address
       January 11, 1985, at the Martin Luther King, Jr.
       Nonviolent Social Change, Inc., Atlanta, Georgia
PUBLR: San Francisco, CA (2015 Steiner St., San Francisco
       Project, c1985.
DESCR: iv, 11 p. ; 24 cm.
SERIE: The Hunger Project papers, 0743-6416 ; no. 3 (March
NOTES: Keynote address at the National Action Symposium on
       Hunger, sponsored by the Martin Luther King, Jr.
       Nonviolent Social Change and the Hunger Project.
SUBJT: Poor—Developing countries
AAUTH: Martin Luther King, Jr. Center for Nonviolent Socia
AAUTH: Hunger Project.
SERIE: Hunger Project papers. no. 3
OCLC# 02706924
——Type DS to Display item availability S
>
```

Figure 2.28: PALS, labeled display

```
To select another button, press TAB.              (c
To see the next page of information, press RETURN now.

HELP     GOBACK      STARTOVER
FORWARD  BACKWARD    REQUEST      LIKE        OPTIONS

         THIS IS ITEM NUMBER 2 OF THE 4 YOU FOUND IN THE C
COMDSC MK 42240
   Publisher number: MK 42240 CBS Masterworks
 Date/place capture: 1974——
 Date/place capture: 1976——
Form of composition: sp ov
  Instr/voices code: ka01 oe
  Instr/voices code: oa
    Personal author: Gershwin, George, 1898-1937.
      Uniform title: Instrumental music. Selections
              Title: Rhapsody in blue = Rhapsodie en bleu
                     ; An American in Paris = Un Americai
                     overtures [sound recording] / George
                     [overture] arrangements by Don Rose.
   Publication info: New York, N.Y. : CBS Masterworks, [1
      Physical desc: 1 sound disc : digital ; 4 3/4 in.
       General note: CBS Masterworks: MK 42240.
```

Figure 2.29: Unicorn, labeled display (1)

```
To select another button, press TAB.                    (c
To see the next page of information, press RETURN now.

HELP            GOBACK          STARTOVER
FORWARD         BACKWARD        REQUEST         LIKE            OPTIONS



              THIS IS ITEM NUMBER 2 OF THE 4 YOU FOUND IN THE C
        General note: The 1st work for piano and reduced (
                      piano part consisting of the 1925 pi
                      George Gershwin; the 2nd work a symp
          Performers: George Gershwin, piano, Columbia Jaz
                      New York Philharmonic (2nd work) ; B
                      (3rd work) ; Michael Tilson Thomas,
        General note: "Consists of previously released
material"—Container.
        General note: Compact disc; analog recording.
        General note: Durations: 13:41; 18:22; 38:39.
            Contents: Broadway overtures. Oh, Kay! (7:06)
                      ; Girl crazy (5:41) ; Strike up the
                      thee I sing (4:36) ; Let 'em eat cak
             Subject: Piano with jazz ensemble.
             Subject: Symphonic poems.
             Subject: Overtures, Arranged.
     Personal author: Gershwin, George, 1898-1937. prf
```

Figure 2.30: Unicorn, labeled display (2)

```
To select another button, press TAB.                    (c
To view the next items you found, press RETURN now.

HELP            GOBACK          STARTOVER
FORWARD         BACKWARD        REQUEST         LIKE
OPTIONS

              THIS IS ITEM NUMBER 2 OF THE 4 YOU FOUND IN THE C
     Personal author: Thomas, Michael Tilson, 1944- cnd
     Personal author: Gershwin, George, 1898-1937. Rhapsod
     Personal author: Gershwin, George, 1898-1937. America
     Personal author: Gershwin, George, 1898-1937. Musical
                      1987.
    Corporate author: Columbia Jazz Band. prf
    Corporate author: New York Philharmonic. prf
    Corporate author: Buffalo Philharmonic Orchestra. prf
         Added title: Rhapsodie en bleu.
         Added title: American in Paris.
         Added title: Americain a Paris.
         Added title: Broadway overtures.


COMDSC MK 42240    copies:1
   copy:1             COMDSC      (AV-SERVICE)
```

Figure 2.31: Unicorn, labeled display (3)

3

The Catalog: Interface to the Collection

A good catalog is an interface between the user and the library's collection. It may be more than that, but it must, first and foremost, do that job effectively. Recognizing that the catalog is primarily an interface points up several issues that need to be considered. This chapter covers these issues, summarized here:

- The catalog is a means, not an end, and most users wish to spend very little time at the catalog.

- A good interface should cater both to those who wish to browse through material itself and to those who wish to do preliminary browsing within the interface—recognizing that preliminary browsing, while it can offer new forms of closeness, can't substitute for actual examination.

- If material is not represented at all in the catalog, it ceases to exist for many users.

- Material that is inaccurately represented in the catalog is imperfectly available to many users.

- More complete representation of specific items within the collection, going beyond physical items, will make the interface more useful.

- A good interface should not overwhelm the user with possibly irrelevant information but should encourage the user to locate more possibly relevant material if so inclined.

- A proper interface to specialized material, such as music material and material in non-Roman scripts, requires specialized techniques for appropriate access.

- When extending the catalog to go beyond the physical collection, the primary interface role must be recognized: most users want to get at material that's available here and now.

Catalog: Means, Not End

Generally, library users want to spend as little time as possible at the catalog. They use the catalog to get to the collection: the books and other materials actually on the shelves, in that particular location, at that time.

Perhaps as many as 95 percent of all users[1] have no particular interest in the catalog itself or in exploring the possible information paths available. The 95 percent figure is based on some formal and informal evidence that only about 5 percent of successful catalog

---

1 Where "user" is defined as a particular library user on a particular day with a particular need; the same person may well fall into the important 5 percent on a different day.

searches (that is, searches that retrieve at least one item) result in long displays that aren't default displays, when shorter (brief single-record or multiple-record) displays show call number, status, and enough bibliographic information to identify a book. For many users and uses, even a one-line display with perhaps 50 characters of bibliographic information, plus call number and (ideally) status, will be enough: they'll be off to the shelves. I call these the quick-check searchers.

Quick-Check Searchers

What these users want from the catalog is fairly straightforward, boiling down to one or more of three things:

- **Known-item searching:** Whether a particular item is available (circulation status) and, if so, where to find it (location and call number). Most author-title and many title searches fall into this category.

- **Another book by a favorite author:** What titles by a particular author are currently available—and where they are. Many author searches fall into this category; it's particularly relevant for fiction and such categories of literature as humor and essays.

- **A place to look for something on a subject:** A call number (or, for the mildly persistent searcher, one or more call numbers) to serve as the starting point for shelf browsing. Most subject searches, some title searches (particularly title-word searches) and a few author-title searches (using a known item to get a subject-range pointer) fall into this category.

The behavior of these searchers is rational and proper, frustrating as it may be for catalog designers and subject-access researchers and theoreticians. While the percentage of quick-check searchers may (and perhaps should) be lower in large research libraries, most public and school library users and a

great many academic library users really don't, and shouldn't, want to spend their time at the catalog itself.

Quick-Check Subject Searching

Even for subject searches, where quick-check users will miss much of the potentially relevant material, I would argue that quick-check searching is the most appropriate behavior for most users under most conditions. That's a heretical stance in the online-catalog research community, so perhaps I should clarify what I mean.

Let's say I've just watched the movie *Blaze*, and that, as a result, I'd really like to know something more about Earl Long (or maybe his brother Huey, the Kingfish). Now, I'm in a position typical of most people delving into a new subject. I really don't want to know all the magazine articles, archival materials, and other items available around the country that are somehow related to the Long dynasty; I don't even much care what the "best" material on Earl K. Long is. That may come later, if I find the subject fascinating. For now, I want *something I can pick up, take home, and make sense of.* I need location and status information, but I also need to look at the books.

If there's a name index, I enter "Long, Earl" or, if my memory is working well, "Long, Earl K." (Or I enter "Earl K. Long" and the system fixes it for me.) If there are author and subject indexes, I probably ask for Earl Long as a subject. In that case, chances are I'll get Michael L. Kurtz's *Earl K. Long* or A. J. Liebling's *The Earl of Louisiana*—or, if my library has A. J. Liebling's essay collection that contains the latter and has done good subject indexing, I'll get that collection. I might very well get a pointer to their videocassette of *Blaze* as well; maybe they even have some other nonprint material on Earl Long. I'll jot down one or two call numbers, particularly for items on the shelf, and go looking. Chances are, I'll take the Liebling book.

Did I get the "best" information on ol' Earl? Maybe not. Do I care? Absolutely not. Would I be happier *or better served* if, instead of getting me those call numbers in a two- or three-screen sequence, the catalog took me through a five-minute journey designed to assure that I retrieved all relevant material on Earl? Good grief, no.

That latter statement may be a little clearer if we suppose a slightly more abstruse subject. I've been hearing a lot about ergonomics lately and would like to know a little about it—maybe just enough to know whether my little data-entry sweatshop will be in trouble with OSHA if I don't invest in some wrist pads or buy chairs that cost more than $25.[2] I go to look up "ergonomics" in the catalog. Now, this can get pretty complicated; there are loads of related topics, and much of the most worthwhile material will probably be articles in various medical journals. But this is my first exposure to the subject other than an article in the newspaper about a San Francisco ordinance. I want to know *something*; I not only don't want to know *everything* but couldn't possibly understand most of it.

I look up "ergonomics" in the subject index. If I'm unlucky, I don't get a result (because "Human engineering" is the more commonly used subject heading). Maybe I'm lucky, or maybe I used a word or title-word search because I had no idea whether the word would be used as a subject. percent-2In any case, I've probably retrieved a small handful of items, including Kathlyn Gay's *Ergonomics: Making Products and Places Fit People.* percent0I jot down 620.82 (this is a Dewey-

using public library) and go looking for this or similar books.

Chances are I'll wind up taking home Gay's book or *The Psychology of Everyday Things* (at 620.8). Either one will probably suit me just fine. Oh, I'll miss the books at 613, which I would have found under the subject "Human engineering"—but I'll have something that will get me started. On the other hand, a thorough search technique covering the region's libraries, even without adding articles and nonprint materials, would yield more than a thousand items, including things such as *Biotechnology: Principles and Applications* and *The Gene Business.* Now, the first of those is probably terribly relevant and may even be "the best book" on the subject, *if* I want or can use that depth of information. Articles in medical and other journals would surely be more up-to-date; they would also, almost certainly, be useless for my own current needs.

And that's the key to the heresy: the catalog should serve to meet my current needs as a user—not my hypothetical needs as an ideal researcher. The most common subject cry in public libraries and undergraduate libraries, quite properly, is "Give me *something*, and give it to me *now*."

That's certainly not all there is to say about subject searching. Chapter 7 includes some discussion of the ways in which a good catalog can *and should* provide more and better subject retrieval for those searchers unsatisfied with a quick result.

The Transparent Catalog

The ideal catalog for quick-check searchers is transparent, although that's an impossible ideal. "Transparent," in this case, means that

---

2   No, I don't have a data-entry sweatshop. This example is hypothetical, unlike the first.

the catalog doesn't come between the user and the material—it provides a clear, easy-to-use view of what's there. Characteristics of a transparent catalog for quick-search use include the following:

- Users do not need advance training in order to use the catalog. Anything they need to know (other than what a keyboard and screen are) is at the catalog or, ideally, is part of the catalog itself.

- Users do not need to know library jargon in order to use the catalog effectively.

- Users can start a catalog session, enter a search, and retrieve call number and status information within two or three minutes, and with very few steps or intermediate screens.

- Users are aware that more information on the retrieved items is available, but providing that awareness does not slow down the user who just wants to get in, check something, and get out.

If quick-check searchers find that the catalog is responsive and occasionally tells them something they didn't know, they will appreciate the library more, probably use it better, and possibly be ready to make "better" (more intensive) use of the catalog when that's appropriate.

Let's say I go to my local library to see whether there's anything by Richard Condon I haven't read yet. If I know that the catalog is quick and easy to use, I may pause to search for Condon rather than going directly to the mystery shelves. If I do, I may learn that Condon's books are split between mystery and straight fiction—and that he writes under some other names. Now I'm delighted: there's a whole new range of slightly crazed writing for me to look at! Somewhere in the back of my mind, I'll be more supportive of the library—and will certainly use the catalog more in the future.

But if it takes me ten minutes or ten screens to find out what Condon titles are available, I'll probably forget the whole thing and just go to the shelves, at least in any but the largest public libraries. Who needs the hassle?

The Best Compliments are No Complaints

This is really very sad, of course. Here you've committed enormous resources to installing this wonderful new online catalog, with state-of-the-art features. You're sitting there proudly near the terminal cluster; you may even be wandering the area as part of a "get acquainted with the catalog" program. And you'd sure like it if people would use the catalog and come tell you how great it is.

Here's how you know how great the catalog is: lots of people use the terminals; lots of them use it for just a minute or two, jotting down something on a slip of paper (which you've naturally provided next to the terminal, if you don't provide printers); they go to the shelves and find material; and they don't either start muttering at the terminal or look helpless. They don't come up to you and start with "That damn catalog" or "Whatever happened to the card catalog?"

Congratulations. You're succeeding. And, of course, being part of a user-oriented library, you'll be there to help out when some-one *does* look a little puzzled. More about that in chapter 7.

Serving the Five Percent

Fortunately for the future of online catalog designers and researchers, some library searchers aren't quick-check searchers. Perhaps 5 to 10 percent of public library users and possibly a much higher percentage of academic library users need more than what's described above. They need to be able to explore a topic or person, to find the most appropriate material or information, and retrieve that material or information.

Most of the rest of Part I is really about the 5 percent, whom you might call "serious catalog searchers." Probably 90 percent of the effort required to design and define a good catalog will be devoted to meeting the needs of this 5 percent, just as probably 90 percent of the information in MARC records is needed by only 5 percent of the searchers.

That's appropriate, and is not unique to this situation. A library that serves the 95 percent well and completely fails to serve the 5 percent is a failing library—particularly since those 5 percent will almost certainly represent a much larger percentage of people who use the library (remember that a "searcher" or "user" is defined in terms of the needs of a particular day) and will include many who directly support the library.

The 5 percent need rich access to complete information. They will increasingly appreciate access beyond traditional book-level bibliographic information and will make good use of your library's efforts to go "beyond the walls." They need catalogs that can work with them to explore the library universe—and there's no likelihood that we'll run out of new ideas for improving such catalogs.

Fail to serve the 5 percent, and your library and its catalog are seriously inadequate. But you need to remember—and this is the whole extent of my subject-access heresy above—that you must not abandon the 95 percent in order to serve the 5 percent. If you insist that every searcher should gain the benefit of advanced subject-searching techniques, you are insisting that every searcher become part of the 5 percent. They will not do that—and they will resent you (or at least the catalog) for attempting to force them to. Fail

to serve the 95 percent, and you are failing disastrously: in effect, for most users, your library ceases to have a catalog.

Shelf and Catalog Browsing

Even though most users will prefer to browse the bookshelves, a good catalog should help them to browse your collection in a variety of ways. To support shelf browsing, all you need to do is assure that call numbers show up on the first screen of the default single-record display and maybe even on the multiple-record display. That's more difficult when your library has several branches, possibly with different call numbers for the same item and probably with different location and related information. It's still feasible, at least to some extent; some systems in Part II show clever approaches to providing this information.

Catalog browsing can take several forms: call numbers (browsing the "virtual shelf"), author, title, subject or some combination of searches—but in each case, the user should be able to do two things rapidly and without special training:

- Move within the overall set of information with no possibility of getting lost;

- Look at more information for any single record or series of records within the set, preferably going from one record to the next with a single command or keystroke.

Browsing the catalog can't compare to browsing the shelves, in those cases where all the wanted material is actually on contiguous shelves. Shelf-browsers get to skim through items, seeing at once whether they're appropriate; it will be decades (if ever) before that will be plausible for most catalogs.

But catalog browsing can offer several advantages over shelf browsing, for the simple reason that the desired material (and information) won't always be on contiguous shelves. For example:

- A user can browse through all of a library's works by and about Martin Luther King, Jr., which may include dozens of videocassettes, sound recordings, microfilm materials, and maybe even computer files as well as books, although few libraries will find it reasonable to intershelve all those media.

- A serious searcher can browse through not only those items entirely devoted to Martin Luther King, Jr., but also magazine articles on King, books containing chapters on King, archival materials at a nearby university, and one-of-a-kind materials around the world that could, if necessary, be scanned and transmitted to this library's Ariel™[3] document-delivery workstation.

- I can assemble a virtual bookshelf including *Blaze*; books about and by Earl K. Long; books about and by Huey Long; Randy Newman's *Good Old Boys* (a particularly relevant sound recording); some recordings by Hank Williams, Sr., Dr. John, and others; maps of Louisiana and Maryland from the late 1950s; photographs of Earl Long and Blaze Starr; articles from the CD-ROM *Time Almanac* on the Long dynasty; a recording of an Earl Long press conference that's been digitized and is available for downloading; Blaze Starr's autobiography and a current work on the sociology of exotic dancing—and, probably, dozens of related works in each of these areas. I can then browse through this "bookshelf," determining which works I really want to deal with and which are available, and print out a finding list for the resulting group. Or, if I'm lazy and a trifle unscrupulous, I can just turn the whole mess into a bibliography for an article or book without actually bothering to look at all the material.

That's browsing with a vengeance—and the final scenario really isn't all that improbable in the relatively near future. At that point, of course, I'm well into the 5 percent—but don't tell me that I'm just searching for facts, because that's not true. (The Randy Newman record and Hank Williams, Sr. record add little or nothing to the "facts" about the Longs but certainly help to round out the understanding I'm trying to achieve.)

Summing up: the catalog can't compete with the shelves, when all the user wants is to look at a few books. But the catalog can provide enormously powerful browsing, far beyond what's possible at the shelves. It should support both—particularly since dial-in and other remote users can't go to the shelf for even the simplest browsing.

Completeness

If it isn't in the online catalog, it isn't in the collection. Maybe that's all that needs to be said about completeness, the absolute need to carry out full retrospective conversion.

In past years, a number of prominent librarians have argued that older materials don't need to be in the online catalog at all—or, in a related vein, that subject access isn't needed for material more than ten years old. There are probably some libraries for which those statements make sense—but those libraries should also assiduously discard any material more than ten years old. By excluding them from the catalog, or leaving crucial access out, the library is effectively hiding the material in any case. Why leave it to rot on the shelf? Why not burn it and have done with it?

---

3 Ariel is RLG's document-transmission system, likely to become the standard for the field.

Humanists will be appalled at the suggestion that older material doesn't count; so should most scientists. It's a rare discipline that reinvents itself every decade; even in solid-state electronics and bioengineering, there are important works more than a decade old. Humanities scholars already suffer from the fact that access to material published within the past quarter-century is so much better than for older material. The older material is at the heart of humanities scholarship, and is at the heart of the library's role as cultural memory.

I think the case is straightforward for most libraries and most librarians: if you don't understand the need for full and complete retrospective conversion, you're not a librarian, you're a factmonger.

Full and complete: that means older material should be *fully* represented, with access as complete as for contemporary material. Full and complete also means that "less-serious" material deserves proper treatment. If your library includes fiction, it should be fully represented in the catalog. If you're enhancing nonfiction records with chapter titles and the like, shouldn't you be enhancing fiction records to provide access to key characters and themes and to the stories in collections?

Full and complete also means accurate. Ideally, completeness and accuracy should also mean bringing older subject headings up to date and dealing with items cataloged using older rules. Accuracy may count for even more in the online catalog, since erroneous records may be inaccessible. It's a pleasant fantasy that online access techniques obviate the need for care and for authority records— but, if anything, quite the opposite is true. Full, complete, accurate databases form the necessary foundation for truly worthwhile library catalogs.

Those databases will accept and, as needed, restore full, accurate MARC records. Whether the records are stored in MARC format or translated to some other format isn't relevant, as long as the translations are invisible, reversible, and reliable. There's no need to say much more about MARC, except that any catalog that doesn't fully accept MARC-format records has no legitimacy in the general library field. You can go beyond MARC, you can add alternative sources, but the dominant format for accurate exchange of complex bibliographic information is MARC. It has been for two decades, and will continue to be for some time to come. Accept no substitutes.

Intellectual Access

Once the catalog includes all of the library's material, the library should begin to provide better access to the *intellectual* items contained within the *physical* items. The library should also consider providing deeper access to the items, which isn't quite the same thing.

It's important to distinguish access to intellectual items from access to full text; they're not the same thing. Access to intellectual items is primarily the provision of "In" analytics, e.g.:

- author, title, and subject access to individual papers within a collection or conference proceedings;

- author, title, and subject access to articles within periodicals;

- composer, artist, title, and subject access to pieces within a classical collection (recording or score) or songs on a popular recording or in a popular songbook.

Deeper access to material includes such possibilities as access to chapter names within monographs, access to tables of contents or indexes, and other such possibilities.

Broader access to material, although incredibly expensive and difficult, actually carries out the full tenet of complete representation of a collection. Think of it as completing the catalog. Deeper access doesn't expand the represented collection but expands the number of access points to that collection. Think of it as enhancing the catalog. Both are useful, both are expensive, and both raise some difficult issues.

Relevance and Overload

Perhaps the most obvious issue relating to completing and enhancing the catalog is the issue of information overload—the tendency of a rich catalog to provide more items than the user can (or chooses to) cope with. Directly related to information overload is relevance, as usually expressed in terms of recall and precision.

I've already said that a catalog should provide ways to help the user locate more possibly relevant information on request, and will get back to that in other chapters. For now, let's look at recall, precision and information overload, particularly for the 95 percent.

First, the usual definitions. *Recall* is the ability to find everything needed—to locate all the material relevant to a given request. Generally, the broader the search result, the higher the recall. Mathematically, recall can be stated as:

$$Recall = \frac{Relevant-retrieved}{Relevant-available}$$

noting that *Relevant-retrieved* is not necessarily equal to *Total-retrieved*, the actual size of the result. *Precision* is the ability to find *only* what is wanted—to locate only the material

relevant to a given user making a given request. Mathematically, precision can be stated as:

$$Precision = \frac{Relevant-retrieved}{Total-retrieved}$$

Perfect retrieval would have a total score of 2.00, or 200 percent: retrieving everything that's relevant, and nothing that isn't relevant. Except under very special circumstances, it's fair to say that perfect retrieval isn't possible. For most cases, some balance must be achieved between recall and precision, noting that techniques that improve recall frequently damage precision, and vice-versa. It's even tempting to say (and may be true in most cases) that the sum of recall and precision never exceeds a certain fixed limit in even the best systems, and that the limit isn't all that high—perhaps not much more than 100 percent.

Indeed, many searchers would consider a combined *and balanced* sum of 100 percent to be respectable: that is, retrieving half of what's relevant, with half of what you retrieve being relevant. If you could achieve a balanced sum of 160 percent (80 percent recall with 80 percent precision), you should be absolutely delighted. The problems arise when precision and recall become seriously unbalanced. Information overload sets in when recall substantially exceeds precision or when the result set is simply overwhelming for the particular user regardless of its relevance.

Some observers have stated that it's always better to improve recall. So what if searchers have to winnow out a little more chaff? At least they're being presented with all the needed information. This viewpoint may seem beguiling at first, but quickly falls apart in reality. At the extreme, there's an easy way to assure 100 percent recall, at least within a single collection: shut down the catalog altogether, and simply point people to the shelves.

Everything the collection has that could be relevant to their search needs is somewhere in that mass: that's 100 percent recall.

Sound unappealing? If so, then you can forget 100 percent recall. And if the above sounds unappealing or even horrendous, think twice about your dreams of full-text access to all the world's texts. Not only will it *not* provide 100 percent recall unless several billion librarians add hundreds of terabytes[4] of indexing to the hundreds of terabytes of full text, but the yield for any plausible search will resemble the entire collection of a typical branch library.

Full-text access to all the world's texts *will not* provide 100 percent recall for most searches—and the items you'll miss (assuming you're immortal, thus able to deal with the recall) may include the most important items. After all, names for concepts frequently get added *after* the seminal papers on the concepts are written. That's a fundamental flaw in "relevance ranking" by word counting as well: hack works and "year's progress" reviews are more likely to score high on key words than are seminal articles.

Of course it's absurd to point someone at the stacks and say, "What you need is somewhere in there." At the other extreme, it's frequently possible to provide 100 percent precision, but the recall ratio may be quite low. Whether or not that's a problem depends on the user's needs. Quick searchers want 100 percent precision and frequently get it; by and large, they don't care whether their recall ratio is 10, 20, or even 1 percent. It's easier to find "something about x" than to find "everything about x," and you're a lot less likely to need to wade through "lots of things about y, z, and aa."

The point at which information overload sets in—the point at which the user starts to give up—depends on the user, the total result size, and the precision ratio. My own guess is that any precision ratio much lower than 30 to 50 percent for any result size much larger than 10 or 20 items will cause many users to start giving up. Formal and informal studies suggest that users rarely look at more than 15 to 30 items in a result set—and I'd guess that if only 2 or 3 of the first 15 look interesting, the user is less likely to go on to 30.

Unfortunately, true relevance for a given user doesn't depend just on appropriateness of subject matter. It also depends on appropriateness of reading level and assumed background, and possibly on currency. If I retrieve 20 items from a search on ergonomics, of which all 20 have something to do with ergonomics, but I can only make sense of 2 of the items, then for me, the results show 10 percent precision: 90 percent of the items retrieved are irrelevant *for my use*. And if I retrieve a thousand items with no good way to reduce the number, then I'll probably give up or ask for help: the result is too large for precision to matter.

As libraries enhance and expand their online catalogs, they must be sensitive to the issue of information overload. Librarians may be more prone to information overload than some other professionals. Just because you're suffering from information overload, however, you're neither required nor entitled to inflict it on your users.

Non-Roman Material

A user dealing with non-Roman materials may not be able to accurately and precisely

---

4 A terabyte is one million million bytes (or a trillion bytes), or a thousand gigabytes.

locate the needed materials if the catalog provides access only in romanized form.

It's really that simple: if all you provide is the romanized information, you're not providing full access to the material. The process of romanization collapses enough variations so that some meaningful distinctions can no longer be made. Romanization can also introduce differences that do not exist in the original script. In either case, access suffers.

The examples and details of the problem are too complex for this particular book, but it's not a hypothetical issue. Without the ability to key searches in the original scripts and retrieve bibliographic records with those scripts displayed, precise access to the materials can't be assured.

What's the solution? For now, there are some library catalogs that can index and display some non-Roman character sets, and there will be more in the future. In the future—perhaps five to ten years away for most systems—we will see the establishment and implementation of a universal character code encompassing all character sets. That code, currently called Unicode and likely to emerge as part of an international standard, may double the uncompressed storage requirements in some systems but will permit standardized storage and communication of all characters.

That isn't the whole answer, of course. Once you add non-Roman characters, you must deal with non-Roman normalization rules for indexing and retrieval, and you must provide techniques for keying non-Roman searches. That won't be easy, and it's not likely to happen outside the libraries that need it most, at least not for a few years.

Other Problem Cases

Non-Roman materials are not the only cases where it's difficult to make the catalog into a clear window to the collection. Music librarians have struggled with online access for years, with varying degrees of success. There are other (perhaps smaller) categories where traditional access doesn't yield good results.

The difficulties with music are too numerous and intricate to detail here, even if I had the expertise to do so. Immediate problems include the totally nondistinctive nature of most classical music titles (try retrieving "Symphony in A"—particularly in a keyword-only system that doesn't index words of one letter); the fact that pieces are so likely to be parts of collections in sound recordings, where the collection itself has no particular significance and may have no apparent title; the unsearchable nature of the flat and sharp signs in some catalogs; the uselessness of subject searching for most music materials; and others.

The only advice I can offer here is that those who are developing online catalogs, selecting them for a library, and customizing them for the library should listen to their music librarians and, if possible, involve them in the decision-making teams. Their complaints are valid; their experience may be invaluable. Solving their problems may also solve or avoid some other problems—such as retrieving material on "C++," the object-oriented version of the "C" computer language, without getting all the material on "C" itself.

The Here and Now

Most libraries should use their catalogs to go "beyond the walls," and later chapters will touch on some aspects of that extension. Increasingly, a library's catalog can provide an indirect interface to materials in the region, in a consortium of libraries or, directly or through gateways, to hundreds or thousands of libraries around the country and around the world.

But first, provide an excellent interface to the here and now, the material actually available at a given location. Make sure that users can readily narrow their searches to include only those materials. Most users want something now: not tomorrow, not a week from now, but now. Sometimes, they *need* something now—and it doesn't matter that you can provide them with something "better" in a few days.

Let them know that more is available. Ease their way into a broader world of resources. But don't force them to deal with the broader world; that may be inappropriate, even hopeless.

Conclusion

Tomorrow's catalog will be much more than a set of bibliographic records for the books, films, records, scores, and serial titles housed in a single location. Tomorrow's catalog will provide thoughtful ways to encourage users to probe deeper into a topic, finding more of the related material. That's all to the good.

Still, now and for the foreseeable future, the majority of library users have little interest in spending time at the catalog and little need to explore topics in any depth. They need quick access to limited information, a clear and easy window on the collection at hand. While the catalog should do much more than this, it must first do this well.

4

The User Interface, "Integrated Systems," and Shared Computers

While the online catalog serves as the most visible aspect of library automation, you need much more to provide effective support. This book focuses on the visible interface; the full scope of library automation is too broad to cover here, but it's impossible to deal with the online catalog in a vacuum.

Your library must obviously use some other aspects of library automation to support an online catalog. You must be creating or acquiring machine-readable bibliographic records in order to display them. If you are to provide circulation status—an important advantage of online catalogs—you must have an automated circulation system that works together with the online catalog. If you have automated acquisitions support, you will have information on which items are on order, which are being processed, and (perhaps) which you have explicitly decided not to order; that can also be valuable information for the online catalog. Serials check-in and binding support may enable you to provide accurate, up-to-date holdings information as part of the online catalog, which will become more important as you add article-level access.

These functions should work together to strengthen one another and to make the online catalog more valuable. Other functions may add even more value. If your catalog can provide access to other online catalogs, you may be able to offer interlibrary borrowing or circulation requests from the online catalog, although this can pose new problems. If you can work out control, copyright, and funding issues, you may soon be able to link article-level access to document-delivery systems, ordering facsimile copies of articles from the online catalog.

The Visible and the Whole

The online catalog is, in effect, the visible aspect of the whole panoply of library automation activities. Its success reflects the success of the whole. Because all the pieces work together, a rallying cry for the past decade or so has been "integrated online systems," the idea that all aspects of library automation should be part of a single system.

In one sense, an integrated system offers distinct advantages. Clearly, users should be able to find out whether items are currently available. Clearly, you serve users better if you let them know what's on order and being processed, as long as that processing is efficient. Clearly, users with access to article-level information should be able to find out whether you have not only the periodical but the issue—and, if not, how they can acquire the article. And clearly, time should not be spent rekeying this information. Thus, from the perspective of user service, integration is obviously the right way to go.

Integration: Philosophy, Not Machinery

You need to think in terms of integration. That does not mean that you must acquire a single set of hardware and software that serves all your library automation needs. In some cases, that may be the thing to do; in many other cases, it is neither the most effective nor the most economical way to proceed.

Integration for library automation is ultimately a question of philosophy and standards, not of machinery. The most obvious standard to support integrated automation has already been mentioned: the MARC formats and specifically USMARC within the United States. You can acquire cataloging information from the Library of Congress, OCLC, RLIN, WLN, any number of CD-ROM vendors, and others; integrating all the diverse bibliographic information is almost trivial because all the suppliers use USMARC.

Would you accept a local online catalog system that could only use records derived from that vendor's bibliographic resource (whether online or CD-ROM)? Probably not: you'd be putting yourself at the mercy of one vendor, and with USMARC, there's no excuse for such a limitation. Assuming that your entire local system must come from a single vendor, and accepting proprietary methods of

any sort that rule out any possibility of later multivendor systems, similarly limits your future and puts your library at risk.

Standards exist and are being developed that will make interchange of other forms of library information more straightforward, and even now systems designers can usually figure out ways to convey needed information from one system to another. You can achieve functional integration without necessarily using a single "integrated system."

That's an important consideration as you think about the future of your library's automation plans. A true integrated system need not consist of only one supplier's software and need not reside in a single computer. If you can achieve functional integration, where information is available to each aspect of the system as it is needed, you have an integrated system.

Single System vs. Linked Systems

Which is better—a single-supplier system or linked systems that can be integrated through careful planning? It depends on your library and the state of your current systems. For many libraries, the single-supplier system will offer easier planning and fewer difficulties in dealing with suppliers. Using a single supplier may, however, mean giving up the advantages of certain systems and possibly replacing well-functioning systems.

We don't expect every library to be equally deep in all aspects of collection development and service. Why should we expect every vendor to be equally expert at all phases of library automation? Just because Vendor C offers the slickest acquisitions and fund-accounting systems I've ever seen doesn't mean that Vendor C will also offer the best online catalog for my particular library.

Linking involves its own difficulties, but for some libraries it will provide the best combination of services. More to the point, given economic realities, it will allow you to improve different aspects of your library automation at different rates, as time and funding permit. You may not need automated acquisitions at this point, or may find a book supplier's services more than adequate; meanwhile, you can acquire a first-rate online catalog knowing that you can eventually add bibliographic information for on-order items to the catalog. Or, if your existing online catalog continues to meet your needs and was designed for the future, you can add that sensational new circulation system and see the results reflected in your catalog.

Right now, linking is more difficult than buying a single-source integrated system, but that's changing. On one hand, some standards are evolving for exchange of non-bibliographic information; on the other hand, vendors are finding it increasingly useful to make such linkages available. That's why you see more and more announcements of alliances among competitors. Even though two companies may both offer online catalogs and circulation systems, they can recognize that, for some libraries, the most sensible solution will be Company A's online catalog and Company B's circulation system. Since each company would rather have half of a library's business than none of it, the alliance is a reasonable strategy.

What does all this have to do with designing an effective catalog for your library? Basically, the following:

- The best online catalogs provide circulation status, on-order information, and in-process information.

- Article-level bibliographic information is more useful if it is linked to issue-level holdings information, such as can be provided through serials control systems.

- As catalogs are extended "beyond the walls" of the library, they should be linked to systems to provide for interlibrary borrowing, circulation, or document delivery.

- Just as no single catalog is ideal for every library, no single acquisitions or serials system is ideal for every library.

- For some libraries, the best balance of systems—given library needs, library funds, and other issues—can be achieved by linking disparate systems into a functionally integrated whole.

Shared Computers

Just as your library automation support need not reside entirely in a single computer, it's not always necessary for your online catalog to have a computer entirely to itself. The trend is *away* from sharing, for good reasons. In the past, you may have shared a campus or city computer, running your online catalog and other automation functions as part of a time-sharing system. In the future, it's likely that you will have at least one computer, and possibly several, devoted to your online catalog.

Shared computers can offer cost savings, but they also create several problems, some of which specifically relate to using the same computer for library and nonlibrary functions. Others, discussed in the next two sections of this chapter, also relate to using the same computer and databases for the online catalog and for other library-automation functions.

Problems that arise when sharing a computer with nonlibrary functions can include the following, among others:

- **Scheduling difficulties:** Good libraries have more extended hours than most other campus or city services. The online catalog requires full service whenever the library is open (and, possibly, even when it isn't); that means that computer support staff must be available and that the computer can't be devoted to batch processing at a level that damages catalog response time.

- **Priority and power difficulties:** Good online catalogs require solid, well-balanced computing power—particularly efficient time-sharing and telecommunications support and efficient database management and retrieval. A library can't serve its users if that power isn't available on the first two days of the month because the shared computer is being used for accounting and payroll processing. Additionally, successful catalogs require ever more power—because more library users make heavier demands on the catalogs and because libraries will expand and enhance catalog services. That power may not be available on a shared computer, and the library may lack sufficient clout to force needed upgrades.

- **Economic difficulties:** Many college and university campus computing centers have offered "excess" computing power to libraries at heavily discounted rates, sometimes free. The same may be true for city and school computers. As other agencies find more use for the excess power, and as libraries find that they require power beyond the excess level, the discounts may disappear and libraries may find themselves unable to afford the shared computing environment.

- **Inability to change or need to change:** A library sharing a computer may find its ability to select suitable software hampered in one of two ways. On one hand, if the library provides crucial financial support for the shared computer, the larger agency may resist any library move to change systems if the new system requires a different computer. Although the

change may make good sense to the library for service and financial reasons, it may not be feasible politically. On the other hand, if the library is a secondary partner in the shared-computer center, the superior agency may decide to change systems (either computers or underlying operating systems) even though the change will damage the library's automation support.

Do these factors mean that libraries should avoid sharing computers with other agencies? Ten years ago, the answer would have been no—because, for many libraries, shared computers were the only way to gain enough computing power. Today, the answer is increasingly yes: in most cases, if a library needs to share a computer, it should be part of a library consortium. At least in that case the computer is entirely devoted to library needs.

Security

One potential problem arises for every online catalog and becomes more important for an integrated system and even more important on a shared computer. That problem is security—assuring that online catalog users don't gain access to sensitive information and that they don't change information or otherwise damage the system.

About the only cases where libraries really don't need to worry about security are single-station CD-ROM catalogs with no hard disks and sealed CD-ROM drives. No user can change a CD-ROM under any circumstances; chances are, no user will be able to do much damage to anything on such a system (other than pure physical vandalism).

More typical online catalogs can be (and usually are) designed for adequate security. If PCs are used as terminals, typically they can be set up so that any attempt to break out of or exit the online catalog will yield an immediate return to the online catalog. With "dumb" terminals, the only issue is whether it's possible to get beyond the online catalog interface through the terminal.

Surprisingly, the answer may be yes. With intelligent system design, the most a computer vandal will be able to do is change some help screens or the sign-on message at a specific terminal, damage that can easily be repaired. If the system is not well designed, there's more chance that an enterprising user could change circulation records or shut down the entire system. (The chances of actual damage are very slight with any well-designed system, however.)

When you add dial-up access or use PCs as terminals, security issues become more significant. That's particularly true if you provide staff with dial-up access to more sensitive aspects of an integrated system. In the latter case, there are some minimal protections that *must* be taken:

- Dial-in access to anything other than the online catalog *must* require a password.

- The library must insist that staff members change their passwords regularly—possibly even disabling any password in use for more than a given number of days.

- Staff members must be advised on good password protocol, which includes never posting the password at a terminal and using something other than common short words as passwords.

- Dial-up access to anything other than the online catalog should be anonymous, at least until the password is provided. That is, the sign-on message should not say "Urban Library Cataloging System: Account?" but something much more neutral—e.g. "Account?" by itself—or even just "?"

- Any password system should be self-limiting, typically disconnecting after three in-

correct password (or nonexistent account) attempts, and should log and report failed attempts to access the system.

Other, more substantial measures are available; planners wishing to provide dial-up and Internet access to a system may wish to look further into system security measures. For example, you could permit dial-in access to functions other than the online catalog only on a call-back basis: that is, the staff member dials in, provides an appropriate password, and hangs up, after which the library computer dials back a known telephone number for the user—and, of course, logs the connection time and number.

If the online catalog is the only system on a computer and runs as a read-only system, calling up information from the linked circulation system but unable to change such information or the database itself, security will be less problematic.

Shared computer systems represent a special problem. Most libraries want to provide as much access as possible, which means permitting dial-up and Internet access without the use of account numbers or passwords. But computer centers worry about unauthorized access to operating systems that generally aren't very secure. Unless your library can convince the computer center (and yourself) that it is totally impossible to break out of the online catalog and into the shared operating system, the computer center is unlikely to permit anonymous access. You can't really blame them: they know that there are bad people out there, people who will damage crucial systems either out of malice or just for the intellectual challenge.

I don't advocate paranoia, but you must exercise some healthy caution when implementing any online catalog. You're providing access to a powerful computing capability, one that relies on a database that may be worth more than the computer itself. Maintaining open access while assuring that no harm comes to the database, the computer or other functions on the computer requires foresight. You need to ask the right questions and be sure that the answers are legitimate.

One aspect of system security should be a standard part of every online catalog: regular backup procedures, with off-site storage of backups at regular intervals. Failing to back up catalog and other data is an invitation to disaster.

Privacy

You need to consider two different issues when thinking about privacy concerns: the privacy of a particular user in terms of what he or she is doing at the online catalog, and protecting the privacy of other users—both from one another and from agencies such as the FBI and local police. The second issue is part of security and can be dealt with in a fairly straightforward manner:

- While circulation-status information should be available at any online-catalog terminal or dial-in port, the online catalog (as a public interface) should not include information on *who* has any given item— and staff should not be able to use public terminals to acquire such information.

- Circulation systems (and, thus, online catalogs) should never retain historical records on who borrowed given items; such records are a fishing license for law-enforcement agencies, which will generally find a way around shield laws.

- While statistical records of circulation patterns can be valuable, care must be taken to assure that user-related records are kept at a sufficiently general level that they cannot be used to reveal specific borrowing activity. You should not retain such patterns unless you have clear and ethically reason-

able uses for them. For example: while you certainly wish to know how frequently large-print materials circulate (and which kinds of large-print material circulate most frequently) so that you can plan your large-print collection, there's no good reason to retain records that correlate age of borrower, sex of borrower and zip code of borrower with the specific large-print volumes borrowed. If your large-print collection is heavily used, why do you care how old the readers are or their sex? In general, the more detailed your statistical records, the more they can infringe on privacy.

- While you may wish to allow users to check their own current charge lists, presumably by scanning charge-card bar codes or typing in passwords, *the bar code or password should be cleared* as soon as the information is given. Most users won't explicitly end a session when they're done; don't give the next user access to the personal information.

The first issue—privacy of the online-catalog user—is more complicated. For example, is it reasonable to log complete search sessions? It can be valuable as a way of examining why searches fail and planning help screens, training materials, or improvements to the user interface. For a catalog with hard-wired terminals and anonymous dial-in, it should not be a privacy matter.

But what if your catalog offers services beyond searching, services that may require self-identification? Is it really acceptable to say "Well, if they want to use those services, they should recognize that that information may be logged"? A better solution might be to establish a logging system that immediately detaches search strategies from time, date, and terminal, thus preventing any link between the searches and the self-identified user.

The library's concern for privacy should also influence its attitudes toward possible access improvements. One PACS-L participant suggested that libraries could save client profiles—records of successful searches, with the user's telephone number. When another user does somewhat similar searches, the catalog software could spot the similarities and provide the telephone number of the first user to the second user. Now, think about that idea: should a library (particularly a public or academic library) even contemplate such a service? Would it be acceptable if such profiles are saved only after the express consent of users? Would such consent be required for every search session, or could it be given once and assumed thereafter?

I regard the concept as so fundamentally invasive that libraries should steer clear of it. There are enough agencies involved in diluting the privacy of our purchasing patterns, income, magazine subscriptions, and the like. Should libraries encourage people to give up the privacy of their own thoughts and research interests? It's not acceptable to say, "Well, it's voluntary; if people don't want their interests known, they can say no." Perhaps a library could maintain an "interests database" as an auxiliary service—but such a database would contain only those interests that users had explicitly added. Records of searches can be used in many ways. If such a service is added to a system, the "second user" will sometimes be a recruiter for some cause, a law-enforcement agent, a "lonely heart," or someone skilled at using search patterns to reveal supposed personality characteristics or traits. Libraries ought not reveal who has charged out certain items; they surely should not reveal who has considered certain topics!

Conclusion

Think in terms of functional integration: make your online catalog the user's window to the whole range of library activities. Functional integration can be based on a single hardware and software system, but that isn't necessary, and it's frequently not ideal for a given library. Integration means that catalog users can see whether an item has been checked out (and when it's due and how many holds it has); that article searchers can find out whether your library has the journal issue they need (and, if not, how they can acquire it); and that people interested in a new item can find out whether you've ordered it or whether it's sitting waiting to be processed.

Integrated systems, whether single or linked, involve more security and privacy issues than standalone online catalogs, but every catalog requires some attention to security and privacy. Shared computers raise more difficult issues and may be increasingly unattractive for libraries as time goes on.

Privacy and security need attention not only when implementing a system but when thinking about ways to improve it. You need to know how your system is used in order to make it more valuable—but you do not need to tie specific usage to specific users, and in general should avoid such links. Libraries exist to promote access to cultural memory and information; they should not be in the business of making public the interests of specific users.

5

Design Principles for Online Catalogs

Today's and tomorrow's online catalogs should offer interesting new designs, but those designs should be based on established design principles. This chapter and those that follow deal with a variety of design issues that can or should affect every library considering an online catalog and every vendor upgrading a system design.

System Ergonomics

Your catalog should be pleasant to use, not only for the bulk of users who spend less than three minutes at the catalog but also for serious searchers who may spend an hour or more using the system. While some ergonomic factors may seem irrelevant for your library, you'll find more people using the system for longer periods as you add features and information to the catalog.

Display Characteristics

Displays must be legible to be useful. Catalog users should not have to squint to read a display or guess at the characters on the display. Good display legibility involves at least five factors, the last two of which may be software or hardware issues:

- The display must be large enough so that characters can be read easily by library users with a relatively wide range of visual acuity but not so large (or badly designed) that characters turn into patterns of separate dots.

- The display must be visible—that is, free from glare and reflections and situated so that it is not in direct sunlight.

- The display should be kept reasonably clean; cathode-ray tubes (the display of choice in most situations) do attract dust and need regular cleaning for maximum legibility.

- Text must stand out clearly on the screen—that is, it must not fade into the background for any typical user. That requires judgment in using highlighting, color, and other special effects.

- Characters must be distinct and clear. Users should be able to distinguish characters without thinking. A microcomputer-based graphics display may require care in selecting a character set. For example, some character sets make no visible distinction between a lowercase *ell* (l) and an uppercase *i* (I); others don't adequately differentiate between the lower-case *ell* (l) and the *one* (1). Very poor displays may not even be clear enough to differentiate between the *zero* (0) and capital *oh* (O), lowercase *bee* (b) and *six* (6), or *zero* (0) and *eight* (8).

Legible displays need not be expensive: for example, $80 amber monochrome displays for MS-DOS computers will work quite well. (For Macintosh-based front ends or systems, the display itself is quite good, but some Macintosh screen fonts are poor choices for online catalogs, lacking the necessary distinctions between characters.) When a library goes beyond simple text to display in-place diacritics (particularly Vietnamese tone marks appearing together with diacritics) and non-Roman character sets, high-resolution displays (preferably with larger screens) will be required, at a considerably higher price.

During the mid-1980s, we were told that amber-on-black text was much more ergonomically sound than other color combinations for monochrome displays. That particular piece of accepted wisdom seems to have faded away, although it continues to be true that amber-on-black text can achieve high contrast and legibility without extreme brightness because the human eye is unusually sensitive to amber. It was always the case that some green displays were better than some amber displays, and while some users prefer amber, others find the displays painful to the eyes.[1]

These days, paper-white (black text on off-white background) displays seem to be the rage. They can be very effective but must be tested under actual library lighting. Some paper-white displays flicker noticeably under the fluorescent lighting used in many libraries; some will flicker regardless of the lighting conditions. When the background is mostly bright, any flicker is much more noticeable than when it is mostly dark. Flickering displays will distract all users and give headaches to users who spend much time at the catalogs.

Questions about the healthfulness and safety of video displays have been raised for years and seem no closer to resolution now than in the past. A skeptic would note that the kind of health and safety challenge changes every few years, as previous challenges are shown to be unfounded—e.g., now that we know there's no ionizing radiation from a properly made display, maybe the 60Hz electric current is a problem. Note that most shielding devices are expensive and of unproven worth—and are really intended for cases where you're sitting at a display most of the day.

If you want to be cautious about display safety, you can start by using monochrome displays (which have far lower emissions of all types than color displays), which will save money in any case. Beyond that, your terminal clusters should be designed so that no user's face is within three feet of the *back* of another display (or, ideally, the side). If your workstations leave enough room for books and notepads used by both right-handed and left-handed users, you should achieve this spacing in any case. In other words, user-friendly workstation design will take care of most terminal safety issues.

Keyboards and Other Devices

Every user interface requires a display-equivalent to provide results to the user and a keyboard-equivalent to provide requests to the system. Almost always, the keyboard-equivalent will actually be a keyboard, possibly supplemented by a touch screen or mouse.

The characteristics of a good input device are the same now as they were in 1987:

- **"Familiarity.** The best device is one that most users have used in other settings. If it

---

1 Since this is largely a matter of personal preference, I'll admit to favoring amber—and cheerfully move on from amber to color. On a color monitor, I typically use bright-white text on a medium-blue or deep-blue background.

is not familiar, a device must have such an obvious design and use that a user can learn to use it within seconds.

- **"Ease of use.** The device should make it equally simple to enter menu choices and complex commands.
- **"Sturdiness.** The device should be difficult to break and impossible to misuse in a way that makes the system fail.
- **"Speed.** The device should not slow the user down.
- **"Clarity.** Input should not be ambiguous."[2]

Those characteristics add up to a standard QWERTY keyboard for most libraries, with standard keyboard separation, thickness, key design and travel, and so on. (See *Patron Access* for more discussion.) Specially labeled keys offer some advantages, but pose problems for remote users. (Chapter 8 notes evolving standard function-key definitions.) For an academic library on an all-Macintosh campus, a mouse is a natural addition—and for most institutions with high computer usage, a mouse may be a natural addition in the near future.

A pointing device, mouse or otherwise, can make a user interface faster for some purposes, although it can't replace a keyboard entirely. Unfortunately, the mouse itself is *not* an immediately obvious device if a user has no experience with it, as various salespeople and trainers can attest. The scene in *Star Trek IV* where Scotty tries to use the mouse as a voice-command device or microphone illustrates one kind of misunderstanding; the apparently true story of a person waving the mouse in the air and wondering why nothing happens illustrates a more common problem.

What about touch screens? Early library experience with touch-screen online catalogs

was sufficiently problematic that they are in bad repute. Touch screens gather dirt and grime much faster than other displays, making them harder to read. The limited recognition accuracy of a touch screen usually requires widely-spaced choices. Touch screens typically require more steps for a specific result than do keyboard systems.

All that may still be true, but it's also true that at least one fairly dazzling touch-screen-*and*-keyboard user interface has been introduced in the Library of Congress reading rooms. The interface doesn't offer as much power as their keyboard-based command-driven systems, but it is easy to approach and quite delightful, at least at first glance. Only experience will show whether it can change the dismal reputation of touch screens.

Speed and Responsiveness

One signature line in an electronic message about online catalogs included the following summation: "Three things are important in an online catalog: speed, speed and speed." In connection with a discussion of imaging systems, Steve Cisler noted that "a casual user of an interactive information system such as a videotex terminal, videodisc station or even an OPAC will begin to get impatient after 7 seconds; a devoted scholar who can get the information in no other way may be more patient."[3] Or, as I said at the LITA Screen Design preconference in June 1991, speaking of the increasingly computer-comfortable population: "Every user who's comfortable with a PC is also comfortable with a keyboard. . . . That comfort and knowledge gives you more flexibility in designing a user interface. But users who are comfortable with PCs also expect

---

2 Walt Crawford. *Patron Access: Issues for Online Catalogs.* (Boston: G. K. Hall, 1987), 77-78.

3 Steve Cisler. "Re: Document Imaging Systems." PACS-L message, July 19, 1990.

performance from their systems. When you do something at the keyboard, you expect something on the display *right now!*"

Absolute speed matters a great deal, and it's not always easy to achieve in a catalog, particularly as the size and uses of the catalog grow. That's always been true; it's probably also true that today's users are considerably less patient than those of years past. Once you start to use a personal computer, it's not acceptable to say, "Well, computers just don't work quickly." Users know better than that.

Perhaps as important as sheer speed is *where* slowdowns occur and the overall responsiveness of the system. A user will probably accept a brief delay for a search, particularly if the system provides feedback to indicate why it's taking a while. But the user won't be so forgiving if it takes five seconds or more to display the next record in a list, the next screen in a browse or, particularly, the next screen for a long record. The user will also become impatient very rapidly if the system doesn't respond to commands. It's one thing to say "Please wait: now searching," but it's quite another for the screen to sit unchanged for thirty seconds. At that point, the user may be inclined to think the command was not accepted, which can lead to other unexpected consequences as the user strikes Enter repeatedly.

The worst thing about response time is that it does not degrade smoothly. Every multiuser system has a "knee," a point at which gradually worsening response suddenly gets much worse very rapidly. That's not unique to library catalogs or computer systems; it's an inherent part of queuing theory, and can happen in other situations.

Queuing theory can help predict the point at which a response knee will occur, but only if you know all characteristics of the computer and the software thoroughly, including the mix of searches to be done. You find the knee by hitting it: when your system suddenly slows to a crawl, you've found the knee.

Need it be said that an online catalog that requires two minutes to process a simple title search is unacceptable? A library with nothing but in-house terminals can prevent computer slowdowns, of course, by limiting the number of terminals—but if the catalog is in demand that simply substitutes human queuing for computer queuing. Once you have human queuing, the system ergonomics are shot: how can a thoughtful subject searcher track down a topic when other users are breathing down her neck?

Sound and Other Feedback

One fundamental aspect of good user-interface design for online catalogs is that "the user can't make a mistake." That is, while the system can counsel the user on more effective ways to do something, even suggesting that the user check spelling, it should never use the dreaded word "Error."

That may be all that needs to be said about the use of a beep or other sound as user feedback. For a public terminal, sound feedback represents bad ergonomics in two respects. First, it draws attention to the user, who appears to have done something wrong; it could discourage further exploration. Second, it adds an inappropriate noise to the library, one that can be confused with other electronic noises (such as those used in a circulation system).

User feedback should be private (it should not draw the attention of other users); it should be constructive (not pointing out errors but showing possible improvements); it should be neutral (not witty or anthropomorphic, and certainly not condemning); and most of all it should be appropriate. Beeps are inappropriate in a library catalog. Messages of encouragement (e.g., "You're doing great!") may be helpful in special training environments but have no place in a library. Color used as feedback must be used cautiously and sparingly.

Workstation Issues

The public-terminal workstations[4] in a library should accommodate users comfortably and provide space for possessions and notebooks. Workstations should be designed so that both left-handed and right-handed users can take notes while using the catalog. Some workstations should be wheelchair accessible and comfortable not only for wheelchairbound users but for older and less mobile users as well. Workstations should be designed so that users have some degree of privacy, but also so that librarians can help users at the terminals if needed.

A library should have enough workstations at appropriate locations—but how many are enough and what constitutes appropriate depend on the library. Most libraries will strive to avoid lines of users waiting for terminals—at worst, people shouldn't have to wait for a terminal more often than they had to wait to get to the section of a card catalog they wanted. The online catalog is better than the card catalog in this respect: ten people can be searching simultaneously for works by Thomas Pynchon, which isn't possible at the card catalog.

Some libraries provide terminals at standing-height stations, presumably to encourage quick searching. Ideally, some workstations will be standing-height and some will be equipped with chairs for extended use.

Some libraries with standing-height terminals have found that users bring over stools so they can be more comfortable.

One school of thought says that terminals should be scattered throughout the stacks and in all areas of a library so that users can find them whenever they might want them. There's a lot to be said for that approach—but there's also much to be said for having most terminals within eyesight of librarians so they can spot users who appear to need help. Remember that a mediocre catalog coupled with concerned, alert, user-oriented public-service librarians will probably perform better than a superbly designed catalog when no librarians are available. Good librarians provide the finishing touch for any good catalog.

Printers

Should the library provide printers at every workstation, at some workstations, or not at all? As usual, there's no easy answer and no single answer is right for all libraries.

The advantages of printers are quite clear. With good user-interface design, a user can gather a list of desired items and print out a quick finding list, including accurate call numbers. As catalogs are enhanced and expanded, there will be more reasons to need printed output. Users will benefit from being able to print out finding lists, particularly since copying down call numbers isn't trivial, especially in very large libraries. When we studied every transaction in the University of California, Berkeley main stacks for an academic quarter,[5] we found that mistranscribed call numbers accounted for more service failures than did the combination of misshelved books, lost books, and books not yet returned

---

4 Places where people work at terminals, as opposed to very powerful personal computers.

5 In the early 1970s, in an unpublished study.

to the shelves. Transcription errors happen in every library.

The disadvantages of printers are also clear. Some of them are noisy and produce poor-quality listings, although the ink-jet printers used these days are very nearly silent and produce acceptable quality. But ink-jet printers are expensive to run, with supply costs averaging five cents or more per page. Continuous-form ink-jet printers tend to jam, particularly as users tear off partial sheets; sheet-fed printers waste paper and need to be resupplied frequently. Although they also waste paper to some extent, laser printers may provide the best combination of low noise, moderate per-page costs, and relatively infrequent need to replace paper and printing mechanisms—but laser printers are expensive and bulky and can emit enough ozone to be mildly irritating in poorly ventilated areas.

Screen Density and Sparseness

The rest of the design principles in this chapter relate to what appears on the screen rather than to the screen itself or the other physical attributes of the catalog.

First, screens should not be crowded: the online catalog should not take up every available spot on the screen. Crowded screens, like crowded print pages, are harder to read and understand than sparsely filled screens.

Well-designed print pages usually devote 45 to 60 percent of the page to white space; a page with text covering more than 60 percent of the surface will be difficult to read. Screens are inherently more difficult to read than printed pages, and the guidelines for density are correspondingly lower. Some have suggested that 15 percent is the ideal density for a screen: roughly 300 characters on a standard 25-line by 80-character screen. That

may be an appropriate density for menus, opening screens and fill-in-the-blank search prompt screens, but it is too low for effective use in most areas of an online catalog.

A more realistic figure is 30 percent— that is, 600 characters or about 100 words. That's a good target for a single-screen help message: 100 words is a good-size paragraph and probably about the right amount of information for quick help. It turns out to be a realistic figure for most single-record displays as well, if other readability guidelines are followed. If you do some counting in the examples in Part II, you'll find that very few single-record displays exceed 30 percent density by very much.

The Case for High Density

Cardlike displays with wide text lines can exceed 30 percent density on long records; browse screens that take up all available lines with one-line records can also exceed 30 percent, sometimes by quite a bit. Those are two cases in which high density may be reasonable in some catalogs.

The two best cases for high density are when it permits all needed information to be displayed on a single screen, and when it provides for faster and more effective remote use of a catalog. The first case is difficult: is it better to make a single-record display open, easy to follow, and easy to read, or is it better to design the display so that 90 percent of records will fit on a single screen? The advantages of openness are clear, but so are the advantages of taking in all the information about a record at once. At least one library explicitly decided to use a wide cardlike display rather than a well-spaced labeled display for precisely that reason: they concluded that their users would benefit more from seeing all the information at once than from seeing labels and good spacing. They have an excellent point.

As long as catalogs are used locally and on displays, white space is essentially free: transmitting new screens should take almost no time, and the number of characters will be the primary factor in transmission time. That's also true for dial-up and network users, as long as terminal emulation protocols are used and display overhead isn't too high. But that raises other issues—for example, good display signposts (discussed below) may require two or three lines of text, and prompting may take another two or three lines. If those lines are repeated on every display, sparse displays may require significantly more transmission time than crowded displays.

In practice, most crowded displays are also scrolling designs, catalogs that do not assume screen clearing and cursor placement as part of terminal functionality. In such cases, the urge to use every line effectively is much stronger; fortunately, such limited terminal functionality is disappearing. Even VT100 emulation—one of the most prevalent and least powerful forms of terminal emulation, present in almost every telecommunications package—provides for screen clearing, top-to-cursor clearing, cursor-to-bottom clearing, line clearing and direct cursor addressing; that's enough to eliminate most transmission overhead and encourage more open displays.

Readability

The text should be as readable on the screen as it is in a book—but reading a screen is not the same as reading a book. Still, some of the same principles apply, *specifically* to online tutorials and help messages, where the user is reading a screen from top to bottom. With browsing and single-record displays, more trade-offs come into play: typically, the user is scanning for information, not reading as one would read prose.

Line Length

Readability studies consistently show that text should contain no more than 60 to 65 characters per line. That's true of print, and it's equally true on the screen. It's an excellent guideline for all extended text and works well for labeled displays as well. If record text will occupy no more than 60 to 65 characters, 14 to 19 characters (on a standard screen) are available for labels. That avoids most of the messy abbreviations sometimes used for short labels. If ADDITIONAL AUTHORS: is the right label to use, devote columns 1 to 20 to labels: the label will just fit.

Even with cardlike displays, a 65-character line seems to be quite enough. Using some white space on both sides of the text makes the display clearer and more readable.

The exceptions are single-line summary displays and columnar location, call number and status displays. Columnar information, if well organized and labeled, can use the full width of the screen to good effect; single-line summary displays typically require the full line in order to be useful.

White Space

White space can serve to organize elements of a display and ease the user's task of recognizing elements—but only when it's used intelligently. Intelligent use includes spaces or dashed lines between signposts and bibliographic displays and between bibliographic displays and prompts or function-key labels. Intelligent use can include blank lines between separate parts of a single-record display or between multiple records when each record occupies more than one line. Intelligent use of white space can make a help screen more useful.

Part II includes many examples of effective white space, and a few where additional white space would clarify information and make it easier to use. You can judge where white space would enhance a display. In your own catalog, a little experimentation will usually show where white space is most effective.

Naturally, white space in search results increases the space requirements for the results. Just as a library may elect to stay with a card format to conserve space, so a library may elect not to add space between elements of a labeled display in order to conserve space.

One fairly straightforward guideline about white space: double-spaced text is typically *not* an effective use of white space, particularly when text is meant to be read. Double-spacing reduces the coherence of a paragraph, turning it into a series of separate lines (which is one reason typesetters and proofreaders prefer double-spaced text); it also takes up white space that could be used to better effect around the margins and between paragraphs and logical groups of text.

Capitalization

While capitalized text can be used effectively as a highlighting technique, it is well established that capitalized text is substantially more difficult to read than mixed-case text. CAPITALIZED TEXT LACKS ASCENDERS AND DESCENDERS; ALL THE LETTERS ARE THE SAME HEIGHT AND HAVE LESS INDIVIDUAL CHARACTER.

Thus, while capitalized labels work very well (particularly when that is the only form of highlighting), capitalized index entries in browse screens become difficult to scan: the user must slow down to make sense of the words. If a system is unable to display headings in the original mixed case, it might even

be preferable to display them in all lower case (except for an initial capital letter). Thus, while

`King, martin luther, jr., 1929-1968 — religion`

does look a bit strange, it's much easier to scan than

`KING, MARTIN LUTHER, JR., 1929-1968 — RELIGION`

Some of the examples in Part II make this clear: when you put several lines of capitalized text together, readability suffers.

Highlighting Techniques

Modern catalogs, particularly CD-ROM catalogs and others with PCs as terminals, can use many different kinds of highlighting. You can have bright and dim text—or, on some screens, 32 shades of gray or 256 different colors. You can have reverse-video text or blinking text. You can have capitalized text. Some modern systems can use italic text, boldface text, or text in entirely different typefaces. Text can be underlined or boxed; you can use special characters to set text apart. You can use windows with background shading, icons, three-dimensional buttons, and other devices to make elements of the screen stand out.

If you do all of the above in a single display, you may attract the Nintendo set but you won't have an effective, intelligible display. I call it the arcade-game syndrome—and it's surprisingly easy to turn a coherent display into an arcade game. (Just one chunk of blinking text will probably do it, quite apart from antagonizing your users.) At the other extreme, it's possible to have an effective, coherent, well-liked user interface that has no highlighting whatsoever—no boldface, no reverse video, no capitalized text.

Several of the catalogs in Part II use no highlighting. Several use some advanced techniques, not always visible on the printed page. One or two of the catalogs use a range of colors to help organize information; we were unable to print an equivalent range of grays.

What's best? In general, any highlighting technique except blinking text will work well if used sparingly—and every highlighting technique will suffer when more than two or three are used in the same display. If you plan to use reverse-video to highlight menu choices and other cursor-controllable options (e.g., selecting a field for related-record searching), you should not use a similar highlighting technique for other purposes. If you're using capitalized labels in a display, think twice about making the labels reverse video or boldface: do you really need double emphasis?

I'm writing this while looking at a screen with six different color schemes on it—two colors in each of five informational and control areas, and two or more (up to sixteen) in the editing screen. On the other hand, the program doesn't use capitalization, blinking, or boldface, and it uses reverse video only in very specific cases. Is this too much highlighting? For a program I use every day, probably not. For an online catalog, probably so.

When it comes to highlighting, less is more—and, sometimes, the optimum number of highlights may be zero.

Limiting the Choices

Most people can deal with seven choices in short-term memory, give or take two. That's well established, and it suggests that online catalogs should, in general, offer no more than nine options at any one time. If you're at all typical, you can "grok" a set of seven to nine index names, headings, command choices, or whatever, taking them in almost instantly—

whereas you have to pause over a longer set, reading through it to see what you need.Choices, limiting

One of the reasons Disneyland works as well as it does, at least in the original design, is that you never have more than three choices at any one time. When you make one of those three, there may be three more—but you're never confronted with dozens of options at once.

That's a little too simple for an online catalog, to be sure; seven to nine, however, is usually workable. The ninth choice may be "Other," or subchoices may be layered below several of the choices, but most people will be able to handle such a scheme more readily than one that shows too many choices at once. A pull-down menu may have more than nine options, but the best ones will group those into groups of nine or less. There may be more than nine things going on in a screen at once, but they should be grouped so that the user never has to focus on more than nine at a time.

When More Is Better

The exception, for many systems, is heading and other multiple-item browse screens. As Part II shows, quite a few systems display as many headings as will fit within the screen, sometimes up to 16 at once. The advantage is that users can see more options at a time and have fewer keystrokes to deal with the list. The disadvantage is that each screen is somewhat more difficult to comprehend.

Some systems deliberately limit multiple-result screens to nine per screen, even when that leaves several blank lines on the screen. To my eye, the results support the "seven plus or minus two" principle: I find such displays easier to read. You may not, and your users may not care; in any case, browsing isn't really reading.

Control Options

How should users be able to control the catalog—and should there be more than one option? Increasingly, the answer to the second question will be yes for a great many libraries. Users will be able to key pure commands if they know the (common) syntax; users will be able to use pull-down menus or follow prompted sequences; users will be able to use movable highlight bars to select items; function keys will carry out a number of common actions; and users may be able to select items with pointing devices.

The basic principle here is that if multiple options are available, they should be used intelligently and "openly." If you can use a pointer to select an index, you should be able to use the pointer to select a field for related-record searching or a heading from a browse list. If you can use pull-down menus for some things, you should be able to use them for almost everything. And if you accept a command language at all, it should be able to accomplish everything that the other options can accomplish. Don't make the experienced typist go looking for the mouse or function keys—and if you use both a mouse and function keys, the user should certainly be able to click on the function-key labels as an alternative to pressing the keys.

The Three-Minute Guideline

At least one control methodology should be simple and apparent enough that a typical user can sit down and achieve results within 3 minutes. That's probably about as much time as a user is prepared to devote to learning a catalog, at least in a public library. Academic users may devote a little more time and are more likely to accept training—after all, it's the only game in town. Still, if a user can

perform a simple search in 3 minutes, the system probably has clear control options.

Obviousness

A good online catalog is obvious: you can see how it works almost immediately; it tells you where you are and how you got there; and, in most cases, it gives you easy ways to find out where you can go from here.

Chapter 6 discusses how it works in some detail. For now, a few words on telling users where they are and where they can go may be useful. It's important to note that these guidelines are more controversial than most others. Signposts (how you got here) and prompts or options (where you can go) take up space, possibly lots of space. Some designers will argue, with support from users, that the space isn't justified.

Look through the examples in Part II. Some have no signposts; others have few (if any) prompts; some have neither. More systems seem to lack good signposts than to work without prompts; it's not clear whether that's the right balance.

Signposts

Signposts tell you where you are and how you got here. "How you got here" typically has two elements: your most recent search (if you've done a search) and your most recent action (if something other than a search). Many online catalogs provide the first signpost, which should include the index (if any) and the search term—but several, while providing that signpost on multiple-result displays, drop it on single-record displays.

Relatively few online catalogs echo the most recent action: how did you get to this particular place? Perhaps that's sensible; after all, you should know what you just did. It also eliminates certain problems in systems that don't do everything by command, since menu choices, function keys, and pointers can be difficult to echo as signposts.

The virtue of a latest-action signpost is that it reassures the user that the online catalog has acted on a command. That virtue may not be sufficient to justify another line of the screen. On the other hand, positional signposting (described below) can be on the same line as latest-action signposting.

The other aspect of a signpost, where you are, or positional signposting, can include the total size of the current result set, the set number (if there is one), which record or records are being displayed, and possibly other information. It's always useful to provide the size of the current result set, even on single-record displays; that's something users tend to forget rapidly.

The other key use for signposting occurs when a supportive catalog takes action on the user's behalf or suggests such an action. If the user's subject search has been turned into a title word search, a signpost should make that clear. If the user's search for Samuel Clemens has been redirected to Mark Twain—without noting this change and asking for confirmation—it is critical that a signpost say what's been done. Here, there seems to be little disagreement: every catalog I've seen that does such redirection also announces that it has occurred.

One of the most troublesome signposting issues occurs when items are retrieved based on elements that do not display as part of the default single-record or multiple-record display. A user may wonder why the records are there. Should the catalog redefine the multiple-record display to include the retrieving element (as sometimes happens) or should catalog designers assume that troubled users

will take the time to look at a full-record display?

Options and Prompts

How much should the catalog say about what you can do next? Part II shows a wide range of possibilities, from systems that say nothing at all to systems that carry a full menu on the screen at all times.

It's easy (although possibly incorrect) to say that a system with no prompting at all is user hostile, leaving the poor searcher in the lurch. This tends to happen after a result has been displayed. On the other hand, such systems tend to be open command-driven systems in which you can take any action at any time. That gives the users much more power, but means that any set of prompts will either be incomplete or will take up too much of the screen.

Indeed, some heavily prompted systems do appear to lose much of the screen to menus or function-key matrices. These systems are more crowded while providing less information. While perhaps friendlier for the total novice, they may be slower and clumsier for all other users.

Pull-down menus and function keys can substitute for prompts. For many catalogs over the next few years, these methods will provide a straightforward solution to a complex problem. On the other hand (in online catalog design, there's *always* another hand), pull-down menus fail the obviousness test: like pointing devices, their functionality is obvious only after you've been introduced to them.

Models and Metaphors

Users form their own mental models of how a catalog works. If those models match reality, the users will be effective catalog users. If the models are incorrect, users will be frustrated. Model building is an inherent part of learning to use any new system. First, you try to relate the new situation to an old one, creating a metaphor. Then, you try to establish a consistent schema, creating a model. Neither practice is necessarily conscious.

Coherence, the theme of chapter 6, is crucial to the model-building process. If a system design is incoherent and muddled, the user's model will inevitably be incorrect: what the user learns from one search process will be useless in another aspect of catalog use.

Metaphors can substantially ease learning, but an inappropriate metaphor may cut short the user's ability to make the most of a new system. That said, we must consider the only really obvious metaphor for an online catalog: the card catalog.

The Danger of the Card Metaphor

As a general guideline, online catalogs should not suggest catalog cards or card catalogs as metaphors. There are at least two good reasons for this:

- The card-catalog metaphor is extremely limiting, because a good online catalog offers a wealth of searching and display possibilities far beyond those of a card catalog, particularly as the online catalog is expanded and enhanced.

- Online catalogs make lousy card catalogs. There are a few things that you can do faster and more easily in card catalogs than in online catalogs; when faced with the card-catalog metaphor, users will remember the superior aspects of the card catalog more than its drawbacks.

The question of what card catalogs do better than online catalogs formed the basis for a long and sometimes rather silly many-sided debate on PACS-L in mid-1991. Part of the problem with the debate is that a few people on the "online side" chose to characterize the "card side" (the assertion that card catalogs do *some* things better than online catalogs) as a "preference for card catalogs." It was nothing of the sort, of course. Others on both sides made universal assertions based on their own preferences or, worse, on their own experiences.

What it boiled down to, for most of those on the card side, is that you can thumb through a tray of catalog cards (800 to 1000 cards) quite rapidly, glancing at levels of information as you need them. Online catalogs don't, and probably can't, support such rapid scanning with immediate full-record access as needed. It's a special case, to be sure: you must first succeed with the card catalog's fairly restrictive retrieval schemes, and there must be enough relevant cards to make such browsing worthwhile—and you must understand what's on the cards. Still, that's something that online catalogs don't do as well.

The answer is to avoid the card metaphor. I shudder whenever someone uses the phrase "online card catalog," but that phrase still pops up.

The Case for Familiarity

It's hard to ignore the benefits of familiarity. Even though research suggests that most users really don't understand most of the information on a catalog card, they've still had experience with it. That may not be true much longer; within a decade or two, we'll have millions of users who have *never* used a card catalog. Then, of course, the faulty metaphor won't matter.

In the meantime, the balance is difficult. Is it better to maintain a link with the familiar catalog-card image (a very space-efficient display, if not a particularly self-evident one), even though it may limit users' perspectives on what the catalog can do—or should online catalogs steer clear of any link to the card catalog? Fortunately, this may be a transitional problem. Unfortunately, it's another problem with no ready solution.

Conclusion

Even within the basics, there are few easy answers. Should you use labels, right-justified with left-justified text, one field to a line? Absolutely—unless it makes more sense for you to display records in a different manner. Should you avoid putting more than 600 characters on a screen? Absolutely—most of the time. Should you avoid using half a dozen different devices to highlight and organize? Generally, yes—but with contemporary window-oriented color interfaces, it's a rough question to answer. Knowing the general principles will help you to decide when it makes sense to ignore them.

6

Coherent Interface Design

Coherent design always strengthens a catalog. Good online catalogs make sense to new users and continue to make sense as users become more experienced. Coherent catalogs make learning and exploration easy because users can apply what they've learned in one area to work in another area. A coherent system isn't just the result of putting all the pieces together—it is the result of forethought, planning and an overall vision.

Coherence requires several things, one of which is that the user interface be consistent with the underlying hardware and software engine. It's tempting to try to improve a user interface by putting a pretty face over existing software—but if the existing software won't actually support the model that the user interface presents, the system won't perform consistently and will disappoint users.

The relatively sparse sets of screens and commentaries in Part II won't always tell you whether a design is truly coherent; using one of the systems for an hour or two probably will. Some of the commentaries do tell something of the bases for system designs. One in particular deserves your reading in conjunction with this chapter: John Kupersmith's commentary on UTCAT, the catalog of the University of Texas at Austin, in chapter 43. Each of the commentaries contributes to the wider understanding of online catalogs, to be sure, and you should definitely read all of them—even if the chapter title tells you all you want to know about the catalog itself. In the case of UTCAT, however, Kupersmith provides an unusually valuable and well-written perspective.

The Mutter Test

On the few occasions that I've done hands-on evaluation of an online catalog, I've found one test to be a good indicator of overall system coherence: the mutter test. A catalog passes the mutter test if I, as a first-time user, am able to start using the system, carry out some basic searches, look through some records and maybe advance to more complex searching without starting to mutter to myself. If I can get all the way through a half-hour searching session without muttering, the system passes—and it's almost certainly a coherent system.

Essentially, there's only one passing grade for the mutter test: I don't start to mutter. For a typical catalog user, that may be satisfactory: the catalog functions well enough to stay out of the way. If I'm specifically approaching the catalog as an object of study, I'll try to determine what I like about the catalog—but it's passed the most important test.

If there's only one passing grade, there are several gradations of failure, particularly for a normal catalog user. How long does it take before I start muttering? Does muttering proceed to swearing under my breath—or, as in at least one real case, to the point where I'm tempted to put my fist through the terminal? That's serious failure. For a typical user, the effective response will be to ignore the catalog altogether unless there's no alternative.

One of the most insidious failures of the mutter test, and a sure sign of incoherent design, is when I'm doing fine for a few minutes and suddenly mutter "What the hell?" What's happened is that the model of system behavior I've established up to this point suddenly doesn't work.

I should add that an actual user may start to mutter for different reasons, ones that have nothing to do with coherence. If the catalog offers dismal response time, a user will be unhappy. While coherence is critical, it doesn't make up for inadequate computer power.

An Overall Vision

The basis for coherent design is design itself. That may seem fatuous, but it's an important principle: there's a difference between designing a system and assembling a system. Every coherent online catalog must begin with an overall vision, a grand design, a sense of what the catalog should be and how it should function. That overall vision may be a set of principles for the catalog, an overall sketch, a software sketch of how the system will look, or possibly just a paragraph or two describing the catalog as a whole. The key, in every case, is that there is a single unifying vision, an overall design, and that the catalog carries out that design.

How does that overall vision arise? That depends on the particular situation:

- **Point of entry:** The vision may be a fresh start for a new commercial vendor, a library building its own system, or an organization completely replacing an existing design. Alternatively, it may be a vendor's basis for a substantive revision or a library's preparation for implementing a selected commercial system.

- **Working styles:** An overall vision may begin as one designer's broad view, fleshed out through discussions with the rest of those involved in the design process; it may be hammered out in committee meetings, then cast into an overall view; or it may be synthesized by one person or a group of people after detailed analysis of all the factors needed for a successful catalog. I believe that the best overall visions read as though written by one person; that doesn't mean they come from one person. It is, however, generally true that it's more difficult for a committee to arrive at a single coherent vision, because there's a tendency to get bogged down on details—and that "committee designs" can lack overall coherence.

- **Developmental and political styles:** Although it would always seem preferable to work down from an established overall vision, that isn't always possible. Sometimes, it's necessary to develop an overall vision after some of the pieces are already in place. Unless there's sufficient flexibility to change some of the pieces based on the overall vision, however, those pieces will force the overall design—and may make a coherent vision impossible.

This may all sound vague; that's because it is. I can't give you a set of guidelines for developing an overall vision. I can say that coherent design is just as important when your library is determining how it will implement a selected commercial system as it is when you're developing a new system. When you're implementing a commercial system, you must coordinate two visions. First you must thoroughly understand the grand design that underlies the commercial system (assuming that there is one). Then you must build your own library-specific design that incorporates and reflects that design. Failure to reflect the underlying design will lead to an incoherent implementation; failure to establish a library-specific vision will make coherent implementation difficult.

Bringing It All Back Home

After the visionary leader or committee produces the overall vision and promulgates it with suitable fanfare, the implementers take over, turning it into reality. But it isn't always quite that simple. You can anticipate that problems will arise along the way, either because the overall vision was too broad or because some elements turn out to be impractical.

At that point, it's important to return to the overall vision and attempt to refine it—not to set it aside with a "yes, but." If the vision is embodied in a set of principles, it should be possible to overcome the impracticalities with minor changes in those principles. That may require testing the new principles against other parts of the implementation; that's better than creating exceptions to the principles. An exception to a well-established set of principles will stand out from the rest of the catalog; it will draw attention to itself as an inconsistency.

Sometimes, an overall vision can be turned into a system with little or no alteration; that's the best outcome. Naturally, it's best to develop an overall vision in a manner that provides for some flexibility during implementation. An overall vision should be just

that: a grand design, a set of principles, or both.

Functional Consistency

Good user interfaces are internally consistent. They don't fight with the user, and they don't behave one way in one area and a different way in a seemingly comparable area. The key phrase here is *seemingly comparable*: the system should be consistent *from the user's perspective.*

If a system requires that you press Enter after keying a single-letter command at one point but acts immediately on a direct keystroke in a seemingly similar situation, it's inconsistent. If a system accepts function keys for certain commands at some points but won't accept the function keys *for the same commands* at other points, it's inconsistent. In both cases, the user's increasing comfort with the catalog will be shattered: they won't understand what's going on.

Consistent functionality and consistent control options for the user seem fundamental to good user-interface design. If your system supports a pointer, it should *always* support a pointer for apparently equivalent purposes. If your system accepts commands, it should *always* accept commands—and it should accept and act on any command that makes sense from a user's perspective within the current situation.

Displays should also behave in a consistent manner—but here the situation gets complicated. Consistency is important, but so is user efficiency; there are cases in which consistency may be inconsiderate.

The Case for Inconsistency

Your online catalog provides a browsable name authority display as the result of any name search. A single keystroke moves from a highlighted line to a brief display of the result set—and another keystroke or command moves from there to individual record displays.

But what if a selected name only represents a single item? Should the system still display a brief result set consisting of a single entry? That's consistent, but inconsiderate (unless, of course, your catalog's brief result is designed to be a sufficient end result for most searchers).

What about multi-index or Boolean searches? Should they still yield something like an authority display? Probably not; such a display doesn't have any bearing on the result. The ideal result is direct display of a single record.

Consistency should always work on the user's behalf. That doesn't mean blindly doing the same thing every time, regardless of whether it makes sense. It does mean always behaving the same way within a given context. If the context is clearly different, the behavior can be different—and a user can certainly understand why a single-record result might skip some intervening display steps. This assumes that your single-record display includes enough signposts so that the user will understand what has happened; if not, the results will be apparently inconsistent.

Consistent Language

Use the same words to mean the same things. That goes for labels, commands, menus and help screens. Linguistic variety is great for novels, but awful for the kind of terse, immediately understood text that belongs in an online catalog. Preparing a master vocabulary list and checking all the help screens, tutorials, and other text against the list may be

irritating, but it's a way to improve the coherence of your catalog.

As with functionality, language should be consistent from the user's perspective. If two things differ slightly from a librarian's or system designer's perspective but look the same to a user and don't occur in the same setting, you should call them the same thing. A browse of a name authority file and a browse of a title index aren't really the same from a library perspective or, probably, in terms of implementation—but it makes sense to have the two displays look the same and to call them both browses.

Consistency also requires clarity and unambiguity. Sets of options should be distinctive; a user shouldn't have to guess whether (to use an imaginary example) they should look for a name in the author index or the person index, or whether "subject" or "topic" will give them the best access to books about something.

Predictability

Coherent catalogs are predictable: once a user has done one kind of work on the catalog, the user will be able to predict how other things will work.

Predictability makes learning easy and encourages advanced use of a catalog. A predictable catalog may get by with fewer prompts and menus than an incoherent catalog; once the user's made something work, he or she can guess how other things might work—and they'll frequently be right.

When designing or implementing a catalog, think about predictability in terms of patterns. If some commands can be abbreviated to their first three letters, can all other commands be abbreviated the same way—or are some short terms not straight abbreviations? If you accept first-letter versions of some commands, what are the exceptions— and do they make sense? If there's a default index, is there also a default display? Predictability may begin with an overall vision, but it continues by paying attention to the details.

Extensibility

Your one-site books-and-serials online catalog is fully coherent, consistent, predictable. What happens when you add videocassettes? No problem. What about article-level access? What about the Boolean access you didn't implement immediately?

It's one thing to prepare a coherent overall vision for a static system; it's another to prepare an extensible design that maintains coherence for the long run. Successful online catalogs have rarely been static in the past, and few will be static in the future. You will be adding new features, new kinds of data, new methods of access.

Perhaps the greatest weakness in pure-menu systems is lack of extensibility. If you keep adding new choices to the menus, the menus soon become inconsistent and unwieldy. An observer will soon spot the "new bits," the pieces that have been grafted on to the old system. Many users will find themselves lost or uncomfortable within the new areas.

If there's one safe prediction for today's and tomorrow's online catalogs, it is that they will change and grow. Coherent designs must allow room for growth without disrupting the overall design. That isn't easy, but it is important, unless you're ready to redo your entire system when it's time to expand.

User Control

Coherent catalogs always keep the user in control. That means at least three things:

- Users should be able to take any meaningful action at any point, even if that action does not currently appear as a prompt or menu choice.
- There should always be a direct link between the user's action and the catalog's reaction. If the system doesn't provide direct feedback for the command as a signpost, it should at least be clear that the command has been carried out (or why it has not been carried out). If the user is ignored, the system has gained control.
- The system should not take actions not requested by the user—and if the system takes actions designed to help the user, there should be a clear, openly stated explanation of those actions.

Does that mean that a system shouldn't turn a subject search into a title word search if there are no subject headings? Not necessarily—as long as the subject search isn't clearly stated as a search against subject headings. It does mean that a system shouldn't prepare a derived-key search from the user's full-text search, then present results that don't reflect the search.

How does a user know whether results reflect the search? A few systems in Part II offer some possible answers, but there are no easy or universal answers. *Some* displays should always show the text that caused retrieval—but that won't always be the default display, and the nature of retrieval may not always be obvious. For example, will users understand that a subject word search for "Central America" may yield a record that has one subject heading containing the word "Central" and another subject heading containing the word "America"—but is not about Central America at all?

No Surprises

The system should not surprise the user, at least not in terms of action-reaction links. If the user searches for an author by the "wrong" entry, it's appropriate to provide a cross-reference and highlight the "right" form, ready for one-key retrieval. It may even be appropriate to retrieve records based on the "right" form—but only with an appropriate explanation of what's happened. Otherwise, the user has lost control.

The issue of user control makes me wonder about systems that, in the case of zero-result word searches, throw away some portion of the search in order to yield a result. In controlled demonstrations, such systems do an impressive job of getting what the user really wanted despite the user's faulty memory. But how well do such devices work in real life—and do they keep the user in control?

The Trade-offs in Contextual Coherence

The principles suggested in this brief discussion are important for making an online catalog easy to learn and encouraging users to use it more actively. They are not without exceptions and difficulties, of course.

Perhaps the greatest difficulty with deliberately coherent and consistent designs is that expanded and enhanced catalogs begin to provide multiple contexts, and what works in one context may not work in another. Providing the same commands, indexes and displays for full-text encyclopedia retrieval as for bibliographic retrieval may be inappropriate and self-defeating. Worse yet, what works for dictionary or encyclopedia access may not work as well for literary full texts—and it's possible that what works for access to books and films won't work nearly as well for access to articles.

This book treats a given online catalog as a single context; most users will see it that way. But that single context may increasingly serve as a mask for many subcontexts, and the single overall context may become too restrictive for the elements.

There are no easy answers for this problem. For now, it's enough to say that consistency continues to be important, but that contextual shifts must be considered.

No Single Standard

By now, it should be clear that this book won't say "Good online catalogs look like this and work like that." Even if all libraries had essentially the same kinds of collections and users, that wouldn't be a reasonable statement.

There have been calls for librarians to work together to design the best next-generation library catalog, then get vendors to build it for them. this makes sense only if you assume that there is such a thing as *the* best next-generation catalog. Otherwise, any such effort would either be unproductive or potentially deceptive, if a vendor produced such a catalog and assumed that libraries would buy it.

I believe that the sampling of current catalogs in Part II provides conclusive proof that coherent designs can take many different forms—and that no single design is superior for all libraries and all situations. Next-generation catalogs will generally be evolutionary, not revolutionary, and the seeds of many of them are represented in Part II. Many of the approaches are valid, coherent, thoughtful, and probably quite successful.

It's reasonable to say that *one example* of a good online catalog (for some libraries, in some situations, with some user populations) would look like this and work like that. It's not reasonable to generalize from that example. There is no single standard; I don't believe there ever will be. Some may find that unfortunate. As a believer in change and evolution, I find it heartening.

Conclusion

Coherent online catalogs (or systems of any sort) reflect single unified visions. Good online catalogs must remain coherent, which means that the visions must be open ended. Coherent catalogs are consistent and predictable. They are not all the same, however. Coherence, consistency, and predictability must be viewed from the user's perspective. The next chapter discusses some aspects of user-centered design, one key to any truly excellent online catalog.

7

User-Centered Design

Your online catalog should serve your users. Its design should center on their needs. A design that serves your users well should also serve the library staff well; an interface designed primarily to serve staff needs may not meet the needs of your users.

Knowing Your Users

Do you know who your users are? Do you know what they expect of the library, what they want from the catalog, and what they bring to the catalog? Every library is different (some dramatically so), but every library needs to consider its user base.

The users of today aren't the same as the users of 1981, when the major studies of online catalogs were done. Many more of them are comfortable with computers (and, thus, with keyboards and displays). While the numbers will vary enormously, I'd be surprised if a typical public library doesn't find that at least 25 percent of its users are comfortable with computers. The percentage will be higher among younger users and even higher in many academic and special libraries, nearing 100 percent in some cases.

Being comfortable with computers isn't the same as being computer literate, assuming that the latter phrase has any meaning. Library users should not need to be computer experts or even experienced users to make effective use of a library catalog. However, users who are at ease giving commands through a keyboard and seeing responses on a display will take to an online catalog more readily than those who are not. Users at ease with computers, particularly younger users, will also be less fearful of damaging the online catalog and more willing to play with it, thereby learning to use it effectively.

Beyond general comfort with computers, the specific nature of computer experience depends on the particular libraries. For example, some academic libraries can confidently assume that nearly all of their primary users will not only know how to use a mouse but will understand the Macintosh interface, because the campus uses the Macintosh as a standard and required computer. Such libraries should take advantage of that knowledge, since it serves as a considerable shortcut in making the catalog familiar.

Technophobes

Every public, school, and academic library will have some technophobic users. Some of these users will regard those damn machines as the ruination of the library. They knew how to find the right cards in those elegant wooden cabinets and now they're lost. You're forcing them to stare at this malevolent machine, which will probably catch fire or start beeping at them if they don't do exactly what it wants them to. Even among those who had no love for card catalogs or experience with them, there will be some who just don't take to computers and who resent being asked to use them.

You can't design an online catalog with technophobes in mind, but good user-centered design may help to keep the phobia from getting worse. Most probably, it will have no effect: the technophobes just won't use the catalog.

The only thing I can really say about technophobes is that they may not be who you expect. Many people probably assume that retired people will be helpless when it comes to computers. That's a bad assumption; as senior centers in Menlo Park, California, and elsewhere have found, many people over sixty will take to computers as readily as people in any other age range—perhaps more readily than in some other age ranges. Sad to say, there's very good reason to believe that the tendency toward technophobia may peak in my generation: people in their forties and fifties. That's particularly true among businessmen,[1] some of whom associate typing with secretarial labor, which they see as menial, and who think of computers as mysterious machines in sealed rooms that run their lives.

The good news? Technophobia, at least fear of computers, appears to be a declining trait—not surprisingly, since it's a trait with poor survival value. Most schoolchildren grow up much more comfortable with keyboards and displays than they are with card catalogs; those who read should take to

today's and tomorrow's online catalogs with a vengeance.

Understanding Your Users

Attitude toward computers is just one variable for users. Others that will influence a user-centered design include age distribution (particularly as it affects typical visual acuity), extent and nature of handicapped population, and the uses to which the library and the catalog will be put. None of these factors will necessarily determine the overall shape of an online catalog, but they should all be considered when working out the design and implementation.

Attempting to understand your users is not the same thing as asking them what they want in an online catalog or testing online catalog designs through a panel of users. You may achieve more by studying their behavior than by asking them for direct advice, but you should also pay attention to their comments. Naturally, you should also review some of the existing research on user behavior. In doing so, however, you must pay careful attention to *where* the research was done, *when* it was done, and the full set of circumstances under which it was done—and you should not automatically assume that the conclusions reached in a study are justified by the study.

There is absolutely no reason to assume that public library users will have the same needs or exhibit the same searching behavior as students and faculty at large libraries. For that matter, there's no reason to assume that users at small academic libraries will behave the same way. The size of the collection, the nature of the catalog and the backgrounds and needs of the users all play a part in how systems are used. That's also true for public

---

1 I'm using business*men* deliberately: the gender is part of this particular situation.

libraries, of course: catalog use within a 20,000-title neighborhood branch library will probably be much different than within a 200,000-title main library—and use within a University town will certainly be different than use within a farm town. Not better or worse, just different.

Help

Every catalog user needs help once in a while, and the catalog itself should be ready to provide such help. Help can include a number of different provisions, some of them part of the catalog and some of them external to it. How you provide help will, in part, depend on your user population. Unfortunately, no matter how much you provide and how well you provide it, it won't always reach people when they need it.

Some principles for designing online help seem fairly straightforward, and haven't changed much in the last few years:[2]

- Catalog users should be able to ask for assistance at any point while using an online catalog, and the first level of assistance should come from the catalog itself.

- Forms of assistance should include context-sensitive help, explanations of any part of the system (tutorials), and information about the current searching session.

- Help text of all sorts should be prepared as carefully as other system text and should be consistent with the rest of the system.

- Context-sensitive help screens work best when they are self-contained, with a topic fitting on a single screen. Context-sensitive help should incorporate the user's actual command when appropriate.

- Help, and particularly context-sensitive help, may work better within a partial-screen window over the existing display than as an entirely separate display.

- Users should be able to leave a help or tutorial screen or window with a single keystroke, restoring the previous screen; they should also be able to take any other legitimate action while viewing the help text. In particular, a user should be able to key in a search while viewing information on how that search operates.

- Repeated mistakes can be interpreted as calls for help.

- Brief lessons on any aspect of an online catalog should always be available but never required. Such lessons should be well indexed so users can find the lesson they need.

- Users should be able to see a summary of specific information about their current search session, if session-specific information is meaningful.

Part II includes quite a few examples of different sorts of help and tutorial, some more effective than others. One recent trend in interactive help systems doesn't appear often (if at all) in these examples but will almost surely improve help systems in the future: hypertext techniques to provide multilayered help as needed by the user.

Context-sensitive help may include highlighted words and phrases. Tabbing or pointing to one of those words or phrases and pressing a function key (or clicking a mouse) will lead through a hyperlink to a brief tutorial on that word or phrase—which, in turn, will have other highlighted words and phrases. The use of hyperlinks will make clear single-screen (or partial-window) explanations even more functional because curious users or those who need deeper information can use the highlights to explore.

---

2 More discussion of each of these points will be found in *Patron Access: Issues for Online Catalogs*, pp. 150–156.

A good hypertext help system needs a clear way to retrace steps and highlight words. It should also, as with all other help, offer the alternatives of escaping from any depth directly back to the pre-help screen, or taking any legitimate action from any depth of help.

Unfortunately for today's catalogs and those of the next few years, hypertext help systems are no more immediately obvious than most icons. An increasingly high percentage of PC users (of whatever variety) will be familiar with the concepts, because so many of today's best commercial programs include hypertext help systems. If help is available through a function key (as it generally should be), a strong case can be made that, if that function key is pressed while context-sensitive help is on the screen the next screen should explain the hyperlinks and how to use them. Call it "help about help." "Explain help" should also explain hyperlinks, if they are used.

Hyperlinks aren't the only way to provide easy access to in-depth assistance, and they shouldn't be the only provision. An index to explanations should also be available, from which topics can be called up by highlighting, pointing and clicking or keying an Explain command.

There's one fundamental problem with online help, no matter how carefully it is written or how cleverly it makes use of the user's command. Most people won't ask for help, even when they run into trouble. There are several reasons for this: for example, they've tried using help and it doesn't solve their problems; it interrupts their work; and there's too much information to remember when they leave the help screen.[3] Those problems can be overcome wholly or in part by good design, but that won't entirely solve the problem.

Knowing that the best help screens will mostly go unused and unread doesn't mean a library can ignore them. It's reasonable to assume that users will be somewhat readier to use help screens in the future; in any case, they can be invaluable for the few who take advantage of them. For remote users, discussed in chapter 11, online help may be the lifeline: unlike local users, they can't rely on the ultimate help system, a good librarian.

Training

Academic libraries have an advantage, since they can urge that students receive some training in effective library use, including use of the online catalog. Good bibliographic instruction certainly makes life easier for students and staff, and many colleges and universities provide effective instruction, either through separate courses or through sessions integrated into other courses.

It's been suggested that all libraries should stress bibliographic instruction as a way of making the catalogs and collections more valuable. While that is an interesting idea, I find it hard to imagine the circumstances under which any public library could get a significant percentage of its users to attend classes on using the catalog. I also wonder how successful academic libraries can be in seeing that faculty members and staff receive bibliographic instruction—or that the campus users, in general, retain any significant portion of the instruction they receive.

Training can certainly be useful; for entering students, it can be an enormous boon. But very few libraries can reasonably assume that their users will arrive at the catalog with an understanding of how it and the library work. To a great extent, users will learn as

---

3   Anne Lipow offered these reasons at the LITA Screen Design Preconference, June 1991; they are all quite valid.

they use—and if that's not possible, they won't be effective catalog users.

Paper Materials

Just because many or most users won't be prepared before they reach the catalog, don't assume that all catalog training must be part of the system itself. Some users will prefer to learn entirely from the catalog, while others would rather have some sort of paper as an aid. Good paper materials help to make a catalog easy to learn and use; the best paper materials will help occasional users to become fairly expert catalog users.

Four varieties of paper training material come immediately to mind: "cheat sheets," flip charts, brochure-size overviews, and full-size manuals. Full-size manuals will serve little if any part in most catalog self-training systems: they're too much to deal with on the spot, few libraries can pay for mass production of book-size manuals, and few users will buy them or read them. The other three varieties can be useful, and many libraries should integrate them into a self-training system.

A cheat sheet may be the most difficult item to produce; for some systems, it will be nearly impossible. The key characteristics of a cheat sheet are these:

- It is a single sheet of paper printed on one or both sides, preferably small enough to fit into a shirt pocket.

- It can be produced cheaply enough to be given away. Users can be encouraged to take cheat sheets with them—but the sheets don't have so much blank space that they're useful as notecards; they're likely to be too expensive for that sort of use.

- It provides enough information to let a new user start a session, carry out the most common searches, display results in the most useful formats, and learn how to do more with the catalog.

- It may (but need not) list all possible commands. It may (but need not) list all available indexes. It will show enough about primary searches so that users will typically enter them correctly—but it will not show every detail of searching strategies.

Good cheat sheets are graphically attractive, terse, and informative. Those who can successfully design them should be honored; it's not an easy task.

Flip charts should provide comprehensive information about the online catalog, arranged as a series of brief descriptions (amply illustrated with actual screen captures) on a series of small pages with clear, brief headings. Descriptions can point to other descriptions, but it should be possible for a user to flip to Searching for People (for example) and get enough information to carry out a successful name search, right on the one small page.

Flip charts are usually mounted to or stationed at or near the terminals themselves; they're designed to be used while searching. They may use laminated stock or other means to make them work well, and they will typically be too expensive to give away. Some libraries may, however, elect to reproduce the contents of a flip chart on plain paper stock or in some other manner that does make them available to users, free or at a nominal price.

Flip charts may contain much of the same text as online tutorials—but, unlike the online text, flip charts should contain actual screen images. Nothing relates the printed page to the catalog itself as surely as seeing a screen image on the page. If your catalog can be accessed using a personal computer (either MS-DOS or Macintosh), you can capture the screens and print them; that's how Part II came about. Almost every library with an online catalog, PCs, and desktop publishing equipment should have screen-capture software.

A brochure can be an expanded cheat sheet, a reformatted flip chart, or an introduction to the catalog in a different format. Ideally, it should be cheap enough for wide distribution. It should include screen captures where appropriate. It can be a single sheet of paper folded into three or four minipages, or it can be a small saddle-stitched (stapled) booklet. It may cover just the online catalog, or it may include commentary about the library and its collections.

A few libraries are producing effective training materials, including brochures, cheat sheets, and flip charts. More should do so. Many users would rather read a little bit before sitting down at the keyboard, and many others will find their keyboard work reinforced by the reading.

Forgiveness

User-centered catalogs "forgive" user confusion, whenever that's possible. Forgiveness can take many forms and be quite powerful. It can also involve difficult decisions, since some aspects of forgiveness may tend to close off future options for a catalog or lead to apparent inconsistency within a catalog. Forgiveness is one key aspect of user friendliness— but it's certainly possible for a catalog to be too user friendly.

Forgiveness can include many different aspects of a user interface, such as the following:

- **Command synonyms and abbreviations:** A command-driven system should be able to accept clear, unambiguous synonyms for verbs, index names, and display names—e.g., "view" or "see" for **Display;** "get," "search," or "locate" in lieu of **Find;** "?" instead of **Help;** "author" or "person" for a **Name** index; "topic" or "about" for a **Subject** index. Synonyms always increase the likelihood that a command will succeed—but they can foreclose future extension of the catalog, since words may already be used. Shortened forms of verbs, index names, and display names should usually be acceptable down to an unambiguous lower limit—but making that limit too low will do more to foreclose expansion capabilities than anything else. Every time a system recognizes a single-letter verb, it eliminates $1/26$ of all possible future verbs, and the same is true for index names or display names.

- **Default (unnamed) indexes, displays, and display ranges:** Many catalogs should have indexes and displays that are used when no index or display names are provided. A default index should be designed so that most searches will yield useful results; examples might be unified phrase indexes or unified word indexes. Most online catalogs currently provide default multiple-record and single-record displays. Good online catalogs also assume a display range when a display is requested without such a range; usually, the range should equal the result size.

- **Command error correction based on spelling or syntactic analysis:** While tricky, this form of correction can be quite useful—but, in every case, the user should be told what's happening. Which of the following error corrections[4] are reasonable, and which go too far?
  Your command: FIMD TITLE FOUNDATION'S EDGE was interpreted as the command: Find Title FOUNDATIONS EDGE

---

4 Taken from *Patron Access*, pp. 132-134, 178.

Your command: GET MYTHICAL MAN MONTH BY BROOKS was interpreted as the command: Find Title MYTHICAL MAN MONTH & Name BROOKS

Your command: ANYTHING ABOUT ABRAVANEL? was interpreted as the command: Find Subject ABRAVANEL

Your command: BYZANTIUM BY A. MILLER was interpreted as the command: Find Name MILLER, A and Title BYZAN-TIUM

Your command: DO YOU HAVE AR-THUR MILLER'S BYZANTIUM was inter-preted as the command: Find Name MILLER, ARTHUR and Title BYZAN-TIUM

- **Recasting of failed searches or prompt-ing for possibilities:** This can include treating a zero-result subject search as a title-word search (as is done in at least one system in Part II); transposing author names; using a spell-checking subroutine to identify and correct possible spelling er-rors; retrying Boolean searches (including multiword searches) with some portion of the search omitted; Soundex or other pho-netic search strategies; and prompting for various strategies. A catalog could also retry a failed search with assumed right truncation, if the catalog does not already provide autotruncation. Some strategies will work very well; some may cause more confusion than assistance. One general as-sertion seems reasonable: any time the user's search is modified, the user should be alerted to that fact.

- **Providing Boolean expansion, particu-larly for zero-result searches:** A Boolean expansion screen (showing the results of each term within the Boolean search) may or may not be helpful when some result is found. It would appear to be generally helpful when no result is found, since it may highlight a spelling error.

- **Providing "relevance-ranked" responses for Boolean searches with no full result or all Boolean searches:** If there are five terms in a Boolean search (e.g., a word search with automatic ANDing), give back a list showing the number of records with four of the five present, then the number with three of the five, and so on. Such a list might break out each partial combination.

- **Providing immediate and obvious "es-cape" and "undo" capabilities:** A user should be able to abandon a search when he or she immediately recognizes that something is wrong—and a catalog might be more forgiving by pausing when a search exceeds a given threshold and ask-ing whether the search should be contin-ued. The threshold should be set high enough so that at least 95 percent of all searches will be carried out uninterrupted. Users should also be able to undo their most recent action. The Escape key is the obvious choice for both of these functions, assuming that such a key is available.Undo

These are a few aspects of forgiveness; there can be many others. Even within this set, it seems clear that some techniques go too far, making catalog use somewhat of a guess-ing-game. On the other hand, one principle can be stated unequivocally for any user-ori-ented catalog: *the user should never be left at a zero-result search with no offer of assistance.* Browse-oriented indexes avoid this problem, of course, since there's no such thing as a zero-result search, but the problem still arises for multiword and multi-index Boolean searches.

Stressing Success

Many types of forgiveness can be couched in terms of stressing success—trying to make sure that, whenever possible, catalog searches succeed. As always, however, stressing success isn't as simple as taking every avenue to assure nonzero results. Sometimes, success *means* finding nothing—if the library doesn't have what you're looking for, and you have looked for it knowledgeably. Success also means finding *only* the items you're really looking for, without having to plow through hundreds of items that are of no interest.

That's only significant because some forgiving strategies can hamper accurate, narrow searching. Automatic truncation appears to be a useful idea—but some users would like to have a way to "turn it off," to say that, for this search, they want exactly what they ask for and no more. That's particularly true if automatic truncation is at the character level as opposed to the word level: for example, if you want books about cats and know enough to say "Find Word CAT or CATS," you really don't want the first part of that clause to return every book with "Catalog" in a title or subject heading. Should there be a clear "nontruncation" symbol?

The same can be said for strategies that revise and reissue a zero-result search. As long as the user is told that this has happened, and that it happened because the original search yields no results, then it seems OK—unless the revised search bogs down the system and takes several minutes to return a response. Perhaps a more user-friendly mechanism would be to note the zero result and ask for permission to submit the revised search.

There are no easy answers, particularly since most studies show that too many searches fail. A library should consider not only its users but the size and nature of its collection when evaluating how far to carry forgiveness and measures to assure success. Some balancing may yield the friendliest solution for all your users.

Related Records

Tomorrow's user-centered catalogs should encourage users to follow the path of related records by making it easy to do so—and, perhaps, by broadening the definition of related records. A few catalogs already support rapid retrieval of related records; more will do so in the future, sometimes by intuitive or immediate means.

On a Macintoshed campus or in a library where most users are comfortable with pointers (call them mice, for short), I'd like to see a catalog where the following is possible from any single-record display:

- You can move the mouse cursor to any field in the record (any personal name, corporate name, subject, title or uniform title, series—maybe even a note field or the publisher's name) and that field will be highlighted, or you can select some portion of a field by usual click-and-drag means;

- Once a field or partial field is highlighted, you can either click once, bringing up a dialog box asking what you want to do with the text (with the options being, say, "Search for this," "Edit first" and "Cancel")—or you can double-click and the system will go do it or, if the field isn't something that's normally searchable, ask you for some clarification or offer some possibilities. (In a catalog that doesn't index notes, for instance, a clicked note field could be used as a set of words for an all-index word search, particularly if relevance-ranked search results are provided and the search engine is powerful enough for this sort of thing.)

Is that possible? Certainly. Is it realistic? Possibly not. More conservatively, however, there should be an easy way to search on any field that would plausibly be indexed: subjects, series statements, authors and titles. Easy ways can include moving a highlight bar with cursor keys (if each field is on a new line) or selecting from numbered fields; a slightly more cumbersome method involves asking for related records first, then selecting from a new screen that numbers each potential candidate.

Should related-record searches be browse oriented or yield direct results? If the former is provided, then it should be equally easy to select the call number, yielding a shelf browse.

One key aspect of forgiveness when supporting related-record searching: it should be easy to abandon or undo the related-record search.

I know of no negative aspects to supporting related-record searching, and it has clear benefits for most users. Most libraries thinking about new catalogs and user interfaces should plan for fast, easy related-record searching—and such searching should support *all* kinds of related records, not only subjects. Many users can make good use of immediate access to all books in the same series as this, all videos by the same producer as this one, all recordings and scores for this particular title, and so on.

If one extreme of related-record user friendliness is the ability to point and click to related records, the other extreme, which should disappear over the next few years, is the catalog interface that doesn't allow open searching from a record display. If you can't even search a subject heading from a title-retrieved record display, the catalog is getting in your way. That's unreasonable.

Sets and Review

One interesting idea for a user-centered catalog may be problematic for most libraries, unless some secondary issues can be worked out. That idea, derived directly from online databases and found in a few catalogs, is that search results should be numbered, and that it should be possible to review result sets (the review showing the search and the result size for each set) and make use of them. Uses for old results include restoring them for display or using them as part of new search arguments.

The advantages are clear: numbered sets allow users to explore different search strategies and return immediately to ones that have been most useful, and by combining sets, users can arrive at particularly worthwhile final-result sets for printing, downloading, mailing to the user's electronic address, or further study. Add to these features the ability to delete records selectively from a result set, and you have a powerful tool for advanced users.

There's one big problem for most libraries: people rarely end their search sessions neatly. Most catalog users simply leave the catalog as soon as they're finished. Which means that the next user at that terminal will be faced with a group of result sets that he or she never asked for.

One partial solution is to use a time-out, returning the catalog to an opening screen after a certain amount of inactivity. The stored result sets could be cleared at the point of timing out. But time-outs can be tricky. If set aggressively—as low as three minutes in some libraries, apparently—they will abandon a session while a user is thinking about the next move or, possibly, checking some notes. If set conservatively, perhaps at 15 minutes, chances are another user will begin searching before the time-out.

On balance, set numbering and review capabilities still seem to increase the user friendliness of a system. It may make sense to urge that people begin their session by selecting the Start command or function key, and maybe there's no particular harm in presenting some people with the results of other people's searches. Because privacy may be a factor, however, users should also be reminded that they can (and should) press Start or Stop at the end of their session, to clear out their stored sets.

Improving Subject Access

Most commentators on online catalogs will assert that subject access is woefully inadequate in every existing catalog and that, as the dominant form of searching, major efforts must be taken to improve it.

The forgiveness strategies mentioned in this chapter will certainly help to improve subject access, and there are other strategies as well. On the other hand, it's easy to get carried away with wonderful subject access, to the detriment of a balanced, efficient, effective catalog.

First, there's the assertion that most searching is subject searching. Within academic libraries, that's probably true—although the published figures do not consistently demonstrate the truth of the statement. Within public libraries, it's far less probable. A great deal of catalog use in public libraries will be for purposes other than subject retrieval.

None of this means that subject access shouldn't be studied and improved. It does mean that improved subject access must be viewed as part of a catalog, not as the dominant issue in catalog design. That's particularly true when dealing with strategies that explore the topical aspects of bibliographic data in depth—when what the user really wants is a call number and status information.

"Is That Enough?"

One excellent suggestion regarding advanced strategies for better subject access is that it should be offered *after* a user has viewed a search result—perhaps in the form of a question such as "Does this satisfy your needs?," "Is that enough?," or something of the sort.[5]

If a user really just wants something general on a topic, chances are the user will either say "Yes" or ignore the question entirely. If a user isn't entirely happy, the question at least offers the possibility (actually a probability) that there may be other material on the topic. Once a "No" answer is received, a variety of advanced techniques could swing into action.

Such techniques could include the following (none of them my ideas) as well as many others:

- Using the call number(s) of the result to display the subject associated with the related class number, then progressing to related class numbers and related subject headings.

- Using thesauri to convert keyed subject terms, expanding them into clusters of synonyms and creating word or subject searches as appropriate. Thesauri to map keyed terms into the language of approved subject headings could also be useful.

- Given sufficient computer power, the whole set of words within a result or result set could be used to search a universal word index (including enhanced and full-text records), with the results then being returned only above a certain "relevance limit" cutoff.

- Easy movement from unit records to enriched authority records, including scope notes, biographical information, etc.

---

5   This is not my idea, although I wish it were. Anne Lipow mentioned it during the reception following the June 1991 LITA Screen Design Preconference, after I took issue with her elaborate ideas for improving user results, including some form of computer dialogue. She said she'd accidentally omitted the statement that the new techniques should be *offered* to the user, not brought into play automatically, and that a question after a result was found might be the best way to do it. Given that modification, my public disagreement with her ideas vanished.

Some of these strategies seem likely to move rather rapidly from an inadequate result to a flood of largely useless information, particularly if all elements of records are indexed and full-text systems become part of the catalog. Still, with sufficient software and hardware power and ingenious design, optional improved subject access could make library materials much more useful.

Browsing at All Levels

There are several different kinds of browsing. A user-centered design should support as many as possible, as easily as possible. We've already discussed heading browses as part of index support. There are two approaches to heading browses: one that simply opens a complete index, starting at the searched key; another that yields a set of headings as a result, allowing browsing only within that set. Both have their virtues.

Shelf browsing—browsing the call number index—should be particularly easy and somewhat open ended. Most users in small and medium-size libraries will prefer to browse the physical shelves, but large libraries and remote use may make that impractical.

There's also record browsing, and some catalogs are deficient in this area. If I'm looking through a set of *Rhapsody in Blue* recordings for those based on the original score, I may need to browse through long displays for each record. A surprising number of catalogs won't let me do that; I'll have to return to the brief multiple-record display between each pair of records. That shouldn't be necessary in a well-designed catalog.

But what if I want to jump back to the multiple-record display? I shouldn't have to step back through each record, either; few catalogs have this sort of infelicity.

Backing Out

It's one thing to jump back from single-record displays to the multiple-record list. But what about going one step further: going back from a multiple-record list to a heading list? That can be quite useful, but it's rarely straightforward. It does pose some problems in terms of clear implementation, although theoretically a Back up or Escape function could proceed through any number of layers.

User Feedback

One good user-centered addition to an online catalog is the ability to send feedback to the system. Several catalogs currently offer a function that opens an editing screen and allows a catalog user to send either a signed or an anonymous message. It's good to allow users to get problems off their chests—and such feedback can also yield ideas for improving the catalog or other aspects of the library.

User feedback works if the library pays attention to it. Signed user feedback should be answered; anonymous user feedback should be recognized and dealt with. Some libraries have bulletin boards with selected questions or comments posted together with responses; it's also possible to have a message-review facility that provides both messages and responses in a browsable or searchable facility.

On the other hand, offering user feedback but not responding to it is worse than not offering it at all. If there's no such function, users won't have any expectations. If they take the time to prepare messages but never see any indication of response, they will assume that the library staff doesn't care what they think. That's not a sign of a user-centered library or catalog.

Functions Beyond Searching

Some user-centered catalogs offer functions beyond searching. Some are directly search related, such as the ability to print bibliographies or download records to diskette. Others relate to the library in general, such as the ability to renew items, request holds, suggest orders, request interlibrary loans or even charge items out. A messaging facility can serve not only for user feedback but to accommodate some of these related functions.

Some added functions require that users identify themselves, possibly by passing a lightpen over their bar-coded library card, or passing a magnetic-striped library card through a reader, or keying in their borrower ID. The problem with any such function is that it removes the anonymity of a searcher—and, if the searcher proceeds to leave the catalog, it can attach that searcher's identity to the next user.

This needs careful design. One solution is to require that identification be provided for *each* specific function, with the identification being removed from the system as soon as the function has been carried out. That can be cumbersome, but it appears to be the most straightforward protection against privacy and identification problems.

Conclusion

Every good catalog is user centered. User-centered design involves many facets and trade-offs; a catalog that's ideally suited to intense subject searchers may be nearly useless for casual quick-check users. In any case, a library should attempt to understand its users before locking in a system design.

8

Common User Access and Common Command Language

While future online catalogs will generally be based on existing designs, some trends will help to define more accessible and more useful catalogs. This chapter deals with two such trends: one that will make catalogs more accessible to most computer users, another that will make catalogs more accessible to users of other catalogs and online databases.

The first trend, which goes by many names, is now obvious within most microcomputer software, although not yet common in online catalogs. The second trend, which is library specific, is already beginning to appear in a number of online catalog designs and will surely grow.

This chapter provides only brief discussions of the two trends, Common User Access and Common Command Language. Articles and books have been written about Common User Access and the variations on that theme; many articles have appeared on Common Command Language, and the NISO standard (Z39.58) has finally been adopted.

Common User Access

What do Ventura Publisher for DOS, PC-File Version 6, PC Tools Version 7.1, Quattro Pro and Microsoft Word Version 5.5—all DOS programs—have in common with each other and with most Windows 3 programs (and, to a lesser extent, most Macintosh and most XWindows/Unix programs)? While varying substantially, they all sport user interfaces based on a common set of guidelines that allows users who have encountered a program that employs them to use almost any other such program. IBM calls those guidelines Common User Access, or CUA; the basic principles originated within Xerox PARC, and Macintosh design principles, based on those created at Xerox PARC, are sufficiently similar to discuss simultaneously.

Online catalogs using CUA-compliant interfaces have just begun to appear. While a CUA-compliant interface does very little for a first-time computer user, there are several million people who have already used CUA-compliant or CUA-equivalent programs, and there will surely be tens of millions more, since most DOS programs are moving toward CUA compliance with or without Windows.

The most important aspect of CUA compliance for an online catalog is that it provides a rich organizational structure that provides the equivalent of extensive prompting without taking up too much of the screen. (It does take up some of the screen, to be sure: perhaps four to six lines vertically, and one or two columns horizontally.) That structure also provides a logical basis for the user interface which, while perhaps constraining in some ways, leaves considerable room for individual creativity and versatility.

CUA doesn't solve all your design problems; it doesn't make new users into searching experts; and it won't help much for complete computer novices. But it can be useful, at least when your equipment supports it properly.

A Brief Description of CUA

CUA-compliant systems have a top row of words that activate pull-down menus. File is always on the left, Edit is always next to it, and Help is always the rightmost choice. Typically, one or more lines of environmental information—e.g., what the program is or what file is open, perhaps where you are in a file—appear below the pull-down menus; within an online catalog, these lines would be ideal for contextual signposts such as the current search and result size.

Menus can be activated with a pointer, the Alt key and a distinctive letter (which is highlighted when Alt is pressed), or F10 and a cursor key. Menu options may have submenus (normally indicated with a distinctive icon or string after the option) or dialog boxes (similarly indicated). The Escape key will escape from a current menu or submenu without taking action. In many cases (when multiple options or areas are available), Tab moves from option to option (or area to area) clockwise, while Shift-Tab moves counterclockwise. Enter is used to pull down a menu when a pointer isn't available, to select a submenu option in lieu of a pointer, and to indicate completion of a dialog box—but not, typically, to finish off a particular text string within a dialog box.

CUA-compliant systems generally have at least one and possibly two scroll bars for moving within data sets or displays and, fre-quently, one or two lines of additional information at the bottom of the screen—for example, a bottom line that amplifies the currently highlighted menu option or provides brief information on the current state of the system or possibly provides labels for function keys.

Finally, CUA-compliant systems always use F1 for Help, should use F10 to call up the menus with Alt as an alternative, and, if fully compliant, will use F3 to exit the program. There's more to full CUA than this, but those are the essentials, particularly since there are at least two levels of CUA implementation.

CUA Without Graphics

If you're a Mac user, you'll read that description and say that it sounds like the Mac graphical user interface (GUI) but with function keys added and without icons. In fact, full CUA is a GUI, or WIMP, interface—that is, it uses windows, icons, menus and pointers. IBM's CUA also offers a rich set of choices: every pointer-activated action can be performed by a keyboard equivalent, as can every function key.

The classic CUA situation involves a color screen with high-resolution graphics and a mouse; the Macintosh equivalent may not include the color screen. Windows itself is a full CUA system, as are most Windows-based programs. Icons can definitely play a part in CUA.

But you don't need icons for the most important parts of CUA—in fact, you don't even need graphics beyond the character graphics provided by standard PCs. (Macintoshes always run as graphics machines, so the issue is irrelevant.) Indeed, the nearly CUA-compliant Microsoft Word 5.5 that I'm writing this book with is currently in pure-character mode; except for Ventura Publisher (which would be absurd without graphics), all of the

DOS programs noted in this chapter will also run in character mode.

All of these programs will also run without color, although the screens are somewhat more confusing in monochrome.[1] Effective use of color allows the environmental portions of the interface to "fade away," drawing the user's attention to the work area.

All but Ventura Publisher can even be used effectively without a mouse—although it's certainly true that once you've used a mouse in most of these programs using the program with only a keyboard seems clunky. On the other hand, if you have a problem maintaining steady, fine control of hand movement, the ability to substitute keystrokes for mouse usage can be a blessing: you can be absolutely certain that you're choosing the right thing.

As many programs have demonstrated, you don't even need true graphics to do effective windows, such as the partial-screen windows that might well be used for context-sensitive help or for search prompting without deleting the current result set.

Are Icons Worth the Trouble?

You can't really have icons if you don't use a true graphical interface. But does that really matter? With very few exceptions outside of graphics-oriented programs, most of them irrelevant for online catalogs, what have you seen an icon do other than provide window-dressing for the textual label beneath it?

I've been looking at a number of icon-using systems and have seen two tendencies outside of graphics software itself. At the system level, most icons are either identical or wholly arbitrary, saying nothing intuitive about the thing they represent. For example,

if anyone tries to tell me that a capital X with a slanted L attached to it somehow represents "spreadsheet," I'd say they're crazy. Note the index icons in the MacLAP system: they're identical, except that the index currently in use is shown by an open drawer—presumably extremely helpful for people who can't read the label to the left of the search statement. How would that system be lessened or made harder to use if the five icons with labels were replaced with five boxed index names, perhaps with the currently active one in reverse video? Note that Emory's Macintosh front end for DOBIS does just that: the icons are simply boxed words, which can be done just as effectively with or without graphics.

I'm not saying that icons are wholly useless, or even that their only use is within graphics programs such as drawing, painting, CAD, and desktop publishing. That's probably not universally true, and someone might yet show me an online catalog that truly gains effectiveness and speed through the use of icons, without requiring special training to understand the icons.

At this point, however, I think it's reasonable to say that at least 90 and probably 99 percent of the value of a CUA-compliant or graphical user interface can be achieved without using icons and without using bit-mapped graphics. If you add image retrieval to your online catalog, you will probably need true graphics, and you can make the CUA-compliant interface a little snazzier (but probably no more useful).

Staying Out of the Way

This discussion does not lead to an assertion that all good online catalogs of the future will be CUA-compliant and will use pull-down

---

1   The exception is Ventura Publisher, which on my system runs in black on white, using color only for one exception condition or for actual color within a document.

menus, windows, and pointers. That's nonsense; there are many good models for online catalogs, and an online catalog can be almost immediately obvious without using CUA as a model.

On the other hand, you should at least design your next implementation so that it stays out of the way of CUA-experienced users. You can do that by *not* using function key F1 for anything *other* than Help—and, preferably, using F1 to call up help at any time. Other steps include using Alt and a letter as a way of activating menus or selecting menu options—or at least not using Alt-letter combinations for entirely different purposes—and using Escape to back out of situations, which is a good idea in any event. And if you have something that looks like a scroll bar, it should be a scroll bar; otherwise, make sure it doesn't look like one.

If I had to, I'd guess that most PC-based, Mac-based and workstation-based online catalogs introduced after 1991 will probably use CUA-compliant or other graphic interfaces, and that a growing percentage of mainframe-based and mini-based systems will also do so. The advantages are real, with or without Windows or an equivalent system.

Don't Forget the Typists

Libraries and companies implementing CUA-compliant systems should remember that for experienced searchers and good typists it's faster to key a command string than to navigate through menus with a pointer. Because—unlike most personal computer software—the online catalog normally doesn't accept user keyboard entry within the active window, why not provide a command-line option for those who prefer it? CUA offers a choice of control methods; good future online catalog designs can offer an even wider choice, catering to novices with pull-down

menus and experts with a functional command line.

Common Command Language

When there's both a command line and effective CUA-compliant or menu-driven functionality, the chances are increasingly good that the command line will recognize Common Command Language (CCL), either as the only command language or as a legitimate alternative to the native language of the catalog.

CUA comes to us from the computer industry and is slow to make its presence felt in online catalogs. CCL comes from our own field and was already being widely implemented even as NISO struggled to finalize the American National Standard, ANSI/NISO Z39.58.

Common Command Language specifies a syntax and set of verbs or command words for most actions related to interactive information retrieval and display. While originally designed for online database work, most or all of its provisions apply equally well to online catalogs. The syntax and some of the commands used in CCL have been used in library-related systems for more than a decade, going back to Stanford University's BALLOTS and its descendant, RLIN II.

Status of CCL

It has taken surprisingly long for CCL to reach approval as an American National Standard—possibly because it is clearly an important standard for the future of database systems and online catalogs, and possibly because the already approved ISO 8777 includes some features that seem unfortunate to American users. In 1986, when I was writing *Patron Access*, I mentioned the current version (the standards committee began work in

almost always have exactly as good an interface as the local user. But design trends favor fancier catalogs, for which these problems can arise.

"What Red Key Was That?"

What is a remote user to do when the prompts on a screen are "Press purple up/down arrow to select title then blue E for display with holdings, red F for MARC display, orange M for more titles or yellow Z for new search"?[2] A clever user might guess that the colors are irrelevant and use regular keyboard entries—and the user might or might not be right. But what if the prompt says "Press the Help key" or "Press the red key"?

That's an obvious case in which the text of the interface no longer matches the reality of the interface. There are others—including, depending on the communications technique, any instruction to use a function key or click on something with a pointer.

When a remote user has nothing more than ASCII communications to a catalog or, slightly more helpful, VT100 terminal emulation, there are substantial limits on the complexity of the user interface. Some things just won't work well, or at all.

Transmission Overload

Contemporary user interfaces tend to employ a significant portion of the screen to keep the user oriented: signposts to show where they are and how they got here, menus or prompts to show where they can go, and possibly the overhead associated with Common User Access. That means transmitting many more characters for each new screen, unless ways can be found to avoid retransmitting un-

changed characters. For a user with a 1,200 bps modem, that means up to four seconds transmission time for each screen; it's still two seconds at 2,400 bps. Let's assume that anyone with a 300 bps modem will give up in frustration and spend the $50 to $100 to upgrade.

True graphical user interfaces increase the transmission overload problem substantially. A complete PC text screen requires 2,000 characters, or 4,000 including attributes such as boldface or reverse video (or up to sixteen colors). At a ridiculous extreme, surely pointless for any real catalog, a true-color 1024-by-768 screen without data compression would need 2,359,296 characters—requiring just over four minutes to transmit at 9,400 bps. Even a more plausible case isn't wonderful: a 16-color (or 16-gray-scale) 640-by-480 graphics screen, assuming effective data compression of 3:1, still takes up 51,200 characters and would require more than 20 seconds to transmit at 2,400 bps (with no data compression it would take more than a minute). When you have catalogs that require four to six screens (or more) to get from starting a search to seeing the complete result, that makes remote use extremely annoying.

We're told that we'll all have essentially unlimited communications bandwidth to (essentially) everywhere at little or no cost. Modems will become irrelevant because we'll have optical fibers and digital data links everywhere. That would solve the transmission-overload process—but planning your next catalog on the basis of universal high-speed interconnection in the next few years is about as good an idea as planning your next building on the basis that print will die by the year

---

2 That's not an imaginary example. See Joseph R. Matthews, *Public Access to Online Catalogs*, 2d ed. (New York: Neal-Schuman, 1985), p. 117.

2000. Even if NREN or some equivalent does make high-speed usage-insensitive digital communications available to every library in the country during this decade—surely not a safe bet—that won't bring high-speed communications into the home. A full-fledged graphics screen will still be a pretty sizable chunk of data to send to a remote user, particularly when you send 6 of them for one search and 40 of them to display 20 records.

Approaches to Remote Use

These problems have solutions, some better than others. One easy solution to the transmission-overload problem is to retain scrolling interfaces and keep overhead to a minimum. That's probably not the best solution. Some other possibilities follow.

Vanilla or Converted Interfaces

One approach being used in several catalogs, some noted in Part II, is to have two flavors of interface: one for local users and one for remote users. The two flavors can be logically consistent, but the remote version calls for control-key combinations and reduces the amount of overhead.

That's not a bad solution, and for many libraries it may be the only appropriate short-term solution. The remote user doesn't have as nice an interface, but at least the interface makes sense.

Library-Supplied Software

Should libraries get into the end-user software business? I'd be surprised if some libraries aren't already in that business; for example, the University of Southern California and Dartmouth are surely headed in that direction, if not there already. Special library-supplied software for the most popular PC platforms could provide users with an interface at least as sophisticated as the one in the library, while maintaining efficient communications. For all its faults, that's how Prodigy works; otherwise, the graphics wouldn't be feasible at all.

A library in the software business has several other problems to contend with, including maintenance. On the other hand, the library wouldn't necessarily have to create the software; it could also come from the catalog vendor or some third party. The library might add some local text and support files and distribute the software, free or at a nominal cost. Library-supplied software could mitigate the features problem and the transmission overload problem at the same time.

Online Personal Assistance

Finally, beyond good help screens and tutorials—even more important for invisible users—libraries might consider having "online librarians" who could respond directly to problems at the user interface, possibly even using hooks built into the library-supplied software to see what the nature of the problem is.

Would users be more inclined to ask for help if they know they could pass their request along to a live person? Possibly. It wouldn't help those who are befuddled but unready to ask for assistance—and I don't recommend that librarians or computers should monitor usage patterns and jump in with assistance when it seems to be needed. (It's plausible for a computer to provide help when an error occurs or is repeated; but remote users should not be given any reason to think that their catalog use is being monitored by the library itself—and it shouldn't be.)

Z39.50 and
the Unknown Interface

What happens when invisible users work with robust user interfaces—but those user interfaces aren't what you use in the library? That can and will happen as Z39.50 and related standards move to separate the database (server) from the user interface (client). Your remote connections will be server connections. Remote users may use any number of different interfaces to work with your catalog, assuming that index and retrieval differences can be negotiated.

That's fine as long as everything goes well. But what happens when you get a message saying "The text after TITLE-NOTE on this record doesn't make sense to me. Can you help?"—and you know that there's no such label as TITLE-NOTE in your catalog? What happens when someone calls up frantically and says, "I double-clicked on the series statement to get more records like it, and now my computer's locked up"—and your catalog doesn't support mice?

That's the dark side of the client/server model as it applies to future catalog use. I don't know of any easy solution to the problem. It will surely test the patience of online librarians and those handling telephone calls. The advantages of the model will be regarded as outweighing the disadvantages, I believe, but you may well have to deal with a future in which you can't be sure just how your catalog looks to a given user. Probably not in 1993, possibly not in 1995, but quite possibly before the turn of the century.

Personal Interfaces and
Personal Catalogs

One great advantage of remote use with a client/server model, if and when the transmission-load problems are solved, is that it will allow users to have their own interfaces and, potentially, to have their own needs and preferences respected by online catalogs.

Catalog theoreticians and researchers are properly concerned with the other side of improving subject access and taking library catalogs beyond the walls: the tendency to get too large a result after you get past no result at all. Many users have personal preferences that can help to reduce the result sets or at least present them in "most useful" order. Those preferences are personal, however, not universal.

There are problems with storing personal preferences as part of a catalog. At least two come immediately to mind:

- If the person using the catalog is identified, there is a much greater chance that the user's confidentiality can be compromised.

- If the identified person leaves a terminal without restoring default preferences, *which will frequently happen*, the next user (who may not have a preference profile) may get unexpected results.

Those problems don't arise when the personal preferences are stored as part of a program *on the user's own computer*. In that case, a preferences profile can be transmitted as part of the client/server negotiations. The preferences aren't stored on the central system and aren't necessarily connected to a named user—only to a currently active port. The preferences affect only this particular remote site; thus, they can't confuse another user.

Many of us who have been exposed to FBI and other inquiries into borrowing habits must twitch when people suggest that user preferences be stored and used in online catalogs. The risk to privacy is too great, quite apart from the confusion that can arise. But if those preferences reside on a floppy you carry with you, or in a file on your own computer—or, perhaps, on a magnetic stripe on the back of your library card—the problems seem to be minimal.

Conclusion

Chances are, your library currently serves some invisible catalog users or will serve them in the future. You may never be able to serve them as effectively as you serve on-site users, but you can come very close.

You need to think about the different categories of remote users and how each category needs to be served. It isn't fair to local users to hold their speed and convenience hostage to catalog browsers 3,000 miles away; it also shouldn't be necessary.

None of the problems raised in this chapter are unsolvable. The most intractable problem is the reality that good personal library service always improves an online catalog.

12

Expanding the Online Catalog

Good online catalogs must first offer access to all of the information provided on card catalogs and should do so in a demonstrably superior way. Good catalog designs will also work in an open-ended manner because they can potentially offer much more than card catalogs.

Quite a few online catalogs already go beyond the original boundaries in a number of ways; some examples appear in Part II. Some theoreticians have argued that expanding the catalog in various ways is more important than completing the primary catalog, and for some libraries that may be legitimate. In general, however, expansion should come after complete retrospective conversion and design of coherent user interfaces.

The milestone recognizing fairly widespread implementation of expanded catalogs came in June 1989, with the publication of *Information Technology and Libraries*, vol. 8, no. 2, "Special Issue: Locally Loaded Databases in Online Library Systems." This issue included not only discussions of how several libraries have expanded their catalogs but several different analyses and opinions on how catalog expansion and enrichment should proceed. There have been many other articles, before and since, but this journal issue provides a useful gathering of well-written articles. Some of the articles raise possible expansions, enhancements, and access techniques not covered in this book; I refer you to the issue.

A library can expand the catalog in many different ways, including the following:

- **Article-level access:** access to the actual works within collected works—particularly periodicals, but also conference proceedings and edited collections of papers

- **Enhanced access:** richer access to works within the library through means as simple as adding entries to reflect local interests or as elaborate as adding searchable indexes and tables of contents

- **Community information:** access to nonbibliographic information relevant to a library's users as members of a campus or other community

- **Local databases:** special bibliographic and nonbibliographic databases created within the library or related agencies

- **Full-text resources:** using the catalog as an access and reading device for various documents in machine-readable form

- **Images and sound:** providing the equivalent of "full text" for nonprint resources, particularly those resources that can't normally be circulated

- **Broadening access:** providing access to more collections through a single user interface

- **Gateways:** using the catalog as a mechanism to access other systems, without attempting to use the same user interface

After looking at each of these briefly, it makes sense to consider some questions related to expanded catalogs; as with most other issues, there's more than one right answer.

Finally, what do you call this information service—generically, and for your own particular library?

Access to Articles

Most libraries have always offered some intellectual access to articles in some of their periodicals and to some periodicals they don't hold. We have gone from print services, such as *Readers' Guide to Periodical Literature* and the many scientific abstracting and indexing services, to a huge array of online- and CD-ROM–based services, with some intermediate sources such as *Magazine Index* on microfilm.

The most common trend in expanding online catalogs is probably increased article-level access, most frequently by mounting commercially produced article indexes as part of, or indirectly available through, the online catalog. That trend seems likely to continue as more index producers establish licensing provisions and as more catalogs add ways to support article-level access.

Theoretically, article-level access is no different from bibliographic access to books, records, and films. Access points can be the same, the USMARC formats support articles fully (typically as monographs with "In" fields) and searching techniques can be equivalent. The only real difference, theoretically, is that locational information must include not only a call number but a location within that call number (volume, issue, and page range)—and that for those libraries that circulate

bound periodical volumes circulation status is at a gross level: it's not the article that counts but rather the bound volume.

Realistically, however, there are some issues to consider, including the following:

- Subject access for articles frequently does not use Library of Congress subject headings and may differ for each periodical database. Thus, integrated subject searching across physical-item and article-level databases may not work very well. Some periodical databases lack authority control for names and subjects.

- Periodical databases will usually include titles the library does not actually hold. This automatically puts the library into the intellectual-access business, where document delivery is an additional step. That's really nothing new—print indexes had the same problem—but it becomes a more apparent issue when a single system provides access to items held and not held.

- Libraries must establish the links between the vendor-supplied indexing and their own holdings, location, and status information, and must determine what to say about unheld items. (Some catalog designs now make such links essentially automatic.)

- While article-level records *can* follow standard MARC form and can be fully equivalent to (and searchable comparably to) physical-item records, many databases have more idiosyncratic structures and contents.

- Database licensing restrictions may mean that fully integrated searching (including articles as part of "regular" searches) may not be feasible, for several reasons—including the fairly common restriction that article-index access must be limited to members of a campus community or to in-house terminals.

- Integrated searching across multiple periodical indexes may yield significant duplication and cause a variety of retrieval peculiarities.

- Commercial (and noncommercial) services will provide access to *some* of the article-level information in a library but rarely all of it—unless the library elects to tailor its collection to the indexes, a rather novel approach to collection development and maintenance.

- Internal development of article-level information, either by a single library or as a cooperative project, is certainly feasible but, to date, has rarely been attempted. The major exception, CARL's UnCover, is a dramatic step forward but does not provide subject access. It may, however, be a harbinger of increased efforts in future years, either to supplement or supplant commercial abstracting and indexing sources.

Note that periodical databases need not actually be mounted locally to be searchable through the local catalog. Transparent gateways can be established so that one or more remote databases can function as though they were part of the local catalog, including automatic links to local call number information. It's conceivable to treat CD-ROM databases as part of the online catalog, although the difference in retrieval speed may be troublesome.

Practical Implementations

Most current implementations of article-level access within online catalogs do not integrate the article databases. You can't issue a single search for Martin Luther King, Jr., and retrieve not only books about him but also articles about him. Instead, you must select article information separately and repeat your search (quite possibly using different rules). Typically, if six different sources of periodical information are present, you must select one of the six; you can't search them all as a single unit.

That may change, at least for multiple databases from a single vendor and, eventually, across all periodical databases available within a single catalog. Will periodical access become fully integrated with other access? That's a more difficult question, particularly given variations in access and, perhaps most important, the issue of data overload (discussed near the end of this chapter).

If your catalog doesn't already offer access to some article-level information, chances are it will in the future. That expansion is actually a partial return to the original aim of the catalog: access to *all* of a library's collection. Perhaps not single-search access (for a while, at least), and certainly not without some problems along the way, but this form of expansion is overwhelmingly positive in its effects on the catalog's usefulness and in making the library's collections fully available.

Enhanced Access

Article-level access provides some level of intellectual access to works not currently represented in the catalog; it broadens the user interface to cover more of the collection. Another potential expansion of the online catalog enhances records for books and other items by adding searchable information from tables of contents, indexes, or possibly other sources.

For those books that are actually collections of separate articles, stories, poems, plays and the like, adding access to elements of the tables of contents is equivalent to providing article-level access: it provides access to the intellectual works contained within the physical works. Such expansion is no more controversial than the addition of periodical indexes—although, given financial realities, it may be less probable. The same goes for sheet-level access to sets of maps and piece-level access to sound recordings that contain more than one piece and collections of scores: that's not controversial, it's just expensive. Indeed, it's more controversial *not* to consider such access, as it leaves part of the collection inaccessible.

Enhanced access carries another agenda, however: to offer richer subject access to whole works—or to offer subject access to portions of works, providing access to "information" rather than the work as a whole. The means seem straightforward enough—providing searchable indexes and searchable chapter headings (and, possibly, headings within chapters). It should be recognized, however, that this is a different form of expansion and carries with it some assumptions that require discussion. Rather than broadening the window to cover more of the library's collection, it is deepening the access to some portion of the collection.

That may be a good thing, as long as it doesn't come at the expense of appropriate access to all materials. It is neither an inexpensive nor a straightforward process, and raises some real questions of both data overload and significance.

Does the inclusion of a topic or personal name in a book's index mean that the book offers any useful information on that topic or person? Certainly not, as you can demonstrate by going through almost any book's index and looking up some of the references. Current norms for index building mean that many index entries are essentially useless; filtering by page range will help, but may also eliminate useful items. If you wanted to learn more about Charles Ammi Cutter and used a fully enhanced catalog for a campus with a library-school library, can you imagine the result? (I'd venture a guess that it would be hundreds of titles, and possibly thousands—including this book, thanks to the mention on this page.)

That's a data-overload issue, but there is also an intellectual issue here: is it reasonable to treat elements of a work as independent pieces of information? It's frequently meaningless to do so, because a paragraph or even a chapter may be sensible only in the context of the work as a whole. It may also be an affront to the author's intentions; most book writers do not think of their books as simply collections of independent paragraphs. On the other hand, it can also be valuable and valid—for some books and other works.

Libraries are slower to provide enhanced access than broadened access. I believe they are allocating their resources properly. Enhanced access may be valuable as an additional step, but it requires careful thought.

Campus and Community Information

Many public libraries maintain community information and referral files. These make useful additions to the online catalog, although they don't naturally function as part of a bibliographic database. They become another service, directly accessible through all the library's terminals.

Academic libraries may also provide information on services available to students, and can also offer other campus information resources. As campuses move to campuswide networks, the library catalog is a natural resource on the networks. The library may also be a natural focus for organizing campus information and making it available with the kind of access tools librarians understand best.

Making community or campus information available on a catalog expands access to these traditional local reference sources. It does not appear to raise new questions, except those of organizing, retrieving, and displaying the information within the catalog.

Local Databases

The expanded catalog may also include databases built by the library that would not have been included in a card catalog, or that might have been represented in a separate card catalog. Examples include song indexes, sheet music indexes, indexes to architectural slides or illustrations, television scripts, government publications or pamphlets in vertical files. Quite a few libraries index their campus or local newspaper; that index can become part of the online catalog. The library catalog may also include records for computer files not actually available in the library but housed elsewhere on campus. The catalog could even include the "tough questions answered" file that many libraries now keep at reference desks.

Some of these examples represent nothing more than expansion of the catalog to make more of the library's collection available. That's true of song indexes and government publication listings, for example. Should they be separate files in the online catalog, or should they become part of the primary catalog? That's a decision that involves cataloging and access issues and can only be made on a local basis. Logically, there's no compelling reason that such databases should be kept separate—but practically, separate access may be the only realistic course.

The advantages of putting local databases on the online catalog are clear: all the retrieval power of the catalog can be applied to the local information, users have better access to more of the collection, and collection use will probably increase. When mounting such a database, some attention should be paid to descriptive and other standards. Just as with book cataloging, the online catalog doesn't work magic: it won't create order out of chaotic information. To the contrary, it's likely to make disorderly information more apparent.

Broadening Access

All the areas covered so far expand the traditional functions of a library catalog but retain its essential nature. The catalog provides bibliographic information at some level, showing people what resources may be available to meet certain needs. As discussed to some extent in chapter 11, online catalogs are increasingly broadening access by offering information on other collections as well.

That's a valuable addition, as long as it isn't imposed on the user against his or her will. The user must be able to locate material in the current collection first, moving on to other material as required. The easiest way to do that is to treat the local catalog and other catalogs as separate databases, but it's certainly not the only way, and perhaps not the best way. It may even be sensible to handle locations as "scoping" elements, with the default scope being the local collection.

An ideal situation might offer several graduated levels of inclusiveness. At the highest level, the user retrieves only those items in the local collection. At a second level, the user retrieves items that are known to be available within half a day or less—items at other libraries within the same campus or within a short drive. At the third level, much broader regional access is provided, perhaps including everything to which the user has legitimate primary access. The lowest level includes everything. A user could potentially choose to cast the initial net as widely as possible, or could say that all searches should integrate the first and second level and stop there. As with any such user-specific retained options, such scoping should automatically revert to a default when the terminal "times out" and should be clearly visible as part of the search-result display process. Examples in Part II show this process in action; many libraries understand the issues involved and have acted on them intelligently.

There are two basic differences between a catalog representing many collections and a catalog with gateways to other catalogs:

- The user will always know that gateway access represents some other collection, because explicit action must be taken to use the gateway;

- The user may need to understand different search syntax in order to use the gateway effectively.

Otherwise, such gateways provide yet another way to broaden intellectual access—if not necessarily physical access—to sources of information and enlightenment. Depending on the library, this broadening may have a very high priority; it will eventually play some role in almost every library.

Full-Text Resources

Now we move beyond the bibliographic role of a catalog into providing the final product. Some libraries have begun to add full-text resources to their catalogs, such as the *Academic American Encyclopedia*, various dictionaries, or the complete works of Shakespeare. Some visionaries see this as the beginning of the "electronic library," where all resources are stored digitally and delivered to terminals; others see it as an interesting marginal addition of new ways to access certain kinds of information.

From a logistical standpoint, the clearest aspects of full-text provision are the following:

- It makes more sense when a catalog is part of a campuswide network; otherwise, extensive full-text provision can bog down access to terminals.

- Full-text access does need to be kept separate from bibliographic access, to avoid instant and overwhelming data overload.

- Full-text access may require different searching techniques and different display techniques. Hypertext will add another aspect to full-text access.

- The screen continues to be a mediocre medium for long-term reading and understanding. Full text on the online catalog makes more sense for reference works than for narrative works.

- Copyright provisions will be important for recent material; online access to full text over a campuswide network would appear to be republication or mass uncontrolled copying.

Libraries contemplating full text sources as part of the online catalog should consider the costs and the benefits. What are the benefits of full-text access? Are the benefits sufficient to balance the cost and difficulties? Should library users be encouraged to treat works as collections of words rather than as complete entities, or is this an antiliterary, anti-intellectual tendency? At its most extreme, the question could be placed: does full-text access improve scholarship or denigrate scholarship and literacy?

I'm not sure of the answers, and suspect that they depend on the institution, its users and the particular full text in question. I *am* sure that provision of full text within online catalogs is not an unmixed blessing.

These qualms deal with full text *already available in print*. There are now, and will be in the future, cases where electronic transmission substitutes for print, quite often for perfectly legitimate reasons. Here, if the library is to provide the material at all, it will be through electronic means. Full-text retrieval may not be the only or the most effective way to retrieve such material, but it certainly makes sense that such material should be made available through the online catalog (as a separate resource, of course). Making electronic journals available through an online catalog seems perfectly reasonable and raises few of the questions posed by making, say, Norman Mailer's *Of a Fire on the Moon* available through an online catalog. In the first case, the screen is clearly the medium of choice. In the second, the book itself would appear to be the medium of choice.

Images and Sound

More than one catalog vendor is adding image capabilities, and several libraries have begun different kinds of experimental or production access to images in conjunction with or as part of online catalogs. Provision of digitized sound is less well reported, but seems a likely future trend as well.

The issues are much more complex in these areas than for full text, because images and sound can play roles in access itself—and because images and sound may offer access that could not otherwise be provided. At the same time, images and sound place substantial loads on system storage and transmission capabilities and might better be provided through ancillary systems in some libraries.

Sound as a retrieval mechanism? Certainly, for music collections. It may be far-fetched, it may be difficult to achieve, but one way to deal with difficult retrievals would be to accept notes themselves as part of a search argument, or to play portions of scores or recordings as part of the "display" option.

In addition to its uses for retrieval, digitized sound may be the most feasible way to provide access to many sound recordings, assuming that copyright and performance-right issues can be dealt with. With the possible exception of compact discs, music collections do not include *any* original sound recordings that can be circulated without some potential loss of quality. For historic disk and cylinder recordings (and these days, all analog disk recordings are becoming "historic" to some degree), the potential is all too clear: to play is to damage. Audiocassette copies are themselves far from permanent and generally degrade the original sound to a significant degree.

It's fair to say that using the online catalog to store and transmit a historic recording of Bach's Mass in B Minor—or any other sound recording—poses serious storage and transmission problems with today's technology. Assuming current audio compact disc quality, the audio information alone (without any of the error correction that makes CD work) comes to 1.4 *million* bits per second. That's 176,400 characters or just less than a third of a full-length book, *each second*. That data rate does not pose a problem for optical fiber, but optical fiber (and the systems to drive it) is not widely used to connect online catalog terminals in-house, much less remote terminals.

Similar problems, although much less severe, arise when dealing with still images. They require a fair amount of storage space and transmission bandwidth, and they require high-resolution graphics displays to show clearly. They might be useful for retrieval—and perhaps more importantly, digital display can make available the millions of historic photographs, prints, films, posters, and other images that can't be circulated without certain damage.

But should those images actually be stored and transmitted as part of the online catalog itself—or should the catalog provide links (direct or indirect) to another system? The same question arises for sound—and, to an even greater extent, for video and motion pictures, which require substantially greater data-storage requirements than audio.

One System or Several?

This question arises for many aspects of the expanded catalog. Right now, most libraries run several online systems, including CD-ROM workstations of various sorts in addition to the online catalog. The AVIADOR project provides access to Avery Library's architectural drawings using RLIN bibliographic records—but access is through a link between the catalog and the videodisk player, not by digitizing the drawings themselves and making them part of the same catalog. It will be increasingly feasible to create your own visual archives on optical disks in the future, but it may be more realistic to provide that information by a separate or linked system, rather than as part of the catalog itself.

It will be a few years (or decades) yet before we all have unlimited-bandwidth telecommunications and essentially free storage. It may be a few years after that before you can provide instantaneous access to unlimited quantities of bibliographic or full text, no matter how complex or clumsy the search. In the interim, libraries must make realistic choices. How do you provide the best service to the most people and the special services that a few users need? One system may be the answer, but that's not a safe assumption—at least not for the next few years. Perhaps the catalog should continue to point more than to provide.

One Logical Database or Several?

Should the catalog be a single searchable database or several separately searchable files? Here again, the library must balance theoretical advantages against practical problems. Practically, larger databases increase response problems, large-result problems, and other access problems. That is also, unfortunately, true when you combine many different periodical indexes into a single searchable whole. In this case, homonyms—or, rather, words with different meanings in different fields—become much more of a problem as more fields appear together. Searching also becomes more problematic because most databases don't follow the reasonably consistent rules used for library cataloging.

The case for treating all physical materials equally seems fairly clear, as long as users can limit their searches to suit their needs. Logically, articles in serials should have the same treatment—but practically, separate files may be more reasonable.

One Interface or Several?

Finally, should your catalog use a single search-and-display system for everything—or should the interface be tailored to the information? Here, I think, the split comes between bibliographic information (including articles) and nonbibliographic or full-text information. Well-designed search-and-display systems should serve articles, books and films equally well, and that equality of treatment emphasizes the intellectual equality that underlies it. A book isn't "better" than an article—and *Rhapsody in Blue* certainly isn't "better" as a separate recording than as part of a 70-minute Gershwin collection—they're just housed differently.

Full text isn't the same thing. It may well be searchable using the same syntax (although possibly different index names), but the display should reflect the nature of the text, not the nature of bibliographic data. Dartmouth's contribution to Part II shows this; they have sensibly adjusted their displays to suit their full-text resources. They have, however, retained an overall unity; in effect, while the interface isn't identical, it's so compatible that the user needs no new training. I find Dartmouth's implementation sufficiently convincing to argue that, if full-text additions make sense in the online catalog, a compatible user interface is both achievable and reasonable.

Intellectual Access and Document Delivery

Although a few libraries have customized the periodical databases they've acquired, loading only those portions corresponding to the local collection, most libraries will provide the entire database. That's certainly true for CD-ROM workstations, where the library typically has little choice in the matter.

When you provide intellectual access, and particularly when you make it easy and effective access, you instigate demand for access to the thing itself. How do you satisfy that demand?

That problem is being solved, although not without cost and effort, by a number of related efforts that may all, eventually, work together. The Research Libraries Group is providing one key piece of a reasonably universal solution through its Ariel™ document transmission software and through the work it is doing to resolve related problems. Ariel is being adopted by some other agencies interested in providing documents on demand;

with luck, it can become a widely used de facto standard methodology.

Ariel works as a high-technology, high-resolution, low-cost form of telefacsimile; it combines a full-page scanner (typically a Hewlett-Packard ScanJet Plus), a personal computer and Ethernet network, and a Hewlett-Packard LaserJet III printer. One low-cost circuit board is added to the PC; RLG supplies modestly priced software that handles data compression of the scanned image and scheduling and control of transmitted and received images. Images are transmitted over the Internet, although other transmission means will become feasible as required. The images can be stored on hard disk; little or no development would be required to archive them to optical disk instead.ScanJet.

With Ariel or a similar system in place at the user's library and at some supplier's location, the user's need for a document can be translated into an order that will result in a plain-paper laser-resolution copy of the original article, delivered in a few hours. The process isn't free: copyright fees must be paid, and the supplier will naturally expect some fee for the service. But the process can be reasonably priced, the copy quality is very high, and the copies are durable—indeed, using acid-free paper, they might be considered archival.[1]

Ariel isn't the only game in town. Some database suppliers have been supplying articles on demand for years, either through distributed optical disks or through on-demand fax transmission or overnight mail. The new software and off-the-shelf hardware simply provide a fast, economical, legal way to provide articles when and where they're needed. If scholars on your campus—or users in your community—need only five or ten articles a year from a journal that would cost $200 to

---

1 Toner appears to be an extremely durable agent, once properly fused.

$400 a year for a subscription, $7.50 to $10 for an on-demand article copy is a bargain.

Data Overload

Aside from philosophical questions of full-text access to narrative works and practical questions of computer power, data storage, response time, and transmission speed, the primary problem in the expanded catalog is data overload: the provision of more results than the user can reasonably cope with.

Some anecdotal evidence suggests that users don't believe that they look at more than 15 results, but they actually look at up to 30. The classic criterion for database searchers is "the perfect 20 results." In other words, even when we're looking for information on a subject, we probably don't want to deal with more than roughly two dozen items.

Unfortunately, online catalogs tend either to produce no result or to produce too large a result. We have many suggestions, most of them worthwhile, on dealing with zero results. What do we do about results that are too large?

There are a number of possible techniques, some noted elsewhere in this book. The key thing is to recognize that data overload can be a problem, and that most users neither want nor can use all of the information related to a given topic.

The first criterion should probably be this: *Give the user what he or she asks for—and no more, unless that's not enough.*

It's commendable to ask whether the result seems to be sufficient. It's unfortunate to depart from the user's request in order to achieve a broader result, particularly when the request itself does result in some retrieval.

Expanded catalogs make this issue more significant. Full access to all of the intellectual works in a collection will increase result sizes by several times in many libraries—by many times (perhaps as many as 50 times) in some. If result sizes are too large in a database of one million books, records and films, what will they be when 15 million article citations are added?

When you provide full access to everything in the collection, you must provide clear, efficient, effective tools so that users can make sense of that access. Otherwise, your catalog fails the user just as surely as if the catalog lacked half of the information.

In the worst case, a single user interface providing full-text access to all written material held in every American library would yield such large results to almost any inquiry that it would be virtually useless. If my local branch library had such a catalog, I'd just give up and walk over to the shelves, where I might have a chance of finding something I wanted to read—and I'd call colleagues if I needed to find something on a particular topic. The universal catalog is the useless catalog. Somewhere in the middle, we must maintain usefulness while enriching access.

Naming the Catalog

What constitutes a proper ending to this informal series of essays on contemporary catalog issues? What better than an issue of absolutely no known significance in the real world—and yet one that some libraries and librarians spend significant time and energy on: What do you call the online catalog? The issue works at two levels:

- What's the appropriate generic term for online catalogs, particularly as they expand to become broader information resources?

- How does a given library go about naming its particular online catalog?

If your answer to either or both questions is either "Who gives a ☞✳✻□▼⊞?" or "Get a life!"—well, then, you're on the right track. Go on to Part II, and thanks for reading this far. If you feel that these are serious issues, I can only ask: Why?

To me, the most comfortable term is "catalog"—and "online catalog" only when you need to make some distinction between that and a card catalog. For most users in most libraries by the turn of the century, "catalog" will do just fine.

Some people are more comfortable with "online information system" or something of the sort, particularly as they add more resources to the catalog. That's fine, if that's what you want, but it does take away the comfortable, traditional term "catalog." Of course, if you're uncomfortable with "library" as a term, preferring, say, "information center" or something of the sort, then you will surely prefer a term other than "catalog." But to me, a catalog with bells, whistles, and *Academic American* is still a catalog: it's the library's primary set of pointers to resources.

What should you call your particular catalog? Well, how about "the catalog" or maybe "it." My sense is that most public libraries and school libraries take exactly that approach: if they give the catalog a name at all, it's something like "The Xx Public Library Online Catalog." In other words, "the catalog." Not MetroCat or CityAccess or some other name, possibly resulting from a competition: just "the catalog."

That may even be the coming thing in colleges and universities. Look at Part II; note how many of the examples *don't* include a special local name. Leave out the locally developed systems: for the University of California, Dartmouth, Purdue, Rensselaer, University of New Brunswick, and University ·

of Texas at Austin, a local name seems only reasonable, because the system is truly local.

If your library finds that a special name makes the catalog more appealing or simply more fun, by all means hold your competitions and come up with some marvelous name for it. You'll hear advice to avoid feline names; such advice can be cheerfully ignored as being wholly irrelevant. If you can find someone (person, company, or foundation) to kick in a big chunk of the catalog's costs, that should make the decision easy!

Given the number of difficult decisions a library needs to make while implementing an online catalog, perhaps the issue of choosing a name is significant after all: you really do need something to relieve the tension and pressure. The name really shouldn't matter, and probably won't (unless you make some dreadful mistake in choosing one)—but then, insignificant issues have their places too.

Just don't give users a bad time if they're using your catalog and persist in calling it "the catalog" or "the machine." That's what it is.

Conclusion

As a science-fiction reader (which I am) or as a proper futurist (which I am not), I should tell you that today's local online catalog is just the beginning of an expansion that will eventually make it part of a universal information network, making every fact and opinion equally accessible to everybody. Oh, and as virtual realities rather than text, because text will be recognized as obsolete and limiting.

If you find that conclusion exciting, good luck to you. You'll need it, because universal access realistically means no access at all. Real-world catalogs will expand in a number of ways, some more valuable than others. The best libraries will keep doing what they do uniquely well, while adding new services and resources. Catalogs play a central role in that process. Controlled, coherent, planned expansion makes sense; throwing everything in because it's feasible does not.

Part II

Examples of Online Catalogs

The chapters that follow combine brief informed commentaries on 32 different online catalogs with more than 750 screens from those catalogs. In every case, the commentary comes either from a user of the catalog under discussion or from a vendor representative. Those contributors also captured the screen images used, typically submitting more images than actually appear here (MacLAP is the single exception).

Using These Chapters

These chapters can be used to see the variety of catalog and user-interface approaches currently in use, to gather ideas for your own catalog screens and to think about what works and what doesn't work.

These chapters do not constitute a complete survey of the online catalog market and should not be used as tools in making purchase decisions. That would be inappropriate for several reasons:

- Although every known online catalog vendor was invited to participate or was initially represented by a contributor, several did not respond, and some contributors were unable to meet contribution deadlines. Thus, this is not a complete repre-

sentation of the commercial marketplace. In particular, it is lacking several CD-ROM–based systems.

- Systems change. With the exception of the two prototype versions represented here, these chapters represent systems as they were in the summer and fall of 1991. By the time this book is published, some systems will have evolved; most systems will continue to evolve over time.

- Most chapters represent a particular institution's version of a system. As systems become increasingly flexible, institutional choices may cause marked differences in the appearance and functionality of the same underlying system.

- While these chapters provide excellent introductions to the workings of the online catalogs represented, they don't show the speed of operation, the integration with other system aspects, the quality of service personnel, or any of the other "invisible" aspects of a system. Additionally, these chapters show only the online catalog aspects; many of the systems provide many other important functions for libraries.

Choice of Screens and Commentary

Contributors did not work in a vacuum. Each contributor received a brief set of notes, including suggested searches and the elements that I wanted to see covered (a slightly modified form of those notes appears at the end of this introduction). Some chapters follow the order of those notes in the commentary; some do not. Most chapters include the searches suggested in the notes; some do not. Most of the latter cases are catalogs for special libraries and other collections where the suggested searches would not be workable.

It is fair to say that these notes caused a number of contributors to examine their catalogs more closely than they had done for some time; in at least two cases, the catalogs were actually revised because of the notes.

About the Screens

Screens in these chapters came from the contributors, who used a variety of methods to capture and manipulate them. The contributors chose which screens to submit (and, in some cases, recommended screens to be included in this book—recommendations that were consistently followed), and it can be assumed that these screens portray the systems accurately. Some warnings must be attached to that assumption.

The variety of capture methods means that the quality of text in many screen images is *not* indicative of the quality of text as it would appear on an actual terminal. That is particularly true for screens captured on MS-DOS computers running in text mode, the case for most chapters. Although characters may appear too thick or even closed up in some screens, it's fair to assume that they would be perfectly normal on an actual terminal.

Most screens were captured either on Apple Macintosh computers or on MS-DOS (IBM-compatible) computers. In most cases, the computers were running terminal emula-

tion software—essentially functioning as dumb terminals. Most Macintosh-based screens represent the actual screen fonts, because Macs always run in graphic mode. However, Macintoshes used as terminals may use very different typefaces than other terminals on the same catalog.

Some of these systems use color or many shades of gray to organize and emphasize information. While some screen images do show three or four different shades of gray, there's a direct trade-off between number of gray shades (which must be simulated in print) and clarity of the text; as a result, most shades were normalized to black and white. Similarly, color interfaces generally appear here in much simplified form.

Several contributions came with text files representing screens. After some experimentation, I have chosen to use Bitstream's Swiss Monospaced for these figures rather than the more traditional Courier. Although Swiss Monospaced is sans serif and the character set on most MS-DOS displays and many terminals is (lightly) serifed, Swiss Monospaced is much more typical of actual screen appearance than Courier. In one case (Dynix), the text files lose highlighting that would be present on the screen. In most other cases, the systems do not use highlighting.

Screen Image Sizes

Most screen images have been reproduced in the largest size that would allow three images to fit on a page, with normal margins and captions. That size varies depending on the height-to-width ratio of the original image (*always retained as submitted*), which is not always the same as the height-to-width ratio of a terminal screen (except for Macintosh screens). The size also varies in order to retain appropriate multiples or fractions of the submitted size, thus retaining optimum clarity.

Some screens are printed two to a page for easier reading and examination. After some experimentation, I found that, in most cases, a substantially larger image was easier to read even if the larger image was not accurately scaled.

Some screen images represent less or more than an actual screen. Where less than a 24-line or 25-line screen appears, it is because the interface scrolls and only part of the screen was significant for this purpose. Where more than a 25-line image appears, it is because the contributor used software magic to provide "expanded screens." Note that for INLEX, 27-line HP terminal images had to be captured in 25-line form, thus frequently losing a "More information" indicator from the original screens.

Peculiarities

The complex process of capturing, sending, converting, and printing screen images has resulted in peculiarities in some images. Where screens use shaded backgrounds, some banding or moiré effects may appear because the shading does not scale correctly. These effects are artifacts of the book and will not be present on the actual screens. As already noted, you can assume that the text in many images will be clearer on the screen than it is in the images.

In one or two cases, for various reasons, highlighting may have simply disappeared or have been transformed, possibly in a peculiar manner. In the particular case of the NOTIS contribution, conversion difficulties result in boldface words or characters appearing in regular text but with odd spaces before or after the words or characters. These spaces are also

artifacts of software conversion problems and not part of the actual screens.

The Catalog Collection

Most contributors submitted quite a few more screens than would fit in this book—typically twice as many. Most readers don't need to see that many screens, and they couldn't be included in this book while retaining a reasonable publication price. Some of you—vendors, consultants, libraries planning to change systems or modify the user interface, and library schools—may want the additional information. Some of you may also want to see all the screens more clearly.

For those reasons, *The Catalog Collection* is also available. *The Catalog Collection* contains all of the text in the 32 chapters that follow (and, in some cases, some additional text) and all or almost all of the screen images that were submitted by contributors. That can mean as few as five additional screens (InfoTrax) or as many as 45 (LS/2000).[1] Additionally, most screens in *The Catalog Collection* are printed at half-page size.

The 1992 edition of *The Catalog Collection* is more than 840 pages long and includes more than 1,400 screens. Current plans call for updating *The Catalog Collection* annually and providing an update service for purchasers. Additions to *The Catalog Collection* will be reflected in later editions of *The Online Catalog Book*.

The Catalog Collection does not include Part I of this book and does not include a glossary or index. It is not bound or offset printed but rather photocopied and provided in a three-ring binder. It is also roughly three

---

1   The MacLAP contribution is identical in both books, apart from page numbers; the 13 screens submitted appear at half-page size in both books.

times as expensive as *The Online Catalog Book*.

The Catalog Collection, ISBN 0-8389-7594-1, is available exclusively through the Library and Information Technology (LITA), a division of the American Library Association. Price is $150 per copy, $135 for LITA members, including shipping for prepaid orders. Send orders to ALA Publishing Services, Order Department, 50 East Huron Street, Chicago, IL 60611-2729. Include check or money order, or card number and expiration date for MasterCard, Visa or American Express. Specify the title (*The Catalog Collection*) and ISBN (0-8389-7594-1). Or call 1-800-545-2433, or fax orders to 1-312-944-2641.

Future Contributions

If you use or provide an online catalog that isn't represented here, or a major upgrade to one of the catalogs that is represented here, you may wish to consider contributing to a future edition of *The Catalog Collection*—and, possibly, to the next edition of *The Online Catalog Book*.

If *The Catalog Collection* continues to be published, systems will be added or revised no more frequently than annually—and less frequently if the number of contributions does not justify new editions. Candidates for new and revised chapters may be submitted at any time, but must be received by December 31 for inclusion in the next year's edition. If contributors wish to review the chapter before it appears in print, contributions must be received by November 30.

If and when the next edition of *The Online Catalog Book* is prepared, catalog examples will be taken from the current version of *The Catalog Collection*.

The notes that follow provide most of the information needed to prepare a contribution. Potential contributors should, however, contact me before preparing contributions—and *must* contact me before contributions can be accepted, because a copyright assignment statement must be included with each contribution. Contact me through LITA: Walt Crawford, *The Catalog Collection*, ℅ LITA, 50 East Huron Street, Chicago, IL 60611.

The Online Catalog Book:
Information for Contributors

Thanks for volunteering to contribute to *The Online Catalog Book*. By combining your experienced perspective on your online catalog with other similarly knowledgeable perspectives, the examples section of the book should provide librarians and vendors with an extremely useful, varied source of inspiration for better user interfaces and online catalogs.

The screen images and commentary that you provide should show what's special about your system, but the book should provide reasonably direct comparisons between different user interfaces. These notes should help assure that such comparisons are possible, while leaving room for you to focus on particular points of interest. *Please read through these notes before starting to capture screens.*

These notes use a box □ to mark points where you will probably want to capture a screen image. You may find it convenient to check off the boxes as you're working your way through sessions. Your system may require more screens than are suggested in order to show the options or information available, and some boxes won't apply to your system; these are only general guidelines.

You can keep this information—but the final sheet *must be signed, witnessed, and returned along with your final contribution.*

NOTE: *The final sheet does not appear as part of this chapter. Portions of the following text have been revised since the original notes went out.*

Introduction and Techniques

After reading through these notes, you will be using screen-capture software to capture representative screens from your online catalog. You will also be preparing a brief commentary on your online catalog and its special features to provide background for the screen images and clarify areas in which the images are not self-explanatory (or in which you'd need too many images to make your point).

You will be submitting the screen images on one or more diskettes, preferably accompanied by printed versions of the screens. You will submit your commentary either in machine-readable form (on diskette or via Bitnet) or in written form. You will also submit a paragraph about yourself and the copyright assignment form at the end of these notes.

If you meet the deadline, your submission is appropriate, and space allows:

- I will be using some portion of your screens and some portion of your commentary, possibly edited for clarity, as the bulk of a brief chapter in *The Online Catalog Book*.

- I may use some of the screens and/or commentary within other chapters of the book.

- You will be credited (and thanked) for your contribution.

- You will receive a copy of the finished book.

- I will be using most or all of the screens and commentary within *The Catalog Collection*, and you will be able to purchase a half-price copy of the first edition of that work in which your contribution appears.

Screen-Capture Software

You must have screen-capture capabilities for your online catalog—that is, the ability to capture not only the text within a screen but also highlighting and graphic devices, if any. It must be possible to submit screens as MS-DOS or Macintosh files (one file per screen) in a manner that will make it possible to use them as graphic images within Ventura Publisher.

Preferred Modes
For MS-DOS systems (and systems from which you will be converting material to MS-DOS form), the preferred modes are TIFF (Tagged Image File Format), PCX (PC Paintbrush format) and IMG (GEM bitmapped format). *Most screen-capture programs should support one or more of these formats as output, directly or through conversion.*

For Macintosh systems, the preferred modes are TIFF and any mode that can be converted to TIFF on a Macintosh. Macintosh Paint files can also be converted. If at all possible, submit Macintosh files on MS-DOS diskettes.

Other Possibilities
Other possible MS-DOS formats include EPS (Encapsulated PostScript); CGM; the AutoCAD SLD format; the DXF format (Drawing Interchange Format) used by a number of CAD programs; HPGL (Hewlett-Packard Graphics Language), preferably with the HP 7475A plotter chosen as the output device; the .PIC format created by Lotus 1-2-3 and some other programs; and the GEM line-art format.

Macintosh PICT files can be converted, but only if they are pure vector or pure raster; the results for pure vector may not be workable. Similarly, while Encapsulated PostScript files can be handled, they tend to cause difficulties.

Limitations and Notes
The book will be printed in black ink on permanent paper. There will be no color printing. Any color screens will be translated to shades of gray in a way that may not best represent the original. You're probably better off controlling that conversion at your end. You can comment on specific colors used within screens, if you think it's important.

Final images used for *The Online Catalog Book* will typically be printed at no more than 16 picas (2⅔ inches) high and a proportional width. Some images may be printed larger (and most used in *The Catalog Collection* will be), but in no case will a standard screen image be printed at much more than 25 picas (4⅙ inches) high or 41 picas (6⅚ inches) wide.

Submission of Screen Images

Send the screen image files on one or more diskettes: either 5¼ or 3½ inches, either double-density or high-density, with high-density 3½ inches preferred in terms of diskette handling.

If it's practical to do so, send printed versions of the screens as well, labeled to tell me which file is which image. You can also include captions with the printed versions.

You can mark up to ten screen images as ones that *must* be included, and up to ten more as images that you feel strongly *should* be included. I will honor the first specification (assuming that your contribution is used) and, if possible, the second.

You will typically be sending something like 25 to 50 screen images. If your contribution is accepted, at least fifteen images will be used within the chapter (unless your system is included only as a variant on another system). How many images are used in all, and whether images are used elsewhere in the book, depends on a variety of factors. Typically, all relevant screens will be used for *The Catalog Collection.*

In most cases, you should be able to include all of the files on one or two diskettes. A single 1.44MB diskette should have room for 30 to 50 screens.

If you need to have the diskette(s) returned to you at the end of the project, please let me know when you send them. Unless you indicate that the diskette(s) must be returned, I will retain them.

If your catalog does not use highlighting of any sort, you may elect to submit the screens as ASCII text. Please contact me first.

Submission of Commentary

Your commentary should provide a brief, coherent discussion of your catalog and its particular strengths, relying on screen images rather than restating information that the images contain. The commentary should be in your own voice, using whatever style you consider appropriate.

The commentary should be at least 1,000 words long, and can be as long as you feel it needs to be. I'm unlikely to use more than 3,000 to 4,000 words on even the most interesting system. If possible, I'll edit by selecting sentences, paragraphs, and sections rather than massively rewriting what you submit.

You can submit the commentary via Bitnet/Internet (to BR.WCC@RLG.BITNET) or you can include it as another file with the images or on a separate diskette.

For MS-DOS computers, Microsoft Word (not Word for Windows) is ideal, but Ventura Publisher can convert files from most versions of WordStar, WordPerfect, XyWrite, Multi-Mate, and Xerox Writer 2. If you use Lotus Manuscript, DisplayWrite, Volkswriter, Office Writer, WordStar 2000, Samna Word or any other program that can produce DCA Revisable Form Text export files, I can use them as well. If using Word for Windows, export regular Word files.

If in doubt or if using a word processor that doesn't produce files equivalent to one of these, export the file in plain ASCII, which every word processor should be able to do; leave blank lines between paragraphs.

For Macintosh computers, plain ASCII is best.

An accompanying printed version will be helpful.

Deadlines

Proposed contributions for a given year's edition of *The Catalog Collection*—which will form the basis for the next edition of *The Online Catalog Book,* if any—must reach me by *December 31* of the previous year. If you wish to see the draft chapter before it is published, the contribution must reach me by *November 30* of the previous year.

Address

All diskettes and accompanying materials should be sent to me at RLG: Walt Crawford, c/o RLG, 1200 Villa Street, Mountain View, CA 94041-1100. Bitnet/Internet messages should be sent to BR.WCC@RLG.BITNET. Phone: (415) 691-2227 (direct). Fax: (415) 964-0943.

And now, on to the fun part . . .

You know your online catalog. Now that you've slogged through the details that will make this all work, the rest should be fun; you get to present some of the more interesting parts of your system to help inspire librarians for years to come. Enjoy!

Part 1: Common Information

Starting Out

☐ Show the opening screen or screens; indicate how it is reached (time-out? Start key, Stop key?).

☐ If there's an initial "quick-start" information screen for new users, show it or them.

☐ Show a context-sensitive help screen (if you have them) while carrying out the searches and displays.

☐ Show the online tutorial for Boolean logic, if you have one, or some other interesting online tutorial.

Rhapsody in Blue; [Author and Subject]: Martin Luther King, Jr.

If your database has appropriate information, use both of these searches as appropriate. *Don't do all the steps for both.* Do all of them for *Rhapsody in Blue* (if that works) and interesting ones for Martin Luther King, Jr.; if your database won't give good results with *Rhapsody in Blue*, do the full sequence for Martin Luther King, Jr.

- If the database includes a fair number of sound recordings, use George Gershwin's *Rhapsody in Blue* as the basis for this sequence (assuming you'll get at least two performances). If there are enough different versions so that the final result will be more than six items, narrow the result to compact disc versions.

- Use Martin Luther King, Jr. (as both author and subject), in all media. If the final result will be more than six items, narrow the result to items in English, published between 1980 and 1985.

Search Process
- ☐ Show the most efficient means of locating the CD versions of George Gershwin's *Rhapsody in Blue*.

- For Martin Luther King, Jr.,
  ☐ show authority information, if it's available and interesting (which form is used?).
  ☐ show the best search or easiest search to get the results suggested above.

Multiple-Result Display(s); Sorting Options
- ☐ Show the first screen of one of the multiple results, in default order.
- ☐ Show other sort orders if available.

Single-Result Display(s): All (Labeled, Citation, Short, Long, MARC)
Show each available display option, e.g.:
- ☐ brief
- ☐ labeled
- ☐ long
- ☐ brief with holdings
- ☐ citation-style
- ☐ MARC tagged

If you have it, use CBS Masterworks MK 42240 (Gershwin on piano, Michael Tilson Thomas conducting); if not, use one that "looks interesting."
- ☐ Show long and labeled display options for an "interesting" book or visual material by or about Martin Luther King, Jr.; if you're not using *Rhapsody in Blue*, show all of them.

Status Information &c.
- ☐ Show the status information for one of these items, if available.
- ☐ Show how you'd recall the item, if that's possible.
- ☐ Show how you'd check it out, if that's possible.
- ☐ Find something with multiple locations and copies; show how the information is displayed.

Related Works
- ☐ Can you get other George Gershwin works easily from the single-record result?
- ☐ Other things conducted by the same conductor?
- ☐ Other works on one of the same subjects as the Martin Luther King, Jr. item you displayed?

Error Handling
- ☐ What happens if you try to display a record beyond the end of the result set, e.g., "item 12" when there are only 10 items?
- ☐ What happens if you make a spelling error in searching, e.g., Martin Luther Kign, Jr., or *Rapsody in Blue?*

NOTE

Many of the questions or aspects covered below may already be covered in these first two processes, in which case they should not be repeated.

Boolean Logic and Approximate Information

- ☐ Show aspects of Boolean logic support not already covered, e.g., multiple title words, author-title searching, etc.
- ☐ There's a book something like *Fire on the Moon*. Do you have it? (Actually *Of a Fire on the Moon* by Norman Mailer.) How did you find it?

Known-Item Searching

☐ Show me the fastest possible route to a full (labeled or otherwise) display of *Vineland* by Thomas Pynchon. (If you don't have that, try *Foundation and Empire* by Isaac Asimov, or some other known item.)

Browsing

If you haven't already done so, and your system supports it,

☐ Show me a browse screen of authors in the vicinity of Thomas Pynchon, with that name highlighted.

☐ Subjects like Desktop publishing? (Is there a hierarchical display?)

☐ "Shelflist browsing" in the area of Z678.9 or 686.2?

☐ Other interesting browse capabilities?

Display of Nonbook Information

Show the "best" display options (long labelled is good, if available) for three or four of these, as appropriate for your collection:

☐ Microsoft Works or some other commercial software *or*

☐ a fully cataloged machine-readable database

☐ a videocassette or (better) videodisk, e.g. *Field of Dreams*

☐ a score or collection, e.g., *The Compleat Beatles* or J. S. Bach's Mass in B Minor (and how did you find the latter?)

☐ any interesting map

☐ a serial such as *PC/Computing*, and the search required to find it (note the slash!)

☐ an archival record, if available in your catalog

Leaving the Catalog

☐ Show any special aspect to ending a session.

Part 2: Special Areas

This includes anything interesting about your catalog that hasn't already been covered. For example:

☐ *Unusual indexes and access points*—what they are and how they work (some combination of screens and commentary).

☐ *Maneuvering: help, tutorials, commands*—aspects of the user interface not really covered above.

☐ *Alternative modes*—if your catalog offers more than one mode of operation, show parts of both (or all three, etc.) and discuss how people move between them.

☐ *Citations*—if your catalog offers any article-level information, show one or two typical items (or one item in all available display formats).

☐ *Other forms of information*—show examples of, and discuss, additional forms of information available through the online catalog.

☐ *Printing*—if there are special provisions for printing (formatted bibliographies? offline printing? screen printers only?), note them. Illustrate if appropriate.

☐ *Downloading*—if there are special provisions, mention them.

☐ *Electronic reference*—can patrons submit reference questions through an online catalog interface? If so, how does it work?

☐ *Anything else*—but only parts of the system designed for use by patrons, not those reserved for staff.

(The submission page, which includes a copyright assignment, followed in the original mailing.)

13

The Assistant
at Arkansas Supreme Court Library

Jacqueline S. Wright and Timothy N. Holthoff

The authors of this chapter are the librarian and assistant librarian at the Supreme Court Library in Little Rock, Arkansas. The library serves judges, lawyers and the general public seeking information about state and federal laws. The collection consists primarily of law materials and a large selection of Arkansas state and federal government documents. Also included are a number of general reference materials such as dictionaries, directories, histories, and the like.

The searches used in this chapter are different from those recommended for this book because of the special character of the collection. However, we have attempted to address the same issues.

Overview

The Assistant is an online integrated catalog by Library Automation Products, Inc. It is designed to operate on single microcomputer units or networked workstations. It is programmed in "C" for speed. Menus and pop-up windows are elegantly designed for the untutored user. In the most complicated search the user is never allowed to get lost. The Escape key is always available to go back a step.

Starting and Stopping

The opening screen is available to patrons at all times (Figure 13.1). It shows the search fields in the window on the right and a help window on the bottom. It may be used with a color or a monochrome monitor.

If a patron attempts to exit the catalog a window appears with a flashing statement that access is denied (Figure 13.2). When a key is touched the catalog is again ready for a search.

Searching

A search field may be selected using the cursor. Author, title and subject fields take the user to the appropriate place in the alphabet within the selected list. From there the user may cursor up or down through the entire alphabetic array.

Keyword fields allow the person to find any word within the field. An author, for instance, may be found using either the first or last name in the author keyword field.

The author keyword field may also be used when there are several authors of the same name but the user does not know which one to select. In Figures 13.3 through 13.6 the user is looking for a monograph about the law of evidence written by Weinstein.

Three Weinsteins resulted from the Author search in Figure 13.3. But by selecting the author keyword field, the catalog takes the user directly to any work created by any author with the last name Weinstein (Figures 13.4 and 13.5). Notice also that the system truncates; therefore only part of the word needs to be keyed.

The user may cursor to the desired record and view it by touching the Enter key; or may select any record then use the Page Up or Page Down keys to view the others in succession. When the last record is reached the system tells the viewer (Figure 13.6).

Errors

A spelling error in the author, title, or subject fields takes the user to that part of the alphabetic array (Figure 13.7). Such an error in a keyword field usually results in no record found (Figure 13.8). The search term remains on display so the user has an opportunity to find the error.

Known Titles

A title search for a known title, *The Law of Real Property*, results in three possible hits (Figure 13.9). This is not unusual in a law library because multiple editions are commonplace and all previous editions are kept in the active collection. The patron may select a record then follow the directions in the help window to cursor up or down to the other records (for example, Figure 13.10).

Works By and About a Person

Blackstone, the ancient English law writer, was selected as a substitute for Martin Luther King, Jr. (not represented in the collection). The patron may use a combination of author, title, and subject; or author keyword, title keyword, and subject keyword fields to find works by or about a person, but a more efficient search is done using the global keyword search (Figure 13.11). This will find the word "Blackstone" anyplace in any of the records in the catalog. Five records are found and the titles are displayed in the window (Figure 13.12).

A look at the Blackstone subject headings shows two authorities (Figure 13.13). Notice that when the result is longer than the 45-character window the remainder may be viewed below the window by moving the cursor.

Display

Records may be displayed three ways. The familiar catalog card format has been shown. We will go back for another look at *The Law of Real Property* to see the other formats. The second format, a long record, includes some information not shown on the card format, such as when it was last updated. Also, the search terms are highlighted on the long record (Figure 13.14). The setup permits changes in the labels. For example, "Collation" could be presented as "Pagination" or "PAGINATION." The third screen is the MARC format (Figure 13.15). The user may change the display by touching the F1 key.

We are not able to show circulation information because this library, like many law libraries, does not circulate the collection. We do, however, have duplicate titles housed in a number of different locations. These are indicated by a call number prefix and/or a location in the catalog. This information is displayed on the long form of the record. Weinstein's *Evidence* is a good example. Because the record is longer than the screen we followed the help window directions and scrolled down to see the remainder (the second screen appears as Figure 13.16).

Boolean Logic and Approximate Information

Boolean connectors may be used to narrow the search when the terms may call up too many records. An example is an author keyword (when the last name of the author is known) combined with a global keyword.

After the first search term is entered (Figure 13.17), the user may select "and," "or," "not," a date restriction or "location" to delimit a search (Figures 13.18 and 13.19).

Another way this search may be done is using the command line search. This way all of the words and connectors may be keyed in at once without selecting from the menu. The search above is formatted as shown in Figure 13.20. The parenthetical "A" indicates the first word is an author. The second word defaulted to a global keyword because no indicator was used.

The indicators *are* case sensitive; therefore if lowercase letters are used for the indicators "(A)" the result will be a "no hit."

The system keeps the command line searches in memory indefinitely so that the user may return to make changes.

This system allows flexible searching for records where the words in the title may not be remembered exactly.

Browsing

Shelflist browsing is useful to our patrons. They may find only one book using other search methods, but may find others by using the shelflist. Once there, the patron may page through the records to examine the collection.

The same routine may be used with the subject field. We paste a shelflist card with the trac-

ings in the front of each of our monographs. This allows the user who has found something of interest to use the assigned subject headings as convenient entries into the online catalog.

Nonbook Information

Information about nonbook items is limited only by the imagination of the cataloger. We have cataloged such things as a CD-ROM disc, maps, serials, and we include the tables of contents for a few locally published serials.

Saving Information

Lists of titles retrieved may be saved to disk or to the printer. The output includes full title, author, call number and location. They are displayed alphabetically by title. A sample printout appears in Figure 13.21.

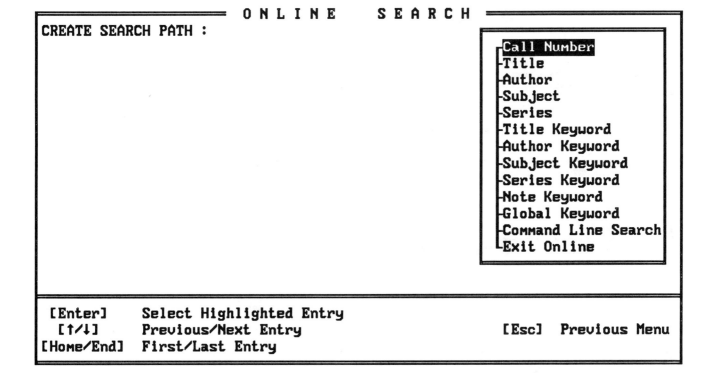

Figure 13.1: Assistant: Main menu

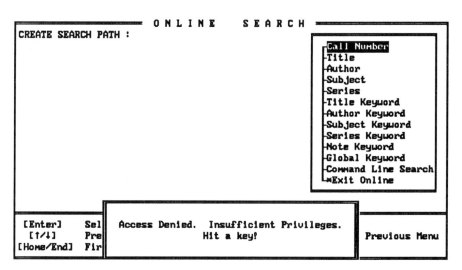

Figure 13.2: Assistant: Password protection

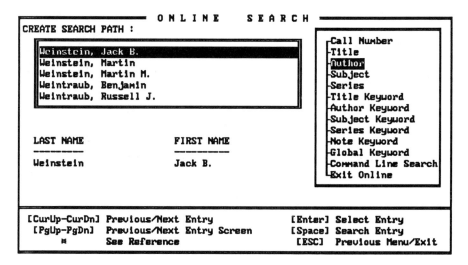

Figure 13.3: Assistant: Author search (browse)

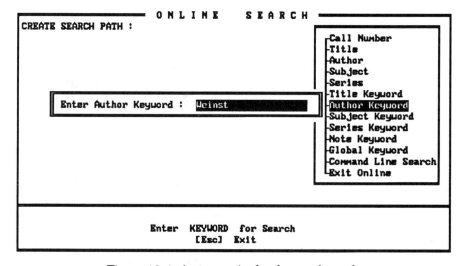

Figure 13.4: Assistant: Author keyword search

```
════════════════ O N L I N E    S E A R C H ════════════════
┌─────────────────────────────────────────────────┐
│ ┌─────────────────────────────────────────────┐ │
│ │ An Analysis of the Tax Reform Act of 1986   │ │      Total Records Found :
│ │ Summary of American law                     │ │
│ │ Weinstein's Evidence                        │ │              3
│ │ *** Last Entry ***                          │ │
│ │                                             │ │
│ └─────────────────────────────────────────────┘ │
│                                                 │
│                                                 │
│                                                 │
│   Title :  An Analysis of the Tax Reform Act    │
│            of 1986                              │
│                                                 │
│                                                 │
│                                                 │
├─────────────────────────────────────────────────┤
│  [Enter]        Select Highlighted Entry        │
│  [PgUp-PgDn]    Previous/Next Entry Screen       [Esc]   Previous Menu/Exit
│  [CurUp-CurDn]  Previous/Next Entry              │
└─────────────────────────────────────────────────┘
```

Figure 13.5: Assistant: Author keyword result

```
═══════════════════════ DISPLAY ═══════════════════════
Main Title : Weinstein's Evidence
Subtitle   : commentary on rules of evidence for the United States courts
             and magistrates
Authorship : by Jack B. Weinstein and Margaret A. Berger.
Publisher  : M. Bender
City       : [New York]
Date       : 1975                      Year  : 1975
Collation  : 5v. in 7 (loose-leaf) ; 26 cm.
Edition    :                           Date Modified: 06/12/75
ISBN/ISSN  :                           LCCN  : 72-97503//r872
Author     : Weinstein, Jack B.
             Berger, Margaret┌──────────────────┐
Subject    : Evidence (Law) -│                  │
Add. Title : Evidence.       │  Last  Record    │
                             │  Hit a key!      │
   Location                  └──────────────────┘
├─────────────────────────────────────────────────┤
│   [F1]        Toggle Display Format      [Alt-F]  Save to File
│   [↑/↓]       Scroll Record Up/Down      [Alt-P]  Print Record
│ [PgUp/PgDn]   Previous/Next Record        [Esc]   Previous Menu
```

Figure 13.6: Assistant: End-of-result message

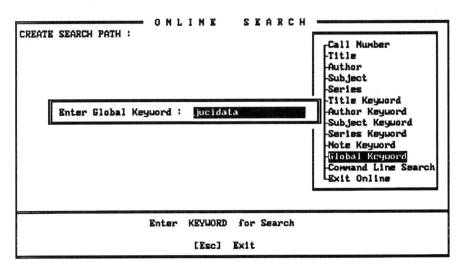

Figure 13.7: Assistant: Spelling error

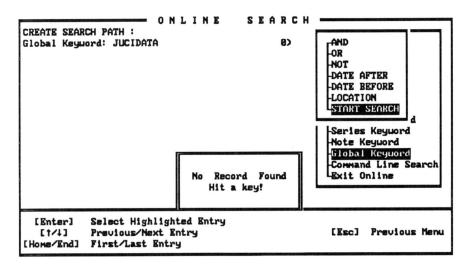

Figure 13.8: Assistant: Result of spelling error

Figure 13.9: Assistant: Title search and result

```
══════════════════ DISPLAY ══════════════════
        Tiffany, Herbert Thorndike
KF          The law of real property / by Herbert Thorndike Tiffany.-- 3d ed.
570      -- Wilmette, Ill., : Callaghan, 06.
.T54        6 v. 25 cm.
1939

            Spine title: Tiffany real property.
            Published in Chicago (1939-<1975 >>.
            Kept up to date by pocket supplements and revised vols.


            1. Real property - United States.   I. Callaghan and Company. II.
         Jones, Basil. III. Tiffany real property. IV. Title.




──────────────────────────────────────────────
      [F1]        Toggle Display Format        [ALT-F]  Save to File
  [PgUp-PgDn]     Scroll Record Up/Down        [ALT-P]  Print Record
[CurUp-CurDn]     Previous/Next Record         [ESC]    Previous Menu
```

Figure 13.10: Assistant: First of three titles

```
═══════════ O N L I N E    S E A R C H ═══════════
CREATE SEARCH PATH :
Global Keyword: BLACKSTONE                   ┌─AND
                                             ├─OR
                                             ├─NOT
                                             ├─DATE AFTER
                                             ├─DATE BEFORE
                                             ├─LOCATION
                                             └─START SEARCH
                                                              d
                                             ├─Series Keyword
                                             ├─Note Keyword
                                             ├─Global Keyword
                                             ├─Command Line Search
                                             └─Exit Online


──────────────────────────────────────────────
    [Enter]       Select Highlighted Entry
  [Home-End]      First/Last Entry                [Esc]  Previous Menu
[CurUp-CurDn]     Previous/Next Entry
```

Figure 13.11: Assistant: Global keyword search

```
====================== O N L I N E    S E A R C H ======================

   ┌──────────────────────────────────────────┐
   │ The comic Blackstone                      │
   │ Commentaries on the laws of England       │      Total Records Found :
   │ A fragment on government                  │              5
   │ Paralegals                                │
   │ Rape and its victims                      │
   └──────────────────────────────────────────┘



      Title :   The comic Blackstone




   [Enter]    Select Highlighted Entry       [Alt-F]  Search List to File
     [↑/↓]    Previous/Next Entry            [Alt-P]  Search List to Printer
 [PgUp/PgDn]  Previous/Next Entry Screen      [Esc]   Previous Menu
```

Figure 13.12: Assistant: Global keyword result

```
====================== O N L I N E    S E A R C H ======================
 CREATE SEARCH PATH :                              ┌────────────────────┐
   ┌──────────────────────────────────────────┐    │ ┌Call Number        │
   │ Blackstone, William, - Sir, - 1723-1780. -│    │ ├Title              │
   │ Blackstone, William, Sir. - Commentaries--│    │ ├Author             │
   │ Blasphemy - Connecticut                   │    │ ├Subject            │
   │ Blood alcohol                             │    │ ├Series             │
   │ Bolivar, Simon, - 1783-1830               │    │ ├Title Keyword      │
   └──────────────────────────────────────────┘    │ ├Author Keyword     │
                                                    │ ├Subject Keyword    │
                                                    │ ├Series Keyword     │
     Subject : Blackstone, William, - Sir, -        │ ├Note Keyword       │
               1723-1780. - Commentaries on the     │ ├Global Keyword     │
               laws of England                      │ ├Command Line Search│
                                                    │ └×Exit Online       │
                                                    └────────────────────┘

      ×         See Reference              [Enter]  Select Entry
    [↑/↓]       Previous/Next Entry        [Space]  Search Entry
 [PgUp/PgDn]  Previous/Next Entry Screen     [Esc]  Previous Menu/Exit
```

Figure 13.13: Assistant: Subject browse

```
══════════════════════════ DISPLAY ══════════════════════════
║ Main Title : The law of real property                       ║
║ Authorship : by Herbert Thorndike Tiffany.                  ║
║ Publisher  : Callaghan                                      ║
║ City       : Chicago, Ill.,                                 ║
║ Date       : 1940                       Year  : 1940        ║
║ Collation  : xxxvi, 1219 p. 23 cm.                          ║
║ Edition    : New abridged ed           Date Modified: 10/20/89 ║
║ Author     : Tiffany, Herbert Thorndike                     ║
║              Callaghan and Company                          ║
║              Zollman, Carl.                                 ║
║ Subject    : Real property - United States                 ║
║ Note       : Spine title: Tiffany real property.           ║
║ Add. Title : Tiffany real property.                        ║
║                                                             ║
║ Location   : Main Library                                  ║
║ Call Number: KF 570 .T54 1940          Copy #/Volume:      ║
╠═════════════════════════════════════════════════════════════╣
║    [F1]        Toggle Display Format    [Alt-F]  Save to File ║
║    [↑/↓]       Scroll Record Up/Down    [Alt-P]  Print Record ║
║ [PgUp/PgDn]    Previous/Next Record     [Esc]    Previous Menu ║
═══════════════════════════════════════════════════════════════
```

Figure 13.14: Assistant: Full display, book

```
══════════════════════════ DISPLAY ══════════════════════════
║ 050 ▌aKF 570 .T54 1940                                      ║
║ 100 ▌aTiffany, Herbert Thorndike                            ║
║ 245 ▌aThe law of real property /▌cby Herbert Thorndike Tiffany. ║
║ 250 ▌aNew abridged ed                                       ║
║ 260 ▌aChicago, Ill., ▌bCallaghan ▌c1940                     ║
║ 300 ▌axxxvi, 1219 p. 23 cm.                                 ║
║ 500 ▌aSpine title: Tiffany real property.                  ║
║ 650 ▌aReal property - United States                        ║
║ 710 ▌aCallaghan and Company                                ║
║ 700 ▌aZollman, Carl.                                        ║
║ 740 ▌aTiffany real property.                               ║
║                                                             ║
║                                                             ║
║                                                             ║
║                                                             ║
╠═════════════════════════════════════════════════════════════╣
║    [F1]        Toggle Display Format    [Alt-F]  Save to File ║
║    [↑/↓]       Scroll Record Up/Down    [Alt-P]  Print Record ║
║ [PgUp/PgDn]    Previous/Next Record     [Esc]    Previous Menu ║
═══════════════════════════════════════════════════════════════
```

Figure 13.15: Assistant: MARC display, book

```
═══════════════════ DISPLAY ═══════════════════
ISBN/ISSN  :                    LCCN  : 72-97503//r872
Author     : Weinstein, Jack B.
             Berger, Margaret A.
Subject    : Evidence (Law) - United States
Add. Title : Evidence.

  Location                 Total
                           Copies
  Main Library               1
  COURT OF APPEALS LIBRARY   1

Location   : Main Library
Call Number: KF 8935 .W39          Copy #/Volume: 2

Location   : COURT OF APPEALS LIBRARY
Call Number: KF 8935 .W39          Copy #/Volume:
────────────────────────────────────────────────────
   [F1]       Toggle Display Format     [Alt-F]  Save to File
  [↑/↓]       Scroll Record Up/Down     [Alt-P]  Print Record
[PgUp/PgDn]  Previous/Next Record       [Esc]   Previous Menu
```

Figure 13.16: Assistant: Lengthy full display (2)

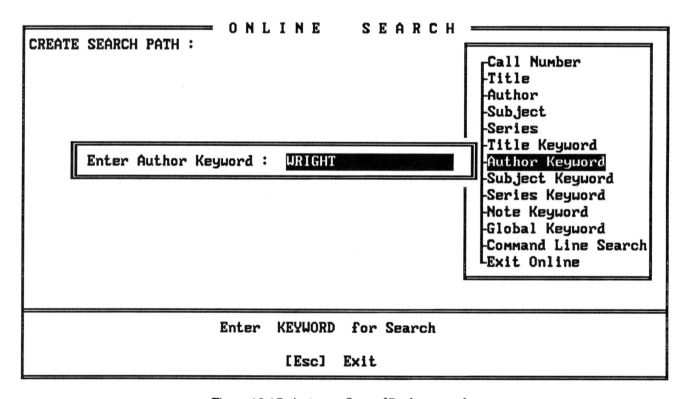

```
═══════════ O N L I N E   S E A R C H ═══════════
CREATE SEARCH PATH :                    ┌─Call Number
                                        ├Title
                                        ├Author
                                        ├Subject
                                        ├Series
                                        ├Title Keyword
   ┌──────────────────────────────┐     ├Author Keyword
   │ Enter Author Keyword :  WRIGHT│     ├Subject Keyword
   └──────────────────────────────┘     ├Series Keyword
                                        ├Note Keyword
                                        ├Global Keyword
                                        ├Command Line Search
                                        └Exit Online
────────────────────────────────────────────────────
              Enter  KEYWORD  for Search

                    [Esc]  Exit
```

Figure 13.17: Assistant: Start of Boolean search

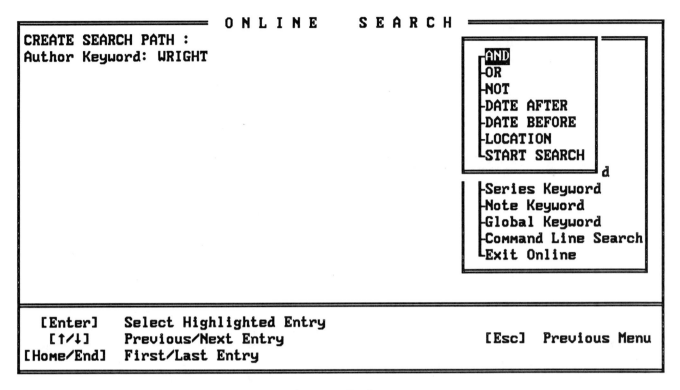

Figure 13.18: Assistant: Boolean prompt menu

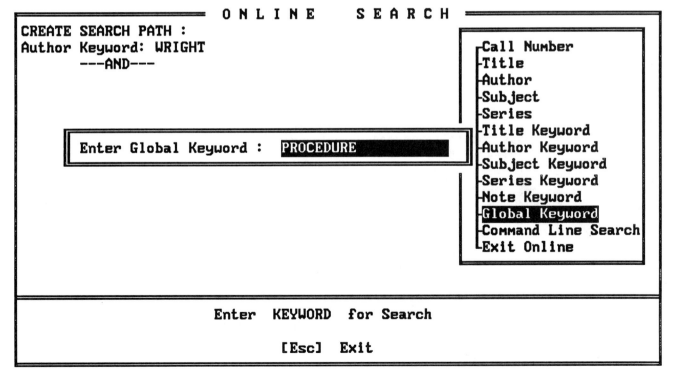

Figure 13.19: Assistant: Finishing Boolean search

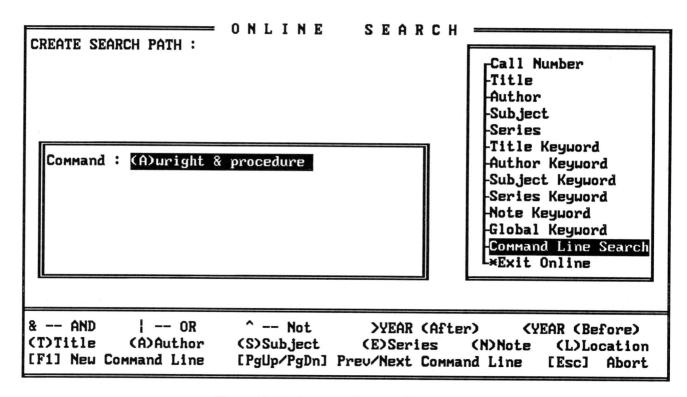

Figure 13.20: Assistant: Command line search

```
Main Title : Arkansas appellate advocacy institute.
Call Number: RR/KFA4155 .A74          Location: Main Library

Main Title : Federal practice and procedure
Author     : Wright, Charles Alan.
Call Number: KF 8840 .W68             Location: Main Library

Main Title : Handbook for appellate advocacy in the
             Arkansas Supreme Court and Court of Appeals
Author     : Wright, Jacqueline S.
Call Number: RR/KFA4155 .W73          Location: Main Library

Main Title : law of federal courts
Author     : Wright, Charles Alan.
Call Number: KF 8840 .W7 1983b        Location: Main Library
```

Figure 13.21: Sample printout

14

BiblioTech®
in a Corporate Library

Stephen C. Lucchetti

BiblioTech® (BT) is the name of the integrated online library system incorporating the online catalog of materials held by Ford Motor Company information centers.[1] Information centers currently indexed in BiblioTech include the Technical Information Section (located in the Scientific Research Laboratory), Electronics Technical Center's Learning Center, and the Quality Education Training Center. Included in the catalog are records for books, journals, journal articles, book analytics, government documents, and audiovisual materials.

BiblioTech requires VT100 terminal emulation. Users come in as DEC VT100 terminals or as PCs or Macintoshes emulating a VT100 using XTalk, ProComm, QModem, etc.

Access

The Technical Information Section's online catalog is authorized for Ford employee use *only*. Access to the system is via dial-up modem (2,400 bps maximum), terminal servers, Ford DECNet,

Internet and Sytek. Searching is available 23½ hours a day, seven days a week, 12:30 A.M. to midnight. In order to provide maximum access to the system, routine system maintenance (except for emergencies) is done on Tuesday mornings from 7:30 to noon as needed.

Figure 14.1 is the first menu users see. The default selection at this screen starts the online catalog. Note that users can also choose to download a bibliography, get Help about the system, or start one of the networked CD-ROM products. A modification of this menu is also available at any time and from *anywhere* within the online catalog by pressing the keystroke sequence Esc-Q.[2]

Starting BiblioTech

Users are encouraged to view the keyboard help (#2) on the master browsing menu (Figure 14.2). One hint for VAX VMS users is that the numeric keypad in BiblioTech has been modeled after the keypad used by the EDT editor. While connected to the online catalog keypad PF1 PF2 gives general help and keypad PF2 gives context-specific help about available options (Figure 14.3). Those

---

1   BiblioTech is a registered trademark of Comstow Information Services, Harvard, Massachusetts. All BiblioTech screens are copyright © 1990 Comstow Information Services. Used with permission. The name BiblioTech is frequently abbreviated as BT in this chapter.

2   Throughout this chapter, "Esc-" followed by a character indicates that the Escape key is pressed, followed by the character noted. These options are discussed later in this chapter.

not using a "real" VT100 terminal must consult their terminal emulator manual for VT100 key locations or contact Technical Information Section's staff for assistance.

BiblioTech is a truly online catalog. Additions, deletions, and corrections to records are made in real time. A user looking for information on a specific topic may get information now and significantly different information 20 minutes from now if new material has been added to the catalog. Item status on the holdings screen may show an item as **In** now but **Out** several minutes from now if someone has checked out the item.

Basic Search Strategy

BiblioTech is searched by browsing specific indexes or via Boolean logic (Figure 14.2). Option 3 (catalog browsing) prompts the user to specify both an index and a display mode. In Figure 14.4, title index and index scan have been marked. The system next asks where to begin scanning the title index. In this case book titles beginning with the word "*Megatrends*" are being searched (Figure 14.5).

BiblioTech now begins displaying titles starting with the word "megatrends" (Figure 14.6). If an entry is *not* located for the specific access point, BT shows the **next** index entry. For each entry BT assigns a reference number AND gives the frequency of usage for that term. In our case all the frequencies are "1" because they are for specific titles. The index may be scanned by pressing the up or down arrow keys or more information on a specific title may be viewed by entering a reference number and then specifying either short or full display.

Short citation display (Figure 14.7) includes information on 3 or 4 specific items. Included in this display are index entry, what the item is (book, document/report, periodical, journal article, book analytic), author, title, publication date, and call number. The index may be scanned for other materials by pressing the arrow keys, or a specific entry may be expanded by entering the reference number and selecting full display.

Figures 14.8 and 14.9 show part of the full information display for the book *Megatrends:2000*.

The holdings screen (Figure 14.9) displays information about which branches own an item, how many copies, format, in-house status, and shelving location. In this case note that two branches are reporting as owning the item. The Engineering and Research Library (Technical Information Section) has two copies one of which is **Out** and the other is **In** but only for reference use. The Learning Center is reporting as having a single copy **On order** but which will be circulatable when received and processed. All material ordered for the library is controlled by BiblioTech and has at least minimal records entered into the system when ordered. Note again that the up and down arrow keys allow a browser to move through an index now looking at full citations.

Other indexes from the BT browsing menu (Figure 14.4) are searched in the same fashion as the title index. Note the existence of indexes for both subject word and subject heading. Also note the presence of a call number index. The call number index allows users to find a single *interesting* book and then take the call number for that book and electronically walk through the library looking for similar books. Specifically located in this way are those books that are always in circulation due to heavy demand and might only rarely if ever be found in the stacks with a manual search.

Figures 14.10 and 14.11 show two of the BT screens for a journal. Full display, page 2 (Figure 14.10), displays holdings information as the first note in the scope note. Note that the copy screen (Figure 14.11) tells you what branches subscribe to a journal, how many copies, format, etc. A particularly valuable bit of information displayed on the holdings screen is the last issue received.

Boolean Searching

Searching with the logical operators AND, OR, and AND NOT is available through Boolean Searching, option 4 on the BT main menu (Figure 14.2). In this mode one first chooses a search option (Figure 14.12) then follows the directions in setting up the search. Figure 14.13 shows how to search for a videocassette version of *Megatrends*. A single term is placed on each line, then a Boolean operator is selected. The figure also shows the results, indicating that a single record was found. Selecting the display option takes one into the BT display mode, which functions as in index searching.

When a Boolean subject search is performed all words in both the subject and title index are searched and the system automatically truncates all entries. In this specific example neither "megatrends" nor "videocassette" was entered in its entirety. Note that truncation makes it easier to search for conference proceedings (where one isn't ever too clear about what the title really will be) and for materials where you don't really know what the title is. For example, suppose someone was looking for a book title something like *Ten new directions for* . . . Each word is too common to search on the title word index. However Boolean subject searching quickly finds two books with these three words in the title. *Ten new directions* is the beginning of the subtitle for *Megatrends*.

Authority and Thesaurus Control

BiblioTech supports authority and thesaurus control for personal name, corporate name, subject heading, and series title. Figure 14.14 shows the BT input screen for scanning a subject heading with the subject Ford entered. Pressing Return at this screen takes the user to a display screen for Ford as a subject heading. Entering "Ford" and then pressing Esc-T takes the user into the subject heading thesaurus at the term FORD. Figure 14.15 shows a subject heading thesaurus screen starting at the term Ford.

The thesaurus supports the following relationships: NT (narrower term), BT (broader term), RT (related term), USE (don't use this term), UF (used for), and SN (scope note). In this case "Ford Motor Co." is *not* an acceptable term and refers to "Ford Motor Company." Entering the appropriate number on the thesaurus screen allows entries to be plucked from the screen and automatically input into the search field at which Esc-T had been pressed.

Bibliography Creation

While searching BiblioTech custom bibliographies may be created by pressing Esc-F, selecting an item(s) to be written to the ASCII file and specifying a file name (Figure 14.16). BT then informs the user what the actual bibliography will be named (Figure 14.17). Individual items, all items currently displayed on a screen, all items indexed to a specific term, or all items in a Boolean generated set can be saved to a bibliography. The name of the bibliography may be changed each time Esc-F is pressed or the default of the last name may be taken. Figure 14.25 shows what a BiblioTech bibliography looks like. Downloading of bibliographies will be discussed later.

Esc-Q Options[3]

At any point in BiblioTech, pressing Esc-Q pauses BiblioTech and gives users the ability to select a number of options, as in Figure 14.1. The default here (pressing Return) takes the user back to BT exactly where they had been, whether at a menu or deep within a specific record.

Help is a TIS-written program based on the VAX help system. It provides structured help about BiblioTech, Ford information centers and information centers around Michigan (Figure 14.19). Figures 14.20 and 14.21 demonstrate part of how a user can go deeper and deeper into the help program, receiving more and more detailed information.

Bibliography is chosen to download ASCII formatted bibliographies saved in BiblioTech or in any of the networked CD-ROM databases. Figures 14.22 and 14.23 demonstrate portions of the program flow. Once the program prompts for a file name to download it pauses and instructs users to turn on their printer function or to turn on their file-save utility. At that point, once Return is pressed the file scrolls across the screen in ASCII format for printing or saving. When done scroll-

---

3 Esc-Q options are programs customized by the Ford Motor Company, Technical Information Section. These programs demonstrate the abilities of BiblioTech and the VAX VMS operating system to pause operation of one program, execute another program, then return to the home operation.

ing, the program posts a reminder to turn printing or file-save off. Bibliographies are maintained for a minimum of 24 hours before being deleted.

CD-ROM Databases

Using third-party hardware and software, TIS has implemented network access to CD-ROM databases. The only user requirement is VT100 (or equivalent) terminal emulation. Our system translates all CD-ROM PC program screen writes into VT100 screen draw commands, and in turn translates all VT100 keyboard sequences into PC keystroke sequences.

After selecting the CD-ROM option from the Esc-Q menu the user is presented with a menu of available CD-ROM databases (Figure 14.24). Once a specific database has been selected help on that database and on keystroke sequence translations is presented so that users are aware of how to enter, move around, save bibliographies, and exit the CD-ROM program. Figures 14.25 through 14.29 show portions of the screen progression as Engineering Index (Compendex) is selected, XTALK is indicated as the terminal emulator, and the first EI searching screen appears. Note that for users who have already viewed help a route around help is described.

While connected to a CD-ROM all printing is spooled to a file on our system. When a user exits, the system looks to see if printing has occurred. If printing has been done, the user is asked to supply an 8-character name for the bibliography. The name of the specific CD-ROM is then prefixed to the supplied name and the user may then use the bibliography option from the system menu to download the ASCII data file into his or her own system. Printouts are in whatever format the program and/or the user have specified.

When exiting the CD-ROM program users back through menus accepting default options until they are returned to BiblioTech *exactly* where they had been prior to pressing Esc-Q. This provides a tremendous amount of synergy. A user may perform a Boolean subject search in BT and then begin scanning the set of documents located. In the course of looking at books they might find a 1985 book on exactly what they are looking for. Very quickly they can start Engineering Index and look up that author to see if the author has published anything more recent. When done with EI they can they return to BT and continue browsing in the specific set for other relevant information.

Mail

Another BT main menu option is mail. Mail is an implementation of the VAX VMS mail utility. In the future mail-help will be rewritten so that users get the type and amount of help appropriate for low-level users. To date, users have been encouraged to send information about problems, difficulties, or comments to us via e-mail. In the future we hope to use mail more for transmittal of search requests, document delivery and interlibrary loan requests, etc.

Exiting

Users exit at the main menu (Figure 14.2) by selecting option 1. As they exit they are asked if they really want to exit or if they would like to restart BiblioTech.

```
                    Ford -- Technical Information Section
                           System Startup Options

PRESS
KEY      OPTION                    ACTION

<CR>                      Start BiblioTech

 B      BIBLIOGRAPHY     Print a BiblioTech or CDROM bibliography

 C      CDROM            ENGINEERING INDEX, Applied Science & Technology
                            Index, or Business Periodicals Index searching
                            using CD-ROM optical disk databases.

 E      EXIT             EXIT/LOGOFF system

 H      HELP             Help about BiblioTech, Ford information centers
                            using BT, document delivery, etc.

***     NOTE: Pressing <Escape>Q while in BiblioTech allows you to branch to
              a menu providing access to the CD-ROM program, get HELP, or print a
              bibliography.
Please select (<CR>,B,C,E,H) :
```

Figure 14.1: BiblioTech: Initial screen

```
BiblioTech Library System (version 5.0)          Master Searching Menu
                                                 General Help
  MASTER SEARCHING MENU

  Displays the options for several methods of searching through the
  on-line catalog.

  For assistance with the menu options for the Master Searching Menu, exit
  from Help and press <PF2> at the "Selection:" prompt.




Press RETURN key to exit help facility
```

Figure 14.2: BiblioTech: Master searching help

```
BiblioTech Library System (version 5.0)          Master Searching Menu
                                                 Specific Help
  MENU SELECTION

  Displays the menu options for searching through the on-line catalog.

    1. To exit from BiblioTech and return to the VAX/VMS system level,
       exit from Help and select "1. exit," then press <RETURN>.

    2. For descriptions of special individual key, control key and escape
       key functions, exit from Help and select "2. keyboard help," then
       press <RETURN>.

    3. To browse the on-line catalog, exit from Help and select "3.
       catalog browsing," then press <RETURN>.

    4. To perform more precise searching with Boolean operators, exit
       from Help and select "4. catalog boolean searching," then press
       <RETURN>.

    5. To use the VAX/VMS MAIL utility, exit from Help and select "5.
       VAX/VMS MAIL," then press <RETURN>.
Press RETURN key to exit help facility
```

Figure 14.3: BiblioTech: Specific help

```
FORD Online BiblioTech Library System          Catalog Browsing Menu

        Indexes:                    Display Modes:

        1. computer ID (CID)        1. index scan
        2. personal name            2. short citation
        3. corporate name           3. full citation
        4. title
        5. word in title            Display Mode:  1
        6. subject heading
        7. word in subject heading
        8. report no.
        9. series title
        10. word in series
        11. call number (shelf list)
        12. report identifier
        13. ISBN
        14. ISSN

        Index:  4_


Press M. or (CTRL/Z) for Master Searching Menu.
```

Figure 14.4: BiblioTech: Catalog browsing menu

```
FORD Online BiblioTech Library System          Catalog Browsing

                        Title

Enter starting position:   MEGATRENDS_____








Press (CTRL/Z) for Catalog Browsing Menu.
```

Figure 14.5: BiblioTech: Title browse entry

```
FORD Online BiblioTech Library System          Catalog Browsing
                  Scanning the Title index

Ref. no. Freq.     Index entry
   1      1     MEGATRENDS 2000: TEN NEW DIRECTIONS
   2      1     MEGATRENDS. (VIDEOCASSETTE)
   3      1     MEGATRENDS: TEN NEW DIRECTIONS TRAN
   4      1     MEKHANIZM ZHIDKOFAZNOGO OKISLENIIA
   5      1     MELTING AND CRYSTAL STRUCTURES.
   6      1     MELTING OF PLASTICS BY THE USE OF R
   7      1     MELTING POINT TABLES OF ORGANIC COM
   8      1     MEMBERSHIP DIRECTORY.
   9      1     MEMBERSHIP DIRECTORY: AMERICAN PHYS
  10      1     MEMBRANE - BASED WATER - AND ENERGY
  11      1     MEMBRANE PROCESSES IN INDUSTRY AND
  12      1     MEMBRANE SCIENCE AND TECHNOLOGY: IN
  13      1     MEMBRANE TECHNOLOGY AND INDUSTRIAL
  14      1     MEMBRANE ULTRAFILTRATION TO TREAT L

M. Master Menu 1. - 14. display citation 20. scan forward 21. scan back  1_
(S)hort or (F)ull citation?    S
Press (CTRL/Z) to re-enter choice.
```

Figure 14.6: BiblioTech: Title browse

```
┌──────────────────────────────────────────────────────────────────────┐
│FORD Online BiblioTech Library System              Catalog Browsing     │
│                    Short citations -- Title                            │
│1. MEGATRENDS 2000: TEN NEW DIRECTIONS   Book            CID: 23707     │
│   Naisbitt, John  Megatrends 2000: ten new directions for the 1990s.  John Na*│
│   1990  CIR 306.0973 N151                                             │
│                                                                        │
│2. MEGATRENDS. <VIDEOCASSETTE>          Document/report    CID: 21748   │
│   Megatrends. <Videocassette> 1985                                    │
│                                                                        │
│3. MEGATRENDS: TEN NEW DIRECTIONS TRAN   Book            CID: 3535      │
│   Naisbitt, John  Megatrends: ten new directions transforming our lives.  Joh*│
│   1982  CIR 306.0973 N15                                              │
│                                                                        │
│4. MEKHANIZM ZHIDKOFAZNOGO OKISLENIIA    Book            CID: 2938      │
│   Denisov, Evgenii Timofeevich.  Liquid-phase oxidation of oxygen-containing  │
│      compounds / E. * 1977  CIR 547.23 D39                           │
│                                                                        │
│M. Master Menu   1. - 4. display citation  20. scan forward  21. scan back   1_│
│(I)ndex or (F)ull citation? F                                          │
│Press <CTRL/Z> to re-enter choice.                                     │
└──────────────────────────────────────────────────────────────────────┘
```

Figure 14.7: BiblioTech: Short citations, title

```
┌──────────────────────────────────────────────────────────────────────┐
│FORD Online BiblioTech Library System              Catalog Browsing     │
│                        Title Search                                    │
│Full citation: Book                                        Page 1      │
│CID: 23707                    Key: MEGATRENDS 2000: TEN NEW DIRECTIONS  │
│Call no.:CIR 306.0973 N151                                             │
│                                                                        │
│Security class.:                                                       │
│Main author:      Naisbitt, John                                       │
│Title statement:  Megatrends 2000: ten new directions for the 1990s.  John│
│                  Naisbitt and Patricia Aburdene.                      │
│Publisher:        Morrow                                               │
│Place of pub.:    NY                                                   │
│Pagination:       384 p.                                               │
│                                                                        │
│Pub. date:        1990              Edition:                           │
│ISBN:             0-688-07224-0     OCLC:                              │
│Vendor No.:                                                            │
│                                                                        │
│M. Master Menu        4. prev record      7. change index/mode         │
│2. display pg. 2      5. next record      8. display copies            │
│3. display pg. 3      6. short citation   9. index scan          2_    │
│Press <DOWN> arrow to scan forward, <UP> arrow to scan back.           │
│Press <CTRL/Z> once to change start, twice for Catalog Browsing Menu.  │
└──────────────────────────────────────────────────────────────────────┘
```

Figure 14.8: BiblioTech: Full display, book (1)

```
┌──────────────────────────────────────────────────────────────────────┐
│FORD Online BiblioTech Library System              Catalog Browsing     │
│                        Display Copies                                  │
│Megatrends 2000: ten new directions for the 1990s.  John Naisbit*  Page 4│
│CID: 23707                                Call no. CIR 306.0973 N151    │
│                                                                        │
│                        Branch: EngResLib                              │
│                                                                        │
│Copy acc. no. Fmt. Status Use Site Part number  Vol. number  Vol. date │
│no.                        loc.                                         │
│──── ──────── ──── ────── ──── ──── ───────────  ──────────── ──────────│
│1    839381   H    OUT    CIRC BOOK                                     │
│2    123456   H    IN     REF  REFO                                     │
│                                                                        │
│                        Branch: LearningCentr                          │
│                                                                        │
│Copy acc. no. Fmt. Status Use Site Part number  Vol. number  Vol. date │
│no.                        loc.                                         │
│──── ──────── ──── ────── ──── ──── ───────────  ──────────── ──────────│
│1             H    ON ORDER CIRC REFO                                   │
│M. Master Menu 1. more 2. short citation 3. full citation 4. browsing menu│
│Press <DOWN> arrow to scan forward, <UP> arrow to scan back.         1 │
│Press <CTRL/Z> once to change start, twice for Catalog Browsing Menu.  │
└──────────────────────────────────────────────────────────────────────┘
```

Figure 14.9: BiblioTech: Holdings display, book

```
FORD Online BiblioTech Library System          Catalog Browsing
                            Title Search
Full citation: Periodical                              Page 2
CID: 84                    Key: JOURNAL OF THE AMERICAN CERAMIC SOC
Call no.:
 Series nos.:
 Scope notes:    HOLDINGS: v.18- 1935-.!Reports on the development,
                 fabrication, and application of advanced ceramic and
                 composite materials of technological and commercial
                 potential.

 Subject headings: Ceramics!Periodicals




M. Master Menu        4. prev record        7. change index/mode
1. display pg. 1      5. next record        8. display copies
3. display pg. 3      6. short citation     9. index scan           3_
Press <DOWN> arrow to scan forward, <UP> arrow to scan back.
Press <CTRL/Z> once to change start, twice for Catalog Browsing Menu.
```

Figure 14.10: BiblioTech: Serials display (2)

```
FORD Online BiblioTech Library System          Catalog Browsing
                           Display Copies
American Ceramic Society. Journal. <Current>            Page 4
CID: 84

Branch: EngResLib                            Last issue: AUGUST

Copy acc. no. Fmt. Status Use Site Part number  Vol. number Vol. date
no.                           loc.
---- --------- ---- ------- ---- ---- -------------- -------------- ----------
1             P    IN            JOUR

Branch: ElecTechCntr                         Last issue: AUGUST

Copy acc. no. Fmt. Status Use Site Part number  Vol. number Vol. date
no.                           loc.
---- --------- ---- ------- ---- ---- -------------- -------------- ----------
1             P    IN            JOUR

M. Master Menu 1. more 2. short citation 3. full citation 4. browsing menu
Press <DOWN> arrow to scan forward, <UP> arrow to scan back.         1
Press <CTRL/Z> once to change start, twice for Catalog Browsing Menu.
```

Figure 14.11: BiblioTech: Holdings display, serial

```
FORD Online BiblioTech Library System        Catalog Boolean Searching
Number of records in master set = 0


To start search, type name or number of
option.                                      Options:
                                             --------
Type HELP for help.                          1. SUBJECT
                                             2. DATE
                                             3. PERSON
                                             4. CORP
                                             5. TYPE
                                             6. DISPLAY
                                             7. HELP
                                             8. COMBINE
                   1_____




Press M. or <CTRL/Z> for Master Searching Menu, <ESC><W> for master set
```

Figure 14.12: BiblioTech: Boolean searching menu

```
FORD Online BiblioTech Library System          Catalog Boolean Searching
Number of records in master set = 1

   Type any word or phrase (term) on the first line and each additional term
   on a separate line. When you have finished typing all of your terms, press
   <RETURN>. The system then prompts you to select a boolean operator. Press
   <PF2> for additional help.  Press <ESC><W> to display current master set.

Subject Search:
   MEGATREN_____           3    _____
   VIDEOCASS_____          502   _____

                    _____      _____
                    _____      _____
Total records selected  _____    1    _____


M. Master Menu  1. Display full citations  2. Continue/new criteria
3. Reset master set  4. Save master set              1

Press <CTRL/Z> for Catalog Boolean Searching screen.
```

Figure 14.13: BiblioTech: Boolean search results

```
FORD Online BiblioTech Library System                    Catalog Browsing

                              Subject headings

Enter starting position:    FORD_____









Press <CTRL/Z> for Catalog Browsing Menu.
```

Figure 14.14: BiblioTech: Subject entry

```
FORD Online BiblioTech Library System              Thesaurus Maintenance
          Subject Heading Thesaurus - Authorized terms with relationships

1. Ford   (not dated)
   SN:  Use to identify products of the Ford Motor Company.  For information
        on the company, use Ford Motor Company

2. Ford automobiles  (05/04/87)
   SN:  Used primarily for historical materials covering several Ford
        vehicles.  Use specific model, e.g. Ford Model I, when possible.

3. Ford Edsel   (01/16/90)
      UF:  Edsel automobile

4. Ford Escort   (11/27/90)
      UF:  Escort

5. Ford family   (not dated)

M. Master Menu     1. - 5. to select term    20.change start
Press <DOWN> arrow to scan forward, <UP> arrow to scan back.
Press <CTRL/Z> to select a new starting position.                    _
```

Figure 14.15: BiblioTech: Subject thesaurus (1)

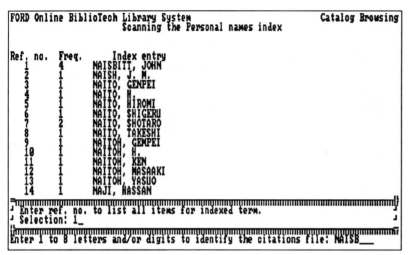

Figure 14.16: BiblioTech: Name for bibliography

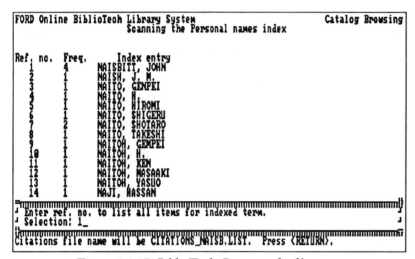

Figure 14.17: BiblioTech: Response for filename

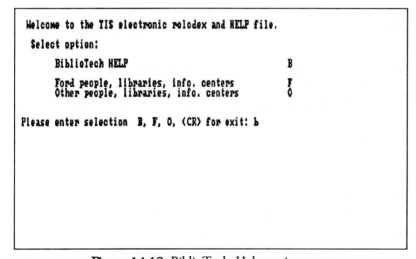

Figure 14.18: BiblioTech: Help, main menu

```
HELP

      HELP has been designed to offer help in using the online technical
          information system available through Ford Motor Company's
          Technical Information Section (TIS).
      Help on a listed topic may be selected by entering either the
          full name of the topic or the minimal numbers of letters to
          uniquely identify the topic.
      Enter a question mark (?) at any time to redisplay the most recently
          displayed text.
      To exit HELP continue pressing <ENTER> until the menu reappears.


  Additional information available:

  BiblioTech Book_Delivery        CDROM      Connect_Req          CTIS
  Doc_Delivery         DPTC       ETC        Help      Holdings  Mail
  Online_searches      Problems   Registration         Terminal_Req
  TIS


Press RETURN to continue ... tis
```

Figure 14.19: BiblioTech: Help for BT, level 1

```
TIS

      TIS (Technical Information Section) is located in Room E2174 of the
      Scientific Research Laboratories in Dearborn, Michigan, at the
      corner of Village and Military Roads.  TIS holdings currently
      loaded into BiblioTech include: ALL books in collection; ALL
      Journal titles in collection (approximately 700 Journals currently
      received); ALL SRL Learning Center materials; technical reports
      added to collection after May 7, 1986; selected Journal articles
      (mostly management related).

      For additional assistance select a topic from the list below:



  Additional information available:

  Qualifiers
  /Holdings  /Hours    /Loans     /Phone_Numbers       /Staff

Press RETURN to continue ... /loans
```

Figure 14.20: BiblioTech: Help for TIS

```
TIS

  /Loans
        TIS materials circulate to all registered Ford personnel.

      Specific loan periods:
                   Books     ==)  3 weeks
                   Reports   ==)  3 weeks
                   Journals  ==)  NO CIRCULATION

TIS Subtopic?
```

Figure 14.21: BiblioTech: Help for TIS/Loans

```
================================================================
 If you created a bibliography while in BiblioTech using <ESC><F>
       or while connected to one of the networked CD-ROM
       programs your bibliography may now be typed out for viewing,
       printing, or downloading .


       Press any character (and return) to view a directory
              of viewable bibliographies.

              Press return to exit.


================================================================
==>: 1
```

Figure 14.22: BiblioTech: Bibliography (1)

```
Total of 10 files.
================================================================
         Enter full name of bibliography to be printed out.

         Press return (with no file named) to EXIT.
================================================================
==> : citations_naisb.list
================================================================
         Toggle printer and/or file save on!

    When ready to receive bibliography press return!

         Press any character, and return to EXIT.
================================================================
==> :
```

Figure 14.23: BiblioTech: Bibliography (3)

```
BiblioTech citations listing
09/20/91 10:55:12

Book                                              CID: 3535
   CIR 306.0973 N15
   Naisbitt, John. Megatrends: ten new directions transforming our lives.
       John Naisbitt. New York, Warner Books, 1982. 290 p. ; 24 cm.

   Includes bibliographical references and index.

Book                                              CID: 6760
   CIR 658.4 N25
   Naisbitt, John. Re-inventing the corporation: transforming your job
       and your company for the new information society.  John Naisbitt,
       Patricia Aburdene. New York, Warner, 1985. xi, 308 p.

   Authors describe an important new trend most observers have missed:
   increasingly severe labor shortages that will create a tight labor
   market for the rest of this century.  The book shows the reader how
   to evaluate his present company in terms of the future.  It gives
   the questions, answers, guidelines, and examples which will enable
   reader to be prepared for the new information society.
```

Figure 14.24: BiblioTech: Bibliography (4)

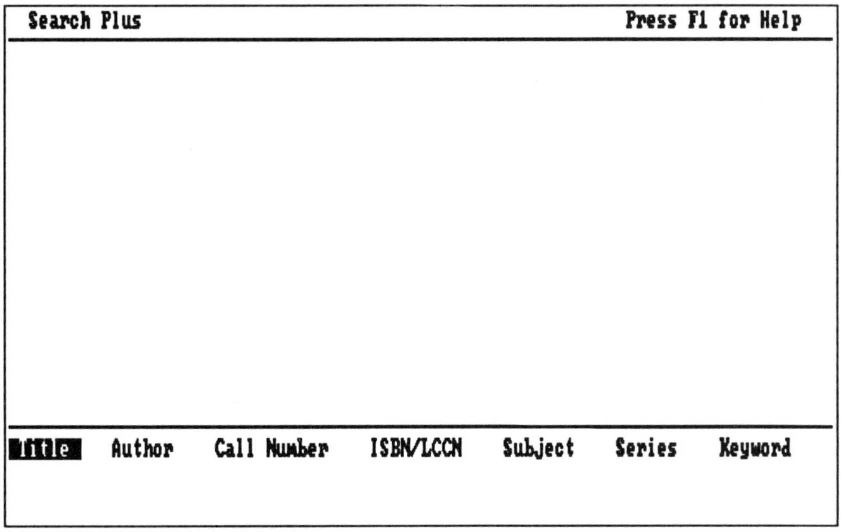

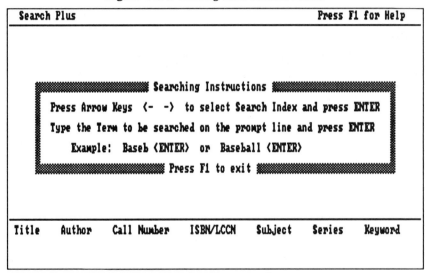

Figure 16.4: Catalog Plus: Search screen

Figure 16.5: Catalog Plus: Search instructions

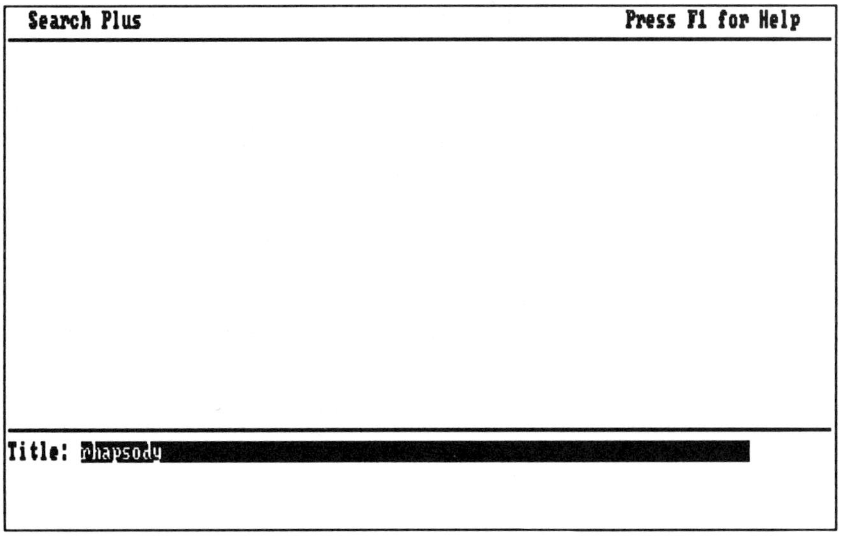

Figure 16.6: Catalog Plus: Title search

```
Search Plus              Titles              Press F1 for Help

  1  Revolution in Central America
  1  Revolution in civil rights
  1  Revolution in nineteenth-century thought
  1  Revolutionaries: agents of change
  1  The revolutionary age of Andrew Jackson
  1  Revolutionary nonviolence
  1  The Revolutionary War
  1  The revolutions in Spanish America : the independence movements of 1808-
  3  Rhapsody in blue
  1  Rhapsody in blue [sound recording]
  1  Rhapsody in blue [sound recording] : An American in Paris / George Gersh
  1  A rhetoric case book
  1  The Rhine
  1  The Rhinemann exchange
  1  Rhode Island
  1  RHODE ISLAND - CHECK VERTICAL FILE FOR MORE INFO ABOUT THIS SUBJECT : AS
```

Figure 16.7: Catalog Plus: Title search browse

```
Search Plus        List is Sorted by Author        Press F1 for Help

Call Number        Title

SR GER 144         Fiedler conducts Gershwin [sound re
SR GER 29          Rhapsody in blue [sound recording]
SR GER 86          Rhapsody in blue [sound recording]











Title: Rhapsody in blue
```

Figure 16.8: Catalog Plus: Titles, sorted result

```
Search Plus        List is Sorted by Author        Press F1 for Help

SR
GER
144
          TITLE: Fiedler conducts Gershwin [sound recording]
    ADDED TITLE: Rhapsody in blue
         AUTHOR: Gershwin, George, 1898-1937
      PUBLISHED: New York: RCA, 1987.
       MATERIAL: 1 compact disc: digital; 4 3/4 in.
           NOTE: Boston Pops Orchestra; Earl Wild, pianist.
        SUBJECT: Orchestral music
        SUBJECT: Concertos (Piano)
        SUBJECT: Piano with orchestra
    ADDED ENTRY: Wild, Earl
    ADDED ENTRY: Fiedler, Arthur, 1894-1979
    ADDED ENTRY: Boston Pops Orchestra

                                            (continued)

Title: Rhapsody in blue
```

Figure 16.9: Catalog Plus: Long display (1 of 2)

```
 Search Plus        List is Sorted by Author        Press F1 for Help

SR
GER
144
             TITLE: Fiedler conducts Gershwin [sound recording]
            AUTHOR: Gershwin, George
         PUBLISHED: RCA, 1987.
          MATERIAL: 1 compact disc.


Copies Available: SR GER 144   (DESK)




_____
Title: Rhapsody in blue
```

Figure 16.10: Catalog Plus: Brief display

```
 Search Plus        List is Sorted by Author        Press F1 for Help

SR
GER
144   ▓▓▓▓▓▓▓▓▓▓▓▓▓▓▓▓ Searching Instructions ▓▓▓▓▓▓▓▓▓▓▓▓▓▓▓▓

      Press ENTER to toggle between BRIEF and FULL record formats

      Press  N  to display next or  L  to display last record
             in a single heading or term

Copie   Press    ↑ ↓  PgUp  PgDn Keys to move the screens

      Press ESC to return to the previous screen

      ▓▓▓▓▓▓▓▓▓▓▓▓▓▓▓▓ Press F1 to exit ▓▓▓▓▓▓▓▓▓▓▓▓▓▓▓▓


_____
Title: Rhapsody in blue
```

Figure 16.11: Catalog Plus: Help for display

```
 Search Plus               Subjects              Press F1 for Help

1  Kikuyu tribe
1  Kilimanjaro, Mount (Tanzania)
2  Killilea, Karen, 1940-
1  Kimbrough, Emily, 1899-
1  King Island Native Community
1  King Philip's War, 1675-1676
1  King snakes
1  King William Island, Canada
7  King, Martin Luther, Jr., 1929-1968
2  King, Stephen, 1947-
1  King, Stephen, 1947----Interviews
1  King, Stephen, 1947---Criticism and interpretation
1  King, Stephen, 1947---History and criticism
1  King, Stephen--History and criticism
2  Kings and rulers--Biography
1  Kings and rulers--Biography--Addresses, essays, lectures
_____


```

Figure 16.12: Catalog Plus: Subject result browse

```
 Search Plus        List is Sorted by Call No.      Press F1 for Help

Call Number        Title

323.4 K            I have a dream : the story of Marti
323.4 M            Martin Luther King, Jr : his life,
B Kin              King : a biography
B Kin              Let the trumpet sound : the life of
B Kin              Martin Luther King, Jr : a document
B Kin              My life with Martin Luther King, Jr
B King             Martin Luther King




 Subject: King, Martin Luther, Jr., 1929-1968

```

Figure 16.13: Catalog Plus: Subject result list

```
 Search Plus        List is Sorted by Call No.      Press F1 for Help

323.4
K
          TITLE: I have a dream : the story of Martin Luther King in text and
                 pictures
      PUBLISHED: New York: [1968].
       MATERIAL: 96 p. illus., ports. 28 cm.
           NOTE: "Parts of this book appeared originally in Time and Life
                 magazines."
        SUBJECT: King, Martin Luther, Jr., 1929-1968

No Copies Available.




 Subject: King, Martin Luther, Jr., 1929-1968

```

Figure 16.14: Catalog Plus: Long display, book

```
Search Plus              Call Numbers            Press F1 for Help
────────────────────────────────────────────────────────────────
 1  684 M           Fundamental wood turning              Milton, Archi
 1  684 Newman      Woodcraft : basic concepts and skills Newman, Thelm
 1  684 O           Woods and woodworking for industrial art Olson, Delmar
 1  684 S           Complete book of wood finishing       Scharff, Robe
 1  684. S          Working in wood : the illustrated manual Scott, Ernest
 1  684.1 S         Contemporary furniture making for everyo Shea, John
 1  684.8 H         Operation of modern woodworking machines Hjorth, Herm
 1  684.8 H         Modern machine woodworking             Holtrop, Wil
 1  686.2 S         Gothic and English alphabets          Solo, Dan
 1  688 M           Historic models of early America      Maginley, C.J
 1  688.7 L         The shop on High Street : the toys and g Loeper, John
 1  690 Macaulay    Pyramid                               Macaulay, Dav
 1  690 Macaulay    Unbuilding                            Macaulay, Dav
 1  690 N           The craftsman in America              National Geog
 1  690.69 K        Careers in the building trades        Kasper, Sydne
 1  691.7 C         Steel beams & iron men                Cherry, Mike
────────────────────────────────────────────────────────────────
```

Figure 16.15: Catalog Plus: Call number browse

```
Search Keywords                   ESC: Search Plus Main Menu
────────────────────────────────────────────────────────────────
Results           Words/Phrases              Searchable Fields

            ┌─────────────────────────────┐
            │ foundation                  │     All Fields
            └─────────────────────────────┘
                        AND
            ┌─────────────────────────────┐
            │ empire                      │     All Fields
            └─────────────────────────────┘

            ┌─────────────────────────────┐
            │                             │
            └─────────────────────────────┘

Limiters:   ┌─────────────────────────────┐
            │ Publishing Year from: 1900  to: 1991 │
            │ Reading Level from:   0.0   to: 14.9 │
            └─────────────────────────────┘
────────────────────────────────────────────────────────────────
<F1> Help <F3> New Search <F5> View Stop Words <F7> View Keywords <F10> Search
     Use <ESC> to Stop a Search and <TAB> to select Searchable Fields
```

Figure 16.16: Catalog Plus: Keyword search

```
Search Keywords                          ESC: Search Plus Main Menu

Res▓▓▓▓▓▓▓▓▓▓ Keyword Searching Instructions ▓▓▓▓▓▓▓▓▓▓▓elds
    ┌──────────────────────────────────────────────────┐
    │ Boolean Operators:                               │
    │     OR combines search terms into a larger set   │
    │     AND limits a search by requiring each term to be present │
    │     NOT limits a search by requiring a term to NOT be present │
    │                                                  │
    │ The "*" character is used for truncation:        │
    │     teach* finds any words that start with the root teach │
    │          Example: teacher, teachers, teaching    │
    │                                                  │
    │ The "?" character is used as a Wildcard character: │
    │     wom?n finds all words that share the same specified characters │
    │          but allows another character to replace the ? character │
    │          Example: woman, women                   │
    │                                                  │
    └▓▓▓▓▓▓▓▓▓▓▓▓▓▓ Press F1 to exit ▓▓▓▓▓▓▓▓▓▓▓▓▓▓▓──┘

<F1> Help <F3> New Search <F5> View Stop Words <F7> View Keywords <F10> Search
```

Figure 16.17: Catalog Plus: Help, keyword search

```
Search Keywords                          ESC: Stop the Keyword Search

Results              Words/Phrases              Searchable Fields

36 Match(es)   │foundation                │        All Fields

                        AND

76 Match(es)   │empire                    │        All Fields


               │                          │


     Limi│ 18 Match(es) found, press <ENTER> to view them │



Search =  foundation AND empire
```

Figure 16.18: Catalog Plus: Keyword search result

```
Search Keywords                          ESC: Return to Keyword Search

    9  The Foundation trilogy : three classics of science fiction  1982
    9  Foundation's edge                                           1982












Search =  foundation AND empire
```

Figure 16.19: Catalog Plus: Titles from keywords

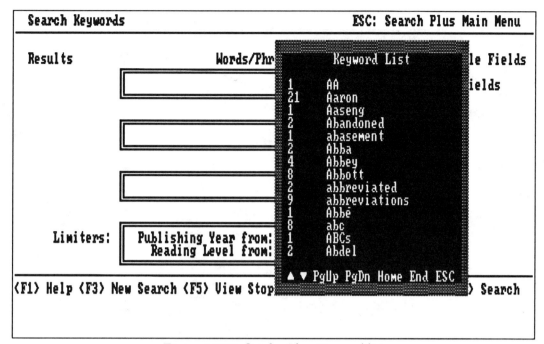

Figure 16.20: Catalog Plus: Keyword list

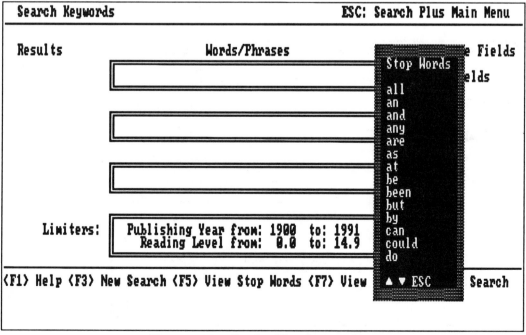

Figure 16.21: Catalog Plus: Stopword list

```
MARC Editor                                    ESC: Add/Update Items Menu
Cat. Source  040    _aDLC
                    _cDLC
                    _dIMchF
LC Call      050 0  _aPS3551.S5
                    _bA6 1982
LC Dewey     082 0  _a813/.54
                    _219
ME:Pers Name 100 10 _aAsimov, Isaac,
                    _d1920-
Title        245 14 _aThe Foundation trilogy :
                    _bthree classics of science fiction /
                    _cby Isaac Asimov.
Publication  260 0  _a[Garden City, N.Y. :
                    _bDoubleday,
                    _cc1982]
Phys Desc    300    _a227, 227, 225 p. ;
                    _c22 cm.
Note:General 500    _aEach work has special t.p.
Note:Content 505 0  _aFoundation -- Foundation and empire -- Second foundation
                          1 Copy
Search: 1) Title   4) Series       A)dd Another Item    N)ext Item
        2) Author  5) Subject      U)pdate This Item    L)ast Item
        3) Call #  6) ISBN/LCCN    R)emove This Item    V)iew/Add Copies
```

Figure 16.22: Catalog Plus: MARC display (partial)

```
                    +** MIDDLETOWN HIGH SCHOOL LIBRARY +**
                         Books About Drug Abuse

Today's Date: Aug 27,1991                                      Page 1
_____


362.2       Berger, Gilda
Berger         Crack, the new drug epidemic!.  London ;New York:  F.
            Watts, 1987.
               Discusses the manufacture and sale of crack, explains
            the dangers of crack use and addiction, and describes
            efforts to treat addicts and end the crack trade.

362.2       Berger, Gilda
Berger         Drug abuse : the impact on society.  New York:  Watts,
            1988.
               Discusses drug abuse and its impact on modern society
            in such areas as crime, family life, and the work place.



_____
  Scanning Record: 3        |    Press <ENTER> to pause, <ESC> to exit
```

Figure 16.23: Catalog Plus: Subject bibliography

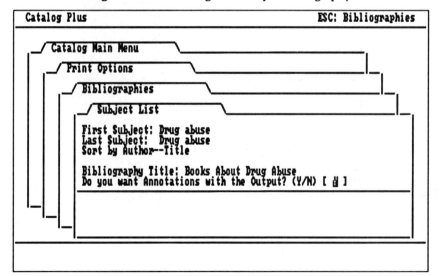

```
Catalog Plus                                     ESC: Bibliographies

   / Catalog Main Menu
     / Print Options
       / Bibliographies
         / Subject List

           First Subject: Drug abuse
           Last Subject:  Drug abuse
           Sort by Author--Title

           Bibliography Title: Books About Drug Abuse
           Do you want Annotations with the Output? (Y/N) [ N ]
```

Figure 16.24: Catalog Plus: Print options

17

CL-CAT
Cal Poly's Polycat

*Brian Williams and
Ilene F. Rockman*

The traditional CLSI CL-CAT in-house environment is a Wyse 60 amber terminal with a labeled function-key keyboard. The accompanying screens were downloaded to a Macintosh; thus, the highlighting that would be bright amber and the letters that would be low intensity amber are shown as black.

Additionally, CL-CAT ports can be configured for one of several user defined "languages." In other words, some of the text shown on the screen can be modified to reflect the needs of the user. In particular, Cal Poly has a modification for the remote user that translates what would normally be function-key command prompts, such as browse or keyword, into their standard keyboard equivalents, control-w or control-k. The accompanying screens illustrate both in-house and remote languages for these and other commands.

Searching

The typical CL-CAT search begins with the user-defined welcome screen (Figure 17.1).

A browse search will display a range of alphabetically related items with retrieval postings and relevant cross-references from authority control on the browse screen (Figure 17.3). A keyword search will just give the postings for the search terms on the search history screen. Figure

17.4 shows the retrieval from the browse search of Martin Luther King, Jr., as a subject. This search can also be limited by date (which is shown), or by language or format.

An author search in browse mode will also display cross-references from authority control (Figure 17.5).

Displays

The brief record display (Figure 17.6) shows one-line bibliographic descriptions with the author, title, format, and publication date. These are user-defined categories. The copy-availability screen (Figure 17.7) is title specific and includes both the brief record and status information. (All labels are user defined and can include circulation status, call number, and permanent location for all copies of an item.)

The full-record format (Figure17.8) is a longer labeled display, and the MARC record is also available (Figure 17.9), by entering an "m." There are no screen prompts for the MARC record.

Figure 17.10 shows a Boolean keyword search of King as subject combined with a title word of "dream," limited to media (that is, non-print); in this case, the search yields a single result, displayed immediately in a copy-availability display. Figure 17.11 shows the full display for the videocassette *I Have a Dream*.

Errors and Help

In a keyword search with a spelling error there will probably be no retrieval (Figure 17.12), while in a browse search, the system places you at the closest match in an alphabetical list of all headings that share the same context as the search term entered (Figure 17.13).

Pressing Help at this point displays the help screen for the search history screen (Figure 17.14). Some predeveloped help screens are provided, but most libraries will rewrite their own. Some are context sensitive and others are not. Figure 17.15 is an example of an advanced searching help screen; Figure 17.16 is a Boolean help screen.

Known Items, Partial Knowledge and Browsing

If a patron knows only part of a title, those known details can be input in any order as title keys in a keyword search (Figure 17.17). Spelling and spacing are important, capitalization is not. The patron would then select the item from the retrieval listed on the brief-references screen.

A known item can be located by entering as much detail as desired in any field at the same time. When a single title is retrieved, CL-CAT goes directly to the copy-availability screen instead of the brief-reference screen.

A browse search of "Desktop Publishing" (Figure 17.18) displays some related headings as "also found under". A browse search for a call number, Z678.9, appears in Figure 17.19. Note that the requested item normally appears mid-screen in a browse.

Truncation and Restriction

Figure 17.20 shows the process that CL-CAT uses for truncation (indicated by $). Rather than processing the result of a truncated search, the system asks the user to select the specific terms desired. The user is presented each option with the number of postings included in parentheses so that a specific decision can be made to include a term with the truncated root.

Remote Access

Upon login, remote users of the system see an additional screen (Figure 17.21), not provided in CL-CAT by CLSI but inserted by Cal Poly's modified front end to the system. This provides some additional information on the system when the user logs in. Remote access to Cal Poly's Polycat is available via the Internet at library.calpoly. edu or 129.65.20.21. Telnet to this address and follow the instructions on the screen. Note that ctrl-D is used to disconnect from Polycat remotely and that VT100 emulation is required for correct screen formatting.

Screen printing is available at some of the terminals in the library.

```
Welcome to the Robert E. Kennedy Library online Catalog.
    IF YOU CANNOT FIND A PARTICULAR ITEM IN THE ONLINE
           CATALOG PLEASE CALL REFERENCE
                  (805) 756-2649

    You May Search the Catalog Using Any of the Methods
    Listed Below.  Choose By Pressing the Corresponding
    Number Key.  You may Request Assistance at Any Time
By Pressing the CTRL Y Key.
    TO SEARCH BY:    (1)   SUBJECT

                     (2)   AUTHOR

                     (3)   TITLE

                     (4)   AUTHOR AND TITLE

                     (5)   ALL CATEGORIES
```

Figure 17.1: CL-CAT: Welcome screen

```
                        SUBJECT SEARCH




TYPE SUBJECT WORD(S)

SUBJECT=king, martin luther jr


PRESS
        CTRL W To See Alphabetic Listing of Subjects.
        CTRL K To Find Your Word(s) as Part of a Subject.
```

Figure 17.2: CL-CAT: Subject search

```
                          HEADING BROWSE
SEARCH TERM(S): SUBJECT = KING, MARTIN LUTHER JR
NO.      HEADINGS                                    REFERENCES FOUND
---   ---------------------------------------------------  ---------
      King, Martin Luther.
 1.      FOUND UNDER:King, Martin Luther, Jr., 1929-1968.        45
      King, Martin Luther, 1899-1965
 2.      FOUND UNDER:King, M. Luther (Martin Luther), 1899-1965.  1
 3.   King, Martin Luther, Jr., 1929-1968.                       45
 4.   King, Martin Luther, Jr., 1929-1968.                        1
 5.   King, Martin Luther, Jr., 1929-1968--Assassination.         6
 6.   King, Martin Luther, Jr., 1929-1968--Bibliography.          2
 7.   King, Martin Luther, Jr., 1929-1968--Biography.             1


Press Line Number(s) to Select One or More Headings.
Then Press 3 to See the Matching References.

Or PRESS: _
N Next Page
P Prev. Page                      Press 3        to Enter Next Search.
CTRL V for Help.                  CTRL O to START OVER.
```

Figure 17.3: CL-CAT: Subject browse display

```
                         SEARCH HISTORY

NO.  SEARCH TERMS                                   REFERENCES FOUND
---  ------------------------------------------------------  ------
 1.   SUBJECT = KING, MARTIN LUTHER JR [HEADINGS SELECTED]        45
 2.   (SUBJECT = KING, MARTIN LUTHER JR [HEADINGS SELECTED]) AND
PUBYR>1980                                                        17
 3.   ((SUBJECT = KING, MARTIN LUTHER JR [HEADINGS SELECTED]) AND
PUBYR>1980) AND PUBYR<1985                                         6








Press Line Number for Brief References.
Or PRESS:

COMPOSE a Search.
HELP for Assistance.                   START OVER Completely.
```

Figure 17.4: CL-CAT: Search history

```
                         HEADING BROWSE

SEARCH TERM(S): AUTHOR = KING, MARTIN LUTHER JR
NO.      HEADINGS                                    REFERENCES FOUND
---      --------------------------------------------------  ----------
         King, Martin Luther.
  1.        FOUND UNDER:King, Martin Luther, Jr., 1929-1968.       10
         King, Martin Luther, 1899-1965
  2.        FOUND UNDER:King, M. Luther (Martin Luther), 1899-1965.  1
  3.      King, Martin Luther, Jr., 1929-1968.                      10
  4.      King, Martin Luther, Jr., 1929-1968.                       1
  5.      King, Mary.                                                2
  6.      King, Mary Elizabeth.                                      2
  7.      King, Mary L.                                              1


Press Line Number(s) to Select One or More Headings.
Then Press 3 to See the Matching References.

Or PRESS: _
1 Next Page
2 Prev. Page                          Press 8         to Enter Next Search.
CTRL W for Help.                       CTRL O to START OVER.
```

Figure 17.5: CL-CAT: Author browse display

```
                        BRIEF REFERENCES

SEARCH TERM(S): (S=KING, MARTIN LUTHER AND PUBYR>1980) AND PUBYR<1985
REFERENCES FOUND:     9                                   Page  1 of 1
NO. AUTHOR               TITLE                          FORMAT    DATE
---------------------------------------------------------------------
  1. Garrow, David J.,    The FBI and Martin Luther King, J  BOOK   1981
  2. Oates, Stephen B.    Let the trumpet sound: the life o  BOOK   1982
  3. McKissack, Pat,      Martin Luther King, Jr., a man to  BOOK   1984
  4.                      Martin Luther King, Jr., Day       MEDIA  1983
  5.                      Martin Luther King, Jr. a prolong  AUDIO  1984
  6. Harris, Jacqueline L Martin Luther King, Jr./          BOOK   1983
  7. Ansbro, John J.      The mind of Martin Luther King, J  BOOK   1982
  8. California. State De  Martin Luther King, Jr., 1929-196 BOOK   1982
  9.                      King the man of vision who fought  MEDIA  1983


Press Line Number to Select Your Choice:

Or PRESS:
                                SEARCH HISTORY to Enter Next Search.

HELP for Assistance.            START OVER Completely.
```

Figure 17.6: CL-CAT: Brief reference display

```
                         COPY AVAILABILITY

SEARCH TERM(S): (S=KING, MARTIN LUTHER AND PUBYR>1980) AND PUBYR<1985
REFERENCES FOUND:   9
          CALL NO:      E185.97 K5 G3
          AUTHOR:       Garrow, David J., 1953-
          TITLE:        The FBI and Martin Luther King, Jr. : from
          PUBLISHER:    1st ed.--New York ; London : W.W. Norton,
          DESCRIPT:     320 p. ;
                                                   Page  1 of 1
    LOCATION             CALL NO.                       STATUS
_____

     STACKS:2ND-5TH FL    E185.97 K5 G3               Not Checked Out




  PRESS YOUR CHOICE:

                               SEARCH HISTORY to Enter Next Search.
                               FULL  Record.
                               RETURN to BRIEF REFERENCES.
  HELP for Assistance.         START OVER Completely.
```

Figure 17.7: CL-CAT: Copy availability screen

```
                           FULL RECORD

SEARCH TERM(S): (S=KING, MARTIN LUTHER AND PUBYR>1980) AND PUBYR<1985
REFERENCES FOUND:   9                                Page  1 of 1
------------------------------------------------------------------------
LOCATION:   Stacks  2d-5th fl
CALL NO:    E185.97 K5 G3
AUTHOR:     Garrow, David J., 1953-
TITLE:      The FBI and Martin Luther King, Jr. : from "solo" to Memphis
PUBLISHER:  1st ed.--New York ; London : W.W. Norton, 1981.
DESCRIPT:   320 p. ;
SUBJECT 1:  King, Martin Luther, Jr., 1929-1968.
SUBJECT 2:  United States. Federal Bureau of Investigation.
QUALIFIER:  Monograph, English, 1981




  PRESS YOUR CHOICE:

                               SEARCH HISTORY to Enter Next Search.
                               COPY Availability.
                               RETURN to BRIEF REFERENCES.
  HELP for Assistance.         START OVER Completely.
```

Figure 17.8: CL-CAT: Full display, book

```
                            MARC RECORD

SEARCH TERM(S): (S=KING, MARTIN LUTHER AND PUBYR>1980) AND PUBYR<1985
REFERENCES FOUND:    9
-----------------------------------------------------------------------
000        00685nam  2200217Ia 45_A0
001        ocm07784646 820113_
005        19890802225100.0_
008        810923s1981    nyu              00110 eng d_
020        #a 0393015092
040        #a EWF #c EWF #d CPS
049        #a CPSM
090        #a E185.97.K5 #b G3
100    10  #a Garrow, David J., #d 1953-
245    14  #a The FBI and Martin Luther King, Jr. : #b from "solo" to
           Memphis / #c David J. Garrow.
250        #a 1st ed.

PRESS YOUR CHOICE:            SEARCH HISTORY to Enter Next Search.
                             FULL Record.
NEXT Page.                   COPY Availability.
                             RETURN to BRIEF REFERENCES.
HELP for Assistance.          START OVER Completely.
```

Figure 17.9: CL-CAT: MARC display, book (partial)

```
                        ALL CATEGORIES SEARCH




    TYPE SEARCH WORD(S)

    su=king and title=dream and for=med


    PRESS
          BROWSE To See a List of Alphabetic Headings.
          KEYWORD To Find Your Word(s) Anywhere.




    HELP for Assistance.              START OVER Completely.
```

Figure 17.10: CL-CAT: Multi-index search w/limits

```
                          FULL RECORD

SEARCH TERM(S): (SU=KING AND TITLE=DREAM) AND FOR=MED
REFERENCES FOUND:   1                                  Page  1 of 2
---------------------------------------------------------------------
LOCATION:   LR & C  2d fl
CALL NO:    128(Vid.C.)
TITLE:      King I have a dream
PUBLISHER:  [s.l.] : MPI Home Video, c1986.
DESCRIPT:   1 videocassette (28 min.) : sd., b&w  with color sequences ; 1/2
            in.
LOCAL NOTE: $19.95.
NOTE 1:     SUMMARY: Presents the famous speech of Martin Luther King given
            at the Lincoln Memorial (Wash. D.C.) on August 28, 1963.
NOTE 2:     VHS Format
SUBJECT 1:  King, Martin Luther, Jr., 1929-1968.
SUBJECT 2:  Afro-Americans--Civil rights--Videocassette.


PRESS YOUR CHOICE: _              SEARCH HISTORY to Enter Next Search.
NEXT Page.                        COPY Availability.

HELP for Assistance.             START OVER Completely.
```

Figure 17.11: CL-CAT: Full display, video (1 of 2)

```
                        SEARCH HISTORY

NO.  SEARCH TERMS                             REFERENCES FOUND
---  ---------------------------------------------------  ------
 1.   SUBJECT=MARTIN LUTHER KIGN                           NONE
```
```













Press Line Number for Brief References.
Or PRESS:


COMPOSE a Search.
HELP for Assistance.                  START OVER Completely.
Press HELP for Hints on Constructing Your Search.
```

Figure 17.12: CL-CAT: Result of error in keyword

```
                          HEADING BROWSE

SEARCH TERM(S): SUBJECT = MARTIN LUTHER KIGN
NO.         HEADINGS                                      REFERENCES FOUND
---  ----------------------------------------------------  ----------
 1.    Martin, Jay.                                             1
 2.    Martin, John, 1789-1854.                                 1
 3.    Martin, Luther, 1748-1826.                               1
 4.    [CLOSEST ENTRY]Martin Luther King, Junior. National
         Historic Site (Atlanta, Ga.)--Pictures.               1
 5.    Martin Luther King Middle School.                        1
       Martin, Marie Francoise Therese, Saint, 1873-1897
 6.       FOUND UNDER:Therese, de Lisieux, Saint, 1873-1897     3



Press Line Number(s) to Select One or More Headings.
Then Press BRIEF to See the Matching References.

Or PRESS:
NEXT Page.
PREVious Page.                          SEARCH HISTORY  to Enter Next Search.
HELP for Assistance.                    START OVER Completely.
```

Figure 17.13: CL-CAT: Result of error in browse

```
The SEARCH HISTORY display automatically appears when you have
conducted a KEYWORD search.

            If you found NO TITLES    Press <START OVER> for a new search.
If you found MORE THAN ONE TITLE    Press line number to see results.
The SEARCH HISTORY display also allows you to compose new searches without
starting over each time.  It also enables you to conduct more sophisticated
searches using more advanced techniques.

To see advanced searching techniques type ADVANCED <RETURN>.

PRESS <RETURN> TO CONTINUE SEARCHING.
```

Figure 17.14: CL-CAT: Help for search history

```
The SEARCH HISTORY screen enables you to expand or narrow your search.
On this screen you can:

    1.  Limit your search by:
            Date - Type LIMDAT <RETURN> for instructions.
            Format - Type LIMFOR <RETURN> for instructions.
            Language - TYPE LIMLAN <RETURN> for instructions.

    2.  Use Boolean logic operators "and", "or", "not".
            Type BOOLEAN <RETURN> for instructions.

    3.  Combine searches already displayed on Search History screen.
            Type COMPOSE <RETURN> for instructions.

    4.  Search by root words.
            Type TRUNC <RETURN> for instructions.

PRESS <RETURN> TO CONTINUE SEARCHING.
```

Figure 17.15: CL-CAT: Help for advanced searching

```
There are three boolean operators:
            AND (all records have both search terms)
            OR  (all records have either search term)
            NOT (all records exclude the second term)

Examples:   Mass media and television (narrows search)
            Mass media or television  (broadens search)
            Mass media not television (narrows search)

Use them in KEYWORD on the search history screen.
Different or similar operators may be used in a single search:

            A=Salinger and T=Catcher
            S=Flowers or Bulbs
            A=Hemingway not T=Sun
```

Figure 17.16: CL-CAT: Help screen for Boolean

```
                            BRIEF REFERENCES

SEARCH TERM(S): TITLE=FIRE MOON
REFERENCES FOUND:    5                                   Page  1 of 1
NO. AUTHOR              TITLE                     FORMAT   DATE
----------------------------------------------------------------------
 1. Dalgliesh, Alice,   The enchanted book/       BOOK     1947
 2. Ginsburg, Mirra.    The Master of the Winds and other  BOOK  1970
 3. Mailer, Norman.     Of a fire on the moon.    BOOK     1970
 4. Mayne, William,     William Mayne's Book of giants; s  BOOK  1969
 5. Smith, Lee,         Me and my baby view the eclipse:  BOOK  1990




Press Line Number to Select Your Choice:

Or PRESS:
                              Press      to Enter Next Search.

CTRL Y for Help.              CTRL O to START OVER.
```

Figure 17.17: CL-CAT: Partial title search, result

```
                         HEADING BROWSE

SEARCH TERM(S): SUBJECT = DESKTOP PUBLISHING
NO.        HEADINGS                                    REFERENCES FOUND
---   ------------------------------------------------- ---------
           Desk calculators
  1.         FOUND UNDER:Calculators.                        37
  2.      Deskey, Donald, 1894-                               1
  3.      Desks--United States--Exhibitions.                  1
  4.      Desktop publishing.                                15
  5.      Desktop publishing--Bibliography.                   1
  6.      Desktop publishing--Computer programs.              2
  7.         ALSO FOUND UNDER:Ventura (Computer program)      1
  8.      Desktop publishing--Library applications.           1


Press Line Number(s) to Select One or More Headings.
Then Press 3 to See the Matching References.

Or PRESS:
  Next Page
  Prev. Page                        Press 3        to Enter Next Search.
 TRL Y for Help.                    TRL O to START OVER.
```

Figure 17.18: CL-CAT: Browse display, subjects

```
                      CALL NUMBER BROWSE

SEARCH TERM(S): CALL NUMBER = Z678.9
NO.     CALL NUMBERS              TITLES          REFERENCES FOUND
---   ----------------------   --------------------------- ---------
  1.    Z678.85 M4              Measuring the quality of library   1
  2.    Z678.85 R6 1988         Are we there yet?: evaluating li   1
  3.    Z678.85 W57             Standards for library service: a   1
  4.    Z678.892 U5 C53(REF)    CLASS forum                        1
  5.    Z678.9 A1 A38           Advances in library automation a   1
  6.    Z678.9 A1 A62 1975      Information roundup: a continuin   1
  7.    Z678.9 A1 A65 1966      The Brasenose Conference on the    1
  8.    Z678.9 A1 B35 1971      Interface: library automation wi   1
  9.    Z678.9 A1 C2 1967       Automation in libraries            1


Press Line Number(s) to Select One or More Headings.
Then Press 3 to See the Matching References.

Or PRESS:
  Next Page
  Prev. Page                        Press 3        to Enter Next Search.
 TRL Y for Help.                    TRL O to START OVER.
```

Figure 17.19: CL-CAT: Call number browse

```
                      ▓MATCHING WORD SELECTION▓

SEARCH TERM(S):   SUBJECT=AGRICULTU$
--------------------------  --------------------------  --------------------------
 AGRICULTURA(2)            AGRICULTURAL(1573)           AGRICULTURE(3268)
 AGRICULTURISTS(23)




The Words Listed Above Match Your Search Term(s).  Select
the Term(s) You Wish to Include, Then Press ▓RETURN.▓

PRESS YOUR CHOICE:                          ▓A▓ to Select All Words.
▓NEXT▓ Word.                                ▓S▓ to Select a Word.
▓PREV▓ious Word.                            ▓E▓ to Eliminate a Word.
▓CTRL Y▓ for Help.                          ▓CTRL O▓ to START OVER.
```

Figure 17.20: CL-CAT: Result of truncated search

```
                      WELCOME TO POLYCAT
          LOGON HELP: 756-5506    SEARCHING HELP: 756-2649

             Function key Equivalents for the Use of POLYCAT

       Key             Function        Description
       ----------      ----------      ----------------------------
       CTRL O          Start Over      Returns you to Welcome Screen.
       CTRL Y          Help            Displays help screens.
       C               Compose         Enter new search term.
       N               Next            Displays next screen.
       P               Previous        Displays previous screen.
       F               Full            Displays record in full format.
       C               Copy            Displays copy availability.
       B               Brief           Displays one line record summary.
       S               Search History  Displays last nine queries.
       CTRL W          Browse          Lists category related retrieval.
       CTRL K          Keyword         Lists occurrences of search terms
       CTRL D          Disconnect      Exit Polycat.

          Use local "Print Screen" to save this screen.
-------------------------------------------------------------------------
Program will continue in 30 seconds -- Please be sure 'autowrap' is set OFF
```

Figure 17.21: CL-CAT: Remote-user help screen

18

Dartmouth College Library
Online System

Katharina Klemperer

The Dartmouth College Library Online System provides access to virtually all items owned by Dartmouth College Library in its eight locations. It also includes some journal indexes (Medline and the MLA Bibliography), some reference works in full text (Grolier's *Academic American Encyclopedia* and the *American Heritage Electronic Dictionary*), and the full texts of several literary works (The plays and sonnets of Shakespeare, and the King James Version of the Bible). New files are continually being added.

The databases in the Online System are mounted with BRS/SEARCH as the search engine and a locally developed user interface. The system takes full advantage of the power of the BRS/SEARCH engine. Any field in the unit record, as well as the entire record, can be searched by keyword. The Boolean operators AND, OR, and AND NOT may be used, as well as positional operators that allow users to find words in adjacent positions. Other features allow users to search for truncated terms or to limit their retrievals after they have completed a search, as illustrated in the accompanying screens.

The user interface was designed for use by novices with no training. The dialogue is constructed so that beginning users are helped along with a tutorial-style menu display, which assists them in constructing commands. As users become comfortable with the command language, they can drop the menus and search more quickly without waiting for the intermediate instructions to appear. There are more than a hundred glossary and help screens that explain the meaning of command words, library terms, and relevant computer terms. The command language matches the Common Command Language Standard with very few exceptions, and the dialogue is designed to be as nonmodal as possible: a user can type any command at any point in the session. For example, a user may type a new search before a display is completed, without exiting the display mode.

The Dartmouth community is fortunate in that virtually every building on the campus, including all offices and residence hall rooms, is connected to the computer center, and hence the library system, by means of the campus network. Because most students own microcomputers that can be used as terminals, and because the system runs 24 hours a day, the Online System is available to its entire user population wherever and whenever it is needed.

The Dartmouth College Information System (DCIS)

To provide state-of-the-art access to information resources for Dartmouth College, the library and

Dartmouth College Computing Services are developing the Dartmouth College Information System (DCIS). DCIS is an information navigation and retrieval tool, whose use will become second nature to the faculty, student body, and staff of Dartmouth College. The project embraces all information resources at the college, from library materials to statistical files in the social sciences to full texts in the humanities such as the *Thesaurus Linguae Grecae*. collections of images such as the photo archives of the college to audio-visual data for instructional purposes.

In the fall of 1991 the first component of the DCIS project was distributed to all the incoming freshmen at the college: a Macintosh application called Online Library, which provides a Macintosh front end to all the databases that are available on the library's BRS server. The Macintosh interface makes use of the advantages of the Macintosh graphical user interface. Users no longer need to learn a command language to access information; they can rely on the intuitive point-and-click operations provided by the mouse, buttons, menus, and windows. The interface is integrated with other Macintosh applications, so that users can save retrieved material into word processors or other programs for subsequent manipulation.

The Macintosh interface is under development at this point and will continue to be enhanced until it provides the full range of functionality that the library system allows. For this reason, most of the screen examples are taken from the terminal version, although both interfaces are used by the public.

Figure 18.1 shows the welcome screen for the system. As illustrated in Figures 18.2 and 18.3, context-sensitive help is available by typing "help" at any screen. Figure 18.4 shows the online tutorial for Boolean logic.

Searching and Displays

Users can rely on menus, being prompted for each new step in a command, or can key in complete commands at once. The following sequence could be used to locate compact disc versions of George Gershwin's *Rhapsody in Blue*. Figure 18.5 shows a direct search for both author and title in a single step, limited by **Lim Type Sound Recording** as a second step (the augmented search result is not displayed completely because it is too long). Note that the search terms are highlighted in the summary result. In this case, the best way to locate compact disc versions is to **Display Location**, resulting in Figure 18.6.

While the default display of a result is not sorted, **Sort Date** will yield Figure 18.7; it is also possible to sort by author, title or any other field in the record. **Sort Date Descending** produces a reverse chronological listing.

Displays

Searches yielding single results automatically show a medium display, as in Figure 18.8. **Display Long** yields a long labeled display (Figures 18.9 through 18.11), using Return to move from screen to screen, "PS" to show the previous screen. **Show Status** yields a status display as in Figure 18.12, part of the status display for an item with many copies. It is not possible to recall or charge an item from the online catalog.

Errors

Attempting to display a record number beyond the end of the result set will yield a brief message as in Figure 18.13. Misspelled searches will yield no result, as in Figure 18.14, but users will be notified of nonexistent words.

Approximate and Known-Item Searching

Title searches look for keywords anywhere in the title, so the search *F TI FIRE ON THE MOON* will yield the result in Figure 18.15. ("On" and "the" are ignored by the system.) The fastest way to find Thomas Pynchon's *Vineland* is an exact-title search (Figure 18.16), although other methods will also work.

Browsing

The browse command returns all index terms that begin with the letters typed by the user. For many indexes, the entire field (with hyphens) is indexed, as well as the individual words. Thus, *BRO AU PYNCHON* yields Figure 18.17. Call number browsing is problematic because periods aren't indexed (although they are displayed in a citation display), so they don't appear in the index display that is produced by a browse. This feature is used mostly by staff.

Nonbook Information

Figure 18.18 shows a search for Bach's Mass in B Minor, using a somewhat different search strategy to search all fields (the general index) and limiting the results to scores. Figure 18.19 shows part of one of the scores.

Unusual Indexes and Access Points

Figure 18.20 is the explain screen for indexes in the Catalog file. (Note, here as elsewhere, that all commands can be abbreviated to three characters and that some can be abbreviated to a single character). Here, menus and paging have been turned off.

Other Resources

The Dartmouth College Library Online System offers consistent access to a wide range of resources. Figure 18.21 shows a search for articles about Ingmar Bergman (in Swedish) in the *MLA Bibliography*. Figure 18.22 shows the use of adjacency searching within the *American Heritage Dictionary*, here looking for all cases in the entire dictionary in which "blow" and "up" appear together. Figure 18.23 shows one of five screens for the long form of the first result. Note that the commands and display formats are consistent with the Catalog file, although labels differ. The phrase "blow up" appears on the fourth of five screens. The Dictionary file can also help with crossword puzzles, using truncation ("?" masks a single letter).

Grolier's Academic American Encyclopedia is available as the Encyclopedia file, with full-text searching. Figure 18.24 shows 15 of the 18 articles that contain the words "nuclear" and "disarmament," with the number of lines in each article.

Some full literary texts are also available. In the Shakespeare Plays file, a user can search for the scene in which the speech "My kingdom for a horse!" was uttered, for example. Similarly, in the King James Bible, users can look for the chapter and verse where the phrase "Blessed are the meek" occurs, as in Figure 18.25.

Other Features

Downloading

Users can display records in EndNote format. If using a Macintosh terminal emulation program, they can then save the text of the display on disk and import them directly into the EndNote™ bibliography management program. Workstation users can download any display onto the workstation disk.

Electronic Reference

Dartmouth College Library offers true electronic reference, done directly by electronic mail. However, the online system does have an electronic suggestion box, which sends suggestions immediately to a reference librarian via electronic mail, who responds if a return address is given. This feature doesn't get used for reference questions (although it could), but the library gets a fair number of suggestions for acquisitions.

Mailing Results

After completing a search, the user can type "mail" to send displays of one or more citations to an electronic mail address.

Connecting to Other Systems

The **Connect** command allows users to connect to other systems on the Internet. All login information is supplied automatically by the Dartmouth system.

Truncation

The "$" symbol masks any number of characters. As previously illustrated, "?" masks a single letter.

Macintosh™ Interface

Figures 18.26 through 18.29 show screens from
the Macintosh interface.

```
                        Welcome to the
                Dartmouth College Library Online System
           Copyright 1987 by the Trustees of Dartmouth College

The MLA BIBLIOGRAPHY file is available for searching.  It contains
citations in the fields of literature, folklore and linguistics.  For
more information, type EXPLAIN MLA.  (11 June, 1991)

CARL UnCover, a database of tables of contents of journals, is
available via the CONNECT command.  Type EXPLAIN CONNECT for
information.  (10 April 1991)

It is now possible to see the circulation status of an item in the CATALOG
file.  Type EXPLAIN SHOW STATUS for information. (10 April 1991)

You are now searching the CATALOG file.  To search another file,
type SELECT FILE.

-----------------------------------------------------------------------
Type one of the following commands, or type HELP for more information:
   FIND   - to search for items    SELECT FILE - to search another file
   BROWSE - to scan the indexes    BYE         - to end your session
->
```

Figure 18.1: Dartmouth: Opening screen

```
Search S1: F SUB BOOLEAN ALGEBRA
Result S1: 46 items in the CATALOG file.

   1. Delvos, F. J.      Boolean methods in interpolation and... 1989
   2.                    Handbook of Boolean algebras /          1989
   3. Karchmer, Mauricio. Communication complexity : a new app... 1989
   4. Schneeweiss, Win... Boolean functions : with engineering... 1989
   5. Dunne, Paul E.     The complexity of Boolean networks /    1988
   6. Colloquium on Al... Algebra, combinatorics and logic in ... 1986
   7. Keenan, Edward L... Boolean semantics for natural langua... 1985
   8. Bell, J. L. (Joh... Boolean-valued models and independen... 1985
   9. Kim, Ki Hang.      Boolean matrix theory and applicatio... 1982
  10. Johnstone, P. T.   Stone spaces /                          1982
  11. Thayse, Andre, 1... Boolean calculus of differences /       1981
  12.                    Kinetic logic : a Boolean approach t... 1979
  13. Levitz, Kathleen.  Logic and Boolean algebra /             1979
  14. Takeuti, Gaisi, ... Two applications of logic to mathema... 1978
  15. Hailperin, Theod... Boole's logic and probability : a cr... 1976
-----------------------------------------------------------------------
Press RETURN to continue display, or type one of the following commands:
   DISPLAY MEDIUM      FIND        SELECT FILE       HELP      PRINT
   DISPLAY LONG        BROWSE      SET MODE BRIEF    BYE
->
```

Figure 18.2: Dartmouth: Subject search

```
Your search,
      F SUB BOOLEAN ALGEBRA

retrieved 46 items in the CATALOG file.  You have displayed
one screen of items.  You may now

Press return to see the next screen
Type FIND to begin a new search.
Type a different DISPLAY command to see more or less information.
Type CLEAN to "paint" your screen again and clean up unwanted characters.
Type SELECT FILE to search another file.
Type SHOW to find out information about your session.
Type SET to change the controls over your session.
Type SUGGEST to send a comment to the system.
Type EXPLAIN for additional help and information.
Type BYE to end your session.

Type EXPLAIN DISPLAY for instructions on the DISPLAY command.
----------------------------------------------------------------------
 Press RETURN to continue display, or type one of the following commands:
    DISPLAY MEDIUM       FIND           SELECT FILE      HELP    PRINT
    DISPLAY LONG         BROWSE         SET MODE BRIEF   BYE
 -> |
```

Figure 18.3: Dartmouth: Context-sensitive help

```
You can combine keywords in a FIND command by using the conjunctions (also
known as Boolean operators) AND, OR and AND NOT.  For example,

FIND TOPIC MUSHROOMS OR FUNGI will retrieve all items containing either the
    word "MUSHROOMS" or the word "FUNGI" in a topic field.
FIND TOPIC POWER AND NOT NUCLEAR will retrieve all items with a topic field
    containing the word "POWER" but not the word "NUCLEAR".

You can also combine different indexes using conjunctions.  For example,

FIND AUTHOR ERNEST HEMINGWAY AND TITLE OLD MAN SEA will retrieve items with
    "ERNEST" and "HEMINGWAY" in an author field, and "OLD," "MAN," and "SEA"
    in a title field.
FIND AUTHOR GAIL SHEEHY AND NOT TITLE PASSAGES will retrieve items by
    Gail Sheehy that do not have the word "PASSAGES" in the title.

For fuller descriptions of conjunctions and related topics, type
    EXPLAIN AND       EXPLAIN OR       EXPLAIN AND NOT      EXPLAIN KEYWORDS
----------------------------------------------------------------------
 Type one of the following commands, or type HELP for more information:
    FIND   - to search for items     SELECT FILE - to search another file
    BROWSE - to scan the indexes     BYE         - to end your session
 -> |
    By pressing BREAK you have interrupted your display
```

Figure 18.4: Dartmouth: Tutorial for Boolean

```
Search S3: F AU GEORGE GERSHWIN AND TI RHAPSODY IN BLUE; LIM TYPE SOUND R...
Result S3: 23 items in the  CATALOG  file.

    1. Watts, Andre.         Andre Watts plays George Gershwin so... 1976
    2. Gershwin, George... Rhapsody in blue ; An American in Pa... 1989
    3. Gershwin, George... Rhapsody in blue ; An American in Pa... 1988
    4. Gershwin, George... Rhapsody in blue sound recording = R... 1988
    5. Gershwin, George... Classic Gershwin sound recording.       1987
    6. Gershwin, George... Levant plays Gershwin sound recordin... 1987
    7. Gershwin, George... Rhapsody in blue ; An American in Pa... 1986
    8.                     Paul Whiteman's historic Aeolian Hal... 1986
    9. Gershwin, George... Rhapsody in blue ; Preludes for pian... 1985
   10. Gershwin, George... Rhapsody in blue : (1924) ; Preludes... 1985
   11. Gershwin, George... Thomas salutes Gershwin! sound recor... 1984
   12. Gershwin, George... Gershwin's greatest hits sound recor... 1984
   13. Gershwin, George... Rhapsody in blue ; An American in Pa... 1981
   14. Gershwin, George... The Gershwin album sound recording      1980
   15. Gershwin, George... An American in Paris ; Rhapsody in b... 1976
----------------------------------------------------------------------
 Press RETURN to continue display, or type one of the following commands:
    DISPLAY MEDIUM       FIND           SELECT FILE      HELP    PRINT
    DISPLAY LONG         BROWSE         SET MODE BRIEF   BYE
 ->
```

Figure 18.5: Dartmouth: Limiting by type

```
Search S3: F AU GEORGE GERSHWIN AND TI RHAPSODY IN BLUE; LIM TYPE SOUND R...
Result S3: 23 items in the CATALOG file.
                                -1-
   Location: Music, Phonotape M/20/W37/A63/1976

                                -2-
   Location: Music, Compact disc M/22/G47/R53/1989

                                -3-
   Location: Music, Compact disc M/1010/G38/R27/1988

                                -4-
   Location: Music, Compact disc M/1000/G47/I67/1988

                                -5-
   Location: Music, Compact disc M/3.1/G47/C62/1987

------------------------------------------------------------------------
Press RETURN to continue display, or type one of the following commands:
    DISPLAY MEDIUM         FIND          SELECT FILE        HELP      PRINT
    DISPLAY LONG           BROWSE        SET MODE BRIEF     BYE
->  |
```

Figure 18.6: Dartmouth: Display Location

```
Search S3: F AU GEORGE GERSHWIN AND TI RHAPSODY IN BLUE; LIM TYPE SOUND R...
Result S3: 23 items in the CATALOG file.

    1.                          Piano roll discoveries. Sound recording 1959
    2.  Gershwin, George ... Concerto in F, for piano and orchest... 1967
    3.  Gershwin, George ... Gershwin's greatest hits.                1970
    4.  Gershwin, George ... The Gershwin album.                      1970
    5.  Gershwin, George ... Rhapsody in blue ; An American in Pa...  1973
    6.  Gershwin, George ... Cuban overture. Rhapsody in blue An...   1975
    7.  Gershwin, George ... Rhapsody in blue; the 1925 piano rol...  1976
    8.  Gershwin, George ... Gershwin plays Gershwin.                 1976
    9.  Gershwin, George ... An American in Paris ; Rhapsody in b...  1976
   10.  Watts, Andre.        Andre Watts plays George Gershwin so...  1976
   11.  Gershwin, George ... The Gershwin album sound recording      1980
   12.  Gershwin, George ... Rhapsody in blue ; An American in Pa...  1981
   13.  Gershwin, George ... Gershwin's greatest hits sound recor...  1984
   14.  Gershwin, George ... Thomas salutes Gershwin! sound recor...  1984
   15.  Gershwin, George ... Rhapsody in blue : (1924) ; Preludes...  1985
------------------------------------------------------------------------
Press RETURN to continue display, or type one of the following commands:
    DISPLAY MEDIUM         FIND          SELECT FILE        HELP      PRINT
    DISPLAY LONG           BROWSE        SET MODE BRIEF     BYE
->
```

Figure 18.7: Dartmouth: Sort by date

```
Search S2: F GEN MK 42240
Result S2: 1 items in the CATALOG file.

                                -1-
   Author: Gershwin, George, 1898-1937.
    Title: Rhapsody in blue sound recording = Rhapsodie en bleu ; An
           American in Paris = Un Americain a Paris ; Broadway overtures /
           George Gershwin.
  Imprint: [New York, N.Y.] : CBS Masterworks, [1988]
 Location: Music, Compact disc M/1000/G47/I67/1988




                                                    I


------------------------------------------------------------------------
Type one of the following commands; or type HELP for more information:
    FIND          DISPLAY LONG       SET MODE BRIEF    PRINT      BYE
    BROWSE        DISPLAY MEDIUM     SELECT FILE       HELP
->
```

Figure 18.8: Dartmouth: Medium display

```
Search S2: F GEN MK 42240
Result S2: 1 items in the █CATALOG█ file.

                             -1-
     Author: Gershwin, George, 1898-1937.
      Title: Rhapsody in blue sound recording = Rhapsodie en bleu ; An
             American in Paris = Un Americain a Paris ; Broadway overtures /
             George Gershwin.
  Collation: 1 sound disc : digital, stereo. ; 4 3/4 in.
    Imprint: [New York, N.Y.] : CBS Masterworks, [1988]
      Notes: Michael Tilson Thomas, conductor. 1st work: George Gershwin (1925
             piano roll); Columbia Jazz Band. 2nd work: New York
             Philharmonic. 3rd-8th works: Buffalo Philharmonic.
             Overtures arranged by Don Rose.
             1st work recorded at 30th Street Studios, New York, 1976. 2nd
             work recorded at Philharmonic Hall, New York, 1974. 3rd-8th
             works recorded at Kleinhans Music Hall, Buffalo, N.Y., 1976.
                                           (Item continues on next screen)
-----------------------------------------------------------------------------
Press RETURN to continue display, or type one of the following commands:
     DISPLAY MEDIUM        FIND            SELECT FILE        HELP     PRINT
     DISPLAY LONG          BROWSE          SET MODE BRIEF     BYE
->
```

Figure 18.9: Dartmouth: Long display, recording 1

```
Search S2: F GEN MK 42240
Result S2: 1 items in the █CATALOG█ file.

             "Consists of previously released material."       I
             Compact disc.
             Durations: 13:41 ; 18:32 ; 38:39.
             Program notes in English, German and French (22 p.) in container.
             Broadway overtures: Oh, Kay! (7:06) -- Funny face (5:50) -- Girl
             crazy (5:41) -- Strike up the band (7:07) -- Of thee I sing
             (4:36) -- Let 'em eat cake (8:19)
       Type: Sound recording
   Subjects: Piano with jazz ensemble.
             Symphonic poems.
             Overtures, Arranged.
             Musical revues, comedies, etc. -- Excerpts, Arranged.
   Other Au: Thomas, Michael Tilson, 1944-
             Gershwin, George, 1898-1937.
                                           (Item continues on next screen)
-----------------------------------------------------------------------------
Press RETURN to continue display, or type one of the following commands:
    PS (previous screen)  DISPLAY MEDIUM  SELECT FILE       PRINT    HELP
    FIND                  DISPLAY LONG    SET MODE BRIEF    BROWSE   BYE
-> |
```

Figure 18.10: Dartmouth: Long display, recording 2

```
Search S2: F GEN MK 42240
Result S2: 1 items in the █CATALOG█ file.

             Rose, Don.
             Gershwin, George, 1898-1937. Rhapsody in blue. 1988.
             Gershwin, George, 1898-1937. American in Paris. 1988.
             Gershwin, George, 1898-1937. Musical comedies. Selections; arr.
             1988.
             Columbia Jazz Band.
             New York Philharmonic.
             Buffalo Philharmonic Orchestra.
   Other Ti: Instrumental music. Selections.
    Pub. no: █MK 42240█
   Location: Music, Compact disc M/1000/G47/I67/1988



-----------------------------------------------------------------------------
Type one of the following commands; or type HELP for more information:
    PS (previous screen)  DISPLAY MEDIUM  SELECT FILE       PRINT    HELP
    FIND                  DISPLAY LONG    SET MODE BRIEF    BROWSE   BYE
->
```

Figure 18.11: Dartmouth: Long display, recording 3

```
Search S4: F TI WEBSTERS THIRD INTERNATIONAL
Result S4: 6 items in the CATALOG file.

  Author: Gove, Philip Babcock, 19
   Title: Webster's third new international dictionary of the English lang...
Location: BAKER PE1625 W36 1961
          Status: Reference item - available for use in library only
         BAKER PE1625 W36 1961 cop. 2
          Status: Reference item - available for use in library only
         BAKER PE1625 W36 1961 cop. 5
          Status: On shelf - if not found, ask at BAKER Circulation Desk
         BAKER SPEC COLL G746w
          Status: Available for use in library only
         DANA PE1625 W36 1961 cop. 3
          Status: Not checked out - if not found ask at Circulation Desk
         DANA PE1625 W36 1961 cop. 4
          Status: Not checked out - if not found ask at Circulation Desk
                                          (Item continues on next screen)
-------------------------------------------------------------------------
Press RETURN for more information, or type any command.


-> |
```

Figure 18.12: Dartmouth: Status with many copies 1

```
Search S8: F AU GEORGE GERSHWIN
Result S8: 95 items in the CATALOG file.

    1. Gershwin, George... Porgy & Bess : [Compact Disc]      On order
    2. Gershwin, George   Girl crazy: [sound recording]       On order
    3. Gershwin, George... Porgy and Bess.                     1935
    4. Gershwin, George... Rhapsody in blue /                  1990
    5. Gershwin, George... Porgy and Bess highlights sound reco... 1989
    6. Gershwin, George... Love walked in /                    1938
    7. Gershwin, George... Nice work if you can get it /       1937
    8. Watts, Andre.      Andre Watts plays George Gershwin so... 1976
    9. Gershwin, George... Rhapsody in blue ; An American in Pa... 1989
   10. Gershwin, George... Porgy and Bess highlights [sound rec... 1988
   11. Gershwin, George... Rhapsody in blue ; An American in Pa... 1988
   12. Gershwin, George... Rhapsody in blue sound recording = R... 1988
   13. Gershwin, George... Gershwin's improvisations for solo p... 1987
   14. Gershwin, George... Classic Gershwin sound recording.    1987
   15. Gershwin, George... Porgy and Bess sound recording       1987
-------------------------------------------------------------------------



->
      Search S8 has only 95 items. You can't display number 99.
```

Figure 18.13: Dartmouth: Error (display range)

```
Search S10: F TI RAPSODY IN BLUE
Result S10: 0 items in the CATALOG file.




















---------------------------------------------------------------------
Type one of the following commands, or type HELP for more information:
   FIND   - to search for items      SELECT FILE - to search another file
   BROWSE - to scan the indexes      BYE         - to end your session
->
   The word RAPSODY cannot be found in the CATALOG file
```

Figure 18.14: Dartmouth: Error (spelling)

```
Search S12: F TI FIRE ON THE MOON
Result S12: 6 items in the CATALOG file.

   1. Vollenweider, An... Down to the moon sound recording /    1986
   2. Willis, Connie.   Fire watch /                            1985
   3. Ellington, Duke,... Duke Ellington and his orchestra (19... 1971
   4. Mailer, Norman.   Of a fire on the moon                   1970
   5. Tolkien, J.R.R. ... Poems and songs of Middle earth soun... 1967
   6. Rogers, Bernard,... Dance scenes.                         1960










---------------------------------------------------------------------
Type one of the following commands; or type HELP for more information:
   FIND         DISPLAY LONG      SET MODE BRIEF   PRINT      BYE
   BROWSE       DISPLAY MEDIUM    SELECT FILE      HELP
-> |
```

Figure 18.15: Dartmouth: Approximate information

```
Search S13: F X TI VINELAND
Result S13: 1 items in the CATALOG file.

                              -1-
   Author: Pynchon, Thomas.
    Title: Vineland / Thomas Pynchon. 1st ed.
  Imprint: Boston : Little, Brown, c1990.
 Location: Baker Stacks PS/3566/Y55/V56/1990




                                                       I


                                     I
--------------------------------------I----------------------------
Type one of the following commands; or type HELP for more information:
   FIND         DISPLAY LONG      SET MODE BRIEF   PRINT      BYE
   BROWSE       DISPLAY MEDIUM    SELECT FILE      HELP
->
```

Figure 18.16: Dartmouth: Known-item search

```
Browse request: BRO AU PYNCHON

  B1    PYNCHON ...................................................  10 items
  B2    PYNCHON-JOHN-1621-1703 ....................................   1 items
  B3    PYNCHON-THOMAS ............................................   5 items
  B4    PYNCHON-WILLIAM ...........................................   2 items
  B5    PYNCHON-WILLIAM-1723-1789 .................................   1 items




 -------------------------------------------------------------------
 Type one of the following commands, or type HELP if you need it:
     FIND        - to search for a term or to start a new search
     SELECT FILE - to search another file
 -> |
```

Figure 18.17: Dartmouth: Browse author

```
Search S27: F GEN BACH B MINOR MASS; LIM TYPE SCORE
Result S27: 8 items in the CATALOG file.

   1. Bach, Johann Seb... Messe in H-moll, BWV 232 = Mass in B... 1965
   2. Liszt, Franz, 18... Variations on the basso continuo of ... 1942
   3. Bach, Johann Seb... Mass in B minor, for soli, chorus an... 1927
   4. Bach, Johann Seb... Mass in B minor, for soli, chorus an... 1927
   5. Bach, Johann Seb... Mass in B minor; for soli, chorus an... 1899
   6. Bach, Johann Seb... Messe, music H moll.                   1856
   7. Bach, Johann Seb... High mass in B minor
   8. Bach, Johann Seb... High mass in B minor




 -------------------------------------------------------------------
 Type one of the following commands; or type HELP for more information:
     FIND          DISPLAY LONG      SET MODE BRIEF    PRINT      BYE
     BROWSE        DISPLAY MEDIUM    SELECT FILE       HELP
 ->
```

Figure 18.18: Dartmouth: Search for score

```
Search S27: F GEN BACH B MINOR MASS; LIM TYPE SCORE
Result S27: 8 items in the CATALOG file.

                              -1-
   Author: Bach, Johann Sebastian, 1685-1750.
    Title: Messe in H-moll, BWV 232 = Mass in B minor, BWV 232. Facsim.
           reproduction of the autograph with a commentary edited by Alfred
           Durr.
Collation: score (188 p.) 12 p. 37 cm.
  Imprint: Kassel, New York, Barenreiter [c1965].
     Type: Score
 Language: lat
 Subjects: Bach, Johann Sebastian, 1685-1750 -- Manuscripts --
           Facsimiles.
           Masses -- To 1800 -- Scores.
 Other Au: Durr, Alfred, 1918- ed.
 Other Ti: Mass S.232. B minor
                                          (Item continues on next screen)
 -------------------------------------------------------------------
 Press RETURN to continue display, or type one of the following commands:
     DISPLAY MEDIUM       FIND         SELECT FILE       HELP      PRINT
     DISPLAY LONG         BROWSE       SET MODE BRIEF    BYE
 -> |
```

Figure 18.19: Dartmouth: Long display, score 1

```
-> e indexes
You can search for words in the following indexes in the CATALOG
Database.  You may use the spelled-out version of the index or the
abbreviation that appears in parentheses.

    General (GEN)     to search for words anywhere in the record
    Author (AU)       to search for any author
    Title (TI)        to search for title words
    Series (SE)       to search for words in the series title
    Topic (TO)        to search for words in titles or subject headings
    Subject (SU)      to search for words in subject headings
    Publisher (PUB)   to search for the publisher name
    Place (PL)        to search for the place of publication
    Notes (NTS)       to search for words in the notes section of a record
    LCCN              to search for Library of Congress Card Number
    ISBN              to search for an International Standard Book Number
    ISSN              to search for an International Standard Serial Number

For more information, type EXPLAIN followed by the index name.
For a list of technical indexes, type EXPLAIN TECH INDEXES.
For a list of fields that can be displayed, type EXPLAIN DISPLAY FIELDS.
For related information, type EXPLAIN FIND or EXPLAIN DISPLAY.

-> |
```

Figure 18.20: Dartmouth: Explain Indexes

```
Search S2: F TOPIC INGMAR BERGMAN; LIMIT LANGUAGE SWEDISH
Result S2: 1 items in the MLA BIBLIOGRAPHY file.

                        -1-
    Author: Steena, Birgitta
     Title: Ingmar Bergmans Laterna Magica
      Type: journal article
    Source: Finsk Tidskrift [20501 Abo, Finland]. 1988; 223-224(2); 78-90.




-----------------------------------------------------------------------
Type one of the following commands; or type HELP for more information:
    FIND          DISPLAY LONG      SET MODE BRIEF    PRINT      BYE
    BROWSE        DISPLAY MEDIUM    SELECT FILE       HELP
-> |
```

Figure 18.21: Dartmouth: Search MLA Bibliography

```
Search S3: F GEN BLOW ADJ UP
Result S3: 3 items in the DICTIONARY file.

    1. blow (1)
    2. dis*tend
    3. dy*na*mite




-----------------------------------------------------------------------
Type one of the following commands; or type HELP for more information:
    FIND          DISPLAY SHORT     DISPLAY MEDIUM    PRINT      BYE
    BROWSE        DISPLAY LONG      DISPLAY CONTEXT   SELECT FILE  HELP
-> 
```

Figure 18.22: Dartmouth: Dictionary search, adj.

```
Search S3: F GEN BLOW ADJ UP
Result S3: 3 items in the DICTIONARY file.
                              -1-
            Word: blow (1)
Part of Speech: verb
Inflected Form: blew, blown, blow*ing, blows.
Part of Speech: intransitive verb
          Sense: 1. To be in motion, as air.
                 2. To move along or be carried by or as if by the wind.
                 3. To expel a current of air, as from the mouth or from a
                    bellows.
                 4. To produce a sound by expelling a current of air, as in
                    sounding a musical wind instrument.
                 5. To breathe hard; pant.
                 6. To burn out or melt, as a fuse.
                 7. To burst suddenly, as a tire.
                                       (Item continues on next screen)
--------------------------------------------------------------------
Press RETURN to continue display, or type one of the following commands:
  DISPLAY MEDIUM    FIND              HELP      SELECT FILE    PRINT
  DISPLAY LONG      DISPLAY CONTEXT   BROWSE    BYE
  ->
```

Figure 18.23: Dartmouth: Definition display (1)

```
Search S2: F GEN NUCLEAR DISARMAMENT
Result S2: 18 items in the ENCYCLOPEDIA file.

   1. Bethe, Hans                                       (51 lines)
   2. Bevan, Aneurin                                    (21 lines)
   3. chemical and biological warfare                  (263 lines)
   4. Einstein, Albert                                 (249 lines)
   5. Garcia Robles, Alfonso                            (20 lines)
   6. nuclear freeze movement                           (30 lines)
   7. public opinion                                   (158 lines)
   8. Russell, Bertrand                                (143 lines)
   9. Stimson, Henry Lewis                              (44 lines)
  10. Sweden                                           (514 lines)
  11. aircraft, military                               (677 lines)
  12. arms control                                     (143 lines)
  13. disarmament                                      (107 lines)
  14. pacifism and nonviolent movements                (224 lines)
  15. United States, history of the                  (2636 lines)
--------------------------------------------------------------------
Press RETURN to continue display, or type one of the following commands:
  DISPLAY MEDIUM    DISPLAY PREVIEW   HELP      SELECT FILE    PRINT
  DISPLAY LONG      DISPLAY CONTEXT   FIND      BROWSE         BYE
  ->
```

Figure 18.24: Dartmouth: Encyclopedia search

```
Search S1: F TEXT BLESSED MEEK
Result S1: 1 items in the BIBLE file.
                              -1-
    Book: Matthew
 Chapter: 5
   Verse: 1 And seeing the multitudes, he went up into a mountain: and when
           he was set, his disciples came unto him:
           2 And he opened his mouth, and taught them, saying,
           3 Blessed are the poor in spirit: for theirs is the kingdom of
           heaven.
           4 Blessed are they that mourn: for they shall be comforted.
           5 Blessed are the meek: for they shall inherit the earth.
           6 Blessed are they which do hunger and thirst after righteousness:
           for they shall be filled.
           7 Blessed are the merciful: for they shall obtain mercy.
           8 Blessed are the pure in heart: for they shall see God.
                                       (Item continues on next screen)
--------------------------------------------------------------------
Press RETURN to continue display, or type one of the following commands:
  DISPLAY LONG       FIND     HELP     SELECT FILE    PRINT
  DISPLAY CONTEXT    BROWSE   BYE
  -> |
```

Figure 18.25: Dartmouth: Bible search

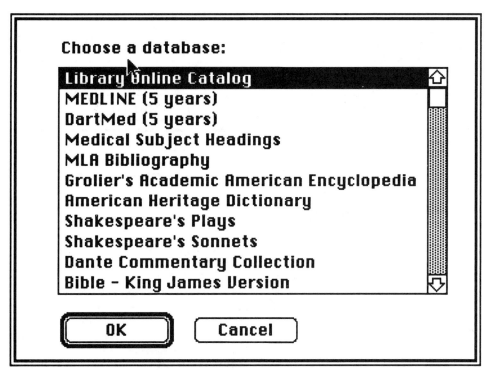

Figure 18.26: Dartmouth: Macintosh version, menu

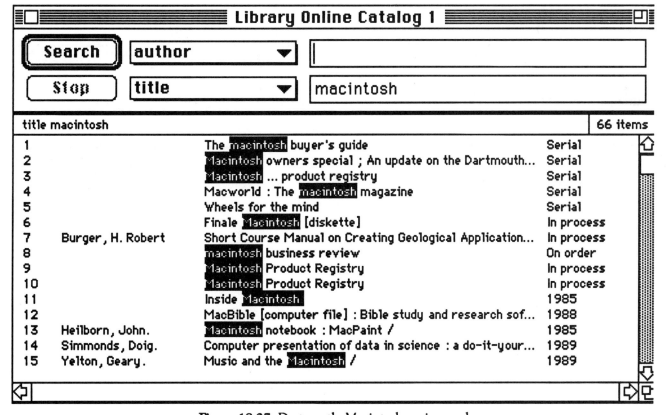

Figure 18.27: Dartmouth: Macintosh, main search

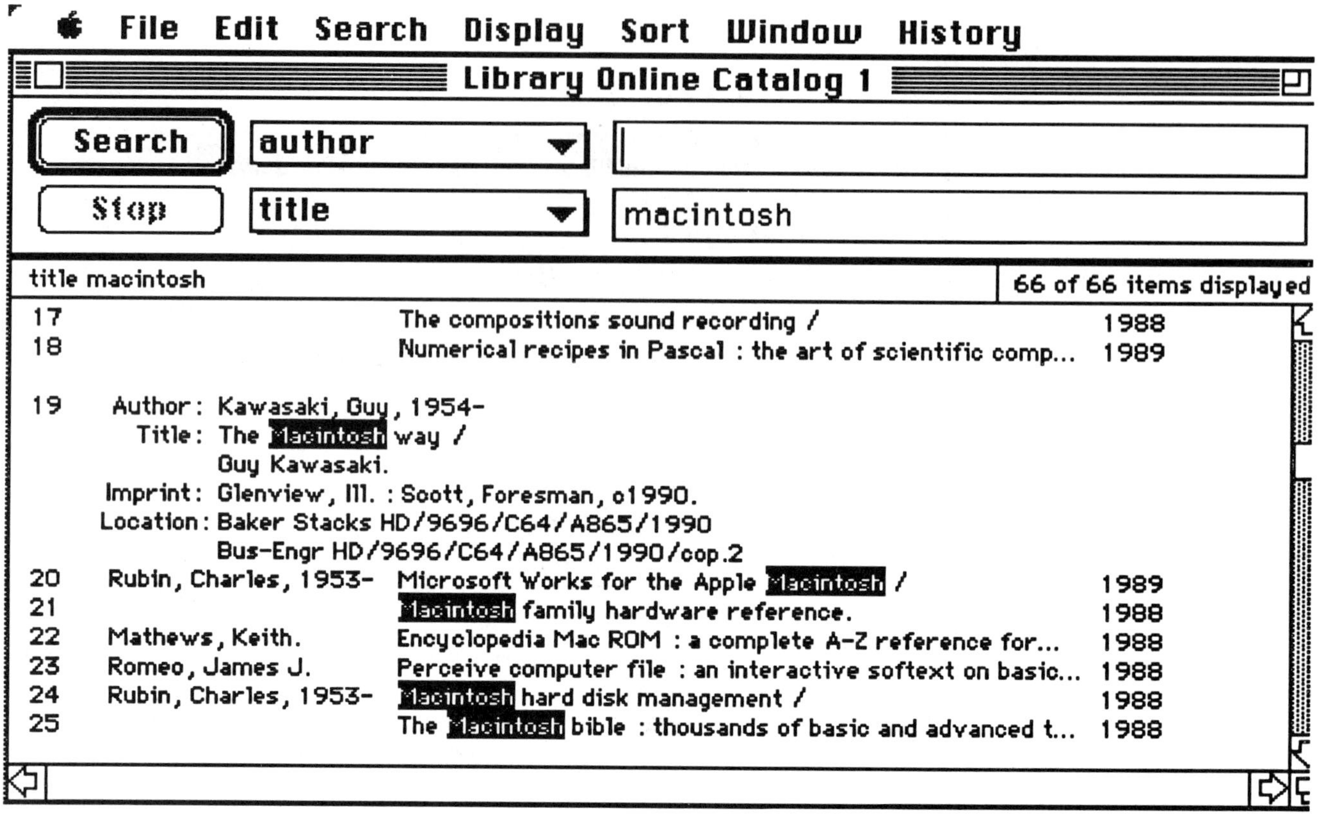

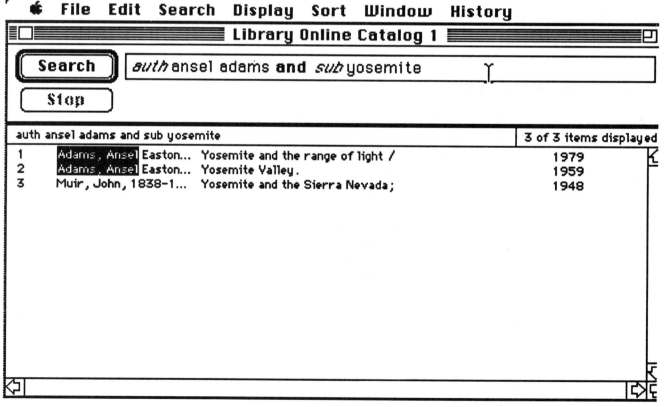

Figure 18.28: Dartmouth: Macintosh, medium view

Figure 18.29: Dartmouth: Macintosh, expert search

19

The Data Research Information Gateway

Carl Grant

In designing a new generation of online catalog for its automation system, Data Research sought to develop a tool that would realize the dream of the "Library without Walls"—a library whose resources are not limited by its physical boundaries.

The design process started with a few fundamental assumptions. First, we assumed that the modern catalog must allow the user to retrieve relevant information from a variety of resources easily. These databases would not necessarily reside at the library, but still must be available in the most current form. Most important, all of these databases should be accessible using the same user interface.

Second, we recognized the dilemma most libraries face regarding the evolution of technology. Despite the clear trend toward windowing among user interfaces for all types of software, the ASCII character-cell terminals that currently dominate the library automation environment are incapable of true windowing, and libraries do not have the financial resources to replace their entire terminal stock. A design challenge, therefore, was developing an interface that mimics critical aspects of windowing and provides a definable evolutionary path to the inevitable switch to true windowing terminals.

The resulting product is the Data Research Information Gateway. At this writing (mid-1991), this product is undergoing thorough field testing with general release expected by 1992.

A Powerful Search Engine to Access Multiple, Diverse Databases

Using the Gateway, information can be retrieved using a variety of techniques, including full keyword access to virtually all of the MARC fields, "term rotation," and a new indexing scheme that allows Boolean searching on the authority indexes.

An extensive indexing table that includes virtually all MARC fields provides the user with a wide variety of starting points for searches. It is possible to search on the size of the work and the number of pages. This same indexing also facilitates browsing through data by allowing users to collect data sets that could not otherwise be perused.

Virtually all current online catalog products use controlled vocabularies for subject and authority fields, but most systems are unable to fully exploit those vocabularies. The Data Research Information Gateway lays claim to "next-generation" status by allowing keyword access on the authority indexes, eliminating the limitations of the controlled vocabulary.

For example, a search on the term "Civil War" will draw not only those headings that start with "Civil War" and the authority record directing the user to "United States—History—Civil War" but also will find any subject heading that contains the search terms, such as "Baton Rouge—History—Civil War." For the user unfamiliar with subject searching, this is a powerful feature that maximizes search results.

"Term rotation" in conducting searches also helps to maximize search results. Users entering "Martin Luther King, Jr.," will, through the power of the software, find the same results as if they had keyed "King, Martin Luther" (Figures 19.2 and 19.3). In addition, the software will attempt to resolve unmatchable terms and reconduct the search. If the user were to enter the search "Martin Luther Knig, Jr." (Figure 19.11), the software would alert the user that the term could not be found and was being eliminated from the search (Figure 19.12). The search would then be reconducted and the results displayed (Figure 19.13).

Keyword searching in the software is also used to maximize search results. An example may be seen in Figures 19.16 and 19.17, wherein the user enters what would appear to be a string search, yet is actually one title in a trilogy. Through extensive keyword indexing of all fields, such successful search results are the norm rather than the exception using this software.

Stop words have never been used in the Data Research system, not because it isn't possible to have stop words, but because the system performance is not affected by their use and, in many instances, their inclusion in a search helps return more meaningful data sets. Searches that include terms such as "the," "a," "on," etc., can result in a large number of hits if the system allows their inclusion, but generally, when combined with other key terms in the search, the result is to narrow the search set. For example, consider the search "fire on the moon" (Figures 19.14 and 19.15).

The Information Gateway also enables the "layering" of searches. This capability allows a searcher to conduct additional searches, and then return to the previous search with the resulting search sets still intact. For example, when a user searches on "Civil War," reference is made to Jefferson Davis in one of the resulting records. The user can then search on "Jefferson Davis." If that search is unprofitable, the user can return to the previous search sets.

To support the increasing trend toward multimedia in libraries, the software is also designed to deal with the display of nonbook information. Such a display is shown in Figures 19.18.

Production note: This chapter represents a work in progress, and some discrepancies may exist in certain figures, e.g. the label "Paging" in Figure 19.18. Such labels may, in any case, be set by each library and may be format dependent. Note also that Figures 19.7 and 19.8 reflect the use of color or boldface to highlight some information; this has been eliminated in other figures for the sake of readability.

Aesthetics, Functionality and Pragmatic Considerations about the User Interface

The interface developed for this version of the catalog is designed with a number of factors in mind including the general presentation, ability to support various types of databases and accommodation of the differing skill sets of users.

Clearly, many interfaces today are trending toward windowing. Yet the fact remains that most libraries do not have terminals to support true windowing and have no idea when they will replace their ASCII character-cell terminals. The cost of this is simply too staggering for most libraries in relation to the benefits derived.

Thus the Data Research Information Gateway is designed to have the characteristics of windowing software while still operating on ASCII character cell terminals. It utilizes such features as the menu bar (Figure 19.3), pull down menus (Figure 19.19) and "windowed" data presentation (Figure 19.4).

Support of various types of databases was also a critical aspect in the design of the interface. Since the late 1970s, Data Research has maintained a nationwide network for libraries. Services on this network have evolved to include access to such databases as the Library of Congress bibliographic file, periodical indexes, full-text files, and the collections of other libraries on the network.

In addition to databases provided on the network, Data Research libraries can offer multiple databases as part of their local operation, including Community Information and Local Periodical Indexes. Data Research has also developed software that allows libraries to offer seamless database access via the Internet. Connection to any of these databases is supported from any node and is done by simply selecting the database from a menu. Once connected the searcher can re-execute a previous search and see the data presented as if it was locally loaded.

The interior layers of the user interface are designed to accommodate the fact that the user is now essentially logged onto a machine thousands of miles away using a file that requires different indexing tables, data labels, and help screens (Figure 19.19). Yet the interface retains the essential elements so that the user is not forced to deal with the new search environment.

Planned implementation of the NISO Z39.50 protocols for information search and retrieval will further this concept and allow the number of databases that can be accessed to expand considerably. Users benefit immensely in that they have access to other libraries and to other resources from a single point. The concept of the catalog as a consolidated entry point to extensive data resources is finally being realized!

Avoiding "Least Common Denominator" Design: An Interface That Adapts to Varying User Skill Sets

The last consideration in the interface design is the varying skill sets of users. Considerable analysis was performed to determine that the interface would accommodate a wide range of users, from novice to experienced searcher. The design includes support of borrower profiles that match library-defined parameters with the search parameters, display formats, fax numbers, and levels of help to be associated with a search session. As this feature evolves, it will also support automatic online notification of the borrower regarding books, articles or services that may be of interest.

Another trend being fulfilled by the Information Gateway is the accommodation of self-service, convenience-type library activities. These may include such things as photocopy requests, placing reserves, interlibrary loan, self-service circulation, and imaging.

In the currently released version of the Data Research Online Catalog, for example, the user may, upon locating a citation of interest, indicate that a reserve should be placed for that item. Once the item is located the system will alert the user via electronic mail or surface mail of the availability and pickup location. Likewise, the user may indicate the desire for a photocopy of a particular article or the need to interlibrary loan an item for their use.

Self-service circulation, although not a direct part of the Information Gateway, is a logical extension of the module. With the increased ability to locate information independent of the librarian comes the desire to be able to check the item out the same way. A self-service circulation station is also in testing at Data Research and is expected to be released in late 1991.

Finally, image delivery to the user is also of increasing interest. The test version of the Data Research Information Gateway links to third-party imaging products. If the user is utilizing a terminal capable of image delivery, the image can be displayed. Alternatively, if the user is on a standard ASCII terminal, the image may be directed to a suitable printer for retrieval by the user.

In summary, this module attempts to meet the real-world demands for a functionally rich module capable of maximizing the retrieval of relevant information while working within the parameters of existing hardware. It allows links with information resources formerly considered beyond both the physical and financial reach of the library. It vastly improves the access points to the data without adding additional layers of confusion for the user. It provides complete and comprehensive delivery of all types of information and images to a user at any location they choose. In short, it allows the construction of the "library without walls."

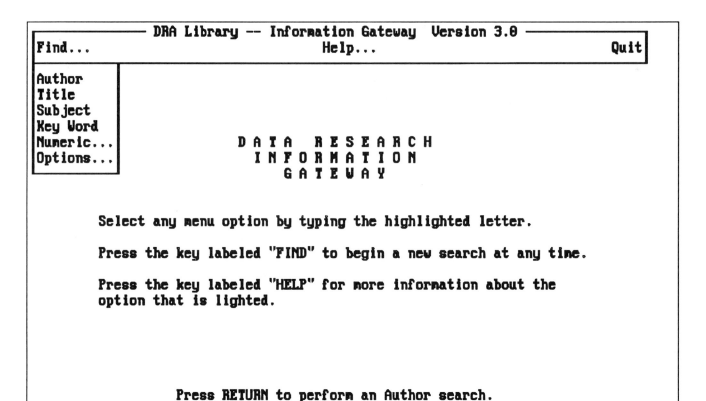

Figure 19.1: DRA: Opening screen

Figure 19.2: DRA: Author search

```
┌─────────────── DRA Library -- Hit List Display ───────────────┐
│┌─────────────────────────────────────────────────────────────┐│
││Select        Page        Find...        Help...    Backup       Quit││
│└─────────────────────────────────────────────────────────────┘│
│You searched AUTHOR for: Martin Luther King, Jr.               │
│                  6 Author headings found              Page 1   │
│1  King, Martin Luther, Jr., 1929-1968. (6 Titles)             │
│2  Martin Luther King, Jr. Center for Nonviolent Social Change. (1 Title)│
│3  Task Force to Review the FBI Martin Luther King, Jr., Security and│
│   Assassination Investigations. (0 Titles)                    │
│4      Search for United States. Task Force to Review the FBI Martin Luther│
│       King, Jr., Security and Assassination Investigations. (1 Title)│
│5  United States. Dept. of Justice. Task Force to Review the FBI Martin Luther│
│   King, Jr., Security and Assassination Investigations. (0 Titles)│
│6      Search for United States. Task Force to Review the FBI Martin Luther│
│       King, Jr., Security and Assassination Investigations. (1 Title)│
│7  United States. FBI Martin Luther King, Jr., Security and Assassination│
│   Investigations, Task Force to Review the. (0 Titles)        │
│8      Search for United States. Task Force to Review the FBI Martin Luther│
│       King, Jr., Security and Assassination Investigations. (1 Title)│
│Next                                                           │
│                                                               │
│                                                               │
│    Make a selection from the hit list to see title or holdings information.│
│       Press RETURN to make a selection from the hit list.     │
└───────────────────────────────────────────────────────────────┘
```

Figure 19.3: DRA: Author search result

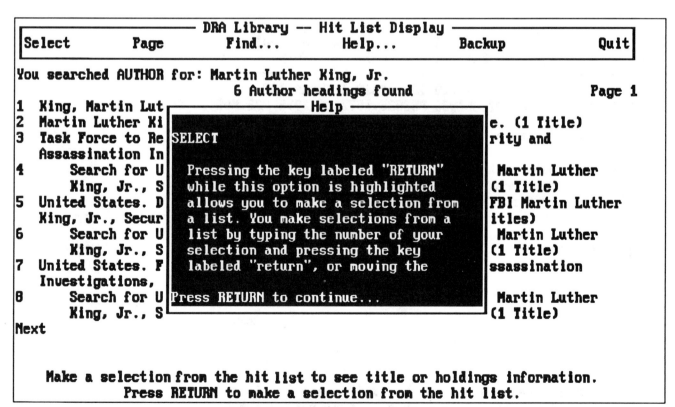

Figure 19.4: DRA: Context-sensitive help

```
┌──────────── DRA Library -- Titles Display ────────────┐
│Select      Page       Find...       Help...      Backup       Quit│
└───────────────────────────────────────────────────────┘
You searched AUTHOR for: Martin Luther King, Jr.
                    6 Titles Found                          Page 1
1  King, Martin Luther, Jr., 1929-1968. Stride toward freedom; the Montgomery
   story. [1st ed.]. New York, Harper. 1958.
2  King, Martin Luther, Jr., 1929-1968. A testament of hope: the essential
   writings of Martin Luther King, Jr. 1st ed. 1986.
3  King, Martin Luther, Jr., 1929-1968. Where do we go from here: Chaos or
   community? [1st ed.]. New York, Harper & Row. 1967.
4  King, Martin Luther, Jr., 1929-1968. Why we can't wait. [1st ed.]. New York,
   Harper & Row. 1964.
5  King, Martin Luther, Jr., 1929-1968. The words of Martin Luther King, Jr.
   New York: Newmarket Press. 1983.
6  Speaking for America[Sound recording :] twelve national leaders talk about
   their visions for America. 1975.



        Make a selection from the hit list to view holdings information.
      Enter a number OR highlight a number and press RETURN to make a selection.
```

Figure 19.5: DRA: Title list from author search

```
┌──────────── DRA Library -- Holdings Display ────────────┐
│Select      Page      Find...     Full     Help...      Backup       Quit│
└─────────────────────────────────────────────────────────┘
                    BIBLIOGRAPHIC INFORMATION
   Call Num:  PS3525I1972G61936 PS3525.I1972 G6 1936 PZ3.M69484 Go

     Author:  Mitchell, Margaret, 1900-1949.

      Title:  Gone with the wind.
  Published:  New York, Macmillan, 1936.
     Paging:  1037 p. 22 cm.
────────────────────────────────────────────────────────────
                    LOCATIONS WITH HOLDINGS
1    Ellett Brch                                              Page 1




        Make a selection from the list to see holdings information.
          Press RETURN to make a selection from the hit list.
```

Figure 19.6: DRA: Holdings display, book

```
 ┌─────────────── DRA Library -- Holdings Display ───────────────┐
 │Find...          Full          Help...         Backup      Quit│
 ├───────────────────────────────────────────────────────────────┤
 │▓▓▓▓▓▓▓▓▓▓▓▓▓▓▓▓▓▓▓BIBLIOGRAPHIC INFORMATION▓▓▓▓▓▓▓▓▓▓▓▓▓▓▓▓▓▓▓│
 │  Call Num:  E185.97K5A251986 E185.97.K5 A25 1986              │
 │                                                               │
 │    Author:  King, Martin Luther, Jr., 1929-1968.             │
 │                                                               │
 │     Title:  A testament of hope : the essential writings of Martin Luther │
 │             King, Jr. / edited by James Melvin Washington.   │
 │   Edition:  1st ed.                                           │
 │  Published: San Francisco : Harper & Row, c1986.            │
 │    Paging:  xxvi, 676 p. ; 25 cm.                            │
 │                                                               │
 │     Notes:  Includes index.                                  │
 │     Notes:  Bibliography: p. 654-661.                        │
 │  Subjects:  Afro-Americans--Civil rights.                   │
 │  Subjects:  United States--Race relations.                  │
 │Other Entry: Washington, James Melvin.                       │
 │                                                               │
 │      LCCN:    85045378                                        │
 │                                                               │
 │                                                               │
 └───────────────────────────────────────────────────────────────┘
Press RETURN for more, OR any other key to end Full Bibliographic Display.
```

Figure 19.7: DRA: Full display, book

```
 ┌─────────────── DRA Library -- Holdings Display ───────────────┐
 │Find...          Full          Help...         Backup      Quit│
 │───────────────────────────────────────────────────────────────│
 │                  BIBLIOGRAPHIC INFORMATION                    │
 │  Call Num:  E185.97K5A251986 E185.97.K5 A25 1986            │
 │                                                               │
 │    Author:  King, Martin Luther, Jr., 1929-1968.            │
 │                                                               │
 │     Title:  A testament of hope : the essential writings of Martin Luther │
 │             King, Jr. / edited by James Melvin Washington.  │
 │   Edition:  1st ed.                                          │
 │───────────────────────────────────────────────────────────────│
 │ THE LIBRARY HAS NO HOLDINGS OF THIS TITLE.  SEE LIBRARIAN FOR ASSISTANCE. │
 │                                                               │
 │                                                               │
 │                                                               │
 │                                                               │
 │                                                               │
 │▓Enter the SUBJECT you wish to locate:▓▓▓▓▓▓▓▓▓▓▓▓▓▓▓▓▓▓▓▓▓▓▓│
 │▓ Martin Luther King, Jr.▓▓▓▓▓▓▓▓▓▓▓▓▓▓▓▓▓▓▓▓▓▓▓▓▓▓▓▓▓▓▓▓▓▓▓│
 │▓and press RETURN when complete OR press EXIT cancel.▓▓▓▓▓▓▓▓│
 └───────────────────────────────────────────────────────────────┘
```

Figure 19.8: DRA: Subject search

```
┌──────────── DRA Library — Hit List Display ────────────┐
│ Select      Page        Find...      Help...    Backup        Quit │
└────────────────────────────────────────────────────────┘
You searched SUBJECT for: Martin Luther King, Jr.
                   14 Subject headings found                 Page 1
1  King, Martin Luther, Jr., 1929-1968. (LC) (17 Titles)
2  King, Martin Luther, Jr., 1929-1968. (AC) (4 Titles)
3  King, Martin Luther, Jr., 1929-1968 — Assassination. (LC) (2 Titles)
4  King, Martin Luther, Jr., 1929-1968 — Assassination — Juvenile
   literature. (LC) (1 Title)
5  King, Martin Luther, Jr., 1929-1968 — Bibliography. (LC) (1 Title)
6  King, Martin Luther, Jr., 1929-1968 — Juvenile literature. (LC) (6 Titles)
7  King, Martin Luther, Jr., 1929-1968 — Quotations. (LC) (1 Title)
8  King, Martin Luther, Jr., 1929-1968 — Religion. (LC) (1 Title)
Next




        Make a selection from the hit list to see title or holdings information.
          Press RETURN to make a selection from the hit list.
```

Figure 19.9: DRA: Subject result

```
┌──────────── DRA Library — Titles Display ────────────┐
│ Select      Page        Find...      Help...    Backup        Quit │
└────────────────────────────────────────────────────────┘
You searched SUBJECT for: Martin Luther King, Jr.
                   17 Titles Found                         Page 1
1  Ansbro, John J. Martin Luther King, Jr.: the making of a mind. Maryknoll,
   NY: Orbis Books. 1982.
2  Bennett, Lerone, 1928. What manner of man; a biography of Martin Luther
   King, Jr. Chicago, Johnson Pub. Co. 1964.
3  Bennett, Lerone, 1928. What manner of man; a biography of Martin Luther
   King, Jr. [3d rev. ed.]. Chicago, Johnson Pub. Co. 1968.
4  Davis, Lenwood G. I have a dream; the life and times of Martin Luther King,
   Jr. Westport, Conn., Negro Universities Press. 1973.
5  Garrow, David J., 1953. Bearing the cross: Martin Luther King, Jr., and the
   Southern Christian Leadership Conference, 1955-1968. 1986.
6  Garrow, David J., 1953. The FBI and Martin Luther King, Jr.: from "Solo" to
   Memphis. 1st ed. New York: W.W. Norton. 1981.
7  Great Americans: Martin Luther King, Jr.[videorecording]. 2nd ed. Chicago,
   IL: Encyclopaedia Britannica Educational Corporation. 1982.
8  In remembrance of Martin[videorecording /]. Dallas, Tex.: Idanha Films;
   Alexandria, Va.: PBS Video [distributor]. 1986.
Next
        Make a selection from the hit list to view holdings information.
      Enter a number OR highlight a number and press RETURN to make a selection.
```

Figure 19.10: DRA: Title list from subject search

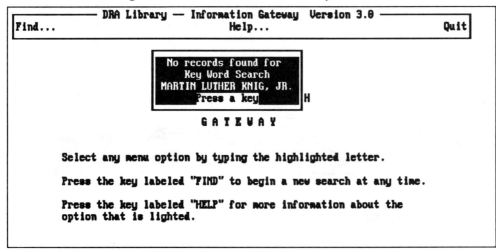

Figure 19.11: DRA: Result of spelling error

```
┌─────────────── DRA Library -- Information Gateway  Version 3.0 ───────────┐
│Find...                              Help...                          Quit│
├──────────────────────────────────────────────────────────────────────────┤

              ┌──────────────────────────────────────────────┐
              │          KNIG is not in the dictionary.      │
              │This word will be eliminated from your search.│
              │Press the key labeled "RETURN" to continue,   │
              │OR any other key to re-enter your search.     │
              │              Press a key                     │
              └──────────────────────────────────────────────┘


        Select any menu option by typing the highlighted letter.

        Press the key labeled "FIND" to begin a new search at any time.

        Press the key labeled "HELP" for more information about the
        option that is lighted.



│                                                                          │
└──────────────────────────────────────────────────────────────────────────┘
```

Figure 19.12: DRA: Action taken, spelling error

```
┌─────────────────── DRA Library -- Hit List Display ──────────────────────┐
│Select        Page        Find...        Help...      Backup        Quit│
├──────────────────────────────────────────────────────────────────────────┤
You searched SUBJECT for: Martin Luther Knig, Jr.
                     14 Subject headings found                    Page 1
1  King, Martin Luther, Jr., 1929-1968. (LC) (17 Titles)
2  King, Martin Luther, Jr., 1929-1968. (AC) (4 Titles)
3  King, Martin Luther, Jr., 1929-1968 -- Assassination. (LC) (2 Titles)
4  King, Martin Luther, Jr., 1929-1968 -- Assassination -- Juvenile
   literature. (LC) (1 Title)
5  King, Martin Luther, Jr., 1929-1968 -- Bibliography. (LC) (1 Title)
6  King, Martin Luther, Jr., 1929-1968 -- Juvenile literature. (LC) (6 Titles)
7  King, Martin Luther, Jr., 1929-1968 -- Quotations. (LC) (1 Title)
8  King, Martin Luther, Jr., 1929-1968 -- Religion. (LC) (1 Title)
Next




      Make a selection from the hit list to see title or holdings information.
         Press RETURN to make a selection from the hit list.
└──────────────────────────────────────────────────────────────────────────┘
```

Figure 19.13: DRA: Search result after error

```
┌─────────────────── DRA Library ── Holdings Display ───────────────────┐
│┌─────────────────────────────────────────────────────────────────────┐│
││Find...        Locations      Full        Help...       Backup    Quit││
│└─────────────────────────────────────────────────────────────────────┘│
│                       BIBLIOGRAPHIC INFORMATION                        │
│   Call Num:  PS35251972G61936 PS3525.1972 G6 1936 PZ3.M69484 Go        │
│                                                                        │
│    Author:  Mitchell, Margaret, 1900-1949.                             │
│                                                                        │
│     Title:  Gone with the wind.                                        │
│ Published:  New York, Macmillan, 1936.                                 │
│    Paging:  1037 p. 22 cm.                                             │
│────────────────────────────────────────────────────────────────────── │
│NO HOLDINGS AT THIS LOCATION.  SELECT LOCATIONS FOR HOLDINGS AT OTHER LOCATIONS.│
│                                                                        │
│                                                                        │
│                                                                        │
│                                                                        │
│ ┌────────────────────────────────────────────────────────────────────┐│
│ │Enter the TITLE you wish to locate:                                  ││
│ │≫Fire on the Moon                                                    ││
│ │and press RETURN when complete OR press EXIT to cancel               ││
│ └────────────────────────────────────────────────────────────────────┘│
└────────────────────────────────────────────────────────────────────────┘
```

Figure 19.14: DRA: Search with incomplete title

```
┌─────────────────── DRA Library ── Holdings Display ───────────────────┐
│┌─────────────────────────────────────────────────────────────────────┐│
││Find...            Full         Help...          Backup          Quit ││
│└─────────────────────────────────────────────────────────────────────┘│
│                       BIBLIOGRAPHIC INFORMATION                        │
│   Call Num:  TL799M6M26                                                │
│                                                                        │
│    Author:  Mailer, Norman.                                            │
│                                                                        │
│     Title:  Of a fire on the moon / [by] Norman Mailer.               │
│   Edition:  [1st ed.]                                                   │
│ Published:  Boston : Little, Brown, [1970].                            │
│────────────────────────────────────────────────────────────────────── │
│  THE LIBRARY HAS NO HOLDINGS OF THIS TITLE.  SEE LIBRARIAN FOR ASSISTANCE.│
│                                                                        │
│                                                                        │
│                                                                        │
│                                                                        │
│                                                                        │
│                                                                        │
│                                                                        │
│                 Press RETURN to search the database.                   │
└────────────────────────────────────────────────────────────────────────┘
```

Figure 19.15: DRA: Results of incomplete search

```
┌─────────── DRA Library ── Information Gateway  Version 3.0 ───────────┐
│Find...                            Help...                        Quit │
└───────────────────────────────────────────────────────────────────────┘


                    D A T A   R E S E A R C H
                    I N F O R M A T I O N
                         G A T E W A Y


        Select any menu option by typing the highlighted letter.

        Press the key labeled "FIND" to begin a new search at any time.

        Press the key labeled "HELP" for more information about the
        option that is lighted.

   ┌─────────────────────────────────────────────────────────────────┐
   │Enter the TITLE you wish to locate:                                │
   │>>Foundation and Empire                                            │
   │and press RETURN when complete OR press EXIT to cancel             │
   └─────────────────────────────────────────────────────────────────┘
```

Figure 19.16: DRA: Title search

```
┌─────────────── DRA Library ── Holdings Display ─────────────────┐
│Find...            Full           Help...        Backup      Quit │
└──────────────────────────────────────────────────────────────────┘
                     BIBLIOGRAPHIC INFORMATION
     Call Num:  PS3551S5A61981

      Author:  Asimov, Isaac, 1920-

       Title:  The Foundation trilogy : Foundation, Foundation and Empire,
                Second Foundation ; The stars, like dust ; The naked sun ; I,
    Published:  New York : Octopus/Heinemann, c1981.
   ─────────────────────────────────────────────────────────────────
   THE LIBRARY HAS NO HOLDINGS OF THIS TITLE.  SEE LIBRARIAN FOR ASSISTANCE.




        Press RETURN to view the bibliographic information in FULL screen mode.
```

Figure 19.17: DRA: Title result, internal phrase

```
┌─────────────────── DRA Library ── Holdings Display ───────────────────┐
│ Find...            Full            Help...           Backup         Quit│
├───────────────────────────────────────────────────────────────────────┤
│░░░░░░░░░░░░░░░░░░░░░░░░░BIBLIOGRAPHIC INFORMATION░░░░░░░░░░░░░░░░░░░░░░░░│
│    Call Num:  VIDEO 1179                                               │
│                                                                       │
│       Title:  In remembrance of Martin videorecording / WNET-TV, New York.│
│   Published:  Dallas, Tex. : Idanha Films ; Alexandria, Va. : PBS Video│
│               [distributor], 1986.                                    │
│      Paging:  1 videocassette (60 min.) : sd., col. ; 1/2 in.         │
│                                                                       │
│       Notes:  Made in cooperation with Martin Luther King Jr., Center for│
│               Nonviolent Social Change.                               │
│     Credits:  Creator and director, Kell Kearns.                      │
│                                                                       │
│  Annotation:  Records the tributes to the life and accomplishments of Dr.│
│               Martin Luther King Jr. which took place in Atlanta, Georgia, on│
│               the first federal holiday honoring Dr. King's birth.    │
│                                                                       │
│    Subjects:  King, Martin Luther, Jr., 1929-1968.                    │
│    Subjects:  Afro-Americans--Civil rights—United States. Civil rights│
│                                                                       │
│ Press RETURN for more, OR any other key to end Full Bibliographic Display.│
└───────────────────────────────────────────────────────────────────────┘
```

Figure 19.18: DRA: Full display, video (1 of 2)

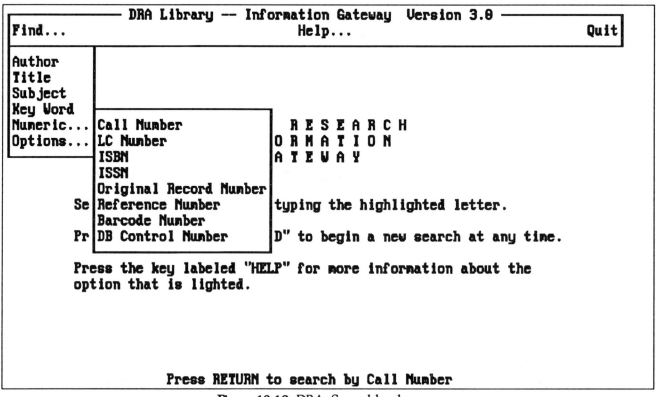

Figure 19.19: DRA: Second-level menu

20

DOBIS at Emory

Selden S. Deemer

Although DOBIS is the Rodney Dangerfield of online systems, since 1986 Emory University has done a great deal of polishing on the basic system. The total number of DOBIS systems worldwide is approaching 200, with rapid growth in Japan, where a Japanese-language version has been developed.

DOBIS runs under CICS in a standard IBM mainframe environment. About 90 percent of the program modules are written in PL/1; a few time-critical routines are written in 370 Assembly language. DOBIS is its own database manager.

The Emory DOBIS OPAC is currently an "open" system, with no identification required from either dial-in or Internet users. We have designed our system to meet the needs of a "lowest common denominator" of equipment. Only full-screen display (VT100 or IBM3163 with ALA support) is required of dial-in users. Internet users must have tn3270 support. Because of the full-screen requirement, 2400 bps is the minimum acceptable communications speed for dial-in users.

Highlighting (which may appear as a different color on color monitors) is the only display attribute that is used for information purposes; we do not use color per se to add information content to screen displays.

Our development effort has been biased toward "naive" users, on the assumption that a large portion of our users have either never used the system before, or use it so infrequently that they do not become expert in its use.

Help

The F1 key returns to the main menu from any context. The F2 key calls context-sensitive help screens throughout the system. The design of the help screens was an entirely local development, involving both library and computing staff members. Our goal was to provide clear, concise help screens that avoided jargon. All help screens follow a consistent layout that uses highlighting sparingly and keeps density low to avoid information overload.

Menus and Commands

DOBIS has a well-defined user interface, with given elements of a screen always appearing in the same locations. Although the system is menu driven, offering choices from either numbered lists or single-letter command codes, experienced users can "chain" search commands to eliminate wading through multiple screens. A command chain always begins with the slash "/" character, and each link in the is separated by a slash. Typing *//sear* takes a user into searching from anywhere in the system. Thus *//sear/1/gershwin* will search the author index for "gershwin."

Keyword Indexing

DOBIS uses KWIC indexing to generate multiple added access points from multiple surnames, corporate and conference names, all titles, and all subject headings. Because of the KWIC indexing, the role of stopwords is different than in many systems. A stopword prevents generation of an added entry; it does not prevent a user from searching under it. We have defined separate stopword lists for common languages, such as English, French, German, etc. Search terms are not case sensitive, but punctuation and spacing are significant. With the exception of multiple surnames, personal authors' names must be entered as they are stored: last name, first name.

Additional Databases

In late 1990 Emory introduced access to a locally mounted ABI/INFORM database, running under modified DOBIS software. We expect ABI/INFORM to be the first of multiple reference databases, including a campus phone book, etc. For performance and security reasons, reference databases are run in a separate CICS region. Access to ABI/INFORM is restricted to current Emory students, faculty, and staff, who are required to signon using an ID number and password.

About the Screens

The screens in this submission were generated on a Macintosh SE, running Yale's TinCan terminal emulation software. I have defined common OPAC searching functions as on-screen "buttons."

TinCan supports IBM "ALA" terminal emulation, with options to display diacritical marks super/subimposed, or side by side. TinCan also supports logging screens to disk files, preserving the extended ALA character set. Since the Macintosh handles extended characters in a different fashion, these files can be displayed and edited properly only with TinCan's built-in text editor.

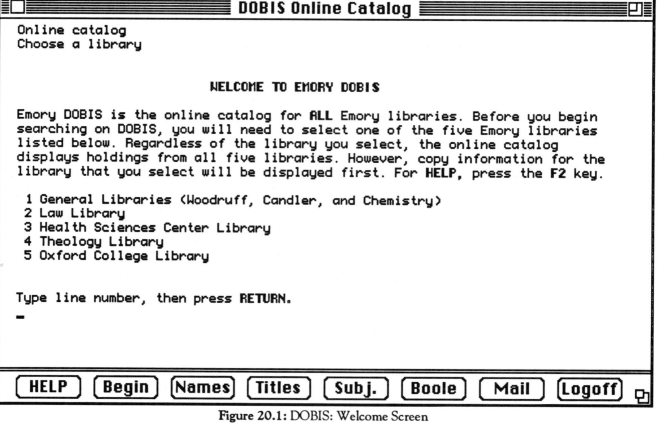

Figure 20.1: DOBIS: Welcome Screen

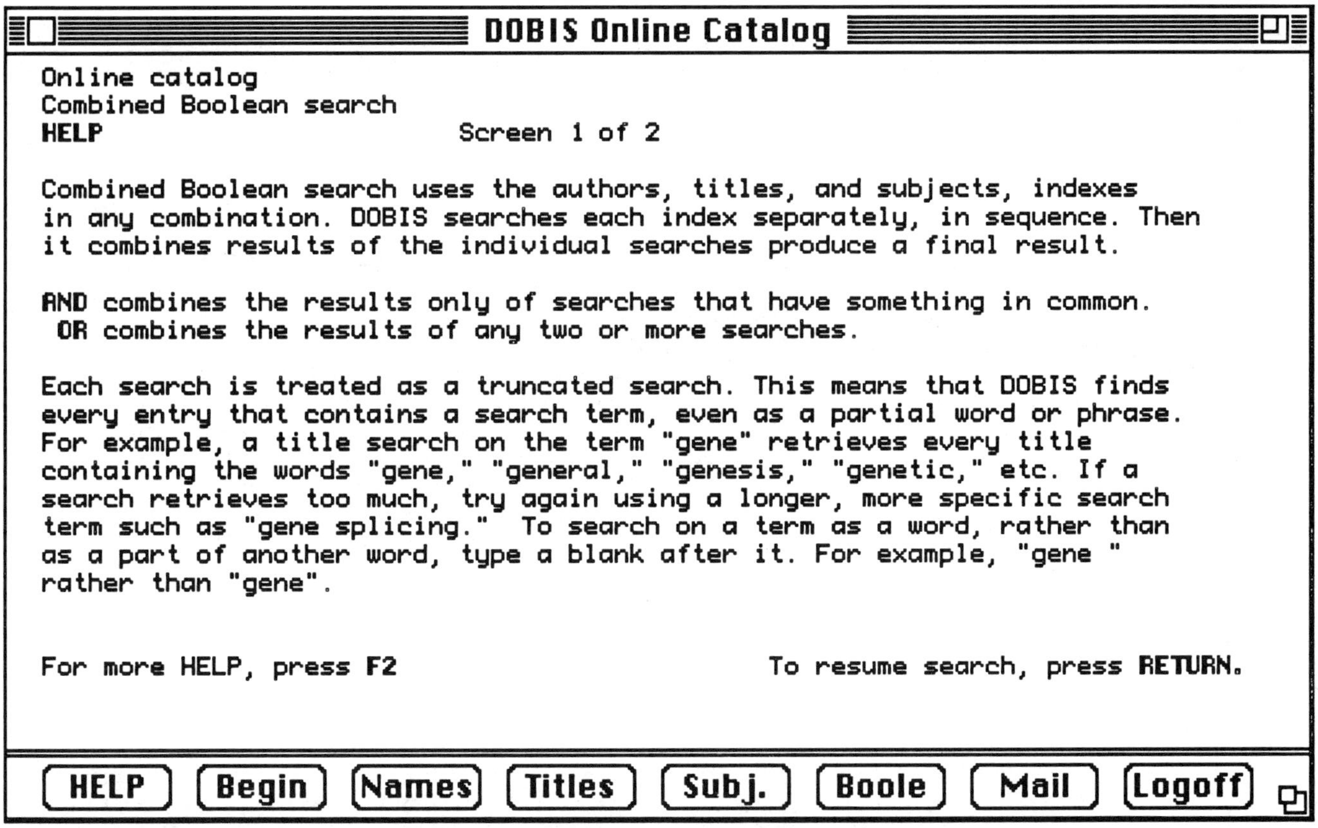

```
╔════════════════════ DOBIS Online Catalog ═════════════════════╗
║                                                                ║
║  Online catalog                                                ║
║  Combined Boolean search                                       ║
║  HELP                      Screen 1 of 2                       ║
║                                                                ║
║  Combined Boolean search uses the authors, titles, and         ║
║  subjects, indexes in any combination. DOBIS searches each     ║
║  index separately, in sequence. Then it combines results of    ║
║  the individual searches produce a final result.               ║
║                                                                ║
║  AND combines the results only of searches that have           ║
║  something in common.                                          ║
║   OR combines the results of any two or more searches.         ║
║                                                                ║
║  Each search is treated as a truncated search. This means      ║
║  that DOBIS finds every entry that contains a search term,     ║
║  even as a partial word or phrase. For example, a title        ║
║  search on the term "gene" retrieves every title containing    ║
║  the words "gene," "general," "genesis," "genetic," etc. If a  ║
║  search retrieves too much, try again using a longer, more     ║
║  specific search term such as "gene splicing." To search on a  ║
║  term as a word, rather than as a part of another word, type a ║
║  blank after it. For example, "gene " rather than "gene".      ║
║                                                                ║
║  For more HELP, press F2            To resume search, press    ║
║                                     RETURN.                    ║
║                                                                ║
╠════════════════════════════════════════════════════════════════╣
║  [ HELP ] [ Begin ] [Names] [ Titles ] [ Subj. ] [ Boole ]     ║
║           [ Mail ] [Logoff]                                    ║
╚════════════════════════════════════════════════════════════════╝
```

Figure 20.2: DOBIS: Boolean help (1 of 2)

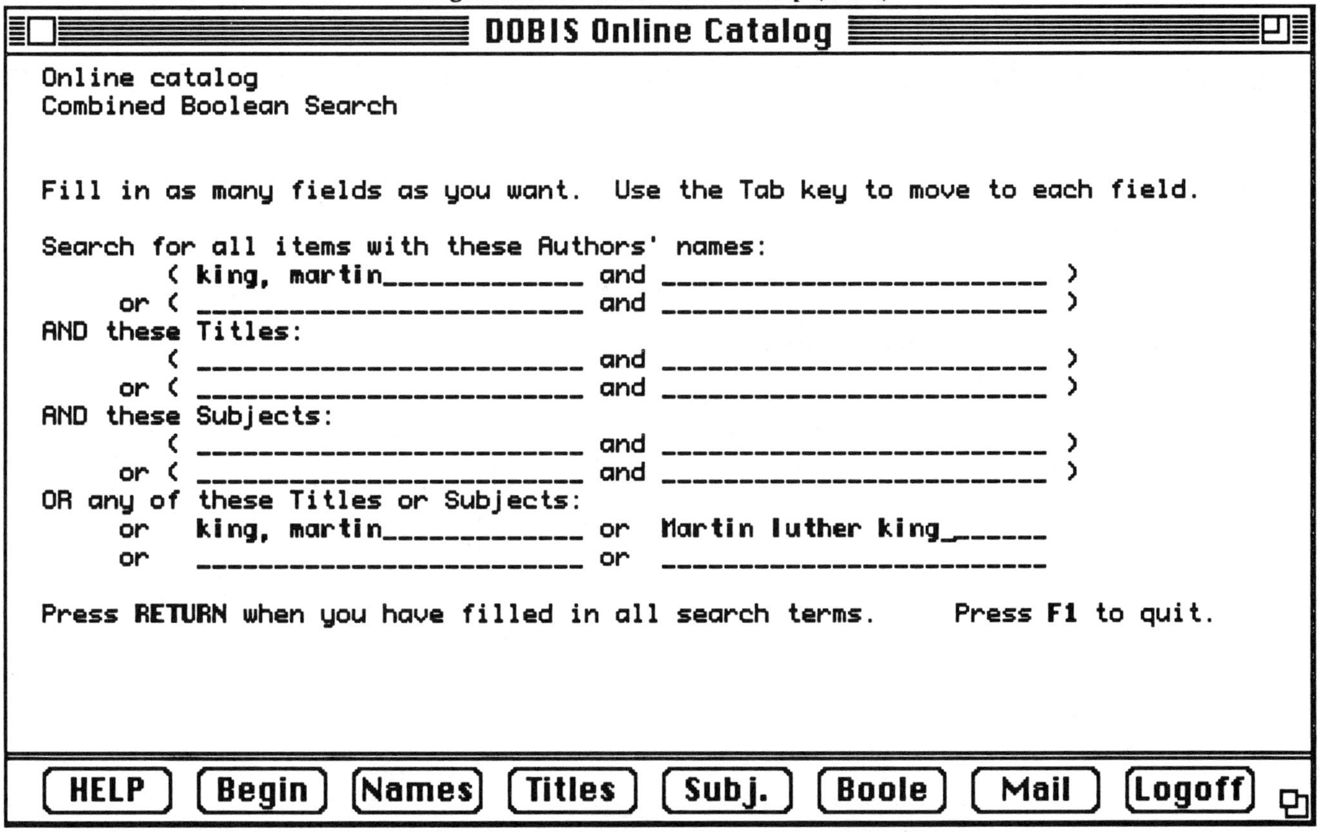

```
╔════════════════════ DOBIS Online Catalog ═════════════════════╗
║                                                                ║
║  Online catalog                                                ║
║  Combined Boolean Search                                       ║
║                                                                ║
║                                                                ║
║  Fill in as many fields as you want.  Use the Tab key to move  ║
║  to each field.                                                ║
║                                                                ║
║  Search for all items with these Authors' names:               ║
║       < king, martin_____ and _____ >        ║
║    or < _____ and _____ >              ║
║  AND these Titles:                                             ║
║       < _____ and _____ >              ║
║    or < _____ and _____ >              ║
║  AND these Subjects:                                           ║
║       < _____ and _____ >              ║
║    or < _____ and _____ >              ║
║  OR any of these Titles or Subjects:                           ║
║    or    king, martin_____ or Martin luther king_____  ║
║    or    _____ or _____                ║
║                                                                ║
║  Press RETURN when you have filled in all search terms.        ║
║  Press F1 to quit.                                             ║
║                                                                ║
╠════════════════════════════════════════════════════════════════╣
║  [ HELP ] [ Begin ] [Names] [ Titles ] [ Subj. ] [ Boole ]     ║
║           [ Mail ] [Logoff]                                    ║
╚════════════════════════════════════════════════════════════════╝
```

Figure 20.3: DOBIS: Boolean search screen

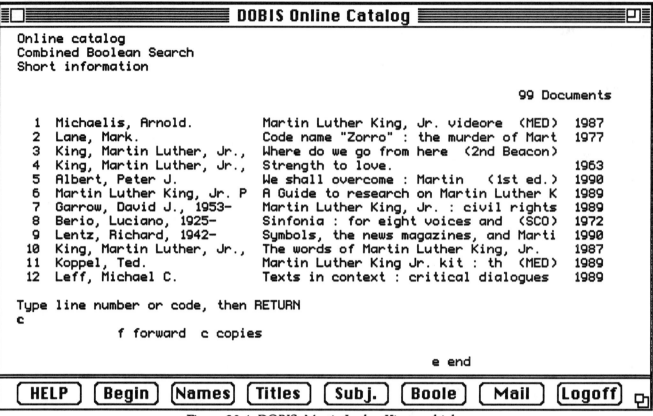

Figure 20.4: DOBIS: Martin Luther King, multiple

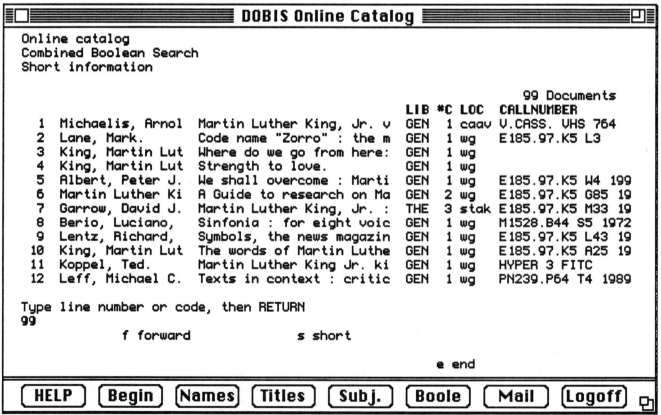

Figure 20.5: DOBIS: Martin Luther King, mult./loc

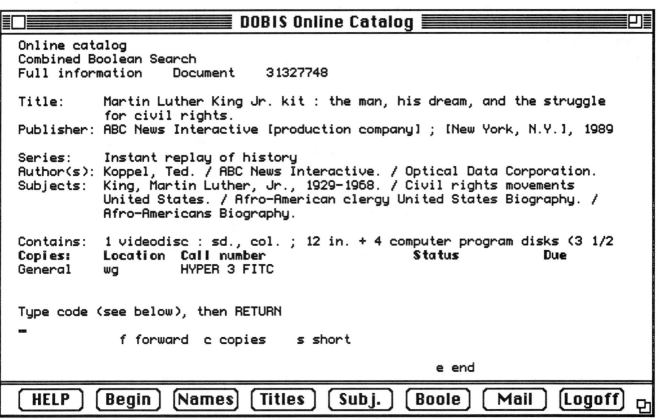

Figure 20.6: DOBIS: Long display, videodisc (1)

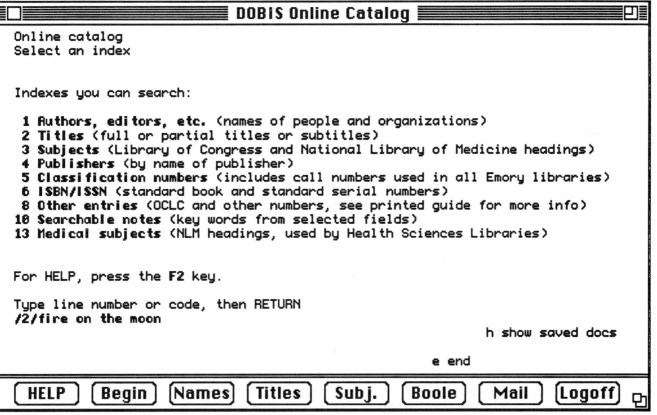

Figure 20.7: DOBIS: Search menu

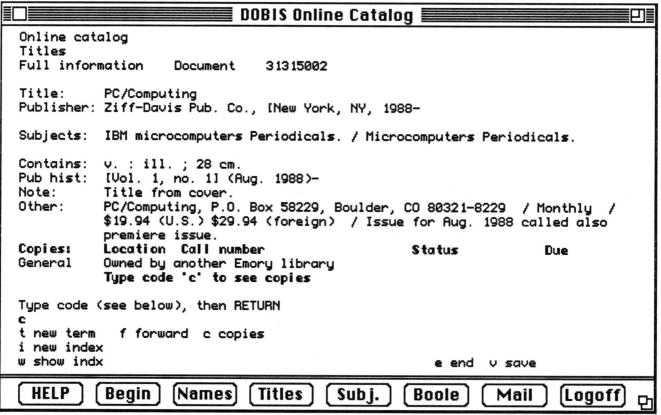

```
▤▢▥════════════ DOBIS Online Catalog ════════════▥▤
   Online catalog
   Titles


    1  /                        Fire on the earth : Anselm Kiefer and the postmode  1
    2             Of a  fire on the moon.
    3                        Fire on the mountain                                    3
    4              The  fire on the mountain, and other Ethiopian stories            1
    5   ------------------ Fire on the prairie; The story of Wheaton College.        1
    6              The  fire opal                                                    1
    7  /                        Fire over the islands : the coast watchers of the    1
    8              The  fire people.                                                 1
    9                        Fire protection guide on hazardous materials.           1
   10  / to the enemy : the  fire raid on Tokyo.--------------------------------------
   11  / g local government  fire rates : the costs and benefits
   12  / gods : the Shingon  fire ritual
   13  /            Vedic  fire sacrifice and the Eucharist : transcendence a
   14       Fire science for  fire safety

   Type line number or code, then RETURN

   ¯
   t new term    f forward                                    h show saved docs
   i new index   b backwrd                                    u truncatd search
                                                e end

  ┌──────┐ ┌───────┐ ┌───────┐ ┌────────┐ ┌───────┐ ┌───────┐ ┌──────┐ ┌────────┐
  │ HELP │ │ Begin │ │ Names │ │ Titles │ │ Subj. │ │ Boole │ │ Mail │ │ Logoff │
  └──────┘ └───────┘ └───────┘ └────────┘ └───────┘ └───────┘ └──────┘ └────────┘
```

Figure 20.8: DOBIS: Title browse

```
▤▢▥════════════ DOBIS Online Catalog ════════════▥▤
   Online catalog
   Titles
   Full information    Document    31315002

   Title:      PC/Computing
   Publisher:  Ziff-Davis Pub. Co., [New York, NY, 1988-

   Subjects:   IBM microcomputers Periodicals. / Microcomputers Periodicals.

   Contains:   v. : ill. ; 28 cm.
   Pub hist:   [Vol. 1, no. 1] (Aug. 1988)-
   Note:       Title from cover.
   Other:      PC/Computing, P.O. Box 58229, Boulder, CO 80321-8229  / Monthly  /
               $19.94 (U.S.) $29.94 (foreign)  / Issue for Aug. 1988 called also
               premiere issue.
   Copies:     Location  Call number              Status         Due
   General     Owned by another Emory library
               Type code 'c' to see copies

   Type code (see below), then RETURN
   c
   t new term    f forward   c copies
   i new index
   w show indx                                 e end   v save

  ┌──────┐ ┌───────┐ ┌───────┐ ┌────────┐ ┌───────┐ ┌───────┐ ┌──────┐ ┌────────┐
  │ HELP │ │ Begin │ │ Names │ │ Titles │ │ Subj. │ │ Boole │ │ Mail │ │ Logoff │
  └──────┘ └───────┘ └───────┘ └────────┘ └───────┘ └───────┘ └──────┘ └────────┘
```

Figure 20.9: DOBIS: Long display for serial

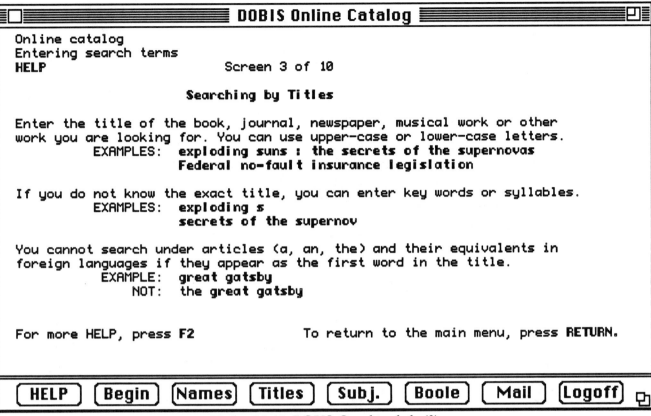

```
┌─────────────────────────────────────────────────────────────────────┐
│ ≣▣□≣══════════════ DOBIS Online Catalog ══════════════▣≣             │
│                                                                       │
│ Online catalog                                                        │
│ Entering search terms                                                 │
│ HELP                       Screen 3 of 10                             │
│                                                                       │
│                      Searching by Titles                              │
│                                                                       │
│ Enter the title of the book, journal, newspaper, musical work or other│
│ work you are looking for. You can use upper-case or lower-case letters.│
│          EXAMPLES:  exploding suns : the secrets of the supernovas    │
│                     Federal no-fault insurance legislation            │
│                                                                       │
│ If you do not know the exact title, you can enter key words or syllables.│
│          EXAMPLES:  exploding s                                       │
│                     secrets of the supernov                           │
│                                                                       │
│ You cannot search under articles (a, an, the) and their equivalents in│
│ foreign languages if they appear as the first word in the title.      │
│          EXAMPLE:  great gatsby                                       │
│              NOT:  the great gatsby                                   │
│                                                                       │
│                                                                       │
│ For more HELP, press F2           To return to the main menu, press RETURN.│
│                                                                       │
│ [ HELP ] [ Begin ] [ Names ] [ Titles ] [ Subj. ] [ Boole ] [ Mail ] [ Logoff ] │
└─────────────────────────────────────────────────────────────────────┘
```

Figure 20.10: DOBIS: Searching help (3)

```
┌─────────────────────────────────────────────────────────────────────┐
│ ≣▣□≣══════════════ DOBIS Online Catalog ══════════════▣≣             │
│                                                                       │
│ Online catalog                                                        │
│ Authors, editors, etc.                                                │
│                                                                       │
│                                                                       │
│   1                    Pyman, Avril.                              1   │
│   2                    Pynchon, Thomas.                           8   │
│   3                    Pynchon, William, 1590?-1662.              1   │
│   4                    Pynchon, William, 1723-1789.               1   │
│   5   ──────────────── Pyne, Jemima.──────────────────────────── 1   │
│   6                    Pyne, Stephen J., 1949-                    5   │
│   7                    Pyne, Timothy.                             1   │
│   8                    Pyne, W. H. (William Henry), 1769-1843.    1   │
│   9                    [Pyne, William Henry] 1769-1843.           1   │
│  10   ──────────────── Pyne, Zoë Kendrick.──────────────────────  1   │
│  11                    Pyner, David A.                            1   │
│  12                    Pynn, R.                                   2   │
│  13                    Pynoos, Jon.                               2   │
│  14                    Pynoos, Robert S., 1947-                   1   │
│                                                                       │
│ Type line number or code, then RETURN                                 │
│                                                                       │
│ t new term    f forward                      h show saved docs        │
│ i new index   b backwrd                      u truncatd search        │
│                                     e end                             │
│                                                                       │
│ [ HELP ] [ Begin ] [ Names ] [ Titles ] [ Subj. ] [ Boole ] [ Mail ] [ Logoff ] │
└─────────────────────────────────────────────────────────────────────┘
```

Figure 20.11: DOBIS: Author browse: Pynchon

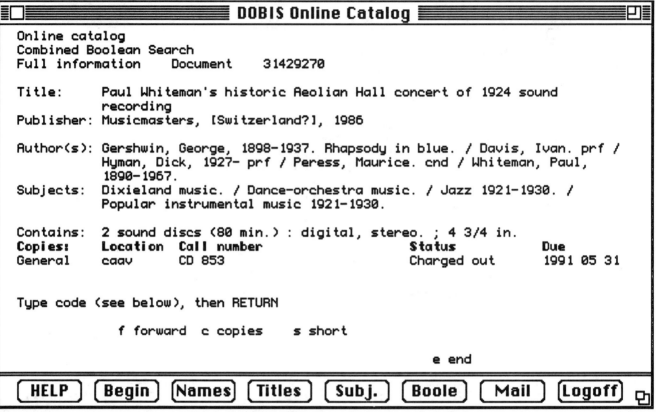

Figure 20.12: DOBIS: Long display, recording (1)

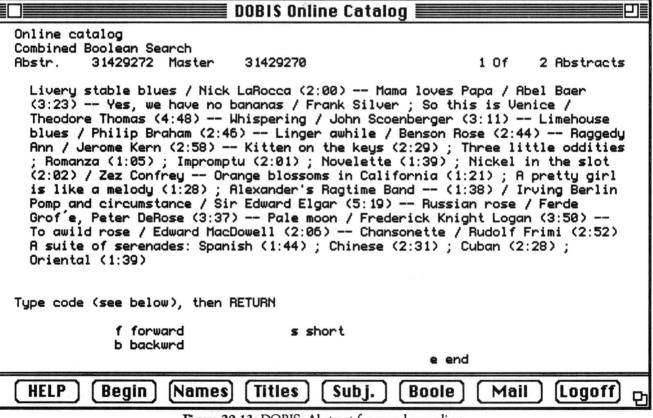

Figure 20.13: DOBIS: Abstract for sound recording

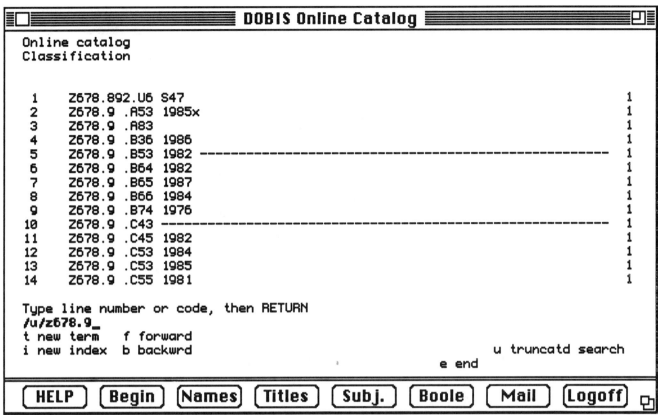

Figure 20.14: DOBIS: Call number browse

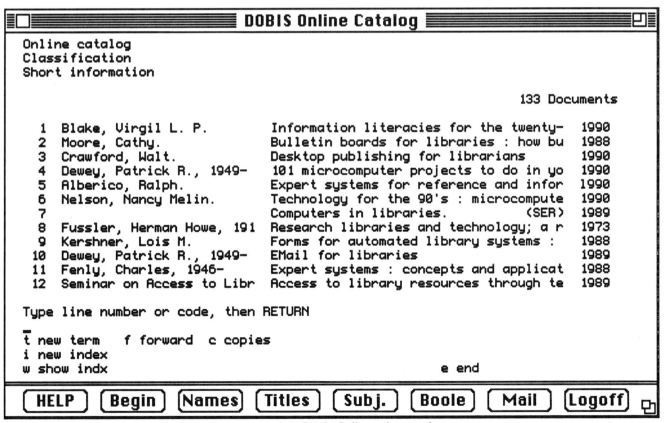

Figure 20.15: DOBIS: Call number result set

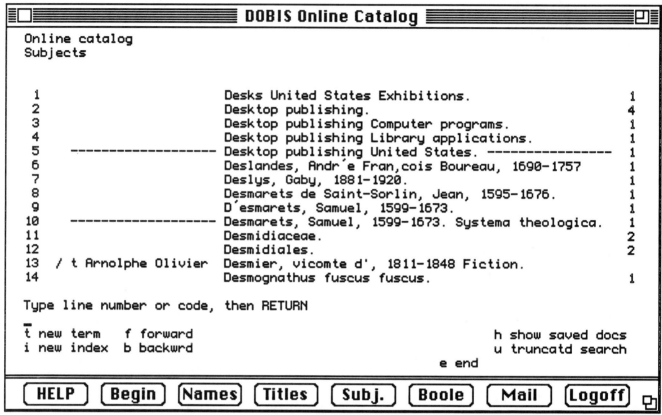

Figure 20.16: DOBIS: Subject browse

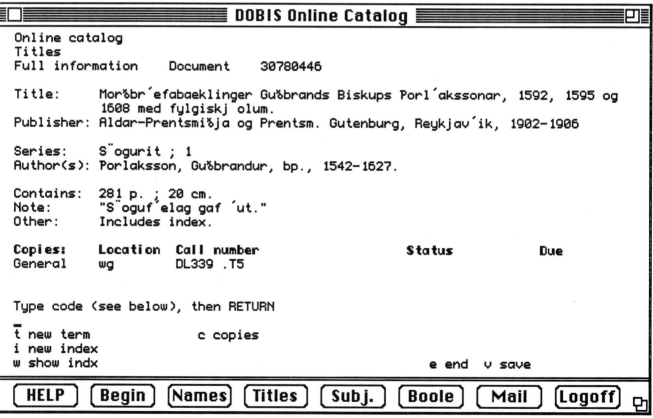

Figure 20.17: DOBIS: Book display, special chars.

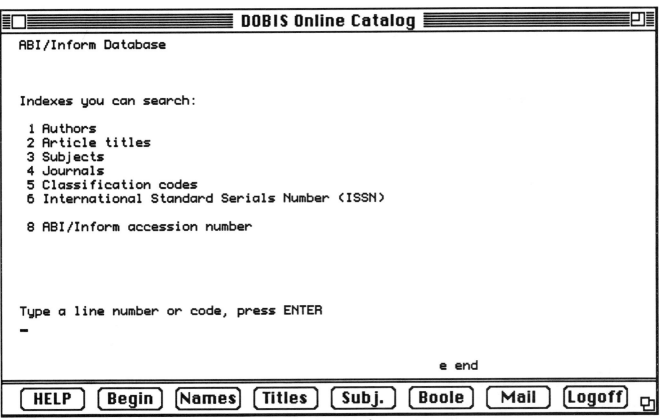

Figure 20.18: DOBIS: ABI/Inform, main menu

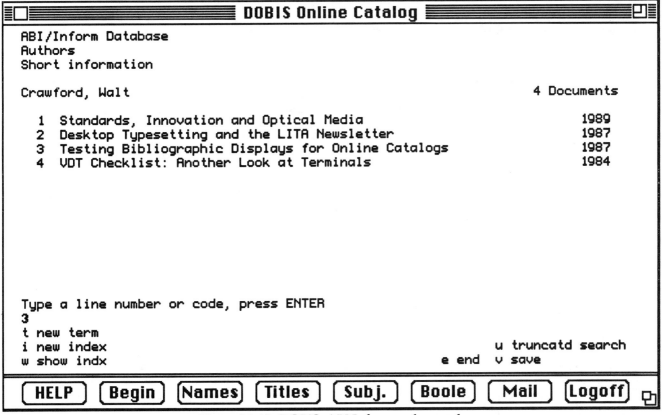

Figure 20.19: DOBIS: ABI/Inform, author result

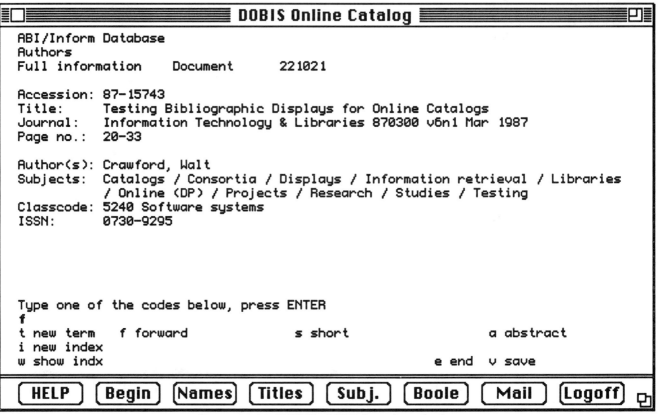

Figure 20.20: DOBIS: ABI/Inform, long display

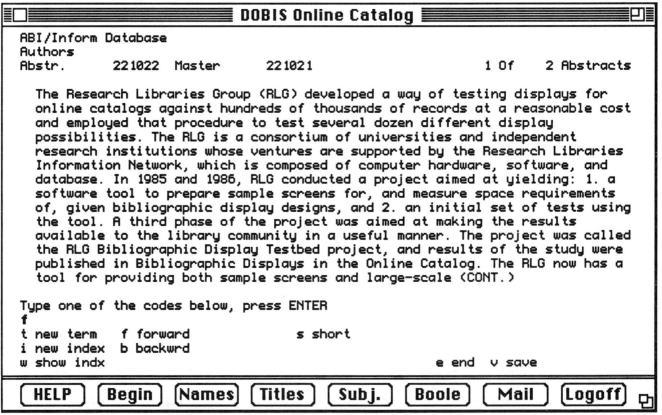

Figure 20.21: DOBIS: ABI/Inform, abstract (1)

21

Dynix
University of Dayton

Mary Ann Walker

The University of Dayton, a private Catholic university, implemented the Dynix online catalog in December 1987. The Dynix software from Dynix Libraries, Inc., of Provo, Utah, was chosen for its ease of use and its versatility. Dynix Release 130 is the version in use at Dayton. The online catalog software supports both authority control and keyword searching of indexes. It runs on many hardware platforms. The hardware selected at Dayton was a Prime 9755 with nearly 2 gigabytes of storage. Currently, there are 75 terminals and 30 Internet and dial-in ports supported by the Prime.

University of Dayton

The University of Dayton has an enrollment of nearly 10,000 students: 6,000 undergraduates and 4,000 graduate students. The institution has Schools of Education, Engineering and Law, as well as a College of Arts and Sciences. The university, through its Research Institute, is heavily involved in basic and applied research in the areas of materials science, human factors engineering, optics, biology, physics, thermodynamics, combustion engineering, and mathematics .

The Roesch Library, the university's main library, houses collections of books, journals, government documents, and microform collections that are included in the Dynix online catalog. The library's holdings consist of over 850,000 volumes and nearly 3,000 active journal titles. The School of Law Library's collection, which exceeds 165,000 volumes, is part of the Dynix system. Moreover, the Marian Library, which contains the world's largest collection of printed works on the Virgin Mary, has been inputting their holdings into the online catalog. The Marian Library's resources include 65,000 books and manuscripts in more than 50 languages. This specialized theological library also has extensive collections of religious art, national and regional bibliographies, and works on the history of the book. Both the Law Library and the Marian Library were implemented as branches in the Dynix software so that each library could maintain a distinctive online catalog and circulation operation.

Logging On

Patrons who come to the library are presented with an opening menu of Dynix search choices (Figure 21.1). If the catalog terminal is at a screen other than the opening menu, the patron can press a color-coded function key Start Over to return to the opening menu. In addition to five primary searches, choices point to additional searches, (Figure 21.2) or specialized features of the OPAC that will be discussed later.

231

To login to the Dynix catalog, a remote user must type in the following sequence: "LOGIN PUB02 (return), Password? PUBLIC (return)." The remote user is then requested to choose one of three terminal types—ADDS Viewpoint, DEC VT100, or ANSI. Additionally, those patrons who dial-in via telephone lines must set their communications software to 300, 1,200, or 2,400 bps, even parity, and full duplex.

Welcome, Help and Tutorials

The Dynix welcome screen (Figure 21.3) guides the user to help screens—i.e., type a question mark and return to find help. The help screens at this level are of a general nature. They give short explanations of the commands used in the online catalog as well as instructions for logging off the catalog. Dynix does provide more elaborate in-context help screens when the user is viewing any particular menu (e.g., Figure 21.4). With the 130 Release, it is now possible to enter the help screens during a search and type "RS" (Review Search) for a listing of the search strategy used during the search.

Currently, the University has no online tutorial for Boolean logic. However, Dynix software allows us to modify and add help screens and we plan to write such a tutorial in the near future.

Title Search and Display

The university library at present has no sound records nor compact discs in its collection. The patron can search for the title *Rhapsody in Blue* by using search #2 Title.

After selecting "2" from the menu, the help screen (Figure 21.5) is presented to the patron. A standard help screen comes with the system, however, the library can easily modify the screen with more appropriate examples for their patrons. After typing in the words of the title, a summary listing is presented to patrons (Figure 21.6). The search entered appears near the top of the screen.

One or two lines of command prompts appear at the bottom of each screen, with content depending on the screen being displayed. Commands for starting over ("SO") and for accessing help ("?") are always displayed.

Full Displays

At the full bib record (Figures 21.7 through 21.9) the bottom right-hand corner indicates that there is more information on the next screen. The command line also changes to allow the patron to move Back to the summary screen; search for Related Works; place a hold on the book (PH); and see copy status if there is more than one copy of the work. At the top of the bib record is displayed the collection code and call number of the first available copy of the book. This information is taken from the holdings record (Figure 21.10).

If the Roesch Library's copy of a book is checked out and the Law Library has an available copy, the Law Library copy will display on the bib record. If all copies are checked out; or if all available copies at this location are checked out, a message will appear on the bib record. A patron can place a hold only if all copies at a particular location are either checked out or are set to trace. No holds are permitted if the book has a status of "checked in" or a status of "lost."

The labels used in the full bib display are limited to ten characters and can be determined by the library. The library can also select the order in which fields are displayed. At Dayton, subjects are displayed before notes but after added authors and added titles. With Release 130, changes to the bib displays are done by Dynix representatives. When Release 140 is implemented, clients will be able to change their own bib displays without Dynix intervention.

A patron may toggle to the MARC format of a full bib record by pressing the letter "M." This is a hidden command in the online catalog. But once a screen displays in MARC format, the command line indicates that M = nonMarc. An example of a MARC record is Figure 21.11 for the title *Rhapsody in Blue*.

Martin Luther King, Jr., as Author and Subject

An author-search help screen (Figure 21.12) displays for author searches. The summary screen (Figure 21.13) displays the search at the top of the screen. Along the right side of the screen, the number of titles for each selection is listed. By choosing #3, a bib summary listing of the eight titles appears (Figure 21.14).

In this particular instance, one would choose only the Martin Luther King entry. In a subject keyword search or LC subject heading search the patron may wish to select several headings. Dynix software allows you to choose consecutive numbers 1-3, or discrete numbers 5, 7, at any summary screen.

Dr. King as an author has no birth and death dates. As a subject, four of the eight headings have included " Jr. — 1929–1968" in the heading. Dynix software displays "see references" and "related references." So, for example, "desktop publishing" refers directly to the heading "Electronic publishing." Related references can be chosen directly from the display or included in a set.

Keyword Searching

Figure 21.15 is an example of a keyword search using truncation—*COMPUT?*. If an excessive number of hits are retrieved, the system prompts the user to choose additional words to narrow the search. In Release 130, keywords are stopworded if the search retrieves more than 4,000 records. With Release 140 due out in December, 1991, Dynix has assured clients that the search algorithm will be rewritten. Keyword searches of even one-letter words will be supported. Thus, keyword searches on terms such as "vitamin A" will be permitted. As Dynix keyword searching performs today, stopwords are a problem. For instance, the term "legal" was stopworded after the load of the law library tapes. Words such as education, united, states and history are also stopwords.

Figures 21.16 and 21.17 demonstrate part of the title keyword search for Norman Mailer's *Of a Fire on the Moon*. In title keyword searches it is not now possible to search two letter words. I entered the words "fire" and "moon" at the beginning of the search. The second screen prompts the user for the first letter of the author's last name. By entering the author's last name, the user is taken directly to the full bib display for *Of a Fire on the Moon* (not shown).

Related Works

At the full bib screen, it is possible to perform a related works search (Figures 21.18 and 21.19). For this particular record, the related-works function could lead the user to books on subjects related to this work or to other works by Norman Mailer. If this book were part of a series, the related-works function could be used to list other books in the same series. Depending on the record, the related-works function can lead the user to a list of works by the author, coauthors, a list of titles in the series, or a list of works on related subjects.

Great Books Database

Figures 21.20 and 21.21 display the menu and a sample citation for the Great Books Database. This database was created locally. Dynix software provides a hook by which the program can be called. The database consists of personalized reviews of books by University of Dayton faculty. Broad subject categories that parallel the curricula of the university are assigned the reviews.

Reserve Materials

Patrons can search for reserve materials in the catalog. Searches are available by instructor, course number, title, title keyword, and author. Dynix software allows the inclusion of personal copies as well as the listing of periodical articles. Because the Dynix system has authority control of the author field, those reserve materials that are personal copies have three asterisks typed after the author's name. Thus on the *Report of New Authority Headings*, cataloguers can easily distinguish those headings that were created by the reserve materials versus those headings generated from the load of MARC records. Figure 21.22 displays materials placed on reserve for a particular course. Note that personal copies are designated.

Other Notes

At the university, the vast majority of government documents are kept in a separate documents collection. They are not cataloged. Yet, librarians felt that government documents should appear in the online catalog. Dynix bibliographic short entry was chosen as the method for inputting the documents—federal and state. Only the SuDocs number and the title of the documents are input into the catalog as those fields are not under authority control.

Patron Information

Patron information is available on the catalog. The patron must input her or his bar code. Then the system prompts the patron for his or her telephone number. Even though the requirement of indicating a telephone number can be troublesome for some patrons. Dynix instituted a two-tier procedure for accessing patron information because of concerns for patron privacy. A menu of patron information appears that allows one to view items currently checked out, library blocks, books that are being held at the library, and address information.

Production note: these screens were captured as text and do not show highlighting, although Dynix does use highlighting for some purposes.

```
04 MAY 91                  UNIVERSITY OF DAYTON                    04:55PM
                           PUBLIC ACCESS CATALOG

                            Welcome to DOC
                  University of Dayton Online Catalog
                   Choose one of the searches below:

                     1.   SUBJECT
                     2.   TITLE
                     3.   KEY WORD(S) in Title
                     4.   AUTHOR
                     5.   Library of Congress SUBJECT Headings
                     6.   Reserve Room Materials
                     7.   GREAT BOOKS Database
                     8.   Additional Searches
                     9.   Review Patron Record
                    10.   Print Saved Bibliography
                    11.   Logoff


    Enter your selection (1-11) and press <RETURN> :
    Commands:  ? = Help, BB = Bulletin Board
```

Figure 21.1: Dynix: Opening menu

```
04 MAY 91                    UNIVERSITY OF DAYTON                    04:55PM
                            PUBLIC ACCESS CATALOG

                        Welcome to the online catalog.
                 Please select one of the following search methods.

                            1.  SERIES
                            2.  CALL NUMBER
                            3.  GOV. DOCUMENT NUMBER
                            4.  ISBN/ISSN Number
                            5.  OCLC NUMBER
                            6.  Previous Search Menu
                            7.  Logoff




    Enter your selection (1-7) and press <RETURN> :
    Commands:  ? = Help, BB = Bulletin Board
```

Figure 21.2: Dynix: Additional searches

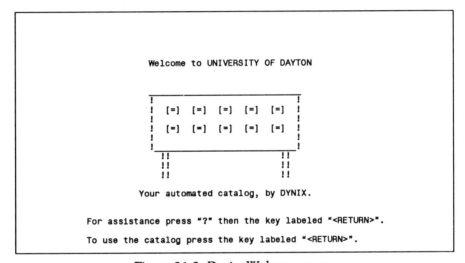

Figure 21.3: Dynix: Welcome screen

```
Lev 3 HELP for:            What Searches are Available          SCREEN 2 OF 4


                    ********* KEYWORD SEARCHES *********

    A KEYWORD search finds important words that you specify.

    For example, in a title keyword search, it will find library

    materials which have that word anywhere in their titles, whether

    it is the 5th word or the 30th word.




    Press <RETURN> for next screen :
    Commands:  SO = Start Over, A = Addt'l Topics, P = Previous Screen,
               <RETURN> = Next Screen, CS = Command Summary, Q = Quit Help
```

Figure 21.4: Dynix: Search help

```
06 MAY 91                   UNIVERSITY OF DAYTON                    09:17PM
                            PUBLIC ACCESS CATALOG


                                   TITLE



          Examples:
                       GONE WITH THE WIND    (Complete title)
                       FROM HERE TO          (OK to shorten title)






     Enter EXACT TITLE and press "RETURN" :   RHAPSODY IN BLUE

     Commands:   SO = Start Over, ? = Help
```

Figure 21.5: Dynix: Title search help screen

```
06 MAY 91                   UNIVERSITY OF DAYTON                    09:18PM
                            PUBLIC ACCESS CATALOG

     Your Search:rhapsody in blue
      #   TITLE (May be truncated)
       1. Rhapsody /

       2. Rhapsody; a dream novel;

   >   3. Rhapsody in blue /

       4. Rhapsody on the Sursum corda /

       5. Rhapsody : op. 11, no. 1 : for piano solo /

       6. Rhapsody : op. 11, no. 2 : for piano solo /

       7. Rhapsody : op. 11, no. 3 : for piano solo /



     Enter a line number for more detail :
     Commands:   SO = Start Over, B = Back, P = Previous Screen,
                 <RETURN> = Next Screen, ? = Help
```

Figure 21.6: Dynix: Title search, summary result

```
06 MAY 91                   UNIVERSITY OF DAYTON                    09:18PM
                            PUBLIC ACCESS CATALOG

     Call Number    Circulating Collection           Status : checked In
                    ML 96.5 .G4 R5


        AUTHOR      1) Gershwin, George,   1898-1937.

     ADD AUTHOR     1) Grofe, Ferde,   1892-1972.
                    2) Sultanof, Jeff.

         TITLE      Rhapsody in blue /

                    George Gershwin.

       EDITION      Gershwin 50th anniversary ed., commemorative facsim. ed.


                              - - - - More on Next Screen - - - -

     Press <RETURN> to see next screen :
     Commands:   SO = Start Over, B = Back, RW = Related Works, C = Copy status,
       PH = Place a Hold, <RETURN> = Next Screen, ? = Help
```

Figure 21.7: Dynix: Full display, score (1)

```
06 MAY 91                    UNIVERSITY OF DAYTON                    09:18PM
                             PUBLIC ACCESS CATALOG

Call Number   Circulating Collection              Status : checked In
              ML 96.5 .G4 R5
Continued...
PUBLISHER       Secaucus, N.J. (265 Secaucus Rd., Secaucus 07094) :   Warner
                Bros. Publications,   c1987.
   # PAGES      1 score (64 p.) :   port. ;   23 x 31 cm.

   SUBJECTS     1) Grofe, Ferde, - 1892-1972.
               2) Gershwin, George, - 1898-1937 - Manuscripts -
            Facsimiles.
               3) Grofe, Ferde, - 1892-1972 - Manuscripts - Facsimiles.
               4) Piano with orchestra - Scores.
               5) Music - Manuscripts - Facsimiles.

     NOTES     1) For piano and orchestra; orchestration by Ferde Grofe.

                                       - - - - More on Next Screen - - - -

Press <RETURN> to see next screen :
Commands:  SO = Start Over, B = Back, RW = Related Works, C = Copy status,
   PH = Place a Hold, <RETURN> = Next Screen, ? = Help
```

Figure 21.8: Dynix: Full display, score (2)

```
06 MAY 91                    UNIVERSITY OF DAYTON                    09:18PM
                             PUBLIC ACCESS CATALOG

Call Number   Circulating Collection              Status : checked In
              ML 96.5 .G4 R5
Continued...
               2) Line reproduction of the manuscript at the Library of Congress
            in the hand of Ferde Grofe.
               3) Prefatory material in English by Jeff Sultanof: p. 3-9.

                                       - - - - End of Title Info - - - -








Press <RETURN> to see Copy status :
Commands:  SO = Start Over, B = Back, RW = Related Works, PH = Place a Hold,
   F = First page, ? = Help
```

Figure 21.9: Dynix: Full display, score (3)

```
06 MAY 91                    UNIVERSITY OF DAYTON                    09:19PM
                             PUBLIC ACCESS CATALOG

Author Gershwin, George,   1898-1937.
  Title Rhapsody in blue /                            Holds:  0

   CALL NUMBER                         STATUS        LIBRARY
1. Circulating Collection              checked In    Roesch Library
   ML 96.5 .G4 R5








Choose a command :
Commands:  SO = Start Over, B = Back, PH = Place a Hold, ? = Help
```

Figure 21.10: Dynix: Holdings display

```
11 MAY 91                    UNIVERSITY OF DAYTON               09:18AM
                             PUBLIC ACCESS CATALOG
                                                        DYNIX #: 389919
cmI
001    16928473
020     $c $25.00
028 32 FS0004 $b Warner Bros. Publications
040    WEL $c WEL $d OBE $d IUL $d CPL $d DAY
041 0   $g eng
045 1   $b d1924 $b d1926
048     $b ka01 $a oa
049    DAYY
090    ML96.5.G4 $b R5
100 10 Gershwin, George, $d 1898-1937.
245 10 Rhapsody in blue / $c George Gershwin.
250    Gershwin 50th anniversary ed., commemorative facsim. ed.
254    Manuscript full score.
260 0  Secaucus, N.J. (265 Secaucus Rd., Secaucus 07094) : $b Warner Bro
       s. Publications, $c c1987.
                             - - - - More on Next Screen - - - -

Press <Return> to see next screen :
Commands:  SO = Start Over, B = Back, M = nonMarc, C = Copy Status,
               N = Next Screen, PH = Place a Hold, ? = Help
```

Figure 21.11: Dynix: MARC display

```
06 MAY 91                    UNIVERSITY OF DAYTON               09:20PM
                             PUBLIC ACCESS CATALOG



                                   AUTHOR



        Examples:
                     ASIMOV, ISAAC   (Author's full name)
                     HEMINGW         (Note: OK to shorten name)








Enter author LAST NAME FIRST and press "RETURN" :   KING, MARTIN LUTHER

Commands:  SO = Start Over, ? = Help
```

Figure 21.12: Dynix: Author search help screen

```
12 MAY 91                    UNIVERSITY OF DAYTON               04:15PM
                             PUBLIC ACCESS CATALOG

   Your search: king martin luther
       AUTHOR (May be truncated)                              Titles
    1.  King, Martha L.                                          3

    2.  King, Martin L.                                          1

 >  3.  King, Martin Luther.                                     8

    4.  King, Mary C.                                            1

    5.  King, Mary Ellen Tyson, 1945-                            1

    6.  King, Mervyn A.                                          2

    7.  King, Michael, 1942-                                     2


Enter a line number :
Commands:  SO = Start Over, B = Back, P = Previous Screen,
              <Enter> = Next Screen, ? = Help
```

Figure 21.13: Dynix: Author search result, summary

```
06 MAY 91                    UNIVERSITY OF DAYTON                    09:22PM
                             PUBLIC ACCESS CATALOG

  Your search: King, Martin Luther.
     AUTHOR/TITLE (truncated)                        CALL #
  1.  Small, Mary Luins.          c1969.           E185.97.K5 D42
         Creative encounters with "Dear Dr. King..." : a handbook of discussion

  2.  King, Martin Luther.        [1968,           BX6452 .K5
         Strength to love.

  3.  King, Martin Luther.        [1958]           E185.89.T8 K5
         Stride toward freedom; the Montgomery story.

  4.  King, Martin Luther.        c1986.           E185.97.K5 A25
         A testament of hope : the essential writings of Martin Luther King, Jr

  5.  King, Martin Luther.        [1968,           E185.97 .K5
         The trumpet of conscience

                               - - - - 8 titles, More on next screen - - - -
  Enter a title number for more detail :
  Commands:  SO = Start Over, B = Back, <RETURN> = Next Screen, ? = Help
```

Figure 21.14: Dynix: Author search, title summary

```
11 MAY 91                    UNIVERSITY OF DAYTON                    09:29AM
                             PUBLIC ACCESS CATALOG

  COMPUTABILITY COMPUTABLE COMPUTATION COMPUTATIONAL          Total=612
  Searching ...                                       Running total

  (COMPUTABILITY COMPUTABLE COMPUTER COMPUT)                  612




  There were no results for that combination.

  SUBJECT headings matched    612

  To narrow the search, enter more words.
  Or, press "D" and <Return> to see all 612 SUBJECT headings.

  Type additional word(s) :
  Commands:  SO = Start Over, B = Back, D = Display, ? = Help
```

Figure 21.15: Dynix: Result of truncated keyword search

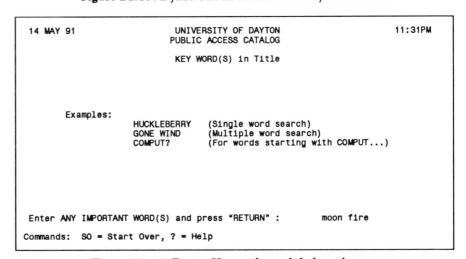

```
14 MAY 91                    UNIVERSITY OF DAYTON                    11:31PM
                             PUBLIC ACCESS CATALOG

                             KEY WORD(S) in Title




          Examples:
                     HUCKLEBERRY     (Single word search)
                     GONE WIND       (Multiple word search)
                     COMPUT?         (For words starting with COMPUT...)




  Enter ANY IMPORTANT WORD(S) and press "RETURN" :          moon fire

  Commands:  SO = Start Over, ? = Help
```

Figure 21.16: Dynix: Keyword search help and entry

```
14 MAY 91                 UNIVERSITY OF DAYTON                11:31PM
                          PUBLIC ACCESS CATALOG

                           KEY WORD(S) in Title




   You may enter first letter of author's last name, then press <RETURN>.

        Example:     T    (for Mark Twain)


   If you don't know the author's name, press <RETURN>.



 Enter ANY IMPORTANT WORD(S) and press "RETURN" :  MOON FIRE
 Enter author's name :          mailer
 Commands:  SO = Start Over, <Return> = Any Author, ? = Help
```

Figure 21.17: Dynix: Completion of keyword search

```
14 MAY 91                 UNIVERSITY OF DAYTON                11:32PM
                          PUBLIC ACCESS CATALOG

                Related Works

    AUTHOR      1. Mailer, Norman.

    SUBJECTS    2. Space flight to the moon

                3. Project Apollo

                4. Astronauts — United States

                5. United States — Civilization — 1945-




                                  - - - End of Related Works - - -

 Enter a number to see related works :
 Commands:  SO = Start Over, B = Back, ? = Help
```

Figure 21.18: Dynix: Related-works menu

```
Your search:  Related works for: Astronauts — United States
   AUTHOR/TITLE (truncated)                    CALL #
 1.                            1962.           TL789.8.U6 M52
      We seven,

 2. Baldwin, James, 1924-      1979.           D411 .V5 SEPT., '79, NO.2
      A Black author speaks out

 3. Mailer, Norman.           [1970]           TL799.M6 M26
      Of a fire on the moon.

 4. O'Leary, Brian, 1940-      1970.           TL789.85.04 A3
      The making of an ex-astronaut.

 5. Wolfe, Tom.               1979.            D411 .V5 SEPT., '79, NO.2
      Astronauts are real people.

                            - - - - 5 titles, End of List - - - -
 Enter a title number for more detail :
 Commands:  SO = Start Over, B = Back, ? = Help
```

Figure 21.19: Dynix: Related-works result

```
11 MAY 91              UNIVERSITY OF DAYTON              09:34AM
                       GREAT BOOKS DATABASE

        A list of books which members of the UD faculty
              consider important, often fundamental.

           Choose one of the searches below:

                    1.  Authors
                    2.  Titles
                    3.  Recommending Professors
                    4.  Fiction & Other Literature
                    5.  Arts & Humanities
                    6.  Business
                    7.  Education
                    8.  Engineering
                    9.  Law
                   10.  Sciences
                   11.  Social Sciences
                   12.  Return to the Public Access Catalog

        Enter your selection (1-12) and press <RETURN>:
```

Figure 21.20: Dynix: Great Books database menu

```
 11 MAY 91                     Fiction                      09:36AM

     Cervantes Saavedra, Miguel de
       Don Quixote

       New York, Modern Library, 1930
     PQ6329.A2 1930A
     Roesch Library, 5th. Floor

     This book is dedicated to the knight errant in all of us. It is
     especially inspirational to those individuals who devote much of
     their lives to crusading for unpopular and losing causes. Like
     Don Quixote's contemporaries, some may regard such crusades as
     madness, but the world is a better place for the effort.
     Conformity, comfort and taking the easy way is a recipe for
     stagnation and death of the spirit. Is it not preferable to
     sometimes choose the road less travelled, although it may lead to
     bruises and ridicule? Ride on, Don Quixote!


                      Recommended by:  Dennis Turner
                                       Law
       Press <RETURN> to continue.
```

Figure 21.21: Dynix: Great Books record display

```
 11 MAY 91               UNIVERSITY OF DAYTON                09:38AM
                         PUBLIC ACCESS CATALOG

   Your search:   ENG 102
       AUTHOR                TITLE (truncated)            CALL#
    1.                       The killers                  Hanging
    2. Carver, Raymond.      Cathedral : stories /        PS3553.A
    3. Crews, Frederick C.   Random House Handbook        Personal
    4. Farrelly, James ***   A practical guide to research paper   Personal
    5. Hemingway, Ernest,    In our time; stories         PS3515.E
    6. Kelly, William J.     Models in Process            Personal
    7. McDonald, Daniel ***  The language of argument     Personal
    8. Moffett, James.       Points of view               Personal
    9. Ramage, John D. ***   Writing arguments: a rhetoric with   Personal
   10. Seyler, Dorothy U. *  Read, reason, write          Personal
   11. Seyler, Dorothy U. *  Read, Reason, Write          Personal
   12. Troyka, Lynn (Quitma  Handbook for writers         Personal
   13. Twain, Mark,   1835-  The complete short stories and famo  PS1302 .
                         - - - - 13 titles, End of List - - - -



   Enter a title number for more detail :
 Commands:  SO = Start Over, B = Back, ? = Help
```

Figure 21.22: Dynix: Reserve books, course summary

22

Geac 9000
IRIS at Rutgers

Melinda Reagor and
Robert T. Warwick

The Integrated Rutgers Information System (IRIS) is a Geac 9000-based catalog. The circulation status of items displayed in the catalog is drawn from a separate circulation module running on a Geac 8000. The database currently contains approximately 820,000 full bibliographic records from a number of sources (CAPTAIN [an early local MARC-based system], RLIN, OCLC, Utlas) for materials cataloged or converted over the past 18 years. It includes an additional 130,000 brief records for circulating items that are still awaiting full conversion from their manual records. All formats except AMC (Archival and Manuscript Control) are represented at present; plans to load all AMC records are nearing completion. Tape loads include current CJK (Chinese, Japanese, Korean) cataloging records; loading of a retrospective CJK tape is also planned. Although complete CJK records are loaded and stored, at this time only transliterated tags are displayed.

Starting Out

The opening screen (Figure 22.1) is reached under several conditions. When library staff turn on the terminals each day, they select the catalog from a menu screen. Thereafter, the opening screen is returned to at time-out during a search session (currently set at 300 seconds) or when a patron types "end" to end a search. When a dial-in patron connects to the catalog, this is the first screen that is presented following a notice of successful connection.

The news screens (e.g., Figure 22.2) is reached by pressing Send at the opening screen. The news changes as appropriate, particularly when capabilities or services are changed or added. While there is great flexibility to the number of screens possible, effort is made to keep the length of the news manageable. A screen with current information about library hours at the major branches is a more-or-less permanent feature of the news.

The end of the news leads to a screen from which three processes, or modules, can be selected by number or mnemonic (Figure 22.3). Selection of the CATalog is prompted. When the CATalog is selected, the patron is presented with an initial search screen listing the basic search options available (Figure 22.4).

By entering "new user" at the opening screen, the patron can reach new user help screens. These two screens provide a basic overview of searching. Once New User is selected, both screens must be viewed before control is returned to the patron. Exit from them leads to the news screen(s).

243

Context-sensitive help screens are provided throughout the search process. For example, on a brief display, typing "help" leads to an explanation of the contents of a brief display (Figure 22.5). The capability of asking for help at any point is explained on the first of the two New User help screens. Help is not automatically prompted on each screen where context-sensitive help is actually available.

There are six screens of online tutorial information for Boolean logic. After a patron selects Boolean (BOL) from a list of options on the choose search screen, he is offered the three options of prompted Boolean (SRC), advanced Boolean (ABS) or more details on how to use Boolean operators (MOR). After selection, each of the three paths offers additional explanation; SRC also offers a context-sensitive help screen.

Search Process

Rhapsody in Blue on Compact Disc

A prompted Boolean search for George Gershwin's *Rhapsody in Blue* yielded 13 citations (Figures 22.6 and 22.7). Limiting the search to media recordings narrowed the result to 10 citations; a review of each of the 10 citations showed that none is a CD. If the patron is not a 19-year-old who has never owned an LP, it might occur to him to limit the search further to publication dates only after the advent of CD technology (1984), yielding 2 citations. There is no easier way to limit to CDs.

Martin Luther King, Jr. as Author or Subject

A search for Martin Luther King, Jr., whether as an author or a subject, was conducted using the advanced Boolean mode (ABS). The advanced mode is required because the easier template mode (SRC) permits only Boolean AND searches among different indexes. The advanced mode allows Boolean OR searches among different indexes.

The initial search conducted yielded 132 citations. Once it was limited to items in English published between 1980 and 1985, the search yielded 24 citations (Figures 22.8 and 22.9). Displaying the results in author-title order (Figure 22.10) or in subject-title order (Figure 22.11) reveals that the catalog lacks authority control. The two forms for Martin Luther King, Jr., that were valid at different times (i.e., King, Martin Luther and King, Martin Luther, Jr., 1929–1968) are separated by the heading for his father (King, Martin Luther, 1899–1984).

Multiple-Result Displays and Sorting Options

There are four sort options. The default display order, as retrieved (DAR), displays results in record number order (Figure 22.12) that may appear random to a patron. The display in author-title order (DAT) appears in Figure 22.10, the display in subject-title order (DST) in Figure 22.11. The remaining option is to display in title-author order (DTA) (Figure 22.13).

In all options, the displayed elements do not necessarily match the search terms that were entered. The titles are always 245s (or 240s for recordings or scores when present). The authors and subjects are always those that occur first in the retrieved record. Only Boolean searches have sort options.

Single-Result Displays

Citation 3 from Figure 22.11 is used to show all available single-record display options. All brief displays include holdings. Both brief and full displays are labeled. The long-labeled display (FUL) is shown in Figure 22.14 (partial). The brief display with holdings (Figure 22.16) is the default display. A MARC-tagged display of the bibliographic record (e.g., Figure 22.15) is available. Tagged holdings can be requested from the MARC bibliographic display.

Status and Other Information

Status information for item holdings, pulled from the circulation module, is available on the brief display (Figure 22.16).

Patron recalls and checkout are not available through the catalog, but rather through the staff-mediated circulation module. However, a patron can select patron at the select process screen (Figure 22.3) to find out what is currently checked out to him.

Multiple locations and copies appear in Figure 22.16.

Related Works

Without doing another search, there is no easy path from a single-record result to other works by George Gershwin, to other things conducted by the same conductor, or to other works on one of the same subjects as the Martin Luther King, Jr., item displayed.

Error Handling

Attempting to display a record beyond the end of the result set generates an error message (Figure 22.17)

Spelling errors in non-Boolean searches go unrecognized as such, yielding search results in the index area of the misspelling (Figure 22.18). Spelling errors in Boolean searches that produce results nonetheless also go unrecognized. Spelling errors in zero-hit Boolean searches prompt suggestions for revising the search (Figure 22.19), including a suggestion to check the spelling.

Boolean Logic

Boolean searches allow for truncated search terms (Figure 22.20). When using truncated terms, all of the matching full terms (up to a maximum of 64) will be displayed in the result list with their respective frequencies (Figure 22.21, partial).

Approximate Information

A Boolean search for "something like *Fire on the Moon*," using the title words "fire" and "moon" (Figure 22.22), yields one citation for this imperfectly remembered (as opposed to known) item.

Known-Item Searching

A title search for Thomas Pynchon's *Vineland*, for example, using the chaining feature (/) to combine the search type and search term yields an index display of titles beginning with "vineland." At this point, chaining the only entry that matches the title (1) with a request for the specific

display (**ful**) is the quickest way to a full labeled display of the record for the known item. Were this sequence entirely known at the start of the search, the entire sequence could be chained at the beginning (**til/vineland/1/ ful**).

Browsing Examples

An implicitly truncated author search for "pyn" allows browsing authors in the vicinity of "Thomas Pynchon," but all matches are highlighted.

Subjects near "Desktop publishing" can be browsed by entering "desktop" as an implicitly truncated subject; search results include the subject heading "Desktop publishing" and its subdivisions. Note that the arrangement of index entries is strictly character based, without regard for subdivision placement; the supplied screen is thus only apparently hierarchical.

"Shelflist browsing" in the area of Z678.9 is achieved by entering that character string as a call number search and scanning the resulting index display (Figure 22.23). As with other indexes, browsing the individual records corresponding to the call numbers indexed requires record-by-record selection from the index screen.

Nonbook Information

Geac supports separate customized indexing and display of fields for each separate site-defined format. Rutgers has chosen to define only the eight MARC formats as used by the national utilities.

The full-labeled record for Computer Library (Figure 22.24, partial) represents a fully cataloged machine-readable database. The full-labeled record for J.S. Bach's Mass in B Minor (Figure 22.25, partial) represents a score. It was retrieved using a prompted Boolean search limited to scores. Note that Rutgers has indexed single letters and numbers in its keyword indexes, particularly to allow for easier retrieval of music materials. The search result included four citations; a full-labeled display is provided for one of them.

Special Areas

While IRIS has no unusual indexes or access points, all the standard indexes available on RLIN are also available on IRIS (e.g. those described above, LCCN, ISBN, publishers' numbers). Rutgers made a conscious attempt to correlate IRIS with RLIN to minimize the dislocation when staff move between the two systems.

Commands can be chained during a search or display request—including beginning a new search—without returning to a menu. Mnemonic commands are unique, allowing them to be properly interpreted at any time by the system.

In addition to the patron information mentioned above, IRIS makes available information about selected materials on reserve when Reserve is selected from the select process screen (Figure 22.3). It is also possible to load external databases from commercial vendors into IRIS and make them available as additional options on the select process screen. When external databases are implemented in this fashion, they use the same search and display features as the catalog, presenting a consistent interface to users.

Rutgers is currently testing this enhancement, using the *Computer Database Index* from Information Access Corporation (IAC), but has not made it available to the public at this time. It is available only from staff terminals that have access to test systems.

IRIS has a very small list of Boolean stopwords, consciously tailored to RLIN's. When one of them is used as a Boolean search term, Geac provides a message that the term is "NI" (not indexed) and requires the user to reenter the search without the stopword. In the non-Boolean phrase indexes, only initial "a," "an," and "the" are stopwords and are ignored.

In addition to limiting searches by publication date, media, and language, patrons may also limit by Rutgers branch library locations. As many locations as desired can be selected. When a search has been limited to specific locations, only holdings from the specified locations will appear on the brief display. Other Rutgers holdings do not show.

In-library terminals are assigned to specific locations. When searching on a terminal assigned to a specific location, holdings information is rearranged to display that location's holdings first. Other locations' holdings follow.

```
@99 TECHNICAL AND AUTOMATED  - IRIS LIBRARY SYSTEM -  ALL *INTRODUCTION

                     RUTGERS UNIVERSITY LIBRARIES
        ** Welcome to IRIS - INTEGRATED RUTGERS INFORMATION SYSTEM **
IRIS is a computerized database that contains records for books and other
materials catalogued for the Rutgers University Libraries system from 1972
onward.  If you do not find an item in IRIS, check the card catalogue or the
Rutgers Union List of Serials.
        - type  CAT  to search the library catalogue.
        - type  RES  to find out about items on reserve.  You must press
                     the CAPS LOCK key before selecting RES or PAT.
        - type  PAT  to find out about the loans, fines or holds on your
                     patron record.  PAT is available only at terminals
                     with light pens.
        - type  NEW USER  for an overview of searching.
        - type  COMMAND HELP  for an overview of commands.
        - type  END  to end your search.  Dial-in users must type END
                     before hanging up.

     Press the SEND key to view library news  (<CR> if dialing in).


Now issue one of the above commands to begin; to exit type END: _
```

Figure 22.1: Geac 9000: Welcome screen

```
┌─────────────────────────────────────────────────────────────────────┐
│ 099 TECHNICAL AND AUTOMATED  - IRIS LIBRARY SYSTEM -  ALL * NEWS      │
│                                                                       │
│          LIBRARY HOURS: APRIL 26, 1991 - MAY 14, 1991                 │
│                                                                       │
│                  Monday-Thursday    Friday      Saturday    Sunday    │
│                                                                       │
│ Alexander     8 am - 1 am      8 am - midnite 9 am -midnite 11 am- 1 am│
│ Art           9 am - midnite   9 am -10 pm    9 am - 5 pm   1 pm - midnite│
│ Camden        8 am - midnite   8 am - 5 pm    9 am - 5 pm   11 am - 7 pm│
│ Chemistry  8:30 am - midnight  8:30 am -10 pm 10 am - 6 pm  noon - midnight│
│ Douglass      8 am - 1 am      8 am - 1 am    9 am - 1 am   9 am - 1 am│
│ Kilmer        8 am - 1 am      8 am - 1 am    9 am - 1 am   9 am - 1 am│
│ LSM           8 am - 1 am      8 am - 1 am    9 am - 1 am   9 am - 1 am│
│ Math       8:30 am - midnight  8:30 am -10 pm 10 am - 6 pm  noon - midnight│
│ Newark Dana   8 am - midnite   8 am - 9 pm    10 am - 6 pm  noon - 10 pm│
│                                                                       │
│                                                                       │
│ Ask at the reference desk for other library hours.                    │
│                                                                       │
│                                                                       │
│                                                                       │
│ Press SEND to continue _                                              │
└─────────────────────────────────────────────────────────────────────┘
```

Figure 22.2: Geac 9000: News screen (3)

```
┌─────────────────────────────────────────────────────────────────────┐
│ 099 TECHNICAL AND AUTOMATED  - IRIS LIBRARY SYSTEM -  ALL *SELECT PROCESS│
│                                                                       │
│                                                                       │
│                                                                       │
│                                                                       │
│ Which process do you wish to select?                                  │
│                                                                       │
│          1. CAT - Search the library catalog                          │
│                                                                       │
│          2. PAT - Find out about your fines, loans, holds, patron record│
│                                                                       │
│          3. RES - Find out about items on reserve                     │
│                                                                       │
│                                                                       │
│                                                                       │
│                                                                       │
│                                                                       │
│ Enter number or code: CAT                        Then press SEND      │
└─────────────────────────────────────────────────────────────────────┘
```

Figure 22.3: Geac 9000: Process selection

```
┌─────────────────────────────────────────────────────────────────────┐
│ 099 TECHNICAL AND AUTOMATED  - IRIS LIBRARY SYSTEM -  ALL *CHOOSE SEARCH│
│   What type of search do you wish to do?                              │
│                                                                       │
│          1. TIL - Title, journal title, series title, etc.            │
│                                                                       │
│          2. AUT - Author, illustrator, editor, organization, etc.     │
│                                                                       │
│          3. SUB - Subject heading assigned by library.                │
│                                                                       │
│          4. NUM - Call number, ISBN, ISSN, etc.                       │
│                                                                       │
│          5. BOL - Boolean or keyword search.                          │
│                                                                       │
│          6. LIM - Limit your search to a portion of the catalogue.    │
│                                                                       │
│                                                                       │
│                                                                       │
│ Enter number or code: _                          Then press SEND      │
└─────────────────────────────────────────────────────────────────────┘
```

Figure 22.4: Geac 9000: General search screen

```
099 TECHNICAL AND AUTOMATED  - IRIS LIBRARY SYSTEM -  LIN *BOOLEAN SEARCH-HELP

     The system has just shown you a brief citation, which includes call numbers
and location information.

     The symbol * is used to separate multiple authors and titles.
     The symbol ▸ is used when there is too much information to fit on one line.

     To return to your brief citation, type  PS  for  PREVIOUS SCREEN .

     In addition, you may use one of the following codes:

          FUL - to see an expanded version of your citation
          CAT - to begin another search
          IND - to see an alphabetical list of titles
          FOR - to see next citation in your list
          BAC - to see previous citation in your list
          REV - to revise current search string.




Enter code: _                                        Then press SEND
```

Figure 22.5: Geac 9000: Context-sensitive help

```
099 TECHNICAL AND AUTOMATED  - IRIS LIBRARY SYSTEM -   ALL *PROMPTED BOOLEAN

Enter one or more words. Use OPTION 1 or 2, but not both.
 OPTION 1
   All Indexes :
 OPTION 2
   Author  Index : gershwin                                            AND
   Title   Index : rhapsody blue_                                      AND
   Subject Index :
 Published After:     (year) Before:      Language:ALL       Media:ALL


Use Option 1 or Option 2, but not both.

    OPTION 1 EXAMPLES:   All Indexes:  ECONOMICS
                         All Indexes:  ENVIRONMENT* TECHNOLOGY
      OPTION 2 EXAMPLE:  Author  Index:  RUTGERS
                         Title   Index:  PINELANDS
                         Subject Index:

     To exit this screen without doing a boolean search, move the cursor
next to "All Indexes" and enter a  /  followed by a command.  For
example.  /CAT  will start a new search:  /HELP  will give you more
```

Figure 22.6: Geac 9000: Two-index Boolean search

```
099 TECHNICAL AND AUTOMATED  - IRIS LIBRARY SYSTEM -   ALL *BOOLEAN RESULTS

  # WORD                   AUTHOR     TITLE     SUBJECT      TOTAL

  1 BLUE                       0       786          0         786
  2 GERSHWIN                 236         0          0         236
  3 RHAPSODY                   0       122          0         122






  ----------------------------------------------------------------
  Your search has found    13 CITATIONS from     1,144 word occurrences.

    DAR - display as retrieved        REV - Revise current search request
    DAT - display in author/title order  CAT - begin a non-Boolean search
    DTA - display in title/author order  DST - display in subject/title order
    ABS - advanced Boolean search     CMD - see additional commands

  Enter Command: DAR                                   Then press SEND
```

Figure 22.7: Geac 9000: Boolean result summary

```
099 TECHNICAL AND AUTOMATED  - IRIS LIBRARY SYSTEM -  LIN *ADVANCED BOOLEAN

   Identify each word as a  T: Title word,  A: Author word, or  S: Subject word.

   Use operators and symbols as needed: & or blank means AND, / means OR,
   ! means BUT NOT, - joins words in a phrase, * gives a word any ending,
   () groups words in a search request.

   Some examples:   T:GENTRIFICATION
                    T:HAMLET A:SHAKESPEARE
                    T:DIRECT-MAIL
                    S:ROBOT*

   For help enter BOL/MOR/
Qualified by : Date Language . Use the SHO/ command for details

Enter Search Request :<a:luther a:king>/<s:luther s:king>_
```

Figure 22.8: Geac 9000: Advanced Boolean search

```
099 TECHNICAL AND AUTOMATED  - IRIS LIBRARY SYSTEM -  LIN *BOOLEAN RESULTS

 # WORD                        AUTHOR    TITLE    SUBJECT      TOTAL

 1 KING                         1,995      0       2,096       4,091
 2 LUTHER                         461      0         331         792




-----------------------------------------------------------------------------
Your search has found    24 CITATIONS from      4,883 word occurrences.

   DAR - display as retrieved          REV - Revise current search request
   DAT - display in author/title order CAT - begin a non-Boolean search
   DTA - display in title/author order DST - display in subject/title order
   ABS - advanced Boolean search       CMD - see additional commands

Enter Command: DAR                                    Then press SEND
```

Figure 22.9: Geac 9000: Boolean result summary

```
099 TECHNICAL AND AUTOMATED  - IRIS LIBRARY SYSTEM -  LIN *BOOLEAN SEARCH

                                                matches    24 titles
Ref# Author                      Title                          Date
   1 Ansbro, John.               Martin Luther King, Jr. : the m>  1982
   2 Clausen, A. W.              Poverty in the developing count>  1985
   3 Garrow, David J., 1953-     The FBI and Martin Luther King,>  1983
   4 Garrow, David J., 1953-     The FBI and Martin Luther King,>  1981
   5 Garrow, David J., 1953-     The Martin Luther King, Jr. FBI>  1984
   6 Hanigan, James P.           Martin Luther King, Jr. and the>  1984
   7 King, Martin Luther.        King, Malcolm, Baldwin : three >  1985
   8 King, Martin Luther, 1899-  Daddy King : an autobiography /   1980
   9 King, Martin Luther, Jr., 1929-> Strength to love /           1984
  10 King, Martin Luther, Jr., 1929-> Strength to love /           1981
  11 King, Martin Luther, Jr., 1929-> The words of Martin Luther King> 1983
  12 Lincoln, C. Eric <Charles Eric>> Martin Luther King, Jr. : a pro> 1984
                  THIS IS THE START OF YOUR SEARCH RESULT LIST

Type a number to see more information -OR-
   FOR - move forward in this list      CAT - begin a new search
   ALL - remove all search limits       SHO - display current search limits
   REV - revise current search          CMD - see additional commands
Enter number or code: FOR                             Then press SEND
```

Figure 22.10: Geac 9000: Multiple, author-title

```
099 TECHNICAL AND AUTOMATED  - IRIS LIBRARY SYSTEM -  LIM *BOOLEAN SEARCH

                                         matches    24 titles
   Ref# Subject                    Title                      Date
      1 Afro-American Baptists -- Sermo> Strength to love /    1984
      2 Afro-American Baptists -- Sermo> Strength to love /    1981
      3 Afro-Americans -- Civil rights.  King, Malcolm, Baldwin : three >  1985
      4 Kennedy, John Fitzgerald, Pres.>  Of Kennedys and Kings : making >  1980
      5 Kennedy, John Fitzgerald, Pres.>  Of Kennedys and Kings : making >  1980
      6 King, Martin Luther.       The FBI and Martin Luther King,>  1983
      7 King, Martin Luther.       The FBI and Martin Luther King,>  1981
      8 King, Martin Luther.       Let the trumpet sound : the lif>  1982
      9 King, Martin Luther.       Let the trumpet sound : the lif>  1985
     10 King, Martin Luther.       Martin Luther King, Jr. and the>  1984
     11 King, Martin Luther.       Martin Luther King, Jr. : the m>  1982
     12 King, Martin Luther.       Martin Luther King, Jr.--to the>  1985
                    THIS IS THE START OF YOUR SEARCH RESULT LIST


   Type a number to see more information -OR-
     FOR - move forward in this list    CAT - begin a new search
     ALL - remove all search limits     SHO - display current search limits
     REV - revise current search        CMD - see additional commands
   Enter number or code: FOR                      Then press SEND
```

Figure 22.11: Geac 9000: Multiple, subject-title

```
099 TECHNICAL AND AUTOMATED  - IRIS LIBRARY SYSTEM -  LIM *BOOLEAN SEARCH

                                         matches    24 titles
   Ref# Title                      Author                     Date
      1 Of Kennedys and Kings : making >  Wofford, Harris.      1980
      2 Daddy King : an autobiography /  King, Martin Luther, 1899-  1980
      3 Of Kennedys and Kings : making >  Wofford, Harris.      1980
      4 The FBI and Martin Luther King,>  Garrow, David J., 1953-  1983
      5 The FBI and Martin Luther King,>  Garrow, David J., 1953-  1981
      6 Let the trumpet sound : the lif>  Oates, Stephen B.     1982
      7 Martin Luther King, Jr. : the m>  Ansbro, John.         1982
      8 Builders of the dream : Abraham>  Oates, Stephen B.     1982
      9 The Martin Luther King, Jr. FBI>  Garrow, David J., 1953-  1984
     10 Martin Luther King, Jr. : a pro>  Lincoln, C. Eric <Charles Eric>>  1984
     11 Martin Luther King, Jr. and the>  Hanigan, James P.     1984
     12 King, Malcolm, Baldwin : three >  King, Martin Luther.  1985
                    THIS IS THE START OF YOUR SEARCH RESULT LIST


   Type a number to see more information -OR-
     FOR - move forward in this list    CAT - begin a new search
     ALL - remove all search limits     SHO - display current search limits
     REV - revise current search        CMD - see additional commands
   Enter number or code: FOR                      Then press SEND
```

Figure 22.12: Geac 9000: Multiple, default order

```
099 TECHNICAL AND AUTOMATED  - IRIS LIBRARY SYSTEM -  LIM *BOOLEAN SEARCH

                                         matches    24 titles
   Ref# Title                      Author                     Date
      1 Builders of the dream : Abraham>  Oates, Stephen B.     1982
      2 Daddy King : an autobiography /  King, Martin Luther, 1899-  1980
      3 The ethics of Martin Luther Kin>  Smith, Ervin.         1981
      4 The FBI and Martin Luther King,>  Garrow, David J., 1953-  1983
      5 The FBI and Martin Luther King,>  Garrow, David J., 1953-  1981
      6 King, Malcolm, Baldwin : three >  King, Martin Luther.  1985
      7 Let the trumpet sound : the lif>  Oates, Stephen B.     1982
      8 Let the trumpet sound : the lif>  Oates, Stephen B.     1985
      9 Martin Luther King /           Shuker, Nancy.         1985
     10 Martin Luther King, Jr. : a pro>  Lincoln, C. Eric <Charles Eric>>  1984
     11 Martin Luther King, Jr. and the>  Hanigan, James P.     1984
     12 The Martin Luther King, Jr. FBI>  Garrow, David J., 1953-  1984
                    THIS IS THE START OF YOUR SEARCH RESULT LIST


   Type a number to see more information -OR-
     FOR - move forward in this list    CAT - begin a new search
     ALL - remove all search limits     SHO - display current search limits
     REV - revise current search        CMD - see additional commands
   Enter number or code: FOR                      Then press SEND
```

Figure 22.13: Geac 9000: Multiple, title-author

```
099 TECHNICAL AND AUTOMATED  - IRIS LIBRARY SYSTEM -  LIM *BOOLEAN SEARCH

                                              Citation  3 of  24
    AUTHOR King, Martin Luther.
     TITLE King, Malcolm, Baldwin : three interviews / by Kenneth B. Clark, with
           new introduction.
   EDITION 1st Wesleyan paperback ed.
 PUBLISHER Middletown, Conn. : Wesleyan University Press ; Scranton, Pa. :
           Distributed by Harper & Row, 1985.
   DESCRIP viii, 65 p. : ports. ; 21 cm.
     NOTES Rev. ed. of: The Negro protest. 1963.
 OTHER AUT X, Malcolm, 1925-1965. * Baldwin, James, 1924- * Clark, Kenneth
           Bancroft, 1914- * Baldwin, James, 1924- Negro protest.
  SUBJECTS Afro-Americans -- Civil rights. * Afro-Americans -- Interviews. *
           United States -- Race relations.
   LC CARD   83823490
      ISBN 0819560901 (pbk. : alk. paper) :

    BRF - see locations and call numbers   CIT - return to your citation list
    FOR - see next citation in list        BAC - see previous citation
    CON - see next screen                   CAT - begin a new search
    REV - revise current search             CMD - see additional commands
 Enter code: _                                      Then press SEND
```

Figure 22.14: Geac 9000: Full display (partial)

```
099 TECHNICAL AND AUTOMATED  - IRIS LIBRARY SYSTEM -  LIM *MARC RECORD DISPLAY

                                              Citation  3 of  24
    001    NJR005252763
    008    841127s1985    ctuc          00010 eng
    010     $a  83823490
    020     $a0819560901 (pbk. : alk. paper) :$c 0.95
    035     $bRLINNJR$c084-B33244
    040     $dCStRLIN$dNJR
    043     $an-us---
    050    0 $aE185.61$b.K533 1985
    090     $aE185.61$b.K533 1985$103/13/89 CT$h05/28/87 N$h01/07/87 N$h10/27/86
           N$h11/18/85 CT$h11/15/85 C$h11/07/85 CTZ
    099     $aE185.61.K533 1985
    100    10$aKing, Martin Luther.
    245    10$aKing, Malcolm, Baldwin :$bthree interviews /$cby Kenneth B. Clark,>

    BRF - see locations and call numbers   FUL - see complete citation
    CIT - return to your citation list     FOR - see next citation in list
    BAC - see previous citation            CON - see next screen
    HOL - display holdings                 CMD - see additional commands
 Enter code: CON                                    Then press SEND
                **CONTINUED ON NEXT SCREEN**
```

Figure 22.15: Geac 9000: MARC display (partial)

```
099 TECHNICAL AND AUTOMATED  - IRIS LIBRARY SYSTEM -  LIM *BOOLEAN SEARCH

                                              Citation  3 of  24
    AUTHOR King, Martin Luther.
     TITLE King, Malcolm, Baldwin : three interviews / by Kenneth B. Clark, with>
   EDITION 1st Wesleyan paperback ed.
 PUBLISHER Middletown, Conn. : Wesleyan University Press ; Scranton, Pa. :
           Distributed by Harper & Row, 1985.

               Loan    Call              Cpy
 Location      Type    Number            #     Status

 CAMDN         NIGGIN  E185.61.K533 1985  1    In Library
 ALEX          STACKS  E185.61.K533 1985  2    On Loan        91-06-02 24:00
 ALEX          STACKS  E185.61.K533 1985  3    In Library
 DANA          STACKS  E185.61.K533 1985  1    In Library
 DANA          STACKS  E185.61.K533 1985  2    In Library

    FUL - see complete citation          CIT - return to your citation list
    FOR - see next citation in list      BAC - see previous citation
    CAT - begin a new search             REV - revise current search
    CMD - see additional commands
 Enter code: _                                      Then press SEND
```

Figure 22.16: Geac 9000: Brief display, holdings

```
099 TECHNICAL AND AUTOMATED  - IRIS LIBRARY SYSTEM -  LIM *BOOLEAN SEARCH

   Ref# Subject                        Title                          Date
      3 Afro-Americans -- Civil rights.  King, Malcolm, Baldwin : three >  1985
      4 Kennedy, John Fitzgerald, Pres.>  Of Kennedys and Kings : making >  1988
      5 Kennedy, John Fitzgerald, Pres.>  Of Kennedys and Kings : making >  1988
      6 King, Martin Luther.             The FBI and Martin Luther King,>  1983
      7 King, Martin Luther.             The FBI and Martin Luther King,>  1981
      8 King, Martin Luther.             Let the trumpet sound : the lif>  1982
      9 King, Martin Luther.             Let the trumpet sound : the lif>  1985
     10 King, Martin Luther.             Martin Luther King, Jr. and the>  1984
     11 King, Martin Luther.             Martin Luther King, Jr. : the m>  1982
     12 King, Martin Luther.             Martin Luther King, Jr.--to the>  1985
     13 King, Martin Luther.             Roots of resistance : the nonvi>  1985
     14 King, Martin Luther, 1899-       Daddy King : an autobiography /   1988



 Type a number to see more information -OR-
   FOR - move forward in this list      BAC - move backward in this list
   CAT - begin a new search             ALL - remove all search limits
   SHO - display current search limits  CMD - see additional commands
 Enter number or code: _                            Then press SEND
               YOUR NUMBER IS NOT INCLUDED IN CURRENT LIST
```

Figure 22.17: Geac 9000: Message for error above

```
099 TECHNICAL AND AUTOMATED  - IRIS LIBRARY SYSTEM -  ALL *TITLE SEARCH

   Your title: rapsody in blue                  matches  no   titles
   Alphabetically close headings are listed below

                                                  No. of citations
                                                  in entire catalog
    1 Rapsodije iz proslog srpskog zivota : memoary /               1
    2 El rapto del santo grial, e, El caballero de la verde oliva /  1
    3 El raptor de la hija de Lope de Vega.                         1
    4 Raptors.                                                      1
    5 Raptors. 1969.                                                1
    6 Rapunzel /                                                    1
    7 Rapunzel, a story by the brothers Grimm, with pictures by Felix H>  1
    8 Rapunzel's revenge : fairytales for feminists.                1
    9 Rapunzel [Sound recording]                                    2
   10 Raquel                                                        1
   11 Raquel, the Jewess of Toledo.                                 1

 Type a number to see more information -OR-
   FOR - move forward in this list      BAC - move backward in this list
   CAT - begin a new search

 Enter number or code: FOR                          Then press SEND
```

Figure 22.18: Geac 9000: Result of spelling error

```
099 TECHNICAL AND AUTOMATED  - IRIS LIBRARY SYSTEM -  ALL *BOOLEAN RESULTS

  # WORD              AUTHOR    TITLE    SUBJECT     TOTAL

  1 BLUE                 0       786        0         786
  2 RAPSODY              0        0         0          0




  ---------------------------------------------------------------
             No CITATIONS found.
             Revise search request - Check spelling,  try other keywords
   REV - Revise current search request - CAT - begin a non-Boolean search
   ABS - advanced Boolean search        SRC - prompted Boolean
   HLP - for complete help menu


 Enter Command: REV                                 Then press SEND
```

Figure 22.19: Geac 9000: Spelling error, Boolean

```
099 TECHNICAL AND AUTOMATED  - IRIS LIBRARY SYSTEM -  ALL *ADVANCED BOOLEAN

   Identify each word as a  T: Title word,  A: Author word, or  S: Subject word.

   Use operators and symbols as needed:  & or blank means AND,  / means OR,
   ! means BUT NOT,  - joins words in a phrase,  * gives a word any ending,
   () groups words in a search request.

   Some examples:    T:GENTRIFICATION
                     T:HAMLET A:SHAKESPEARE
                     T:DIRECT-MAIL
                     S:ROBOT*

   For help enter BOL/NOR/


Enter Search Request :t:trunc*!t:searc*_
```

Figure 22.20: Geac 9000: Truncated title search

```
099 TECHNICAL AND AUTOMATED  - IRIS LIBRARY SYSTEM -  ALL *BOOLEAN RESULTS

   # WORD                    AUTHOR     TITLE     SUBJECT      TOTAL

   1 SEARCH                     0       1,553        0         1,553
   2 SEARCHED                   0           3        0             3
   3 SEARCHER                   0           8        0             8
   4 SEARCHERS                  0           5        0             5
   5 SEARCHES                   0          16        0            16
   6 SEARCHING                  0         161        0           161
   7 SEARCHINGS                 0           2        0             2
   8 SEARCHLIGHT                0          25        0            25
   9 SEARCHLIGHTS               0           3        0             3


Your search has found  17 WORDS

   REV - Revise current search request    CAT - begin a non-Boolean search
   FOR - move forward in this list        TOT - see total, skip rest of list
   ABS - advanced Boolean search          SRC - prompted Boolean
   HLP - for complete help menu

Enter Command: FOR                                      Then press SEND
```

Figure 22.21: Geac 9000: Truncated-search results

```
099 TECHNICAL AND AUTOMATED  - IRIS LIBRARY SYSTEM -  ALL *CALL NUMBER SEARCH

   Your call number: z678.9             matches at least  10  numbers

                                                    No. of citations
                                                    in entire catalog
    1 Z678.9.A1A3 1984                                      1
    2 Z678.9.A1A62 1975                                     1
    3 Z678.9.A1A83 1983                                     1
    4 Z678.9.A1A83 1985                                     1
    5 Z678.9.A1A94 1988                                     1
    6 Z678.9.A1B3                                           1
    7 Z678.9.A1B35 1971b                                    1
    8 Z678.9.A1C2 1967                                      1
    9 Z678.9.A1C5                                           1
   10 Z678.9.A1C5 1978                                      1


Type a number to see more information -OR-
   FOR - move forward in this list      BAC - move backward in this list
   CAT - begin a new search

Enter number or code: FOR                              Then press SEND
```

Figure 22.22: Geac 9000: Shelflist browse

```
                                                    Citation   1 of   1
     TITLE Computer library [computer file]
   EDITION Version 2.20
 PUBLISHER New York : Ziff Communications, 1988-1991.
   DESCRIP Computer laser optical disks ; 4 3/4 in. + user's guide (various
           pagings : ill. ; 20 cm.)
     NOTES Publication span: [Vol. 1] (Sept. 1988-) * Description based on:
           September 1988. * Contains Lotus Bluefish Searchware version 2.31.
           Lotus Bluefish Searchware allows you to search for and retrieve
           information from the Computer Library periodicals database. * CDRM
           381300. * Monthly, with disks covering 12 months. * System
           requirements: IBM PC/XT or AT, COMPAQ or other fully compatible
           computer ; minimum of 512K RAM installed ; minimum of 500K available
           space on hard disk ; DOS 3.1 or higher ; CD-ROM drive card and CD-ROM
           drive ; Microsoft MS-DOS CD-ROM extensions or compatible High Sierra>


  BRF - see locations and call numbers    IND - return to index
  CON - see next screen                    CAT - begin a new search
  CMD - see additional commands

Enter code: CON                                          Then press SEND
                   **CONTINUED ON NEXT SCREEN**
```

Figure 22.23: Geac 9000: Computer-file display (1)

```
                                                    Citation   2 of   4
    AUTHOR Bach, Johann Sebastian, 1685-1750.
     TITLE Masses, BWV 232, B minor. Latin * Messe in h-Moll BWV 232 = Mass in B
           minor / Johann Sebastian Bach ;Faksimile-Lichtdruck des Autographs mit
           einem Vorwort herausgegeben von Alfred D|rr.
 PUBLISHER Kassel : Bdrenreiter, 1983.
   DESCRIP 1 score (188, 15 p.) ; 38 cm.
    SERIES Documenta musicologica. Zweite Reihe, Handschriften-Faksimiles ; 12 *
           Documenta musicologica. 2. Reihe, Handschriften-Faksimiles ; 12.
     NOTES For solo voices (SATB), chorus (SSATB), and orchestra. * Title from
           colophon. * Reproduced from the holograph in the Staatsbibliothek
           Preussischer Kulturbesitz, W. Berlin. * Commentary in German with
           English translation. * At head of series t.p.: Association
           Internationale des Bibliothhques Musicales, Archives et Centres de
           Documentation Musicaux, Internationale Gesellschaft f|r>


  BRF - see locations and call numbers    CIT - return to your citation list
  FOR - see next citation in list         BAC - see previous citation
  CON - see next screen                    CAT - begin a new search
  REV - revise current search             CMD - see additional commands
Enter code: CON_                                         Then press SEND
```

Figure 22.24: Geac 9000: Score (partial)

23

IMPACT™
Auto-Graphics' CD-ROM Patron-Access Catalog System

Joel M. Lee

Auto-Graphics' IMPACT™ CD-ROM patron-access catalog system was introduced at the Baltimore County Public Library in early 1987. It replaced the library's computer-output-microfilm (COM) catalog, which itself superseded a computer-produced book catalog. The massive storage capabilities and moderate cost of CD-ROM, combined with the ease of use and affordability of microcomputer software and equipment, have made CD-ROM technology an effective and attractive medium for library catalogs.

CD-ROM catalogs provide faster and more powerful retrieval techniques than card or COM catalogs. They can be installed and distributed easily to multiple locations without the costly telecommunications, equipment and maintenance costs typically associated with mini- or mainframe computer based online catalogs. IMPACT catalogs often serve as backups to online systems.

The IMPACT system's design, architecture, and special functional features make it suitable for all kinds of libraries and library groups. IMPACT users include public, academic, school and special libraries throughout North America, many of them members of state, provincial, regional, or local consortia.

IMPACT Design, Architecture, and Functionality

The IMPACT system's design is rooted in the premise that the patron-access catalog must always be immediately accessible to the novice user, without training, tutorials, or manuals. The IMPACT interface has been designed to be appealing and easy to use, while the search software ensures accurate and comprehensive information retrieval employing sophisticated searching techniques.

The IMPACT system's architecture is modular. This structure lets libraries select the particular functional modules they require and for the intended use of each catalog station. An IMPACT CD-ROM catalog is customized to each organization's needs, not only in the selection of software modules but also in the construction and indexing of the bibliographic database. An extensive array of customizing features is built into the software, primarily through the System Administration module, to support many profiling options at the workstation level.

Finally, the IMPACT system accommodates the special applications of state, provincial, regional, and local library networks and consortia in addition to those of individual and multibranch libraries. Many features in such modules as Location Scoping, Interlibrary Loan, and Cataloging were designed with the particular structures and operating procedures of library cooperative organizations in mind.

IMPACT Retrieval System

Software Characteristics

Several key characteristics distinguish the IMPACT software:

- a menu approach to the system, incorporating the use of function keys to perform most system functions
- on-screen prompting for available options and the keys that initiate them
- the function-key map, a layout displayed at the left of the screen while searching, which changes at different steps in the search process
- context-sensitive help screens always available by pressing the F9 key
- cross-references that lead users from one form of heading to another and to related subjects; cross-referenced terms can be searched without retyping

Screen Saver

To preserve monitor life the IMPACT software features a "screen-saver" function. If the workstation is left in the middle of a search, the system will automatically return to the opening welcome screen (Figure 23.1) after a period of inactivity at the keyboard. Before returning to this screen, the IMPACT software displays an alert that the search will shortly be lost and the display returned to the welcome screen. If the workstation is still inactive, the screen darkens and the message "PRESS ANY KEY TO BEGIN" is displayed. The time-out periods can be modified using the System Administration module.

Character Set

IMPACT supports the complete expanded ALA (now NISO Z39) ASCII character set, which includes both special characters and the diacritical marks used in many languages (e.g., á ç è ö), and is used to encode USMARC records. These marks need not be entered in searching.

On-screen record displays will include diacritics over or under the appropriate characters. Special characters that cannot be displayed on screen in their proper form are translated into an alternate character which does appear, so that all characters are represented on the screen.

Help Messages

Context-sensitive help messages are available at every point in the system (e.g., Figure 23.2). Pressing F9 will retrieve a help text appropriate to the point at which help was sought. Pressing F9 again will exit from the help message.

Forms of Heading

The forms of heading used in the database have a direct effect on search results. An option Auto-Graphics offers when building the database is authority control, a process that normalizes name and subject headings in the catalog to current form. If authority control has not been applied to the database, there will be inconsistencies in the catalog due to errors or changes in cataloging rules and subject headings. If authority control has not been performed, the user may have to search under multiple forms of the name or subject to achieve greater comprehensiveness. (Some of the illustrations here are from databases to which authority control processing has not been applied.)

Searching Levels

The IMPACT search software is modular as well. Patron level for alphabetical searching is the most basic access level, and several number search key options, such as ISBN/ISSN, LCCN or Publisher's Number for Music, can be selected for premastering. Expert level provides keyword searching capability, while Research level searching adds such advanced search techniques as explicit Boolean operators.

Alphabetical Searching

Patron level, or "Find By" mode, supports a browsing, dictionary approach to database searching through author, title, and subject indexes plus a combined index of all three. The search key is chosen from the opening welcome screen. Entries in any index are displayed alphabetically with cross-references marked with an X (see "Display Options," below). No matter what is typed, a matched list is always displayed with the highlight positioned at the point in the database closest to what was entered. The user can scroll up or down through the database from that point. Figure 23.3 shows an author search; Figures 23.4 and 23.5 show subject and author browse results, with cross-references in Figure 23.4.

Cross-References

Cross-references are searched by highlighting the unauthorized term and pressing Enter. Resulting "see" references for names and subjects are noted on-screen with the message "Your Library Uses" and the authorized form (Figure 23.6). The proper form can be then searched without retyping by highlighting it and pressing Enter.

"See also" references appear at the beginning of matched lists under the heading Also Writes As for names (Figure 23.7) or Related Subjects for subjects (Figure 23.8); the referenced name or subject can be searched without retyping.

Keyword Searching

Expert level, or "Keyword" or "Word Search" mode, provides keyword access to author, title, and subject indexes, plus the "Allword" index combining all three. Unlike in Find By mode, words are retrieved regardless of their position or sequence within a field, so that search words can be entered in any order. If no match for the search is located, the system will display a "No Matches Found" message (Figure 23.9). This is an optional search module. Figure 23.10 shows a keyword title search; Figure 23.11 shows the results.

Number Key Searching

In number key searching, or "Find by Number," any optionally indexed number fields (e.g., LCCN, ISBN, ISSN, Publisher's Number for Music, SuDocs number) can be searched (Figure 23.12). The call number option permits browsing the database in shelf list order. If an exact number match is entered, the search will retrieve the full

record display for the matching record. If no match is located, the system will display a "No Matches Found" message.

Research Level

IMPACT's optional Research level supports advanced searching techniques, including explicit use of the Boolean operators to broaden and narrow keyword searches, wildcard and truncation characters, and qualifiers for date, language, or media type. While the search is being entered, headings (author, title, subject, combined) are selected and Boolean operators AND, OR, and NOT chosen by pressing the F3 key (Figures 23.13 through 23.15).

When a search is begun in Research level, the "Wordometer" appears, tallying results of the search in process. If no match is located, the system will display a "No Matches Found" message. Display options are identical to those for keyword search results.

Location-based Searching: Scoping

Location scoping allows up to five subsets of the database to be searched. For example, if the catalog station is located at a branch of a main library, and if branch level information is included in the database, the catalog station can be profiled to search only the holdings of that branch. By pressing F1 at the search entry screen users can expand searching to different or overlapping subsets of the database at the second, third, fourth, and fifth scoping levels.

The Location Scoping Profile, including libraries' scoping level membership and headings, is defined in the System Administration module (Figure 23.16 shows a search with scope displayed).

Library News

Available from the opening welcome screen as selection F9, this optional feature allows the library to present information of interest on a local, regional, or system level. The contents of this bulletin board are entirely at the discretion of and are written by the library staff. Up to eight categories are available; these choices are displayed on the function-key map after entering library news. Pressing F9 again will exit library news. Library news text (e.g., Figure 23.17) is created and modified using the System Administration module.

Display, Printing and Saving Options

The software includes a number of options for record display, printing, and saving to disk.

Display Options

IMPACT software provides multiple levels or formats for the display of search results. The appropriate level is employed automatically to a particular search. In general, three display levels are possible with any given search:

- **Matched list:** This format will display up to sixteen headings per screen that match the search entered (Figure 23.18). If more headings were matched, users can scroll down to view them. The heading, either author, title, subject, or call number, is shown along with a number corresponding to the number of titles filing under that heading. For call number searching, the corresponding title appears instead of the number of titles (Figure 23.19). Cross-references are indicated by an X in the matched list.

- **Brief-record display:** If multiple titles file under a given heading, this format will display the heading, number of titles filing under the heading, and title, author, publication date, and call number for up to four titles (Figure 23.20). Users may scroll in this format to view additional titles.

- **Full-record display:** This format displays full bibliographic information, as defined by the library, for a single title (Figure 23.21). The heading by which the title was retrieved, the number of titles filing under that heading, and the number of the current title within that list are also displayed. Full-record displays are presented in a labeled format. They may optionally be viewed in the MARC format by pressing Alt-M, which acts as a toggle between patron and MARC displays (Figure 23.22). For each format, **More** will appear at the bottom of the screen if there are additional screens or

lines. **End** will appear on screen if no further screens or lines follow. Locations are presented under a heading defined in the Location Scoping Profile (Figure 23.23).

Holdings Display Option for Serials

A special option, designed for lender selection in interlibrary loan, can be profiled for serials collections where multiple holdings are displayed. If active, the F7 key label reads "Who Owns This." If only one library within the search scope owns the item, one window will open listing the library's symbol and its holdings. If more than one library owns the item, two windows open, as illustrated in Figure 23.24. The window at left lists for all holding libraries the library code. The window at right lists holdings associated with the highlighted library code.

Printing Options

Printer-equipped workstations can print any record retrieved in a search. Screen images can be printed using the DOS Print Screen function, while brief-record displays can be printed, and a complete record image can be printed individually, using the Print Record keys or the Choose mode function.

Saving Options

IMPACT software lets users save (download) one or more records to disk in ASCII Text or MARC format for preparing bibliographies or use in other systems. Records can be saved at either the brief- or full-record display. Use of this capability to save records is optional and is "turned on" using the Choose mode feature. When record saving begins, the system prompts the user for format and disk-drive designation for stored records. The user presses F8 Choose title to save a selected record.

Other IMPACT Modules

The IMPACT system's modular architecture allows libraries to select the particular modules applicable to the intended use of each catalog station. Public-access catalog stations might be equipped only with the searching software modules, while the same CD catalog with additional equipment and software may be used "behind the desk" for more functions. Some software modules have specific hardware requirements, and all require the appropriate indexing on the IMPACT CD-ROM disc itself. (Additional discussion and screens omitted. Details are available from Auto-Graphics, Inc., 3201 Temple Avenue, Pomona, CA 91768-3200; [800] 776-6939; fax [714] 595-3506.)

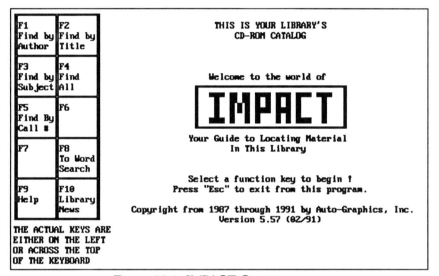

Figure 23.1: IMPACT: Opening screen

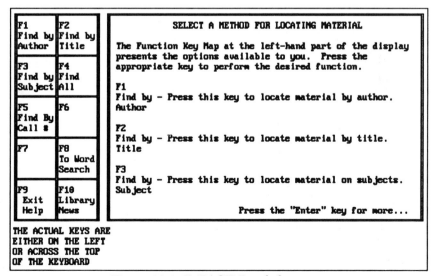

Figure 23.2: IMPACT: First help screen

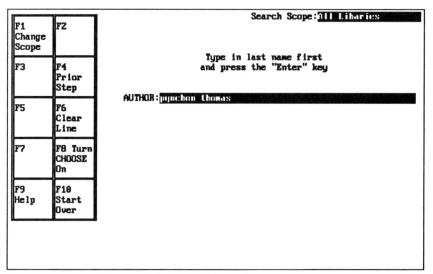

F1 Change Scope	F2
F3	F4 Prior Step
F5	F6 Clear Line
F7	F8 Turn CHOOSE On
F9 Help	F10 Start Over

Search Scope: All Libraries

Type in last name first
and press the "Enter" key

AUTHOR: pynchon thomas

Figure 23.3: IMPACT: Author search entry

SEARCH SCOPE: All System Libraries

F1	F2
F3	F4 Prior Step
F5 Prnt This Display	F6
F7	F8
F9 Help	F10 Start Over

SUBJECT HEADINGS	NUMBER OF TITLES
▶Seat belts, Automobile	X
Seat work	X
Seathl, Chief, 1790-1866	X
Seating (Furniture)	X
Seating (Furniture)—United States—History—17th century—Catalogs.	1
Seating (Furniture)—United States—History—18th century—Catalogs.	1
Seatlh, Chief, 1790-1866	X
Seats	X
Seattle, Chefe, 1790-1866	X
Seattle, Chief, 1790-1866.	1
Seattle, chief of the Suquamish and allied tribes, d. 1866.	2
more	

Using the arrow keys, move the pointer to an individual heading and press the "Enter" key if you wish to see additional detail; or select a function key.

Figure 23.4: IMPACT: Subject browse with x-refs

F1	F2
F3	F4 Prior Step
F5 Prnt This Display	F6
F7	F8
F9 Help	F10 Start Over

AUTHOR HEADINGS	NUMBER OF TITLES
▶Pynchon, Thomas.	5
Pyne, Mable.	1
Pyne, Mable (Mandeville)	1
Pyne, Mable (Mandeville), 1903-	3
Pyne, Polly.	1
Pyne Press.	2
Pyne, Stephen J.	1
Pyne, Stephen J., 1949-	1
Pyne, William H.	1
Pynn, Leroy, 1906-	1
Pynoos, Jon, comp.	1
Pyrde, Duncan.	1
Pyre, James Francis Augustin, 1871-1934.	1
Pyron, Nona.	1
more	

CHOOSE-Drive A:
Using the arrow keys, move the pointer to an individual heading and press the "Enter" key if you wish to see additional detail; or select a function key.

Figure 23.5: IMPACT: Browse for author Pynchon

```
┌─────┬─────┐
│F1   │F2   │                                              NUMBER OF
│     │     │          CROSS REFERENCED HEADINGS            TITLES
│     │     │                                             ─────────
├─────┼─────┤   Seat belts, Automobile
│F3   │F4   │     Your Library Uses
│     │Prior│   ▶ Automobiles—Seat belts.                      1
│     │Step │       end
├─────┼─────┤
│F5 Prnt│F6 │
│This │     │
│Display│   │
├─────┼─────┤
│F7   │F8   │
│     │     │
│     │     │
├─────┼─────┤
│F9   │F10  │
│Help │Start│
│     │Over │
└─────┴─────┘
CHOOSE-Drive A:
Using the arrow keys, move the pointer to an individual heading and press the
"Enter" key if you wish to see additional detail; or select a function key.
```

Figure 23.6: IMPACT: Subject "see" reference

```
                                            SEARCH SCOPE:All System Libraries
┌─────┬─────┐
│F1   │F2   │                                              NUMBER OF
│     │     │          CROSS REFERENCED HEADINGS            TITLES
│     │     │                                             ─────────
├─────┼─────┤   ▶Blixen, Karen, 1885-1962.                    13
│F3   │F4   │     Also Writes As
│     │Prior│       Dinesen, Isak, 1885-1962.                 26
│     │Step │         end
├─────┼─────┤
│F5 Prnt│F6 │
│This │     │
│Display│   │
├─────┼─────┤
│F7   │F8   │
│     │     │
│     │     │
├─────┼─────┤
│F9   │F10  │
│Help │Start│
│     │Over │
└─────┴─────┘
Using the arrow keys, move the pointer to an individual heading and press the
"Enter" key if you wish to see additional detail; or select a function key.
```

Figure 23.7: IMPACT: Name "see also" reference

```
┌─────┬─────┐
│F1   │F2   │                                              NUMBER OF
│     │     │          CROSS REFERENCED HEADINGS            TITLES
│     │     │                                             ─────────
├─────┼─────┤   ▶Water                                        104
│F3   │F4   │     Related Subjects
│     │Prior│       Drinking water.                            3
│     │Step │       Erosion.                                  15
├─────┼─────┤       Floods.                                   11
│F5 Prnt│F6 │       Fresh Water                                1
│This │     │       Geysers.                                    2
│Display│   │       Glaciers.                                  34
├─────┼─────┤       Hail.                                      2
│F7   │F8   │       Hydraulic engineering.                     6
│     │     │       Hydrotherapy                               5
│     │     │       Ice.                                       7
├─────┼─────┤       Lakes.                                    12
│F9   │F10  │       Moisture.                                  1
│Help │Start│         more
│     │Over │
└─────┴─────┘
CHOOSE-Drive A:
Using the arrow keys, move the pointer to an individual heading and press the
"Enter" key if you wish to see additional detail; or select a function key.
```

Figure 23.8: IMPACT: Subject "see also" reference

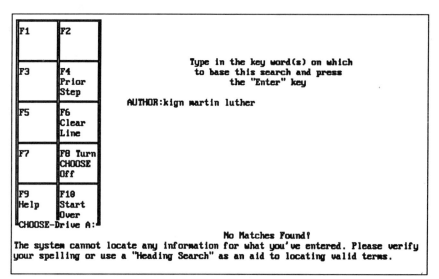

Figure 23.9: IMPACT: Spelling error, word search

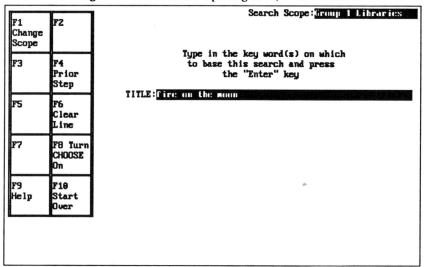

Figure 23.10: IMPACT: Keyword title search

F1	F2	
F3	F4 Prior Step	YOU TYPED:fire on the moon
		Title 1 of 1
F5 Print Record	F6	FORMAT: book
		LOCATION: ADCX ANTX CARX GOUX MASX NCLS NOFX POTX
		WATX 629.4
		MASX NCLS POTX WATX 629 .4 MAIL
		010 629.4/Mail|Space Flight To The Moon|Proje
		ct Apollo|Astrnt
		015 629.4 Ma
		015 629.45 Mai
F7	F8 CHOOSE Title	CONTROL NBR: 60150907
		LC CARD NBR: 01-039099
		AUTHOR: Mailer, Norman
		TITLE: Of a fire on the moon
F9 Help	F10 Start Over	SUBJECT: U. S. National Aeronautics and Space
		Administration.
CHOOSE-Drive A:		more Press ALT/m for MARC Display
Select a function key to continue		

Figure 23.11: IMPACT: Result of title word search

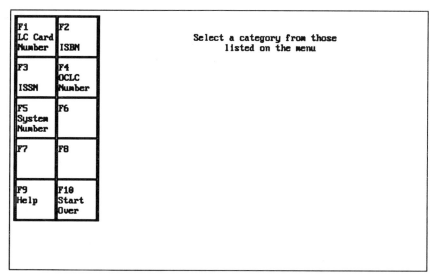

Figure 23.12: IMPACT: Number search key screen

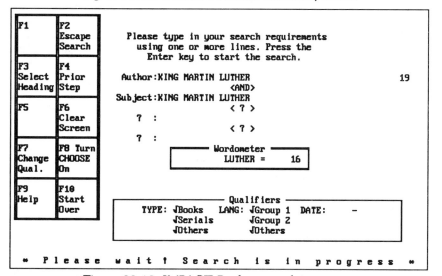

Figure 23.13: IMPACT: Boolean search in process

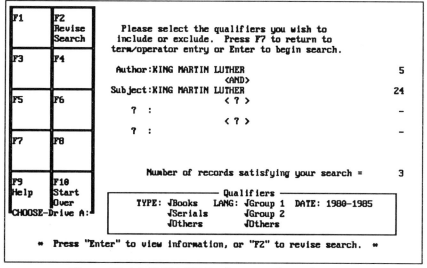

Figure 23.14: IMPACT: Boolean search result screen

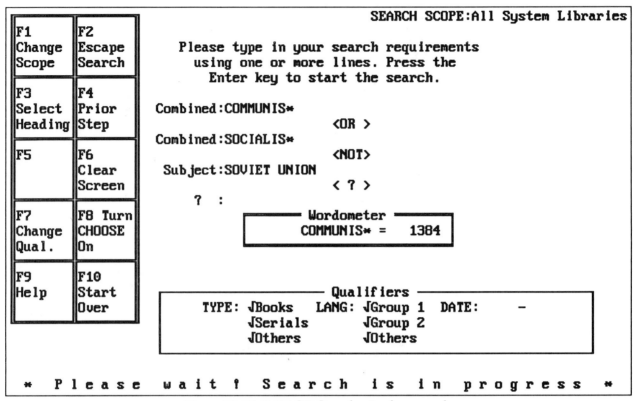

Figure 23.15: IMPACT: Complex Boolean search

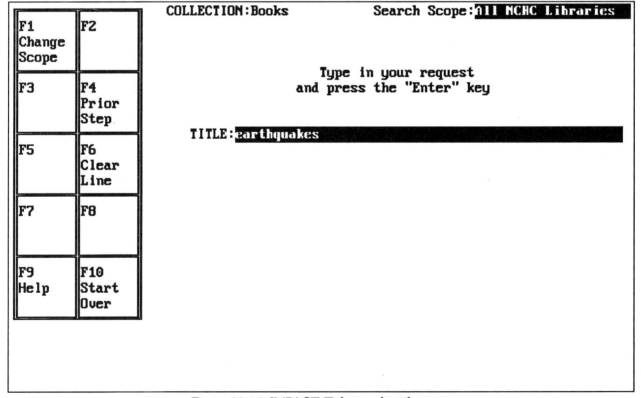

Figure 23.16: IMPACT: Title search with scope

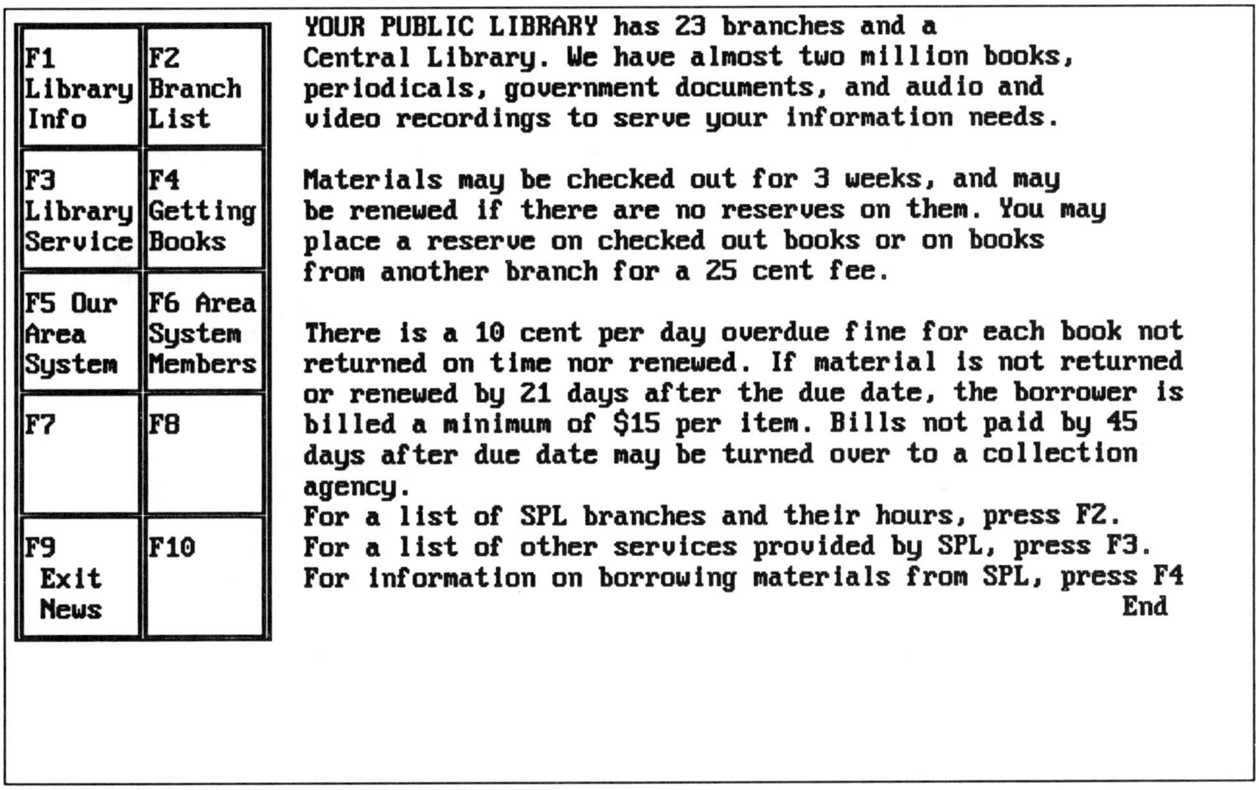

F1 Library Info	F2 Branch List
F3 Library Service	F4 Getting Books
F5 Our Area System	F6 Area System Members
F7	F8
F9 Exit News	F10

YOUR PUBLIC LIBRARY has 23 branches and a
Central Library. We have almost two million books,
periodicals, government documents, and audio and
video recordings to serve your information needs.

Materials may be checked out for 3 weeks, and may
be renewed if there are no reserves on them. You may
place a reserve on checked out books or on books
from another branch for a 25 cent fee.

There is a 10 cent per day overdue fine for each book not
returned on time nor renewed. If material is not returned
or renewed by 21 days after the due date, the borrower is
billed a minimum of $15 per item. Bills not paid by 45
days after due date may be turned over to a collection
agency.
For a list of SPL branches and their hours, press F2.
For a list of other services provided by SPL, press F3.
For information on borrowing materials from SPL, press F4
End

Figure 23.17: IMPACT: Library news

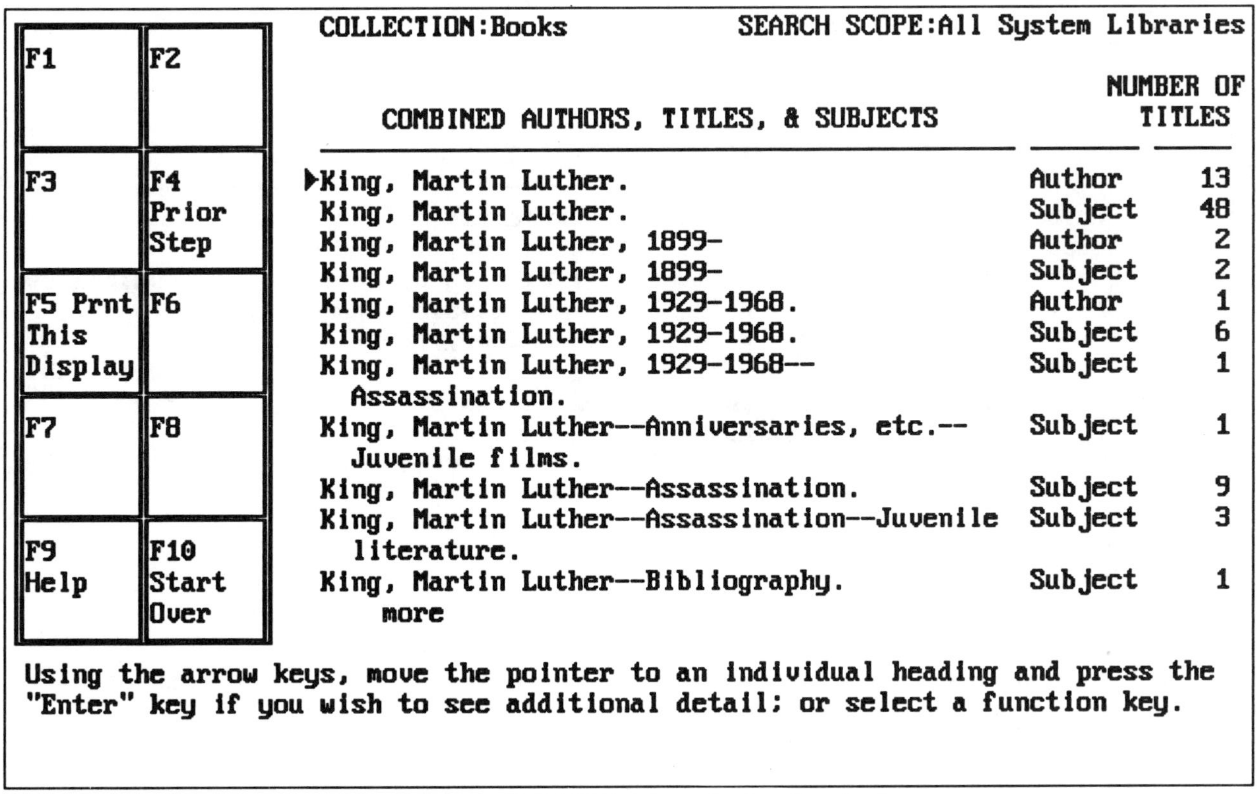

F1	F2
F3	F4 Prior Step
F5 Prnt This Display	F6
F7	F8
F9 Help	F10 Start Over

COLLECTION:Books   SEARCH SCOPE:All System Libraries

COMBINED AUTHORS, TITLES, & SUBJECTS		NUMBER OF TITLES
▶King, Martin Luther.	Author	13
King, Martin Luther.	Subject	48
King, Martin Luther, 1899–	Author	2
King, Martin Luther, 1899–	Subject	2
King, Martin Luther, 1929-1968.	Author	1
King, Martin Luther, 1929-1968.	Subject	6
King, Martin Luther, 1929-1968-- Assassination.	Subject	1
King, Martin Luther--Anniversaries, etc.-- Juvenile films.	Subject	1
King, Martin Luther--Assassination.	Subject	9
King, Martin Luther--Assassination--Juvenile literature.	Subject	3
King, Martin Luther--Bibliography. more	Subject	1

Using the arrow keys, move the pointer to an individual heading and press the
"Enter" key if you wish to see additional detail; or select a function key.

Figure 23.18: IMPACT: Multi-index heading display

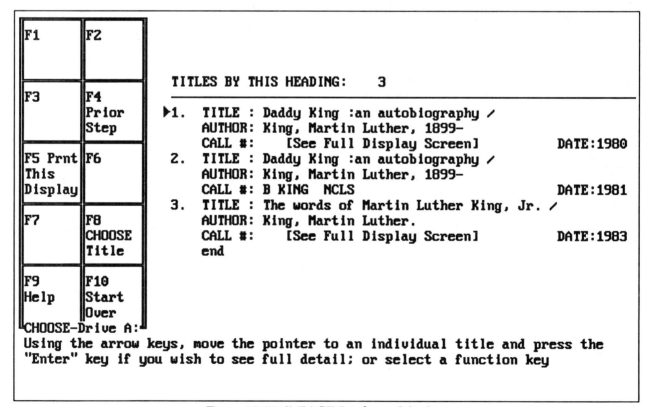

```
                                        SEARCH SCOPE:All System Libraries
┌─────┬─────┐
│F1   │F2   │                CALL NUMBER                    TITLE
│     │     │           ─────────────────────     ─────────────────────────────
├─────┼─────┤         ▶R  686.2                   Graphic arts encyclopedia /
│F3   │F4   │             686.2                   How a book is made /
│     │Prior│          Q  686.2                   Mastering graphics : design and p
│     │Step │             686.2                   Printing it; a guide to graphic t
├─────┼─────┤          Q  686.2                   Slinging ink : a practical guide
│F5 Prnt│F6 │          q  686.2 A733 1945         Notes on modern printing
│This │     │          R  686.2 Ame               American national standard proof c
│Display│   │             686.2 Arn               Ink on paper 2; a handbook of the
├─────┼─────┤             686.2 B                 Printing it; a guide to graphic t
│F7   │F8   │          q  686.2 B192 1977         Art and reproduction : graphic re
│     │     │             686.2 B353              Getting it printed : how to work
│     │     │          q  686.2 B365 1986         Getting it printed : how to work
├─────┼─────┤             686.2 B593 1969         A bibliography of printing : with
│F9   │F10  │             686.2 B658t 1982        Typographic years : a printer's j
│Help │Start│          more
│     │Over │
└─────┴─────┘
Using the arrow keys, move the pointer to an individual title and press the
"Enter" key if you wish to see full detail; or select a function key
```

Figure 23.19: IMPACT: Call number browse matched

```
┌─────┬─────┐
│F1   │F2   │
│     │     │          TITLES BY THIS HEADING:     3
│     │     │          ───────────────────────────────────────────────────────
├─────┼─────┤        ▶1.  TITLE : Daddy King :an autobiography /
│F3   │F4   │            AUTHOR: King, Martin Luther, 1899-
│     │Prior│            CALL #:   [See Full Display Screen]        DATE:1980
│     │Step │         2.  TITLE : Daddy King :an autobiography /
├─────┼─────┤            AUTHOR: King, Martin Luther, 1899-
│F5 Prnt│F6 │            CALL #: B KING  NCLS                       DATE:1981
│This │     │         3.  TITLE : The words of Martin Luther King, Jr. /
│Display│   │            AUTHOR: King, Martin Luther.
├─────┼─────┤            CALL #:   [See Full Display Screen]        DATE:1983
│F7   │F8   │            end
│     │CHOOSE│
│     │Title │
├─────┼─────┤
│F9   │F10  │
│Help │Start│
│     │Over │
└─────┴─────┘
CHOOSE-Drive A:
Using the arrow keys, move the pointer to an individual title and press the
"Enter" key if you wish to see full detail; or select a function key
```

Figure 23.20: IMPACT: Brief record display

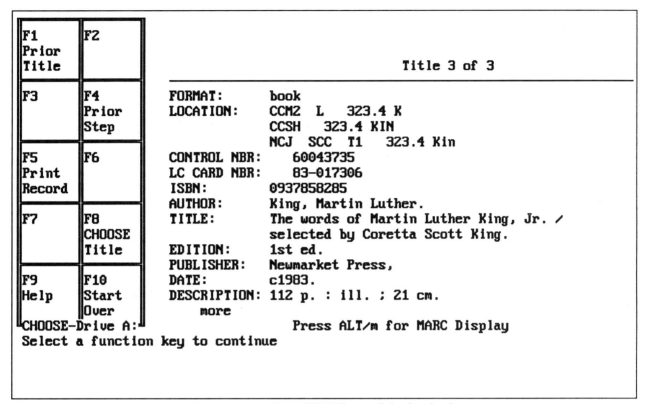

Figure 23.21: IMPACT: Full record display, book

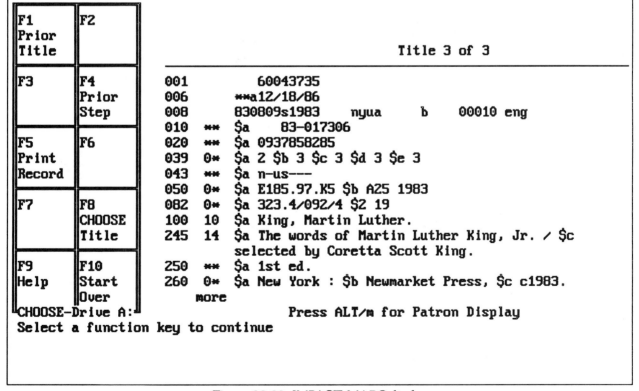

Figure 23.22: IMPACT: MARC display

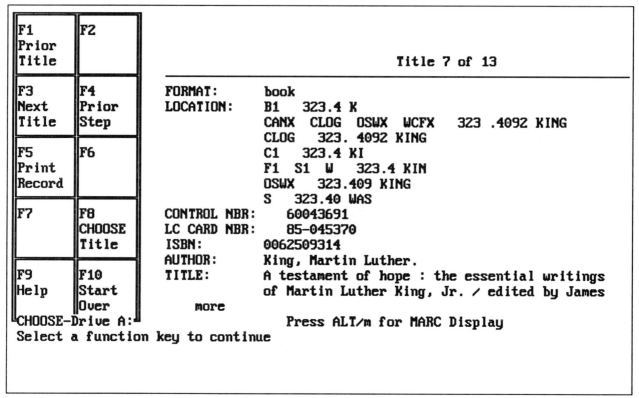

Figure 23.23: IMPACT: Multiple locations

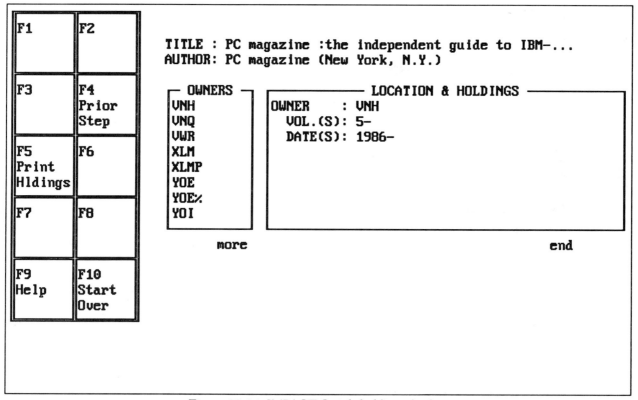

Figure 23.24: IMPACT: Serials holdings display

24

InfoTrax
Rensselaer Polytechnic Institute

Polly-Alida Farrington, Marilyn Moody, Irving E. Stephens, and Joseph Thornton

InfoTrax was developed in-house by Rensselaer Polytechnic Institute library staff using the SPIRES database management system on an IBM 3081 mainframe. SPIRES (Stanford Public Information Retrieval System) software is available through the SPIRES consortium, a not-for-profit organization made up of users of SPIRES. SPIRES is a hierarchical database management system.

InfoTrax is available to all campus users and serves as a campuswide information system by including campus information files as well as library related information. InfoTrax is also available through the Internet and through dial access. Development of the system began with the catalog and acquisitions system. The catalog was released in 1984. The circulation system was completed in 1987, and the first commercial database, the IEEE (Institute of Electrical and Electronics Engineers), was mounted in 1988. The first campus information file, the Rensselaer Polytechnic Institute Campus Directory, was mounted in 1989.

Initial menu screens show the user three possible menu selections: library, research, and campus. The user can easily move among different files on the system. The user interface is command driven, and we have sought to keep the commands close to Common Command Language standards. Commands are consistent from one database or file to another. Only selected fields are displayed to the public and most of these fields are indexed and searchable. Because of this, the system supports the construction of complex Boolean searches.

Commands

Unusual commands of InfoTrax include:

- **Browse.** The browse command allows you to select an item from the database and then electronically browse the shelves around that item.
- **Scan.** The scan command lists words or numbers (but not phrases) that are alphanumerically adjacent. This is useful for looking at the contents of an index when you are not sure of the spelling of a word and for showing the shelf order for call numbers.

Other useful commands support searching by material type, language, date, publisher, collection location, special numbers (report, ISBN, LC card number, etc.) and exact title. Truncated searching is also supported.

Displays

Search results can be displayed and printed in a number of formats. For example, in the Catalog database records may be displayed in brief, call and detail format.

Brief format displays one line with the author and title. The call format displays the author, title, call number, publication date, and item status. The detail format is the most complete and gives authors, title, series title, subjects and notes, publication date, and an item's status information. Fields displayed in each database differ.

InfoTrax Databases

Campus: A directory of campus addresses and telephone numbers of faculty, students and staff. It is searchable by name, department or major, building, job title or class designation.

Career: A directory of alumni willing to advise students about employment and career decisions. It is searchable by name, major or field of interest, geographic location and company name.

CAT (Catalog): The Library's bibliographic database, used to access its cataloged collections.

CJO (Current Job Openings): A text file displaying open positions on campus. Job descriptions for listed jobs are displayed after the line number of a job title is entered.

Class: This file lists the materials available for specific courses available at the Library's Reserve Desk. Displays show materials in descending order of currency (that is, most recent first). The file is searchable by faculty name, course title, course "nicknames," and catalog numbers. Most materials are uncataloged copies of homework problems, practice tests, lecture notes, or videos of lectures. When cataloged library materials appear, their "temporary location" displays in the library's Catalog file.

CUR (ISI's Current Contents Search): A bibliographic database produced from the weekly tapes received from the Institute for Scientific Information, which provides cover-to-cover indexing of more than 6,700 research journals. It is searchable by author, article and publication title, discipline, language, and keywords. The records are linked to the library's journal holdings. The use of this database is restricted to Rensselaer-affiliated users.

Grants: A database containing announcements prepared by the Office of Contracts and Grants about current and pending research opportunities from governmental and private agencies. It is searchable by program title, keywords in summaries, sponsoring agency, and filing dates.

Hours and Updates: A text file containing brief announcements about library programs and services. No searchable indexes are provided, but the "headlines" of entries display at the start of the file to inform users of contents.

IEEE (Institute of Electrical and Electronics Engineers): A bibliographic database of citations and abstracts for all publications of the IEEE. Searchable by author, article and publication title, assigned subject terms, keywords in abstracts, and dates. Journal article citations are linked to library serial holdings information.

ITS (Information Technology Services): A group of text files containing policies, access hours, class schedules, and pricing information for our campus computing services. The files are selected from a menu displayed after choosing "ITS".

Message: A simple messaging facility enabling on-site and remote users to send comments, suggestions or questions to the library. Messages are retrieved daily and routed to appropriate staff for reply.

News and Communications: A full-text database of news and press releases about Rensselaer prepared by the Office of News and Communications. It is searchable by title and text keywords as well as by date.

Request Service: A group of functions available to remote users to initiate photocopy, interlibrary loan, book loan, book renewal, and directory update requests. Users may view their personal loan records but cannot directly change loan or borrower data. Registration with the library is required and continuing access depends on compliance with library policies; e.g., these services are not available to persons with unsettled bills, etc.

Undergraduate Research Program: A special directory file containing the names of faculty whose ongoing research projects may provide job or study opportunities for undergraduates. Searchable by faculty name, department, and research interest.

```
                        Welcome to InfoTrax
                Rensselaer Libraries' Information System
                         (Copyright 1989)



       To look for LIBRARY INFORMATION.........type LIBrary

       To look for RESEARCH DATABASES..........type RESearch

       To look for CAMPUS INFORMATION..........type CAMpus




       Type one of the category names from the list above and press RETURN
  :
```

Figure 24.1: InfoTrax: Welcome screen

```
  : lib

                        LIBRARY INFORMATION



            FILE                                TYPE

       CATALOG...............................CATalog
       ARCHITECTURE SLIDES...................SLIdes
       CLASS RESERVE MATERIALS...............CLAss
       LIBRARY HOURS & UPDATES...............HOUrs
       To send us a MESSAGE..................MESsage



       Use the CURrent Contents or IEEE files to locate
       articles in recent journals or IEEE publications.


       Type one of the file names from the list above and press RETURN
       Press BREAK to return to the MAIN menu
  :
```

Figure 24.2: InfoTrax: Library information

```
: help commands

        FIND            Initiate a search
        AND, AND NOT    Narrow a search
        / (slash)       In Catalog only, narrow a search by material
        OR              Expand a search
        BACKUP          Undo the last AND or OR command
        BROWSE          Browse the stacks from a terminal
        SCAN            Examine entries in an index alphabetically
        BRIEF           Display item information in a condensed format
        CALL            Display enough information to locate the item
        DETAIL          Display all available information about an item
        PRINT           Print your search results
        TERSE           Turn file introductions 'off'
        TERSE OFF       Turn file introductions back 'on'
        NEWS            Displays Library bulletins (if any)
        BOOKS           Selects the BOOKS file for searching
        MUSIC           Selects the MUSIC file for searching
        CATALOG         Selects the CATALOG file for searching
        JOURNALS        Selects the JOURNALS file for searching
        HOMEWORK        Selects the HOMEWORK file for searching
        SLIDES          Selects ARCHITECTURE SLIDES file for searching
*
*    --More--     Press RETURN to continue
```

Figure 24.3: InfoTrax: Help commands

```
: find about martin luther king and (date > 1979 and date < 1986)
*
*
* Results: 3
*
*       3 BOOK(s)
*
*
*          Type BRIEF to display your result
*
*
*    CATALOG selected
*    Type command, then press RETURN    (BREAK to restart, enter STOP to quit)
*
:
```

Figure 24.4: InfoTrax: Martin Luther King search

```
: brief


NO. DATE  TITLE                                BY

   1 1985  Martin Luther King, Jr. resource guide.  University of the State
   2 1982  Let the trumpet sound : the life of Mart  Oates, Stephen B.
   3 1981  Martin Luther King Jr., National Histori  United States.


*
*          Use CALL or DETAIL to display your search result in more detail.
*
*
*          CATALOG selected
*          Type command, then press RETURN   (BREAK to restart, enter STOP to quit)
*
:
```

Figure 24.5: InfoTrax: Brief display

```
: call 1

    ****************************************************************

        BY:   University of the State of New York. Division of Civil Rights ...
      TITLE:  Martin Luther King, Jr. resource guide.
   PUBLISHED: University of the State of New York, State Education Dept.,
              Division of Civil Rights and Intercultural Relations, 1985.
    CALL-NO:  NY DOC UNI 146-4 MARLK 86-70053

    BARCODE    COLLECTION  DESCRIP.  COPY  STATUS      DUE DATE
    ---------- ----------  --------  ----  ----------- --------
    2066866Y   NY DOC                      AVAILABLE
*
*       ----- Record 1 of 3 -----
*
*       CATALOG selected
*       Type command, then press RETURN   (BREAK to restart, enter STOP to quit)
*
:
```

Figure 24.6: InfoTrax: CALL display (book)

```
: det 1

    ****************************************************************

            BY:   University of the State of New York. Division of Civil
                  Rights and Intercultural Relations.
         TITLE:   Martin Luther King, Jr. resource guide.
     PUBLISHED:   Albany, N.Y. : University of the State of New York, State
                  Education Dept., Division of Civil Rights and
                  Intercultural Relations, 1985.
       SUBJECT:   King, Martin Luther.
                  King, Martin Luther -- Study and teaching -- Outlines,
                  syllabi, etc.
                  Civil rights workers.
       CALL NO:   NY DOC UNI 146-4 MARLK 86-70053
       OCLC NO:   13047677
   DOCUMENT NO:   UNI 146-4 MARLK 86-70053
   DESCRIPTION:   80 p. : ill., portraits ; 28 cm.
         NOTES:   Bibliography: p. 56-60.

    BARCODE       COLLECTION  DESCRIP.  COPY  STATUS        DUE DATE
    ----------    ----------  --------  ----  ------------  --------
    2066866Y      NY DOC                      AVAILABLE
 *
 *      ----- Record 1 of 3 -----
```

Figure 24.7: InfoTrax: DETAIL display (book)

```
: call 5

    ****************************************************************

           BY:   United States. Congress. Office of Technology Assessment.
        TITLE:   Application of solar technology to today's energy needs.
    PUBLISHED:   Congress of the United States, Office of Technology Assessment :
                 for sale by the Supt. of Docs., U.S. Govt. Print. Off., 1978-
     CALL-NO:    ARCH TJ810 .U57 1978 / HOLDINGS: v. 1
                 US DOC Y 3.T 22/2:2 So4 / HOLDINGS: v. 1-2

    BARCODE       COLLECTION  DESCRIP.  COPY  STATUS        DUE DATE
    ----------    ----------  --------  ----  ------------  --------
    329355R       ARCH        v.1             AVAILABLE
    10000801A     US DOC      v.1             AVAILABLE
    10025701G     US DOC      v.2             AVAILABLE
 *
 *      ----- Record 5 of 5 -----
 *
 *      CATALOG selected
 *      Type command, then press RETURN    (BREAK to restart, enter STOP to quit)
 *
 :
```

Figure 24.8: InfoTrax: CALL with multiple locs

```
: det 5
*
*           ERROR!   Use HELP to get the correct syntax for your last command
*
*
*       CATALOG selected
*       Type command, then press RETURN    (BREAK to restart, enter STOP to quit)
*
:
```

Figure 24.9: InfoTrax: Out-of-Range error

```
: find about martin luther kign
*
*           Zero results.
*
*           You may want to try the SCAN command
*           (Type HELP SCAN for assistance)
*
*       CATALOG selected
*       Type command, then press RETURN    (BREAK to restart, enter STOP to quit)
*
:
```

Figure 24.10: InfoTrax: Spelling error

```
: find t fire moon
*
*
* Results: 1
*
*       1 BOOK(s)
*
*

  ***************************************************************

            BY:  Mailer, Norman.
         TITLE:  Of a fire on the moon.
       EDITION:  (1st ed.)
     PUBLISHED:  Boston, Little, Brown (1970)
       SUBJECT:  Space flight to the moon.
                 Project Apollo.
                 Astronauts -- United States.
                 United States -- Civilization -- 1945
       CALL NO:  TL799.M6 M26
       OCLC NO:  101602
   DESCRIPTION:  vii, 472 p. 22 cm.

  BARCODE      COLLECTION  DESCRIP.  COPY  STATUS        DUE DATE
  ----------   ----------  --------  ----  ------------  --------
  795852-                                  ON-LOAN       03/08/91
*
*       ----- Record 1 of 1 -----
*
```

Figure 24.11: InfoTrax: Title-word search, result

```
: browse 2
      BY : Pynchon, Thomas.
   TITLE : The crying of lot 49
    DATE : 1986
 CALL-NO : PS3566.Y55 C79 1986
 ========================================================
      BY : Pynchon, Thomas.
   TITLE : Gravity's rainbow
    DATE : 1987
 CALL-NO : PS3566.Y55 G7 1987
 ========================================================
      BY : Hume, Kathryn, 1945-
   TITLE : Pynchon's mythography : an approach to Gravity's rainbow
    DATE : 1987
 CALL-NO : PS3566.Y55 G7348 1987
 ========================================================
      BY : Moore, Thomas, 1946-
   TITLE : The style of connectedness : Gravity's rainbow and Thomas Pynchon
    DATE : 1987
 CALL-NO : PS3566.Y55 G736 1987
 ========================================================
 *            To continue Browsing, enter    <f>orward or <b>ack
 *            else enter any valid InfoTrax command
 :
```

Figure 24.12: InfoTrax: Author browse

```
    ***********************************************************
              BY:   Gullahorn-Holecek, Barbara.
                    WGBH Educational Foundation.
           TITLE:   Artists in the lab
      TITLE-NOTE:   WGBH Educational Foundation.
       PUBLISHED:   New York : Time Life Video, 1981.
         SUBJECT:   Computer art.
                    Computer graphics.
                    Computer animation.
                    Computer music.
         CALL NO:   GRAPHIC :VIDEO N7433.8 .A78x
        MATERIAL:   Videocassette
     DESCRIPTION:   1 videocassette (ca. 60 min.) : sd., col.; 3/4 in.
           NOTES:   Writer, producer, director, Barbara Gullahorn-Holecek.
                    A program on the use of computers in the arts.
          SERIES:   Nova
                    Nova series.

  BARCODE     COLLECTION  DESCRIP.  COPY  STATUS       DUE DATE
  ----------  ----------  --------  ----  -----------  --------
                                          Available
 *
 *    ----- Record 4 of 4 -----
 *
```

Figure 24.13: InfoTrax: Detail, video

```
: find t b minor mass and by bach
*
*
* Results: 2
*
*      2 MUSIC (Phonos & scores)
*
*
*         Type BRIEF to display your result
*
*
*      CATALOG selected
*      Type command, then press RETURN    (BREAK to restart, enter STOP to quit)
*
: det


   ***********************************************************

              BY:  Bach, Johann Sebastian, 1685-1750.
                   Stader, Maria.
                   Topper, Hertha.
                   Haefliger, Ernst, 1919
                   Fischer-Dieskau, Dietrich, 1925
                   Engen, Kieth.
                   Richter, Karl, 1926
                   Munchener Bach-Chor.
                   Munchener Bach-Orchester.
           TITLE:  Mass in B minor, BWV 232
                   Masses, BWV 232
      TITLE-NOTE:  Johann Sebastian Bach.
       PUBLISHED:  (West) Germany : Archive Production, (1961)
```

Figure 24.14: InfoTrax: Detail, recording (1)

```
         SUBJECT:  Masses.
         CALL NO:  PHONO G BACH MAS S77
         OCLC NO:  2744680
        MATERIAL:  Sound Recording
                   Music
*
*    --More--      Press RETURN to continue


     DESCRIPTION:  3 sound discs (122 min.) : analog, 33 1/3 rpm, stereo ; 12
                   in.
           NOTES:  Sung in Latin.
                   Ed. recorded: Werke, Jg. 6 (Leipzig : Bach-Gesellschaft,
                   1856).
                   Program notes in English, German, and French, by Georg von
                   Dadelsen, and text, with German, English, and French
                   translations ((16) p. : ill.) and supplementary notes (on
                   card) laid in container.
          SERIES:  Archive Production, 9th research period: The works of Johann
                   Sebastian Bach. Ser. C: Masses and Magnificat
                   Archive Production, 9th research period. Ser. C.

   BARCODE     COLLECTION  DESCRIP.  COPY  STATUS       DUE DATE
   ----------  ----------  --------  ----  ------------ --------
   100263331   PHONO                       AVAILABLE
*
*    ----- Record 1 of 2 -----
```

Figure 24.15: InfoTrax: Recording (2)

```
****************************************************************

          TITLE:  Time.

        CALL NO:  051 T58
    LIBRARY HAS:  * hardcopy until microfilm received-
                        (Inquire at Reserve Room, 1st Floor)

                  * vol.35 1940 - vol.94 1969, vol.96 1970 - vol.112 1979
                        (3rd Floor)

                  * vol.105 1975 - vol.106 1975, vol.113 1979-
                        (Microfilm Area, 1st Floor)

        CALL NO:  ARCH  (Shelved in Alphabetical Order)
    LIBRARY HAS:  * current year-
                        (Architecture Library, Greene Building)

    LATEST REC'D:  Vol.137,No.9  Mar 04,1991
           NOTE:  Current title began with v. 1-  Mar. 3, 1923-
  EARLIER TITLE:  Literary digest (New York, N.Y. : 1937)
         EDITOR:  Hadden, Briton
                  Luce, Henry Robinson
        OCLC NO:  1767509          ISSN:  0040-781X
*
*     ----- Record 2 of 3 -----
*
*     CATALOG selected
*     Type command, then press RETURN   (BREAK to restart, enter STOP to quit)
*
:
```

Figure 24.16: InfoTrax: Detail, serial

```
*     CAREER selected
*     Type command, then press RETURN   (BREAK to restart, enter STOP to quit)
*
: find major technical writing
*
*
* Results: 3
*
*        Type BRIEF to display your result
*
*
*     CAREER selected
*     Type command, then press RETURN   (BREAK to restart, enter STOP to quit)
*
: det

  ****************************************************************

       Alum's code:  196
            Degree:  M.S., Technical Communications, RPI, 1984
                     B.S., Journalism, Glassboro State, 1982
             Major:  Communications, Technical Writing
          Employer:  AT&T - Bell Labs
          Location:  West Long Branch, NJ
          Industry:  Communications
         Job Title:  Technical Publications Specialist ||
Previous Experience:  Part-time writer for Charles B. Slack Medical
                      publishers
Focus Alumni Netwrk:  No
              Note:  Available for winter and spring visits.
*
*     ----- Record 1 of 3 -----
*  Press RETURN for next record or BREAK to quit DETAIL Display
```

Figure 24.17: InfoTrax: Career database

```
*
: find name holmes
*
*
* Results: 2
*
*         Type BRIEF to display your result
*
*
*
*     CLASS RESERVES selected
*     Type command, then press RETURN   (BREAK to restart, enter STOP to quit)
*
: det


   NUMBER :  65442
   COURSE :  Advanced Numerical Computing
     NAME :  Holmes, M.
 LOCATION :  FOLSOM LIBRARY RESERVE DESK

             Please request items 1-99 by COURSE NAME and ITEM NUMBER,
                            100- by PROFESSOR NAME and ITEM NUMBER.

 ITEM-No.  TYPE        DESCRIPTION

      353  BOOK        Strang, - An analysis of the finite element method
      352  BOOK        Mitchell, - Computational methods in partial
      351  BOOK        Burden, Richard - Numerical analysis
      350  BOOK        Lapidus, Leon. - Numerical solution of partial
      350  BOOK        Lapidus, Leon. - Numerical solution of partial
      150  EXAM        Exam 2 - Fall 1990
*
*    ----- Record 1 of 2 -----
* Press RETURN for next record or BREAK to quit DETAIL Display
```

Figure 24.18: InfoTrax: Class reserve database

```
*     GRANTS selected
*     Type command, then press RETURN   (BREAK to restart, enter STOP to quit)
*
: det 1

   ------------------------------------------------------------------------

      Sponsor:  U.S. DEPARTMENT OF INTERIOR   (USDOI)
        Title:  The Coastal Geology Program
     Abstract:  This program is intended to increase scientific understanding
                of the physical processes affecting the Nation's coastal
                and wetlands. Current field investigations are underway in
                Louisiana, Alabama, Mississippi and Southern Michigan, with
                additional work to begin in Western Louisiana, East Texas,
                and the Great Lakes region. Cost sharing is strongly
                encouraged.
      Contact:  S. Jeffress Williams  703-648-6511
 Reference No:  None
     Deadline:  Applications accepted at any time

   For further information request File Number 332 for Sponsor USDOI
   at Contracts and Grants Office - ext. 6283.
*
*    ----- Record 1 of 3 -----
*
*     GRANTS selected
*     Type command, then press RETURN   (BREAK to restart, enter STOP to quit)
*
```

Figure 24.19: InfoTrax: Grants database

```
*      NEWS selected
*      Type command, then press RETURN    (BREAK to restart, enter STOP to quit)
*
: find about science technology studies
*
*
* Results: 7
*
*          Type BRIEF to display your result
*
*
*      NEWS selected
*      Type command, then press RETURN    (BREAK to restart, enter STOP to quit)
*
: bri


  NO. TITLE                                                          DATE

   1 RENSSELAER TO SPONSOR "TEACH-IN" ON MID-EAST CULTURE AND POL...  02/15/91
   2 DISCUSSION SERIES TO BE HELD                                    02/05/91
   3 RENSSELAER NEWS & IDEAS (story ideas for science, technology... 11/--/90
   4 Rensselaer News & Ideas                                         10/--/90
   5 INVITATION TO REPORTERS TO "YANKEE INGENUITY," A SYMPOSIUM O...  09/14/90
   6 OTHER STORY IDEAS SENT TO REPORTERS PLANNING TO ATTEND "YANK... 09/14/90
   7 Story Ideas for Science and Technology Editors                  07/--/90


*
*          Use DETAIL to display your search result in more detail.
*
*
*      NEWS selected
*      Type command, then press RETURN    (BREAK to restart, enter STOP to quit)
*
```

Figure 24.20: InfoTrax: Campus news

```
*      URP selected
*      Type command, then press RETURN    (BREAK to restart, enter STOP to quit)
*
: find name mark holmes
*
*
* Results: 1
*

   ----------------------------------------------------------------------

              Name:  HOLMES, MARK H
                     Professor
           Address:  310 Amos Eaton Hall
             Phone:  6891
            E-mail:  holmesm@turing.cs.rpi.edu
            School:  Science
        Department:  Mathematics
 Research Interest:  Symbolic computing
*
*      ----- Record 1 of 1 -----
*
*      URP selected
*      Type command, then press RETURN    (BREAK to restart, enter STOP to quit)
*
:
```

Figure 24.21: InfoTrax: Undergrad research program

25

INLEX
at Waukesha Public Library

J. Howard Pringle

The INLEX online catalog provides an intuitive, easy-to-learn and easy-to-use means of access to a library's materials collection. The system is designed so that a user does not have to rely on a knowledge of computers; he or she simply uses the basic keyboard and eight labeled function keys that change with the progress of the search. As a result of the system's design, the user has superior access to library collections. Users never receive negative search results such as "No Match Found" nor suffer the subsequent frustration. The system responds to searches by displaying the closest match it can find, along with indexed entries coming just before and just after the closest match. The software package itself is very flexible and can be readily modified to provide a wide variety of search option types, retrieved-data formats, key labeling and functionality. The result is a system that has been extremely well received.

The hardware platform for the INLEX software is the Hewlett-Packard 3000 family of mini-computers, which can support a few terminals or several hundred. Most installations use a simple terminal to host configuration. However, the INLEX system shows a fair amount of flexibility as it can be accessed by PCs running terminal emulation under MS-DOS or Microsoft Windows, or by Apple Macintoshes. Waukesha is currently using a mix of terminals and MS-DOS PCs to access the catalog and other modules and will be accessing the system under Windows in the near future. Any type of personal computer with communications software may be used to access the dial-in version of the INLEX online catalog.

Searches and Displays

The following sample searches will illustrate the basics of how the system works and how its ease of use has broken down the resistance of many self-proclaimed computer avoiders.

The first screen a user sees is illustrated in Figure 25.1. The initial screen introduces the user to the basic design of the INLEX online catalog: two lines of instructions at the top of the screen and a row of labeled boxes corresponding to the function keys on Hewlett-Packard (or compatible) terminals along the bottom. Both the instruction lines and the labeled boxes change as a search progresses, providing context-sensitive instructions and additional search or retrieval options. To initiate a search, a user presses the function key on the keyboard corresponding to the type of search listed in the labeled box on the screen.

Subject Search

Figure 25.2 illustrates what happens when the user presses the Subject Search key and enters a subject. This user is looking for materials about Martin Luther King, Jr., and has entered only that individual's last name and the initial of his first name. Entering the complete name would take the user more directly to the actual subject but, as a result of the INLEX software's placing all search results within the context of an authority or title list, the user, even if unable to provide a first name or part of the last, would be able to quickly move to the correct entry without further narrowing the search or entering additional information. Figure 25.2 also introduces the Start Over and Step Back keys. These keys appear on each screen the user sees after initiating a search and allow the user to either backtrack through a search one step at a time or start a new search from scratch.

Browsing

When the user presses the function key corresponding to Search Catalog he or she retrieves the screen illustrated in Figure 25.3. This figure provides a good illustration of what a user sees whenever a search is initiated in the INLEX system. The highlighter (reverse bar in the illustration) is located over the entry that provides the closest possible match to the information entered by the user. The user also sees those entries on either side of the highlighter and is able to browse line by line or screen by screen, forward or backward to any point anywhere in the authority (or title) list. The movement of the highlighter itself to an entry allows the entry to be selected for further examination.

The placement of the user within a list of selections provides a number of significant benefits. The user can gain a realization of the scope of the information—subject breakdowns, etc.—on his or her topic. If he or she ends up with a list that bears little resemblance to what was believed to have been entered, it is easy to quickly check the original search for accuracy. And, he or she will encounter what we call the serendipity factor. This factor is the realization of the scope of the library's holdings and the possibility of further exploration brought on by exposure to a wide variety of entries beyond that originally searched. Many users like this ability to browse the listings as it provides them a similar (and, to some, comfort-ing) practice with which they are familiar from skimming through the card catalog.

When the user has located a topic, moved the highlighter to it, and now wishes to view a list of the titles on that topic, he/she presses the function key corresponding to List Titles and the screen illustrated in Figure 25.4 is displayed. From this listing of titles, the user is able to move the highlighter to the title he or she wishes to check. As the highlighter bar is moved from entry to entry, libraries with multiple sites have the option of displaying a message indicating whether or not copies are owned at the library where the searching is being performed. This eliminates the user's need to request further copy information if she knows she only wants to search for material owned by the library in which she's standing. As Waukesha is a single-site library, this feature has not been implemented.

Single-Record Displays

Figure 25.5 illustrates a labeled entry with multiple copies, showing the item's call number, location and availability, along with the information normally found on a catalog card. All of the labeling, which fields are displayed, the screen layout, and how the availability status is displayed are set by the library and can easily be changed. It is also possible to change some of the displayed information on a terminal-by-terminal basis.

If a user does not wish to look at the entire entry for the titles listed on Figure 25.4 and simply wants more detailed copy information, he or she can press the Call Number key and will retrieve a display illustrated by Figure 25.6. The copy information provided is similar to that provided with the full display but contains additional information on media type and the holding library name. In multibranch installations it is possible to set the system so that Full Display will display those copies specific to the branch originating the search and Call Number will display all holdings for all branches.

As a side note, the labeling of the keys can easily be modified so that each installation can provide the key labeling most suitable to their site. For example, in most sites Call Number is labeled Display Copies. Waukesha relabeled the key in order to make more obvious to the user the option of going right to the call number instead of having to retrieve the entire bibliographic record display.

A MARC record display, as illustrated in Figure 25.7 (partial), is not something most members of the public are interested in seeing, but library staff do make use of this display. The INLEX system makes the display of MARC records optional and Waukesha has chosen to make the MARC display available on staff terminals but not on public terminals.

Error Handling

In the previous discussion of placing a user's search results in a list, the advantages of this method for handling the incorrect entry of information were mentioned. Figure 25.8 illustrates what would happen if a user were to enter "Kign" instead of "King." The system will place the user as closely as possible to the search entered while retaining a copy of the original search strategy on the input line. A user, upon being presented with the illustrated results, could easily check the original search for correctness and either retype the search or, as frequently happens if the result is not too far distant from the desired result, simply page down or up to the correct entry.

Other Searches

Figures 25.9 through 25.11 illustrate the sequence for an author search of books *by* Martin Luther King, Jr. The same basic search procedure illustrated in the subject search, including the same sequence and labeling of keys, apply for author searches. Throughout the system function keys retain their positions and labeling so that the user, after performing a couple of searches, will instinctively know the locations of the keys for certain functions.

In addition to the basic author, subject, and title searches, users are able to search a number of additional indexes and to perform a variety of keyword searches on a variety of indexes. The actual types of searches available are specified by the library and can be made available on a terminal-by-terminal basis. Waukesha permits additional searching by call number and a variety of numeric indexes including ISBN, LCCN, ISSN, and Superintendent of Documents (SuDocs) number. Some of these searches are illustrated later in this document.

Keyword searching is a particularly useful search technique, and the INLEX system provides a relatively straightforward method of conducting both basic and advanced Boolean searches. Again, the local library can determine the nature and scope of searches available on a terminal-by-terminal basis.

Figure 25.12 illustrates the initiation of a keyword search for a title that the user believes contains the terms "fire" and "moon." The user selects Keyword Search from the initial selection screen, enters the keywords, presses the keyboard's Return key and the system provides the screen in Figure 25.12. If so desired, right truncation is possible by simply typing in a word root and a "+" sign.

Figure 25.12 shows the basis for Boolean combines. The system has searched the indexes for occurrences of the words "fire" and "moon" and provided the number of hits for each word in the titles, subject authorities, name authorities (Waukesha indexes only corporate and conference authors for keyword searching) and within any notes fields that the library has specified to be indexed. At this point, a user could browse the entire list of 368 titles containing the word "fire" or he or she could attempt to narrow the search by combining terms with Boolean operators.

The user moves the highlighter to the first word of the combining operation and presses the Combine Words key. Figure 25.13 shows how the selected word is highlighted, a letter "s" for selected is placed next to it and the number of results from the selection is displayed. The next step is to choose the other word(s) to use in the combination.

The user has decided to use the AND operator and to stay within the title index. However, if desired, the user may combine terms across any of the indexes. He or she may also change the type of operator to an OR or NOT at any stage of the search by simply pressing the Change Oper'tn function key. The user may also, if so desired, add a new word into the search or remove a word or result at any time during the search. In Figure 25.14, however, the user has ANDed the words "fire" and "moon" in the title index and has come up with a single title that contains both of the words. Given many user's unfamiliarity with Boolean operators and the occasional complexities of keyword combining, INLEX added an interactive Help feature in late 1991.

Figure 25.15 illustrates the consistency of the user interface within the catalog by showing that once a user has results from the keyword/Boolean search, the means of viewing the result are the same as viewing the results of any other kind of search.

Known-Item Searching

As illustrated previously, the INLEX software emphasizes browse mode searching. This works very well in easing the transition from card catalog to online catalog in public libraries where the library is frequently unable to provide a great deal of transition training (and the public is unwilling to attend it). This is not to say that access to materials can be gained only by browsing a list of selections. As illustrated in Figure 25.16, users entering specific information will be taken directly to a specific entry where they can go through the usual procedure to obtain call numbers, etc.

Other Searches and Browses

The user can search and browse local call number (shelf) lists (Figure 25.17) and perform a variety of other numeric searches, including Superintendent of Documents number, ISBN, ISSN, OCLC number, and LCCN among others. These searches can also be limited to staff-only use if desired. Users browsing the call number list find a feature unique to this kind of search. At the top of the screen display under the item's call number, users are provided with status information on each item as it is highlighted during the user's browse through the call number list. The user is not required to press any other keys to retrieve the information. This capability can considerably speed up the process of checking the status of a multicopy item if the user knows the call number.

Nonbook Information

The INLEX system integrates all types of information into a single MARC database and searching for nonbook materials is conducted in the same fashion as searching for books.

Figure 25.18 shows part of the display of a motion picture in the collection. It can be seen that the display is very similar to book materials with changes and tracing dictated by cataloging practice. The entry in the initial title list will bring out the fact that this item is a video recording, not a book or other type of item.

Figures 25.19 illustrates partial displays of a music score of Mozart's *Magic Flute*. The displays emphasizes the media type and the complete contents, although we are unable to provide multiple screen illustrations due to space constraints.

Other Features

The INLEX online catalog has a number of features beyond those described above. All screens may be printed on attached terminal printers if so desired, although Waukesha does not provide printers and, as a result, the function key corresponding to the Print key has been removed from its usual position on the screen in all of the searches illustrated above. The catalog has a Bulletin Board module that allows staff to create listings of library or community events, new acquisitions, etc. (Figure 25.20). From the Bulletin Board screen the user is able to access a complete catalog tutorial that shows the user the variety of searches possible in the system, how to navigate through the screens along with some shortcuts and general hints.

Non-English Searching

The Bulletin Board screen also reveals one of the system's more unique offerings: access to foreign language searching. The INLEX system supports up to six different languages on a single terminal, including a simplified vocabulary for children, at one time. The user simply selects the language of choice from the display screen by depressing a function key. Implementing one or more of the foreign languages is the library's choice. When a language is selected all of the instruction lines, key labels, and descriptive information in displays are translated into the language of choice. As with the English language version of the catalog, all instruction lines, key labels, and display information, and formats can easily be changed to meet local needs.

Figure 25.21 shows the Spanish language initial selection screen. Note that this screen has some types of searches disabled, illustrating how a terminal can have certain types of searches disabled while other terminals may concurrently have the searches enabled.

A search is initiated in the same manner as in the English catalog, and the process of selecting an author and displaying titles, catalog entries, and call numbers remain the same. The search and retrieval procedures and function-key labels remain consistent with the English language version. The functional interface is the same regardless of the module being accessed.

Authorities

The INLEX system maintains full MARC authority records, as well as nonauthorized/locally created authority records and cross-references. All types of cross-references (e.g., broader, narrower, etc.) appear in the online catalog. If a user searches on an invalid subject heading, such as "juvenile diabetes," the system will respond with a display of the appropriate cross-reference, such as SEE "Diabetes in children," highlighting the valid term and the number of titles attached to it. The user is not made to perform a second search using the valid term. Full authority records themselves

may also be displayed; however, most libraries choose this option only for their staff terminals.

Conclusion

To wrap up, the INLEX online catalog module provides a high degree of flexibility in functional availability, display options, security and its ability to meet local conditions. It is a powerful, easy to use and learn, intuitive software product. Since enhancements are continually being released, it's important to note that some of the above information may be obsolete by 1992. Online catalog enhancements currently under development at INLEX include:

- The addition of another function-key option on the initial search screen which offers automatic ANDing. The user could then enter two or more search terms for any type of search (e.g., author, title, subject) and see results for each term as well as combinations of terms.

- The display of additional elements of information on entries listed on title display screens. The system currently shows author/title/year of publication/edition elements. This is to be expanded.

- The ability to perform keyword phrase searches such as "Wall Street," "New Zealand," etc.

Production note: INLEX normally uses a 27-line HP display, but the screen-capture software used is only able to capture 25 lines. As a result, some displays lack the "More on Next Screen" message that normally appears when a record requires more than one screen.

```
INLEX/3000 ver. 20.0      Waukesha Public Library        THU, AUG 8, 1991
Press the function key corresponding to the type of search you want to perform.
For example, press f1 to search by an author's name, f2 for a title search, etc.
```

| AUTHOR SEARCH | TITLE SEARCH | SUBJECT SEARCH | | 1 N | 1 | LOCAL CALL # | KEYWORD SEARCH | NUMERIC SEARCHES | ITEM SEARCH |

Figure 25.1: INLEX: Catalog selection screen

```
Type a subject (e.g. STAR WARS). DON'T USE "A" "AN" OR "THE" AS A FIRST WORD.
The first part of a subject (STAR) is OK. Then press SEARCH CATALOG (f1).
```

SUBJECT   king, m

SUBJECT   No. of Titles

| SEARCH CATALOG | | | 5 | 23 | | START OVER | STEP BACK |

Figure 25.2: INLEX: Subject search entry screen

```
Up & down arrows move selection bar (highlighted). NEXT or PREV keys show next
or previous screens. LIST TITLES (f1) lists titles by AUTHOR or about SUBJECT.
```

SUBJECT   king, m

SUBJECT	No. of Titles
SEE Henry VIII, King of England, 1491-1547	8
King Kong (Motion picture)	1
King, Larry, 1933-	5
King, Larry, 1933—Audio-visual aids.	1
King, Larry, 1933—Health	1
King, Larry L—Biography	1
King, Martin Luther, 1899-1984	2
King, Martin Luther, Jr., 1929-1968	59
King, Martin Luther, Jr., 1929-1968—Anniversaries, etc.	2
King, Martin Luther, Jr., 1929-1968—Assassination	6
King, Martin Luther, Jr., 1929-1968—Audio-visual aids.	1
King, Martin Luther, Jr., 1929-1968—Fiction	1
King, Martin Luther, Jr., 1929-1968—Iconography	1

| LIST TITLES | | MARC DISPLAY | | 5 N | 16 | NEW SEARCH | | START OVER | STEP BACK |

Figure 25.3: INLEX: Result from subject search

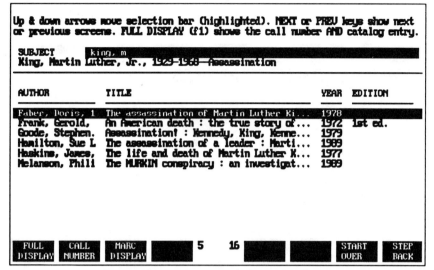

Up & down arrows move selection bar (highlighted). NEXT or PREV keys show next
or previous screens. FULL DISPLAY (f1) shows the call number AND catalog entry.

SUBJECT   king, m
King, Martin Luther, Jr., 1929-1968—Assassination

AUTHOR	TITLE	YEAR	EDITION
Faber, Doris, 1	The assassination of Martin Luther Ki...	1978	
Frank, Gerold,	An American death : the true story of...	1972	1st ed.
Goode, Stephen.	Assassination! : Kennedy, King, Kenne...	1979	
Hamilton, Sue L	The assassination of a leader : Marti...	1989	
Haskins, James,	The life and death of Martin Luther K...	1977	
Melanson, Phili	The MURKIN conspiracy : an investigat...	1989	

| FULL DISPLAY | CALL NUMBER | MARC DISPLAY | | 5 | 16 | | | START OVER | STEP BACK |

Figure 25.4: INLEX: Title list on a subject

To see more of the catalog entry (if it is on more than one screen), press
the NEXT key or the PREV key.

SUBJECT   king, m
Haskins, James, The life and death of Martin Luther K... 1977

CALL NUMBER	921 K585H	NonFicti	AVAILABLE
	÷ 921 K585H	CHILDREN	AVAILABLE
	÷ 921 K585H	CHILDREN	AVAILABLE
	÷ 921 K585H	CHILDREN	AVAILABLE

AUTHOR   Haskins, James, 1941-
TITLE   The life and death of Martin Luther King, Jr. / James Haskins.
PUBLICATION   New York : Lothrop, Lee & Shepard, c1977.
DESCRIPTION   176 p. : ill. ; 22 cm.

NOTE   Includes index.
NOTE   A biography of a man who dedicated his life to the cause of
              civil rights, which also reexamines unanswered questions
              concerning his assassination.

| | CALL NUMBER | MARC DISPLAY | | 5 | 16 | | | START OVER | STEP BACK |
| | | | | | N | | | | |

Figure 25.5: INLEX: Full display, multiple locs.

If there is more than one screen full of copies, use the NEXT or PREV to
look at the other screen.

SUBJECT   king, m
Haskins, James, The life and death of Martin Luther K... 1977

LIBRARY	CALL NUMBER	LOCATION	STATUS	MEDIA
Waukesha	921 K585H	NonFicti	AVAILABLE	Book
Waukesha	÷ 921 K585H	CHILDREN	AVAILABLE	Book
Waukesha	÷ 921 K585H	CHILDREN	AVAILABLE	Book
Waukesha	÷ 921 K585H	CHILDREN	AVAILABLE	Book

| FULL DISPLAY | ITEM DETAIL | MARC DISPLAY | | 5 | 16 | | | START OVER | STEP BACK |
| | | | | | N | | | | |

Figure 25.6: INLEX: Location display, multiple

To see more of the catalog entry (if it is on more than one screen), press
the NEXT key or the PREV key.

SUBJECT   `king, m`
Haskins, James, The life and death of Martin Luther K...   1977

```
5.7466      11/14/1987 23:82   11/14/1987 23:82   ot
LDR ————cam 22———— i 4588
881   ocm82818869 $
885   19878227155145.8$
888   778228a1977    nyua     j         88118beng $
818   $a   77883157 /AC $
829   $a8688418823.$a8688518828$blib. bdg.$
835   $a(CaOTULAS)1455613986$
848   $aDLC$cDLC$da.c.$dWIU$
843   $an-us——$
849   8$aWIU$c1$aWIU$c2$c3$c4$
858 8 $aE185.97.K55$hH336
882   $a323.4/892/4$aB$a92$
892   $a9215$bN585H$
188 18$aHaskins, James,$d1941-$
245 14$aThe life and death of Martin Luther King, Jr. /$cJames Haskins.$
```

| FULL DISPLAY | DISPLAY COPIES | | | 5 16 N | | | START OVER | STEP BACK |

Figure 25.7: INLEX: MARC display, book (partial)

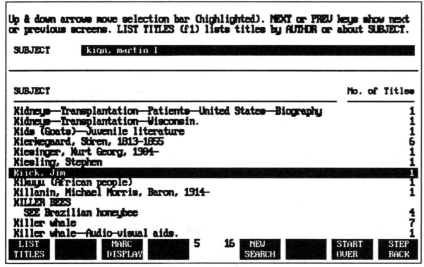

Up & down arrows move selection bar (highlighted). NEXT or PREV keys show next
or previous screens. LIST TITLES (f1) lists titles by AUTHOR or about SUBJECT.

SUBJECT   `kiqn, martin l`

SUBJECT	No. of Titles
Kidneys—Transplantation—Patients—United States—Biography	1
Kidneys—Transplantation—Wisconsin.	1
Kids (Goats)—Juvenile literature	1
Kierkegaard, Sören, 1813-1855	6
Kiesinger, Kurt Georg, 1904-	1
Kiesling, Stephen	1
Kiick, Jim	1
Kikuyu (African people)	1
Killanin, Michael Morris, Baron, 1914-	1
KILLER BEES	
SEE Brazilian honeybee	4
Killer whale	7
Killer whale—Audio-visual aids.	1

| LIST TITLES | MARC DISPLAY | | 5 16 | NEW SEARCH | | START OVER | STEP BACK |

Figure 25.8: INLEX: Spelling error and result

Up & down arrows move selection bar (highlighted). NEXT or PREV keys show next
or previous screens. LIST TITLES (f1) lists titles by AUTHOR or about SUBJECT.

AUTHOR   `king, m`

AUTHOR	No. of Titles
King, Judith E	1
King, Karen	1
King, Larry, 1933-	6
King, Larry L	6
King, Laura B., 1953-	1
King, Laurel.	1
King, Marian	1
King, Martin Luther, 1899-1984	2
King, Martin Luther, Jr., 1929-1968	9
King, Mary	2
King, Melinda	1
King, Michael	1
King, Mike	1

| LIST TITLES | MARC DISPLAY | | 5 16 N | NEW SEARCH | | START OVER | STEP BACK |

Figure 25.9: INLEX: Results of author search

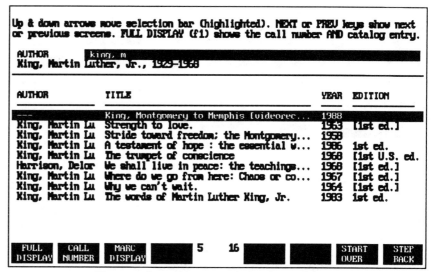

Figure 25.10: INLEX: Title list for an author

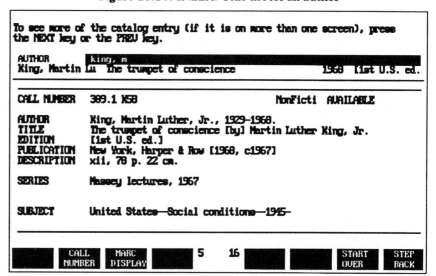

Figure 25.11: INLEX: Long display, book

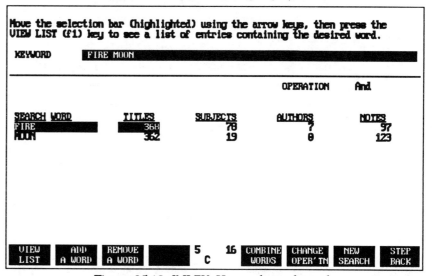

Figure 25.12: INLEX: Keyword search result

Move the selection bar (highlighted) using the arrow keys, then press the
VIEW LIST (f1) key to see a list of entries containing the desired word.

KEYWORD   FIRE MOON

| | | OPERATION | And |

RESULTS   368

SEARCH WORD	TITLES	SUBJECTS	AUTHORS	NOTES
FIRE	368s	78	7	97
MOON	362	19	8	123

| VIEW | ADD | REMOVE | | 5 | 16 | COMBINE | CHANGE | NEW | STEP |
| LIST | A WORD | A WORD | | C | | WORDS | OPER'TN | SEARCH | BACK |

Figure 25.13: INLEX: Selecting words, operators

Move the selection bar (highlighted) using the arrow keys, then press the
VIEW LIST (f1) key to see a list of entries containing the desired word.

KEYWORD   FIRE MOON

| | | OPERATION | And |

RESULTS   1

SEARCH WORD	TITLES	SUBJECTS	AUTHORS	NOTES
FIRE	368s	78	7	97
MOON	362a	19	8	123

| VIEW | ADD | REMOVE | | 5 | 16 | COMBINE | CHANGE | NEW | STEP |
| LIST | A WORD | A WORD | | C | | WORDS | OPER'TN | SEARCH | BACK |

Figure 25.14: INLEX: Achieving a Boolean result

Up & down arrows move selection bar (highlighted). NEXT or PREV keys show next
or previous screens. FULL DISPLAY (f1) shows the call number AND catalog entry.

KEYWORD   FIRE MOON
RESULTS TITLES

| AUTHOR | TITLE | YEAR | EDITION |
| Mailer, Norman. | Of a fire on the moon. | 1970 | [1st ed.] |

| FULL | CALL | MARC | | 5 | 16 | | | START | STEP |
| DISPLAY | NUMBER | DISPLAY | | C | | | | OVER | BACK |

Figure 25.15: INLEX: Titles from keyword search

Up & down arrows move selection bar (highlighted). NEXT or PREV keys show next
or previous screens. FULL DISPLAY (f1) shows the call number AND catalog entry.

TITLE   VINELAND

AUTHOR	TITLE	YEAR	EDITION
Peter, Adeline.	Vincent Van Gogh	1974	
Bitossi, Sergio	Vincent Van Gogh	1987	
Gogh, Vincent v	Vincent van Gogh; paintings and drawi...	1969	
Wollstonecraft,	A vindication of the rights of woman...	1975	1st ed.
Pryor, Bonnie.	Vinegar pancakes and vanishing cream	1987	
Osborn, Paul.	The vinegar tree, a play.	1931	
Pynchon, Thomas	Vineland	1990	1st ed.
Cravens, Richar	Vines	1979	
—	The Vineyard Bible : a central narrat...	1988	
Burns, James Ma	The vineyard of liberty : the America...	1982	1st ed.
Fegan, Patrick	Vineyards and wineries of America : a...	1982	
Aardema, Verna.	The Vingananee and the tree toad : a...	1983	
Dumas, Alexandr	VINGT ANS APRES	1958	

| FULL DISPLAY | CALL NUMBER | MARC DISPLAY | | 5   16 C | NEW SEARCH | | START OVER | STEP BACK |

Figure 25.16: INLEX: Result of known-item search

Up & down arrows move selection bar (highlighted). NEXT or PREV keys show next
or previous screens. FULL DISPLAY (f1) shows the call number AND catalog entry.

CALL NUMBER   686.2
Waukesha NonFicti AVAILABLE   Book

CALL NUMBER	AUTHOR	TITLE	YEAR
686 L514b	Lee, Marshall	Bookmaking : the...	1979
686 M58	Middleton, Be	The restoration of...	1972
686 Sp3	Spector, Marj	Pencil to press :...	1975
686 Sw44i	Swerdlow, Rob	Introduction to g...	1979
686 W436	Weiss, Harvey	How to make your...	1974
686.1 Se32p	Seeger, Nancy	A printmaker's gu...	1981
686.2 B353g	Beach, Mark.	Getting it printed...	1986
686.2 B62	Pierpoint Mor	Art of the printed...	1973
686.2 F62B	Fleishman, Se	Printcrafts for f...	1977
686.2 H97	Hutchison, Ho	Mimeograph operat...	1979
686.2 M23	McNaughton, H	Proofreading and...	1973
686.2 R36	Rice, Stanley	Book design : text...	1978
686.2 Sp3	Spencer, Herb	New alphabets A to...	1974

| FULL DISPLAY | ITEM DETAIL | MARC DISPLAY | | 5   16 C | NEW SEARCH | | START OVER | STEP BACK |

Figure 25.17: INLEX: Call number browse

To see more of the catalog entry (if it is on more than one screen), press
the NEXT key or the PREV key.

TITLE   SHE WORE A YELLOW RIBBON
—   She wore a yellow ribbon [videorecord...   1985

CALL NUMBER	VIDEO 791 She wore a yellow ribbon AudioVis AVAILABLE
TITLE	She wore a yellow ribbon [videorecording] / RKO Radio Pictures, inc.
PUBLICATION	[S.l.] : RKO Home Video, 1985.
DESCRIPTION	1 videocassette (VHS) (93 min.) : sd., col. ; 1/2 in.
SERIES	Film classics
NOTE	Videorecording of the 1949 motion picture.
NOTE	Producers, John Ford, Merian C. Cooper ; screenplay, Frank Nugent, Laurence Stalling, direcor, John Ford.
NOTE	John Wayne, Joanne Dru, John Agar.
NOTE	The story of a U.S. Calvary captain's last days in service on the western frontier in 1876.

| | CALL NUMBER | MARC DISPLAY | | 5   16 C | | | START OVER | STEP BACK |

Figure 25.18: INLEX: Full display, video (partial)

```
To see more of the catalog entry (if it is on more than one screen), press
the NEXT key or the PREV key.

TITLE       MAGIC FLUTE
Mozart, Wolfgan  The magic flute = Die Zauberflöte : o...  1944
```

```
CALL NUMBER   782.1 M87                    NonFicti  AVAILABLE

AUTHOR        Mozart, Wolfgang Amadeus, 1756-1791.
TITLE         The magic flute = Die Zauberflöte : opera in two acts / by
              Wolfgang Amadeus Mozart ; words by Carl Ludwig Giesecke and
              Emanuel Schikaneder ; English version by Edward J. Dent ; vocal
              score by Erwin Stein.
UNIFORM TITL  Die Zauberflöte. Vocal score. English & German
PUBLICATION   [s. l.] : Boosey & Hawkes, [c1944]
DESCRIPTION   200 p. ; 28 cm.

SERIES        The Royal edition of operas


SUBJECT       Operas—Vocal scores with piano
```

```
        CALL    MARC              5    16              START   STEP
       NUMBER  DISPLAY               C                  OVER    BACK
```

Figure 25.19: INLEX: Full display, score

```
INLEX/3000 ver. 20.0     Waukesha Public Library      THU, AUG 8, 1991

To scan the Library News listings press the NEXT or PREV keys. To use the
COMPUTER CATALOG press key f1.  For the CATALOG TUTOR please press key f2.



                     L I B R A R Y    N E W S


           A brief list of what's new and of interest at the library.

A NEW ALL TIME RECORD BUSINESS MONTH!!!
July 1991 set a new all-time record month for the number of books checked out
at the library. 185,543 items were checked out; an 18.5% increase over July
of 1990. At the same time more than 180,000 books were checked back in. This
is the first time the Library has surpassed 180,000 checkouts in a month in
its history. For the whole year of 1991, Library business is up 9.2% over 1990.
>>> Remember, the Library goes back to regular Saturday hours (9 a.m. to 6 p.m.)
    on September 7.
END OF LIBRARY NEWS
```

```
COMPUTER CATALOG              1    1       ESPANOL
CATALOG  TUTOR                   N
```

Figure 25.20: INLEX: Library news/bulletin board

```
INLEX/3000 ver. 20.0     Waukesha Public Library      THU, AUG 8, 1991
Oprima la tecla de funcionamiento que corresponde al tipo de busqueda que
desea ejecutar. Por ejemplo, oprima F1 para buscar el nombre de un autor, etc.
```

```
BUSQUEDA BUSQUEDA BUSQUEDA       1    1                    BOLETIN
 AUTOR    TITULO    TEMA            N                      MENSAJES
```

Figure 25.21: INLEX: Spanish initial screen

26

INNOPAC Online Catalog at the University of Nevada

Carol A. Parkhurst and Myoung-ja Lee Kwon

The INNOPAC online catalog was developed by Innovative Interfaces, Inc., based in Berkeley, California. The University of Nevada System Libraries' INNOPAC systems were installed in 1989 in two locations: one in Las Vegas and the other in Reno. The two systems serve the entire university system including two universities, four community colleges, and the Desert Research Institute libraries. The online catalog is fully interfaced, providing full bibliographic records, circulation status, serials check-in and on-order information in the public catalog. Although the acquisitions and serials control systems are on separate computers, the system is fully integrated from a user's perspective. Recently Innovative introduced a system configuration whereby all of the functions are performed by one UNIX machine. The company introduces new and enhanced features periodically, making the system dynamic and ever expanding.

The opening screen for the Las Vegas catalog (Figure 26.1) lists the basic indexes under which users can begin a search. The library controls the text of the three lines at the top and bottom of the screen. With the next software release (Release 7—in beta test at this writing), menus and options can be in different languages, including Chinese. When a terminal is left idle for a library-determined length of time, it reverts to

the opening screen. For dial-up (either telephone dial or networked) terminals, the library can set a time-out to disconnect the terminal completely. The opening screen for dial-up terminals has an option to **Disconnect**. By pressing the Escape key or **N** for **New Search**, the opening screen can be called up at any time. Users must return to this screen when they wish to search a different index.

From the Las Vegas opening screen, users can search the catalog by author (**A**), title (**T**), subject (**S**), call number (**C**) or keywords (**W**). The indexes, and the fields and subfields to be included in each index, are chosen by the library. Reserve lists by professor or course name may be found by choosing **R** and various library-related information is found by selecting **I**. A library may choose to load additional databases (e.g., journal indexes) or make access to external databases available through the **Connect to another Database (D)** option.

Although there is no online tutorial, when a user chooses an index, the screen shows what to type and gives a simple example (Figure 26.3). Whenever appropriate, the screen displays a menu at the bottom of the screen from which to choose the next step. The menu is context sensitive. For example, if one is in the author search mode, **A** is **Another search by author**; if in the subject search mode, **A** is **Another search by subject**. The first screen of a multiple-search result gives no menu option for backward browsing but allows forward browsing. In a multiple hit screen, there is a menu choice for limiting the search. Each option is preceded by a single character which, when pressed, selects that option without requiring the Enter key. If the terminal has a local printer attached, the option to print is available on most screens.

There are two modes of public-access catalog searching: the first (Figure 26.1) has a short list of indexes to search; the second mode includes additional indexes such as bibliographic utility record numbers, ISSN/LC card numbers, Government Documents numbers, etc. By pressing the Shift + key any time during a search, users can go into the second mode of searching (Figure 26.2). In the second mode, complete bibliographic records are displayed without status information. In addition to the information normally displayed in the first mode, all other MARC fields are included. Complete order records and check-in records may be displayed. Generally, users stay in the first searching mode.

With Release 7, a user may create a list of records for export. The bibliographic list can be added to at any time during a search and can be exported to another system in any of three formats: MARC, ASCII text, or PBS ProCite.

Searching

Choose A for an author index search from the opening screen. At the author prompt type "gershwin george" (Figure 26.3). The system is sensitive to word order (except in the keyword index), but not to punctuation or upper and lower case. Apostrophes are ignored; all other punctuation marks are treated as spaces. The search "gershwin george" brings up 47 entries displaying titles in groups of eight alphabetically by title (Figure 26.4). The library may choose a default display for this screen of either title and location or title and call number.

From the browse screen (Figure 26.4), a user can jump to a specific title by name or number of entries. Choosing the option to **Jump** and typing "rhapsody in blue" moves the browse display to

entries starting with this title. This is the best way to do an author-title search. To display a single record, type the line number (Figure 26.5). From the single record display, you can go back to the browse screen, where all of Gershwin's works were listed, by pressing **R**, or go forward or backward to bring up a bibliographic record of the next or previous numbers without going back to the browse screen. If you try to display a record beyond the end of the result set, the terminal simply beeps and nothing happens.

A comprehensive search for works by and about Martin Luther King, Jr., must be done in both the author and subject indexes. Typing "king martin" in the author index results in several choices (not shown); choosing **1** distinguishes Martin Luther Jr. from Sr. (Figure 26.6); then choosing **2** results in all books written by Martin Luther King, Jr. (Figure 26.7).

Subject Search and Limits

A search for Martin Luther King, Jr., in the subject index results in 50 entries. By choosing to Limit, the result set may be limited by one or more characteristics (Figure 26.8). The instructions on the screen lead the user through the formulation of a limiting request. At any point, the user may choose to find the items that match the limited search criteria or may continue to narrow or expand the search. Limiting the Martin Luther King search by English **Language** (Figure 26.9) and further by **Year of publication** after 1979 and **Year of publication** before 1986 results in ten entries (Figure 26.10).

Shelflist Browse and Related-Record Searching

From any bibliographic record display, one can choose a shelflist display of nearby items sorted by call number. Selecting **Z** for **Show items nearby on shelf** will display the title and location of items with call numbers that file immediately before and after the one originally selected (Figure 26.11).

To look up other works with the same subject, the user can choose **S** for **Show items with the same subject** (Figure 26.12). If the record has more than one subject heading, the user types the number of the desired subject heading and the corresponding subject-heading browse screen will display. If the user was searching in any index other than the subject index, this will change the index setting. If a user wants to go back to the original search, he has to return to the opening screen by pressing **N** for **New Search** and type in the original search.

Rotated Subject Headings

INNOPAC allows the library to "rotate" its subject headings so that access to the subject is provided through every subdivision in subfields ‡t, ‡x, and ‡z, except those that the library specifies not to rotate because they occur so frequently. A search for "Nevada" captures all subject headings with Nevada in any position, e.g.:

Accountants—Nevada
Adult Education—Nevada—Reno
Nevada—Road Maps

Other Aspects of Searching

When a user keys a very general search such as **United**, INNOPAC reports the number of items it is finding as it searches. It offers the option of stopping the search at any time and continuing or displaying the items found so far (Figure 26.13).

When a user keys an unauthorized subject or name heading for which there is an authority record, INNOPAC tells the user that the heading is "Not used in this library." INNOPAC displays the correct heading and asks whether to continue the search under that heading (Figure 26.14). INNOPAC also accommodates "see also" references to guide users to search under related headings (Figure 26.15).

If a search is keyed in any index for which there are no matching entries and no authority record, INNOPAC displays a browse screen with entries that would file immediately before and after the search string (Figure 26.16).

The Reno INNOPAC catalog has two subject indexes, one for Library of Congress subject headings and one for National Library of Medicine subject headings. It also has two call number indexes, one for LC call numbers and the other for Dewey call numbers and other local call numbers.

INNOPAC will index call numbers using any of these schemes so that they file in correct shelflist order: LC classification logic, Dewey classification logic, SuDocs logic, NLM logic or character by character. The user may search for a specific call number or may key in a partial call number such as Z678.9 to browse the call number index.

Keyword Searches, Synonyms and Truncation

The keyword index is built from title, corporate/conference author, contents note and subject fields of the library's choice. Searching by keywords generally produces a more comprehensive result than a title index search, since the contents note field and corporate/conference authors fields are indexed in addition to title fields.

In indexing keywords, the system automatically drops any articles, one-letter or two-letter words and other library-selected stopwords. In keyword searching, truncation is not automatic. You may, however, explicitly request truncation by keying an asterisk (*) after the word. Searching for "cat*" will retrieve all words that begin with the letters "c-a-t."

If a user knows only a few words from a title, the keyword index can be used. Typing the words "moon" and "fire" results in a single entry, Norman Mailer's *Of a Fire on the Moon*. The Boolean operator AND between the words is implicit and need not be typed. By keying an OR between terms, you are asking for records that contain either the first term or the second term. When both AND and OR Boolean operators are used in one search, INNOPAC processes all AND operations before it processes any OR operations. Figure 26.17 illustrates how INNOPAC processes a complex Boolean expression.

INNOPAC has automatic synonym control, which allows you to search for the word "color" and automatically retrieve all the entries which contain either the word "color" or the word "colour" (Figure 26.18). Each library sets up the pairs of words that it wants as synonyms for this purpose.

With the exception of the keyword index, the system searches a string of words from left to right, with automatic truncation. Therefore, the more complete the information, the more specific the search result. For example, an author search for "smith" will retrieve all of the Smithsonians as well as the Smiths. To get to a specific title and avoid automatic truncation, type in the search ending with a vertical bar (|). In all indexes except the keyword index, a search may be done on one or more letters or numbers.

Displays

The system offers four levels of record display: brief display with holdings information for serials or multivolume sets (not shown); labeled display with comprehensive bibliographic information that can be in multiple screens; labeled display with complete bibliographic information including all fixed and variable length fields (Figure 26.20). A MARC-tagged record display (Figure 26.19) may be made available in the public search mode at the library's option.

The default screen display for a single-hit result is the labeled display with comprehensive bibliographic information. Since the default screen display already includes holdings information, the brief screen display with holdings information is not often selected. When determining the default screen display format for bibliographic records, the library can choose the fields and subfields to be displayed, the wording of the labels, and the order of the information. Recognizing that users make use of subject headings to expand their searches, we display subject headings right after publication information.

Holdings and Status Information

Holdings information for multiple volume sets or serials is displayed in two ways: summary holdings information in the bibliographic record under the highlighted label **Library Has**, and detailed holdings information for individual volumes with location, call number, and circulation availability status in the boxed window in the middle of the screen (Figure 26.21). Due to the finite number of spaces on one line, the library can only use about 18 letters to describe location. The call number display is limited to approximately 25 characters. The library can define and set its own status mes-

sages, e.g., "NOT CHECKED OUT," "MISSING," "LIBRARY USE ONLY," etc.

When displaying individual volumes with status information, users can choose to display volumes chronologically or in reverse order, i.e., recent receipts first. Users can display more volumes on the screen or can **Find a specific volume/copy**. For currently received serials, current check-in information is the default display. To view the most recently received volumes or issues, the user can choose to display a check-in card format which also includes information on volumes sent to the bindery (Figure 26.22). Records for materials which have been ordered show the status as ON ORDER, IN PROCESS, or others as appropriate.

At the library's option, a public user may be allowed to request an item. After you select the **Request** option, the system asks you for your name, your library ID number, and any special instructions. The staff can review these requests at any time. This option is not used in the Nevada catalogs.

Reserve List

By pressing **R** at the opening screen, INNOPAC will guide users to search for materials on course reserve by professor's name or course name. Items for a specific course (Figure 26.23) can be sorted by author or by location.

Library Information and User Options

By choosing **I** at the opening screen, users can view up to nineteen screens of information about the library, its hours, circulation policies, dial-up information, etc. (Figure 26.24). Also, users are able to type in titles for the library to consider purchasing or may make general suggestions. Choosing the **Additional items the library should acquire** option results in the user being prompted for author, title, other information, the user's name, and the user's address. Choosing the **Suggestions** option offers blank lines into which patrons can key suggestions. The suggestions are read by library staff.

Journal Article Index

By selecting **D** for **Connect to another Database** at the opening screen (Figure 26.1), a user can search any additional databases the library has loaded on INNOPAC or chooses to make available through dial-up. When you choose this option, INNOPAC displays a menu of the databases to which it is possible to connect. The UNLV Library loaded the Wilson *Social Sciences Index*. This database covers article citations from 1986 to date. "Welcome to Social Sciences Index" (Figure 26.25) is the opening screen for this database, which is independent from the Las Vegas library catalog. All searching conventions are identical to those of the online catalog. Because this is a journal citation database, each record is brief: author, title, journal title in which the article appears with volume and pages, year, subject, and ISSN (Figure 26.26). Similar options are available, such as **S** for **Show items in the same subject, F** for **Forward browse,** or **B** for **Backward browse.** One of the nice features about this database is that a table of contents for a particular volume of a journal can be displayed. When searched by journal title, a browse screen is displayed with volume indication, and when a single volume is chosen, the system displays a table of contents in alphabetical order by title. Since there is no connection between the library catalog database and the *Social Sciences Index* database, the system does not provide information on whether the library owns the journal a user may want. To determine if the library owns a particular issue, the user has to quit out of this database, move to the online catalog's opening screen (Figure 26.1), and search under the title of the journal.

```
            Welcome to the Online Catalog of
      James R. Dickinson Library/CCSN Learning Resource Centers
  University of Nevada, Las Vegas/Community College of Southern Nevada

        You may search for library materials by any of the following:


                    A > AUTHOR
                    T > TITLE(Book/Journal)
                    S > SUBJECT
                    C > CALL NO

                    W > KEYWORDS (title, corp.author, etc.)
                    R > RESERVE Lists
                    I > Library INFORMATION
                    D > Connect to another DATABASE
                    B > Disconnect

              Choose one (A,T,S,C,W,R,I,D,B) :

  The online catalog contains all library materials processed since 1981
          and some information converted from the card catalog.
     Please consult other catalogs or ask a librarian for assistance.
```

Figure 26.1: INNOPAC: Opening screen

Figure 26.2: INNOPAC: Second search mode

Figure 26.3: INNOPAC: Author search screen

Figure 26.4: INNOPAC: Browse result for author

```
You searched for the AUTHOR: gershwin george

AUTHOR      Gershwin, George, 1898-1937.
TITLE       Piano music. Selections.
            Rhapsody in blue ; Preludes for piano ; Short story ; Violin
               piece ; Second rhapsody for orchestra with piano ; For Lily
               Pons ; Sleepless night ; Promenade : walking the dog [sound
               recording] / Gershwin.
PUBL INFO   New York, N.Y. : CBS Records, p1985.
SUBJECT     Piano with jazz ensemble.
            Piano music.
            Piano with orchestra.
DESCRIPT    1 sound disc : digital ; 4 3/4 in.
SERIES      CBS Records masterworks.
NOTES       First work for piano and jazz band; 3rd, 4th, 6th, and 7th works

        LOCATION           CALL #                      STATUS
   1 > UNLV Nonbook        M22.G47 T46x - Compact Disc  NOT CHCKD OUT

M > MORE BIBLIOGRAPHIC Record    N > NEW Search
R > RETURN to Browsing          A > ANOTHER Search by AUTHOR
F > FORWARD browse              Z > Show Items Nearby on Shelf
B > BACKWARD browse            O > OTHER options
Choose one (M,R,F,B,N,A,Z,S,P,O)
```

Figure 26.5: INNOPAC: Labeled display (recording)

```
You searched for the AUTHOR: king martin luther
2 entries found, entries 1-2 are:                    LOCATIONS
King Martin Luther
    1  —> See KING, MARTIN LUTHER, 1899-1984
    2  —> See KING, MARTIN LUTHER, JR., 1929-1968




Please type the NUMBER of the item you want to see, or
R > RETURN to Browsing          P > PRINT
N > NEW Search                  L > LIMIT this Search
A > ANOTHER Search by AUTHOR
Choose one (1-2,R,N,A,P,L)
```

Figure 26.6: INNOPAC: Author result, cross-ref

```
You searched for the AUTHOR: king martin luther jr 1929 1968
9 entries found, entries 1-8 are:                     LOCATIONS
King Martin Luther Jr 1929 1968
    1  I have a dream : the life of Martin Luther King.   UNR Film Lib
    2  The measure of a man                               UNR Main
    3  Strength to love                                   UNR Main
    4  Strength to love                                   WNCC (Carson)
    5  Stride toward freedom : the Montgomery story       UNR Main
    6  A testament of hope : the essential writings of M  UNR Main
    7  The trumpet of conscience                          UNR Main
    8  Where do we go from here: Chaos or community?      UNR Main




Please type the NUMBER of the item you want to see, or
F > Go FORWARD                  P > PRINT
N > NEW Search                  L > LIMIT this Search
A > ANOTHER Search by AUTHOR    J > JUMP
Choose one (1-8,F,N,A,P,L,J)
```

Figure 26.7: INNOPAC: Result set for author

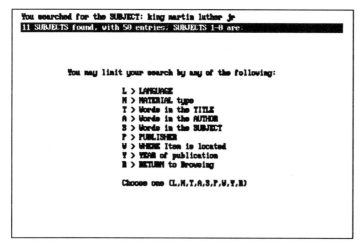

```
You searched for the SUBJECT: king martin luther jr
11 SUBJECTS found, with 50 entries; SUBJECTS 1-8 are:



           You may limit your search by any of the following:

                       L > LANGUAGE
                       M > MATERIAL type
                       T > Words in the TITLE
                       A > Words in the AUTHOR
                       S > Words in the SUBJECT
                       P > PUBLISHER
                       W > WHERE item is located
                       Y > YEAR of publication
                       R > RETURN to Browsing

                   Choose one (L,M,T,A,S,P,W,Y,R)
```

Figure 26.8: INNOPAC: Search limit options

```
You searched for the SUBJECT: king martin luther jr
11 SUBJECTS found, with 50 entries; SUBJECTS 1-8 are:
   LANGUAGE =


                 E > English
                 F > French
                 G > German
                 I > Italian
                 S > Spanish
                 J > Japanese
                 U > Russian
                 B > Basque
                 R > RETURN to Previous Screen

                 Choose one (E,F,G,I,S,J,U,B,R)
```

Figure 26.9: INNOPAC: Language limit screen

```
You searched for the SUBJECT: king martin luther jr LIMITED TO English AND ..
10 entries found, entries 1-8 are:                     LOCATIONS
King Martin Luther Jr 1929 1968
     1 The FBI and Martin Luther King, Jr. : from "Solo"  UNM Main
     2 Let the trumpet sound : the life of Martin Luther  UNM Main
     3 Martin Luther King                                 UNCC (Carson)
     4 Martin Luther King, Jr. : the making of a mind     UNM Main
     5 Martin Luther King, Jr.—to the mountaintop         UNM Main
     6 Of Kennedys and Kings : making sense of the sixti  UNM Main
King Martin Luther Jr 1929 1968 Assassination
     7 At the river I stand : Memphis, the 1968 strike,   UNM Main
King Martin Luther Jr 1929 1968 Iconography
     8 A lasting impression : a collection of photograph  UNM Main







Please type the NUMBER of the item you want to see, or
F > Go FORWARD            A > ANOTHER Search by SUBJECT    J > JUMP
R > RETURN to Browsing    P > PRINT
N > NEW Search            D > DISPLAY Title and Author
Choose one (1-8,F,R,N,A,P,D,J)
```

Figure 26.10: INNOPAC: Subject result with limits

Figure 26.11: INNOPAC: Shelflist browse

Figure 26.12: INNOPAC: Related-subject search

Figure 26.13: INNOPAC: Long-search report

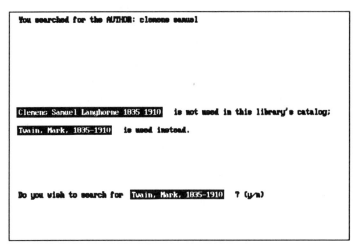

```
You searched for the AUTHOR: clemens samuel




Clemens Samuel Langhorne 1835 1910   is not used in this library's catalog;
Twain, Mark, 1835-1910   is used instead.



Do you wish to search for Twain, Mark, 1835-1910   ? (y/n)
```

Figure 26.14: INNOPAC: Authorized-form message

```
You searched for the SUBJECT: rocks
5 entries found, entries 1-5 are:                          LOCATIONS
Rocks
  1  --> See Also BRECCIA
  2  --> See Also PETROLOGY
  3  --> See Also ROCKS, SILICEOUS
  4  --> See Also ROCKSLIDES
  5  --> See Also STONE








Please type the NUMBER of the item you want to see, or
R > RETURN to Browsing            P > PRINT
N > NEW Search                    D > DISPLAY Title and Author
A > ANOTHER Search by SUBJECT     L > LIMIT this Search
Choose one (1-5,R,N,A,P,D,L)
```

Figure 26.15: INNOPAC: See-also references

```
You searched for the SUBJECT: tumr
Your SUBJECT not found, Nearby SUBJECTS are:

  1   Tumors Testis Congresses  ............................  1 entry
  2   Tumors Testis Diagnosis  .............................  1 entry
  3   Tumors Throat  .......................................  1 entry
  4   Tumours --> See TUMORS  ..............................  1 entry
      Your entry  Tumr  would be here
  5   Tumuli --> See MOUNDS  ...............................  1 entry
  6   Tun Huang Hsien Art Buddhist China  .................  1 entry
  7   Tun Huang Hsien Art Chinese China  ..................  1 entry
  8   Tun Huang Hsien Cave Temples Buddhist China  ........  1 entry






Please type the NUMBER of the item you want to see, or
F > Go FORWARD                    A > ANOTHER Search by SUBJECT
B > Go BACKWARD                   P > PRINT
N > NEW Search                    O > OTHER options
Choose one (1-8,F,B,N,A,P,D,T,J,O)
```

Figure 26.16: INNOPAC: Result of keying error

```
                      WORD : supreme court challenge death penalty
SUPREME        is in 374   titles.
COURT          is in 855   titles.
CHALLENGES     is in 251   titles.
DEATH          is in 1341  titles.
PENALTY        is in 32    titles.
Both "PENALTY" and "CHALLENGES" are in 0 title. Therefore "CHALLENGES" is disca
Adding "SUPREME" leaves 0 title. Therefore "SUPREME" is discarded.
Adding "COURT" leaves 0 title. Therefore "COURT" is discarded.
Adding "DEATH" leaves 27 titles.

There are 27 entries with PENALTY & DEATH.
Do you want to see items found? (y/n)
```

Figure 26.17: INNOPAC: Complex Boolean processing

```
You searched for the WORD: color
658 entries found, entries 68-75 are:                        LOCATIONS
   68  The Behavioral significance of color        Life & Hlth Sci
   69  Good news for modern man; Today's English version  WNCC (Carson)
   70  The Lindisfarne Gospels : three plates in colour  UNR Special Coll
   71  Bibliography of water colour painting and painter  UNR Main
   72  Bird behavior                                UNR Main
   73  Black Africans and native Americans : color, race  UNR Main
   74  The Black elite : facing the color line in the tw  UNR Main
   75  Black is the color of the cosmos : essays on Afro  UNR Main




Please type the NUMBER of the item you want to see, or
F > Go FORWARD       A > ANOTHER Search by WORD      L > LIMIT this Search
B > Go BACKWARD      P > PRINT                       J > JUMP
N > NEW Search       D > DISPLAY Title and Author
Choose one (68-75,F,B,N,A,P,D,L,J)
```

Figure 26.18: INNOPAC: Synonym control

```
You searched for the TITLE: community junior college research
001   2571944
005   19881286219730.0
008   761122d19761981dcugr1p        uuua0eng dcas a
010   77649419 //r82
012   21b9111
022   03616975
030   CCROD
035   (CaOTULAS)152815832
035   1472830|bWULS
040   NSD|cNSD|dDLC|dOCL|dNSD|dOCL|dNSD|dNST|dDLC|dNST|dUNL
042   nsdp|alc
043   n-us——
049   UNLP
082   370.1/543/0973

 LOCATION         CALL #                        STATUS
1 > UNLV Periodicals  LB2328 .C685               LIB USE ONLY

D > DISPLAY Holdings            M > NEW Search
M > MORE BIBLIOGRAPHIC Record   A > ANOTHER Search by TITLE
R > RETURN to Browsing          Z > Show Items Nearby on Shelf
F > FORWARD browse              O > OTHER options
Choose one (D,M,R,F,M,A,Z,S,T,O)
```

Figure 26.19: INNOPAC: MARC display (partial)

```
You searched for the TITLE: community junior college research
B12467868                    BIBLIOGRAPHIC Information
LANG: eng          COPIES: 2        BCODE1: s         BCODE3: -
SKIP: 0            CAT DATE: 12-06-88 BCODE2: a        COUNTRY: dcu
LOCATION: unlp
CALL #      LB2328 .C685
TITLE       Community/junior college research quarterly
PUBL INFO   Washington, D.C. : Hemisphere Pub. Corp., c1976-c1981
PUBL INFO   Vol. 1, no. 1 (Oct.-Dec. 1976)-v. 5, no. 4 (July-Sept. 1981)
DESCRIPT    5 v. ; 23 cm
NOTES       Quarterly
NOTES       Title from cover
SUBJECT     Community colleges —United States —Periodicals
SUBJECT     Junior colleges —United States —Periodicals
ALT TITLE   Community junior college research quarterly
CONT'D BY   Community/junior college —0277-6774 (DLC)    82641876
OCLC #      2571944
ISN/LCN     77649419 //r82
ISN/LCN     03616975
 M > MORE BIBLIOGRAPHIC Record     A > ANOTHER Search by TITLE
 R > RETURN to Browsing            S > Record SUMMARY
 F > FORWARD browse                Z > Show Items Nearby on Shelf
 N > NEW Search                    I > Show ITEMS with the same SUBJECT
Choose one (M,R,F,N,A,S,Z,I)
```

Figure 26.20: INNOPAC: Comprehensive display

```
You searched for the TITLE: kritisch ausgape

AUTHOR      Haydn, Joseph, 1732-1809.
TITLE       Symphonies.
            Kritische Ausgabe samtlicher Symphonien = Critical edition of the
                complete symphonies / Joseph Haydn ; Herausgeber, H.C. Robbins
                Landon.
PUBL INFO   [Wien] : Philharmonia : Universal Edition, c1960-c1967.
LIB. HAS    v. 1-107
SUBJECT     Symphonies —Scores.
DESCRIPT    1 miniature score (107 v.) ; 19 cm.

        LOCATION            CALL #                    STATUS
 001 > UNLV Book Stacks   M1000.H3 S9 L3 v.1        NOT CHCKD OUT
 002 > UNLV Book Stacks   M1000.H3 S9 L3 v.2        NOT CHCKD OUT
 003 > UNLV Book Stacks   M1000.H3 S9 L3 v.3        NOT CHCKD OUT
 004 > UNLV Book Stacks   M1000.H3 S9 L3 v.4        NOT CHCKD OUT
 005 > UNLV Book Stacks   M1000.H3 S9 L3 v.5        NOT CHCKD OUT
 ——————————————— 107 volumes/copies to view ———————————————
 I > INFO on more volumes/copies   R > RETURN to Browsing
 V > Find Specific VOLUME/COPY     F > FORWARD browse
 D > DISPLAY Holdings              B > BACKWARD browse
 M > MORE BIBLIOGRAPHIC Record     O > OTHER options
Choose one (I,V,D,M,R,F,B,N,A,Z,S,P,O)
```

Figure 26.21: INNOPAC: Score, multiple volumes (1)

You searched for the TITLE: pc computing

TITLE   PC/Computing
CALL #   JOURNAL STACKS   LOCATIONS Engineering Lib

Boxes 1 to 14 of 24

May 91	Jun 91	Jul 91	Aug 91	Sep 91	Oct 91	Nov 91
ARRIVED	ARRIVED	ARRIVED	ARRIVED	ARRIVED	EXPECTED	E
04-18-91	05-22-91	06-24-91	07-17-91	08-23-91	09-17-91	10-17-91
4:5 1	4:6 1	4:7 1	4:8 1	4:9 1	4:10	4:11

Dec 91	Jan 92	Feb 92	Mar 92	Apr 92	May 92	Jun 92
E	E	E	E	E	E	E
11-17-91	12-17-91	01-17-92	02-17-92	03-17-92	04-17-92	05-17-92
4:12	5:1	5:2	5:3	5:4	5:5	5:6

```
F > Go FORWARD              A > ANOTHER Search by TITLE
L > LINE Display Format     P > PRINT
R > RETURN to Browsing      D > Re-DISPLAY Records
N > NEW Search
Choose one (F,L,R,N,A,P,D)
```

Figure 26.22: INNOPAC: Serial check-in format

R10010063   COURSE Information
PROF/TA   Siegel, Richard
COURSE   PSC 439/639
COURSE   Political Science 439/639
COURSE   Problems of World Politics

NUM	TITLE	AUTHOR
1	Adding green to the international studies curricu	Soroos, Marvin S.
2	Black mist and acid rain - science as fig leaf of	Boehmer-Christiansen, So
3	Contending theories of international relations	Dougherty, James E
4	Deep ecology	Devall, Bill, 1938-
5	Ecology of war and peace	
6	Foreign affairs (Council on Foreign Relations)	
7	Global environmental change	
8	International cooperation : building regimes for	Young, Oran R
9	International environmental affairs	

```
There are 30 items on reserve
A > Sort list by AUTHOR       F > FORWARD
L > Display LOCATION & status R > RETURN to browsing
P > PRINT items               Q > QUIT
Choose one (A,L,P,F,R,Q)
```

Figure 26.23: INNOPAC: Course reserve list

```
*** LIBRARY INFORMATION ***

01 > UNIVERSITY MAIN LIBRARY HOURS FALL '91
02 > HOURS FOR AQUARIUM MICROCOMPUTER LAB
03 > BRANCH LIBRARY LOCATIONS & HOURS FALL '91
04 > MEDICAL, DBI, & MJC FALL '91
05 > COLL.OF ED. LEARNING & RESOURCES HOURS FALL '91
06 > COMM.COLL. LEARNING RES. CTRS. HOURS FALL '91
07 > UNIVERSITY GENERAL LIBRARY PRIVILEGES
08 > UNIVERSITY MAIN LIBRARY LOAN PERIODS
09 > UNIVERSITY BRANCH LIBRARIES LOAN PERIODS
10 > EXPLANATION OF "NOT CHK'D OUT"
11 > WHAT ARE "RESERVE LISTS?"
12 > UNIVERSITY RESERVE MATERIALS AND FINES
13 > UNIVERSITY INTERLIBRARY LOAN
14 > LOOKING FOR MAGAZINE OR JOURNAL ARTICLES?
15 > FOOD, DRINK, SMOKING PROHIBITED
16 > PHOTOCOPYING IN THE UNIVERSITY LIBRARIES
17 > RESPONSES TO YOUR SUGGESTIONS AND COMMENTS
18 > LOCATING LIBRARY MATERIALS IN THE MAIN LIBRARY
A > ADDITIONAL items library should acquire
S > SUGGESTIONS
N > NEW Search
Choose one (01-18,A,S,N)
```

Figure 26.24: INNOPAC: Library information list

```
                    Welcome to SOCIAL SCIENCES INDEX




              A > ARTICLE AUTHOR
              T > ARTICLE TITLE
              S > SUBJECT
              W > KeyWORDS in the title
              J > JOURNAL TITLE

              Q > QUIT


              Choose one (A,T,S,W,J,Q) :

         For Assistance, Please ask at the Reference Desk
```

Figure 26.25: INNOPAC: Social Sciences indexes

```
You searched for the SUBJECT: king martin luther 1929 1968

AUTHOR       Sheridan, Earl.
TITLE        The diminishing soul of black America.

APPEARS IN   Social Theory and Practice v. 14 (Summer '88)  p. 131-49 Soc
               Theory Pract.
YEAR         1988.
SUBJECT      King, Martin Luther, 1929-1968.
             Blacks —Political activities.
             Black leadership.
ISSN         0037-802X.




R > RETURN to Browsing        A > ANOTHER Search by SUBJECT
F > FORWARD browse            S > SHOW items with the same SUBJECT
B > BACKWARD browse           T > Display MARC Record
N > NEW Search
Choose one (R,F,B,N,A,S,T)
```

Figure 26.26: INNOPAC: Social Science result

27

IO+
The Library Workstation at the University of Illinois

Leslie Troutman[1]

IO+ is the name given to the expanded online catalog at the University of Illinois at Urbana-Champaign (UIUC) and at Chicago (UIC).[2] IO+ offers enhanced access to a variety of information resources and services using multifunction, DOS-based, microcomputer workstation software developed by three UIUC faculty members: William Mischo, Tim Cole, and C. C. Cheng. These resources and services currently include ILLINET Online, BRS/SEARCH (used to access locally mounted periodical index databases), CARL Un-Cover, and files or databases created in-house and stored on the microcomputer hard disk. Eventually, IO+ will include ties to optical disk databases (CD-ROM), national bibliographic databases, Internet resources (including remote online catalogs), UIUCNET (the campus fiber-optic network, where users may reach BITNET, campus directories and bulletin boards, etc.) and microcomputer applications software, expert systems, and database management systems.

Notes about the figures: IO+ uses a palette of 16 colors in order to enhance the presentation of information and help users relate various functions with various colors. For the purposes of this presentation, these colors were converted primarily to black on white with an occasional gray. This has resulted in a minor loss of clarity and definition, making the screens look more crowded than they would normally.

In order to show more detail on the IO+ screens, some have been enlarged in a manner that may result in occasional "banding" in gray areas. These are artifacts of the publication process, not part of IO+ itself.

The Online Catalog: ILLINET Online

ILLINET Online is the statewide library computer network for Illinois. It is comprised of OCLC cataloging records contributed by 800 Illinois libraries and, as of the beginning of 1991, contained more than five million bibliographic records and more than eight million authority records. It is the catalog for the forty member libraries of the Illinois Library Computer Systems Organization (ILCSO) and is a resource-sharing tool for nearly 2,500 Illinois libraries of all types. Begun more than ten years ago, ILLINET Online is a unique

---

1   The author gratefully acknowledges the assistance of Tim Cole and William Mischo in the preparation of this chapter.

2   For more information on the history and development of IO+, see William H. Mischo et al., "University of Illinois at Urbana-Champaign," in *Campus Strategies for Libraries and Electronic Information* (Rockport, Massachusetts: Digital Press, 1990): 117–141.

and invaluable bibliographic tool available not only to users within the confines of the library itself but also through a statewide dial access program.

At ILCSO libraries, ILLINET Online is made up of two separate yet linked databases, each with their own distinct command language. The Library Computer System (LCS) component is a short-record database providing call number, location and circulation information. The Full Bibliographic Record (FBR) component, based on WLN software, is the online catalog for the ILCSO libraries, providing entry points by personal and corporate name, title, uniform title, subject, and series. A search defaults to the home library; the eleven dial-access telephone numbers default to one of the five larger libraries in the state. The default library may be changed by the use of scope codes. One may search each of the forty ILCSO libraries individually or as a group. Other possible scopes are for one of the eighteen Regional Library Systems, the four Research and Reference Centers, the Center for Research Libraries or the entire database.

Most of the ILCSO libraries have completed retrospective conversion projects and ILLINET Online contains the complete holdings of these libraries. One exception to this is the University of Illinois at Urbana-Champaign. With more than seven million volumes, UIUC found that a complete retrospective conversion of the entire collection was not economically feasible. While there are LCS (circulation) records for almost everything in the UIUC Library, there are FBR (OPAC) records for only a portion of the collection. At UIUC ILLINET Online contains FBR records for books cataloged after 1975, serials cataloged after 1977, and music and audiovisual materials cataloged after 1979.

Improvements to ILLINET Online keep the database vital in a changing online environment. One of these improvements is a three-phrase restructuring of the LCS database that will bring it into the FBR database environment and will eliminate a host of problems attendant upon working with a nonstandard, noncommercial database management system. It will eliminate the need for two sets of commands since LCS records will be searchable using FBR commands. Toward this end, a new interface is currently under development for ILLINET Online. The restructuring will be completed in the near future.

ILLINET Online: The Interface at UIUC

The microcomputer interface for ILLINET Online currently in place at UIUC was developed by Chin-Chuan Cheng, Professor of Linguistics at UIUC.[3] The interface queries the user in natural language and formulates search commands internally thereby making knowledge of the direct commands unnecessary. For the new or casual user of ILLINET Online this presents obvious advantages. The interface is easily bypassed for those wishing to use the somewhat greater flexibility and power of command mode.

There are five primary search options: (1) author-title; (2) title; (3) author; (4) call number, ISBN, ISSN; and (5) subject. Title searches may be limited to periodical titles, and the user is given the option of supplying a specific volume number or year. In the author search, the user may search either a personal name or a corporate name. The shelf-position search (a subject-area call number search) is an option when the user elects to do a subject search.

The author-title, title, author, call number, and shelf-position searches are initially executed in LCS. With the exception of the latter two searches, the user is given the option of searching FBR if the search is unsatisfactory. In FBR, the author-title search takes advantage of the Boolean capabilities of the system by employing the Boolean AND. Here, and in the title search, titles are searched in FBR as keywords. Corporate author searches in FBR are also keyword searches.

Subject, ISBN, and ISSN searches begin in FBR. The subject search begins by reminding the

3 Chin-Chuan Cheng, "Microcomputer-Based User Interface," *Information Technology and Libraries* 4, no. 4 (December 1985): 346–351.

user that the search will be more successful if Library of Congress subject headings are used. Various modifications are applied to the search string if the initial search is unsuccessful. These include issuing a browse command in the subject authority file to find alphabetically similar headings and searching the entered string as title keywords.

All searches of the interface offer the user the option of searching other ILLINET Online libraries. Items at the forty ILCSO institutions may be charged, saved or renewed depending upon their circulation status. The Intersystems Library Delivery System, a network of vehicles running regularly throughout the state, will deliver materials to the requestor's library in approximately one week. Items from non-ILCSO libraries are readily obtainable through Interlibrary Borrowing since the holding libraries within the state are listed. The ease with which resource sharing at the user level is accomplished is one major benefit of ILLINET Online and the interface.

Article-Level Searching: IBIS

In the summer of 1990, BRS/SEARCH software was purchased jointly by the University of Illinois Libraries at Urbana and Chicago to provide periodical index searching in a mainframe computing environment. Using the microcomputer software written by William Mischo, Beckman Institute and Engineering Librarian and Tim Cole, Assistant Beckman Institute and Engineering Librarian, the Illinois Bibliographic Information System (IBIS), features guided assistance in search strategy formulation; context-sensitive help screens and suggestive prompts; storage of search strategy on diskette and uploading of previously stored strategy; automatic truncation and stopword removal; user-feedback mechanisms to refine search strategy; downloading and printing of citations; search history; display of call number and limited holdings information; and direct command execution within a search performed through the interface.

The interface is constructed with window-based menus and displays that feature selection and refinement menus and an explanation window; there is support for the use of a mouse and

a dial-up version is also available. The capability exists to invoke other microcomputer application packages (e.g., database management systems) from the selection menu, returning to the top level menu upon completion of the application. Future developments include voice-synthesized interaction for the visually impaired user and interactive links with the online catalog and other databases.

In the spring and summer of 1991, while in beta testing, IBIS offers access to the *Current Contents* database. One may elect to search either the latest week of *Current Contents* or the file dating back to January 1990. The user may choose an individual section (e.g., Arts and Humanities or Engineering and Technology) or all seven sections combined. The database may be searched by personal author name, by organization or geographic name, by keywords, by keywords limited only to titles, and by journal title. Other options include limiting articles retrieved to a particular type (e.g., book reviews, literature review articles).

Full Boolean logic is supported and all searches can be refined as required by the user. After retrieving a set, the user may mark specific items for downloading/printing, print/download the entire set, review search history, or retrieve the table of contents of a specific issue. The user may download up to 300 references or print on the attached printer (40 references). By the fall of 1991, the additional option of sending output to a high-speed printer for "off-line" printing or to one's electronic mail box will be in place.

Databases to be added include *Medline* and six Wilson databases (*Applied Science and Technology Index, Biological and Agricultural Index, Business Periodicals Index, Humanities Index, Readers' Guide,* and *Social Sciences Index*). The Illinois Library Computer Systems Organization has purchased a BRS/ SEARCH software license and plans to mount ERIC by fall of 1991 for users across the state. Negotiations between various agencies in the state of Illinois and commercial vendors may result in access to tools such as the *Academic American Encyclopedia*, EPIC, and the Illinois Legislative Status Service. The software will be continually developed in order to take full advantage of the searching capabilities of each new database.

Microcomputer Databases

IO+ features keyword searching of in-house–created databases mounted on the hard disk of the workstation. Limited Boolean searching is also possible. Each library on the UIUC campus is free to determine which types of in-house–created database would best serve their users. Typical files include a list of journals for a specific departmental library or group of libraries (e.g., journals in the Engineering Library or journals in the six libraries of the Arts and Humanities Council); current and retrospective acquisitions lists; help files; faculty information files; library resource guides; and customized bibliographies. If a given file contains call numbers, it is possible to link to the circulation database in order to determine current availability.

Conclusion

As one of the largest academic libraries in the United States, the University of Illinois Library continually strives to maintain its role as a leader in library technology and resource sharing. Through IO+ library users may move beyond the online catalog to a multitude of electronic sources and services. Enhanced access to information by means of the Library Workstation will provide an excellent model for the systems of the future.

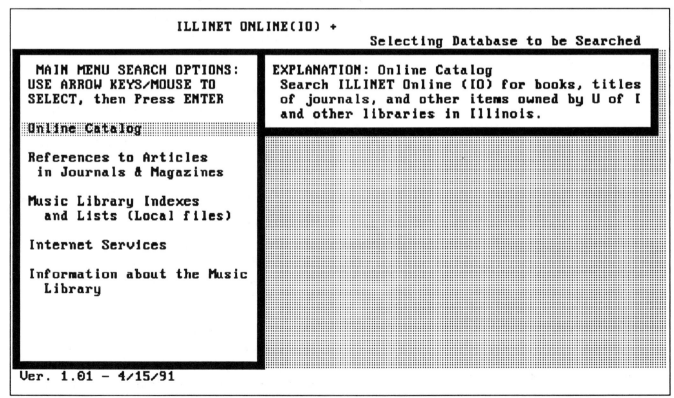

Figure 27.1: IO+: Main menu: ILLINET Online

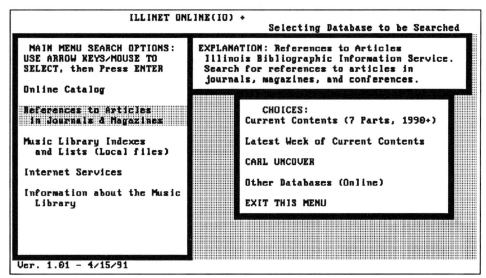

Figure 27.2: IO+: Main Menu: IBIS

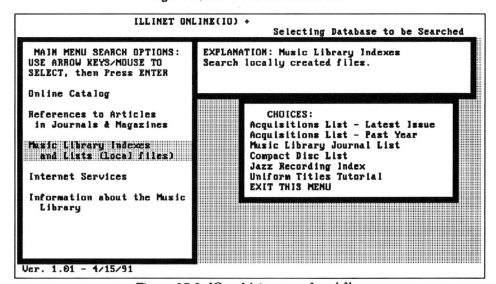

Figure 27.3: IO+: Main menu: Local files

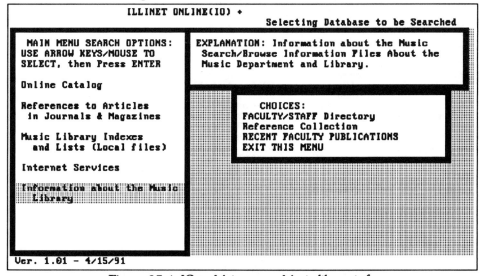

Figure 27.4: IO+: Main menu: Music library info

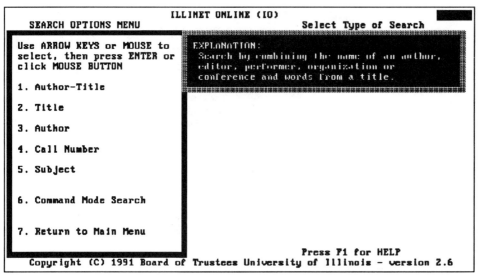

```
                        ILLINET ONLINE (IO)
    SEARCH OPTIONS MENU                    Select Type of Search

   Use ARROW KEYS or MOUSE to    EXPLANATION:
   select, then press ENTER or     Search by combining the name of an author,
   click MOUSE BUTTON              editor, performer, organization or
                                   conference and words from a title.
   1. Author-Title

   2. Title

   3. Author

   4. Call Number

   5. Subject

   6. Command Mode Search

   7. Return to Main Menu

                                    Press F1 for HELP
   Copyright (C) 1991 Board of Trustees University of Illinois - version 2.6
```

Figure 27.5: IO+: ILLINET Online main menu

```
                      Beginning of search
---------------------------------------------------------------------
Type the last name of the author or the first important word of the
organization and then press <ENTER>:  GERSHWIN
Type the first important word of the title and <ENTER>: RHAPSODY
Searching Circulation Records.
Found 18 similar items.
Type another word or name to narrow the search (if none, press <ENTER>):
BLUE
Retrieving the first 18 items...
Searching for exact match.
01 GERSHWIN, GEORGE, 1898-1937      RHAPSODY IN BLUE $NEW YORK          1924
02 GERSHWIN, GEORGE, 1898-1937.     RHAPSODY IN BLUE. AN AMERICAN IN PARIS 1960
04 GERSHWIN, GEORGE,1898-1937.      RHAPSODY IN BLUE
05 GERSHWIN, GEORGE, 18981937.      RHAPSODY IN BLUE, PIANO & ORCHESTRA; A 1927
06 GERSHWIN, GEORGE, 1898-1937      RHAPSODY IN BLUE, PIANO & ORCHESTRA$NY 1924
07 GERSHWIN, GEORGE, 1898-1937.     RHAPSODY IN BLUE$ NEW YORK          1942
08 GERSHWIN, GEORGE                 RHAPSODY IN BLUE AND OTHER GERSHWIN TU 1965
09 GERSHWIN, GEORGE, 1898-1937.     RHAPSODY IN BLUE
10 GERSHWIN, GEORGE, 1898-1937.     RHAPSODY IN BLUE$ COMMEMORATIVE FACSIM 1987
These  9  items match your request.
Type a line number and <ENTER> to see call number and location of that item;
press <S> to see the similar items found in this search or <ENTER> to go on.

Author-Title Search: GERSHWIN RHAPSODY              Press <ESC> to Exit
```

Figure 27.6: IO+: Author-title search, LCS

```
organization and then press <ENTER>:  GERSHWIN
Type the first important word of the title and <ENTER>: RHAPSODY
Searching Circulation Records.
Found 18 similar items.
Type another word or name to narrow the search (if none, press <ENTER>):
BLUE
Retrieving the first 18 items...
Searching for exact match.
01 GERSHWIN, GEORGE, 1898-1937      RHAPSODY IN BLUE $NEW YORK          1924
02 GERSHWIN, GEORGE, 1898-1937.     RHAPSODY IN BLUE. AN AMERICAN IN PARIS 1960
04 GERSHWIN, GEORGE,1898-1937.      RHAPSODY IN BLUE
05 GERSHWIN, GEORGE, 18981937.      RHAPSODY IN BLUE, PIANO & ORCHESTRA; A 1927
06 GERSHWIN, GEORGE, 1898-1937      RHAPSODY IN BLUE, PIANO & ORCHESTRA$NY 1924
07 GERSHWIN, GEORGE, 1898-1937.     RHAPSODY IN BLUE$ NEW YORK          1942
08 GERSHWIN, GEORGE                 RHAPSODY IN BLUE AND OTHER GERSHWIN TU 1965
09 GERSHWIN, GEORGE, 1898-1937.     RHAPSODY IN BLUE
10 GERSHWIN, GEORGE, 1898-1937.     RHAPSODY IN BLUE$ COMMEMORATIVE FACSIM 1987
These  9  items match your request.
Search the remaining 8 items? (Press <Y> if "YES", <ENTER> otherwise.)
Press <ENTER> to search other libraries in the LCS network;
     <X> to expand on this search with the author & title
         in the UNIVERSITY OF ILLINOIS AT URBANA-CHAMPAIGN catalog;
     <E> to end.

Author-Title Search: GERSHWIN RHAPSODY              Press <ESC> to Exit
```

Figure 27.7: IO+: AT search expanded to FBR

```
Search the remaining 8 items? (Press <Y> if "YES", <ENTER> otherwise.)      ████
------------------------------------------------------------------------------
This search may not cover all items in the library.
Found 14 records.
                                            BIBLIOGRAPHIC DISPLAY
     1. Gershwin, George, Rhapsody in blue : (1924) ; Preludes for piano
        (1926) ; Short story : (1925) ; Violin piece : Gershwin melody
        no. 48 ; . . . [sound recording] / p1985. 1 sound disc
        ocm13-225819
     2. Gershwin, George, Rhapsody in blue ; An American in Paris [sound
        recording] / p1981. 1 sound disc (34 min.)    ocm11-240115
     3. Gershwin, George, Rhapsody in blue 1942] minature score (47 p.)
        ocm00-490553
     4. Gershwin plays Rhapsody in blue. [sound recording] [1974] 2 s.
        ocm09-747370
     5. Gershwin, George, Rhapsody in blue / [c1924] 197- printing.
        miniature score (47 p.)   ocm00-889608
These are short records number 1 - 5. Do one of the following:
   Type a line number and <ENTER> to see corresponding full record.
   Press <ENTER> without a number to see the remaining records.
   Press <C> for circulation information.
   Press <O> to search other libraries.
   Press <E> to end this search.

Author-Title Search: GERSHWIN RHAPSODY                    Press <ESC> to Exit
```

Figure 27.8: IO+: Results of AT search in FBR

```
     5. Gershwin, George, Rhapsody in blue / [c1924] 197- printing.    ████
        miniature score (47 p.)   ocm00-889608
------------------------------------------------------------------------------
                                            BIBLIOGRAPHIC DISPLAY
     Gershwin, George, 1898-1937.
     [Rhapsody in blue]
     Rhapsody in blue ; An American in Paris [sound recording] /
Gershwin. Cleveland, Ohio : Telarc Records, p1981.
     1 sound disc (34 min.) : 500 rpm., stereo., compact digital ; 4 3/4
in.
     Second work is a symphonic poem.
     Program notes by Deena Rosenberg and notes on the pianist and
technical information on the recording ([12] p. ; 12 cm.) inserted in
container.
     Eugene List, piano ; Cincinnati Symphony Orchestra ; Erich Kunzel,
conductor.
     Recorded at Music Hall in Cincinnati, Ohio, January 5, 1981.
        1. Piano with orchestra   2. Symphonic poems   3. Compact discs.
  I. Kunzel, Erich. prf  II. Gershwin, George, 1898-1937. American in
Paris. III. List, Eugene, 1918- prf  IV. Cincinnati Symphony Orchestra
prf  V. CD-80058 Telarc  VI. Title.
        ocm11-240115
Wish to see circulation information? (Press <Y> if "YES", <ENTER> otherwise.)

Author-Title Search: GERSHWIN RHAPSODY                    Press <ESC> to Exit
```

Figure 27.9: IO+: Full display, sound recording

```
     Program notes by Deena Rosenberg and notes on the pianist and     ████
technical information on the recording ([12] p. ; 12 cm.) inserted in
container.
     Eugene List, piano ; Cincinnati Symphony Orchestra ; Erich Kunzel,
conductor.
     Recorded at Music Hall in Cincinnati, Ohio, January 5, 1981.
        1. Piano with orchestra   2. Symphonic poems   3. Compact discs.
  I. Kunzel, Erich. prf  II. Gershwin, George, 1898-1937. American in
Paris. III. List, Eugene, 1918- prf  IV. Cincinnati Symphony Orchestra
prf  V. CD-80058 Telarc  VI. Title.
        ocm11-240115
Wish to see circulation information? (Press <Y> if "YES", <ENTER> otherwise.)

CDISCM1010G47R47   GERSHWIN, GEORGE, 1898-1937.
RHAPSODY IN BLUE$ CLEVELAND, OHIO
NOLC   3100134   1981      1   ADDED: 860817   MENG
01   001 BUO   MUQ
PAGE 1 END◆
Print the information? (Press <Y> if "YES", <ENTER> otherwise.)
Do you need help with the symbols? (Press <Y> if "YES", <ENTER> otherwise.)
The call number is CDISCM1010G47R47.  The library has 1 copy.
Line 01:  Copy 1 is in Music--Music Building.
          The loan period is usually building use only.
Press <C> to charge out, <R> to renew, <S> to save, <ENTER> to go on.
Author-Title Search: GERSHWIN RHAPSODY                    Press <ESC> to Exit
```

Figure 27.10: IO+: Circulation record

```
Retrieving the first 10 items...
Searching for exact match.
03 KING, MARTIN LUTHER, 1929-1968.  THE TRUMPET OF CONSCIENCE$NY        1968
06 KING, MARTIN LUTHER, 1929-1968.  LA FORCA D'ESTIMAR$ 8A. EDICIO.$ BARCE 1976
08 KING, MARTIN LUTHER             NOBEL LECTURE BY THE REVEREND DR. MART 1965
10 KING, MARTIN LUTHER, JR., 1929-1 STRENGTH TO LOVE$ 1ST FORTRESS PRESS E 1981
These  4  items match your request.
-----------------------------------------------------------------------------
                               AUTHORITY DISPLAY
  *    8. King, Martin Luther, 1899-1965
       4. King, Martin Luther, 1899-1984.
  *    7. King, Martin Luther, 1929-1968
       3. King, Martin Luther, Jr., 1929-1968.
       5. King, Martin Luther, Jr., 1929-1968. Speeches. Selections.
       6. King, Martin Luther, Jr., 1929-1968. Why we can't wait.
       2. King, Martin Luther, Jr., 1929-1968.--Speeches. Selections.
       1. King, Martin Luther, Jr., 1929-1968.--Stength to love. Catalan
These are headings number 1 - 8. Do one of the following:
  Type a line number and <ENTER> to see corresponding bibliographic records.
  Press <B> to browse--to see more headings.
  Press <I> for an interpretation of the symbols to the left of the headings.
  Press <E> to end this search.

Author Search:    KING MARTIN LUTHER             Press <ESC> to Exit
```

Figure 27.11: IO+: Authority file display (author)

```
     community7 / 1968. 209 p.   ocm00-192942
-----------------------------------------------------------------------------
Type a line number and <ENTER> for circulation information: 4

323.4X585WO   KING, MARTIN LUTHER.
THE WORDS OF MARTIN LUTHER KING, JR$ 1ST ED.$ NEW YORK   83-17306
     2743393   1983       4   ADDED:  840212
01     001 16-4W STX
02     002 3W    UGX
03     003 16-4W STX
04     004 16-4W STV
PAGE 1 END◆
Print the information? (Press <Y> if "YES", <ENTER> otherwise.)
Do you need help with the symbols? (Press <Y> if "YES", <ENTER> otherwise.)
The call number is 323.4X585WO.  The library has 4 copies.
Line 01:  Copy 1 is in Stacks--Circulation Desk/Stacks 2nd Floor Main Library.
          The loan period is usually 16 weeks for faculty - 4 weeks for others.
Line 02:  Copy 2 is in Undergraduate Library.
          The loan period is usually 3 weeks.
Line 03:  Copy 3 is in Stacks--Circulation Desk/Stacks 2nd Floor Main Library.
          The loan period is usually 16 weeks for faculty - 4 weeks for others.
Line 04:  Copy 4 is in Stacks--Circulation Desk/Stacks 2nd Floor Main Library.
          The loan period is usually 16 weeks for faculty - 4 weeks for others.
Press <C> to charge out, <R> to renew, <S> to save, <ENTER> to go on.
Author Search:    KING MARTIN LUTHER             Press <ESC> to Exit
```

Figure 27.12: IO+: Help for circulation info

```
-----------------------------------------------------------------------------
                          Beginning of search
-----------------------------------------------------------------------------
You will have the best results if you use Library of Congress Subject Headings.
Type a subject heading or term to describe the subject:
DESKTOP PUBLISHING
Type a subheading or a qualifying word or phrase.
  (Press <ENTER> if none.)

Press <ENTER> for all or press the corresponding key if the subject is about a
  topic--<T>, person--<P>, organization--<O>, or geographical area--<G>.










Subject Search:  DESKTOP PUBLISHING             Press <ESC> to Exit
```

Figure 27.13: IO+: Subject search, opening screen

```
(Press <ENTER> if none.)                                              ████

Press <ENTER> for all or press the corresponding key if the subject is about a
  topic--<T>, person--<P>, organization--<O>, or geographical area--<G>.
T
This search may not cover all items in the library.
Found 23 headings.
                                           AUTHORITY DISPLAY
      1. Desktop publishing.
      9.    --Catalogs.
      7.    --Computer-assisted instruction.
      4.    --Computer programs.
     10.    --Congresses.
      5.    --Equipment and supplies--Purchasing.
      2.    --Periodicals.
      8.    --United States.
      6.       --Handbooks, manuals, etc.
      3. Desktop publishing.
These are headings number 1 - 10. Do one of the following:
  Type a line number and <ENTER> to see corresponding bibliographic records.
  Press <ENTER> without a number to see the remaining headings.
  Press <B> to browse--to see more headings.
  Press <E> to end this search.

Subject Search:  DESKTOP PUBLISHING                    Press <ESC> to Exit
```

Figure 27.14: IO+: Subject authority display

```
----------------------------------------------------------------------████
                          Beginning of search
----------------------------------------------------------------------
Type the call number (whole or part) and press <ENTER>: 686.2
Searching Circulation Records.
11 686.097423R212/LATHEM, ED/RAY NASH AND THE GRAPHIC ARTS WORKSHOP AT DAR/1987
12 F.686.1M132M/MCCLURE, L/THE MCCLURE PRESS$ SALISBURY, CONN./1984
13 686.1M7780/MOON, GEOR/THE OLDEST TYPE-PRINTED BOOK IN EXISTENCE$ LONDON/1901
14 686.109M612T/MILLER, CO/TECHNICAL AND CULTURAL PREREQUISITES FOR THE IN/1983
15 686.10947N344I/NEMIROVSKI/IVAN FEDOROV, OKOLO 1510-1583$ MOSKVA/1985
16*686.2
17 686.2AD18P1982/ADAMS, J. /PRINTING TECHNOLOGY$ 2ND ED.$ NORTH SCITUATE,/1982
18 686.2AD18P1988/ADAMS, J. /PRINTING TECHNOLOGY$ 3RD ED.$ ALBANY, N.Y./1988
19 686.2AN34D/ANEMA, DUR/DESIGNING EFFECTIVE BROCHURES AND NEWSLETTERS$ DU/1987
1A 686.2B226P/BANN, DAVI/THE PRINT PRODUCTION HANDBOOK$ CINCINNATI, OHIO/1985
1B 686.2B353G/BEACH, MAR/GETTING IT PRINTED$ PORTLAND, OR./1986
Type a line number and <ENTER> to see call number and location of that item;
press <R> to review the 10 similar items just found or <ENTER> to go on.




Shelf Position Search: 686.2                          Press <ESC> to Exit
```

Figure 27.15: IO+: Call number browse

```
----------------------------------------------------------------------████
                          Beginning of search
----------------------------------------------------------------------
F A BACH JOHANN SEBASTIAN--MASSES--B MINOR
                                        SUMMARY DISPLAY
RESULT:    15 bibliographic items.



S 1-4
                                        BIBLIOGRAPHIC DISPLAY

      1. Bach, Johann Sebastian, Mass in B minor. [sound recording] [1968] 3
         sound discs.   ocm03-177001
      2. Bach, Johann Sebastian, Mass in B minor, BWV 232 [sound
         recording] / 1982. 2 sound discs    ocm08-863346
      3. Bach, Johann Sebastian, Mass in B minor [sound recording] BWV 232.
         MHS 1708-1710. 3 sound discs.   ocm03-281464
      4. Bach, Johann Sebastian, Mass in B minor [sound recording] [1954] 3
         sound discs.   ocm05-159877



Type 'HELP' for Help.  Type the Full Command Search String.  Press <ESC> to Exit
```

Figure 27.16: IO+: Command-mode search, author-ut

```
------------------------------------------------------------------
This search may not cover all items in the library.
Found 3 records.
                              BIBLIOGRAPHIC DISPLAY
     1. Ligeti, Gyorgy, 1923- [Requiem. ]Requiem, for soprano, mezzo, 2
        choirs, and orchestra. Lontano, for full orchestra. Continuum,
        for harpsichord. h sound recording Heliodor 2549-011. 2 s. 12 in. 33
        1/3 rpm. microgroove. stereophonic.   ocm02-135659
     2. Ligeti, Gyorgy, 1923- [Requiem. ]Requiem, fur Sopran und
        Mezzosopran, zwei gemischte Chore und Orchester Lontano, fur
        grosse Orchester. Continuum, fur Cembalo Wergo [197-] 1 disc 33 1/3
        rpm. stereo. Title varies:  Continuum Title varies:  Lontano
        ocm14-024843
     3. Ligeti, Gyorgy, 1923- [Instrumental music. Selections ]Konzert fur
        Violoncello und Orchester ; Lontano : fur grosses Orchester ;
        Doppelkonzert fur Flote, Oboe und Orchester ; San Francisco
        polyphony : fur Orchester [sound recording] / Gyorgy Ligeti.
        Mainz : Wergo, p1988. 1 sound disc : digital :   ocm18-809680
These are short records number 1 - 3. Do one of the following:
  Type a line number and <ENTER> to see corresponding full record.
  Press <C> for circulation information.
  Press <O> to search other libraries.
  Press <E> to end this search.

Author-Title Search: LIGETI LONTANO            Press <ESC> to Exit
```

Figure 27.17: IO+: Searching other libraries (1)

```
       Mainz : Wergo, p1988. 1 sound disc : digital ;   ocm18-809680
------------------------------------------------------------------
Searching for catalog information in the LCS network.
This search may not cover all items in the libraries.
Found 4 records.
                              BIBLIOGRAPHIC DISPLAY
     1. Ligeti, Gyorgy, Requiem, for soprano, mezzo, 2 choirs, and
        orchestra. Lontano, for full orchestra. Continuum, for
        harpsichord . . . 2549-011. 2 s.   ocm02-135659
     2. Ligeti, Gyorgy, Lontano, fur grosses Orchester. Lontano, for
        full orchestra. [c1969] score (40 p.)   ocm00-327815
     3. Ligeti, Gyorgy, Requiem, fur Sopran und Mezzosopran, zwei
        gemischte Chore und Orchester Lontano, fur grosse Orchester.
        Continuum, fur Cembalo [197-] 1 disc   ocm14-024843
     4. Ligeti, Gyorgy, Konzert fur Violoncello und Orchester ;
        Lontano : fur grosses Orchester ; Doppelkonzert fur Flote,
        Oboe und Orchester ; San Francisco polyphony : f . . . [sound
        recording] / p1988. 1 sound disc   ocm18-809680
These are short records number 1 - 4. Do one of the following:
  Type a line number and <ENTER> to see corresponding full record.
  Press <L> to see which libraries have the items.
  Press <G> to go on searching additional in-state libraries.
  Press <E> to end this search.

Author-Title Search: LIGETI LONTANO            Press <ESC> to Exit
```

Figure 27.18: IO+: Searching other libraries (2)

```
     4. Ligeti, Gyorgy, Konzert fur Violoncello und Orchester ;
        Lontano : fur grosses Orchester ; Doppelkonzert fur Flote,
        Oboe und Orchester ; San Francisco polyphony : f . . . [sound
        recording] / p1988. 1 sound disc   ocm18-809680
------------------------------------------------------------------
Type a line number and <ENTER> to see which libraries have the item: 2
                              HOLDINGS DISPLAY
        Ligeti, Gyorgy, Lontano,   ocm00-327815
     ******** LIBRARY ********     ********** REGION **********
     1. DePaul U (DP)               Chicago Library System
     2. Roosevelt U (RU)            Chicago Library System
     3. N IL U (NI)                 Northern Illinois Library System
     4. Millikin U (ML)             Rolling Prairie Library System
     5. W IL U (WE)                 Western Illinois Library System
------------------------------------------------------------------
Searching for the item at  DePaul U (DP)

MUS.785.1L723L   LIGETI, GYORGY, 1923-  LONTANO$ MAINZ   70-240799
      58711   1969       1   ADDED: 800621   NENG
01    001 16-3W LPX
PAGE 1 END+
Print the information? (Press <Y> if "YES", <ENTER> otherwise.)
Do you need help with the symbols? (Press <Y> if "YES", <ENTER> otherwise.)
Press <C> to charge out, <R> to renew, <S> to save, <ENTER> to go on.
Author-Title Search: LIGETI LONTANO            Press <ESC> to Exit
```

Figure 27.19: IO+: Searching other libraries (4)

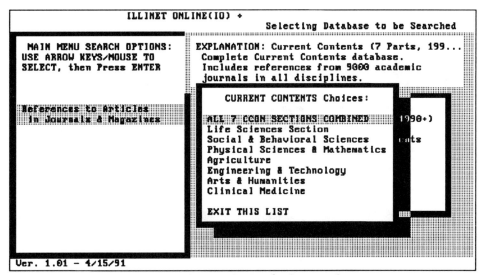

Figure 27.20: IO+: IBIS: Top for Current Contents

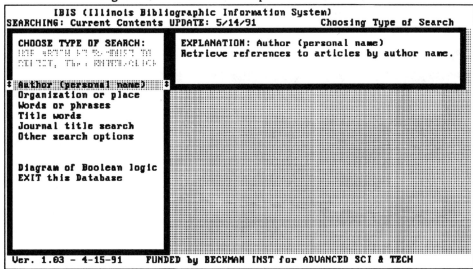

Figure 27.21: IO+: IBIS main menu

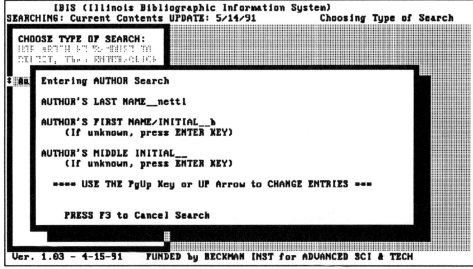

Figure 27.22: IO+: IBIS personal name search

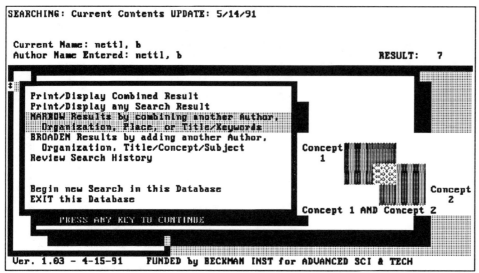

Figure 27.23: IO+: IBIS choices from name result

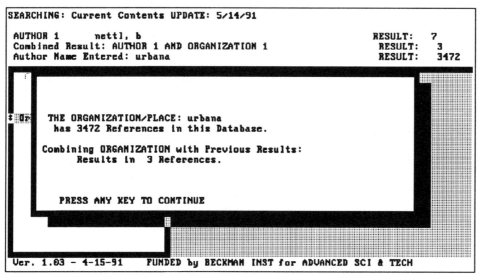

Figure 27.24: IO+: Narrowing IBIS author search

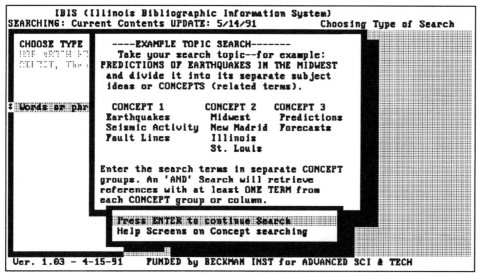

Figure 27.25: IO+: IBIS word or phrase search

```
            IBIS (Illinois Bibliographic Information System)
SEAR                                                          ype of Search
  CH   The most important element of a successful search
  |:|  for references to articles is putting together a
  |:|  useful search strategy. The search strategy consists
       of a series of words or phrases entered by the searcher
       to describe the search topic.

  ‡|||  A typical search topic can be put in a title-like
       phrase. An example search topic might be:

       EARTHQUAKES IN THE MIDWEST AND THEIR EFFECT ON BUILDINGS.

       Many searches to locate periodical article references
       use search strategies that involve several different
       subject areas or concepts. In the example above, the 3
       primary concept terms are:
                1) Earthquakes:
                2) Midwest:
                3) Buildings.
       Note that a word like "EFFECT" does not describe a subjec
         TYPE ANY KEY TO CONTINUE

 Ver. 1.03 - 4-15-91    FUNDED by BECKMAN INST for ADVANCED SCI & TECH
```

Figure 27.26: IO+: Help for word/phrase search (1)

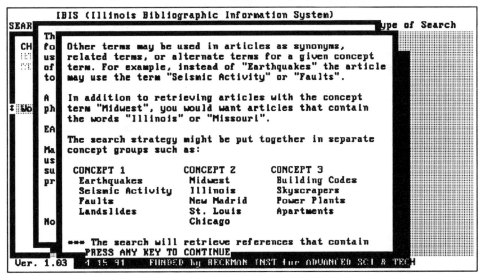

Figure 27.27: IO+: Help for word/phrase search (2)

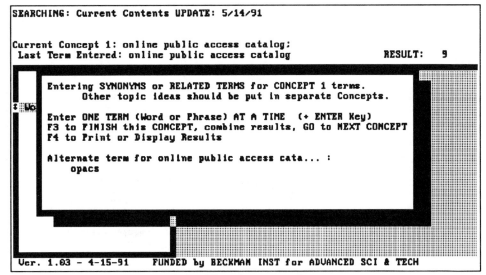

Figure 27.28: IO+: Prompting for synonyms

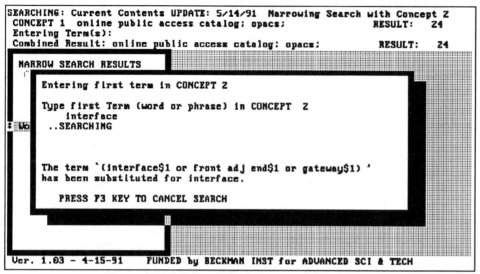

```
SEARCHING: Current Contents UPDATE: 5/14/91  Narrowing Search with Concept 2
 CONCEPT 1  online public access catalog; opacs;         RESULT:   24
 Entering Term(s):
 Combined Result: online public access catalog; opacs;   RESULT:   24
┌──────────────────────────┐
│ NARROW SEARCH RESULTS    │
│    ┌─────────────────────────────────────────────────┐
│    │  Entering first term in CONCEPT 2               │
│    │                                                 │
│    │  Type first Term (word or phrase) in CONCEPT  2 │
│    │      interface                                  │
│ WO │  ..SEARCHING                                    │
│    │                                                 │
│    │                                                 │
│    │  The term `(interface$1 or front adj end$1 or gateway$1) ' │
│    │  has been substituted for interface.            │
│    │                                                 │
│    │     PRESS F3 KEY TO CANCEL SEARCH               │
│    │                                                 │
│    └─────────────────────────────────────────────────┘
└──────────────────────────┘
 Ver. 1.03 - 4-15-91    FUNDED by BECKMAN INST for ADVANCED SCI & TECH
```

Figure 27.29: IO+: Substituting predefined terms

```
        CONCEPT 1 AND CONCEPT 2          2 Refs     SCREEN    1 OF    1
        1 OF  2
JOURNAL TITLE, DATE & ISSUE NUMBER:
  JOURNAL-OF-THE-AMERICAN-SOCIETY-FOR-INFORMATION-SCIENCE.
  1991 MAR V42 N2.
ARTICLE REFERENCE(S) INCL. PAGES, ARTICLE TITLES, AUTHORS, ETC:
  P78 - P98
  SYSTEM DESIGN AND CATALOGING MEET THE USER - USER INTERFACES TO
  ONLINE PUBLIC ACCESS CATALOGS.  (English).  Review.
  YEE-MM.
  UNIV CALIF LOS ANGELES, FILM & TELEVIS ARCH, 1438 MELNITZ HALL,
  405 HILGARD, LOS ANGELES, CA, USA, 90 (Reprint).
  References: 187.
  _:




 Next   Prev   Number   Mark   Change   Print/Downld   TOC   EXIT
    Display Next Reference
```

Figure 27.30: IO+: Results of previous 8 steps

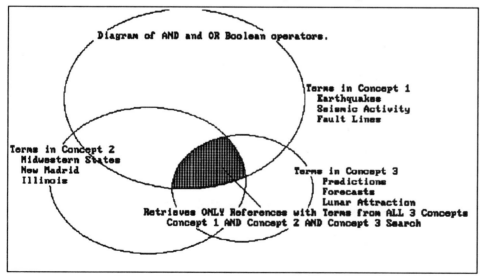

Figure 27.31: IO+: Diagram of Boolean AND

28

Josiah
The Brown University Library Online Catalog

Howard Pasternack

Josiah,[1] the Brown University Library Online Catalog, is based on the BLIS Version of WLN Release 2.2. In the early 1980s, Biblio-Techniques, Inc., a private company in Olympia, Washington, obtained the rights to market a library system using as a nucleus software licensed from the Western Library Network (WLN), then known as the Washington Library Network. The Biblio-Techniques system, which was marketed under the trade name of BLIS, was sold to a number of research libraries, including Brown University and the University of Cincinnati. In 1986, Biblio-Techniques filed for bankruptcy, and Brown University made the decision to continue operation and development of the system using its own resources.

The User-Interface Toolkit

The BLIS system continues to be unique in one major respect. As part of its enhancement of the WLN bibliographic software, Biblio-Techniques provided each customer with a user-interface toolkit. This toolkit enables a BLIS site to design and program a user interface for the online catalog. The WLN system itself uses a command language that is similar in structure to RLIN. With the BLIS user-interface toolkit, a BLIS site can design menus that execute the WLN commands in background.[2] Each BLIS site can decide what type of searches to support, how the screens are to look, how much (or how little) help is to be provided and how scrolling is to be accomplished from screen to screen. The primary limitation in the toolkit is that the WLN command language must support a particular function, so that a BLIS site cannot implement a function if a search cannot be performed using the WLN command language.

Another feature of the toolkit is the ability to program search sequences that can execute automatically in background. Specifically, the programs that execute the user interface have access to the transaction work areas of the system and can evaluate the number of hits for any search. In the event that there are zero hits, an alternate search can be automatically executed. This facility enables a BLIS site to take advantage of the redundant indexing features and linked authority control mechanisms of the WLN sys-

---

1 Josiah is named after Josiah S. Carberry, a mythical professor of psychoceramics (the study of cracked pots) at Brown University. Professor Carberry has been a friend of the library of Brown University for many years.

2 Technically, the BLIS toolkit depends on the WLN command language and the COM-PLETE teleprocessing system from Software A.G. of North America. The COM-PLETE screen mapping facility is used to create the text for the menus.

tem. For example, the user interface can be programmed to search for corporate author keywords in the event that an author phrase search does not retrieve any records. Similarly, a title keyword search can be done automatically when a subject search fails to retrieve records.

Josiah and UCLID

The Brown University user interface is based on a design originally developed at the University of Cincinnati and implemented in Cincinnati's UCLID system. After the Biblio-Techniques bankruptcy, Brown arranged with the University of Cincinnati to install UCLID Version 2.0 on the Brown mainframe. A committee of Brown librarians, faculty, and students then modified UCLID for Brown's own clientele and created Josiah. While UCLID and Josiah have both been revised several times in the intervening years, when placed side by side their similarities are readily identifiable.

Josiah is designed to operate in a networked environment and to be accessible from virtually all devices that can access the Brown campuswide network. A basic design assumption is that most use of the system will be from outside of the Library and that online help needs to be readily available. To accommodate network users, the menus are kept as simple as possible; this simplicity hides some fairly complex search algorithms executed in background.

Moving through Josiah

The opening Josiah screen for terminals in the library is a logo (Figure 28.1); the logo facilitates the automatic logon of library terminals through Brown's ASCII network. Technically, the logo is not part of the interface. The second screen for library users (and the first for most dial-in users) is a Welcome to Josiah screen (Figure 28.2). By pressing the Return key from the welcome screen, the user brings up the Josiah Options Menu (Figure 28.3). The Options Menu serves as the main menu and provides immediate access to Josiah's

two modes of searching: the Search Menu and the Direct Command. The Options Menu also provides access to the Josiah Information Guide (Figure 28.4), a series of help screens providing general information about the system. The most heavily used of the Josiah Information Guide screens is Library Holdings in Josiah (Figure 28.5).

The Josiah Search Menu (Figure 28.6) offers choices to search by author, title, author-title combination (Boolean) or subject. The Direct Command mode of searching enables users to search Josiah using the WLN command language. The language supports bibliographic file searches by author, title, series, subject, year of publication and ISBN/ISSN; authority file searches by author, series, and subjects; direct browse of subject headings and indirect browse of author and series headings; call number browse; and Boolean combinations. While the Direct Command offers more functionality than the search menu, use of the command language requires documentation and training. Most users search Josiah through the search menu, and this aspect of the system is what will be described herein.

Searches and Displays

The Title Search screen (Figure 28.7) is typical of the search entry screens. Brief instructions and examples guide the user in search formulation and entry. If the user wishes, additional help is available by pressing the PF1 key or by typing PF1. The Title Help Menu (not shown) is also typical of the help available in Josiah. By selecting "Display Title Search Help," the user is able to display more detailed help information (Figure 28.8).

A title search for *Rhapsody in Blue* will yield the result shown in Figure 28.9. This screen, known as the multiple-item list, is displayed for all searches with a result of more than one record.[3] To display an individual record, the user types an item number from the list. The resulting record is automatically displayed in a labeled format called the brief record (Figure 28.10). The brief record is also the default display for any search resulting in a single item. A detailed record display (card cat-

---

3 The multiple-item list is in order chronologically by the dates records are loaded into the database. The list cannot be sorted.

alog format) is also available to the user (Figure 28.11). A record with USMARC content designation can be displayed in the Josiah interface by typing "$c," but this feature is not documented for the user (Figure 28.12).[4]

Josiah is designed to provide positive feedback to the user on error conditions, and errors are handled in a number of ways. If the user does not enter a search statement on a search entry screen, the system will respond with a prompt. If the search statement does not retrieve any records, a help menu with **Zero-items Help** is displayed (Figure 28.13). If more than one hundred records are retrieved, Josiah will display a menu with **Too-many Items Help** (Figure 28.14). If the search exceeds Josiah's search capabilities or contains system defined errors, a menu providing guidance about error conditions will display (Figure 28.15). On any menu or record display screen, an undefined command or a request to display an item that does not exist will result in an error prompt.

An interesting feature of Josiah's title search is the pre-programmed search strategy: if a search does not retrieve any records by title, Josiah automatically searches for corporate/ conference author keywords.

The Josiah author search is similar to the title search, but is a phrase search rather than a keyword search. As a consequence, the user must invert personal names. The system, however, automatically supplies right truncation,[5] so the user does not need to enter the full form of an author's name. In the event that the initial search does not retrieve any records, the system is preprogrammed to search the authority file for all authority records that match the search and to display all bibliographic records that are linked to the authority records found. For example, a search for "Dudevant, Amantine" will automatically result in the display of the bibliographic records for "Sand, George" (Figure 28.16). (The screen shown in Figure 28.16 includes asterisks (*) for various for-

eign language diacritics. Josiah includes two character set translations: one for vanilla ASCII terminals and another for terminals that can display diacritics and special characters.)

The most efficient strategy for retrieving a known item when the author and title are known is the author-title search (Figure 28.17), which uses the WLN command language's Boolean search capability. Articles and prepositions are ignored in the title portion of the search.[6] In the event that there are no records that match both the author and title, Josiah displays a menu reporting the results for each individual part of the author-title search (Figure 28.18).

The subject search is a phrase search and is, thus, similar to the author search. The system is programmed to try first the phrase without truncation, and if no records are retrieved, to resubmit the search with right truncation. Another extremely useful feature of the preprogrammed search strategy is the use of a title keyword search if no records are retrieved by subject. After exhausting all subject approaches to finding records, Josiah will try a title keyword search and display a help menu if title records are found. The help file associated with this menu is among the most heavily consulted of the Josiah help screens (Figure 28.19).

Leaving Josiah

A logoff from Josiah is accomplished by pressing the PF10 key and choosing the logoff option from the Josiah Options Menu. Technically, PF9 = Options Menu and PF10 = Logoff are identical; a separate PF key is provided to remind users where the logoff option is located.

Users are generally pleased with Josiah and its ease of use. The primary user requests for enhancements are for the display of circulation status information and for the ability to sort result sets. Because of the lack of vendor support for BLIS and the need to implement circulation, ac-

---

4 Music materials are currently loaded into Josiah in the MARC Books format since WLN Release 2.2 does not support music. When the implementation of WLN Release 2.5 is completed at Brown, music will be reloaded in the proper format.

5 The user can also supply truncation but is not encouraged to do so.

6 This is also true for the title search. The WLN command language includes a stopword list for titles and for corporate/conference author keywords.

quisitions, and serials control, Brown University is planning to migrate to another system in the next two years. Brown is the last library using BLIS, and after Brown completes the migration to a new system, the Biblio-Techniques library system will become a footnote in the annals of library automation history.

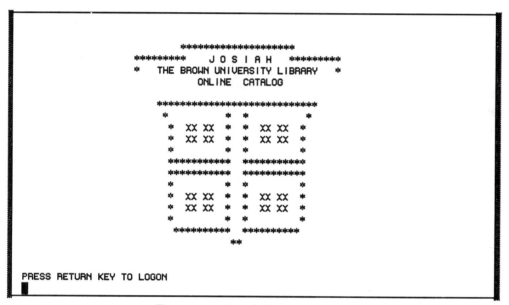

Figure 28.1: Josiah: Opening screen

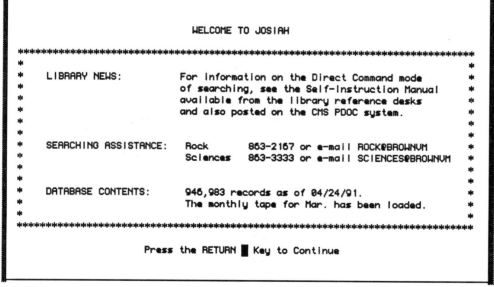

Figure 28.2: Josiah: Welcome screen

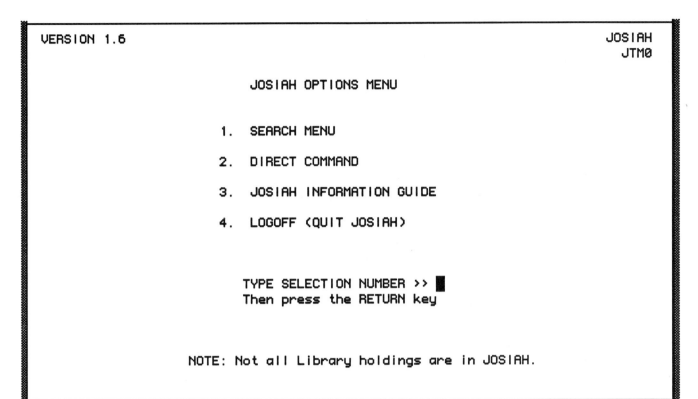

Figure 28.3: Josiah: Options menu

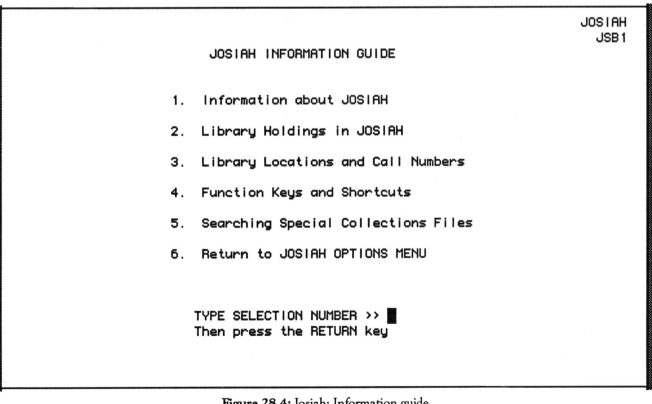

Figure 28.4: Josiah: Information guide

```
                                                                    JOSIAH
                    LIBRARY HOLDINGS IN JOSIAH                        JSB3

JOSIAH contains bibliographic information and call numbers for items cataloged
by the Brown University Library system and the John Carter Brown Library. As of
January, 1991, JOSIAH contained some 925,000 records, or over 65 percent of
the Brown University Library holdings.

FOUND IN JOSIAH:
  1.  Books, periodicals, and other items cataloged since 1974.
  2.  Increasing numbers of older library materials.

NOT FOUND IN JOSIAH:
  1.  Articles from journals and magazines.
  2.  Archives, manuscripts, and broadsides.

The database is growing at the rate of 8,000 items per month -- 3,000 for
current materials and 5,000 for pre-1974 items. Conversion of older materials
is funded by grants from David and Laurance Rockefeller and other donors.

If you can not locate an item in JOSIAH, check the card catalog or see a
Library staff member for assistance.

       ■ JOSIAH INFORMATION GUIDE: Press the RETURN key
```

Figure 28.5: Josiah: Information screen

```
                                                                    JOSIAH
                                                                     JSM2

                    JOSIAH SEARCH MENU


            1.  Start AUTHOR Search

            2.  Start TITLE Search

            3.  Start AUTHOR/TITLE Search

            4.  Start SUBJECT Search

            5.  Return to the JOSIAH OPTIONS MENU




                  TYPE SELECTION NUMBER >> ■
                  Then press the RETURN key



            Press PF1 (F1 on Library Terminals) for HELP
```

Figure 28.6: Josiah: Search menu

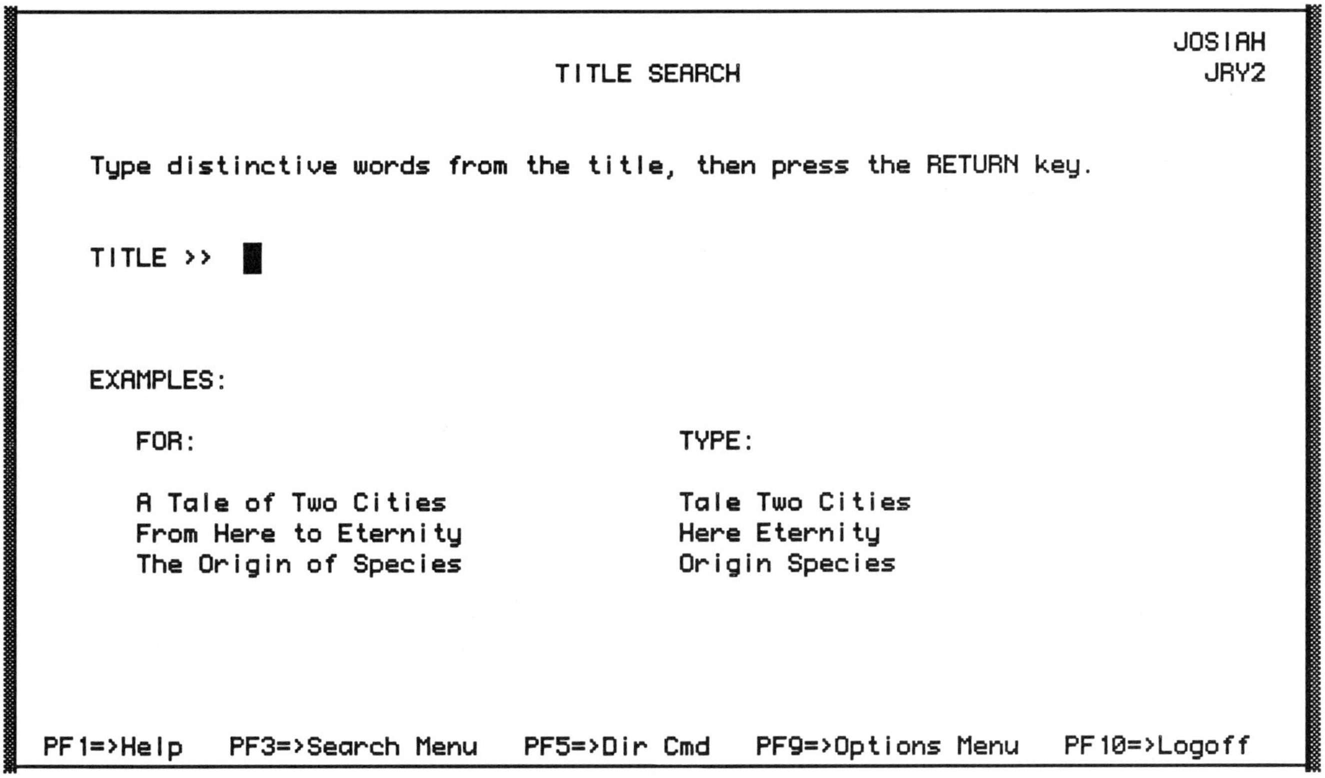

```
                                                              JOSIAH
                        TITLE SEARCH                          JRY2


   Type distinctive words from the title, then press the RETURN key.


   TITLE >>  █



   EXAMPLES:


     FOR:                            TYPE:


     A Tale of Two Cities            Tale Two Cities
     From Here to Eternity           Here Eternity
     The Origin of Species           Origin Species




PF1=>Help    PF3=>Search Menu    PF5=>Dir Cmd    PF9=>Options Menu    PF10=>Logoff
```

Figure 28.7: Josiah: Title search screen

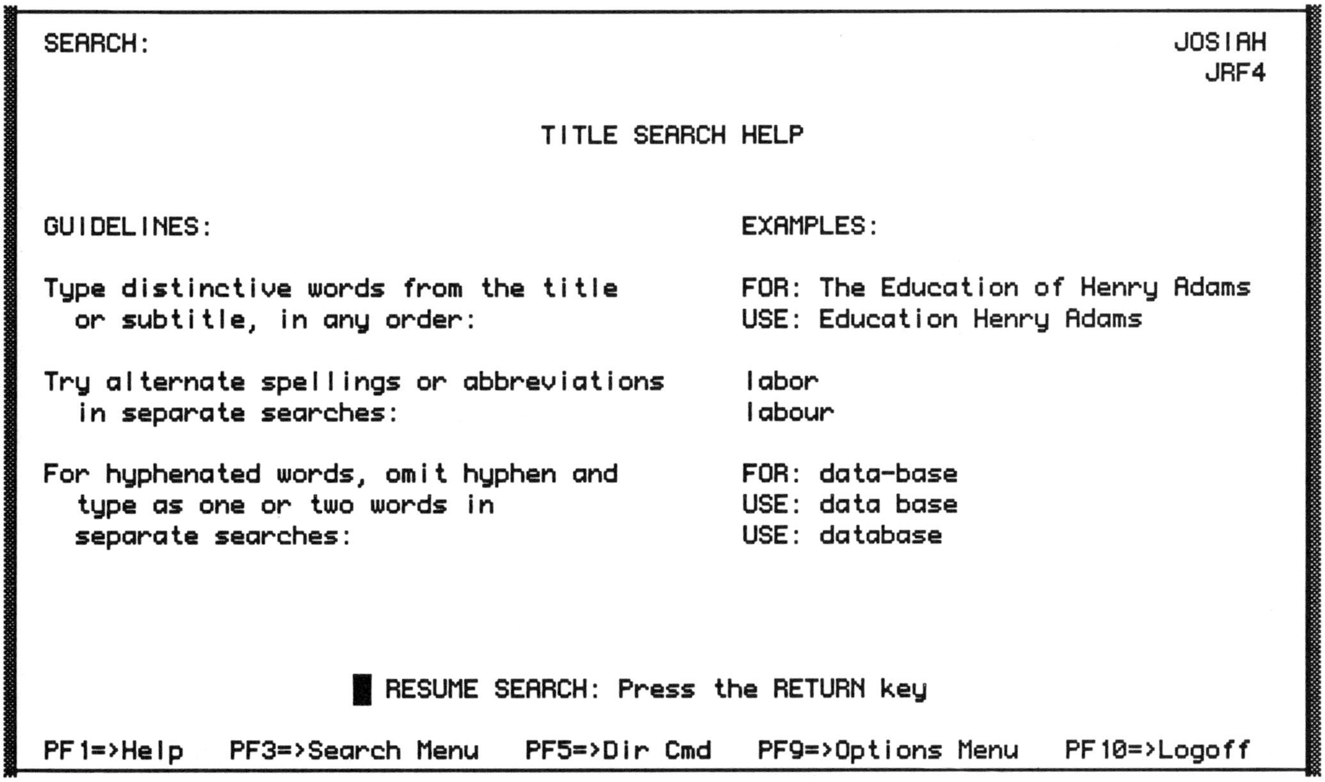

```
SEARCH:                                                       JOSIAH
                                                              JRF4

                        TITLE SEARCH HELP

GUIDELINES:                              EXAMPLES:

Type distinctive words from the title    FOR: The Education of Henry Adams
  or subtitle, in any order:             USE: Education Henry Adams

Try alternate spellings or abbreviations labor
  in separate searches:                  labour

For hyphenated words, omit hyphen and    FOR: data-base
  type as one or two words in            USE: data base
  separate searches:                     USE: database




                █ RESUME SEARCH: Press the RETURN key

PF1=>Help    PF3=>Search Menu    PF5=>Dir Cmd    PF9=>Options Menu    PF10=>Logoff
```

Figure 28.8: Josiah: Title search help

```
SEARCH: RHAPSODY IN BLUE                                      JOSIAH
TOTAL ITEMS FOUND:   16                          MULTIPLE ITEM LIST
                        BEGINNING OF LIST
     1. Gershwin, George,    Rhapsody in blue; {score}         1927
     2. Gershwin, George,    Rhapsody in blue {score}          1942
     3. Gershwin, George,    Rhapsody in blue. {score}         1924
     4. De Luca, Angelo,     Gay journey, rhapsody in blue and grey,  1965
     5. Gershwin, George,    Gershwin songs from "Manhattan" : {score}  1979
     6. Gershwin, George,    Rhapsody in blue / {sound recording}.  1983
     7.                      Paul Whiteman's historic Aeolian Hall conc  1986
     8. Gershwin, George,    Rhapsody in blue ; Concerto in F ; An Amer  1987
     9. Gershwin, George,    Concerto in F ; Three preludes ; Rhapsody  1988
    10. Rattle, Simon,       The jazz album {sound recording} :  1987
    11. Gershwin, George,    Levant plays Gershwin {sound recording}.  1987
    12. Gershwin, George,    An American in Paris ; Concerto in F ; Rha  1988



FOR MORE INFORMATION:
  Type an item number from above OR     N -- Next Screen of Items
  Type a letter from the right:  >> █   P -- Previous Screen of Items
  Then press RETURN                     S -- Start a New Search (Title)

PF1=>Help   PF3=>Search Menu   PF5=>Dir Cmd   PF9=>Options Menu   PF10=>Logoff
```

Figure 28.9: Josiah: Multiple item list

```
SEARCH: RHAPSODY IN BLUE                                      JOSIAH
ITEM    9 OF    16                                     BRIEF RECORD

Author:  Gershwin, George, 1898-1937.
Uniform Title:  Concerto, piano, orchestra, F major; arr
Title:  Concerto in F ; Three preludes ; Rhapsody in blue {sound recording}
   / George Gershwin.
Published:  {S.l.} : Stradivari, p1988.
Physical Description:  1 sound disc : digital ; 4 3/4 in.
Author Names:     1. Krieger, Norman   2. Castagnetta, Grace, 1912-   3.
   Gershwin, George, 1898-1937. Preludes, piano. 1988.   4. Gershwin,
   George, 1898-1937. Rhapsody in blue; arr. 1988.
Subjects:    1. Piano music, Arranged.   2. Piano music.

Location and call number:
 1. ORWIG CD   M37.G47 C6x 1988



FOR MORE INFORMATION:
  Type another item number OR           D -- Detailed Record
  Type a letter from the right:  >> █   M -- Multiple Item List
  Then press RETURN                     S -- Start a New Search (Title)

PF1=>Help   PF3=>Search Menu   PF5=>Dir Cmd   PF9=>Options Menu   PF10=>Logoff
```

Figure 28.10: Josiah: Labeled display (recording)

```
SEARCH: RHAPSODY IN BLUE                                          JOSIAH
ITEM    9 OF   16                                       DETAILED RECORD
                            SCREEN 1 OF 2
    Gershwin, George, 1898-1937.
    {Concerto, piano, orchestra, F major; arr}
    Concerto in F ; Three preludes ; Rhapsody in blue {sound recording}
/ George Gershwin. {S.l.} : Stradivari, p1988.
    1 sound disc : digital ; 4 3/4 in.
    Program notes inserted in container.
    The 1st work a concert transcription of the piano solo by Grace
Castagnetta; 3rd work a solo version by the composer.
    Compact disc.
    CAST:  Norman Krieger, piano.
    Recorded Aug. 1987, RCA Recording Studios, New York.
        1. Piano music, Arranged.   2. Piano music.  I. Krieger, Norman

Continued on Next Screen

FOR MORE INFORMATION:               N -- Next Screen of Record
  Type another item number OR       B -- Brief Record & Call Number
  Type a letter from the right: >> █  M -- Multiple Item List
  Then press RETURN                 S -- Start a New Search (Title)

PF1=>Help   PF3=>Search Menu   PF5=>Dir Cmd   PF9=>Options Menu   PF10=>Logoff
```

Figure 28.11: Josiah: Cardlike display

```
SEARCH: RHAPSODY IN BLUE                                          JOSIAH
ITEM    9 OF   16             SCREEN 1 OF 4                 BRIEF RECORD
    COLLECTION ID: 1

    am   bur90-1016    db   05/22/90  06/14/90  --/--/--  BROWN      BROWN
    007      |a      |sd@fungnnmmned
    035      |a      |(CStRLIN)RLINRIBG90-R1016
    040      |ac     |RPB|RPB
    041 0    |g      |eng
    045      |a      |x2x4
    090      |abi    |M37.G47|C6x 1988|05/22/90 CT
    100 10   |ad     |Gershwin, George,| 1898-1937.
    240 10   |amro   |Concerto,|piano, orchestra,|F major;|arr
    245 00   |ahc    |Concerto in F ; Three preludes ; Rhapsody in blue|
                     {sound recording} /|George Gershwin.

Continued on Next Screen

FOR MORE INFORMATION:               N -- Next Screen of Record
  Type another item number OR       D -- Detailed Record
  Type a letter from the right: >> █  M -- Multiple Item List
  Then press RETURN                 S -- Start a New Search (Title)

PF1=>Help   PF3=>Search Menu   PF5=>Dir Cmd   PF9=>Options Menu   PF10=>Logoff
```

Figure 28.12: Josiah: MARC display

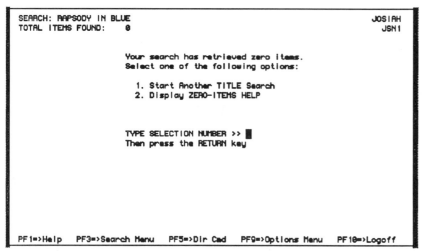

Figure 28.13: Josiah: Zero-result screen

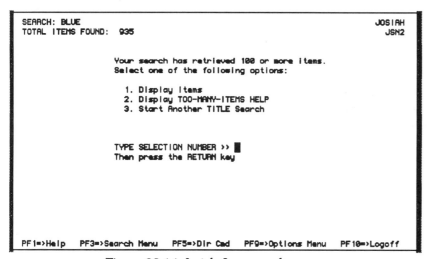

Figure 28.14: Josiah: Large-result screen

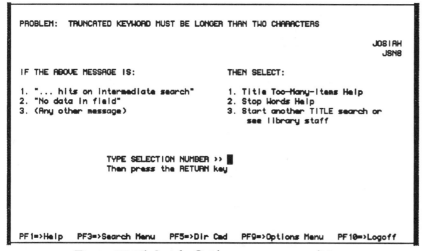

Figure 28.15: Josiah: Guidance on error conditions

```
 SEARCH: DUDEVANT AMANTINE                                           JOSIAH
 TOTAL ITEMS FOUND:    37                                  MULTIPLE ITEM LIST
                                 BEGINNING OF LIST
      1. Sand, George,         Broken chain :                         1959
      2. Sand, George,         *uvres autobiographiques.              1970
      3. Sand, George,         The country waif =                     1977
      4. Sand, George,         Indiana /                              1975
      5. Sand, George,         L*elia /                               1978
      6. Sand, George,         My life /                              1979
      7. Sand, George,         In her own words /                     1979
      8. Sand, George,         Valentine /                            1978
      9. Sand, George,         Mademoiselle Merquem /                 1981
     10. Sand, George,         Correspondance                        1964
     11.                       Gamiani :                              1980
     12. Flaubert, Gustave,    Correspondance /                      1981



 FOR MORE INFORMATION:
    Type an item number from above OR      N -- Next Screen of Items
    Type a letter from the right:  >> █    P -- Previous Screen of Items
    Then press RETURN                      S -- Start a New Search <Author>

 PF1=>Help    PF3=>Search Menu    PF5=>Dir Cmd    PF9=>Options Menu    PF10=>Logoff
```

Figure 28.16: Josiah: Redirected author search

```
                         AUTHOR/TITLE SEARCH                         JOSIAH
                                                                     JRY4

 Use the AUTHOR/TITLE SEARCH when you know both the AUTHOR and the TITLE.

 First, type the author's name and press the RETURN key.
 Then, type distinctive words from the title and press the RETURN key.


      AUTHOR >>


      TITLE  >>



 EXAMPLES:

      AUTHOR >> Shakespeare William    <type last name first>
      TITLE  >> Julius Caesar

      AUTHOR >> American Mathematical Society
      TITLE  >> Transactions

 PF1=>Help    PF3=>Search Menu    PF5=>Dir Cmd    PF9=>Options Menu    PF10=>Logoff
```

Figure 28.17: Josiah: Author-title search screen

```
SEARCH: Author: MAILER                                          JOSIAH
        Title:  MOONFIRE                                        JSN3


          Your search has retrieved the following:

                 0 items for your author/title combination
                41 items for your author alone
                 0 items for your title alone

          Select one of the following options:

                 1. Display AUTHOR Items
                 2. Display TITLE ZERO-ITEMS HELP
                 3. Start Another AUTHOR/TITLE Search
                 4. Start Another Search (SEARCH MENU)



                 TYPE SELECTION NUMBER >> █
                 Then press the RETURN key


 PF1=>Help    PF3=>Search Menu    PF5=>Dir Cmd    PF9=>Options Menu    PF10=>Logoff
```

Figure 28.18: Josiah: Failed author-title info

```
SEARCH: MODERN FRENCH ART                                      JOSIAH
                                                               JRH8

                    SUBJECT-WORDS-IN-TITLES HELP

Your search has retrieved zero items with your subject.

The subjects in JOSIAH are the same as those used in the card catalogs.
For best results, consult the Library of Congress Subject Headings list,
available in the Reference Department.

In addition to using the Library of Congress Subject Headings list,
you may wish to review the items with your subject word(s) in the TITLE.
JOSIAH has automatically retrieved these items for you.

It is possible that some of the TITLE items are relevant to your search. By
reviewing the individual records for these items, you may be able to identify
some useful subject headings with which to try additional subject searches.
If there are no relevant items among the titles, try another SUBJECT search
or see a Library staff member for assistance.

          █ RESUME SEARCH: Press the RETURN key

 PF1=>Help    PF3=>Search Menu    PF5=>Dir Cmd    PF9=>Options Menu    PF10=>Logoff
```

Figure 28.19: Josiah: Subject-words-in-titles help

29

LS/2000
University of North Carolina at Wilmington

Ron Johnson

LS/2000 is an integrated public catalog, cataloging and circulation system that runs on Data General minicomputers under the MIIS operating system. Originally called ILS, it was developed by Avatar to serve medical libraries. In December 1983, OCLC bought ILS, renamed it LS/2000 and established a local system division to market and service the product. In July 1990, Ameritech Information Systems purchased the Local Systems Division, including LS/2000, from OCLC.

Introduction and General Description

LS/2000 has author, subject, title, call number, keyword, and approximately 30 other avenues for searching the bibliographic database. Search group design is part of the initial profiling process.

Users may use a menu of search possibilities (Figure 29.1) or use the command language at search initiation prompts. There are three screens of general help and instructions (e.g., Figure 29.2), and at the bottom of each enter-search-type screen, there is a brief message telling the user how to enter the search (e.g., Figure 29.4). These messages can be edited by library personnel.

Search results are displayed on a summary screen, ten titles at a time, with matching entries

presented in reverse chronological order. Choosing a reference number from the summary display exhibits the full display for that record, which includes author, title, imprint, and all added entries, plus location, call number, and status of each item or volume attached to the bibliographic record.

Full MARC records may be displayed from the summary screen or from the full display. From the full display, one may look at the next full display by entering the command /N (for next). The up-arrow, or caret (^), takes a user one step back in the search. The Enter key takes the user one step forward in the search until the end of the display, then takes the user to the previous summary screen, allowing another choice to be made. Users may also move forward or backward in a search one screen at a time.

LS/2000 does not include Boolean search capabilities. However, if a search results in more citations than a library-defined number, the system activates a limitation option, which allows refining the search, beginning a new search or viewing the citations sequentially without further limitation. Users may employ only system-defined searches to refine a query.

More than a hundred special, medical, public and academic libraries in the United States and the UK have installed LS/2000. Developments made by OCLC Local Systems include Reserve Room, full authority records, linking from separate acquisitions and serial control products, enhanced online catalog user interface, local site controlled parameter/profile maintenance and MARC transfer from OCLC (both first system and PRISM) to local systems products.

Ameritech Information Systems has not yet had a full release cycle but has issued a release developed largely by OCLC, which established circulation consistency for filing transactions and changing functions, corrected a number of system issues, and introduced programs for file transfer from OCLC PRISM and other bibliographic utilities. Most of the energies of Ameritech have been devoted to determining their direction with LS/2000. Development thus far has been products users must purchase, and pay maintenance for, to enhance operation of LS/2000. For instance, the System Access Menu is a new feature, but is not included in Release F software—its purchase and maintenance costs are extra. Customer requests for better system response time have led to the announced development of Encore, a companion system designed to serve as the search engine, offering full Boolean search capabilities for key words and phrases and allowing mounting other databases from tape or CD-ROM. Circulation and bibliographic updates in LS/2000 would be integrated with Encore.

Starting Out

Whether hardwired or on a networked port, all users begin use of LS/2000 by the Enter Search interface. This interface is determined by profiling during the design portion of the installation process. At UNCW, after 5 minutes of inactivity, hardwired terminals revert to this screen; networked terminals log off and automatically disconnect from the network. At the Enter Search screen, users may choose a number to define the search type, enter a keyword, or use the retrieval subsystem command language to initiate a search.

Searching and Displays

Figure 29.3 is a summary screen of the command language structure for online retrieval. LS/2000 is a text-based system. To indicate that the command language is being used, a slash ("/") must precede any command mnemonic. If the command is followed by an equals sign and the argument, the system will perform the entire search without displaying intermediate prompts. Commands may be entered at any "Choice:" or "Enter [search type]" prompt. For instance, "/ti=rhapsody in blue" yields Figure 29.5, displaying four titles in reverse chronological order (as determined by MARC record-generation date). This brief display is called the Search Summary screen. Our library includes the material type in audiovisual call numbers, so users can tell we do not own a compact disc, but just analog recordings of *Rhapsody in Blue*.

Figures 29.6 and 29.7 show the labeled full display for a sound recording. For bibliographic records with many added entries, two or more screens may be required to display the entire record and its accompanying location/call number/status information. The full bibliographic citation, however, remains on the screen for the entire sequence.

LS/2000 has an author index and a title index. A user cannot concurrently search both indexes with a single search argument. Figure 29.8 shows part of the search summary for "Martin Luther King, Jr.," as an author. Only reference numbers 1 to 10 can be chosen from this screen; any reference number 1 to 11 can be chosen from the screen that would follow.

Only LS/2000 sites with full authority records loaded as part of their database can search LC subject headings and subject subdivisions as single arguments. Figures 29.9 and 29.10 show such a search and the direct result.

Choosing reference number 2 from figure 29.10 gives a summary of the subject subdivisions in alphabetical order (Figure 29.11). Reference number 1 includes all the subdivisions and any subject headings not containing subdivisions.

The number of citations that initiates the Limit Search feature is determined by profiling and may be changed by the system administrator. Locally the limit is 41 titles. The King search produced 43 titles, so the narrow search option, which also allows the choice of looking at all titles or of restarting a new search, is invoked (Figure 29.12).

Several choices are allowed for limiting the search (Figure 29.13). Figure 29.14 shows a limitation by year of publication. Once the number of citations falls below the profiled search limit, a user is not given the option of further limiting the search, but all citations are presented for viewing (Figure 29.15).

Figures 29.16 and 29.17 show full "catalog card" display and status information for reference number 1 of figure 29.15. At the end of the full-record display, entering "/D" (command for "display") will show the full MARC record for the title.

Multiple locations are presented in alphabetical order; within locations, in call number order. The title in Figure 29.18 has the latest edition in Library of Congress classification and earlier editions in SuDocs classification. Some location names equate to OCLC holding libraries, but others are unique to the local system. Location names and abbreviations are determined during profiling.

Errors

A typing error in the search argument (Figure 29.19) results in a message that no exact match was found. The closest-match algorithm returns the first occurrence of the last correct letter in the search. In the example, "Kige . . ." is the closest match to "Kign."

One can keep pressing Return until "King" shows up, but it is usually faster to re-enter the search argument: for example, Martin Luther King, Jr., would appear as R418, on the 42nd screen. For multiscreen results, the "No Exact Match" banner appears only on the first screen of the list.

Inexact Title Searching

The keyword "fire" was entered as a search argument (Figure 29.20) The catalog has 435 titles with "fire" in the bibliographic record; 258 of these are with "fire" as a keyword in title (Figure 29.21). This is enough to trigger the Limit Search

feature. The search is limited by entering the keyword "moon." (Figure 29.22, omitting two search screens).

The keyword "moon" appears in 235 bibliographic records, 161 of which are in titles. The system combines the two searches $KW=fire$ AND $KW=moon$ to produce one bibliographic record (Figures 29.23 and 29.24 omitting intermediate screen). This item is temporarily assigned to the Reserve Desk (as indicated by the "*" preceding its location name) because the item is on reserve for course related reading.

Author-Title Searching

The command language is used to query $Author=Pynchon$ and $Title=Vineland$. This formatted search requires the first four letters of the author's last name, a comma, and the first four letters of the first nonarticle word of the title. At the Enter author-title key screen (not shown), a help message tells users how to enter the search argument. This author-title key search yields one bibliographic record (Figure 29.25).

Browsing

A subject search of "publishing" (Figure 29.26) shows the browse feature. Call number searches (Figure 29.27) display in browse format, beginning with the portion entered. To be assured of *not* getting a "No Match" message, the call number should be entered with a hyphen as the last element of the argument. A hyphen may also be used at the end of other searches to call up browsing.

Leaving the System

The command "/EXIT" signs the user off and, if access is via network or modem, disconnects the session from the library's communications equipment. The final message from LS/2000 is:

"YOU ARE LOGGED OFF
GOODBYE
###"

```
PUBLIC CATALOG                                              Searching: UNCW


            Enter the NUMBER of search you wish to perform


                       1 - By LC SUBJECT HEADING - MAIN HEADING ONLY
                       2 - By LC SUBJECT HEADING OR SUBDIVISION
                       3 - By AUTHOR
                       4 - By TITLE
                       5 - For OTHER Searches

                               OR

            Enter a KEY WORD to see possible matches


CHOICE: ████████████████████████████████████████████████


    Enter ? for GENERAL INSTRUCTIONS.  To ENTER, type number then press RETURN.

```

Figure 29.1: LS/2000: General search screen

```
                 HOW TO ENTER SEARCH TERMS

For a specific TOPIC
           IF                              THEN
  - you are unsure of library       Enter a KEY WORD you know
    terminology for the topic

  - you are certain of the Library of   When prompted, enter its first
    Congress subject heading           word or words

For an AUTHOR
    When prompted, enter the author's name in the format: Last, First

For an ORGANIZATION or GOVERNMENT AGENCY or CONFERENCE
    When prompted, enter the first word or words of the
    organization or conference name

For a TITLE
    When prompted, enter the first word or words of the title

More help:   1 - SEARCHING STYLES
             2 - SEARCHING HINTS

Press RETURN to search or enter a number:
```

Figure 29.2: LS/2000: Search help (2 of 3)

```
RETRIEVAL SUBSYSTEM
COMMAND:

GENERAL FUNCTIONS
CL   Choose Location      TD   Time & Date
DE   Detail
RETRIEVAL SUBSYSTEM
ES   Enter Search Screen  KW   Keyword              CC   Software/Hardware
OS   Other Searches       LA   Language             SU   LC Subj Hd or Subdv
AU   Author               LC   LC Card Number       SJ   LC Subj Mn Hd Only
AT   Author/Title Key     MT   Material Type        SF   Subj.-Conference Aut
CU   Call Number          MC   Musical Comp. Type   SC   Subj.-Corporate Auth
CN   Conference Author    MI   Music Inst./Voice    SN   Subj.-Personal Autho
CR   Corporate Author     MP   Music Pub. Number    SV   Subj.-Uniform Title
FA   Faculty Reserves     FC   Fac./Course Reserves TI   Title
MF   Format of Music      ON   OCLC Number          TK   Title Key
SD   Gout. Docs. Number   PN   Personal Author      UT   Uniform Title
IB   ISBN                 RN   Report Number        DI   Dept./Course Reserve
IN   ISSN                 SE   Series
JT   Journal Title        SR   Series Authority


        PLEASE ENTER ONE OF THE ABOVE TWO-LETTER COMMAND CODES
```

Figure 29.3: LS/2000: Command summary

```
┌─────────────────────────────────────────────────────────────────┐
│ PUBLIC CATALOG                               Searching: UNCW      │
│                                                                   │
│                                                                   │
│                                                                   │
│                                                                   │
│  ENTER AUTHOR:                                                    │
│  ▓/TI=RHAPSODY IN BLUE▓▓▓▓▓▓▓▓▓▓▓▓▓▓▓▓▓▓▓▓▓▓▓▓▓▓▓▓▓▓▓▓▓▓▓▓▓▓▓▓▓   │
│                                                                   │
│                                                                   │
│                                                                   │
│                                                                   │
│                                                                   │
│           Enter author's full or partial name in format: Last, First │
│                                                                   │
│                                                                   │
└─────────────────────────────────────────────────────────────────┘
```

Figure 29.4: LS/2000: Title search (command mode)

```
┌─────────────────────────────────────────────────────────────────┐
│ PUBLIC CATALOG                               Searching: UNCW      │
│                                                                   │
│  TITLE:   ▓RHAPSODY IN BLUE▓                                      │
│                                                                   │
│  REF  DATE   TITLES                        AUTHOR      CALL NUMBER │
│  ───  ────   ──────                        ──────      ─────────── │
│  R1   1968   RHAPSODY IN BLUE                          A/V Phonodisc 88 │
│  R2   1967   RHAPSODY IN BLUE              Gershwin, Geo A/V Phonodisc 61 │
│  R3   1959   RHAPSODY IN BLUE              Gershwin, Geo A/V Phonodisc 43 │
│  R4   1959   RHAPSODY IN BLUE; AMERICAN IN PA Gershwin, Geo A/V Phonodisc 43 │
│  (END)                                                            │
│                                                                   │
│                                                                   │
│  CHOICE: R                                                        │
│         Enter a REF number to see the title list; or /ES to restart. │
│                                                                   │
└─────────────────────────────────────────────────────────────────┘
```

Figure 29.5: LS/2000: Search Summary screen

```
┌─────────────────────────────────────────────────────────────────┐
│ PUBLIC CATALOG                               Searching: UNCW      │
│                                                                   │
│  A/V Phonodisc 88                                                 │
│      TITLE:          Paul Whiteman. [Sound recording]             │
│      PUBLISHER:      RCA Victor LPV 555, [1968-                   │
│      PHYSICAL DESC:  discs. 33 1/3 rpm. mono. 12 in.              │
│      SERIES:         Vintage series                               │
│                                                                   │
│      SUBJECTS:       Music, Popular (Songs, etc.) - United States │
│                      Sound recordings.                            │
│      ADDED ENTRIES:  Whispering                                   │
│                      The Japanese sandman                         │
│                      Anytime, anyday, anywhere                    │
│                      My man                                       │
│                      Song of India                               │
│                      Hot lips                                     │
│                      Three o'clock in the morning                 │
│                      I'll build a stairway to paradise            │
│                      Rhapsody in blue                             │
│                      When day is done                             │
│                      What'll I do                                 │
│                      Love nest                                    │
│                                                                   │
│  Press RETURN to continue:                                        │
└─────────────────────────────────────────────────────────────────┘
```

Figure 29.6: LS/2000: Labeled display, recording

```
┌──────────────────────────────────────────────────────────────────────────┐
│ PUBLIC CATALOG                                          Searching: UNCW    │
│                                                                            │
│ A/V Phonodisc 80                                                           │
│     TITLE:         Paul Whiteman.  [Sound recording]                       │
│     PUBLISHER:     RCA Victor LPV 555, [1968-                              │
│     PHYSICAL DESC: discs. 33 1/3 rpm. mono. 12 in.                         │
│     SERIES:        Vintage series                                          │
│     ADDED ENTRIES: Medley from "Anything goes"                             │
│                                                                            │
│                                                                            │
│ LOCATION          CALL#/VOL/NO/COPY              STATUS                     │
│                                                                            │
│ A/V MATERIALS     A/V Phonodisc 80 c.1           Available                 │
│                                                                            │
│                                                                            │
│                                                                            │
│                                                                            │
│                                                                            │
│ (END) Press RETURN to continue or /ES to start a new search:               │
└──────────────────────────────────────────────────────────────────────────┘
```

Figure 29.7: LS/2000: Labeled display, continued

```
┌──────────────────────────────────────────────────────────────────────────┐
│ PUBLIC CATALOG                                          Searching: UNCW    │
│                                                                            │
│                                                                            │
│ PERSONAL AUTHOR:  ▐KING, MARTIN LUTHER, JR., 1929-1968▌                     │
│           FOUND:  11                                                       │
│                                                                            │
│ REF  DATE   TITLES                       AUTHOR        CALL NUMBER          │
│ ───  ────   ──────                       ──────        ───────────          │
│ R1   1990   The Promised land (1967-1968)              A/V VC E185.615 .E9  │
│ R2   1990   Two societies (1965-1968)                  A/V VC E185.615 .E9  │
│ R3   1986   A testament of hope :        King, Martin  E185.97.K5 A25 1986  │
│ R4   1985   Great speeches                             A/V VC PN6121 .G744  │
│ R5   1977   Strength to love /           King, Martin  BX6333.K5 S7 1970z   │
│ R6   1970   Martin Luther King speaks    King, Martin  A/V AC 139           │
│ R7   1968   In search of freedom.        King, Martin  A/V Phonodisc 462    │
│ R8   1967   Where do we go from here:    King, Martin  E185.615 .K5         │
│ R9   1964   Why we can't wait /          King, Martin  E185.61 .K54 1964    │
│ R10  1963   Letter from Birmingham city jail King, Martin E185.61 .K534     │
│ (MORE)                                                                     │
│                                                                            │
│ CHOICE: R                                                                  │
│       Enter a REF number to see details of a title; or /ES to restart.     │
└──────────────────────────────────────────────────────────────────────────┘
```

Figure 29.8: LS/2000: Titles from author result

```
┌──────────────────────────────────────────────────────────────────────────┐
│ PUBLIC CATALOG                                          Searching: UNCW    │
│                                                                            │
│                                                                            │
│                                                                            │
│                                                                            │
│ ENTER LC SUBJECT HEADING OR SUBDIVISION:                                   │
│ ▐KING, MARTIN LUTHER▌                                                       │
│                                                                            │
│                                                                            │
│                                                                            │
│                                                                            │
│      Enter a Library of Congress subject heading or subject subdivision that│
│   describes the topic you wish to search.  Chronological subdivisions (such │
│              as Civil War, 1861-1865) CANNOT be searched.                   │
└──────────────────────────────────────────────────────────────────────────┘
```

Figure 29.9: LS/2000: Subject search

```
PUBLIC CATALOG                                          Searching: UNCW



LC SUBJECT HEADING OR SUBDIVISION:    KING, MARTIN LUTHER

REF    TITLES    LC SUBJECT HEADING OR SUBDIVISION
---    ------    --------------------------------
R1        1    KING, MARTIN LUTHER, 1899-1984
R2       44    KING, MARTIN LUTHER, JR., 1929-1968
(END)








CHOICE: R
        Enter a REF number to select a heading;  or /ES to restart.
```

Figure 29.10: LS/2000: Subject result

```
PUBLIC CATALOG                                          Searching: UNCW



PERSONAL NAME AS SUBJECT:    KING, MARTIN LUTHER, JR., 1929-1968

REF    TITLES    PERSONAL NAME AS SUBJECT
---    ------    ------------------------
R1       44    King, Martin Luther, Jr., 1929-1968
R2        3    - Assassination
R3        2    - Bibliography
R4        1    - Homes and haunts
R5        4    - Juvenile literature
R6        1    - Philosophy
R7        1    - Political and social views
R8        1    - Public opinion
R9        2    - Religion
R10       1    - Songs and music
(END)

CHOICE: R
        Enter a REF number to see the title list; or /ES to restart.
```

Figure 29.11: LS/2000: Subject and subdivisions

```
PUBLIC CATALOG                                          Searching: UNCW
PERSONAL NAME AS SUBJECT: KING, MARTIN LUTHER, JR., 1929-1968    FOUND: 44


Your search has identified many citations. What would you like to do next?



                1. Narrow search

                2. View citations sequentially

                3. Start new search






                Enter one of the numbers above;  or /ES to restart.
CHOICE:
```

Figure 29.12: LS/2000: Search limit screen

```
PUBLIC CATALOG                                    Searching: UNCW
PERSONAL NAME AS SUBJECT: KING, MARTIN LUTHER, JR., 1929-1968      FOUND: 44

             Enter the NUMBER of the limitation search you wish to perform


                      1 - Limit by PUBLICATION YEAR
                      2 - Limit by LANGUAGE
                      3 - Limit by PERSONAL AUTHOR
                      4 - Limit by LC SUBJECT HEADING OR SUBDIVISION
                      5 - Limit by TITLE
                      6 - Limit by CORPORATE AUTHOR
                      7 - Limit by CONFERENCE AUTHOR

                             OR

             Enter a KEY WORD to see possible limiting matches




CHOICE: ███████████████████████████████████████████████
```

Figure 29.13: LS/2000: Search limit options

```
PUBLIC CATALOG                                    Searching: UNCW
PERSONAL NAME AS SUBJECT: KING, MARTIN LUTHER, JR., 1929-1968      FOUND: 44




SHOW TITLES PUBLISHED FROM: 1985


              THROUGH: 1990






         Enter the last year to be included in the search; or /ES to restart.
```

Figure 29.14: LS/2000: Limiting search by date

```
PUBLIC CATALOG                                    Searching: UNCW
PERSONAL NAME AS SUBJECT: KING, MARTIN LUTHER, JR., 1929-1968      FOUND: 44
PUBLICATION YEAR: 1985-1990                                        FOUND: 18

PERSONAL NAME AS SUBJECT:   KING, MARTIN LUTHER, JR., 1929-1968
                 FOUND:  18

REF  DATE   TITLES                        AUTHOR        CALL NUMBER
---  ----   ------                        ------        -----------
R1   1990   The Promised land (1967-1968)               A/V VC E185.615 .E9
R2   1990   Symbols, the news magazines, and  Lentz, Richar E185.97.K5 L43 1990
R3   1990   Martin Luther King, Jr., Nationa
R4   1989   At the river I stand :        Beifuss, Joan JC599.U5 M37 v.12
R5   1989   The MURKIN conspiracy :       Melanson, Phi E185.97.K5 M39 1989
R6   1989   Martin Luther King, Jr. :                   JC599.U5 M37 v.1-3
R7   1989   We shall overcome :                         JC599.U5 M37 v.4-6
R8   1989   The social vision of Martin Luth  Zepp, Ira G.  JC599.U5 M37 v.18
R9   1989   Texts in context :                          PN239.P64 T4 1989
R10  1988   Parting the waters :          Branch, Taylo E185.61 .B7914 1988
(MORE)

CHOICE: R
         Enter a REF number to see details of a title; or /ES to restart.
```

Figure 29.15: LS/2000: Summary from limited search

```
PUBLIC CATALOG                                           Searching: UNCW

A/V VC E185.615 .E942 1990 no.4
    The Promised land (1967-1968) videorecording / Blackside, Inc. ;
        produced, directed and written by Paul Stekler and Jacqueline Shearer.

    King, Martin Luther, - Jr., - 1929-1968
    Race relations - United States.
    Civil rights movements - United States - History.
    Afro-Americans - Civil rights - United States - History.
    Videocassettes.
    Segregation - United States - History.
    Civil rights - United States - History.
    King, Martin Luther, Jr., 1929-1968
    Bond, Julian, 1940-
    Stekler, Paul Jeffrey.
    Shearer, Jacqueline.
    Hampton, Henry, 1940-
    Fayer, Steve, 1935-
    Blackside, Inc.
    PBS Video.
    America at the racial crossroads

Press RETURN to continue:
```

Figure 29.16: LS/2000: Catalog-card display (1)

```
PUBLIC CATALOG                                           Searching: UNCW

A/V VC E185.615 .E942 1990 no.4
    The Promised land (1967-1968) videorecording / Blackside, Inc. ;
        produced, directed and written by Paul Stekler and Jacqueline Shearer.

    The promised land, 1967-1968


NO.  LOCATION        CALL#/VOL/NO/COPY              STATUS

 1   A/V MATERIALS   A/V VC E185.615 .E942 1990 no.4  Available








(END) Select ILL number, RETURN to continue or /ES to start a new search:
```

Figure 29.17: LS/2000: Catalog-card display (2)

```
PUBLIC CATALOG                                           Searching: UNCW

HA202 .S84
    TITLE:          State and metropolitan area data book.
    PUBLISHER:      Washington, D.C. : U.S. Dept. of Commerce, Bureau of the
                    Census : For sale by the Supt. of Docs., U.S. G.P.O., 1980-
    FREQUENCY:      Annual

    SUBJECTS:       United States - Statistics - Periodicals.
    ADDED ENTRIES:  United States. Bureau of the Census.
    HOLDINGS:       1979-


LOCATION        CALL#/VOL/NO/COPY              STATUS

DOCS US         C 3.134/5: 1979 c.1           Available
DOCS US         C 3.134/5: 1982 c.1           Available
REFERENCE COLL  Ref HA202 .S84 1986 c.1       Available




(END) Press RETURN to continue or /ES to start a new search:
```

Figure 29.18: LS/2000: Multiple locations

```
┌─────────────────────────────────────────────────────────────────────────┐
│ PUBLIC CATALOG                                          Searching: UNCW   │
│                                                                           │
│                                                                           │
│                                                                           │
│ AUTHOR:    KIGN, MARTIN LUTHER, JR                                        │
│                                                                           │
│ REF   TITLES    AUTHOR                                                     │
│ ───   ──────    ──────                                                    │
│ R1       2    KIGER, JOSEPH CHARLES                                       │
│ R2       2    KIHL, YOUNG W., 1932-                                       │
│ R3       1    KIHLMAN, BENGT A                                            │
│ R4       2    KIHLSTROM, JOHN F                                           │
│ R5       2    KIHM, JEAN JACQUES                                          │
│ R6       1    KIICK, JIM                                                  │
│ R7       1    KIJEK, JEAN C                                               │
│ R8       3    KIK, JACOB MARCELLUS, 1903-                                 │
│ R9       1    KIKER, B. F                                                 │
│ R10      1    KIKUCHI, CHIHIRO, 1914-                                     │
│ (MORE)                                                                    │
│                                                                           │
│ CHOICE: R                                                                 │
│        Enter a REF number to select a heading;  or /ES to restart.        │
│            No exact match, closest is 'KIGER, JOSEPH CHARLES'             │
└─────────────────────────────────────────────────────────────────────────┘
```

Figure 29.19: LS/2000: Result of error in author

```
┌─────────────────────────────────────────────────────────────────────────┐
│ PUBLIC CATALOG                                          Searching: UNCW   │
│                                                                           │
│                                                                           │
│                                                                           │
│ KEY WORD:   FIRE                                                          │
│                                                                           │
│                                                                           │
│ REF   TITLES    KEY WORD                                                  │
│ ───   ──────    ────────                                                  │
│ R1      434   FIRE                                                        │
│ R2        1   FIRE-ARMS                                                   │
│ R3        1   FIRE-BELL                                                   │
│ R4        1   FIRE-BRAND                                                  │
│ R5        2   FIRE-CLAY                                                   │
│ R6        1   FIRE-DANGER                                                 │
│ R7        6   FIRE-DEPARTMENTS                                            │
│ R8        1   FIRE-DWELLERS                                               │
│ R9        2   FIRE-EATER                                                  │
│ R10       1   FIRE-FIGHTERS                                               │
│ (MORE)                                                                    │
│                                                                           │
│ CHOICE: R                                                                 │
│        Enter a REF number to see search contexts;  or /ES to restart.     │
│                                                                           │
└─────────────────────────────────────────────────────────────────────────┘
```

Figure 29.20: LS/2000: "Fire" as keyword search

```
┌─────────────────────────────────────────────────────────────────────────┐
│ PUBLIC CATALOG                                          Searching: UNCW   │
│                                                                           │
│                                                                           │
│ TERM:  FIRE                                                               │
│                                                                           │
│ REF    TERM APPEARS IN                                                    │
│ ───    ──────────────                                                     │
│                                                                           │
│ R1     45 LC SUBJECT HEADINGS OR SUBDIVISIONS                             │
│ R2      8 AUTHORS                                                         │
│ R3      4 JOURNAL TITLES                                                  │
│ R4     62 CONTENTS NOTES                                                  │
│ R5    258 TITLES                                                          │
│ (END)                                                                     │
│                                                                           │
│                                                                           │
│                                                                           │
│                                                                           │
│                                                                           │
│                                                                           │
│ CHOICE: R                                                                 │
│        Enter a REF number to choose search context; or /ES to restart.    │
│                                                                           │
└─────────────────────────────────────────────────────────────────────────┘
```

Figure 29.21: LS/2000: "Fire" as keyword (2)

```
┌──────────────────────────────────────────────────────────────────┐
│ PUBLIC CATALOG                                    Searching: UNCW  │
│ KEY WORD: FIRE                                        FOUND: 258   │
│                                                                    │
│ KEY WORD:    MOON                                                  │
│                                                                    │
│                                                                    │
│ REF    TITLES    KEY WORD                                          │
│ ───    ──────    ────────                                          │
│ R1      237      MOON                                              │
│ R2        2      MOON'S                                            │
│ R3        1      MOONAM                                            │
│ R4        1      MOONBAH                                           │
│ R5        3      MOONBEAMS                                         │
│ R6        1      MOONBELLS                                         │
│ R7        1      MOONBOW                                           │
│ R8        1      MOONDUST                                          │
│ R9       36      MOONEY                                            │
│ R10       1      MOONEYHAM                                         │
│ (MORE)                                                             │
│                                                                    │
│ CHOICE: R                                                          │
│         Enter a REF number to see search contexts;  or /ES to restart. │
│                                                                    │
└──────────────────────────────────────────────────────────────────┘
```

Figure 29.22: LS/2000: "Moon" as limiting keyword

```
┌──────────────────────────────────────────────────────────────────┐
│ PUBLIC CATALOG                                    Searching: UNCW  │
│ KEY WORD: FIRE                                        FOUND: 258   │
│ WORD IN TITLE: MOON                                   FOUND: 1     │
│                                                                    │
│ WORD IN TITLE:    MOON                                             │
│         FOUND:  1                                                  │
│                                                                    │
│ REF  DATE   TITLES                      AUTHOR      CALL NUMBER    │
│ ───  ────   ──────                      ──────      ───────────    │
│ R1   1970   Of a fire on the moon.      Mailer, Norma TL799.M6 M26 │
│ (END)                                                              │
│                                                                    │
│                                                                    │
│                                                                    │
│                                                                    │
│                                                                    │
│                                                                    │
│ CHOICE: R1/                                                        │
│         Enter a REF number to see details of a title; or /ES to restart. │
│                                                                    │
└──────────────────────────────────────────────────────────────────┘
```

Figure 29.23: LS/2000: Two-word combination

```
┌──────────────────────────────────────────────────────────────────┐
│ PUBLIC CATALOG                                    Searching: UNCW  │
│                                                                    │
│ TL799.M6  M26                                                      │
│     AUTHOR:        Mailer, Norman.                                 │
│     TITLE:         Of a fire on the moon.                          │
│     EDITION:       [1st ed.]                                       │
│     PUBLISHER:     Boston, Little, Brown [1970]                    │
│     PHYSICAL DESC: vii, 472 p. 22 cm.                              │
│                                                                    │
│     SUBJECTS:      Project Apollo (U.S.)                           │
│                    Space flight to the moon                        │
│                    Astronauts - United States                      │
│                    United States - Civilization - 1945-            │
│                                                                    │
│ LOCATION           CALL#/VOL/NO/COPY               STATUS          │
│                                                                    │
│ *RESERVE DESK      TL799.M6 M26 c.1            On Reserve at RESERVE DESK │
│                                                                    │
│                                                                    │
│ (END) Press RETURN to continue or /ES to start a new search:       │
│                                                                    │
└──────────────────────────────────────────────────────────────────┘
```

Figure 29.24: LS/2000: Labeled display, 2-word

```
┌─────────────────────────────────────────────────────────────────┐
│ PUBLIC CATALOG                                  Searching: UNCW   │
│                                                                   │
│                                                                   │
│ AUTHOR/TITLE KEY:   PYNC,VINE                                     │
│                                                                   │
│ REF  AUTHOR/TITLE   TITLES            AUTHOR       CALL NUMBER     │
│ ───   ───────────   ──────            ──────       ───────────    │
│ R1    PYNC,VINE     Vineland /        Pynchon, Tho PS3566.Y55 V56 199│
│ (END)                                                             │
│                                                                   │
│                                                                   │
│                                                                   │
│                                                                   │
│                                                                   │
│                                                                   │
│ CHOICE: R1/                                                       │
│        Enter a REF number to see details of a title; or /ES to restart.│
└─────────────────────────────────────────────────────────────────┘
```

Figure 29.25: LS/2000: Author/Title result

```
┌─────────────────────────────────────────────────────────────────┐
│ PUBLIC CATALOG                                  Searching: UNCW   │
│                                                                   │
│                                                                   │
│ LC SUBJECT HEADING - MAIN HEADING ONLY:    PUBLISHING             │
│                                                                   │
│ REF    TITLES    LC SUBJECT HEADING - MAIN HEADING ONLY           │
│ ───    ──────    ──────────────────────────────────────          │
│ R1      119      PUBLISHERS AND PUBLISHING                        │
│ R2       1       PUEBLO BONITO (N.M.)                             │
│ R3       1       PUEBLO DEL ARROYO (N.M.)                         │
│ R4       1       PUEBLO INCIDENT, 1968                            │
│ R5       47      PUEBLO INDIANS                                   │
│ R6       8       PUEBLOS                                          │
│ R7       1       PUERPERAL PSYCHOSES                              │
│ R8       2       PUERPERIUM                                       │
│ R9       1       PUERTO RICAN DRAMA                               │
│ R10      6       PUERTO RICAN LITERATURE                          │
│ (MORE)                                                            │
│                                                                   │
│ CHOICE: R                                                         │
│        Enter a REF number to select a heading;  or /ES to restart.│
│        No exact match, closest is 'PUBLISHERS AND PUBLISHING'     │
└─────────────────────────────────────────────────────────────────┘
```

Figure 29.26: LS/2000: Subject browse

```
┌─────────────────────────────────────────────────────────────────┐
│ PUBLIC CATALOG                                  Searching: UNCW   │
│                                                                   │
│                                                                   │
│ CALL NUMBER:  Z678.9-                                             │
│                                                                   │
│ REF  CALL NUMBER          TITLES               AUTHOR             │
│ ───  ───────────          ──────               ──────            │
│ R1   Z678.9 .A83          Librarians and online ser Cochrane, Pauline│
│ R2   Z678.9 .B74 1976     COBOL programming :  Brophy, Peter.     │
│ R3   Z678.9 .C53 1985     Microcomputer spreadsheet Clark, Philip M.│
│ R4   Z678.9 .C57          Automation, space managem Cohen, Elaine,│
│ R5   Z678.9 .C65 1967     The computer and th  Cox, Nigel S. M.   │
│ R6   Z678.9 .E86 1985     Essential guide to the li                │
│ R7   Z678.9 .E93 1971     Computers & systems; Eyre, John,        │
│ R8   Z678.9 .F87          Research libraries and te Fussler, Herman H│
│ R9   Z678.9 .G76          Minicomputers in librarie Grosch, Audrey N.│
│ R10  Z678.9 .G77          Minicomputers in librarie Grosch, Audrey N.│
│ (MORE)                                                            │
│                                                                   │
│ CHOICE: R                                                         │
│        Enter a REF number to see details of a title; or /ES to restart.│
└─────────────────────────────────────────────────────────────────┘
```

Figure 29.27: LS/2000: Call number browse

30

MacLAP
at Apple Computer, Inc.

Russ Stephens

The Apple Corporate Library in Cupertino, California, uses CASPR's MacLAP as its online patron-access catalog. This is a Macintosh application that features the familiar and friendly Graphical User Interface (GUI), and is designed to provide patron access to the cataloging and circulation modules of the Macintosh Library System (MLS). The MLS modules may be manipulated by library staff only, but the patron searches the same selected data records entered into MLS via the MacLAP front-end screen (Figure 30.1).

In the Apple Library, this screen is displayed on two machines that are dedicated to MacLAP: one at the front desk (adjacent to reference personnel who may offer search assistance); the other amid the stacks. It is not necessary for patrons to start or search for the MacLAP catalog opening screen themselves. The application is easily launched by library staff each morning as part of opening procedures. Patrons need only walk up to the screen, select a search and type mode, and enter a request.

The MacLAP Interface

The MacLAP interface is easy and fun to use. Patrons may search by clicking upon the preferred search method, in which case the selection is made evident by the open file drawer icon. In the instance of a search by author (Figure 30.1), the word "Author" also appears next to the search field. The material type may also be specified by clicking on the "type" box, and dragging the mouse pointer to the desired code. Examples of type codes are BK (book), VT (videotape), CAS (cassette) and TR (technical report). Selecting type "All" will search on all material types and is particularly useful for subject searches.

The four icons in the top right-hand corner of the screen indicate, from left to right:

- the place to go for help
- commands for hardcopy printing
- disk or file storage of information
- export of information

Clicking on the Help icon gives information on how to use the screen for searches, and includes instruction on Boolean logic. The full Help discussion has been recreated here (Figures 30.2 and 30.3); in the actual online application the patron would use the familiar GUI scroll bar that shows on the screen to the right of the text.

In addition to the standard author, title, or subject searches, MacLAP also allows for call number and keyword searches. The Help feature is especially informative regarding keyword searching, the most powerful feature of MacLAP.

Examples of author, title, and subject searches follow. In addition to call number, author, and title, the number of copies and their circulation status are given as well. If the patron had wanted to search on videotapes only, a selection of "VT" would have been made under "type." Likewise, a specific search for books would have necessitated a selection of "BK." This provides an efficient means of locating specific types of materials.

In addition, any combination of type and search method is possible. In the case of a search that retrieves large numbers of documents, the patron may again use the scrolling feature in order to view all or part of the listing. This feature also serves as an effective browsing tool. The MacLAP search input field is not case sensitive, and there is no need for any attention to shift keys when typing in a search request.

Figure 30.4 shows the results of an author search on all types, with the second citation highlighted. Clicking on the citation will produce a facsimile of a catalog card that gives full bibliographic detail, including the circulation number used by the library staff to locate records in the MLS database (Figure 30.5). For longer records, the system creates a series of cards that may be viewed in succession (Figure 30.6). Multiple-card presentation is made evident by the appearance of the word "Cont..." on the lower right-hand corner of the first card.

Searching and Browsing

In the author search (Figure 30.4), the patron knew the exact spelling of the author's name and searched accordingly. However, this author search, as with all MacLAP searches, could have been truncated for less precision or extended with a comma and the author's first name or initial for greater precision.

Patrons usually search by title when they are confident of search terminology. It is important to note that leading articles ("the," "an" and "a") are omitted in the indexed title field and must be excluded in the search terms. It is not necessary to search on every word in the title; rather, the patron may search on as few words as necessary to bring up the desired item. Boolean operators may not be used in title searches.

Subject searching (Figure 30.7) is done in a similar fashion to author and title searching. It is a powerful browsing tool as well. Boolean operators are allowed and may greatly enhance the subject search process. This greatly facilitates the subject search process and allows the MacLAP subject search to be used effectively.

In order to provide the most efficient means of locating items, the search process may be as general or specific as the patron desires. MacLAP allows for more obscure searches in the database, notably in the "notes" field of the bibliographic record. For example, a software engineer may have heard about a technical report by an alternate number that was not used in the call number or title during the cataloging process. By putting the alternate number in the notes field with an "also numbered as..." reference, it is possible to retrieve the document both ways. It is here that the MacLAP keyword search is extremely effective, since it enables the patron to search on the first 64 characters of any indexed field in the bibliographic record.

In the following example (Figure 30.8), Technical Report STAN-CS-85-1063 has also been numbered HPP-84-6. By searching on the truncated keyword "HPP" it is possible to find this item by its alternate number as well (Figure 30.9). Choosing the type "TR" (Technical Report) may narrow the search even further by excluding other material types.

In the author search on "Baumeister" (Figure 30.6), a keyword search by staff on the familiar reference title "Marks" would also have been effective. This demonstrates full use of the system by librarians and patrons alike.

Boolean Logic

Multiple-keyword searching with Boolean operators is also possible and allows for a high degree of relevance (Figure 30.10). In this search, the patron was interested in books (only) on Macintosh software, but not any items that might include discussions on DOS.

Call Number Searching

Call number searching is also possible on MacLAP (Figure 30.11). This feature may be used after a subject or keyword search, whereby the patron notes the call number of a desired item, and then searches on the main body of the number. This will show all items shelved around the book, the authors and titles of which may then be reviewed for possible relevance. Right truncation is automatic in call number searching, as it is in all MacLAP searches except keyword searching. Keyword searching does not use automatic truncation in order to avoid hits on nonrelevant items. However, right truncation may be forced in keyword searches by adding a question mark (?) to the end of the word.

Printing and Exporting Records

Sets of records may be printed to local or network printers by clicking on the printer icon described earlier. The dialog box will ask the patron to specify the desired record form (Figure 30.12). The patron will also be asked whether or not he or she wants to be prompted after each record or record set is printed. This allows the record form to be changed if necessary. In addition, the system allows for selective record printing within sets of records. The patron may select individual records from record sets by using the mouse and the shift/control buttons on the keyboard. The dialog box also inquires about the inclusion of copy numbers and status on the printout.

Record sets may be saved to local floppy disk files in the same manner. They may also be exported to a disk file in two different formats (Figure 30.13).

Remote Searching

Finally, MacLAP allows for remote searching using AppleTalk® and AppleShare networking services. These may provide library holdings access to many different user groups, as well as provide access from home or other remote sites through normal telephone connections.

To summarize, it is evident that MacLAP's graphical user interface and keyword searching capability are its strongest features. The easy to use icon-driven screen is well liked by patrons, who might otherwise be intimidated by an online catalog that requires some type of written and/or verbal instructions. At the Apple Library, we have found that most users very much prefer to explore MacLAP themselves, sometimes pausing to ask questions that often refer to search strategies. Therein lies the beauty of the system, for it allows the patron the option of independence while at the same time providing a means of searching comprehensively.

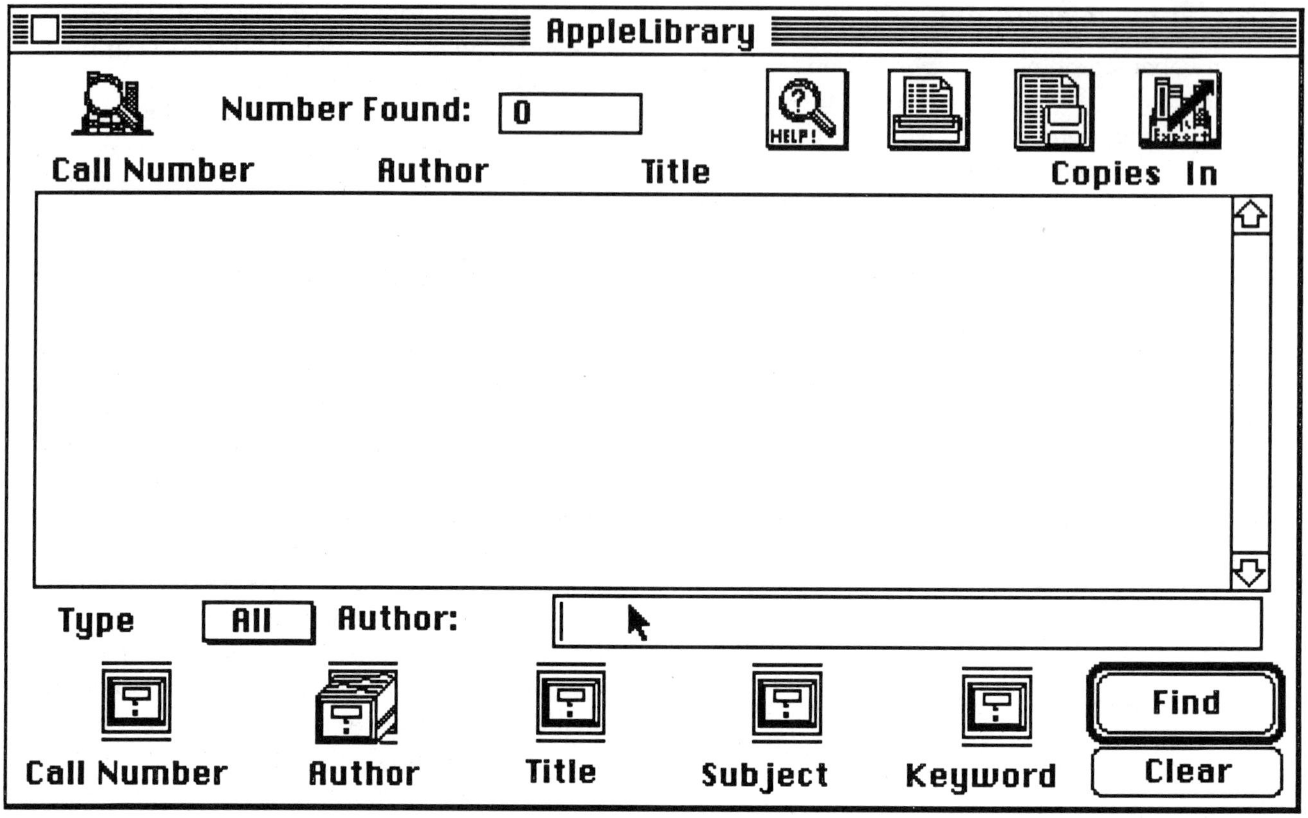

Figure 30.1: MacLAP: Opening screen

```
MacLAP Help

Searching Steps
1. Select a Type of item or All items.
2. Click on a catalog drawer.
3. Enter a search term.
4. Press the Return key or click on the Find button.

About the Catalog Drawers
There are five catalog drawers for searching by Call Number, Author, Title
and Keyword.  Use the Call Number Catalog to search in an area of the
library or for a specific item for which you have the catalog number.
The Author Catalog is used for searching for items written by a specific
author. The Title Catalog is used to search for a particular title.
The Subject Catalog can be great for browsing the library by subject term.
Finally, the keyword catalog is very powerful for searching using
single or multiple keywords

When searching the Call, Author, Title or Subject catalog drawers, enter
the beginning letters or words of your search term.  The more letters you
enter the more accurate your search will be.  Then press Return to Find a
group of records that begin with your search strategy.  If you find too
many items, enter additional letters or words to narrow your search.

When searching the Title drawer, do not enter leading article words at
the beginning of the search term.  Leading articles include 'THE', 'AN',
and 'A'.
```

Figure 30.2: MacLAP: Help text, part 1

```
KEYWORD SEARCHING
Searching by keyword can be very powerful and successful.  A few items
to note about keyword searching:

1. Keyword searches are done on words not phrases.
2. Enter the complete word.  If you want to search all records that
   contain words starting with characters, end the term with a question mark.
   (Example, CAT will return all records with cat in it.  CAT?  will
   return not only all records with cat, but also cats and cattle, etc..)
3. Keyword searching often retrieves unwanted records.  To narrow your
   search use the boolean operator AND.
4. Certain buzzwords lack meaning and are not indexed and cannot be
   used as a search term.  Examples include WHAT, WHICH, WHERE, HOW, WHO
   and THEN.  These are often called STOP words.


BOOLEAN OPERATORS

MacLAP supports the boolean operators AND, OR and NOT.  You can use the
boolean words AND, OR and NOTin the keyword drawer.  In all other drawers
use the character '&' for AND, '▦' for OR and '~' for NOT.  Since the
boolean words are often a part of a title or subject, their use in those
fields would cause an invalid result.  The use of the boolean characters
solves this problem.

The search argument is processed from left to right.  Each term
represents a set of records.  Each set is joined  with the next
set in either an AND, OR or NOT relationship.

The keyword search argument 'Mac?  and Apple not DOS' will be
interpreted as 'Find all records that have the words begining with
the three letters Mac, which also have the word 'Apple' in it, but not
the word 'DOS.'
```

Figure 30.3: MacLAP: Help text, part 2

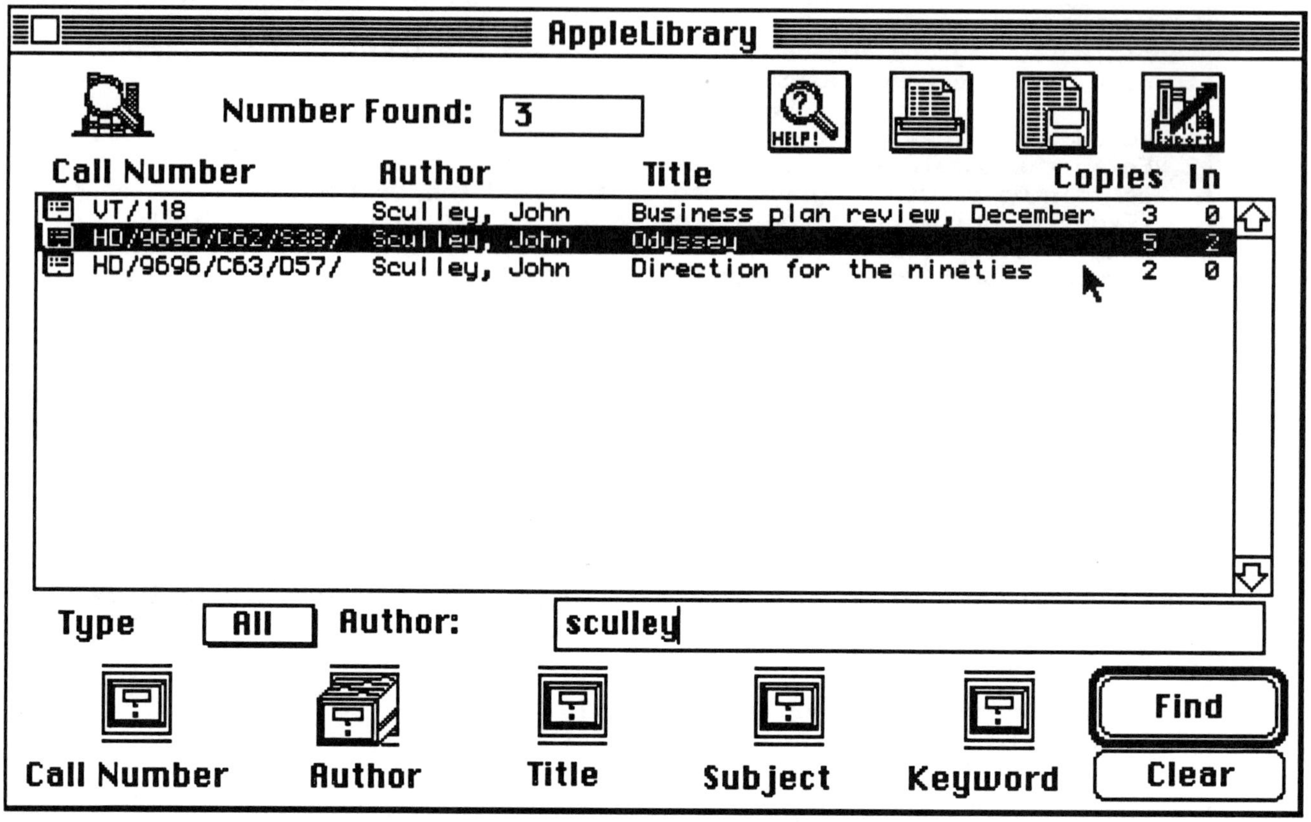

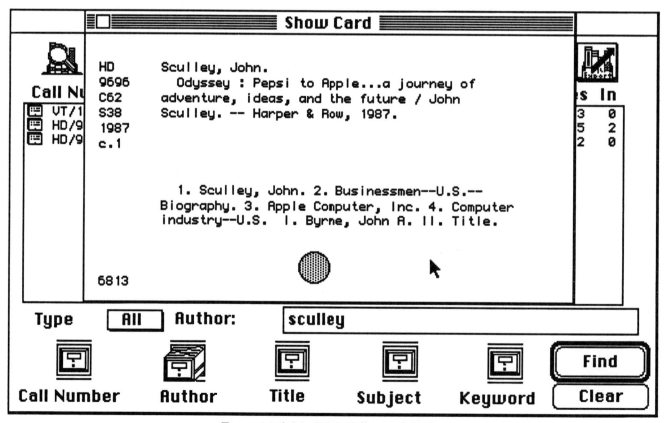

Figure 30.4: MacLAP: Author search and result

Figure 30.5: MacLAP: Full record display

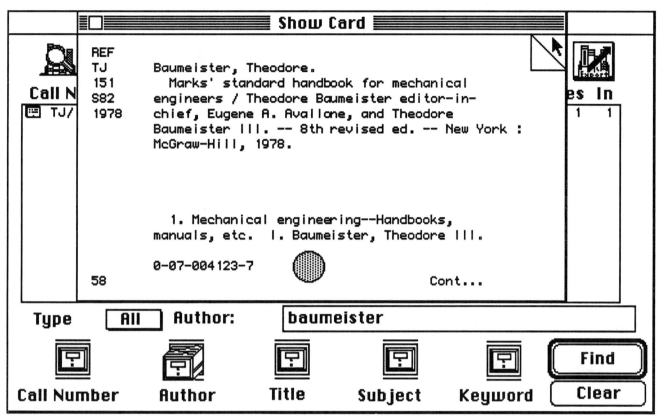

Figure 30.6: MacLAP: Display longer than one card

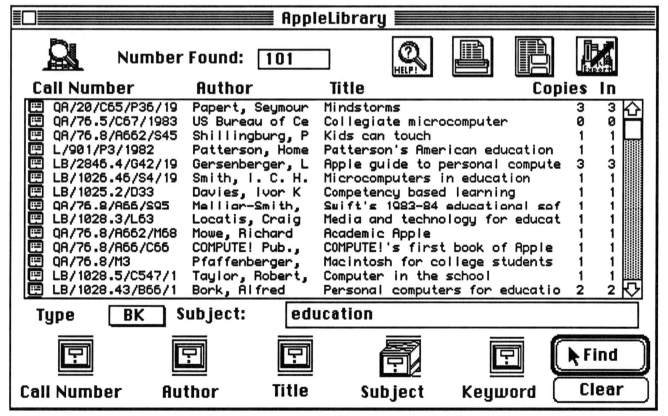

Figure 30.7: MacLAP: Subject search and result

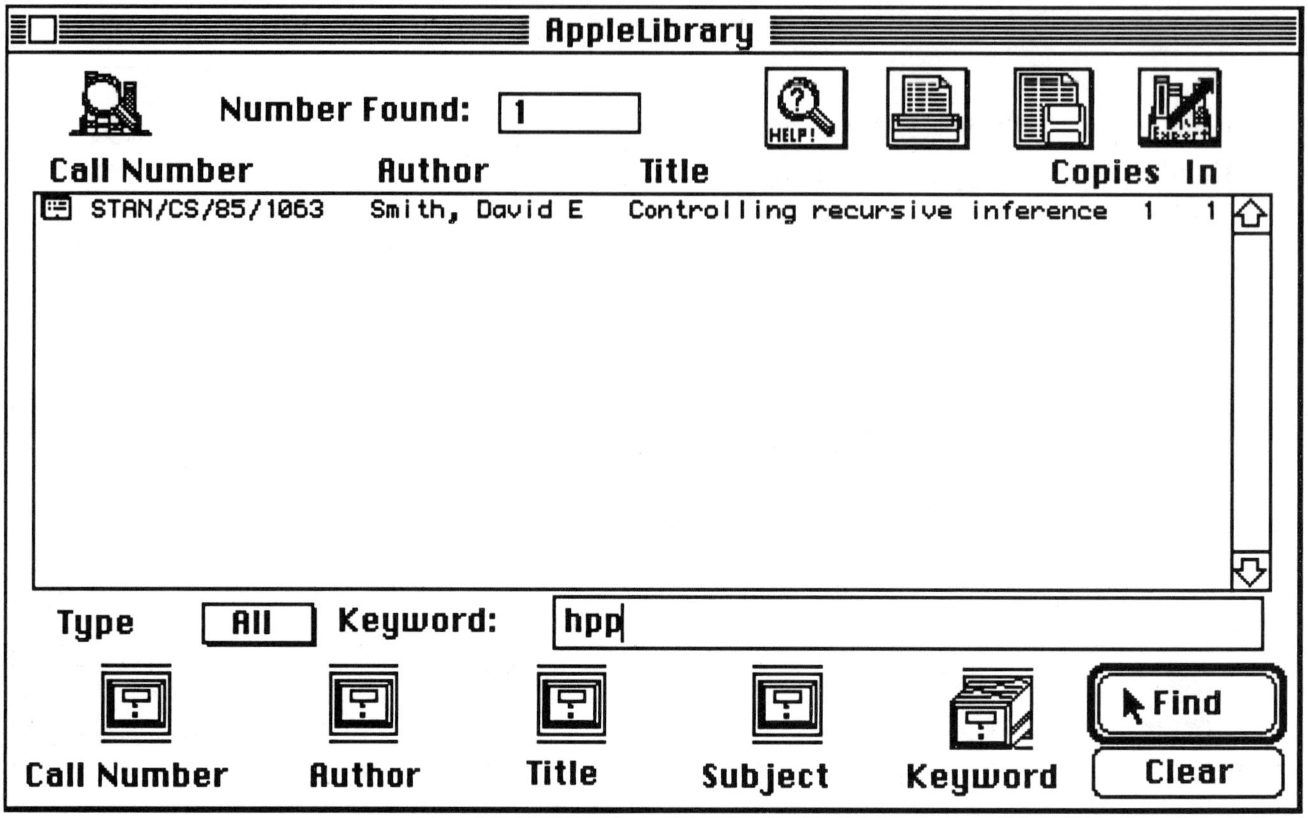

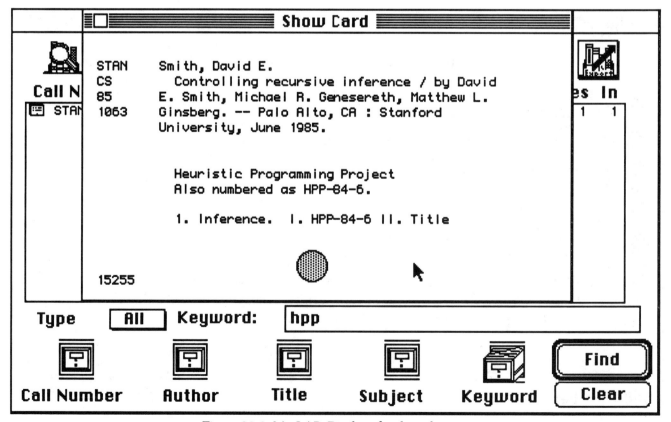

Figure 30.8: MacLAP: Keyword search and result

Figure 30.9: MacLAP: Display of technical report

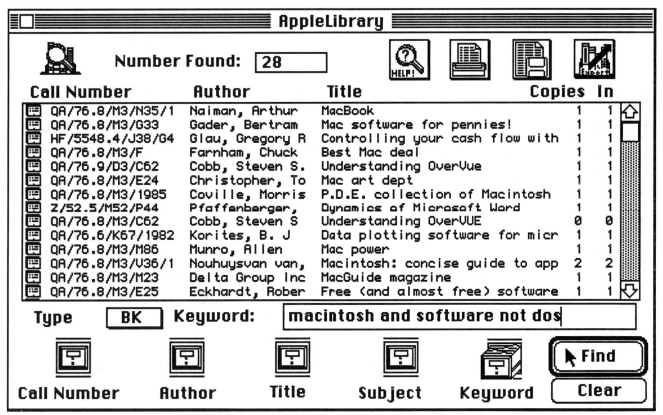

Figure 30.10: MacLAP: Boolean search

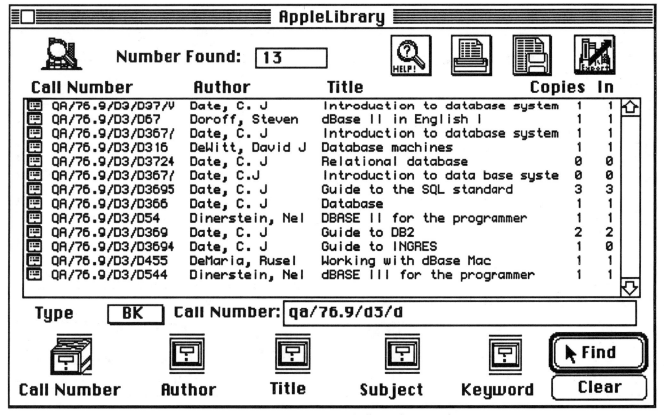

Figure 30.11: MacLAP: Call number search

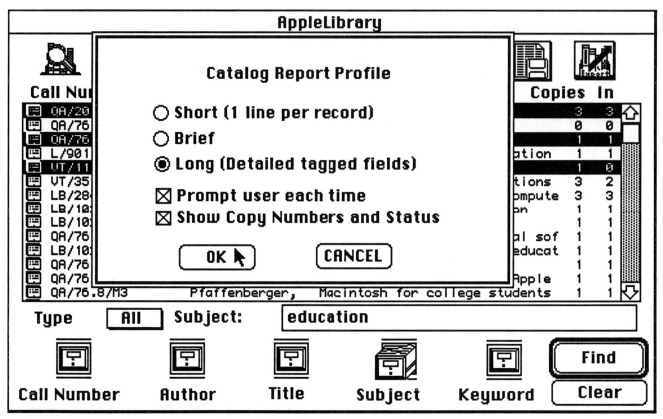

Figure 30.12: MacLAP: Printer dialog box

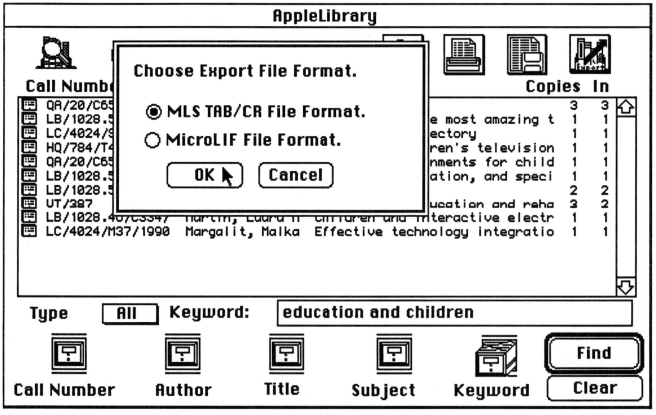

Figure 30.13: MacLAP: Export dialog box

31

MARCIVE/PAC
at Texas A&M

Joni Gomez

MARCIVE/PAC (Patron-Access Catalog) is a microcomputer software system designed for public access to a bibliographic database. Each MARCIVE/PAC is a customized product, designed to meet the needs of a particular library or consortium. Type of access is based on the purpose of the catalog and is tailored to each institution. Parameters set by each library or consortium will determine the look of the finished product, including indexes and how the indexes are constructed as well as screen design and name.

The MARCIVE/PAC installed at the Texas A&M University Library is the HARLiC (Houston Area Research Library Consortium) Union Catalog. When the need for a backup catalog to the online system was recognized, the HARLiC Libraries developed a union CD-ROM catalog of their combined holdings. The HARLiC Catalog combines bibliographic records from academic, public, and medical libraries, using LC, Dewey, and NLM classification. The resulting product contains approximately 1.75 million bibliographic records on multiple CD-ROMs, providing access to more than nine million items, including books, serials, and other materials. Indexes available include author, title, Library of Congress subject heading, medical subject heading, children's subject heading, and call number indexes.

Starting Out

To begin a search, the patron need only sign onto the system and the main menu appears, listing options available (Figure 31.1). The actual options listed are determined by the institution(s) profile. The highlight bar can be moved using the up and down arrow keys. A description of the highlighted option appears in contrast at the bottom of the screen. Function keys labeled F1 through F10 are used to quickly move around within the system. Function keys available at any one time are listed across the bottom. The lower left-hand corner lets the patron know input is required.

At any time, patrons may obtain assistance by pressing F1 for context-specific help (for example, Figure 31.2). For example, at a search screen, the patron might want to know how to use Boolean operators to further define a search. Terms can be enclosed with parentheses and combined with Boolean operators AND, OR, or NOT. The system also allows for truncation of search terms using the asterisk [*], question mark [?], plus [+] or dollar [$].

Search Process

Types of searches available on the HARLiC CD-ROM include title, author, subject, and call number. Subjects are divided into Library of Congress,

355

medical, and children's subject headings. The combined search option allows the patron to precisely define searches by selecting fields (Figure 31.3). Searches can be qualified by format, language, or date. Because of the size of the database the combined search option is the most efficient for locating the CD versions of George Gershwin's *Rhapsody in Blue* (search in Figure 31.3; results and alternative displays in Figures 31.4 through 31.6). The anyword field in the combined search is best for identifying records with Martin Luther King, Jr., as an author or as a subject. (See Figures 31.7 through 31.9.)

Browsing

Patrons can select either browse (F5) or keyword (Enter) search mode. The browse option makes it possible to browse through the author, title, or subject indexes. Terms can be entered and the patron selects F5 for browse. The system will then display the index with the highlight bar at the nearest matching term. In the index, to the left of each term will be a number or an asterisk. The number indicates the number of titles matching each term and the asterisk indicates cross-references are available. (Figures 31.10 through 31.17 show author, subject, and call number browses.)

A convenient feature of MARCIVE/PAC is "list positioning," which allows for rapid movement through the index using the F2 Jump to key.

Display

When a keyword search is conducted, a title list is displayed with the results. The call number of the highlighted title will appear in the upper right-hand corner for the institution at which the search is being conducted. By pressing F3, the patron can see additional holdings for the highlighted title. The location code for each institution, with sublocation when applicable and call number used by that institution, are displayed in a box, highlighted in the center of the screen.

To display the catalog record for a particular title, one need only move the highlight bar to the title and press Enter. Scrolling through the catalog records can be accomplished using the [-] or PgUp

key for previous record and the [+] or PgDn key for next record or the Home or End key.

Search Features

The more words used in a search argument, the fewer the number of matches. When more than one word is used, the system will search using implied AND. Any punctuation or common words will be ignored. For example, entering the search query "fire on the moon" retrieves the bibliographic record, even though the correct title is *Of a Fire on the Moon*.

Errors

When no records match, a screen appears with further instructions (Figure 31.18); Escape or F9 will return you to the last screen and F8 will retrieve the last search argument. The terms entered can then be refined.

Nonbook Information

Nonbook materials are included in the HARLiC Union Catalog (for example, Figure 31.19). The ability to limit by format using the combined search option allows for these items to be readily retrieved.

Leaving the System

MARCIVE/PAC is designed so that the typical patron would not easily be able to exit the program. A combination of keystrokes is required to exit (Figure 31.20).

Printing

MARCIVE/PAC has several output options, including output to a printer, disk or screen. Two choices are made available when using the F7 key. Patrons can print the screen for the current record or go to the print functions menu to print or download as many marked records as desired (Figure 31.21). Records must have been selected by pressing F6 either when the record was displayed or highlighted on the title list. From the print functions menu, patrons may select options for the format of records. The system will return to the default option, call number and title display.

Titles can be cleared from the print menu or by returning to the title list, moving the highlight bar, and pressing F6. (A previewed print list appears in Figure 31.22.)

Additional features

Scoping

Patrons may select the option to limit a search to a particular institution, useful if only locally available items are desired.

Viewpoint

MARCIVE/PAC has the ability to display the entire catalog from the viewpoint of a specified library. Information from the entire catalog is searched with preference given to a particular library. (This and other settable parameters appear in Figure 31.23.)

News and Information

The news and information feature can be used to display the latest news and local information about your library. The HARLiC CD-ROM Catalog uses that area to display location codes for participating institutions.

Parameters

MARCIVE/PAC is designed to run on standard off-the-shelf hardware, allowing flexibility in choosing equipment. Due to different hardware configurations and individual library requirements, MARCIVE/PAC offers the ability to modify the software to meet some of those needs.

Conclusion

MARCIVE/PAC is easy to use with its combination of menus and function keys. Patrons can learn to search quickly. Fast response time, readable displays, and flexible output options all add to patron satisfaction.

```
┌──────────────────── MAIN MENU ────────────────────┐
│                MARCIVE / PAC  Version 5.11         │
│       Copyright (C) 1986-1991 MARCIVE Inc. - All Rights Reserved │
│                                                    │
│             Welcome to the Union Catalog of the    │
│             Houston Area Research Library Consortium (HARLiC) │
│      The MAIN MENU is used to select one of several initial menu items. │
│ Use the ↑↓ arrow keys to highlight the desired item and press the [ENTER] key. │
│                                                    │
│                  ████TITLE SEARCH████              │
│                    AUTHOR SEARCH                   │
│                    SUBJECT SEARCH                  │
│                MEDICAL SUBJECT SEARCH              │
│              CHILDREN'S SUBJECT SEARCH             │
│                 CALL NUMBER SEARCH                 │
│                  COMBINED SEARCH                   │
│                  PRINT FUNCTIONS                   │
│                 NEWS AND INFORMATION               │
│                                                    │
│ ┌Highlighted menu item description:──────────────┐ │
│ │ TITLE SEARCH - Search for specified titles or browse all titles. │ │
│ └────────────────────────────────────────────────┘ │
│                                                    │
│ F1-Help     ↑↓-Move highlight    [ENTER]-Select item │
└────────────────────────────────────────────────────┘
```

Figure 31.1: MARCIVE: Main menu

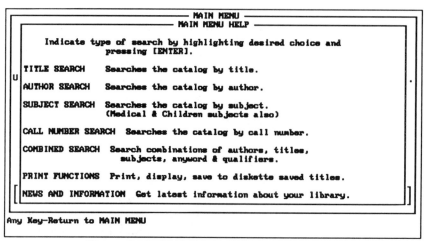

```
┌──────────────────────── MAIN MENU ──────────────────────┐
│ ┌───────────────── MAIN MENU HELP ──────────────────┐   │
│ │      Indicate type of search by highlighting desired choice and   │
│ │                     pressing [ENTER].                             │
│ │                                                                   │
│U│ TITLE SEARCH     Searches the catalog by title.                   │
│ │                                                                   │
│ │ AUTHOR SEARCH    Searches the catalog by author.                  │
│ │                                                                   │
│ │ SUBJECT SEARCH   Searches the catalog by subject.                 │
│ │                  (Medical & Children subjects also)               │
│ │                                                                   │
│ │ CALL NUMBER SEARCH   Searches the catalog by call number.         │
│ │                                                                   │
│ │ COMBINED SEARCH   Search combinations of authors, titles,         │
│ │                     subjects, anyword & qualifiers.               │
│ │                                                                   │
│ │ PRINT FUNCTIONS   Print, display, save to diskette saved titles.  │
│ │                                                                   │
│[│ NEWS AND INFORMATION  Get latest information about your library.  ]│
│ └───────────────────────────────────────────────────┘   │
└─────────────────────────────────────────────────────────┘
Any Key-Return to MAIN MENU
```

Figure 31.2: MARCIVE: Help for main menu

```
┌──────────────────────── COMBINED SEARCH ────────────────────────┐
│   Use the COMBINED SEARCH to search combinations of Authors, Titles, │
│ Subjects (Medical or Children's), or all indexes at once (ANYWORD). The │
│ search may be further qualified by location, format, date, or language  │
│ code. For information on boolean searching press [F1] for Help.         │
│          ┌─Enter combined search request:──────────────────────┐       │
│   Title: │ RHAPSODY                                             │       │
│  Author: │ (GERSHWIN) AND (THOMAS)                              │       │
│ Subject: │                                                      │       │
│ Medical: │                                                      │       │
│Childrens:│                                                      │       │
│ Anyword: │                                                      │       │
│Location: │                                                      │       │
│  Format: │ ▓▓▓▓▓                                                │       │
│    Date: │                                                      │       │
│Language: │                                                      │       │
│          └──────────────────────────────────────────────────────┘     │
│   ┌─Highlighted index description:──────────────────────────────┐      │
│   │ AUTHOR-Searches words in all authors (personal names, agencies, conferences) │
│   └──────────────────────────────────────────────────────────────┘    │
└──────────────────────────────────────────────────────────────────┘
F1-Help  F8-Last search  F10-Main menu   ↑↓-Change Index   [ENTER]-Search
```

Figure 31.3: MARCIVE: Combined search entry

```
┌─COMBINED SEARCH:TITLE-RHAPSODY,AUTH-(GERSHWIN) AND (THOMAS), ▓▓▓▓▓▓▓▓│
│───────────────────────── TITLE LIST ─────────────────── ▓▓▓▓▓▓▓▓│
│                                                          ▓▓▓▓▓▓▓▓│
│ DISPLAY OF 1 THROUGH 2 OF 2 TOTAL RECORDS                ▓▓▓▓▓▓▓▓│
│                                                                  │
│ ▓▓▓▓▓▓▓▓▓▓▓▓▓▓▓▓▓▓▓▓▓▓▓▓▓▓▓▓▓▓▓▓▓▓▓▓▓▓▓▓▓▓▓▓▓▓▓▓▓▓▓▓▓▓▓          │
│ Rhapsody in blue the 1925 piano roll ; An American in Paris.     │
│                                                                  │
│                                                                  │
│                                                                  │
│                                                                  │
│                                                                  │
│                                                                  │
│                                                                  │
│                                                                  │
│                                                                  │
│                                                                  │
│ ↑↓-Move highlight   [ENTER]-Select   PgUp,PgDn-Page   Home-Beginning   End-End │
│ F1-Help F2-Jump F3-Locations F5-Browse F6-Save F7-Print F9-Back F10-Main menu │
└──────────────────────────────────────────────────────────────────┘
```

Figure 31.4: MARCIVE: Title list

```
┌─COMBINED SEARCH:TITLE-RHAPSODY,AUTH-(GERSHWIN) AND (THOMAS),FORMAT-SOUN─┐
└┬TITLE:Rhapsody in blue ; Preludes for piano ; Short story ; Violin piece ;┴┐
 ├──────────────────── CATALOG RECORD DISPLAY ────────────────────────┤

             AUTHOR: Gershwin, George, 1898-1937. cn
              TITLE: Rhapsody in blue ; Preludes for piano ; Short story ;
                     Violin piece ; Second rhapsody for orchestra with piano ;
                     For Lily Pons ; Sleepless night ; Promenade : Walking the
                     dog sound recording / Gershwin.
   PUBLICATION INFO: New York, N.Y. : CBS Masterworks, p1985.
      PHYSICAL DESC: 1 sound disc : digital ; 4 3/4 in. + program notes.
               NOTE: CBS Masterworks: MK 39699.
               NOTE: Title on container spine: Rhapsodies.
               NOTE: First work for piano and jazz band; 3rd, 4th, 6th, and 7th
                     works for piano; last work for piano and orchestra, from
                     the motion picture music for Shall we dance.
               NOTE: Third work reconstructed by, 4th work arr., 6th work
                     realized by Michael Tilson Thomas.
               NOTE: Michael Tilson Thomas, piano and conductor ; Los Angeles
                     Philharmonic.
            SUBJECT: Piano with jazz ensemble.

 ┌──────────────────────────────────────────────────────────────────────┐
 ↑↓-Scroll      PgUp,PgDn-Page     --Previous record      +-Next record
 F1-Help     F6-Save     F7-Print     F9-Back     F10-Main menu
```

Figure 31.5: MARCIVE: Full display, recording

```
┌─COMBINED SEARCH:TITLE-RHAPSODY,AUTH-(GERSHWIN) AND (THOMAS),FORMAT-SOUN─┐
└┬TITLE:Rhapsody in blue ; Preludes for piano ; Short story ; Violin piece ;┴┐
 ├──────────────────── CATALOG RECORD DISPLAY ────────────────────────┤
 │LDR      01339njm  22     Ia 4500
 │001      ocm14186628
 │005      19880308133805.
 │007      sd-fzngnnn---e
 │008      152786s1985    nyuzznn  i        1  N/Amd
 │901      _a 1461025
 │019      _a 13191711
 │024 1    _a 7464396992
 │040      _a GRN _c GRN _d IUL _d OCL _d m/c _d TXN
 │041 0    _g engfreger
 │045 1    _b d1924 _b d1926 _b d1925 _b d1932 _b d1933 _b d1936
 │048      _b ka01 _a oe
 │048      _a ka01
 │048      _b ka01 _a oa
 │049      _a $LIBHLIC
 │100 10   _a Gershwin, George, _d 1898-1937. _w cn
 │245 10   _a Rhapsody in blue ; Preludes for piano ; Short story ; Violin piece ;
 │         Second rhapsody for orchestra with piano ; For Lily Pons ;

 ↑↓-Scroll      PgUp,PgDn-Page     --Previous record      +-Next record
 F1-Help     F6-Save     F7-Print     F9-Back     F10-Main menu
```

Figure 31.6: MARCIVE: MARC display (partial)

```
┌──────────────────── COMBINED SEARCH ────────────────────┐
│   Use the COMBINED SEARCH to search combinations of Authors, Titles, │
│ Subjects (Medical or Children's), or all indexes at once (ANYWORD). The │
│ search may be further qualified by location, format, date, or language │
│ code. For information on boolean searching press [F1] for Help. │
│                                                                       │
│            ┌─Enter combined search request:──────────────────────┐  │
│    Title: │                                                        │  │
│   Author: │                                                        │  │
│  Subject: │                                                        │  │
│  Medical: │                                                        │  │
│Childrens: │                                                        │  │
│  Anyword: │  MARTIN LUTHER KING JR                                  │  │
│ Location: │                                                        │  │
│   Format: │                                                        │  │
│     Date: │  1980-1985                                             │  │
│ Language: │                                                        │  │
│            └────────────────────────────────────────────────────┘  │
│                                                                       │
│  ┌─Highlighted index description:──────────────────────────────────┐ │
│  │ DATE-Searches by publication date                                │ │
│  └────────────────────────────────────────────────────────────────┘ │
└───────────────────────────────────────────────────────────────────────┘
 F1-Help  F8-Last search  F10-Main menu   ↑↓-Change Index   [ENTER]-Search
```

Figure 31.7: MARCIVE: All-index search

```
┌─COMBINED SEARCH:ANY-MARTIN LUTHER KING JR,DATE-1980-1985──── TSU HEARTM
│                        ─ TITLE LIST ─                        BV
│                                                              3785
│ DISPLAY OF 1 THROUGH 16 OF 39 TOTAL RECORDS                  .C69
│                                                              M63
│ Billy Graham and Martin Luther King, Jr. : an inquiry into whi 1979a
│ Charting the course for nonviolent social change : report of the Sixth Annual
│ Dr. Martin Luther King, Jr. : (revised)
│ Echoes from the mountain top : a tribute to Dr. Martin Luther King, Jr.
│ The ethics of Martin Luther King, Jr.
│ The FBI and Martin Luther King, Jr.
│ Great Americans : Martin Luther King, Jr.
│ Great speeches
│ "I have a dream──" the life of Martin Luther King
│ The implications of Dr. Martin Luther King, Jr.'s work and philosophy for the
│ King, Malcolm, Baldwin : three interviews
│ A lasting impression : a collection of photographs of Martin Luther King, Jr.
│ Let the trumpet sound : the life of Martin Luther King, Jr.
│ Let the trumpet sound : the life of Martin Luther King, Jr.
│ Martin Luther King, Jr.
│ Martin Luther King, Jr.
│
│ ↑↓-Move highlight   [ENTER]-Select   PgUp,PgDn-Page   Home-Beginning   End-End
│ F1-Help F2-Jump F3-Locations F5-Browse F6-Save F7-Print F9-Back F10-Main menu
└───────────────────────────────────────────────────────────────────────────────
```

Figure 31.8: MARCIVE: Title list (all-index)

```
┌─COMBINED SEARCH:ANY-MARTIN LUTHER KING,DATE-1980-1985─────────────┐
│┌─TITLE:Echoes from the mountain top : a tribute to Dr. Martin Luther King, ┘│
│├──────────────────── CATALOG RECORD DISPLAY ────────────────────│
│                                                                  │
│            AUTHOR: Dunham, Gerald F.                             │
│             TITLE: Echoes from the mountain top : a tribute to Dr. Martin │
│                    Luther King, Jr. / by Gerald F. Dunhan.      │
│  PUBLICATION INFO: Houston, TX. : Infinity Bound, 1983.         │
│     PHYSICAL DESC: [28] p. : ill. ; 22 cm.                      │
│           SUBJECT: Poetry - Afro-American authors - 20th century.│
│           SUBJECT: King, Martin Luther, Jr., 1929-1968.         │
│  LOCATION/CALL #: HPL ACR-ADU / 811 D917                        │
│  LOCATION/CALL #: HPL ALI-ADU / 811 D917                        │
│  LOCATION/CALL #: HPL BBM-ADU / 811 D917                        │
│  LOCATION/CALL #: HPL CAR-ADU / 811 D917                        │
│  LOCATION/CALL #: HPL CEN-HUM / 811 D917                        │
│  LOCATION/CALL #: HPL COL-ADU / 811 D917                        │
│  LOCATION/CALL #: HPL FIF-ADU / 811 D917                        │
│  LOCATION/CALL #: HPL FRA-ADU / 811 D917                        │
│  LOCATION/CALL #: HPL HEI-ADU / 811 D917                        │
│  LOCATION/CALL #: HPL HIL-ADU / 811 D917                        │
│                                                                  │
├──────────────────────────────────────────────────────────────│
│ ↑↓-Scroll     PgUp,PgDn-Page   --Previous record   +-Next record│
│ F1-Help       F6-Save     F7-Print     F9-Back     F10-Main menu│
└──────────────────────────────────────────────────────────────┘
```

Figure 31.9: MARCIVE: Full display, multiple locs

```
┌──────────────────── AUTHOR SEARCH ────────────────────────────┐
│                                                                │
│┌─Enter the name of the author to be searched:────────────────┐│
││ T PYNCHON                                                    ││
│└──────────────────────────────────────────────────────────────┘│
│                                                                │
│ For KEYWORD SEARCHING:                                         │
│   Enter an author, partial author, initials, or selected words from an │
│   author's name and press the [ENTER] key. Follow the word with an │
│   (*) if you wish to expand the search to all words beginning with those │
│   letters. A list of all authors containing the requested words will be │
│   displayed. For information on boolean searching press [F1] for Help. │
│     Examples:                                                  │
│       SHAKESPEARE W                                            │
│       SHAKESPE*                                                │
│                                                                │
│ For BROWSE SEARCHING:                                          │
│   Enter the author's full name (last name first) and press [F5]. A list of │
│   all authors will be displayed, positioned alphabetically at the requested │
│   author.                                                      │
│     Example:                                                   │
│       SHAKESPEARE, WILLIAM                                     │
│                                                                │
├────────────────────────────────────────────────────────────│
│F1-Help     F5-Browse     F8-Last search    F10-Main menu   [ENTER]-Search│
└────────────────────────────────────────────────────────────┘
```

Figure 31.10: MARCIVE: Author search screen

```
┌─AUTHOR BROWSE SEARCH:Pynchon, Thomas.─────────────────────────────┐
│                      ──── AUTHOR BROWSE LIST ────                  │
│     1 Pynchon, May                                                │
│  ▓▓▓ Pynchon, Thomas.▓▓▓▓                                         │
│     2 Pynchon, William, 1590-1662.                                │
│     1 Pyne, Ann L.                                                 │
│     1 Pyne, Charles H.                                             │
│     1 Pyne, Henry R.                                               │
│     1 Pyne, Kathleen A., 1949-                                     │
│     1 Pyne, Mable.                                                 │
│     1 Pyne, Mable Mandeville.                                      │
│     2 Pyne Press.                                                  │
│     2 Pyne, Ruth M.                                                │
│     1 Pyne, Smith, 1803-1875.                                     │
│     7 Pyne, Stephen J., 1949-                                     │
│     2 Pyne, Timothy.                                               │
│     4 Pyne, W. H. (William Henry), 1769-1843.                     │
│     *Pyne, William Henry, 1769-1843                               │
│     2 Pyne, Zoë Kendrick.                                         │
│     1 Pyner, David A.                                              │
│     1 Pynes, Joan.                                                 │
│                                                                   │
├───────────────────────────────────────────────────────────────────┤
│ ↑↓-Move highlight   [ENTER]-Select   PgUp,PgDn-Page   Home-Beginning   End-End │
│ F1-Help        F2-Jump        F7-Print        F9-Back        F10-Main menu     │
└───────────────────────────────────────────────────────────────────┘
```

Figure 31.11: MARCIVE: Author browse

```
┌────────────────────── SUBJECT SEARCH ──────────────────────┐
│                                                             │
│ ┌─Enter the subject to be searched:──────────────────────┐ │
│ │ DESKTOP PUBLISHING                                     │ │
│ └────────────────────────────────────────────────────────┘ │
│                                                             │
│ For KEYWORD SEARCHING:                                      │
│   Enter a subject, a partial subject, or selected words from a subject and │
│   press the [ENTER] key. Follow the word with an asterisk (*) if you wish to │
│   expand the search to all words beginning with those letters. A list of │
│   subjects containing the requested words will be displayed. For information │
│   on boolean searching press [F1] for Help.                 │
│                                                             │
│      Examples:                                              │
│        ECONOMIC ASPECTS OF WORLD WAR IN FRANCE              │
│        FRANCE ECON* WORLD WAR                               │
│                                                             │
│ For BROWSE SEARCHING:                                       │
│   Enter the full subject heading and press [F5]. A list of all subjects │
│   will be displayed, positioned alphabetically at the requested subject. │
│      Example:                                               │
│        WORLD WAR, 1914-1918 - ECONOMIC ASPECTS - FRANCE     │
├─────────────────────────────────────────────────────────────┤
│ F1-Help    F5-Browse    F8-Last search    F10-Main menu    [ENTER]-Search │
└─────────────────────────────────────────────────────────────┘
```

Figure 31.12: MARCIVE: Subject search screen

```
┌─SUBJECT KEYWORD SEARCH:DESKTOP PUBLISHING─────────────────────────┐
│                     ──── SUBJECT KEYWORD LIST ────                 │
│                                                                   │
│ DISPLAY OF 1 THROUGH 11 OF 11 TOTAL RECORDS                        │
│                                                                   │
│   ▓▓▓▓▓▓▓▓▓▓▓▓▓▓▓▓▓▓▓▓▓▓▓▓                                       │
│     1 Desktop publishing - Bibliography.                          │
│     *Desktop publishing - Computer programs                       │
│     1 Desktop publishing - Equipment and supplies - Purchasing.   │
│     1 Desktop publishing - Handbooks, manuals, etc.               │
│     2 Desktop publishing - Library applications                   │
│     1 Desktop publishing - Problems, exercises, etc.              │
│     2 Desktop publishing - Style manuals.                         │
│     1 Desktop publishing - United States.                         │
│     *Libraries and desktop publishing                             │
│     *Library applications of desktop publishing                   │
│                                                                   │
│                                                                   │
│                                                                   │
├───────────────────────────────────────────────────────────────────┤
│ ↑↓-Move highlight   [ENTER]-Select   PgUp,PgDn-Page   Home-Beginning   End-End │
│ F1-Help    F2-Jump    F5-Browse    F7-Print    F9-Back    F10-Main menu │
└───────────────────────────────────────────────────────────────────┘
```

Figure 31.13: MARCIVE: Subject browse

```
┌─SUBJECT:Libraries and desktop publishing ──────────────────────────────────────┐
│ ──────────────────────── CROSS REFERENCE LIST ────────────────────── │
│                                                                                  │
│ DISPLAY OF 1 THROUGH 1 OF 1 TOTAL CROSS REFERENCE RECORDS                         │
│                                                                                  │
│  *Libraries and desktop publishing                                               │
│                                                                                  │
│         SEE: ▓Desktop publishing - Library applications▓                          │
│                                                                                  │
│                                                                                  │
│                                                                                  │
│                                                                                  │
│                                                                                  │
│                                                                                  │
│                                                                                  │
│                                                                                  │
│                                                                                  │
│                                                                                  │
│                                                                                  │
│ ↑↓-Move highlight   [ENTER]-Select    PgUp,PgDn-Page   Home-Beginning   End-End  │
│ F1-Help            F5-Browse          F9-Back         F10-Main menu              │
└──────────────────────────────────────────────────────────────────────────────┘
```

Figure 31.14: MARCIVE: Subject cross-reference

```
┌─SUBJECT:Desktop publishing──────────────────────────┐ ▓TAMU STK▓
│ ─────────────────────── TITLE LIST ──────────────── │ ▓Z      ▓
│                                                     │ ▓286    ▓
│ DISPLAY OF 1 THROUGH 16 OF 83 TOTAL RECORDS          │ ▓.D47   ▓
│                                                     │ ▓C69    ▓
│ ▓The ABC's of Ventura▓                               │ ▓1989   ▓
│ Achieving graphic impact with Ventura 2.0            │
│ Advanced desktop publishing : a practical guide to Ventura ver More-press F3
│ Advanced Ventura                                    │
│ Computel's quick & easy guide to desktop publishing  │
│ Design for desktop publishing : a guide to layout and typography on the perso
│ Design principles for desktop publishers            │
│ Desktop publishing                                  │
│ Desktop publishing                                  │
│ Desktop publishing bible                            │
│ Desktop publishing bible                            │
│ Desktop publishing, Macintosh edition               │
│ Desktop publishing : producing professional publications
│ Desktop publishing skills : a primer for typesetting with computers and laser
│ Desktop publishing type & graphics : a comprehensive handbook
│ Desktop publishing : using PageMaker on the Apple Macintosh
│ ↑↓-Move highlight   [ENTER]-Select    PgUp,PgDn-Page   Home-Beginning   End-End
│ F1-Help F2-Jump F3-Locations F5-Browse F6-Save F7-Print F9-Back F10-Main menu
└──────────────────────────────────────────────────────────────────────────────┘
```

Figure 31.15: MARCIVE: Title list from subject

```
┌───────────────────── CALL NUMBER SEARCH ─────────────────────┐
│ ┌─Enter the call number to be searched:────────────────────┐ │
│ │ Z678.9                                                    │ │
│ └──────────────────────────────────────────────────────────┘ │
│                                                               │
│                                                               │
│     The CALL NUMBER SEARCH is used to find books by their call number. Enter │
│  a call number or the first part of a call number and press the [ENTER] key. │
│  The requested call number will be used to position a sorted list of all │
│  call numbers.                                                │
│     Examples:                                                 │
│       LA 370.E15                                              │
│       QR                                                      │
│                                                               │
│                                                               │
│                                                               │
│                                                               │
│                                                               │
│                                                               │
│ F1-Help    F8-Last search    F9-Back    F10-Main menu    [ENTER]-Search │
└───────────────────────────────────────────────────────────────┘
```

Figure 31.16: MARCIVE: Call number search

```
┌─CALL NUMBER BROWSE SEARCH:Z678.9────────────────────────────┬─TAMU STK─┐
│              ───────── CALL NUMBER BROWSE LIST ─────────    │ Z        │
│ Z678 .892.U6S47       The River Bend casebook : problems in pub│ 678.9    │
│ Z 678.9 A1 A24        Access: microcomputers in libraries.    │ A1       │
│ Z 678.9 .A1 A3 1984   New information technologies and librarie│ A24      │
│ Z678 .9.A1A34         Advances in library automation and networking. │
│ Z 678.9 .A1 A62 1975  Information roundup : a continuing education session on │
│ Z 678.9 .A1 B35 1971b Interface: library automation with special reference to │
│ Z678 .9.A1C17         Library automation in the nation.       │
│ Z 678.9 .A1 C46 1989  Changing technology : opportunity and challenge : a conf │
│ Z 678.9 .A1 C5        Proceedings.                            │
│ Z 678.9 .A1 C5        Proceedings of the Clinic on Library Applications of Dat │
│ Z 678.9 .A1 C5        Proceedings of the Clinic on Library Applications of Dat │
│ Z 678.9 A1 C5 1974    Applications of minicomputers to library and related pro │
│ Z 678.9 .A1 C5 1975   The use of computers in literature searching and related │
│ Z 678.9 .A1 C5 1977   Negotiating for computer services        │
│ Z678 .9.A1C5 1978     Problems and failures in library automation │
│ Z 678.9 .A1 C5 1979   The role of the library in an electronic society │
│ Z 678.9 A1 C5 1980    Public access to library automation       │
│ Z678 .9.A1C5 1981     New information technologies--new opportunities │
│ Z678 .9.A1C5 1981     Public access to library automation       │
├───────────────────────────────────────────────────────────────────────┤
│ ↑↓-Move highlight    [ENTER]-Select    PgUp,PgDn-Page    Home-Beginning    End-End │
│ F1-Help       F2-Jump       F6-Save       F7-Print       F9-Back       F10-Main menu │
└───────────────────────────────────────────────────────────────────────┘
```

Figure 31.17: MARCIVE: Call number browse

```
┌─TITLE KEYWORD SEARCH:MARTIN LUTHER KIGN JR───────────────────────────────┐
│─────────────────────── TITLE LIST ───────────────────────────────────────│
│   ┌───────────────────────────────────────────────────────────────────┐  │
│   │                                                                     │  │
│   │           NO RECORDS MATCHED YOUR SEARCH AS ENTERED                 │  │
│   │                                                                     │  │
│   │      To return to the search screen, press [F9] or ESC.             │  │
│   │                                                                     │  │
│   │      While on the search screen, you can call your                  │  │
│   │      search back by pressing [F8] Last Search.                      │  │
│   │                                                                     │  │
│   │         You may then                                                │  │
│   │         ─modify your search and press [Enter] to try                │  │
│   │              another keyword search,                                │  │
│   │                           OR                                        │  │
│   │         ─let the system get as close as possible by                 │  │
│   │              pressing [F5] Browse                                   │  │
│   │                                                                     │  │
│   └───────────────────────────────────────────────────────────────────┘  │
│                                                                           │
│                                                                           │
│  F9,Esc-Back    F18-Main Menu                                             │
└───────────────────────────────────────────────────────────────────────────┘
```

Figure 31.18: MARCIVE: Error result

```
┌─COMBINED SEARCH:TITLE-B MINOR MASS,AUTH-BACH,FORMAT-MUS──────────────────┐
│┌TITLE:High mass in B minor.──────────────────────────────────────────────┤
│──────────────────────── CATALOG RECORD DISPLAY ─────────────────────────│
│                                                                          │
│           AUTHOR: Bach, Johann Sebastian, 1685-1758.                     │
│    UNIFORM TITLE: Mass, S.232, B minor.                                  │
│            TITLE: High mass in B minor.                                  │
│ PUBLICATION INFO: New York, Kalmus [n.d.]                                │
│    PHYSICAL DESC: miniature score (219 p.)                               │
│     TITLE SERIES: Kalmus miniature orchestra scores no. 152             │
│          SUBJECT: Masses - To 1800 - Scores.                             │
│ LOCATION/CALL #: UH VTORIA / M2010 .B2 S.232 X3                          │
│                                                                          │
│                                                                          │
│                                                                          │
│                                                                          │
│                                                                          │
│                                                                          │
│                                                                          │
│  ↑↓-Scroll      PgUp,PgDn-Page     ─Previous record      ←Next record    │
│  F1-Help        F6-Save      F7-Print      F9-Back      F18-Main menu     │
└───────────────────────────────────────────────────────────────────────────┘
```

Figure 31.19: MARCIVE: Full display, score

```
┌───────────────────────── MAIN MENU ─────────────────────────────────────┐
│                    MARCIVE / PAC   Version 5.11                          │
│         Copyright (C) 1986-1991 MARCIVE Inc. - All Rights Reserved       │
│                                                                          │
│                    Welcome to the Union Catalog of the                   │
│              Houston Area Research Library Consortium (HARLiC)           │
│        The MAIN MENU is used to select one of several initial menu items.│
│  Use the ↑↓ a┌──────────── EXIT PAC SCREEN ────────────┐e [ENTER] key.   │
│              │                                          │                │
│              │     DO YOU WANT TO EXIT MARCIVE/PAC ?    │                │
│              │     Y - Yes, exit to DOS                 │                │
│              │     N - No, return to MAIN MENU          │                │
│              │                                          │                │
│              └──────────────────────────────────────────┘                │
│                       CALL NUMBER SEARCH                                 │
│                       COMBINED SEARCH                                    │
│                       PRINT FUNCTIONS                                    │
│                       NEWS AND INFORMATION                               │
│                                                                          │
│ ┌Highlighted menu item description:──────────────────────────────────┐   │
│ │  TITLE SEARCH - Search for specified titles or browse all titles.  │   │
│ └────────────────────────────────────────────────────────────────────┘   │
│  Y-Exit  Any other key-Return to MAIN MENU                               │
└───────────────────────────────────────────────────────────────────────────┘
```

Figure 31.20: MARCIVE: Exit prompt

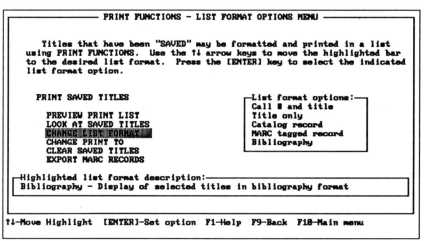

```
┌──────────── PRINT FUNCTIONS - LIST FORMAT OPTIONS MENU ──────────┐
│                                                                  │
│      Titles that have been "SAVED" may be formatted and printed in a list │
│   using PRINT FUNCTIONS. Use the ↑↓ arrow keys to move the highlighted bar │
│   to the desired list format. Press the [ENTER] key to select the indicated │
│   list format option.                                            │
│                                                                  │
│                                       ┌─List format options:─┐   │
│      PRINT SAVED TITLES               │ Call # and title      │   │
│                                       │ Title only            │   │
│         PREVIEW PRINT LIST            │ Catalog record        │   │
│         LOOK AT SAVED TITLES          │ MARC tagged record    │   │
│         CHANGE LIST FORMAT            │ Bibliography          │   │
│         CHANGE PRINT TO               └───────────────────────┘   │
│         CLEAR SAVED TITLES                                        │
│         EXPORT MARC RECORDS                                       │
│                                                                  │
│   ┌─Highlighted list format description:──────────────────────┐   │
│   │ Bibliography - Display of selected titles in bibliography format │ │
│   └────────────────────────────────────────────────────────────┘   │
│                                                                  │
├──────────────────────────────────────────────────────────────────┤
│ ↑↓-Move Highlight  [ENTER]-Set option  F1-Help  F9-Back  F10-Main menu │
└──────────────────────────────────────────────────────────────────┘
```

Figure 31.21: MARCIVE: Print functions menu

```
┌──────────────────────── PRINT DISPLAY ────────────────────────┐
│                                                               │
│ Belfuss, Joan Turner. At the river I stand : Memphis, the 1968 strike, and │
│    Martin Luther King. 1st ed. Memphis : B&W Books, c1985.    │
│    PVAM STACKS HD 5325 .S2572 1968 .M46 1985                  │
│                                                               │
│ Great speeches. [Greenwood, IN] : Educational Video Group, 1985. │
│    UH VTORIA PN6122 .G7 1985                                  │
│                                                               │
│ King, Martin Luther. King, Malcolm, Baldwin : three interviews. Middletown, │
│    Conn. : Wesleyan University Press ; Scranton, Pa. : Distributed by Harper & │
│    Row, 1985.                                                 │
│    HPL CEN-SSC 323.40973 K53                                 │
│    HPL MON-ADU 323.40973 K53                                 │
│    TAMU STX E 185.61 .K533 1985                              │
│    UH ANSTAX E185 .61.K533 1985                              │
│                                                               │
│ Witherspoon, William Roger. Martin Luther King, Jr.—to the mountaintop. │
│    Garden City, N.Y. : Doubleday, 1985.                      │
│    HPL ACR-ADU B K58W                                        │
│    HPL ALI-ADU B K48W                                        │
│                                                               │
├───────────────────────────────────────────────────────────────┤
│ F1-Help F9-Back F10-Main menu ↑↓-Scroll PgUp,PgDn-Page Home-Beginning End │
└───────────────────────────────────────────────────────────────┘
```

Figure 31.22: MARCIVE: Print preview

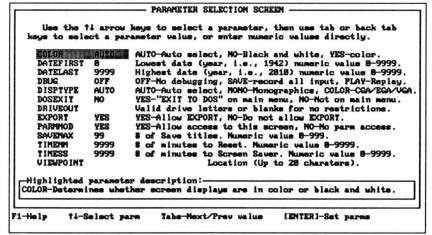

```
┌─────────────── PARAMETER SELECTION SCREEN ───────────────┐
│                                                          │
│     Use the ↑↓ arrow keys to select a parameter, then use tab or back tab │
│   keys to select a parameter value, or enter numeric values directly. │
│                                                          │
│      COLOR      AUTO    AUTO-Auto select, NO-Black and white, YES-color. │
│      DATEFIRST  0       Lowest date (year, i.e., 1942) numeric value 0-9999. │
│      DATELAST   9999    Highest date (year, i.e., 2010) numeric value 0-9999. │
│      DBUG       OFF     OFF-No debugging, SAVE-record all input, PLAY-Replay. │
│      DISPTYPE   AUTO    AUTO-Auto select, MONO-Monographics, COLOR-CGA/EGA/VGA. │
│      DOSEXIT    NO      YES-"EXIT TO DOS" on main menu, NO-Not on main menu. │
│      DRIVEOUT           Valid drive letters or blanks for no restrictions. │
│      EXPORT     YES     YES-Allow EXPORT, NO-Do not allow EXPORT. │
│      PARMMOD    YES     YES-Allow access to this screen, NO-No parm access. │
│      SAVEMAX    99      # of Save titles. Numeric value 0-999. │
│      TIMEMM     9999    # of minutes to Reset. Numeric value 0-9999. │
│      TIMESS     9999    # of minutes to Screen Saver. Numeric value 0-9999. │
│      VIEWPOINT          Location (Up to 20 charaters). │
│                                                          │
│   ┌─Highlighted parameter description:──────────────────┐ │
│   │ COLOR-Determines whether screen displays are in color or black and white. │ │
│   └──────────────────────────────────────────────────────┘ │
│                                                          │
├──────────────────────────────────────────────────────────┤
│ F1-Help    ↑↓-Select parm   Tabs-Next/Prev value   [ENTER]-Set parms │
└──────────────────────────────────────────────────────────┘
```

Figure 31.23: MARCIVE: Parameter selection screen

32

Marquis

Crickett Goodsell Willardsen

Based on a standards-compliant, state-of-the-art processing database, the Marquis Public Access Catalog (PAC) provides a unique graphical interface. Because it runs on a network with database servers, PAC is scalable from a few workstations to several thousand. Marquis PAC accepts, edits, and outputs MARC bibliographic and authority records, including diacritics. It is compatible with bibliographic record services, book jobbers, and other automation systems that output MARC records.

User Interface

With either a mouse or keyboard options, users work with the Marquis PAC system graphically. Graphical tools include pull-down menus and screen "buttons" that users activate either by pointing and clicking with a mouse or by pressing designated keys. Likewise, users can point and click or press keys to single or multiselect items from lists during a search procedure.

Search Process Flow

PAC meets users' objectives—from finding one or more call numbers to compiling lists of titles, authors or subjects—by providing a simple and efficient self-directed path into successful, effective use of the searching system. Each of the following sections explains specific features and functions that PAC provides on its online catalog system.

Beginning in the **Search Options** window, users can conduct a variety of searches to locate library materials. Options include alphabetical searches and keyword searches as well as library-definable searches such as by LCCN, ISSN, ISBN and call number. PAC allows author, title, subject, and series alphabetical searches for which users need not enter a full heading or derived search keys. In alphabetical searches, PAC always matches the search term or terms with the nearest possible entry in the database. Should nothing in the database exactly match the terms, PAC displays entries in the alphabetical neighborhood of the search terms.

Keyword searches are also available by title and subject. Libraries have the option to build keyword indexes for terms that are in more than one field in a bibliographic record. For example, a library can configure the title keyword search so that PAC checks not only the titles but the contents notes for the keywords. To further enhance keyword searches, users can enter multiple terms, truncation symbols and Boolean operators in a search string to broaden or narrow the number of entries found.

From the opening **Search Options** window, PAC progresses through a series of main windows. As users progress through the search windows, PAC displays successive windows so that the title bars of each can be seen. For example, with the **Search Options** window placed in the upper left corner, PAC displays successive windows cascaded down the depth of the title bar plus a little to the right. The subsequently nested windows show users both the path and the original search terms (displayed in each title bar) that led to a given point in the process. Users can back up to various points in the search process by selecting the title bar of a previous window and thereby redirect the search from an intermediate point toward a new direction.

Search Results

The search process leads users to the window that displays the bibliographic information for one or more entries that have been selected from a prior list window. Because PAC offers multiselection capability, users can select more than one item, then view the bibliographic detail of each item by paging forward and backward through the items in a manner similar to a Rolodex file. Although libraries can define what bibliographic detail is displayed, common fields include title, author, subjects, contents, and description.

From the bibliographic display, PAC provides the option to view holdings information for an item. To do so, users proceed to the **Copies** window where PAC displays information such as status, location, call number, and item type. Libraries define the information PAC displays for items.

New Searches

At any point during the search process, users can return to the browsing mode or the search mode. PAC allows users to reopen the **Search Options** window on top of the existing search without closing the existing search windows. Only when users enter a new search string and initiate a new search process does PAC close the previous search windows. However, users can display a list of all previous search strings used in PAC since it was brought up, and from this list select a previous search string to reactivate that particular search process.

Screen Labels

PAC can tailor the appearance and contents displayed in each window to fit the needs of individual libraries. Display options include defining the names and types of search options users encounter

in the opening **Search Options** window and defining the bibliographic and holdings display information PAC provides for items. If desired, libraries can periodically reconfigure existing displays to add to or rename aspects.

Additional Features

Below are brief descriptions of other features that PAC provides to facilitate quick, efficient searches of the library database.

Multiselection Capability

Marquis provides multiselection capability of items in lists through several means:

- list boxes
- multiselection entry boxes in which users can type one or more numbers that correspond with the desired items on the list
- the Select All command option, which highlights and selects all entries in the list
- the Show Selection command option. which displays only those items that users have selected

Bookmarking

Users can use the Bookmarking feature to select bibliographies or item information for later reference or for printing.

Saving to File

Users can save bookmarked information to a specified disk file.

Printing

This feature enables users to print a hard copy of the items shown on a PAC window.

Displaying and Sorting Lists

Users can activate the Display feature to specify the precise bibliographic information (such as title, author, call number and location) that PAC not only displays on the screen but saves or prints.

The Sort feature designates a primary and, if necessary, a secondary category by which PAC orders and displays the list of items on the screen. These categories can include title, author, publication date, call number, and copy location—categories that, like other screen labels, are defined by the individual library.

Search Limiting on Bibliographic Lists

This feature provides additional means for narrowing a search. Once PAC has found and displayed all hits that match the initial search entry, users can activate the Search Limiting feature and search the initial list for only those entries that contain, are equal to, greater than or less than an indexed value such as author, physical description, and edition, among others.

Placing Hold Requests

While searching in PAC, users can select an item and place a hold request on that item.

New Authority Additions

This feature lists new titles, subjects, and authors that have been cataloged in the library database since a library-specified date.

PAC Interaction with Other Marquis Library Systems

Although the other Marquis library systems—cataloging, circulation, acquisitions, and serials—are restricted to library staff use only, librarians can access PAC from any of these systems in order to facilitate tasks in the other systems.

This interaction among the Marquis systems enables libraries to maintain up-to-date files and efficient services for public users. Among the variety of services, Marquis automatically updates the display in PAC lists of cross-references made in cataloging, updates holdings displays in PAC to reflect circulation activities, newly cataloged items and newly-acquired serials, and connects librarians to the list of hold requests users place in PAC which can then be processed in the circulation system.

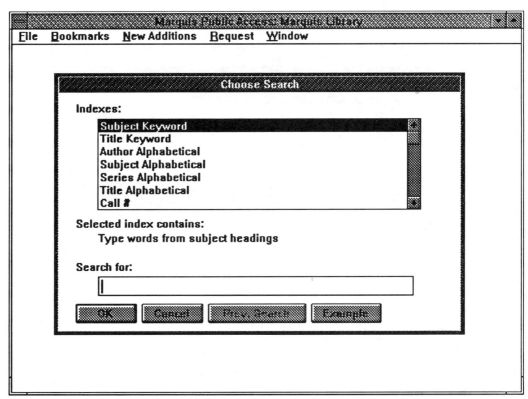

Figure 32.1: Marquis: Opening search screen

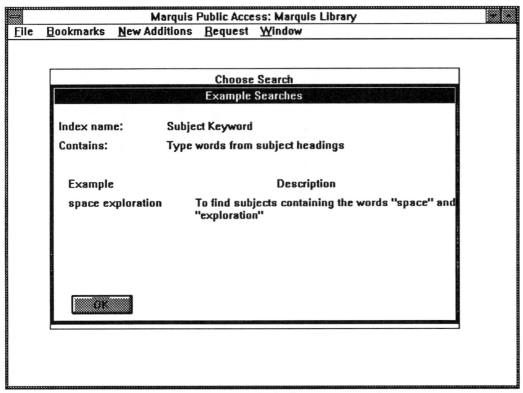

Figure 32.2: Marquis: Help for opening search

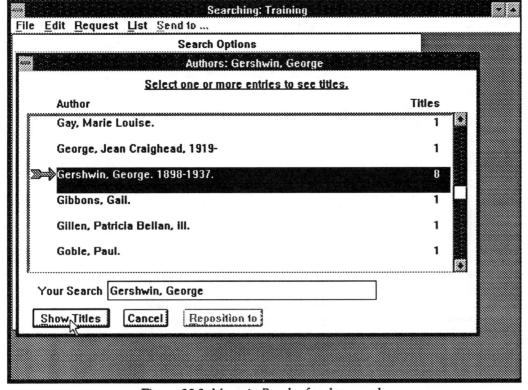

Figure 32.3: Marquis: Result of author search

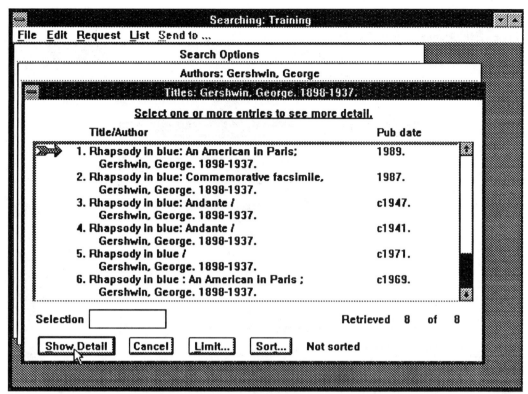

Figure 32.4: Marquis: Titles from author search

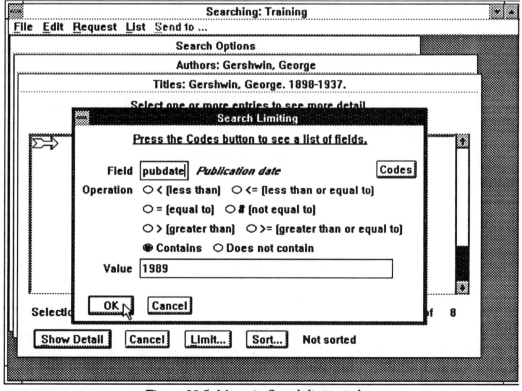

Figure 32.5: Marquis: Search limit window

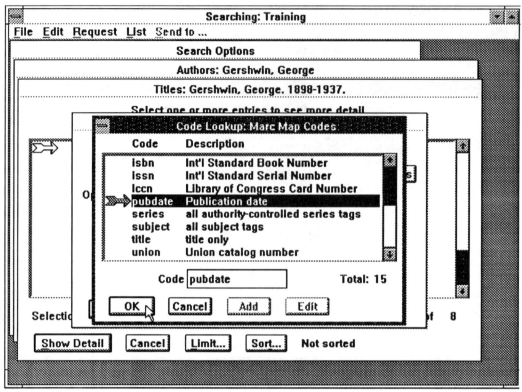

Figure 32.6: Marquis: Code lookup for limits

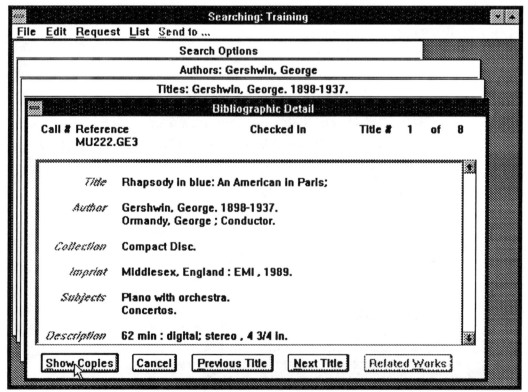

Figure 32.7: Marquis: Display, recording

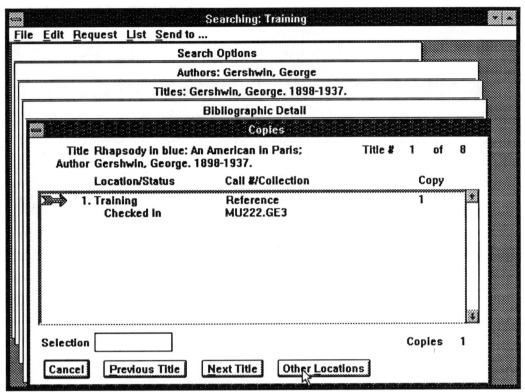

Figure 32.8: Marquis: Holdings display, recording

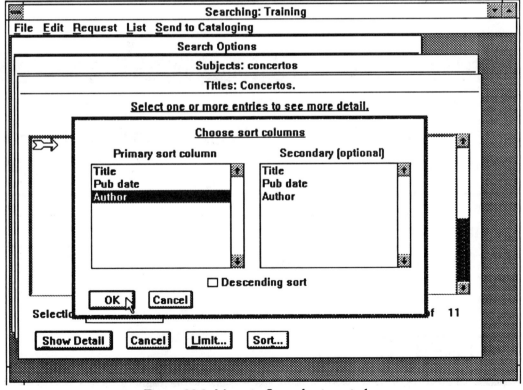

Figure 32.9: Marquis: Sort selection window

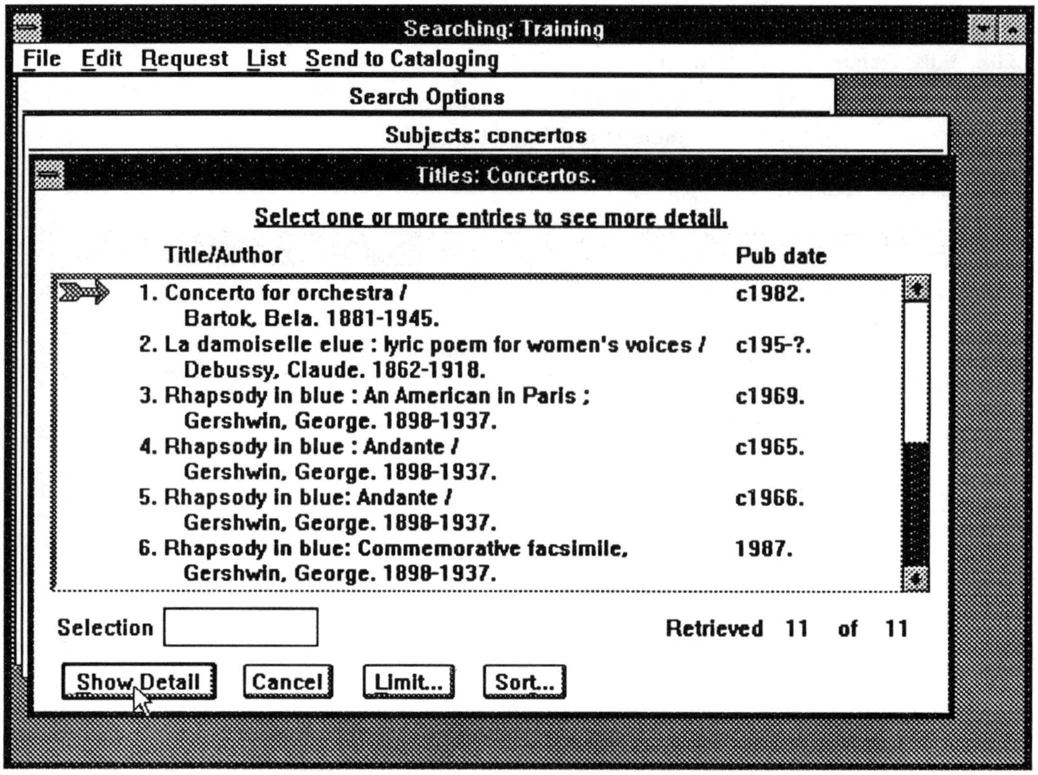

Figure 32.10: Marquis: Titles by author

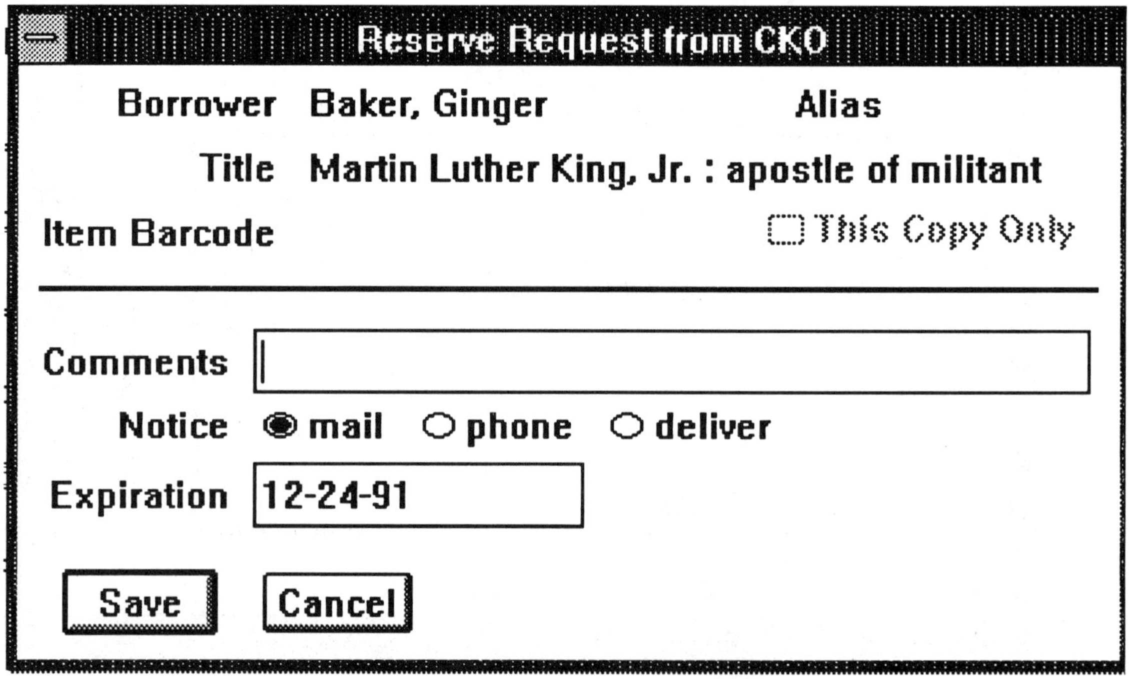

Figure 32.11: Marquis: Hold request

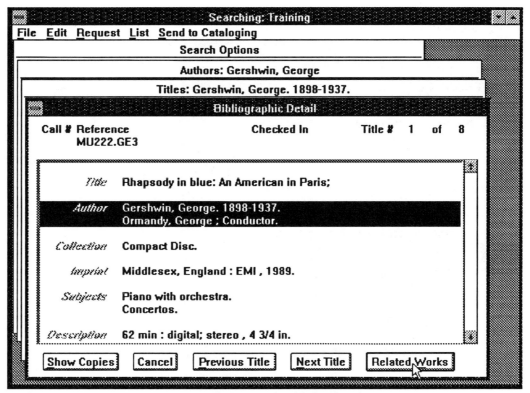

Figure 32.12: Marquis: Highlighted authors

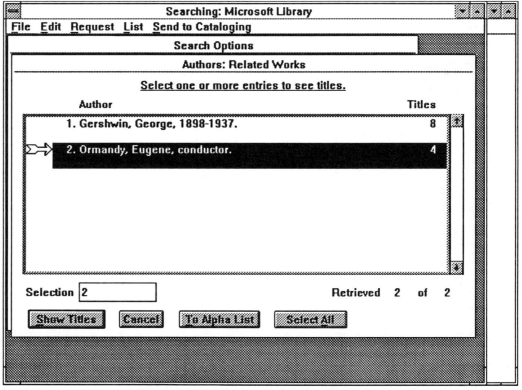

Figure 32.13: Marquis: Related works, author

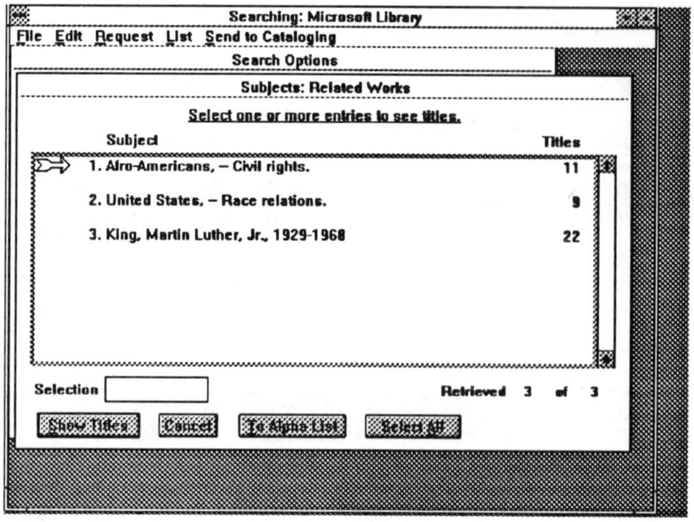

Figure 32.14: Marquis: Related works, subjects

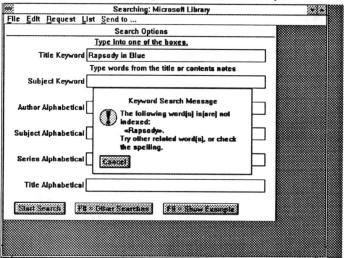

Figure 32.15: Marquis: Result of spelling error

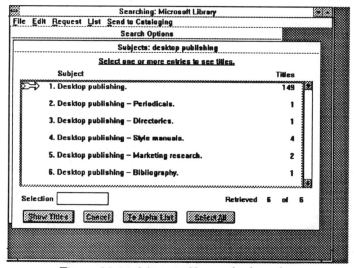

Figure 32.16: Marquis: Keyword subject list

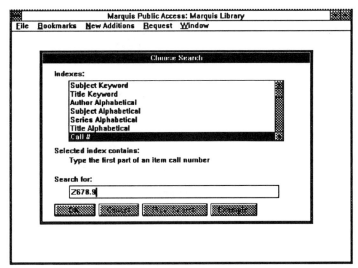

Figure 32.17: Marquis: Initiating call # browse

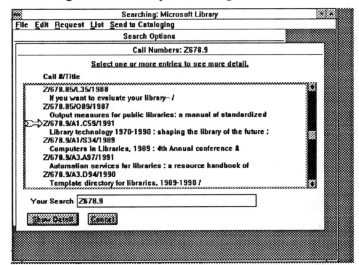

Figure 32.18: Marquis: Call # browse

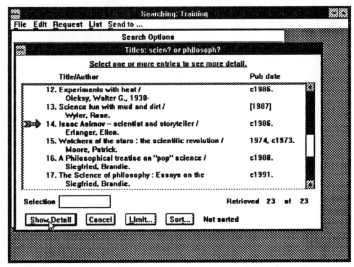

Figure 32.19: Marquis: Truncation and Boolean OR

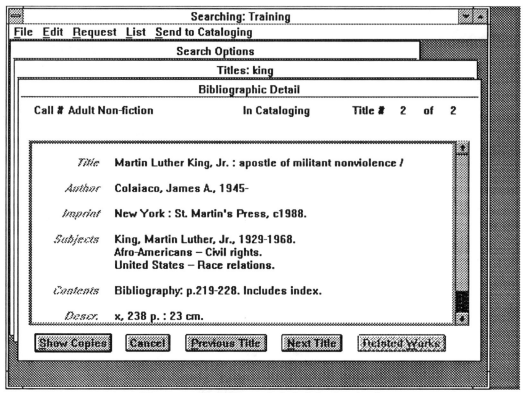

Figure 32.20: Marquis: Labeled display, book

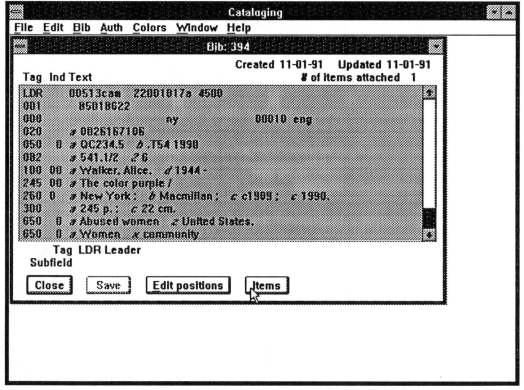

Figure 32.21: Marquis: Tagged MARC display

33

The MELVYL® System
University of California

Genevieve Engel

The MELVYL®[1] system can be used from library terminals at any University of California campus; it is also widely used through campus dial-up connections and through the Internet.

You can reach the system through the Internet using TELNET, for example: TELNET MELVYL.UCOP.EDU or TELNET 31.0.0.13. Once you connect to the system, you will be asked for your terminal type. Enter ? for a list of available types. After entering your terminal type, you will see a message asking you to press Return. This message is also what you will see if you end your session, either by typing "logoff" or "end" or by not typing any commands for ten or twelve minutes so that your session times out.

After you press Return, the MELVYL system welcome screen appears[2] (Figure 33.1). At the welcome screen, you can:

- press Return for a list of databases available (Figure 33.2)
- type "help" (Figure 33.4)
- type any other command

The database menu in Figure 33.2 is also the screen you will see if you type "start" to begin a new session. You can type "start" at any time. If you are using the MELVYL system from a terminal in the University of California libraries, you may find that the previous user's search is still on the screen. Type "start" when you begin a MELVYL session at a library terminal and you will clear any search results or changed settings left by the previous user of that terminal.

From the database menu, you can select TEN, CAT, or PE. The article citation databases listed in the menu are available only to University of California faculty, staff, and students and require passwords for remote access. You can also select OTHER or press Return to see the list of other catalogs and databases accessible through the MELVYL system (Figure 33.3 shows some of them).

You can select any of these systems. The MELVYL system will not require you to enter a password in order to use these systems, but some of the systems have their own password or account requirements. These are marked "account required" in Figure 33.3.

Help and Explain

At any time you can type "help" for information on how to proceed. You can shorten help to "H."

---

1 MELVYL is a registered trademark of the Regents of the University of California.

2 MELVYL system screens copyright 1984, Regents of the University of California.

If you type "help" (or "H") at the MELVYL system welcome screen, you will see Figure 33.4.

You can also type any command at any time. If you type a command at the welcome screen before you have selected a database, you will automatically be in the full catalog (CAT) database. If you select a database, such as TEN, a welcome screen for that database appears (Figure 33.5).

Once you are in a database, you can type "exp guide" for a basic guide to searching the database and displaying search results. Figure 33.6 is the Exp Guide screen for the Ten-Year Catalog (TEN) database.

"Exp" is short for Explain. You can type an "explain" command at any time. Explain Glossary (or Exp Glossary) will list the topics for which Explain information is available.

Search Modes

In the full Catalog (CAT) and the Ten-Year Catalog (TEN) databases, you have a choice of command mode or lookup mode for conducting your search. In the Periodicals (PE) database, only command mode is available. If you will be using the MELVYL system very seldom and you only want to search for monographs, you can select Lookup from the welcome screen for the CAT or TEN database. If you wish to be able to see news and Explain screens, search for periodicals, or limit searches by date, language, form of material, or other limits, you will need to use command mode. Select Command from the database welcome screen, or simply type any command and you will automatically be in command mode.

Searches and Displays

To search for the CD version of George Gershwin's *Rhapsody in Blue*, you can select the TEN database, which contains all the same records as the CAT database for items published in the last ten years. Type a "find" command to do a search (Figure 33.7), then a "display" command to see the search results (Figure 33.8). If you type "display" without specifying a display option, you will see the Short display shown in Figure 33.8.

You can also type "display long" to see the Long display as in Figure 33.9 (the first of three

screens). "Display review" will show the Review display, as in Figure 33.10.

To see specific fields within a record retrieved by your search, type "display" and the field names or abbreviations. For example, "display ti su" displays the title and subject fields (Figure 33.11).

To see a tagged MARC display, type "display marc" (Figure 33.12, first of three screens). To see individual MARC-tagged fields, use the TAGS display and specify which field numbers you want. For example, "display tags 245" displays the 245 field (Figure 33.13).

You can enter a new search at any time, without having to return to the welcome screen (Figure 33.14). You can display records any time you have a search result (Figure 33.15).

Locations

If you do not restrict your result to a specific location, you will get call numbers for all the locations that have the item (Figure 33.16). To see only the records for a specific location, with only the call numbers for that location, use the AT command. For example, typing "at ucb" would restrict your current search (FIND PA KING, MARTIN LUTHER in this case) to items held at the University of California, Berkeley (Figure 33.17).

Errors

Whenever the system can recognize the probable reason for a command it cannot perform, it displays an appropriate message. If it cannot recognize your command at all, for example FID instead of FIND, it will say so ("A MELVYL command cannot begin with FID"). Help is available for all the error conditions the system can detect. When displaying your search results, you can specify record numbers if you only want to see some of the records retrieved. For example, Display 5 shows only record 5; Display 5-10 shows records 5 through 10; Display 2, 3, 4 shows records 2, 3, and 4. If you specify a record number that is higher than the total number of records in your search result (for example, Display 12 when you only have ten records to display), the result will be as in Figure 33.18.

Should you make a spelling error (such as "rapsody" instead of "rhapsody") in your search, the search will proceed as usual, but will probably not retrieve any results, as in Figure 33.19. If you type "help" at this point, a screen suggests checking your search for typing errors (Figure 33.20).

You can edit the words in your search using the Modify command in order to issue a corrected command without retyping the entire search. Type "explain modify" for information.

Boolean Searching

You can combine search words or search indexes using the Boolean operators AND, OR, or AND NOT. Any words or indexes can be combined, for example "find tw floriculture and date current." When you search using an exact index, such as exact subject (XS), every word (including AND, OR, and AND NOT) is treated as part of your search, unless the word is followed by a valid index name. To use Booleans in an exact search, follow each Boolean operator with an index name (Figure 33.21).

Approximate and Known-Item Searching

Use keyword indexes such as title word (TW) and subject (SU) when you are not sure of an exact title or subject heading. To find a book with a title like *Fire on the Moon*, try the search in Figure 33.22.

The words "on" and "the" are ignored in TW searches, so they have been left out of this search command (type "explain stopwords" for information on words ignored in certain indexes). Type "display review" for a quick list of the titles retrieved (Figure 33.23).

If you know the exact title of a work, use the exact title (XT) index in your search. For example, to find *Vineland* by Thomas Pynchon, type "find xt vineland and pa pynchon, thomas." Since only one record is retrieved with this search, it displays automatically without your having to type "display" (Figure 33.24). The automatic display is Short; to see a Long display, you must type "display long."

Browsing

You can use the Browse command to search for headings, rather than for individual records. For example, for a list of all the authors named Pynchon whose works are in the catalog, type "browse pa pynchon." The result screen in Figure 33.25 will display. You do not have to type a "display" command in order to display Browse results.

You can then use any of these names in a personal author (PA) search, or you can use the Select command to search directly from the list of headings, as in Figure 33.26.

Leaving MELVYL

At any time you may end your session on the MELVYL system by typing "end" or "logoff." You will be returned to the message asking you to press Return for the MELVYL catalog. Type "logoff" again to disconnect from the system.

Special Features

In addition to basic indexes for author, subject, title, and periodical-title searching, the MELVYL system includes indexes to search by several number indexes such as ISBN; specialized indexes for music searching, as mentioned above; and indexes to search or limit by date of publication, date an item was added to the catalog, language, and form of materials such as computer file or video. The command "explain indexes" shows the screens in Figures 33.27 and 33.28.

These indexes can be used with the find command in the CAT and TEN databases only. Only some of the indexes are used with the browse command. The ACFIND command mentioned in Figure 33.28 is similar to browse in that it retrieves headings rather than individual records, but it also retrieves authority information such as whether a heading is an AACR2 heading. You cannot select individual records from an ACFIND result as you can with a browse result.

Changing Databases

The PE database uses a separate set of indexes, but the same find and display commands as in the

CAT and TEN databases. To move to the PE database, type "start pe" or "set db pe" at any time. You can then type "explain indexes" for a list of indexes you can use in the PE database. The PE database contains journal titles and call numbers, along with other information about a journal.

The PE database does not contain article citations. Some articles are cataloged in the TEN and CAT databases as "in-analytics" (Figure 33.29).

You can switch from database to database at any time using a "start" or "set db" command. For example, "start cat" brings you to the welcome screen for the catalog database.

The difference between "start" and "set db" is that "start" clears all existing search results and session settings; "set db" does not. If you type "set db cat", you will see a message telling you that you are now in the catalog database; you will not get the catalog database welcome screen.

Changing Modes

You can also switch from command mode to lookup mode and back at any time within the CAT or TEN database by typing "set mode command" or "set mode lookup." You can type "start cat lookup," "start cat command," "start ten lookup," or "start ten command" to clear your searches and settings and start a new session in the database and mode you have specified.

SET and SHOW

The "set" command can be used to change settings such as the date or language of publication. For example, normally all dates in the database are searched; if you wish to restrict all your searches to current dates (in the last three years), you can "set date current." "Explain set" yields two screens, the first of which is shown in Figure 33.30.

To see your current settings at any time, type "show settings."

The show command can be used to see specific settings, for example, "show date" shows you the current date setting. It can also be used to see other information such as news, campus library locations, statistics, and publications you can read online. Figure 33.31 shows the first of three Explain Show screens.

Printing and Downloading

To print or download your search results, use the display command. You can print using a printer attached to your terminal, personal computer, or workstation; set the printer to capture whatever data is sent to your terminal, then issue the display command and the printer will print your search result. Normally, you must press Return at the end of each screen of search results before the next screen is displayed; for printing, you will probably want to use the print or continuous display option to print results continuously on successive pages. "Display print" causes results to be printed continuously with a page break appropriate for paper 11 inches long; "display continuous" prints continuously with no page breaks.

Basic downloading instructions as well as specific instructions for users of UNIX and several microcomputer communications software packages can be seen by typing "show downloading." As with printing, the downloading process consists of setting your system to accept results, then displaying your search results.

Save

Especially helpful when printing or downloading results is the Save command. The Save command puts the records you select into a list which can be displayed later. While you are looking at the results of a search, save the retrievals that you want to print or download by typing "save" and the record number shown at the beginning of the record you want to save, for example, "save 5." You can continue displaying records and saving only those you wish to print or download; additional saved records will be added to your list. You can save records from different searches and even from different databases, and they will be added to the same list. When you have saved all the records you want to print or download, begin the printing or downloading procedure, but type "display list" instead of "display" to capture only the records in the list. The display will look like Figure 33.32.

Related to the save command is the "save set" command, which saves entire search results rather than individual records. Saving sets is especially useful if you have a complicated search and you wish to limit it by another complicated search, or to limit it successively with several separate Boolean operations. For information on sets, type "explain sets."

Comment Command

Your comments and questions on the system are welcome. At any time you can type a "comment" command to send a comment. Send long comments as several comment commands, each about a line long. Figure 33.33 shows a comment being sent to us in two comment commands.

Production note: Some blank portions at the bottoms of screens have been edited out to save space. In each such case, the caption ends with "(edited)."

```
                    Welcome to the University of California's

                           MELVYL* LIBRARY SYSTEM


    ──────────────────── =>> SYSTEM NEWS <<= ────────────────────
         The MELVYL system will be unavailable Sunday morning, August 18
                from midnight to 10 a.m. for system software maintenance.
    ─────────────────────────────────────────────────────────────────────

(c)1984. *Registered trademark of The Regents of the University of California.
================================================================================
OPTIONS:  Choose an option, or type any command to enter the CATALOG database.

   HELP          - For help in getting started.

   [return]      - Press RETURN to choose a database for searching.

   START <db>    - Type START <database name> to begin searching in a database.
->
```

Figure 33.1: the MELVYL system: Welcome screen

```
                         MELVYL SYSTEM DATABASES
                     Select one database from the list below.

Library Databases:

        TEN      For faster searches, type TEN;
                 Ten-Year MELVYL Catalog - materials published from 1981 - 1991.
        CAT      Full MELVYL Catalog - UC libraries and California State Library.
        PE       Periodical Titles - Calif. Academic Libraries List of Serials.

Journal Article Indexes:

        CC       CURRENT CONTENTS - current articles in all subject areas.
        CCT      CURRENT CONTENTS - journal tables of contents in all subjects.
        MED      MELVYL MEDLINE   - articles in medical and life sciences.

Other Systems:
        OTHER    To select other library catalogs and remote information systems.

Shortcut: type any command to enter the CAT database (e.g., FIND or EXPLAIN)
────────────────────────────────────────────────────────────────────────────────
Type the code for one option (e.g., TEN), HELP, or END to end your session.

->
```

Figure 33.2: MELVYL: Database menu

```
OTHER LIBRARY CATALOGS:
These systems may be reached via the MELVYL system but are not part of it.

BOSTON     Boston University                PRINCETON  Princeton University
CARL       Colorado Alliance of Research Libs.  PSU    Penn State University
CMU        Carnegie Mellon University       RPI        Rensselaer Polytech.
DARTMOUTH  Dartmouth College                STANFORD   Stanford University
GLADIS     UC Berkeley                      UDEL       Univ. of Delaware
LIBROS     Univ. of New Mexico General Library  UMD    Univ. of Maryland
NASA       NASA Online Data & Info. Service  UTENN     Univ. of Tennessee
OCEAN      OCEAN Information Center          VATECH     Virginia Tech

ORION      UC Los Angeles  (account required)
EPIC       OCLC, Inc.  (account required)
RLIN       Research Libraries Group  (account required)
_____
OPTIONS:     Choose one option, type HELP, or END to end your session.

             - Type the code for one option (eg., CARL).
             - Press RETURN for more systems.


->
```

Figure 33.3: MELVYL: Other Catalogs (partial)

```
The options for proceeding are:

[return]       - Press RETURN to see the list of MELVYL system databases.  You
                 may then choose a database to search.

START <db>     - If you already know the name of the database you want to
                 search, type START and the database name, eg., START CC.

Any command    - By typing any other valid command, eg., FIND or EXPLAIN, you
                 will enter the CATALOG database.

===========================================================================
OPTIONS:       Choose one option.

  [return]     - Press RETURN to choose a database for searching.

  START <db>   - Type START <database name> to begin searching in a database.

  END          - Type END to end your session.

Or type any command.

->
```

Figure 33.4: MELVYL: Help at welcome screen

```
              Welcome to the MELVYL TEN-YEAR Catalog Database

Contents:    As of 8/16/91, approximately 1,569,116 titles representing
             3,558,500 holdings for materials in the University of
             California libraries, and the California State Library,

Coverage:    Publication dates 1981 through 1991.

                        —=>> NEWS <<=—

             New Exact Other Title index.  Type SHOW EXP46.
UCLA's COLLEGE Library now an option for AT and SET LIBRARY.  Type SHOW NEWS.
_____
OPTIONS:     Type an option and press RETURN, or type any command.

  HELP       - For help in getting started.

  COMMAND    - To use commands and for periodicals; request help any time.
  LOOKUP     - For Lookup Mode—the system leads you through commands.

  START      - To start over or change databases.
  END        - To end your session.
TEN->
```

Figure 33.5: MELVYL: Ten-Year welcome screen

```
GUIDE to searching the MELVYL TEN-YEAR Catalog database:

— Use the FIND command to search for book and periodicals records.  The
   primary indexes for books include:  PA (personal author), CA (corporate
   author), TW (title words), XT (exact title), SU (subject), and XS (exact
   subject).  The main indexes for periodicals are PE (periodical title) and
   XPE (exact periodical title).  For example:

   FIND CA CALIFORNIA HISTORICAL SOCIETY          FIND PA WALKER, ALICE
   FIND SU BACTERIAL GENETICS                     FIND XPE NEWSWEEK

— Use the DISPLAY command to display the records that result from your FIND
   command.  Type DISPLAY (or D) for a short display with author, title, and
   call number.  You can also use LONG, SHORT, or REVIEW options.  For example:

   DISPLAY                 DISPLAY LONG                 D REVIEW

— Type HELP at any time to receive assistance.

— Use an EXPLAIN command at any time to receive an explanation.  For example:

   EXPLAIN FIND      EXPLAIN DISPLAY      EXPLAIN INDEXES      EXPLAIN COMMANDS
TEN->
```

Figure 33.6: MELVYL: Guide screen (Ten–Year)

```
TEN-> find pa george gershwin and tw rhapsody in blue and form cd

   Search request: FIND PA GEORGE GERSHWIN AND TW RHAPSODY IN BLUE AND FORM CD
   Search result:  16 records in the TEN-YEAR Catalog database

   Type D to display results, or type HELP.

TEN->
```

Figure 33.7: MELVYL: Multi–index search

```
TEN-> display
Search request: FIND PA GEORGE GERSHWIN AND TW RHAPSODY IN BLUE AND FORM CD
Search result:  16 records in the TEN-YEAR Catalog database

Type HELP for other display options.

1. SOUND RECORDING
   The Birth of Rhapsody in blue : Paul Whiteman's historic Aeolian Hall
   Concert of 1924 / Reconstructed & conducted by Maurice Peress.  [Ocean,
   N.J.] : Musical Heritage Society, p1987.
      2 sound discs (80 min.) : digital, stereo. ; 4 3/4 in.
      UCR   Music Lib 278 Compact Disc

2. SOUND RECORDING
   Gershwin, George, 1898-1937.
      [Rhapsody in blue.]
      George Gershwin plays Rhapsody in blue : [using the original piano rolls]
   / George Gershwin.  Minneapolis, Minn. : ProArte, p1987.
      1 sound disc (61 min.) : digital, stereo. ; 4 3/4 in.
      Series title:  American artists series.
      UCSD  Central   MU 26017 Music Recording


Press RETURN to see the next screen.
TEN->
```

Figure 33.8: MELVYL: Short display

```
Search request: FIND PA GEORGE GERSHWIN AND TW RHAPSODY IN BLUE AND FORM CD
Search result:  16 records in the TEN-YEAR Catalog database

Type HELP for other display options.

5. SOUND RECORDING

Author:         Gershwin, George, 1898-1937.
Uniform title: Instrumental music. Selections.
Title:          Rhapsody in blue = Rhapsodie en bleu ; An American in Paris = Un
                   Americain a Paris ; Broadway overtures / George Gershwin. [New
                   York, N.Y.] : CBS Masterworks, [1988]
Description:    1 sound disc : digital ; 4 3/4 in.

Publisher No.: MK 42240 CBS Masterworks

Notes:          Overtures arranged by Don Rose.
                "Consists of previously released material."
                Compact disc.
                Durations: 13:41 ; 18:32 ; 38:39.
                Program notes in English, German and French (22 p.) in
                                          (Record 5 continues on the next screen.)
Press RETURN to see the next screen.
TEN->
```

Figure 33.9: MELVYL: Long display, recording (partial)

```
Search request: FIND PA GEORGE GERSHWIN AND TW RHAPSODY IN BLUE AND FORM CD
Search result:  16 records in the TEN-YEAR Catalog database

Type HELP for other display options.

  5. GERSHWIN, George, 1898-1937.
      [Instrumental music. Selections.] CBS Masterworks, 1988. SOUND RECORDING

TEN->
```

Figure 33.10: MELVYL: Review display, recording (edited)

```
Search request: FIND PA GEORGE GERSHWIN AND TW RHAPSODY IN BLUE AND FORM CD
Search result:  16 records in the TEN-YEAR Catalog database

Type HELP for other display options.

5. SOUND RECORDING
Title:          Rhapsody in blue = Rhapsodie en bleu ; An American in Paris =
                   Un Americain a Paris ; Broadway overtures / George
                   Gershwin.
Subjects:       Piano with jazz ensemble.
                Symphonic poems.
                Overtures, Arranged.
                Musical comedies — Excerpts, Arranged.

TEN->
```

Figure 33.11: MELVYL: Fields display (edited)

```
Search request: FIND PA GEORGE GERSHWIN AND TW RHAPSODY IN BLUE AND FORM CD
Search result:  16 records in the TEN-YEAR Catalog database

Type HELP for other display options.

5.       ID 13585   BASE   SB      STS n   REC jm  ENC       DCF a    ENT 900514
         INT        REP    GOV     CNF     FSC     INX       CTY nyu  ILS mu
         MEI 1      FIC    BIO     MOD     CSC d   CON hi    LAN      PD 1988
007      sd_fzngnnmmned  <SB>
028 01   MK 42240 $b CBS Masterworks  <SB>
040      DLC $c DLC $d CStcl $d NhD $d CU-SB  <SB>
041 0    $g enggerfre  <SB>
100 10   Gershwin, George, $d 1898-1937  <SB>
240 10   Instrumental music. $k Selections  <SB>
245 10   Rhapsody in blue = $b Rhapsodie en bleu ; An American in Paris = Un
         Am_ericain _a Paris ; Broadway overtures $h [sound recording] / $c
         George Gershwin.  <SB>
260 0    [New York, N.Y.] : $b CBS Masterworks, $c [1988]  <SB>
300      1 sound disc : $b digital ; $c 4 3/4 in.  <SB>
500      Overtures arranged by Don Rose.  <SB>
500      "Consists of previously released material."  <SB>
                                        (Record 5 continues on the next screen.)
Press RETURN to see the next screen.
TEN->
```

Figure 33.12: MELVYL: MARC display, recording (partial)

```
Search request: F PA GEORGE GERSHWIN AND TW RHAPSODY IN BLUE AND FORM CD
Search result:  16 records in the TEN-YEAR Catalog database

Type HELP for other display options.

5.
245 10   Rhapsody in blue = $b Rhapsodie en bleu ; An American in Paris = Un
         Am_ericain _a Paris ; Broadway overtures $h [sound recording] / $c
         George Gershwin.  <SB>

TEN->
```

Figure 33.13: MELVYL: Selective MARC field display (edited)

```
TEN-> find pa king, martin luther

   Search request: FIND PA KING, MARTIN LUTHER
   Search result:  34 records in the TEN-YEAR Catalog database

   Type D to display results, or type HELP.

TEN->
```

Figure 33.14: MELVYL: Personal-author search

```
TEN-> display 5 long
Search request: FIND PA KING, MARTIN LUTHER
Search result:  34 records in the TEN-YEAR Catalog database

Type HELP for other display options.

5. VIDEORECORDING

Title:        King, I have a dream. Oak Forest, IL : MPI Home Video, [c1986]
Description:  1 videocassette (VHS) (28 min.) : sd., col., b&w ; 1/2 in.

Stock No.:    MP 1350 MPI Home Video

Notes:        Consists chiefly of the speech of Rev. Martin Luther King, Jr.
                 delivered at the Lincoln Memorial, Washington, D.C. on August
                 28, 1963.
              Title from label on cassette.
              "MP 1350".

Subjects:     King, Martin Luther, Jr., 1929-1968.
              Afro-Americans — Civil rights.
              Baptists — United States — Clergy — Biography.
                                        (Record 5 continues on the next screen.)
Press RETURN to see the next screen.
TEN->
```

Figure 33.15: MELVYL: Long display, video (partial)

```
Search request: FIND PA KING, MARTIN LUTHER
Search result:  34 records in the TEN-YEAR Catalog database

Type HELP for other display options.

18. King, Martin Luther, Jr., 1929-1968.
        A testament of hope : the essential writings of Martin Luther King, Jr. /
    edited by James Melvin Washington.  1st ed.  San Francisco : Harper & Row,
    c1986.
            UCB   Main       E185.97.K5 A251 1986
            UCB   Moffitt    E185.97.K5 A25 1986
            UCD   Law Lib    E185.97.K5 A25 1986
            UCD   Main Lib   E185.97.K5 A25 1986
            UCI   Main Lib   E185.97.K5 A25 1986
            UCLA  College    E 185.97 K5 A25 1986
            UCLA  Spec Coll  E 185.97 K5A25 1986
            UCLA  URL        E 185.97 K5A25 1986
            UCR   Rivera     E185.97.K5 A24 1986
            UCSB  Library    E185.97.K5 A25 1986 Also in Black Studies
            UCSB  Library    E185.97.K5 A25 1986 Black Studies Also in Main
            UCSC  McHenry    E185.97.K5 A25 1986
                                    (Record 18 continues on the next screen.)
Press RETURN to see the next screen.
TEN->
```

Figure 33.16: MELVYL: Multiple locations, call#s

```
TEN-> at ucb

   Search request: FIND PA KING, MARTIN LUTHER
   Search result:  9 records at Berkeley or NRLF
                   34 records in the TEN-YEAR Catalog database

   Type D to display results, or type HELP.

TEN->
```

Figure 33.17: MELVYL: Search limit by location

```
display 12

   A DISPLAY command may not include record numbers larger than
   the number of records retrieved.
   Type HELP for more information.

TEN->
```

Figure 33.18: MELVYL: Range error message

```
TEN-> find tw rapsody in blue

   Search request: FIND TW RAPSODY IN BLUE
   Search result:  0 records in the TEN-YEAR Catalog database

   Please type HELP for information on zero search results.

TEN->
```

Figure 33.19: MELVYL: Spelling-error result

```
Your title word search request,
      FIND TW RAPSODY IN BLUE
did not result in any retrievals at all libraries.

Suggestions:

* Check your search request for typing errors.

* Try your search again using only two or three of the most significant
  words in the title.  If you are not sure how to spell a word, leave it out.
  Restricting your search to a few less common title words improves your
  chances of retrieving a book when you do not know the title exactly.

* Truncate search words to pick up spelling variations and related word
  endings.

Or type SET DB CAT to leave the TEN-YEAR database and try your search in
the full CATALOG database.

For more information, type:   EXPLAIN KEYWORDS      EXPLAIN TRUNCATION

TEN->
```

Figure 33.20: MELVYL: Zero–result help

```
TEN-> find xs rural development ecuador or xs rural development colombia

    Search request: FIND XS RURAL DEVELOPMENT ECUADOR # OR XS RURAL DEVELOPMENT
                    COLOMBIA #
    Search result:  33 records in the TEN-YEAR Catalog database

    Type D to display; SHOW SEARCH for other results available for DISPLAY.

TEN-> or xs rural development brazil

    Search request: FIND XS RURAL DEVELOPMENT ECUADOR # OR XS RURAL DEVELOPMENT
                    COLOMBIA # OR XS RURAL DEVELOPMENT BRAZIL #
    Search result:  47 records in the TEN-YEAR Catalog database

    Type D to display; SHOW SEARCH for other results available for DISPLAY.

TEN->
```

Figure 33.21: MELVYL: Exact–index Boolean

```
TEN-> set db cat

    You are now set to the CATALOG database.
    Type HELP for assistance.

CAT-> find tw fire moon

    Search request: FIND TW FIRE MOON
    Search result:  7 records at all libraries

    Type D to display results, or type HELP.

CAT->
```

Figure 33.22: MELVYL: Partial–title search

```
Search request: FIND TW FIRE MOON
Search result:  7 records at all libraries

Type HELP for other display options.

   1. HARRINGTON, Robert.          An appendix to my new system of... 1798
   2. MAILER, Norman.              A fire on the moon : part I of an... 1969
   3. MAILER, Norman.              Of a fire on the moon. 1970
   4. MAILER, Norman.              Of a fire on the moon. 1971
   5. MYERS, John Myers, 1906-     The moon's fire-eating daughter. 1981
   6. MYERS, John Myers, 1906-     The moon's fire-eating daughter. 1984
   7. VAUGHAN, Thomas, 1622-1666.  Euphrates, or The waters of the... 1655


CAT->
```

Figure 33.23: MELVYL: Partial title result (edited)

```
CAT-> find xt vineland and pa pynchon, thomas
Search request: FIND XT VINELAND # AND PA PYNCHON, THOMAS
Search result:  1 record at all libraries

Type HELP for other display options.

1. Pynchon, Thomas.
      Vineland / Thomas Pynchon.  1st ed.  Boston : Little, Brown, c1990.
         UCB    Bancroft   PS3566.Y55 V56 1990
         UCB    Hum Grad   XMAC P997 V56 Modern Authors Collection
         UCB    Moffitt    PS3566.Y55 V56 1990
         UCB    Morrison   PS3566.Y55 V56 1990
         UCD    Main Lib   PS3566.Y55 V56 1990
         UCI    Main Lib   PS3566.Y55 V56 1990
         UCLA   URL        PS 3566 P994v1
         UCR    Rivera     PS3531.Y52 V56 1990
         UCR    Rivera     PS3531.Y52 V56 1990 Spec Coll Eaton
         UCSB   Library    PS3566.Y55 V56 1990
         UCSC   McHenry    PS3566.Y5 V56 1990
         UCSD   Central    IP88-17765
         UCSD   Undergrad  PS3566.Y55 V56 1990

CAT->
```

Figure 33.24: MELVYL: Known–item search (edited)

```
CAT-> browse pa pynchon

Browse request: BROWSE PA PYNCHON
Browse result:  9 personal author headings found

Type D COUNTS to display the number of books with each heading.
Type SELECT and the heading number to search for books with each heading.
Type SHOW SEARCH to see other results available for DISPLAY.

   1.    Pynchon, Adeline (Lobdell)
   2.    Pynchon, John, 1621-1703.
   3.    Pynchon, Joseph Charles, 1815-1889.
   4.    Pynchon, May.
   5.    Pynchon, Thomas.
   6.    Pynchon, Thomas Ruggles, 1823-
   7.    Pynchon, Thomas Ruggles, 1823-1904.
   8.    Pynchon, William, 1590-1662.
   9.    Pynchon, William, 1723-1789.

CAT->
```

Figure 33.25: MELVYL: Author browse (edited)

```
CAT-> select 5

   Search request: SELECT 5 (from BROWSE PA PYNCHON)
   Search result:  19 records at all libraries

   Type D to display; SHOW SEARCH for other results available for DISPLAY.

CAT->
```

Figure 33.26: MELVYL: Selection from browse

```
Use one of the following indexes with the FIND command:

Keyword indexes (word order doesn't matter):
  PA  Personal Author       SU  Subject words     UT  Uniform Title
  CA  Corporate Author      TW  Title Words       SE  Series

Exact indexes (words in exact order):
  XT  Exact Title           XS  Exact Subject     XC  Exact Corporate Author

Searches using exact indexes are usually faster and more precise than searches
using keyword indexes.

Periodicals indexes:
  PE  Periodicals Title words    RPE  Related Periodicals Title words
  XPE Exact Periodicals Titles   XRP  Exact Related Periodicals Titles

Other indexes:
  ADDED index                    DATE index
  FORM index                     LANGUAGE index
  TI  (searched as TW or XT depending on your search words)

More indexes are listed on the next screen.
Press RETURN to see the next screen.  Type PS to see the previous screen.
TEN->
```

Figure 33.27: MELVYL: Explain Indexes (1)

```
Indexes to use with the FIND command, continued:

Nonbook indexes:
  MP  Music Publisher          MK  Music Key          THEMATIC
  GC  Geographical Classification Code                SCALE    Map scale

Number indexes:
  GD    Government Documents Number          RN  Report Number
  ISBN  International Standard Book Number    LN  Local Number
  ISSN  International Standard Serial Number  STOCK NUMBER
  LCCN  Library of Congress Control Number    DLA ID

For information on indexes to use with a BROWSE command, type EXPLAIN BROWSE.

For information on indexes to use with an ACFIND command, type EXPLAIN ACFIND.

For information on options to use with the FIND COMMENTS command, type
EXPLAIN COMMENTS OPTIONS.

For more information on each of the indexes listed in these screens, type
EXPLAIN followed by the index name, for example:
  EXPLAIN PA        EXPLAIN TW        EXPLAIN XS        EXPLAIN MK
There are no more screens to display.  Type PS to see the previous screen.
TEN->
```

Figure 33.28: MELVYL: Explain Indexes (2)

```
Search request: F XT TRANSPORTATION POLICY #
Search result:  42 records at all libraries

Type HELP for other display options.
Type SHOW SEARCH to see other results available for DISPLAY.

5.
Author:        Babcock, Michael W.
Title:         Transportation policy in the 1990s and railroad/motor carrier
                 market shares / by Michael W. Babcock, H. Wade German.
Found in:      Journal of the Transportation Research Forum. Vol. 31, no. 1
                 (1990)
Description:   p. 63-74 ; 23 cm.

Notes:         Includes bibliographical references.

Subjects:      Market share.
               Freight and freightage — Government policy — United States.

Other entries: German, H. Wade.

Call numbers:  UCB   Trans    HE11 .T7 v. 31:1

CAT->
```

Figure 33.29: MELVYL: "In" analytic

```
Use these SET commands to change the default settings that are set at the
beginning of a new session.  These settings determine how the MELVYL system
processes your search requests and displays your retrievals.  Whenever you
change a setting, it remains in effect until you RESET it, or SET it again.

Settings that apply to searches:

    SET ADDED          — changes date setting for items added to the database.
    SET DATABASE       — changes database (CATALOG, MELVYL MEDLINE, etc.)
    SET DATE           — changes publication date setting for book searches.
    SET FORM           — changes form of material (e.g., books, videos, etc.)
                         searched.
    SET LANGUAGE       — changes language setting for searches.
    SET LIBRARY        — changes library setting for searches and displays.
    SET MODE           — changes dialogue mode.

Settings that apply to displays are listed on the next screen.

Press RETURN to see the next screen.
TEN—>
```

Figure 33.30: MELVYL: Explain Set (partial)

```
Use the following SHOW commands to request information.

Shows search information:
    SHOW SEARCH    — shows your current search request and search result.
    SHOW HISTORY   — shows your previous search requests.
    SHOW SETS      — shows searches saved as sets.

Shows setting information:
    SHOW SETTINGS — shows the following settings:
    SHOW DATE      — the date of publication setting.
    SHOW DISPLAY   — the record display option setting.
    SHOW FORM      — the forms of material setting.
    SHOW LANGUAGE — the language setting.
    SHOW LINESIZE — the line length setting.
    SHOW LIBRARY  — the library setting.
    SHOW MODE      — the dialogue mode setting.
    SHOW PAGESIZE — the page length setting.
    SHOW PAGING    — how the display will be paged.
    SHOW REMINDERS— whether reminder messages display or not.
    SHOW TERMINAL — the terminal type setting.
    SHOW TIMEOUT   — length of time before session times out.
                                  (SHOW commands continued on next screen)
Press RETURN to see the next screen.
TEN—>
```

Figure 33.31: MELVYL: Explain Show (partial)

```
List request:   DISPLAY LIST
List size:      2 records in your list

Type HELP for other display options.

  1. (TEN—YEAR FIND result)
     Brown, Carole.
       Bloomsday, the eleventh hour : the quest for the vacant place / Carole
     Brown and Leo Knuth.  Colchester, Eng. : A Wake Newslitter Press, 1981.
          UCB    Main        PR6019.09 U627 1981
          UCSD   Central     PR6019.09 U628 1981

  2. (PERIODICALS result) Newsletter (James Joyce Foundation) <UCB>

PE—>
```

Figure 33.32: MELVYL: List of saved results (edited)

```
TEN—> comment I am logging on to the MELVYL system from my office.  It's very
handy
    Comment received.

TEN—> comment to be able to find out the location of the book I want before I
go to the library.
    Comment received.

TEN—>
```

Figure 33.33: MELVYL: Comment command

34

The NOTIS Online Public Access Catalog

Stuart W. Miller

The following narrative is based on searching using "martin luther king" as the primary search statement for various types of searches. Other searches have been used as appropriate to illustrate functionality and design.

All examples are in black and white. NOTIS can support up to sixteen different colors, depending on: (1) the terminal and/or microcomputer used to access the system; and (2) the controller environment. In a monochrome environment, highlighting is substituted for color. The screen examples supplied use boldface as a substitute for highlighted/color display. (*Editor's note: Due to unusual file conversion problems, boldface does not appear in the figures. Some spacing is also incorrect.*)

Cursors on OPAC screens always appear on the command line. They are represented in the screen examples by an underscore mark (__).

Starting Out

Users typically begin a search session at Figure 34.1. The contents and layout of the introductory screen are determined by each site by typing in text on a template screen in the online system control file. The highlighting in the text is locally defined. Highlighting of the catalog name and Next Command is system supplied.

NOTIS sites typically lock terminals in public areas to OPAC-only searching and the system automatically displays this screen. A locally defined time-out (entered in the online system control file and up to sixteen minutes in length) automatically returns the terminal to this screen should a user display another screen and then leave the terminal. Users can also return to this screen by entering the command "start." The NOTIS OPAC supports the *Common Command Language for Online Interactive Information Retrieval* (NISO standard Z39.58).

Help, news, and tutorial screens are shown later in the sequence. Users may begin any type of search from any screen in the OPAC.

Searches and Displays

An index screen (Figure 34.2) always displays when there are hits on the search statement. Here, the author search "a=king martin" resulted in six hits, two of which are "search under" references. Notice the automatic right-hand truncation and the spacing between distinct headings, indentation for the cross-references, and the grouping of all titles under the one name (the form of heading as established in an authority record).

Hits 3 and 4 have the format identifiers "sound" and "visual," respectively. Every format except for a printed book has such an identifier at the index level. Microforms are also identified. The date of publication appears in the brackets for all format types except serials. For serials, you would see place of publication instead of date.

On this screen, the system highlights all phrases containing the search statement.

Figure 34.3 shows the result of entering line number 1 or 2 from the display shown in Figure 34.2. Notice that the four hits (1 to 4) are identical to hits 3 to 6 on Figure 34.2 and that the system has supplied the complete new search statement. A user could have gone directly to this screen by using the complete name. Highlighting on this screen is identical to to 34.2.

Displays

From Figure 34.3, the user would select a record by typing the line number. Figure 34.4 shows record number 1 from the index. In this example, the default record display type is "brief." The site could have selected the "long" view as the default.

There is a brief and a long view for each of the seven MARC bibliographic formats for a total of fourteen. For each, the labels, the data to display for each label, the amount of data from each field to display to the subfield level, etc., are all determined by each library in the online system control file. Options for label definitions include left or right justification, upper- and/or lower-case, highlighting or color, and order of appearance.

Notice the appearance of the location, call number, and status information—if there is more than one copy, there is a separately numbered line for each. The three labels may also be changed by each site and can appear in upper and/or lower case and be highlighted/color. Status messages are updated immediately as the order or circulation status changes.

Notice, too, how the header and footer of this record differs from the previous screens. The type of record (in this case Music—the name is locally determined and appears in upper- and/or lower-case and may be highlighted) is different for each of the MARC bibliographic format types. A record display always shows the message **Record n of n Entries Found** and what type of view is on the screen. In the footer, the command prompts change according to the type of display. **O Other Options** remains a constant throughout, provid-

ing locally defined text as to what else the user might do at this point in his or her search.

PRI appears as a prompt if the terminal has been defined to the system with an attached printer and if the library has also installed NOTIS's Multiple Database Access System software. Terminals without printers would not display PRI. A formatted citation may be printed by entering the PRI command (or, if using a microcomputer to access the system, the PRI is a downloading command). The citation includes author, title, location, and call number.

By entering "lo" (in either upper- or lowercase) from Figure 34.4, the patron could switch to the "long" view of the record—again, the data display is determined by each library (Figure 34.5, partial). The long view for this record requires three screens (the patron is prompted that the record continues and the top of the display shows the number of the screen, i.e. **Screen n of n**) and the location/call number/status data has been pushed onto the last screen to accommodate the increased amount of data.

Notice that the user can always return to the index or go to the next record in the index by following the command prompts in the footer. The header of the screen tells the user what record number is currently being displayed from all of the items in the index. The index remains until the user enters a new search.

Multiple Copies

Multiple copies always display in the OPAC as shown on Figure 34.6. Each location, each call number, and the status of each display in the order that the copies are identified in a staff-side copy holdings record.

The second location also displays a special note indicating that items there come under special conditions, in this case, **Non-Circulating**. Notice also the difference between the two status messages. **Not checked out** means that the system has found a NOTIS item record (staff use record for circulation) with no active circulation status recorded; the item should be on the shelf. **Check Shelf** means that the system has found no NOTIS item record and so does not know if the item should be on the shelf or not. A subtle, but certainly distinct state of affairs. In this case, the library apparently decided that the copy at Reference Collection would never circulate and so did not create an item record for it. Other status messages are also clear statements of condition, e.g., **Recalled, Overdue**, etc.

All location names are also locally defined in the online system control file—they can utilize upper- and/or lower-case. Here, all uppercase has been used.

Keyword Search

A keyword search (using the ADJ operator, meaning "king followed by martin followed by luther") results in a different kind of index display—sorted in reverse chronological order with hits alphabetized by title within year of publication (Figure 34.7). NOTIS uses the date information in the fixed field of the MARC bibliographic record for this sort.

Here, **forward** would take you to the next index screen beginning with record #15 (the system found 27 hits altogether). (**Forward** in a multiscreen record display takes you to the next record display screen.) Again, to see an individual record, the patron would type the line number.

Guide Screen

Whenever the system finds more than 50 hits for an author, title, or subject search, it presents a summary of search results on a guide screen, showing the total number of entries found and showing the entry that appears on the record in the index range shown on the right (Figure 34.8). Selecting a line number drops the user into an index (as shown in other examples).

This approach provides a "telephone book" arrangement so that the user can quickly scan large retrieval results to determine whether he or she found relevant entries or whether another, more specific search is needed. Notice how many more entries a search under "king" retrieved than a search under "king martin" as used in Figure 34.2.

Title Searches

Figure 34.9 shows the title index that resulted from a title search for "foundation and empire."

Note the similarity to the author index as shown in Figure 34.3. Index displays automatically highlight or color the search statement. In this case, there is an exact hit.

From Figure 34.9, the user would enter 1 to display the record, which has a different title than the one shown on Figure 34.9. If the user were to display the long view of the record, he or she would see *Foundation and Empire* under the **Other Titles** label—in this example, the library has used that label for alternate title fields in the MARC bibliographic record (indexed as titles in NOTIS). The long view also contains a contents note showing the three individual novel titles in this one-volume trilogy.

The library might decide to display alternate titles or contents notes as part of the brief view, particularly if it uses alternate title fields primarily to help patrons locate single titles in collected works or if patrons frequently use keyword searches (since a keyword search would work on a contents note). The change could easily be made in the online system control file.

Help and Explain

Every type of screen in the OPAC has a help screen that displays to a user when he or she enters **h** from that display. Figure 34.10 shows the help screen for a brief view—invoked from a single-record display as shown by information in the header.

The content and layout of all help, explain, news, and introductory screens—any kind of textual screen—are controlled by typing on templates in an online system control file. Each library has complete control over these screens.

Exp is a Common Command Language command used for online tutorials—each help screen has a complementary explain screen.

Any textual screen type in the system can have up to 99 individual screens (or pages). Most sites will never need more than one screen per type, but the generous amount helps with more complex topics such as keyword/Boolean searching.

It is difficult for a user to get "lost" while searching in a NOTIS OPAC. By reading the prompts, she or he can always move around the system in some way. Pressing Enter would redisplay the record from which these screens were reached.

Subject Search

Figure 34.11 is a subject index screen—note that it is identical in structure to the author and title index screens as shown in Figures 34.3 and 34.9 respectively.

Notice here how all "search also" references appear in the beginning. The patron can redirect the search to use those subjects by typing the line number. Subject headings appear with all subdivisions as you move through the index—as shown in Figure 34.12. Here, the user has entered "113" but there are only 112 index entries. The system responds with the message shown.

No Hits

Whenever the system finds no entries for whatever reason, a screen like Figure 34.13 appears (depending upon the type of search). Like all textual screens, each site has control over the text of this screen and can have up to 99 pages of text.

Logging

System logs can be turned on to record the actual search statements entered by patrons. Common mistakes such as spelling errors can be identified. As a corrective, the library could, e.g., add the commonly misspelled name or heading as a 4xx field to the authority record. A user who searched under the misspelled form would then get a cross-reference from which the search could be redirected to the correct form—without retyping or correcting the spelling error.

Multiple Database Access

NOTIS sites with the Multiple Database Access System would see a introductory screen like Figure 34.14 (again, the contents are locally defined) from which the user would select a particular database. The NOTIS OPAC becomes one of those databases. The four-letter labels are locally defined as well. If a user were to enter "opac" from this screen, he or she would then see the OPAC

introductory screen as shown in Figure 34.1. (Figures 34.21 through 34.23 show other databases.)

"News" entered on Figure 34.14 would show a systemwide news screen. "News" entered from the OPAC or other database introductory screens would display the news screen for that database.

Partial Information

Keyword/Boolean searching examines the full MARC bibliographic record. Patrons who are looking for a book with a title "like xxxxx" are best advised to perform a keyword search. Each site selects a default operator—many sites prefer the positional operators WITH or SAME since they simulate natural word searching. AND, OR, XOR, ADJ, NOT, NOTWITH, NOTSAME, SYN, and NEAR are also available.

Call Number Search and Shelflist Browse

Call number searches can be of four types: Dewey (cd=); LC (cl=); SuDoc (cs=); Other (co=). Each site also defines what call number search type will be performed when a user enters "c=." In this library, a c= search is the same as a cl=.

The system drops the user into the index at the point most closely matching the search statement. Notice that no number of entries found appears anywhere, because users can now browse as far forward or as far back in the call number schedule as they wish.

Figure 34.15 shows the initial display. The call number browse feature thus simulates a shelf browse for the patron—and more profitably since the index screens will show all of the items owned by the library, not just what is on the shelf at that moment.

Explain Screens

Each type of searching, record views, etc., has complementary explain screens in the system. Since each type of text screen can have up to 99 "pages," this library has taken advantage of that fact by creating a series of 10 screens to explain keyword searching. Figures 34.16 and 34.17 show the first and sixth screens. The contents of these screens are determined by each site. NOTIS distributes its software with default text screens. Each site may change these by typing over text or adding text on template screens in the online system control file.

Serials Holdings

Figure 34.18 is the brief view for a serial. Since holdings data may be complex, NOTIS puts holdings information on a separate screen. The **HO** command may be combined with one of the location numbers to go directly to that display. **HO** entered by itself will default to the first location. However, using a number only begins the holdings display with that number—the system does not isolate each location on a separate screen as shown on Figure 34.20.

Figures 34.19 and 34.20 show holdings for two locations. For the first location, the library has included a note indicating that earlier volumes are on microfilm, but has not yet entered holdings data for what is held in the **Microform Reading Room** (although it could certainly do so). **Status** refers to order status or circulation status, the latter listing only those pieces with active circulation situations. Also note that the use of call numbers is not required—this library shelves its periodicals by title.

Note the command prompt for **View Record**. This would return the patron to the bibliographic display—brief or long, depending on what view was last displayed.

Other Databases

If a NOTIS site has the Multiple Database Access System installed, the user can switch among the OPAC and the available citation databases. The user can perform searches in the non-OPAC databases in exactly the same manner as he or she would perform an OPAC search. Indexes and record displays look virtually the same, although the labels in record displays will usually differ from those used in the OPAC.

Figure 34.21 shows the result of a subject search in what the library has called WILS—which in this case is a file of several Wilson periodical indexes. Figure 34.22 shows record number 1.

In this database (note that in the upper right-hand corner, we are no longer in NOTISCat, but in WILS), the labels are all in upper case and are right-justified. (In the NOTISCat, they are left-justified and in upper and lower case.) However, everything else looks very similar to the OPAC displays.

Notice the message at the bottom of the screen. If you enter **HO** here, you will see the library's holdings as shown in Figure 34.23.

The patron has opened a window to the library's holdings for the source of the citation. However, the user is still in WILS, not NOTISCat. If the user were to search for the periodical title in NOTISCat, the display would be nearly identical.

Scope or Usage Notes

Users can see the scope or usage notes that appear in authority records as shown in Figure 34.24. This screen would be invoked from the index display.

Search Review

The system automatically saves each unique search to a limit of ten. Whenever the user enters **R(EVIEW),** the review screen displays (Figure 34.25). Entering **EDIT** from the search list screen or any other screen will display the search list with the last search replicated on the command line for editing.

Any search on the list can be reexecuted simply by entering **S1, S2, S3,** etc. S1 is always the last search entered, S2 the next to last, etc. Once the patron has entered the eleventh unique search, the first search entered falls off the list. Keyword searches can be combined with operators, e.g., S6 *and* S3 which then becomes Sn. **EDIT** can also be coupled with a specific search number, e.g., **E2** to reproduce the search statement on the command line for easy editing.

Users with non-OPAC databases can switch between and among any database and the OPAC, and retain the same search list. This allows the user to repeat the same search in any database without rekeying the search. The search clears only when the time-out resets to the introduction screen or the user enters **STOP** (useful for the dial-in user since it will perform system signoff) or **START** to return to the introduction screen.

Conclusion

These examples show the NOTIS catalog as it existed in 1991. Enhancements—including a browse function for all types of searches—will be available in 1992. The most up-to-date information on current online catalog functionality is available from NOTIS' Marketing and Sales Group.

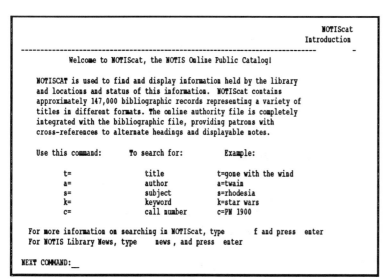

```
                                                    NOTIScat
                                                    Introduction
-----------------------------------------------------------------    -
            Welcome to NOTIScat, the NOTIS Online Public Catalog!

   NOTISCAT is used to find and display information held by the library
   and locations and status of this information. NOTIScat contains
   approximately 147,000 bibliographic records representing a variety of
   titles in different formats. The online authority file is completely
   integrated with the bibliographic file, providing patrons with
   cross-references to alternate headings and displayable notes.

   Use this command:        To search for:        Example:

        t=                     title              t=gone with the wind
        a=                     author             a=twain
        s=                     subject            s=rhodesia
        k=                     keyword            k=star wars
        c=                     call number        c=PN 1900

   For more information on searching in NOTIScat, type      f and press  enter
   For NOTIS Library News, type     news , and press  enter

   NEXT COMMAND:__
```

Figure 34.1: NOTIS: Introductory screen

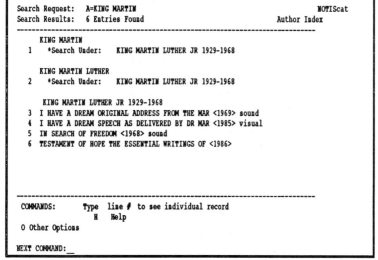

```
   Search Request:   A=KING MARTIN                          NOTIScat
   Search Results:   6 Entries Found              Author Index
   -----------------------------------------------------------------
        KING MARTIN
   1    *Search Under:   KING MARTIN LUTHER JR 1929-1968

        KING MARTIN LUTHER
   2    *Search Under:   KING MARTIN LUTHER JR 1929-1968

        KING MARTIN LUTHER JR 1929-1968
   3  I HAVE A DREAM ORIGINAL ADDRESS FROM THE MAR <1969> sound
   4  I HAVE A DREAM SPEECH AS DELIVERED BY DR MAR <1985> visual
   5  IN SEARCH OF FREEDOM <1968> sound
   6  TESTAMENT OF HOPE THE ESSENTIAL WRITINGS OF <1986>




   -----------------------------------------------------------------
   COMMANDS:     Type  line # to see individual record
                   H   Help
   O Other Options

   NEXT COMMAND:__
```

Figure 34.2: NOTIS: Author index

```
Search Request:   A=KING MARTIN LUTHER JR 1929-1968              NOTIScat
Search Results:   4 Entries Found                        Author Index
------------------------------------------------------------------------
        KING MARTIN LUTHER JR 1929-1968
   1  I HAVE A DREAM ORIGINAL ADDRESS FROM THE MAR <1969> sound
   2  I HAVE A DREAM SPEECH AS DELIVERED BY DR MAR <1985> visual
   3  IN SEARCH OF FREEDOM <1968> sound
   4  TESTAMENT OF HOPE THE ESSENTIAL WRITINGS OF <1986>




------------------------------------------------------------------------
   COMMANDS:       Type  line # to see individual record
                       H   Help
   O Other Options

   NEXT COMMAND:_
```

Figure 34.3: NOTIS: Redirection on author search

```
Search Request:   A=KING MARTIN LUTHER JR 1929-1968              NOTIScat
MUSIC - Record 1 of 4 Entries Found                     Brief View
-----------------------------  Screen 1 of 1  -----------------------------
Author:       King, Martin Luther, Jr., 1929-1968.

Title:        I have a dream <sound recording> : original address from the
              march on Washington, August 1963 / Martin Luther King, Jr.

Published:    New York : 20th Century-Fox Records, <1969?>.
------------------------------------------------------------------------
    LOCATION:              CALL NUMBER:              STATUS:
 1. AV - Dwight Douglas    Record DD35          Check Shelf
    Collection
    (Non-Circulating)



------------------------------------------------------------------------
   COMMANDS:       LO  Long View        H   Help
                   N   Next Record      PRI Print
   O Other Options I   Index

   NEXT COMMAND:_
```

Figure 34.4: NOTIS: Brief view, sound recording

```
Search Request:   A=KING MARTIN LUTHER JR 1929-1968              NOTIScat
MUSIC - Record 1 of 4 Entries Found                     Long View
-----------------------------  + Screen 1 of 3  -----------------------------
Author:       King, Martin Luther, Jr., 1929-1968.

Title:        I have a dream <sound recording> : original address from the
              march on Washington, August 1963 / Martin Luther King, Jr.

Published:    New York : 20th Century-Fox Records, <1969?>.

Description:  1 sound disc (58 min.) : analog, 33 1/3 rpm, stereo. ; 12 in.

Subjects:     March on Washington for Jobs and Freedom, 1963.
              Afro-Americans--Civil rights.

Other authors:  Hentoff, Nat.
                Randolph, A. Philip (Asa Philip), 1889-
                Mays, Benjamin Elijah, 1895-
------------------------------------------------  Continued on next screen  --
   COMMANDS:       BR  Brief View       I   Index
                   F   Forward          H   Help
   O Other Options N   Next Record      PRI Print

   NEXT COMMAND:_
```

Figure 34.5: NOTIS: Long view, recording (1)

```
Search Request:   T=TESTAMENT OF HOPE                         NOTIScat
BOOK - Record 1 of 1 Entry Found                    Brief View
-----------------------------    Screen 1 of 1   -----------------------------
Author:        King, Martin Luther, Jr., 1929-1968.

Title:         A testament of hope

Edition:       1st ed.

Publisher:     San Francisco : Harper & Row, c1986.

Subjects:      Afro-Americans--Civil rights.
               United States--Race relations.
-----------------------------------------------------------------------------
     LOCATION:            CALL NUMBER:              STATUS:
1. GENERAL COLLECTION   E185.97 .K5 A25 1986    Not checked out
2. REFERENCE COLLECTION E185.97 .K5 A25 1986    Check Shelf
   (Non-Circulating)
-----------------------------------------------------------------------------
COMMANDS:        LO  Long View      PRI Print
                 I   Index
O Other Options  H   Help

NEXT COMMAND:__
```

Figure 34.6: NOTIS: Book with multiple copies

```
Search Request:   K=KING ADJ MARTIN ADJ LUTHER                NOTIScat
Search Results:   27 Entries Found                    Keyword Index
-----------------------------------------------------------------------------
      DATE  TITLE:                               AUTHOR:
  1   1986  Bearing the cross : Martin Luther King, Jr  Garrow, David J
  2   1986  Four modern prophets : Walter Rauschenbusc  Ramsay, William M
  3   1986  King remembered                      Schulke, Flip
  4   1986  A testament of hope : the essential writin  King, Martin Luther
  5   1986  To see the promised land : the faith pilgr  Downing, Frederick L
  6   1985  The "I have a dream" speech as de <visual>  King, Martin Luther
  7   1985  Martin Luther King, Jr.--to the mountainto  Witherspoon, William R
  8   1984  Martin Luther King, Jr., a man to remember  McKissack, Pat
  9   1983  A lasting impression : a collection of pho  Tweedle, John
 10   1982  Let the trumpet sound, the life of Martin  Oates, Stephen B
 11   1982  Martin Luther King, Jr <visual>
 12   1982  Martin Luther King, Jr. : the making of a  Ansbro, John J
 13   1981  The FBI and Martin Luther King, Jr. : from  Garrow, David J
 14   1980  Of Kennedys and Kings : making sense of th  Wofford, Harris
-----------------------------------------    Continued on next screen    --
COMMANDS:        Type line # to see individual record
                 F   Forward
O Other Options  H   Help

NEXT COMMAND:__
```

Figure 34.7: NOTIS: Keyword result

```
Search Request:   A=KING                                      NOTIScat
Search Results:   306 Entries Found                  Author Guide
-----------------------------------------------------------------------------
LINE:  BEGINNING ENTRY:                            INDEX RANGE:
  1   KING A ALEXANDER                               1 -  22
  2   KING CAROL A. PROFESSIONAL DINING ROOM MANAGEMENT   23 -  44
  3   KING DAVID B. ESSAYS ON CULTURE AND SOCIETY IN MODERN GERM  45 -  66
  4   KING GRAHAM 1930. GARDEN OF ZOLA EMILE ZOLA AND HIS NOVELS  67 -  88
  5   KING JAMES E. PRIMATE BEHAVIOR                 89 - 110
  6   KING JOHNNY. JOHNNY THE COUNTRY BOY          111 - 132
  7   KING LESLIE J. CITIES SPACE AND BEHAVIOR THE ELEMENTS OF U  133 - 154
  8   KING MARTIN LUTHER JR 1929-1968. TESTAMENT OF HOPE THE ESS  155 - 176
  9   KING PETER 1936. AUSTRALIAS VIETNAM AUSTRALIA IN THE SECON  177 - 198
 10   KING ROBERT HARLEN 1935. READINGS IN CHRISTIAN THEOLOGY  199 - 220
 11   KING STEPHEN 1947. EYES OF THE DRAGON A STORY  221 - 242
 12   KING WAYNE. AUDUBON SOCIETY FIELD GUIDE TO NORTH AMERICA  243 - 264
 13   KINGSBURY HENRY 1943. MUSIC TALENT AND PERFORMANCE A CONSE  265 - 286
 14   KINGSLEY CHARLES 1819-1875. WATER BABIES A FAIRY TALE FOR  287 - 306
-----------------------------------------------------------------------------
COMMANDS:        Type  line # to begin display within index range
                 H   Help
O Other Options

NEXT COMMAND:__
```

Figure 34.8: NOTIS: Guide screen

```
Search Request:    T=FOUNDATION AND EMPIRE                          NOTIScat
Search Results:    1 Entry Found                         Title Index
---------------------------------------------------------------------------
     1  FOUNDATION AND EMPIRE.    ASIMOV ISAAC <1982>




     -----------------------------------------------------------------
  COMMANDS:         Type  line # to see individual record
                    H   Help
     O Other Options

  NEXT COMMAND:__
```

Figure 34.9: NOTIS: Title search

```
Search Request:    T=FOUNDATION AND EMPIRE                          NOTIScat
BOOK - Record 1 of 1 Entry Found                       Brief View Help
----------------------------       Screen 1 of 1   -------------------------------
                           Help for Brief View

    This display gives a    brief  bibliographic description, Library holdings
    information and, for many items, circulation status.  Author, title,
    publisher, series data, and information such as the following are
    provided when appropriate to the item you have selected to view:

    --Description: including number of pages, size of book and illustrations
    --Frequency of publication (for magazines and other serials)
    --Holdings: including copies, locations, call numbers and current issues
    --Circulation information (for ex., charged out, on reserve. etc.)

    For more information about the brief view, type      exp br  and press  enter


     -----------------------------------------------------------------
  COMMANDS:         Press  ENTER to continue

  O Other Options

  NEXT COMMAND:__
```

Figure 34.10: NOTIS: Help for brief view

```
Search Request:    S=AFRO AMERICANS--CIVIL RIGHTS                   NOTIScat
Search Results:    112 Entries Found                     Subject Index
---------------------------------------------------------------------------
       AFRO AMERICANS--CIVIL RIGHTS
         *Search Also Under:
     1     AFRO AMERICANS--POLITICS AND SUFFRAGE
     2     AFRO AMERICANS--SUFFRAGE
     3     BLACK POWER--UNITED STATES
     4     CIVIL RIGHTS WORKERS--UNITED STATES
     5     SELMA MONTGOMERY RIGHTS MARCH 1965

       AFRO AMERICANS--CIVIL RIGHTS
     6  ALONG THE COLOR LINE EXPLORATIONS IN THE BLA <1976>
     7  AND WE ARE NOT SAVED THE ELUSIVE QUEST FOR R <1987>
     8  BEARING THE CROSS MARTIN LUTHER KING JR AND <1986>
     9  BLACK AMERICANS IN THE ROOSEVELT ERA LIBERAL <1980>
    10  BLACK REVOLTS RACIAL STRATIFICATION IN THE U <1976>
    11  BLACKS AND SOCIAL JUSTICE <1984>
     -----------------------------------------------  Continued on next screen    --
  COMMANDS:         Type  line # to see individual record
                    F   Forward          H   Help
     O Other Options    G   Guide

  NEXT COMMAND:__
```

Figure 34.11: NOTIS: Subject search

```
Search Request:   S=AFRO AMERICANS--CIVIL RIGHTS                    NOTIScat
Search Results:   112 Entries Found                    Subject Index
-----------------------------------------------------------------------------
        AFRO AMERICANS--CIVIL RIGHTS--SOUTHERN STATES--HISTORY
 111  FEDERAL LAW AND SOUTHERN ORDER RACIAL VIOLEN <1987>
        AFRO AMERICANS--CIVIL RIGHTS--UNITED STATES
 112  DESEGREGATION FROM BROWN TO ALEXANDER AN EXP <1977>




-----------------------------------------------------------------------------
  COMMANDS:        Type  line # to see individual record
                   B    Back              H   Help
  O Other Options  G    Guide
Number entered does not exist.
NEXT COMMAND:  113
```

Figure 34.12: NOTIS: Error message

```
Search Request:   A=KIGN MARTIN                                     NOTIScat
Search Results:   0 Entries Found            No Author Entries Found
-----------------------        Screen 1 of 1    --------------------------------
                        No Author Entries Found

  Possible reasons are:

  1.  Item may not be in the database, but may be in the card catalog.
  2.  Item is not owned by the library, ask for advice at the Reference Desk.
  3.  The search command or search term(s) were incorrect.

      Please check the following in your search:
      --the command code for author searching is      a=
      --the author's name is spelled correctly
      --numeric '1' must not be alphabetic 'l'
      --the author's last name must be typed first
      --there must not be punctuation in the search

  For more information on author searching, type      exp a and press  enter

-----------------------------------------------------------------------------
  O Other Options

NEXT COMMAND:_
```

Figure 34.13: NOTIS: No-result screen

```
                Alma Mater University Library                  S02E

                     DATABASE SELECTION MENU
   On this terminal, you may search the databases listed below.  Select a
database by entering its four letter label.



       OPAC    Online Public Catalog
       COMP    Compendex Plus (Engineering)
       BUSI    Business Periodicals Index
       PSYC    PsycINFO
       ERIC    Educational Resources
       CART    Current Contents Article File
       CJOU    Current Contents Journal File
       MEDL    MEDLINE
       WILS    Wilson Indexes
       RELI    Religion Indexes
       ACAD    IAC Expanded Academic Index


-----------------------------------------------------------------------------
COMMANDS            H    Help            NEWS  Library System News

Database Selection:_
```

Figure 34.14: NOTIS: Introductory screen for MDAS

```
Search Request:   C=X678.9                                    NOTIScat
                                              Call Number Browse
--------------------------------------------------------------------
    CALL NUMBER:                      TITLE:
 1  X 678.9 A 1 A 34                  Advances in library automation and net
 2  X 678.9 A 1 C 5                   Proceedings
 3  X 678.9 A 1 C 5 1976              The economics of library automation <p
 4  X 678.9 A 1 C 5 1979              The role of the library in an electron
 5  X 678.9 A 1 L 518 1983            Crossroads proceedings of the First Na
 6  X 678.9 A 1 S 34 1986             SCIL 1986 Software/Computer Conference
 7  X 678.9 A 2 M 57 X 1984           Library applications of microcomputers
 8  X 678.9 A 3 D 48 1987             101 software packages to use in your l
 9  X 678.9 A 3 W 33 1986             Directory of microcomputer software fo
10  X 678.9 A 97 1984 X               Automation in Missouri libraries, 1984
11  X 678.9 AL L 321 X VOL 6 NO 3     Library automation at the University o
12  X 678.9 B 64 1982                 Books, libraries, and electronics essa
13  X 678.9 B 66                      The library manager's guide to automat
14  X 678.9 B 66 1984                 The library manager's guide to automat
---------------------------------------------     Continued on next screen   --
COMMANDS:        Type  line # to see individual record
                 F    Forward          H    Help
O Other Options  B    Back

NEXT COMMAND:__
```

Figure 34.15: NOTIS: Call number browse

```
                                                             NOTIScat
                                              Explain Keyword
---------------------------     + Screen 1 of 11  --------------------------------
              Index to EXPLAIN Keyword Searching Series

To find out about:                 Type the following and press        enter:

--Introduction to keyword searching     F 1
--Truncating search terms               F 2
--Boolean and positional operators      F 3
--Qualifying search terms               F 5
--Nested searches                       F 7
--Reviewing searches                    F 8
--Helpful hints                         F 9
--Stopwords                             F 10

   You may also opt to browse these screens sequentially by pressing       enter
   or you may begin a new search from any screen by entering your search below
---------------------------------------------     Continued on next screen   --
O Other Options    F   Forward

NEXT COMMAND:__
```

Figure 34.16: NOTIS: Explain keyword (1)

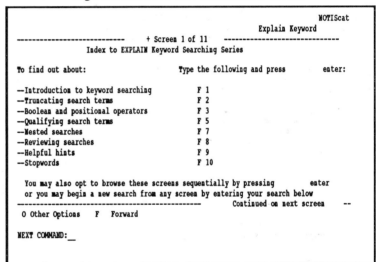

```
                                                             NOTIScat
                                              Explain Keyword
---------------------------     + Screen 6 of 11  --------------------------------
                      Qualifying Search Terms

Keyword searches may be qualified to limit search terms to a field in a
record, such as author, title or subject heading.  A period must precede and
follow the field code.  Some of the qualifiers you may use in NOTIScat are:

   .su. -- to limit search term to subject fields
   .ti. -- to limit search term to title fields
   .au. -- to limit search term to author fields

The form of your search should be:   k keyword.qualifier code.

   For more information on qualifying search terms, press       enter

To return to the Index to EXPLAIN Keyword Series, type      B 5 and press  enter
---------------------------------------------     Continued on next screen   --
O Other Options    F   Forward       B   Back

NEXT COMMAND:__
```

Figure 34.17: NOTIS: Explain keyword (6)

```
Search Request:   T=JOURNAL OF THE AMERICAN DIETETIC AS              NOTIScat
SERIAL - Record 1 of 1 Entry Found                       Brief View
-------------------------------    Screen 1 of 1    ---------------------------
Title:        Journal of the American Dietetic Association.

Published:    Chicago, Ill. : The Association, 1925-
-------------------------------------------------------------------------------
   LOCATION:              CALL NUMBER:              STATUS:
1. CURRENT PERIODICALS    No call number available  Enter     HO for holdings
   (Non-Circulating)
2. REFERENCE COLLECTION   TEMPORARY CONTROL         Enter     HO for holdings
   (Non-Circulating)         NUMBER: AAP6392




-----------------------------------------------------------------
   COMMANDS:        HO  Holdings          H   Help
                    LO  Long View         PRI Print
   O Other Options  I   Index

NEXT COMMAND:_
```

Figure 34.18: NOTIS: Serial, brief view

```
Search Request:   T=JOURNAL OF THE AMERICAN DIETETIC AS              NOTIScat
SERIAL - Record 1 of 1 Entry Found                  Holdings Detail
----------------------------   + Screen 1 of 2   ------------------------------
Title:        Journal of the American Dietetic Association

-------------------------------   Location 1   --------------------------------
LOCATION:      CURRENT PERIODICALS (Non-Circulating)
CALL NUMBER:   No call number available

CURRENT ISSUES:  v.67, no.1-10 (Jan.-Oct. 1991)
                 v. 68, no. 1 (Jan. 1992)
SHELVED AS:      American Dietetic Association Journal.
EXCEPTIONS:      Early volumes on microfiche in Microform Reading Room.
LIBRARY HAS:     v.1-67 (1925-1991)
SUPPLEMENTS:     v.26 Includes the anniversary publication, "Twenty five Years
                 of Service: The American Dietetic Association, 1925-1950."
INDEXES:         v.1-50
STATUS:          v. 26      Being Held for a Patron
-------------------------------------------------- Continued on next screen  --
   COMMANDS:        V   View Record       I   Index
                    BR  Brief View        H   Help
   O Other Options  F   Forward           PRI Print

NEXT COMMAND:_
```

Figure 34.19: NOTIS: Serial holdings display (1)

```
Search Request:   T=JOURNAL OF THE AMERICAN DIETETIC AS              NOTIScat
SERIAL - Record 1 of 1 Entry Found                  Holdings Detail
----------------------------   + Screen 2 of 2   ------------------------------
Title:        Journal of the American Dietetic Association

-------------------------------   Location 2   --------------------------------
LOCATION:      REFERENCE COLLECTION (Non-Circulating)
CALL NUMBER:   TEMPORARY CONTROL NUMBER: AAP6392
STATUS:        In Pre-Order Process




-----------------------------------------------------------------
   COMMANDS:        V   View Record       I   Index
                    BR  Brief View        H   Help
   O Other Options  B   Back              PRI Print

NEXT COMMAND:_
```

Figure 34.20: NOTIS: Serial holdings display (2)

```
Search Request:  S=COCAINE                                               WILS
Search Results:  14 Entries Found                        Subject Index
------------------------------------------------------------------------------
        COCAINE
  1  BACK TO THE DARK AGES <1983>  (RD)
  2  COCAINE KILLER BLIZZARD <1982>  (RD)
  3  COCAINE SOCIETY <1983>  (RD)
  4  COCAINE USE AMONG THE COLLEGE AGE GROUP BIOL <1984>   (ED)
  5  COPING AND THE STRESS INDUCED POTENTIATION O <1983>  (RD)
  6  CRASHING ON COCAINE <1983>  (RD)
  7  DOING COCAINE A VICTIMS ROAD TO RUIN <1983>   (RD)
  8  IDENTIFICATION OF PROGRESSIVE COCAINE ABUSE <1983>   (ED)
  9  KICKING THE COCAINE HABIT <1983>  (RD)
 10  STRUNG OUT AND CALLING IT QUITS <1983>  (RD)
 11  THROWING IT ALL AWAY <1983>  (RD)
 12  WHY CROUCH WAS ARRESTED FOR CHICKEN SOUP POS <1983>  (RD)


------------------------------------------------   Continued on next screen    --
  COMMANDS:        Type  line # to see individual record
                   F     Forward
  0 Other Options  H     Help

  NEXT COMMAND:_
```

Figure 34.21: NOTIS: Subject search/other database

```
Search Request:  S=COCAINE                                               WILS
WILSON RECORD  -- 1 of 14 Entries Found               View Record
------------------------------   Screen 1 of 1    ------------------------------
        AUTHORS:  Kirshenbaum, Jerry.

          TITLE:  Back to the dark ages.

       CITATION:  Sports Illustrated 59:15 Jul 11 '83

       SUBJECTS:  Baseball, Professional--Ethical aspects.
                  Drugs and sports.
                  Cocaine.

      INDEXED IN:  Readers' Guide to Periodical Literature.

           ISSN:  0038-822X.

    ENTRY MONTH:  8307.
------------------------------------------------------------------------------
  COMMANDS:        HO  Holdings        H   Help
                   N   Next Record     PRI Print
  0 Other Options  I   Index
  Held by library--type   HO for holdings information.
  NEXT COMMAND:_
```

Figure 34.22: NOTIS: Record display/other database

```
Search Request:  S=COCAINE                                               WILS
WILSON RECORD  -- 1 of 14 Entries Found               Holdings Detail
------------------------------   Screen 1 of 1    ------------------------------
          TITLE:  Back to the dark ages.
       CITATION:  Sports Illustrated 59:15 Jul 11 '83
---------------------      ASSOCIATED LIBRARY HOLDINGS    ----------------------
Title:         Sports illustrated.
LOCATION:      MAIN
CALL NUMBER:   GV561 .S733
STATUS:        Check Shelf
LIBRARY HAS:   v.1(1954:Aug.16)-v.37(1990:Dec. 30)




------------------------------------------------------------------------------
  COMMANDS:        V   View Record     H   Help
                   N   Next Record     PRI Print
  0 Other Options  I   Index

  NEXT COMMAND:_
```

Figure 34.23: NOTIS: OPAC holdings from a database

```
Search Request:  S=DESKTOP PUBLISHING                          NOTIScat
SERIAL - Record 1 of 17 Entries Found          Heading Information
-----------------------------    Screen 1 of 1   -----------------------------
Desktop publishing

Here are entered works on the use of a personal computer, writing and
graphics software, and page layout software to produce printed material for
publication.









----------------------------------------------------------------------
COMMANDS:            N   Next Record
                    I   Index
 O Other Options    H   Help

NEXT COMMAND:_
```

Figure 34.24: NOTIS: Usage/scope note

```
                                                            NOTIScat
                                               Search List
----------------------------------------------------------------------
Reference searches with "S" followed by the appropriate index number:   "S5"
To execute, use the statement(s) desired:   "S5","S1 AND S5","S1 OR EAR"
To edit, use the EDIT command and the statement(s) desired:   "EDIT S1 AND EAR"
Augment ATS Searches:   "S3 MARGARET", "EDIT S2 MISSISSIPPI RIVER"
                                                        HITS
S1. S =DESKTOP PUBLISHING                                17
S2. T =FOUNDATION TRILOGY                                 1
S3. K =FIRE AND MOON                                      1
S4. K =KING ADJ MARTIN ADJ LUTHER                        27
S5. S =AFRO AMERICANS--CIVIL RIGHTS                      112
S6. A =KING MARTIN                                        6




----------------------------------------------------------------------
 O Other Options   I   Index          H   Help

NEXT COMMAND:_
```

Figure 34.25: NOTIS: Search list

35

PALS
Bridge at the University of Manitoba

Pat Nicholls

PALS is an online integrated library system developed at Mankato State University for the Minnesota State University System and marketed by Unisys Corp. The system was purchased by the University of Manitoba and St. Boniface General Hospital in June 1989. Locally, the system is called Bridge.

The online catalog is the basis of the PALS system and contains the catalog records of 13 campus libraries and 2 hospital libraries. Presently, there is a total of over 710,000 bibliographic records. Bridge is available on the campus network and can be accessed by several hundred terminals on campus. Dial-up access is also available, and the system is accessible on the Internet.

PALS, as installed at the University of Manitoba, does not have any special terminal requirements; a simple ASCII terminal suffices. There is no special color or graphic highlighting and the system is command driven. There is a menu overlay available, and it is possible to set up function keys if the terminals have the capability, but we have not felt these were necessary.

Starting Out and Help

The introductory screen (Figure 35.1) provides a brief introduction to the system, as well as introducing the help screens (for example, Figures 35.2 through 35.4), which are very extensive. There is

also a command to start the system without displaying this introductory screen.

Searching

The system has full keyword searching with most Boolean features. Fields included in the keyword indexes are locally determined. We have chosen to index all author, title and subject fields for the keyword index, plus several note fields such as contents and local use note fields. Keyword searches can be specified as author, title (Figure 35.5), subject (Figure 35.6), series (Figure 35.7) or note (Figure 35.8) keyword searches, or can be generally applied (Figure 35.9). Searches can be narrowed by additional keywords, format, and location, as well as language and date. In addition to keyword searching, PALS provides precise author, title, author-title combination (Figure 35.10), subject searching, and call number searching.

Searches can be truncated and terms within a search can be truncated (Figure 35.11). The truncation key # denotes that one or more letters or one or more terms have been truncated. The ? can be used to indicate truncation of one letter. It can be used within a term or at the end of a term.

Displays and Errors

The default display for public-access terminals is the medium display. Searches that find only one record automatically display the record in this format. For searches retrieving multiple records, the system responds with a prompt that will result in a one-line display of the records found (Figure 35.12). Short (Figure 35.13), medium (Figure - 35.14), long (Figure 35.15), and tagged (Figure 35.16) displays are available in the system in addition to the one-line display.

Attempting to display a record beyond the end of the hitlist results in an error message from the system (Figure 35.17). Error messages such as these are set in the system and not easily changed. Most (e.g.. Display exceeds records matching search — no action taken) are reasonably explicit. An incorrectly keyed search term will typically yield no result.

Upon display of a record, the system prompts with instructions for displaying the availability status of items linked to that record. The display status command (Figure 35.18) tells the patron the specific location of an item that is available on the shelves, when it's due back if it is signed out, how many holds are already on the item, and its reserve ID, if the item is on reserve. Patrons can place a hold on an item that is signed out. When the item is returned, the system generates a notice for the first patron in the hold queue. To recall an item before it is due, the patron must make the request to circulation staff.

Multiple volumes belonging to one title are displayed with the display status command. A summary holdings display is given first with a prompt for more detailed information (Figure 35.19). When the serials-control module is implemented, current issues will be added to this holdings display as they are checked in.

Browsing

All of the indexes, except number indexes, can be browsed to show related entries. This includes the author (Figures 35.20 and 35.21), title, subject (Figure 35.22), and call number (Figure 35.23) indexes. Browsing the subject index shows the subdivisions that have been used for any particular subject heading. Browsing the call number index allows the patron to see the books as they would appear on the shelves, except that they can see several libraries' shelves combined in one sequence. PALS has an authority-control module that provides references from unused names, subject headings, etc., and to related names, etc., but we have not yet implemented it.

Nonbook Materials

We have catalogued many nonbook materials. The appropriate information from the MARC record is displayed for these. Searches can also be limited by these formats if the bibliographic records has been correctly coded. Also included in our catalog are some archival and manuscript materials from the University Archives and Special Collections.

PALS as a Union Catalog

One of the more noteworthy features of PALS is its handling of multiple institutions in one database. Normally, a terminal connected to PALS defaults to searching one institution's catalog. There is also the option of searching another library's catalog or groups of libraries, or the entire system. This can be done as part of a single search or by temporarily changing the search default (Figures 35.24 through 35.26).

Saving Searches

Searches can be saved in sets, to a maximum of ten. Boolean operators can then be used to combine these sets in various ways (Figure 35.27). These sets are retained until cleared by the user or until a new session is begun on that terminal.

Overall, our PALS catalog, Bridge, has been very successful. The availability of circulation information linked to bibliographic records is useful and popular.

```
UML=>begin
BEGIN SESSION ON PALS       09-15-91 10:46:02 ID/WA: P00213/0007  VSN: 90.1

        St. Boniface                    University
        General Hospital                of Manitoba
        Libraries                       Libraries

                        BRIDGE


    Welcome to the online public access catalogue!  The PALS-based catalogue
provides access to the collections of two institutions so users should note
the online prompt to determine which institution they are searching.

    If you are using the system for the first time, type:  HELP

    If you wish to search both libraries in the system, type:  HELP SY

    If you are accessing this system from outside a library, remember that
to leave and return to the campus network, you must type:  $$SOFF

    If you have any questions or require assistance in using the catalogue,
please do not hesitate to approach the Libraries staff.
UML=>
```

Figure 35.1: PALS: Opening screen

```
help
Screen 001 of 001                                       Catalog UML
PALS INSTRUCTIONS:  Basic Help

Explanations are available for most of the system commands.  Type HELP followed
by one of the 2 character codes listed below.  For example, for help on author
searching, enter:  HELP AU

General:                        SE — Sets and Boolean commands
BE — Beginning and ending a session  TR — Truncation of terms or statements
GE — General summary of commands     SY — Searching other institutions
AH — Advanced help summary
CI — Circulation help summary   Narrowing Searches:
NE — News about PALS            NA — Narrowing by additional words
                                DA — Narrowing by publication date
Searching:                      LA — Narrowing by language
AU — Searching by author        FO — Narrowing by format
TI — Searching by title         SH — Narrowing by shelflist locations
TE — Searching by term or topic
SU — Searching by subject       Displaying Results:
CA — Searching by call number   DI — Displaying search results
CO — Searching by author & title PR — Printing offline (Not available)
BR — Browsing the index files   OP — Printing online
```

Figure 35.2: PALS: Basic help

```
>help au
Screen 001 of 001                                              Catalog UML
PALS INSTRUCTIONS:   Searching By Author - Brief Notes

An author search will locate those materials written or edited by individuals,
companies, associations, conferences, or organisations.  The command name
is AU and the correct format is:
          AU last-name first-name middle-name       (for individual authors)
          AU first four words                       (for corporate authors)
For example:
          AU GROVE FREDERICK PHILIP
          AU NAIMARK ARNOLD
          AU PICARD
          AU POETRY SOCIETY OF WINNIPEG

Upon completion of a search command, the system will respond with a count of
the items it has found.  It will also prompt you with a display command.  For
more information on the display command, type HELP DI.

For detailed information on author searching, type HELP AS.

For notes on searching a combination of author and title, type HELP CO.
```

Figure 35.3: PALS: Help for author searches

```
>help tm
Screen 001 of 003                                              Catalog UML
PALS INSTRUCTIONS:   Searching By Term - Detailed Notes

A term search will locate materials which contain the specified terms in the
field being searched.  There are six different term searches and they all use
this format:
     TE  word1 <BO> word2 <BO> word3 <BO> word4...     (General term search)
                    (Where <BO> is a boolean operator:  AND, OR, or NOT)

The six term searches and their commands are:
     TE  (General term search)        NT  (Note term search)
     TT  (Title term search)          RT  (Series term search)
     AT  (Author term search)         ST  (Subject term search)


The TE command is the general term search and it combines all of the other
five term commands.  The TT, ST, NT, RT, and AT commands are all subsets of
the TE command and may be used for a more precise search.  Generally, single
term searches retrieve far too many records to be useful so your term searches
should employ boolean operators in the format shown in the above example.


————Type NS and press NEWLINE, RETURN or ENTER key to get Next Screen
```

Figure 35.4: PALS: Detailed term-search help (1)

```
>tt poverty developing countries
 643 RECORD MATCHES AFTER TERM POVERTY
   5 RECORD MATCHES AFTER TERM DEVELOPING
   3 RECORDS MATCHED THE SEARCH
——Type DI 1-3  to Display the records
>tt fire moon
 398 RECORD MATCHES AFTER TERM FIRE
  NO RECORDS MATCHED THE SEARCH
>
```

Figure 35.5: PALS: Title keyword searches

```
>st poor developing countries
 799 RECORD MATCHES AFTER TERM POOR
  38 RECORD MATCHES AFTER TERM DEVELOPING
  38 RECORDS MATCHED THE SEARCH
——Type DI 1-20 to Display first 20 records
>
```

Figure 35.6: PALS: Subject word search

```
rt discovery hour
  19 RECORD MATCHES AFTER TERM DISCOVERY
  14 RECORDS MATCHED THE SEARCH
——Type DI 1-14 to Display the records
>di
```

Figure 35.7: PALS: Series word search

```
nt fictional biography
    9 RECORD MATCHES AFTER TERM FICTIONAL
Screen 001 of 001  Record 0001 of 0001 UML              Catalog UML
LOCTN: DAFOE ARCHIVES Tc 38
AUTHR: Robertson, Heather, 1942-
TITLE: Sex, politics and the diary : the making of Willie [sound recording]
         : a talk delivered 20 February 1985 in the University of Manitoba
         Libraries Department of Archives and Special Collections Discovery
         hour series / by Heather Robertson.
DESCR: 1 sound cassette (ca. 70 mins.).
NOTES: A study of the making of Robertson's fictional biography of William
         Lyon Mackenzie King.
SUBJT: Robertson, Heather, 1942- Willie
SERIE: Discovery hour series ; 1985/02/20
——Type DS to Display item availability Status
>
```

Figure 35.8: PALS: Notes search and result

```
>te martin luther king
5452 RECORD MATCHES AFTER TERM MARTIN
 393 RECORD MATCHES AFTER TERM LUTHER
  39 RECORDS MATCHED THE SEARCH
——Type DI 1-20 to Display first 20 records
>
```

Figure 35.9: PALS: Term search

```
>co pynchon vineland
Screen 001 of 001   Record 0001 of 0001 UML              Catalog UML
LOCTN: DAFOE MAIN STACKS PS 3566 Y55 V56 1990
AUTHR: Pynchon, Thomas.
TITLE: Vineland / Thomas Pynchon. —
EDITN: 1st ed. —
PUBLR: Boston : Little, Brown, c1990.
DESCR: 385 p. ; 24 cm.
————Type DS to Display item availability Status
>ds
BAR-CODE-ID       LOCATION      COPY  DUE—DATE-TIME  HOLDS  RESERVE-ID
32212004712744    DF 2ND FLOOR   01   08-15-91 17:00  000
>
```

Figure 35.10: PALS: Author-title search

```
UML=>ti dialect# phenom#
Screen 001 of 001   Record 0001 of 0001 UML              Catalog UML
LOCTN: DAFOE MAIN STACKS B 3305 M74 B63
AUTHR: Bologh, Roslyn Wallach.
TITLE: Dialectical phenomenology : Marx's method / Roslyn Wallach Bologh.
       —
PUBLR: Boston : Routledge & Kegan Paul, 1979.
DESCR: xiii, 287 p. ; 22 cm. —
NOTES: Bibliography: p. 275-277.
SUBJT: Marx, Karl, 1818-1883—Methodology.
SUBJT: Methodology
SUBJT: Dialectic
SUBJT: Phenomenology
SUBJT: Marxian economics
SERIE: International library of phenomenology and moral sciences.
————Type DS to Display item availability Status

UML=>tt wom?n
4876 RECORDS MATCHED THE SEARCH
————Type DI 1-20 to Display first 20 records      (or)
Use AND command with additional WORD(s) or LIMITING command to reduce results
UML=>
```

Figure 35.11: PALS: Truncated searches

```
>di
Screen 001 of 001                                       Catalog UML
NMBR DATE ————————————————TITLE———————————————  ————-AUTHOR————-
0001 1981  Charting the course for nonviolent social cha
0002 1935- Crime :   Murder : Accused: Chenault, Marcus ;
0003 1935- Crime :   Murder : Accused: Ray, James Earl ;
0004 1981  The ethics of Martin Luther King, Jr. /       Smith, Ervin.
0005 1982  Martin Luther King, Jr. :   the making of a mi  Ansbro, John J.
0006 1985  Martin Luther King, Jr. :   a guide to help NE
0007 1985  Poverty in the developing countries, 1985 :    Clausen, A. W.
————Type DI NMBR(s) to Display specific records
>
```

Figure 35.12: PALS: Multiple result display

```
>di 7 s
Screen 001 of 001   Record 0007 of 0007 UML                    Catalog UML
LOCTN: AGRICULTURE MAIN STACKS HV 696 F6 H8 no.3 c.1-2
AUTHR: Clausen, A. W.
TITLE: Poverty in the developing countries, 1985 : address delivered on
          January 11, 1985, at the Martin Luther King, Jr. Center for
          Nonviolent Social Change, Inc., Atlanta, Georgia / A.W. Clausen.
          —
————Type DS to Display item availability Status
>
```

Figure 35.13: PALS: Brief display, book

```
>di 7
Screen 001 of 001   Record 0007 of 0007 UML                    Catalog UML
LOCTN: AGRICULTURE MAIN STACKS HV 696 F6 H8 no.3 c.1-2
AUTHR: Clausen, A. W.
TITLE: Poverty in the developing countries, 1985 : address delivered on
          January 11, 1985, at the Martin Luther King, Jr. Center for
          Nonviolent Social Change, Inc., Atlanta, Georgia / A.W. Clausen.
          —
PUBLR: San Francisco, CA (2015 Steiner St., San Francisco 94115) : Hunger
          Project, c1985.
DESCR: iv, 11 p. ; 24 cm.
SUBJT: Poor—Developing countries
SERIE: Hunger Project papers. no. 3
————Type DS to Display item availability Status
>
```

Figure 35.14: PALS: Medium (default) display

```
>di 7 l
Screen 001 of 001   Record 0007 of 0007 UML                    Catalog UML
LOCTN: AGRICULTURE MAIN STACKS HV 696 F6 H8 no.3 c.1-2
AUTHR: Clausen, A. W.
TITLE: Poverty in the developing countries, 1985 : address delivered on
          January 11, 1985, at the Martin Luther King, Jr. Center for
          Nonviolent Social Change, Inc., Atlanta, Georgia / A.W. Clausen.
          —
PUBLR: San Francisco, CA (2015 Steiner St., San Francisco 94115) : Hunger
          Project, c1985.
DESCR: iv, 11 p. ; 24 cm.
SERIE: The Hunger Project papers, 0743-6416 ; no. 3 (March 1985)
NOTES: Keynote address at the National Action Symposium on Poverty and World
          Hunger, sponsored by the Martin Luther King, Jr. Center for
          Nonviolent Social Change and the Hunger Project.
SUBJT: Poor—Developing countries
AAUTH: Martin Luther King, Jr. Center for Nonviolent Social Change.
AAUTH: Hunger Project.
SERIE: Hunger Project papers. no. 3
OCLC#  02706924
————Type DS to Display item availability Status
>
```

Figure 35.15: PALS: Long display, book

```
>di 1 7 t
Screen 001 of 002  Record 0007 of 0007 UML                    Catalog UML
IDL 02706924 UML 891212 UML 1136
LDR      01136nam  22001630a 45 0
001      ocm72706924
008      880530s1985    cau            1  eng d
010        85244434
035   0  #e ag #f r
039   0  2 #b 3 #c 3 #d 3 #e 3
040      MWU #b eng #d UML
043      d——————
046      DLC #c DLC
049   0  UMBA[c.1-2]
050   00 HC59.72.P6 #b C43 1985
055    4 HV696.F6 #b H8
082   0  362.5/09172/4 #z 19
090   0  HV 696 F6 H8 no.3
100   10 Clausen, A. W.
245   10 Poverty in the developing countries, 1985 : #b address delivered
            on January 11, 1985, at the Martin Luther King, Jr. Center for
            Nonviolent Social Change, Inc., Atlanta, Georgia / #c A.W.
            Clausen. —
260   0  San Francisco, CA (2015 Steiner St., San Francisco 94115) : #b
            Hunger Project, #c c1985.
>ns
```

Figure 35.16: PALS: MARC display, book (1)

```
>su poor developing countries
  24 RECORDS MATCHED THE SEARCH
————Type DI 1-20 to Display first 20 records
>di 25
DISPLAY EXCEEDS RECORDS MATCHING SEARCH — NO ACTION TAKEN
>
```

Figure 35.17: PALS: Range error message

```
>di 7 s
Screen 001 of 001  Record 0007 of 0007 UML                    Catalog UML
LOCTN: AGRICULTURE MAIN STACKS HV 696 F6 H8 no.3 c.1-2
AUTHR: Clausen, A. W.
TITLE: Poverty in the developing countries, 1985 : address delivered on
            January 11, 1985, at the Martin Luther King, Jr. Center for
            Nonviolent Social Change, Inc., Atlanta, Georgia / A.W. Clausen.
            —
————Type DS to Display item availability Status
>ds
BAR-CODE-ID      LOCATION      COPY  DUE—DATE-TIME  HOLDS  RESERVE-ID
32212009212716   AG MAIN FLR    01   *ON SHELVES     000
32212009212724   AG MAIN FLR    02   *ON SHELVES     000
>
```

Figure 35.18: PALS: Status display

```
Screen 001 of 001   Record 0001 of 0002 UML                    Catalog UML
LOCTN: ST. JOHNS MAIN STACKS PS 8001 F353
TITLE: 54
PUBLR: Prince George, B.C. : [s.n., 1970]-
DESCR: v. : ill. ; 22-28 cm.
DESCR: [1970]-      . —
NOTES: Sponsored by the College of New Caledonia Student Union.
NOTES: Title from cover.
SUBJT: Canadian literature—20th century—Periodicals.
AAUTH: College of New Caledonia
ATITL: Fifty-four degrees forty minutes north
ATITL: Fifty-four forty
OCLC# 02573759
——Type DS to Display item availability Status
>ds
BAR-CODE-ID      LOCATION      CP DUE——TIME HL HOLDING————— RESERVE-ID
***SUMMARY       type DSD for detail holdngs     1970-71
>dsd
BAR-CODE-ID      LOCATION      CP DUE——TIME HL HOLDING————— RESERVE-ID
32212005617611 SJ MAIN FLR   01 *ON SHELVES      1970
32212005617603 SJ MAIN FLR   01 *ON SHELVES      1971
>
```

Figure 35.19: PALS: Serial holdings

```
>br au pynchon t
Screen 001 of 001                                            Catalog UML
NMBR  COUNT  (AU)——————-INDEX KEY—————     ————————TITLE———————
0001    1   PYMONENKO MYKOLA KORNYLOV    Mykola Pymonenko :
0002*   5   PYNCHON THOMAS
0003    1   PYNE ANN L                   effects of an attention-deman
0004    3   PYNE STEPHEN J
0005    1   PYNE TIMOTHY                 Judicial retirement plans /
0006    1   PYNE ZOE KENDRICK            Giovanni Pierluigi da Palestr
0007    1   PYNER DAVID A                Simplified painless endodonti
0008    2   PYNOOS JON
0009    1   PYNSENT ROBERT B             Julius Zeyer;
0010    1   PYPER NANCY                  Nancy Pyper theatre collectio
0011    1   PYPER T R TERRY              French dictionary of informat
0012    1   PYRA JOSEPH F JOSEPH         Constitutional law, protectio
0013    1   PYRAH LESLIE NORMAN          Renal calculus /
0014    2   PYRAMUS AND THISBE
0015    1   PYRCH RONALD C               heterosexual game /
0016    1   PYRCZ ORVILLE A              Business organization caseboo
0017    1   PYRETHRUM BOARD OF KENYA     Pyrethrum, the natural insect
0018    1   PYRITZ HANS WERNER           Bibliographie zur deutschen L
0019    1   PYRITZ ILSE                  Bibliographie zur deutschen L
0020    2   PYSMENNA LARYSA MYKHAILI
——Type SE NMBR(s) to select entries / BF or BB to browse forward or backward
>se 2
```

Figure 35.20: PALS: Author browse

```
    5 RECORD MATCHES FROM SELECT
————Type DI 1-5  to Display the records
>di
Screen 001 of 001                                         Catalog UML
NMBR DATE ————————————————————TITLE————————————————  ————————-AUTHOR—————————-
0001 1966  The crying of lot 49.                         Pynchon, Thomas.
0002 1973  Gravity's rainbow.                             Pynchon, Thomas.
0003 1984  Slow learner :  early stories /               Pynchon, Thomas.
0004 1963  V.,  a novel.                                  Pynchon, Thomas.
0005 1990  Vineland /                                      Pynchon, Thomas.
————Type DI NMBR(s) to Display specific records
>
```

Figure 35.21: PALS: Records from author browse

```
>br su desktop publishing
Screen 001 of 001                                          Catalog UML
NMBR  COUNT  (SU)—————————- INDEX KEY————————————  ——————————————TITLE——————————
0001    1    DESKS ONTARIO                          All about Ontario desks /
0002*   9    DESKTOP PUBLISHI
0003    1    DESKTOP PUBLISHI LIBRARY APPLIC         Library desktop publishing /
0004    1    DESLANDES M ANDRE FRANCO                Masque et lumieres au XVIIIe
0005    1    DESMARAIS PAUL                          Rising to power :
0006    3    DESMIDIACE
0007    2    DESMIDIALE
0008    1    DESMODORID CLASSIFI                     revision of the marine nemato
0009    2    DESMOSCOLE
0010    1    DESMOSOMAT                              Desmosomatidae (Isopoda, Asel
0011    1    DESMOSTYLI                              Two new Oligocene desmostylia
0012    2    DESNOS ROBERT
0013    1    DESNOS ROBERT CORPS ET                  Etude de "Corps et Biens" de
0014    4    DESNOS ROBERT CRITICIS AND
0015    1    DESNOYER FRANCOIS                       F. Desnoyer, cinquante ans de
0016    3    DESPAIR
0017    1    DESPAIR IN ART                          Gestures of despair in mediev
0018    4    DESPAIR IN LITERATU
0019    1    DESPIAU CHARLES EXHIBITI                Charles Despiau :
0020    4    DESPORTES PHILIPPE
————Type SE NMBR(s) to select entries / BF or BB to browse forward or backward
>
```

Figure 35.22: PALS: Subject browse

```
>br ca Z678.9
Screen 001 of 001                                          Catalog UML
NMBR  COUNT  (CA)———————-INDEX KEY———————   ———————————TITLE———
0001      1  Z 678.88.W45                   Determination of pre-acquisit
0002*     1  Z 678.9.A1A3 1984              New information technologies
0003      1  Z 678.9.A1A34                  Advances in library automatio
0004      1  Z 678.9.A1C5 1965              Proceedings of the 1965 Clini
0005      1  Z 678.9.A1C5 1968              Proceedings of the 1968 Clini
0006      1  Z 678.9.A1C5 1969              Proceedings of the 1969 Clini
0007      1  Z 678.9.A1C5 1970              Marc uses and users :
0008      1  Z 678.9.A1C5 1972              Applications of on-line compu
0009      1  Z 678.9.A1C5 1973              Networking and other forms of
0010      1  Z 678.9.A1C5 1974              Applications of minicomputers
0011      1  Z 678.9.A1C5 1975              use of computers in literatur
0012      1  Z 678.9.A1C5 1976              economics of library automati
0013      1  Z 678.9.A1C5 1977              Negotiating for computer serv
0014      1  Z 678.9.A1C5 1978              Problems and failures in libr
0015      1  Z 678.9.A1C5 1979              role of the library in an ele
0016      1  Z 678.9.A1C5 1980              Public access to library auto
0017      1  Z 678.9.A1C5 1981              New information technologies-
0018      1  Z 678.9.A1C5 1982              Library automation as a sourc
0019      1  Z 678.9.A1C5 1983              Professional competencies—te
0020      1  Z 678.9.A1C5 1984              Telecommunications: making se
————Type SE NMBR(s) to select entries / BF or BB to browse forward or backward
>bf
```

Figure 35.23: PALS: Call number browse (1)

```
ti sys atlas of human anatomy
 11 RECORDS MATCHED THE SEARCH
————Type DI 1-11 to Display the records
SYS>di
Screen 001 of 001                                          Catalog SYS
NMBR DATE  ————————————TITLE————————————   ————————-AUTHOR————-
0001 1989  Atlas of human anatomy /                Netter, Frank H.,
0002 1950  An atlas of human anatomy. —            Anson, Barry Joseph,
0003 1963  An atlas of human anatomy. —            Anson, Barry Joseph,
0004 1971  Atlas of human anatomy,  by Luis Lopez-Antune  Lopez-Antunez, Luis.
0005 1963- Atlas of human anatomy.                 Sobotta, Johannes,
0006 1950  An atlas of human anatomy.              Anson, Barry Joseph,
0007 1959  Atlas of human anatomy
0008 1967  Atlas of human anatomy.                 Spalteholz, Werner,
0009 1983  Sobotta Atlas of human anatomy /        Sobotta, Johannes,
0010 1977  Sobotta/Figge Atlas of human anatomy. — Sobotta, Johannes,
0011 1983  Sobotta Atlas of human anatomy. —       Sobotta, Johannes,
————Type DI NMBR(s) to Display specific records
SYS>di 1
```

Figure 35.24: PALS: Union catalog (1 of 3)

```
Screen 001 of 001                                          Catalog SYS
NMBR DATE  ————————————TITLE————————————   ————————-AUTHOR————-
0001 1989  Atlas of human anatomy /                Netter, Frank H.,
LIBRARIES: SBH UML
————Type DI LIB NMBR to display single record (LIB is one of above libraries)
SYS>di sbh 1
Screen 001 of 001  Record 0001 of 0011 SBH                 Catalog SYS
LOCTN: SBGH MEDICAL QS17 N474a 1989
AUTHR: Netter, Frank H., (Frank Henry), 1906-
TITLE: Atlas of human anatomy / by Frank H. Netter ; Sharon Colacino,
       consulting editor. —
PUBLR: Summit, N.J. : CIBA-GEIGY Corp., c1989.
DESCR: [xx], 514, [1], 36p. : ill.
NOTES: Includes bibliographical references (p. [516]).
NOTES: Med. 87283-91.86-13\2\90
NOTES:  SB 90-39
NOTES:  dlLogin Feb 27/90  94.20
SUBJT: Anatomy—atlases.
————Type DS to Display item availability Status
SYS>di uml 1
```

Figure 35.25: PALS: Union catalog (2 of 3)

```
Screen 001 of 001   Record 0001 of 0011 UML                Catalog SYS
LOCTN: DENTAL QS 17 N474a 1989
LOCTN: MEDICAL RESERVE TEXTBOOK  QS 17 N474a 1989
AUTHR: Netter, Frank H., (Frank Henry), 1906-
TITLE: Atlas of human anatomy / by Frank H. Netter ; Sharon Colacino,
           consulting editor. —
PUBLR: Summit, N.J. : CIBA-GEIGY Corp., c1989.
DESCR: [xx], 514, [i], 36p. : ill.
NOTES: Includes bibliographical references (p. [516]).
NOTES: Med. 87283-91.86-13\2\90
NOTES:  SB 90-39
NOTES:  dlLogin  Feb 27/90  94.20
SUBJT: Anatomy—atlases.
——Type DS to Display item availability Status
SYS>
```

Figure 35.26: PALS: Union catalog (3 of 3)

```
UML=>tt philosophy journal
5116 RECORD MATCHES AFTER TERM PHILOSOPHY
  41 RECORDS MATCHED THE SEARCH
——Type DI 1-20 to Display first 20 records
UML=>sa
WORK AREA SAVED IN SET 3
UML=>fo se
  27 RECORDS MATCHED LIMIT COMMAND
——TYPE DI 1-20 to Display first 20 records
UML=>sa
WORK AREA SAVED IN SET 4
UML=>bo 3 not 4
  41 RECORD MATCHES AFTER SET  3
  14 RECORDS MATCHED THE SEARCH
——Type DI 1-14 to Display the records
UML=>di
Screen 001 of 001                                          Catalog UML
NMBR DATE ——————————————————TITLE—————————————— ————-AUTHOR————-
0001 1973 Exegesis and argument;  studies in Greek phil
0002 1976 Facets of Plato's philosophy /
0003 1973 Martin Heidegger: in Europe and America.    Ballard, Edward G.
0004 1982 The metaphysics of Wittgenstein's Tractatus / Goddard, Leonard.
0005 1975 New essays in the history of philosophy /
0006 1979 New essays on John Stuart Mill and utilitaria
0007 1984 New essays on Aristotle /
0008 1976 New essays on Plato and the pre-Socratics /
0009 1977 New essays on contract theory /
0010 1986 Nuclear weapons, deterrence and disarmament /
0011 1988 Philosophy & biology /
0012 1987 Science, morality & feminist theory /
0013 1988 Select bibliography of journal articles on ph
0014 1986 Women and philosophy :/
——Type DI NMBR(s) to Display specific records
UML=>
```

Figure 35.27: PALS: Saved searches

36

PHOENIX
University of New Brunswick

Judith Aldus and Stephen Sloan

At the University of New Brunswick the library system and the Computing Services Centre have always had a close relationship. PHOENIX was developed as a joint project of both these departments around 1980.[1] Since that time PHOENIX has served the University community well. Now, however, a rewrite is being planned and the next few years should see the emergence of a new PHOENIX.

The catalog system was originally designed as a command-line-only system. However, the Reference staff at the Harriet Irving Library (UNB's main Humanities and Social Science Library) found that they could not provide the amount of instruction required. This was because the library serves as a major provincial resource and has lots of walk-in traffic not associated with the university. To help alleviate this problem, a menu mode for the catalog was developed. Today, the staff at Harriet Irving prefer the menu mode as a default while the branch libraries at Engineering, Education and Science continue to use mainly the command mode. Here we will mainly discuss the command mode as it is the more powerful of the two.

PHOENIX is an IBM 3270 type application. This means that the information displayed changes one full screen at a time, rather than scrolling from bottom to top. When a screen is full, the system requests the user to press the Clear or PF8 key. This prompt will often be visible in the examples.

Starting Out

Figures 36.1 and 36.2 represent the opening screens for the command mode and menu mode respectively. A few notes are needed to explain the items on the menu screen. The bottom line of the display refers to color-coded keys. These were custom designed for the original terminals. While these terminals have been replaced, clear key caps with paper inserts are now used on the newer models.

The reader will also note the listing of eight separate databases on the PHOENIX system. The LIBRARY database is the main one for all libraries on our Fredericton campus (with the exception of the Law Library, which is administratively separate from the other libraries). The other listings are specialized collections. All are MARC format except ENLIST and CLS. CLS will not be covered here (it lists UNB Computing Services publications and is quite small). ENLIST will be discussed

---

1 For a description of the development of PHOENIX see: Clinton, Marshall. "PHOENIX II: An on-line catalogue in a university library" in *Canadian Library Journal*, vol. 39, no. 1 (Feb. 1982): 9–14.

briefly later. Except for the ENLIST demonstration, all searches will be in the LIBRARY database.

Context-sensitive help is not a feature of PHOENIX. However, some online instruction is available. Figure 36.3 shows the explanation that follows the issuing of the *?format* enquiry. Online lessons are provided. Figure 36.5 shows the first of five screens of one such lesson. New lessons are nearly complete and should have replaced the ones shown here by the time this article sees print.

Search and Display

Searches for authors are entered in the form *s/a/lastname, firstname*. The first name will be automatically truncated if just the initial is entered. However, if more than 20 terms result from the truncation, an error message is displayed. Figure 36.5 displays this as well as a successful search for works by Martin Luther King, Jr. At present, PHOENIX has no authority control. It is planned for the next version.

Many users find that BROWSING the author index is more effective than searching. Figure 36.6 shows the results of issuing a *b/a/king, martin* command. The choose command makes the set from items in the listing. In this case we would choose "b."

Browsing is also possible on subjects. Figure 36.7 demonstrates this. Here we have chosen "c" and "b" (actually, a logical OR).

Call number, title, keyword, and periodical indexes are also browsable. Call number browsing is displayed in Figure 36.8.

Searching punctuation is demonstrated in Figure 36.9. The "/" in the title is treated as a space.

Displaying Records

The command for printing records to the screen is *DISPLAY*. It is used in the format *DISPLAY set# format record_numbers*. Formats are short, medium, long, name, title, z (record numbers only) and x (which displays tagged MARC). Defaults are: *last set short format all records*

Terminals not in public areas may send sets to be printed by remote printers either in the library or at Computing Services. This is done by using a *DUMP* command instead of *DISPLAY*. The inability of the present system to provide local printouts is the complaint we hear most often about PHOENIX. However, those users not on public terminals have the option of dumping to either a text file in our mainframe operating system or sending the information to their e-mail account as a message.

Figures 36.10 through 36.13 demonstrate the display format options for a book found in the subject search for works about Martin Luther King, Jr. Figure 36.14 shows the name format for books on Oscar Wilde.

Figure 36.15 displays a UNB publication that has multiple locations and copies.

Display of Nonbook Information

Reproduced here are the long displays for nonbook materials. Figure 36.16 shows a CD-ROM record, Figure 36.17 a collection of scores, Figure 36.18 part of a sound recording, and Figure 36.19 part of an archival record from the BBROOK database. This database is still under development. It will index UNB materials relating to Lord Beaverbrook. It uses full MARC format for the archival records.

One unique aspect of PHOENIX is the ability to search map records by their coordinates. This ability is a little too complex to explain in detail but is illustrated by Figures 36.20 and 36.21. Questions can be addressed to the authors.

Full MARC format is also used in the PAINE database. This file indexes the archives department's newspaper clippings of material relating to the university.

The ENLIST Database

The Engineering Library maintains a "quick and dirty" database that has a simple structure. Known as ENLIST, this database lists materials that could not otherwise be included in the full online catalog. These items include some journal article citations (most notably all the journals of the ASCE), microfiche, books not yet converted from Dewey to LC and pamphlet file material. Although the same command language is used, searching EN-

LIST is somewhat different from searching the LIBRARY database. There is only one index. Words from titles, authors, and keywords are all searched with each search command. Browsing is not supported.

Another unique aspect of ENLIST is that many of the special libraries in Fredericton and professors on campus use it to help organize their own collections. They provide the data in machine readable form. The Engineering Library staff proofs it and adds the records to the database.

Materials owned by this type of user are distinguished by a code in the location field.

A long display for an ASCE journal record is reproduced in Figure 36.22. All fields are included in the index except for call number and notes.

Internet Access

Librarians interested in accessing PHOENIX are welcome to do so through the Internet. Our address is 131.202.1.2. Once connected, choose menu option 8. Remember that this requires TN3270 capabilities and that Telnet will not work.

```
          ***** WELCOME TO THE PHOENIX SYSTEM *****
        FOR THE LATEST DEVELOPMENTS IN PHOENIX, TYPE   NEWS

To learn how to use the PHOENIX system, press the key marked CLEAR and then
press the key marked LESSON. (On terminals outside the Library, type  LESSON.)

If you do not understand a response, type a question mark
If you need help, type  HELP

For information on available databases, type  ?BASES

You are now connected to the LIBRARY data base.
ENTER COMMAND




---x----1----x----2----x----3----x----4---x----5----x----6--- Command Mode --
```

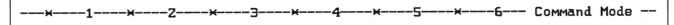

Figure 36.1: Phoenix: Welcome screen

```
                         PHOENIX MENU MODE
Welcome to UNB's online catalogue.  You are now in the LIBRARY database.   To
search in this database, press the GOLD CLEAR key.

To switch databases, type a number and press the GREEN ENTER key.
===>

  DATABASES    NO. OF TITLES   DESCRIPTION
  1 LIBRARY      280983        Material processed since 1977
  2 ENLIST       177624        Applied science and engineering
  3 CLIO          33549        Microfilmed books published before 1900
  4 MMI             998        Micmac-Maliseet Institute
  5 WCL           79389        Ward Chipman Library, U.N.B.S.J.
  6 LAW            8620        Law Library, U.N.B.
  7 CLS             625        Computing Centre documentation.
  8 GLEANER       20632        Index of articles in the Daily Gleaner newspaper




KEYS: RED-COMMAND MODE-PF3 × GOLD-START SEARCH-CLEAR
```

Figure 36.2: Phoenix: Menu screen (menu mode)

```
?format
The DISPLAY command lets you specify the format of the references you want to se
e.  The formats for the references in the Library catalogue are:

    S or SHORT    M or MEDIUM    L or LONG    T or TITLES    N or NAMES

For additional information press the key marked CLEAR then type   LESSON 2

ENTER COMMAND








  ---×----1----×----2----×----3----×----4----×----5----×----6--- Command Mode --
```

Figure 36.3: Phoenix: Help for display formats

```
            LESSON 2 - Finding books on a topic

The SEARCH command is used to find the items in the library which relate
to a subject.  Type S (meaning SEARCH) followed by your topic.

    S FORESTRY          or        SEARCH FORESTRY
    S MOOSE

When you enter a SEARCH command, the system creates a set of references which
contain your term(s).  It tells you how many references there are in the set.

The command:
            S MOOSE
would produce the following response:
            SET 1  12   MOOSE

Here the command S MOOSE has resulted in set number 1, which contains
twelve references with the word MOOSE.

You may search for more than one term at a time:
  ---×----1----×----2----×--- More - Press CLEAR/PF8 ---×----6--- Command Mode --
```

Figure 36.4: Phoenix: Searching tutorial (1 of 5)

```
s/a/king, M
TOO MANY TERMS
     Type  ? for more information.
ENTER COMMAND
?
     More than 20 index terms were found to match a truncated SEARCH term.
This sometimes happens with personal names for which not enough information
has been provided (For example   S SMITH, J).
     You should reenter your search with a longer truncated term, or providing
more information about the personal name.  Alternatively, you can specify the
number of characters to follow the truncated term (For example   S TREE:1).
     For more information type   ?TRUNCATE
ENTER COMMAND
s/a/king, martin
 SET   6        6  KING, MARTIN
ENTER COMMAND




   ---x----1----x----2----x----3----x----4----x----5----x----6--- Command Mode --
```

Figure 36.5: Phoenix: Author search assistance

```
 ID  # REFS   INDEX ENTRY
  a      0    KING, MARTIN
  b      6    KING, MARTIN LUTHER
  c      1    KING, MARY C
  d      1    KING, MARY CATHERINE
  e      1    KING, MARY ELIZABETH
  f      1    KING, MARY L
  g      2    KING, MARY PERRY, 1865-193
  h      1    KING, MARY, TR
  i      1    KING, MAURICE H
  j      1    KING, MAURICE HENRY
  k      1    KING, MAXWELL C
  l      7    KING, MERVYN A
  M      3    KING, MICHAEL
  n      1    KING, MICHAEL J
  o      2    KING, MICHAEL JOHN
ENTER COMMAND




   ---x----1----x----2----x----3----x----4----x----5----x----6--- Command Mode --
```

Figure 36.6: Phoenix: Author browse

```
ID   # REFS    INDEX ENTRY
 a        0    KING, MARTIN
 b       11    KING, MARTIN LUTHER
 c        2    KING, MARTIN LUTHER, JR
 d        1    KING, RICHARD, 1810-1876
 e        2    KING, RUFUS, 1755-1827
 f       23    KING, WILLIAM LYON MACKENZ
 g        1    KING, WILLIAM LYON MCKENZI
 h        1    KING, WILLIAM, 1685-1763
 i        1    KING, WILLIAM, 1768-1852
 j       77    KINGDOM
 k        1    KINGDOMS
 l        1    KINGDON, HOLLINGWORTH TULL
 m        1    KINGENIDAE
 n        2    KINGFISHERS
 o        2    KINGLAKE, ALEXANDER WILLIA
ENTER COMMAND
c cb
 SET   7      13   :CHOOSE C B FROM KING, MARTIN
ENTER COMMAND
 ---x----1----x----2----x----3----x----4----x----5----x----6--- Command Mode --
```

Figure 36.7: Phoenix: Subject browse

```
ID   # REFS    INDEX ENTRY
 a        0    Z678.9
 b        1    Z678.9.A1C53 1985
 c        1    Z678.9.A1C53 1986
 d        1    Z678.9.A1C87 1981
 e        1    Z678.9.A1D15
 f        1    Z678.9.A1I63
 g        1    Z678.9.A1I63 V. 8 NO. 2 J
 h        1    Z678.9.A1J68
 i        1    Z678.9.A1L32
 j        1    Z678.9.A1L325A
 k        1    Z678.9.A1L5 1970
 l        1    Z678.9.A1L518 1983
 m        2    Z678.9.A1M273
 n        1    Z678.9.A1N47
 o        1    Z678.9.A1P7 1973
ENTER COMMAND


 ---x----1----x----2----x----3----x----4----x----5----x----6--- Command Mode --
```

Figure 36.8: Phoenix: Call number browse

```
s contemporary ob gyn
 SET    5       4  CONTEMPORARY OB GYN
ENTER COMMAND
dm4

SET:    5, ITEM:     4 OF     4, RECORD #:   585925
LOCATION:  Main Library.
CALL #:    RG1.C65
LIB.HAS:   v. 2 1973-v. 7 1975,v. {8} 1976,v. 9 1977-v. 17 1981,v. {18} 1981,v
           . 19 1982-v. 30 1987 ;
OTHER:     Contemp. ob/gyn
OTHER:     Contemporary ob/gyn
TITLE:     Contemporary ob/gyn.
IMPRINT:   Oradell, N.J., etc., Medical Economics Co., etc.
COLLATION: v.
COLLATION: v. 1-   Jan. 1973-
ENTER COMMAND



  ---x---1---x---2---x---3---x---4---x---5---x---6--- Command Mode --
```

Figure 36.9: Phoenix: Title search with slash

```
ds7

SET:    1, ITEM:     7 OF     7, RECORD #:   260500
LOCATION: Main Library.
CALL #:   E185.97.K5L45 1970
AUTHOR:   Lewis, David L.
TITLE:    King; a critical biography
DATE:     1970
ENTER COMMAND




  ---x---1---x---2---x---3---x---4---x---5---x---6--- Command Mode --
```

Figure 36.10: Phoenix: Short display, book

```
dm7

SET:    1, ITEM:     7 OF     7, RECORD #:   260500
LOCATION: Main Library.
CALL #:   E185.97.K5L45 1970
AUTHOR:   Lewis, David L.
TITLE:    King; a critical biography by David L. Lewis.
IMPRINT:  New York, Praeger 1970
COLLATION: xii, 460 p.
ENTER COMMAND




  ---x---1---x---2---x---3---x---4---x---5---x---6--- Command Mode --
```

Figure 36.11: Phoenix: Medium display, book

```
d17

SET:      1, ITEM:      7 OF      7, RECORD #:   260500
LOCATION:   Main Library.
CALL #:     E185.97.K5L45 1970
AUTHOR:     Lewis, David L.
TITLE:      King; a critical biography by David L. Lewis.
IMPRINT:    New York, Praeger 1970
COLLATION:  xii, 460 p. illus., ports. 22 cm.
NOTES:      2d ed. published in 1978 under title: King : a biography of Martin
            Luther King, Jr.
NOTES:      Bibliography: p. 417-438.
SUBJECTS:   King, Martin Luther.
SUBJECTS:   Afro-Americans Biography.
SUBJECTS:   Baptists Clergy Biography.
SUBJECTS:   Clergy United States Biography.
ENTER COMMAND



 ----x----1----x----2----x----3----x----4----x----5----x----6--- Command Mode --
```

Figure 36.12: Phoenix: Long display, book

```
dx7

SET:      1, ITEM:      7 OF      7, RECORD #:   260500
001: $a   79095678
036: $a1970$bnyu$dbiography$eeng$fm$ga
090: $aE185.97.K5L45 1970$kMain
100: $aLewis, David L.
245: $aKing;$ba critical biography$cby David L. Lewis.
260: $aNew York,$bPraeger$c1970
300: $axii, 460 p.$billus., ports.$c22 cm.
500: $a2d ed. published in 1978 under title: King : a biography of Martin Luthe
     r King, Jr.
504: $aBibliography: p. 417-438.
600: $aKing, Martin Luther.
650: $aAfro-Americans$xBiography.
650: $aBaptists$xClergy$xBiography.
650: $aClergy$zUnited States$xBiography.
ENTER COMMAND



 ----x----1----x----2----x----3----x----4----x----5----x----6--- Command Mode --
```

Figure 36.13: Phoenix: MARC display, book

```
dn

SET:     1, ITEM:      1 OF     33, RECORD #:     53980
AUTHOR:    Hyde, Harford Montgomery, 1907-
SUBJECTS:  Wilde, Oscar, 1845-1900
OTHER:     Wilde, Oscar, 1854-1900, defendent.

SET:     1, ITEM:      2 OF     33, RECORD #:    111148
AUTHOR:    Wilde, Oscar, 1854-1900.
OTHER:     Jackson, Russell.

SET:     1, ITEM:      3 OF     33, RECORD #:    111722
AUTHOR:    Wilde, Oscar, 1854-1900.
OTHER:     Small, Ian.

SET:     1, ITEM:      4 OF     33, RECORD #:    112112
AUTHOR:    Wilde, Oscar, 1854-1900.
OTHER:     Guillot de Saix, Leon, 1885-

SET:     1, ITEM:      5 OF     33, RECORD #:    115092
 ---×-----1----×-----2----×--- More - Press CLEAR/PF8 --×----6--- Command Mode --
```

Figure 36.14: Phoenix: Name display, Oscar Wilde

```
v 4432431

SET: VIEW, ITEM:      1 OF      1, RECORD #:    443243
LOCATION:  Main Library.
CALL #:    LB2369.N39 1987
LIB.HAS:   copy 1-2
LOCATION:  Archives
CALL #:    LB2369.N39 1987
LOCATION:  Educ Res Ctr
CALL #:    LB2369.N39 1987
LOCATION:  On Reserve in Main Library
TITLE:     Form and format : a guide to the presentation of essays and reports
           / Department of English, University of New Brunswick. —
EDITION:   Multiformat ed. —
IMPRINT:   Fredericton, N.B. : Dept. of English, University of New Brunswick,
           1987.
COLLATION: 54 p. ; 21 cm.
SUBJECTS:  Report writing.
SUBJECTS:   Continuing Reserve   2 copies
OTHER:     University of New Brunswick. Dept. of English.
 ---×-----1----×-----2----×--- More - Press CLEAR/PF8 --×----6--- Command Mode --
```

Figure 36.15: Phoenix: Record with multiple locs

```
d120

SET:    1, ITEM:    20 OF    20, RECORD #:  652119
LOCATION:  Government Documents/CD-ROM
CALL #:    U.S. National Oceanic and Atmospheric Administration
TITLE:     Geophysics of North America {computer file}: CD-ROM.
EDITION:   Release 1.0. —
IMPRINT:   Boulder Co. : National Geophysical Data Center,  1989.
COLLATION: 1 computer laser optical disk ; 5 1/4 in. + 2 computer floppy disks
           + 1 user manual
NOTES:     Computer disks include Tutorial and Access software.
NOTES:     User's manual by Allen M. Hittelman, John O. Kinsfather, Herbert Me
           yers.
NOTES:     Title from laser disk.
NOTES:     System requirements: IBM PC/AT (286 or 386), or compatibles; minimu
           m 450K RAM
SUBJECTS:  Geophysics North America.
OTHER:     Hittelman, Allen M.
OTHER:     Kinsfather, John O.
OTHER:     Meyers, Herbert
   ——×——1——×——2——×—— More - Press CLEAR/PF8 —×——6—— Command Mode —
```

Figure 36.16: Phoenix: Long display, computer file

```
d12

SET:    2, ITEM:    2 OF    2, RECORD #:  301327
LOCATION:  Main Library.
CALL #:    M4.B3 1900z
LIB.HAS:   v. 1,no. 1-11;v. 2,no. 1-11;v. 3, no. 1-11;v. 4,no. 1-11;v. 5,no. 1
           -11;v. 6,no. 1-7, 9-12;v. 7,no. 1-2,4-9;v. 8,no. 1-4,6-8;v. 9,no. 1-
           2, 4-5,6-9;v. 10,no. 1-5;v. 11,no. 2-8,v. 12,no. 1-4,6-11
AUTHOR:    Bach, Johann Sebastian, 1685-1750
OTHER:     Selections
IMPRINT:   New York, Edwin F. Kalmus, {19—}
COLLATION: v. ; 18 cm.
SERIES:    Kalmus study scores
SERIES:    Kalmus miniature orchestra scores
CONTENTS:  {1} to {6} Cantatas, nos. 1-220 (in 67 v.). - {7} Organ (9 v.). - {
           8} Clavier (7 v.). - {9} Masses and sacred choruses (9 v.). - {10} O
           ratorios (6 v.). - {11} Concertos (10 v.). - {12} Fugue, canons, sui
           tes, partitas, Goldberg variations, overtures, sonatas (11 v.)
ENTER COMMAND

   ——×——1——×——2——×——3——×——4——×——5——×——6—— Command Mode —
```

Figure 36.17: Phoenix: Long display, score

```
d14

SET:    2, ITEM:    4 OF    4, RECORD #:  595330
LOCATION:  Educ Res Ctr/A.V.
CALL #:    793 BAC
AUTHOR:    Bach, Johann Sebastian, 1685-1750
OTHER:     Magnificat, BWV 243, D major. Latin.
TITLE:     Magnificat {sound recording} / J.S. Bach. —
IMPRINT:   {Amsterdam} : Philips, 1985.
COLLATION: 1 sound disc (42 min.) : digital ; 4 3/4 in. + 1 booklet.
NOTES:     Philips Digital Classics: 411 458-2.
CONTENTS:  Magnificat, BWV 243 (26 min.) — Jauchzet Gott in allen Landen, kan
           tate BWV 51 (16 min.).
NOTES:     Emma Kirkby, soprano ; Monteverdi Choir ; English Baroque Soloists
           ; John Eliot Gardiner, conductor.
SUBJECTS:  Magnificat (Music)
SUBJECTS:  Cantatas, Sacred
SUBJECTS:  Choruses, Sacred (Mixed voices) with orchestra
OTHER:     Kirkby, Emma.
OTHER:     Gardiner, John Eliot
   ——×——1——×——2——×—— More - Press CLEAR/PF8 —×——6—— Command Mode —
```

Figure 36.18: Phoenix: Long display, recording (1)

```
dx6

SET:     2, ITEM:     6 OF       6, RECORD #:        20
036: $ai1958-1961$fM$gb$jbvk
090: $xCase 3, File 4, 1142-1350$kArchives/Special Collections
130: $a{Lord Beaverbrook Rink (Saint John, N.B.)$f1958-1961}
245: $aSt. John Rink {for} London$f1958-1961.
300: $MCorrespondence$a118 (166 leaves).
300: $MPapers$a10 (33 leaves).
300: $MTechnical drawings$a6 :$bblueprints.
300: $aPamphlets$a1 (12 leaves)
300: $MMaps$a1.
300: $MNewspaper clippings$a1.
520: $aCorrespondence relating to the construction of the Lord Beaverbrook Rink
        in Saint John, N.B.  Also included are:  letters concerning the construct
        ion and operation of the rinks in Newcastle and Fredericton; correspondenc
        e relating to the construction of an Irving gas station on the corner next
        to the Saint John rink; and a New Brunswick government document entitled,
        The Social Services and Education Tax Act and Regulations (1957), with re
        lated correspondence.
---*----1----*----2----*--- More - Press CLEAR/PF8 --*----6--- Command Mode --
```

Figure 36.19: Phoenix: MARC display, archival (1)

```
Maps W070 30 00, n048 00 00
 SET   3      22   W0703000, N0480000
   1  W  70 30 00    W  65 00 00    N  48 00 00    N  45 00 00      500,000
   2  W  70 30 00    W  65 00 00    N  48 00 00    N  45 00 00      500,000
   3  W  71 00 00    W  59 47 00    N  48 02 00    N  43 05 00    1,050,000
   4  W  72 00 00    W  52 00 00    N  60 38 00    N  43 25 00    2,000,000
   5  W  79 30 00    W  63 30 00    N  50 30 00    N  45 00 00    3,000,000
   6  W  79 30 00    W  63 30 00    N  51 00 00    N  45 00 00    3,000,000
   7  W  79 30 00    W  63 30 00    N  52 00 00    N  45 00 00    3,000,000
   8  W  92 00 00    W  56 00 00    N  52 00 00    N  38 00 00    6,500,000
   9  W 105 00 00    W  50 00 00    N  54 00 00    N   5 00 00            0
  10  W 125 00 00    W  67 00 00    N  49 00 00    N  25 00 00    5,000,000
  11  W 126 00 00    W  64 00 00    N  49 00 00    N  23 00 00    7,135,135
  12  W 140 00 00    W  50 00 00    N  80 00 00    N  40 00 00    6,336,000
  13  W 140 00 00    W  50 00 00    N  80 00 00    N  40 00 00   35,000,000
  14  W 140 00 00    W  50 00 00    N  80 00 00    N  40 00 00    6,336,000
  15  W 140 00 00    W  50 00 00    N  85 00 00    N  42 00 00   15,840,000
  16  W 140 00 00    W  50 00 00    N  85 00 00    N  42 00 00    2,000,000
  17  W 141 00 00    W  50 00 00    N  85 00 00    N  42 00 00   15,840,000
  18  W 141 00 00    W  50 00 00    N  85 00 00    N  42 00 00   50,000,000
---*----1----*----2----*--- More - Press CLEAR/PF8 --*----6--- Command Mode --
```

Figure 36.20: Phoenix: Maps by coordinates

```
dx1

SET:     3, ITEM:      1 OF      1, RECORD #:   209894
001: 83269636.C..
034: $aa$b5000000$dW1710000$eW0120000$fN0840000$gN0060000
036: $a1969$bdcu$eeng$fM$ge
090: $aG3301.C55 1969.K5$kMap Room$fnolabel
100: $aKing, Philip Burke,$d1903-
245: $aTectonic map of North America$h{map}.$cCompiled by Phillip B. King. Prep
     ared by U.S. Geological Survey; with collaboration of Geological Survey of
      Canada; Institut of Geology, National University of Mexico; Geological Su
     rvey of Greenland; Danish East Greenland Expedition; and, individual geolo
     gists.
255: $aScale 1:5 000 000 ;$bBipolar oblique conic conformal proj.$c(W 171 00'--
     W 12 00'/N 84 00'--N 6 00')
260: $aWashington, D.C.,$bGeological Survey,$c1969.
300: $acol. map$c186 x 155 cm. on 2 sheets 102 x 164 cm.
500: $a"Contour interval 500 meters."
500: $aIncludes sources of information, 2 index maps, and inset "Lesser Antille
     s and northeastern South America."
 ---*----1----*----2----*--- More - Press CLEAR/PF8 --*----6--- Command Mode --
```

Figure 36.21: Phoenix: MARC display, map

```
ENTER COMMAND
dl1

SET:    1, ITEM:      1 OF      1, RECORD #:      262
LOCATION:  Engineering
CALL #:    ASCE V90 HY1
AUTHOR:    COMMITTEE REPORT
TITLE:     GOOD PRACTICE FOR HIGHWAY PIPELINE CROSSINGS
IMPRINT:   1964
NOTES:     PAPER 3763
ABSTRACT:  CONSTRUCTION HIGHWAYS PIPELINES REPORTS ROADS
ENTER COMMAND




 ---*----1----*----2----*----3----*----4----*----5----*----6--- Command Mode --
```

Figure 36.22: Phoenix: ENLIST, long ASCE record

37

plus
Purdue Libraries Unified System

Alan Alexander-Manifold

The Purdue Libraries Unified System (*plus*) was developed between 1980 and 1988 by the Purdue Library Systems Department (Figure 37.2). It was designed, first and foremost, to be flexible. The system is written in the "C" programming language to run under the UNIX operating system. In the true UNIX tradition, it was developed as a prototype that was successively enhanced from a minimal system to a full online catalog and integrated bibliographic record editing facility.

The *plus* system tries to be all things to all people. It has menus to guide the system through searching and displaying records. It has context-sensitive help and more extensive help screens available through easy commands. It runs on an almost infinite variety of terminals, using the special features of fancy terminals, but functioning in a reasonable and consistent way with the dumbest of terminals. It can be easily tailored so that each user can have information displayed in the most pleasing manner. It is also easy on the programmers; commands are easy to add or extend.

The online public-access catalog portion of *plus* was built on top of a generic framework program, which was designed to provide much of the flexibility. The issue of flexibility affects all online systems, not just catalogs. Thus, the underlying structure of *plus* was designed to give maximum functionality for all parts of a future integrated system.

Menus and Open Commands

The framework program provides a way for the application to define a variety of menus that can be used however the program chooses. A menu in *plus* is nothing more than a "pretty" list of commands. After considerable debate, we decided to print menus on the sides of the screens instead of at the bottom or top (Figure 37.13). We felt that with only 24 lines on a normal screen, giving up 3 or 4 for a menu would have too great an impact, but giving up 20 of 80 columns was okay.

An advanced user can turn off menus, which permits the system to use the full screen for its record displays (Figure 37.16). Each command is available at all times, whether it appears on the current menu or not. For example, a user can start a new author search by entering the "a" command without first displaying the search menu. A user can type a command with or without parameters. For example, if the user simply types "a," the program will prompt for an author. The user could also type "a:king, martin luther" and skip the prompt.

Help and Profiles

The basic framework also supports context-sensitive help, which is linked to the menu that the application chooses to display. In *plus*, the main menu is linked to the main menu help screen. Whenever a help screen is displayed, it always asks the user if more help is desired. If the user signifies that it is, the program displays an index of available help screens (Figure 37.15). The help screens are grouped into logical categories and are numbered for easy access. All help screens are easily modified with any text editor.

The substructure also provides a way to define any number of individual user profiles. These profiles control the commands to which a user has access. Since *plus* is an integrated system, library staff have special profiles defined that permit them to use commands for editing and manipulating records. If a profile prohibits access to a given *plus* command, any help screens associated with that command are also automatically hidden from the user. Currently, only two profiles are defined for public-access users. The first is for public terminals in the libraries. These users have access to all search and display commands, as well as other informational commands. The other public profile is for users who connect to *plus* through the Internet. Because these users must have their own accounts on some other machine on the Internet, they have access to a command to mail the results of their searches to their own account on another computer.

Hardware Independence

One last thing that the controlling framework offers is a high degree of hardware independence. At Purdue, as at most institutions, there is no single accepted standard for terminals. We designed *plus* to use the capabilities of the UNIX operating system to support as wide a range of terminals as possible. This support extends to supporting different protocols for screen clearing, highlighting, and sizing. Every part of *plus*, from the menus to the help screens, is designed to support any terminal type that is defined to UNIX. The system has run on everything from a printing terminal to a windowed workstation. The support for different terminal types extends to the ability to display diacritics, overstrikes, and special characters on those terminals that support such non-ASCII extensions.

Indexes

The three major focuses of an online catalog user are to search, display and manipulate records in the database. *Plus* has special features to support each of these operations. Title, author, corporate author, call number, standard numbers (ISBN, ISSN, LCCN and OCLC), and keyword searching are all available to the public. The standard numbers tend to be most useful to the library staff, but a surprising number of library users are familiar with the ISBN and ISSN. They frequently have citations that include these numbers and are happy to be able to search for them.

The traditional indexes (title, author, corporate author) are all defined as logically as possible. The Systems Department worked with catalogers on which fields should be indexed, then gradually refined the list through interaction with the users after *plus* became available. All indexes are updated immediately when a record is added or changed, so the catalog is always completely up to date. Author and title searches can also be qualified by date and record format by adding a less than sign (<) and the format, year, or range of years.

Keyword searching is limited to the main title field (245) and to the first subdivision of subject headings (Figure 37.8). There is no other access by subject, although this has been frequently mentioned as a desired enhancement. One requirement of all search types is that the user should be able to enter the search exactly as it appears in the record display and get results (Figure 37.14). Thus, punctuation and special characters that are stripped from the index entries are also stripped from the user's search statement to make sure this holds true. Searches that match no records cause the program to display an error message and the search menu (Figure 37.9).

Displays

Searches can be displayed in four different ways. The normal default (unless set otherwise by a user's profile) is to start with the multiple-record display (Figure 37.16, without menu). We wanted to create a display that would allow a number of records to be displayed on the same screen, while giving sufficient information that the user might not need to see a more complete record display. The multiple-record display includes, for each record, the title, author, call number, publication information and locations.

The default for single record displays at a public terminal is the public record display (Figure 37.4). This is a labeled display with similar fields grouped together and blank lines at important places in the display. The user's search is echoed at the top of the screen, along with the number of the current record within that search and the number of the current screen for that record. We wanted to provide as many clues to the users as possible about how they got where they are, and what other things they might do.

Another display, the librarian's record display, is available for anyone who cares to try it (Figure 37.5). On this display, there is a one-for-one correspondence between the labels and numeric MARC tags, so a refined user can determine which field is which without having to memorize all the MARC tags. The final display type is a MARC-tagged record, which is readily available to the public (Figure 37.6). This display type is provided mostly for the library staff and gets little use by the general public. We saw no reason, however, to keep it from the public, if they ever had any use for it.

Extended Search Capabilities

There are several ways to manipulate searches in *plus*. The Boolean operators AND, OR, and NOT are all supported for all search types. Thus, a user can enter a keyword search, then AND it with a call number search (Figure 37.10). Keyword searches can use embedded Boolean operators. If no operator is used, the default is AND. There is an extend-search menu, which, with its help screen, describes all of the Boolean operators (Figure 37.3). Like any *plus* command, however, the Boolean operators can be entered directly, without going through the extend-search menu.

In addition to the Boolean operators, users can save searches that they have already performed (Figure 37.20). The user enters the **sav** command and specifies the name to be used for the search. The search is then retained under that

name until it is removed, or a new session begun. Saved searches can be simple searches or the result of the application of Boolean logic. These saved searches can be restored at any time, or can be used in Boolean operations to refine other searches.

Besides the Boolean commands and the ability to save searches, searches can be printed or mailed to other accounts (Figure 37.21). The print and mail search commands both have options for various print formats. The default is almost identical to the multiple-record display format, but is not broken into screens and uses more columns than on a terminal screen. There are also options for full record printouts in the public, librarian's, and MARC formats. The same options are available for users mailing the results to their own accounts. The mail feature is one of the most popular features of *plus*, as it allows for the easy construction of tailored databases or bibliographies.

Other Features

Several miscellaneous features of *plus* are worthy of mention. In addition to informational commands about library hours and the location of *plus* terminals, the system has an online suggestion box. Users can offer suggestions or comments online, then the suggestions are reformatted, answered and posted online, where they are accessible to all users of the system (Figure 37.19). Several enhancements to *plus* were implemented in response to user suggestions.

A final interesting feature of *plus* is the other systems menu (Figure 37.17). This menu provides commands for connecting to the online catalogs of other nearby institutions. Connections are made across the Internet or other networks where possible, or by dial access if no network connection is available. Before it makes a connection, the program displays a screen giving information about the remote catalog, so the user will know how to search it when it comes up (Figure 37.18). The system then negotiates all network addresses and enters the necessary data to start up the online catalog. The user is kept informed of the progress of the connection but does not have to know anything about how to connect. The system gets out of the way once the remote catalog is ready for searching. The system also provides an easy and consistent way to exit each online catalog. This feature was added to *plus* in early 1988, when such access was not at all common.

The *plus* catalog is no longer in much use, having been abandoned in favor of statewide con-sistency. It is a shame that it could not have been developed further to see if the flexibility that was built into it could have helped it weather some of the upheaval in the library automation world that has found many systems lacking.

```
     P U R D U E   L I B R A R I E S   U N I F I E D   S Y S T E M

             (c) Copyright 1987, Purdue Research Foundation



             The on-line catalog is current as of 07/22/89


             The PLUS online catalog has been replaced.
   There will be no further updates to PLUS, which is updated through 7/22/89




Press <RETURN> to continue, or "h <RETURN>" for help --> █
```

Figure 37.1: plus: Opening screen

```
                    General Information Help Screen
   What is PLUS?   PLUS is a menu-oriented online catalog that is actually
             command-driven.  It was developed by the Purdue Libraries to help
             users find Library material.  PLUS includes descriptions of almost
             400,000 items, including all books cataloged since 1976, many books
             acquired before 1976, and all periodicals in the Libraries.

   Using PLUS:   Once the commands are learned, they may be used to bypass the
             menus.  Follow all commands with a carriage return.  A command and its
             arguments may be given together  by separating the two  with a colon.

             Example:    ENTER OPTION --> t:moby dick


   Getting Help:   Online "help" is available at any time via the HELP command.

             Example:    ENTER OPTION --> h

   When a help screen is displayed, additional help screens may be
   requested by typing 'm' (for more).  You may then select a specific
   help screen by typing its number.

Type 'm' for more help, or press RETURN to continue program --> █
```

Figure 37.2: plus: Help for opening screen

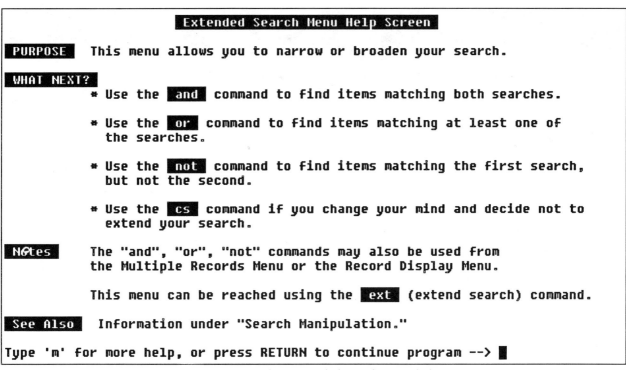

```
┌──────────────────────────────────────────────────────────────────────┐
│           ▄▄▄▄▄ Extended Search Menu Help Screen ▄▄▄▄▄                  │
│  ███PURPOSE███ This menu allows you to narrow or broaden your search.   │
│  ███WHAT NEXT?███                                                       │
│          * Use the  and  command to find items matching both searches.  │
│                                                                         │
│          * Use the  or  command to find items matching at least one of  │
│            the searches.                                                │
│                                                                         │
│          * Use the  not  command to find items matching the first search,│
│            but not the second.                                          │
│                                                                         │
│          * Use the  cs  command if you change your mind and decide not to│
│            extend your search.                                          │
│                                                                         │
│  ███Notes███  The "and", "or", "not" commands may also be used from     │
│               the Multiple Records Menu or the Record Display Menu.      │
│                                                                         │
│               This menu can be reached using the  ext  (extend search) command.│
│                                                                         │
│  ███See Also███ Information under "Search Manipulation."                 │
│                                                                         │
│  Type 'm' for more help, or press RETURN to continue program --> ▌      │
└──────────────────────────────────────────────────────────────────────┘
```

Figure 37.3: plus: Extended search menu help

```
┌──────────────────────────────────────────────────────────────────────┐
│SEARCH   a:king, martin luther<80-85                                     │
│BOOK                      (Screen 1 of 1)            Record     14 of 15  │
│                                                                         │
│      TITLE:  Strength to love / Martin Luther King, Jr.  +───────────────│
│     AUTHOR:  King, Martin Luther.                        | Options:      │
│  PUBLISHER:  Philadelphia : Fortress Press, c1981.       |  nr  Next Record│
│                                                          |  pr  Previous Record│
│   CALL NUM:  252.06 K585s, 1981                          |  ns  Next Screen│
│   LOCATION:  HSSE Library                                |  ps  Previous Screen│
│                copy 1                                    |  mr  Multiple Records│
│                                                          | sav  Save Search│
│   SUBJECTS:  Afro-American Baptists--Sermons.            | ext  Extend Search│
│              Sermons, American.                          |  sm  Search Menu│
│    DESCRIPT:  155, [4] p. ; 22 cm.                        |   q  Quit     │
│       LCCN:  80-2374                                     |   h  Help      │
│        ISBN:  0800614410 : $4.25                         +───────────────│
│                                                                         │
│                                                                         │
│                                                                         │
│                                                                         │
│                                                                         │
│                                                                         │
│ENTER OPTION --> ▌                                                       │
└──────────────────────────────────────────────────────────────────────┘
```

Figure 37.4: plus: Public record display (book)

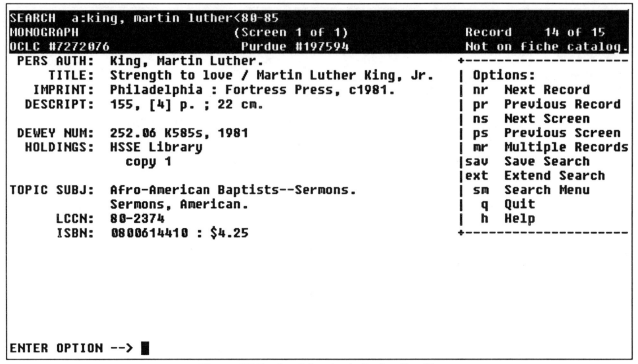

```
SEARCH   a:king, martin luther<80-85
MONOGRAPH                    (Screen 1 of 1)        Record    14 of 15
OCLC #7272076               Purdue #197594         Not on fiche catalog.
  PERS AUTH: King, Martin Luther.                +--------------------
      TITLE: Strength to love / Martin Luther King, Jr.  | Options:
    IMPRINT: Philadelphia : Fortress Press, c1981.       | nr  Next Record
   DESCRIPT: 155, [4] p. ; 22 cm.                         | pr  Previous Record
                                                          | ns  Next Screen
  DEWEY NUM: 252.06 K585s, 1981                           | ps  Previous Screen
   HOLDINGS: HSSE Library                                 | mr  Multiple Records
             copy 1                                       |sav  Save Search
                                                          |ext  Extend Search
 TOPIC SUBJ: Afro-American Baptists--Sermons.             | sm  Search Menu
             Sermons, American.                           | q   Quit
       LCCN: 80-2374                                      | h   Help
       ISBN: 0800614410 : $4.25                          +--------------------




ENTER OPTION --> ▮
```

Figure 37.5: plus: Librarian's display (book)

```
SEARCH   a:king, martin luther<80-85
MONOGRAPH                    (Screen 1 of 2)        Record    14 of 15
OCLC #7272076               Purdue #197594         Not on fiche catalog.
Type: a     Bib lvl: m     Entered: 06/22/82       Used: 06/22/82
Repr:       Enc lvl:       Govt pub:     Lang: eng  Source:       Illus:
Indx: 0     Mod rec:       Conf pub: 0   Ctry: pau  Dat tp: r     M/F/B: 10
Desc: a     Int lvl:       Festschr: 0   Cont: b    Dates: 1981,1977
                                                   +--------------------
010 .. 80-2374                                      | Options:
040 .. DLC#cDLC#dIPL                                | nr  Next Record
020 .. 0800614410 :#c$4.25                          | pr  Previous Record
039 0. 2#b3#c3#d3#e3                                | ns  Next Screen
050 0. BX6452#b.K5 1981                             | ps  Previous Screen
082 0. 252/.0613#219                                | mr  Multiple Records
092 .. 252.06#bK585s, 1981                          |sav  Save Search
049 .. IPL1#c1                                      |ext  Extend Search
100 10 King, Martin Luther.                         | sm  Search Menu
245 10 Strength to love /#cMartin Luther King, Jr.  | q   Quit
260 0. Philadelphia :#bFortress Press,#cc1981.      | h   Help
300 .. 155, [4] p. ;#c22 cm.                       +--------------------
500 .. Reprint. Originally published: Cleveland, Ohio :
       Collins+World, 1977.

ENTER OPTION --> ▮
```

Figure 37.6: plus: MARC display, book (1 of 2)

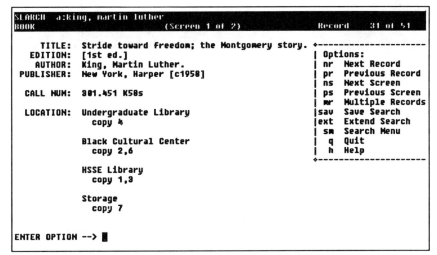

Figure 37.7: plus: Display with multiple locs (1)

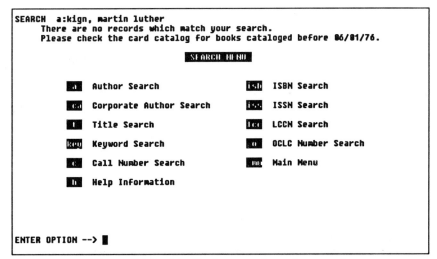

Figure 37.8: plus: Error message (out of range)

```
SEARCH  a:kign, martin luther
        There are no records which match your search.
        Please check the card catalog for books cataloged before 06/01/76.

                         SEARCH MENU

              a    Author Search            isb   ISBN Search

              ca   Corporate Author Search  iss   ISSN Search

              t    Title Search             lcc   LCCN Search

              key  Keyword Search           o     OCLC Number Search

              c    Call Number Search       m     Main Menu

              h    Help Information


ENTER OPTION -->
```

Figure 37.9: plus: Typing error in author search

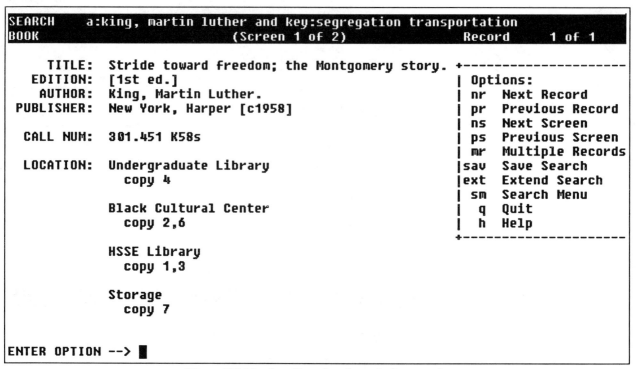

```
SEARCH      a:king, martin luther and key:segregation transportation
BOOK                          (Screen 1 of 2)              Record      1 of 1

      TITLE: Stride toward freedom; the Montgomery story. +------------------
    EDITION: [1st ed.]                                     | Options:
     AUTHOR: King, Martin Luther.                          | nr  Next Record
  PUBLISHER: New York, Harper [c1958]                       | pr  Previous Record
                                                           | ns  Next Screen
   CALL NUM: 301.451 K58s                                  | ps  Previous Screen
                                                           | mr  Multiple Records
   LOCATION: Undergraduate Library                         |sav  Save Search
             copy 4                                        |ext  Extend Search
                                                           | sm  Search Menu
             Black Cultural Center                         | q   Quit
             copy 2,6                                      | h   Help
                                                           +------------------
             HSSE Library
             copy 1,3

             Storage
             copy 7


ENTER OPTION --> █
```

Figure 37.10: plus: Completed two-index search

```
SEARCH  key:fire moon
BOOK                          (Screen 1 of 2)              Record      1 of 1

      TITLE: Of a fire on the moon.                        +------------------
    EDITION: [1st ed.]                                     | Options:
     AUTHOR: Mailer, Norman.                                | nr  Next Record
  PUBLISHER: Boston, Little, Brown [1970]                   | pr  Previous Record
                                                           | ns  Next Screen
   CALL NUM: 629.40973 M281o                               | ps  Previous Screen
                                                           | mr  Multiple Records
   LOCATION: HSSE Library                                  |sav  Save Search
             copy 2                                        |ext  Extend Search
                                                           | sm  Search Menu
             Engineering                                   | q   Quit
             copy 1                                        | h   Help
                                                           +------------------
             Undergraduate Library
             copy 3




ENTER OPTION --> █
```

Figure 37.11: plus: Keyword search for title

```
MULTIPLE RECORDS MENU                              Screen    1 of 32
SEARCH  c:686.2                                            158 records

1     Arnold, Edmund C. / Ink on paper 2; a handbook of t
         686.2 Ar641, 1972      1972, Harper & Row     +-------------------
            Book in:  HSSE                             | Options:
                                                       | ns   Next Screen
2     Auger, Daniel. / La typographie                  | ps   Previous Screen
         686.2 Au42t            1980, Presses Universitair | ss   Select Screen
            Book in:  HSSE                             |dis   Display Record
                                                       |sav   Save Search
3     Barlow, Marjorie Dan / Notes on woman printers in C |ext   Extend Search
         686.2 B249n            1976, Hroswitha Club   | sm   Search Menu
            Book in:  HSSE                             |  q   Quit
                                                       |  h   Help
4     Blumenthal, Joseph / Typographic years : a printer +-------------------
         686.2 B627Z, B627      1982, F.C. Beil
            Book in:  HSSE

5     Broekhuizen, Richard / Graphic communications
         686.2 B785g, 1979      1979, McKnight
            Book in:  HSSE

ENTER NUMBER OR OPTION --> ▮
```

Figure 37.12: plus: Partial call number search

```
SEARCH  t:graduate
A-V MATERIAL                   (Screen 1 of 1)        Record    1 of 165

      TITLE:  The Graduate                        +-------------------
  PUBLISHER:  Criterion 1967                      | Options:
                                                  | nr   Next Record
   CALL NUM:  LD0008                              | pr   Previous Record
   LOCATION:  Film Library                        | ns   Next Screen
                 copy 1                           | ps   Previous Screen
                                                  | mr   Multiple Records
   SUBJECTS:  Moving-pictures                     |sav   Save Search
              Feature films                       |ext   Extend Search
   DESCRIPT:  Laserdisc Sound Color 105 Min. (1 12-inch | sm   Search Menu
              laser videodisc)                    |  q   Quit
                                                  |  h   Help
                                                  +-------------------



ENTER OPTION --> ▮
```

Figure 37.13: plus: Public display, visual mat.

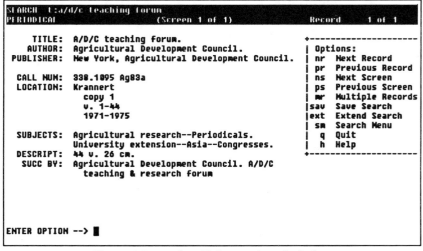

```
SEARCH  t:a/d/c teaching forum
PERIODICAL                     (Screen 1 of 1)        Record    1 of 1

      TITLE:  A/D/C teaching forum.                +-------------------
     AUTHOR:  Agricultural Development Council.    | Options:
  PUBLISHER:  New York, Agricultural Development Council. | nr   Next Record
                                                   | pr   Previous Record
   CALL NUM:  338.1095 Ag83a                       | ns   Next Screen
   LOCATION:  Krannert                             | ps   Previous Screen
                 copy 1                            | mr   Multiple Records
                 v. 1-44                           |sav   Save Search
                 1971-1975                         |ext   Extend Search
                                                   | sm   Search Menu
   SUBJECTS:  Agricultural research--Periodicals.  |  q   Quit
              University extension--Asia--Congresses. |  h   Help
   DESCRIPT:  44 v. 26 cm.                         +-------------------
    SUCC BY:  Agricultural Development Council. A/D/C
              teaching & research forum



ENTER OPTION --> ▮
```

Figure 37.14: plus: Title search with slashes

```
┌─────────────────────────────────────────────────────────────────┐
│                        ▐ HELP SCREENS ▌                          │
│ BASIC SEARCH TYPES --            DISPLAY OPTIONS --               │
│    1. Author Search                 15. Hold Keyword Results On or Off │
│    2. Call Number Search            16. Menus On or Off Command   │
│    3. Corporate Author Search       17. Multiple Records On or Off │
│    4. ISBN Search                   18. Options Menu Command      │
│    5. ISSN Search                   19. Redisplay Screen Command  │
│    6. Keyword Search                                              │
│    7. LCCN Search                GENERAL INFORMATION --           │
│    8. OCLC Number Search            20. General Information       │
│    9. Title Search                  21. Help Command             │
│                                     22. Quit Program Command     │
│ DISPLAY RECORD FORMATS --                                        │
│    10. Librarian Record Display  INFORMATIVE DISPLAYS --          │
│    11. MARC Record Display          23. General Information Command │
│    12. Public Record Display        24. Library Hours Command    │
│                                     25. Library Location Abbreviations │
│ DISPLAYING RECORD(S) --             26. Show Options Command      │
│    13. Display Record Command       27. Suggestion Command       │
│    14. Multiple Records Command     28. Terminal Locations       │
│                                  29. --NEXT SCREEN "ns"--         │
│                                                                  │
│ Type number of help screen desired, or press RETURN to continue program. │
│ HELP SCREEN NUMBER --> █                                         │
└─────────────────────────────────────────────────────────────────┘
```

Figure 37.15: plus: Help screen index (1 of 2)

```
┌─────────────────────────────────────────────────────────────────┐
│ MULTIPLE RECORDS MENU                          Screen    1 of 3  │
│ SEARCH  a:king, martin luther<80-85                   15 records │
│                                                                  │
│ 1      Watley, William Donnel. / Against principalities : an examination of Marti │
│           172.1 K585Z, W29, 1983    1980                         │
│              Book in:  HSSE                                      │
│                                                                  │
│ 2      Beifuss, Joan Turner. / At the river I stand : Memphis, the 1968 strike, a │
│           331.89281363720976819 B396a 1985, B&W Books           │
│              Book in:  HSSE                                      │
│                                                                  │
│ 3      King, Martin Luther / Daddy King : an autobiography      │
│           286.133 K585Z, K585       1980, Morrow                │
│              Book in:  BLAK UGRL                                 │
│                                                                  │
│ 4      Smith, Ervin. / The ethics of Martin Luther King, Jr.   │
│           323.4 K585Z, Sm55         1981, E. Mellen Press       │
│              Book in:  HSSE                                      │
│                                                                  │
│ 5      Garrow, David J. / The FBI and Martin Luther King, Jr. : from "Solo" to Me │
│           323.4482 K585Z, G194      1981, W.W. Norton           │
│              Book in:  BLAK HSSE                                 │
│                                                                  │
│ ENTER NUMBER OR OPTION --> █                                    │
└─────────────────────────────────────────────────────────────────┘
```

Figure 37.16: plus: Multiple records without menu

```
                    ╔═══════════════════════╗
                    ║  OTHER SYSTEMS MENU   ║
                    ╚═══════════════════════╝

     [bsu]  Ball State U. OPAC Catalog      [eis]  Purdue's EIS

     [isu]  Indiana State U. Catalog        [min]  Minnesota U. LUMINA Catalog

     [msu]  Michigan State U. Catalog       [nu]   Northwestern U. LUIS Catalog

     [ndu]  Notre Dame U. UNLOC Catalog     [osu]  Ohio State U. LCS Catalog

     [ugr]  Purdue UGRL/BRS System          [ui]   U. of Illinois LCS Catalog

     [uw]   U. of Wisconsin NLS Catalog     [mm]   Main Menu

     [h]    Help Information                [q]    Quit the Program



ENTER OPTION --> █
```

Figure 37.17: plus: Other systems menu

```
              Notre Dame University NOTIS System Help Screen

The University of Notre Dame's online catalog is called UNLOC.  It is a NOTIS
system with a few local modifications.  The main search types available are:

          TO SEARCH ON            COMMAND          EXAMPLE
          -----------             -------          -------
          AUTHOR                  a                a=bunyan, john
          TITLE                   t                t=dr dobbs journal
          SUBJECT                 s                s=pottery, japanese--edo period
          KEYWORD                 k                k=jesuit$ education america$

AVAILABLE HELP
          To display a help screen about any of the kinds of searching, use
          the search command with no equals sign ("=").  For example, to get
          help on Author searching, type "a".

          You can use the "hs" command to get a list of available help screens.

TO QUIT
          When you are done searching Notre Dame's catalog, type CTRL-D (hold
          down the CTRL or CONTROL key and type 'd').

Press RETURN to continue, ESC to abort: █
```

Figure 37.18: plus: Help screen for Notre Dame

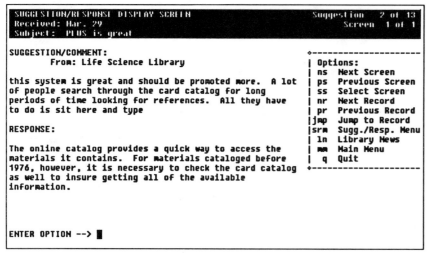

```
SUGGESTION/RESPONSE DISPLAY SCREEN              Suggestion   2 of 13
Received: Mar. 29                               Screen   1 of 1
Subject:  PLUS is great

SUGGESTION/COMMENT:
       From: Life Science Library                +--------------------
                                                 | Options:
this system is great and should be promoted more. A lot | ns   Next Screen
of people search through the card catalog for long | ps   Previous Screen
periods of time looking for references.  All they have | ss   Select Screen
to do is sit here and type                       | nr   Next Record
                                                 | pr   Previous Record
RESPONSE:                                        |jmp   Jump to Record
                                                 |srm   Sugg./Resp. Menu
The online catalog provides a quick way to access the | ln   Library News
materials it contains.  For materials cataloged before | mm   Main Menu
1976, however, it is necessary to check the card catalog |  q   Quit
as well to insure getting all of the available  +--------------------
information.




ENTER OPTION --> █
```

Figure 37.19: plus: Suggestion & response display

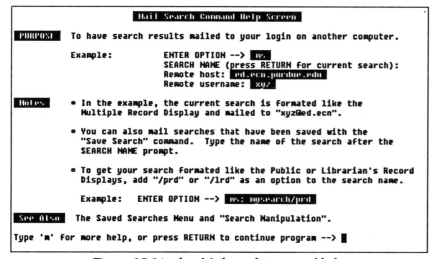

```
SAVED SEARCHES MENU                                  Screen   1 of 2



                         Last Used
       Name      # of Recs  Date      Time    +--------------------
     ----------  ---------  ----------------  | Options:
  1  agecon         144    Apr 25 -  1:00 pm  | rs   Restore Search
  2  alex           347    Jul 12 -  8:55 pm  |rem   Remove Search
  3  arlsal           1    Jan 30 - 12:45 pm  | ms   Mail Search
  4  collections     20    Jan  8 - 11:40 am  |pri   Print Search
  5  donnejohn       80    Jan 11 -  3:07 pm  | ns   Next Screen
  6  drugs          500    Sep  6 - 10:04 am  | ps   Previous Screen
  7  geriatrics     159    May  7 - 12:33 pm  | cs   Current Search
  8  milton          10    Jul 12 -  9:13 pm  | sm   Search Menu
  9  newyork       1809    Nov 16 -  1:52 pm  | mm   Main Menu
 10  ny               3    Nov 16 -  2:00 pm  |  h   Help
                                              +--------------------



ENTER NUMBER OR OPTION --> █
```

Figure 37.20: plus: Saved searches menu

```
              Mail Search Command Help Screen

  PURPOSE    To have search results mailed to your login on another computer.

          Example:        ENTER OPTION --> ms
                          SEARCH NAME (press RETURN for current search):
                          Remote host: ed.ecn.purdue.edu
                          Remote username: xyz

  Notes.    • In the example, the current search is formated like the
             Multiple Record Display and mailed to "xyz@ed.ecn".

            • You can also mail searches that have been saved with the
             "Save Search" command.  Type the name of the search after the
             SEARCH NAME prompt.

            • To get your search formated like the Public or Librarian's Record
             Displays, add "/prd" or "/lrd" as an option to the search name.

             Example:   ENTER OPTION --> ms: mysearch/prd

  See Also   The Saved Searches Menu and "Search Manipulation".

Type 'm' for more help, or press RETURN to continue program --> █
```

Figure 37.21: plus: Mail search command help

38

Resource Librarian

Deanna Petersson

Resource Librarian (RL in figure captions) is a new breed of Library Management Software with a unique graphical user interface. No other software package on the market today provides the same level of multiplatform support on both the Macintosh and the PC. The application is nearly identical in look, feel and functionality on the Macintosh or on any IBM PC or compatible running Windows 3.0 (or higher). Any combination of these machines can be used on the same network, sharing the same data files. Users gain since no retraining is needed to switch from one platform to the other.

Resource Librarian is easy to use, flexible, and can be customized to meet the special needs of an elementary school, high school, special, corporate, or public library. Each library may define types of material, patrons, library schedule, fine rates and other aspects of the software's operation; all screens display the library or company name. Resource Librarian integrates acquisitions, serials, cataloging and circulation, and uses multiple windows for greater flexibility and effectiveness.

A full public-access module, including complete Boolean search capabilities, will be available by the time this book appears. In the meantime, this discussion and the included screens focus on Resource Librarian's current capabilities for searching, browsing, and displaying resource information.

Starting Out

Users begin Resource Librarian by clicking on the Resource Librarian application icon and signing on at an initial logon screen. The security subsystem can restrict patron access to certain functions based on their identification. After completing signon, the user sees a desktop that is typical of graphical user interface (GUI) applications. There is a menu bar at the top of the screen and a tools palette to perform various functions. Clicking on the words "Resource Librarian" in the menu bar brings up a pull-down menu from which users can enter functional areas of Resource Librarian. Time-out and automatic logoff can be provided.

Resource Librarian

Resource Librarian has context-sensitive help throughout. Help for the current function is available by clicking on the "?" on the tools palette or selecting Help from the commands menu. Figure 38.1 shows a typical help window.

Users can control Resource Librarian by clicking on command icons, using pull-down menus to select commands, or using keyboard equivalents specified next to commands. Experienced users will work faster by using keyboard equivalents.

Resource Display

A resource—a book, videocassette, serial, compact disc or other item—can be displayed by clicking on a list of results from any search. The Show detail button yields a scrollable screen providing complete information on the item, as in Figure 38.2. Resource Librarian also provides a number of special displays to support various forms of processing; Figures 38.3 through 38.6 show some of these for *Field of Dreams*. Location and copy information appears when the user clicks Show copies for a selected resource; figure 38.7 shows a multiple-copy location and status display. Figure 38.8 shows the list of subjects for a selected resource. Figures 38.9 and 38.10 show resource detail for a computer program and book, respectively.

Searching and Browsing

Resource Librarian will locate resources by author, title, subject heading, series, call number, ISBN, ISSN, LCCN, and other means. Resources may be located by entering a complete element or part of an element (either **begins with** or **contains**). Whenever a search result has been obtained, the user can choose to print a detailed or summary listing to a file, a printer or one of several other choices.

The **Contains** functionality makes it easy to find resources where part of a searchable field is known. For instance, *Fire on the Moon* would retrieve *Of a Fire on the Moon*, as shown in Figure 38.11. Figure 38.12 shows a search for Isaac Asimov's *Foundation and Empire* using this technique; if the patron was certain of the title, the **Equals** button could have been used (yielding only the first of the two results shown). Figure 38.13 shows the main resource screen for one of the two results, which is actually a sound recording of part of the book.

Resources written by a particular author can be found rapidly by searching for the author and clicking on the **List Resources** button to show the resources. Figure 38.14 shows such a list for Martin Luther King, Jr. Figure 38.15 shows a list of resources with subject headings containing the phrase "Martin Luther King, Jr." Figure 38.16 shows a similar list, reached from a list of subject headings.

Resource Librarian makes browsing easy. Figure 38.17 shows a list of authors in the vicinity of Thomas Pynchon, taken from the authority file. Figure 38.18 shows a shelflist browse.

Boolean Searching

Resource Librarian has partial Boolean capabilities, although no OR is provided. The public-access catalog will have full Boolean search capabilities. For now, a user may run a complex search by specifying the sort (double-clicking on fields in order of preference, clicking to select descending and page breaks if needed) and search criteria (double-clicking on fields, then entering appropriate search criteria in dialog boxes). Figure 38.19 shows such a search; Figure 38.20 shows the results.

Errors

Figure 38.21 shows the result of a spelling error in a search. Resource Librarian provides a descriptive message and an audible beep or dialog box giving even more detailed information. Messages always appear in the same place on the screen. Some problems, such as attempting to display beyond the end of a list, cannot happen because of the point-and-click nature of the interface.

Requests and Queries

Users can submit requests and reference questions, typing information into a notes field. Figure 38.22 shows such a request. The user can also search for resources and add them to the request, as shown in Figure 38.23.

Conclusion

Resource Librarian is constantly being improved. Accuware listens to what our users tell us about the application and how to improve it. This discussion and the screens that follow show only a fraction of Resource Librarian's capabilities to manage information resources. Feel free to call me if you have further questions. Accuware may be reached at (403) 245-0477; the company is located at Suite 300, 914 Fifteenth Avenue S.W., Calgary, Alberta, Canada T2R 0S3.

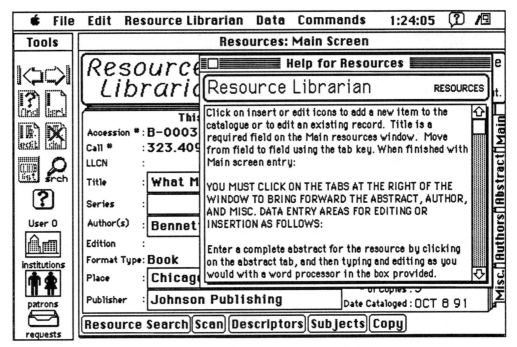

Figure 38.1: RL: Context-sensitive help

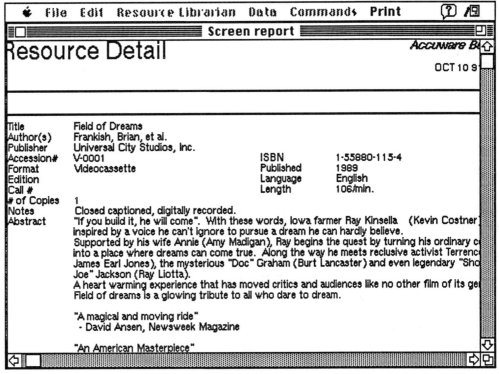

Figure 38.2: RL: Resource detail

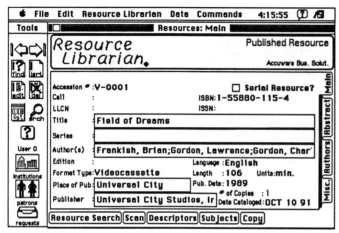

Figure 38.3: RL: Resources main screen

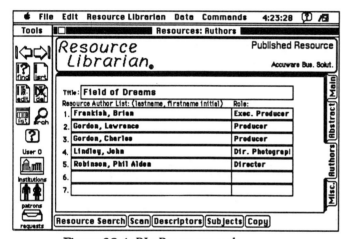

Figure 38.4: RL: Resources author screen

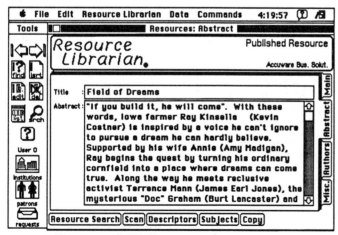

Figure 38.5: RL: Resources abstract screen

Figure 38.6: RL: Resources miscellaneous screen

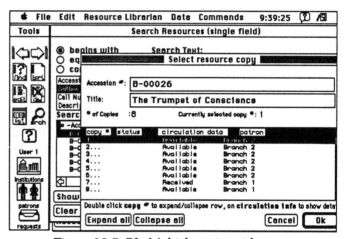

Figure 38.7: RL: Multiple copies with status

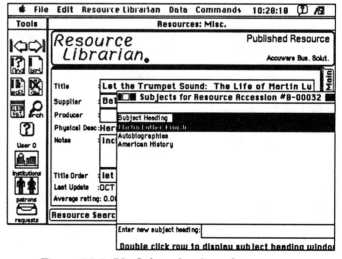

Figure 38.8: RL: Subject headings for a resource

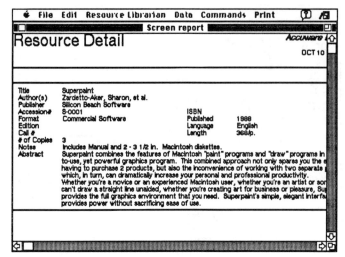

Figure 38.9: RL: Resource detail, data file

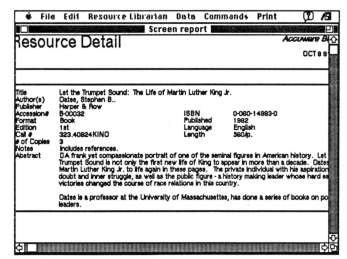

Figure 38.10: RL: Resource detail, book

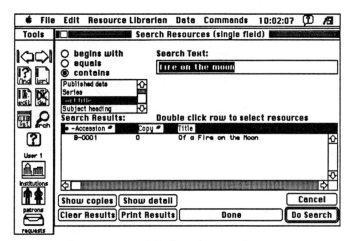

Figure 38.11: RL: Search using Contains

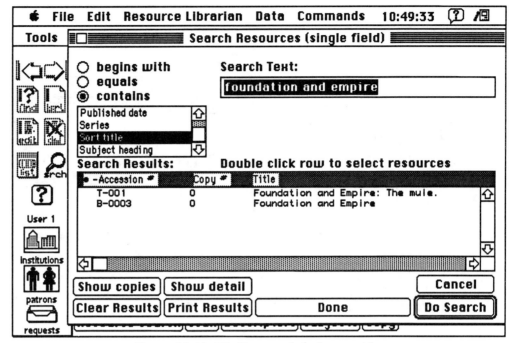

Figure 38.12: RL: Fast search for known title

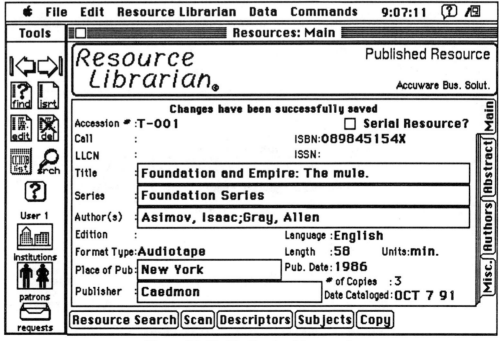

Figure 38.13: RL: Result of fast search

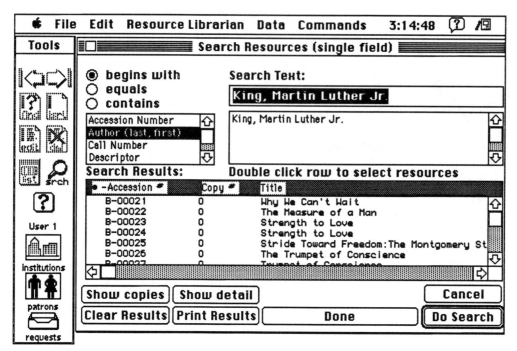

Figure 38.14: RL: Resources for an author

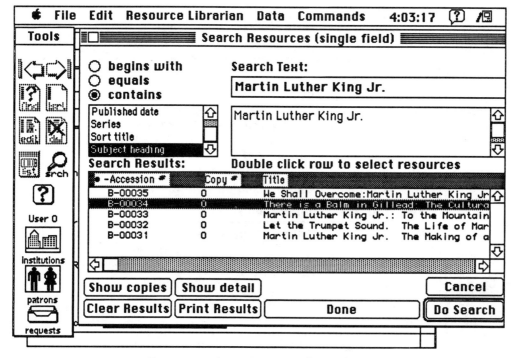

Figure 38.15: RL: Resources for a subject

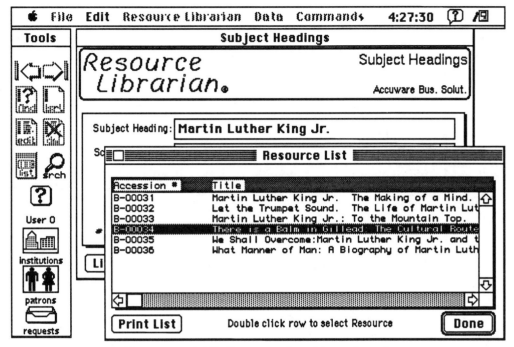

Figure 38.16: RL: Resources for subject, alt. path

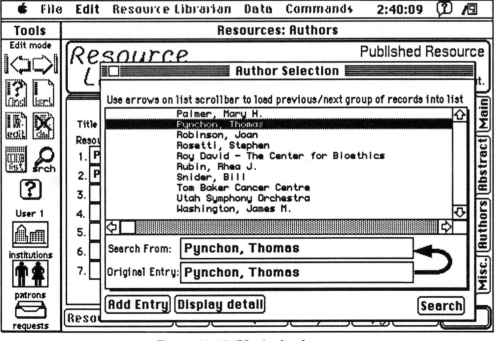

Figure 38.17: RL: Author browse

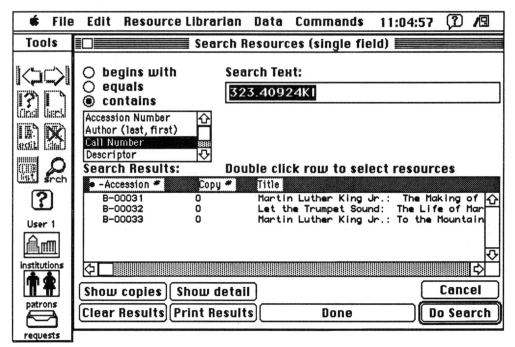

Figure 38.18: RL: Shelflist browse

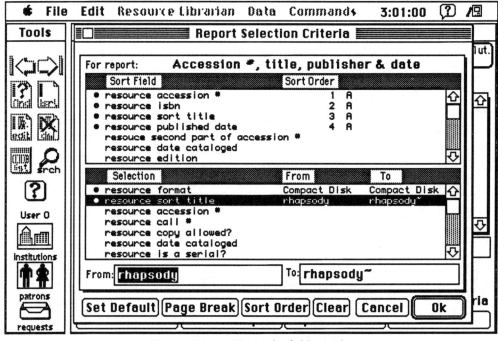

Figure 38.19: RL: Multi-field search

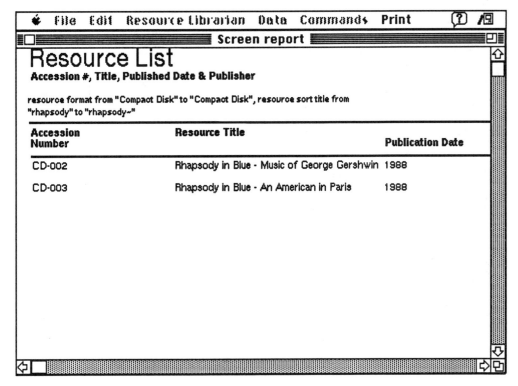

Figure 38.20: RL: Results of multi-field search

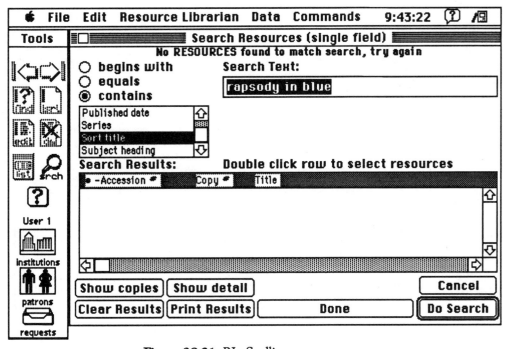

Figure 38.21: RL: Spelling error response

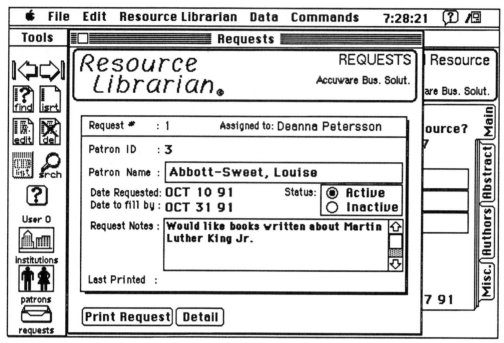

Figure 38.22: RL: Patron request

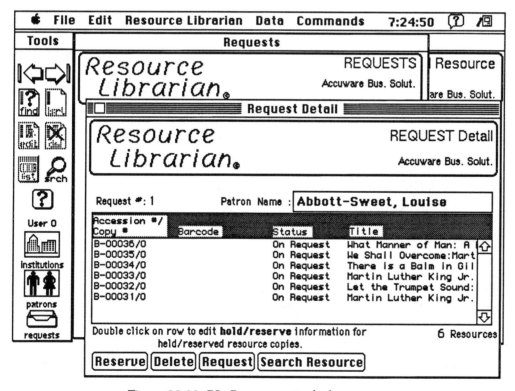

Figure 38.23: RL: Resources attached to request

39

TECHLIBplus

Judy Parr

TECHLIBplus is a product of Information Dimensions, Inc. The sample screens that follow represent the standard (or default) TECHLIBplus catalog. Sites can change all catalog screens. They can define which fields appear on search and display screens, adding to or deleting from the standard screens.

Starting Out

The TECHLIBplus main menu, available from a system menu, provides user access to the online catalog (Figure 39.1). The TECHLIBplus main menu, like other screens, provides online help for those needing guidance, as shown in Figure 39.2. When a user selects the online catalog from the TECHLIBplus main menu, the TECHLIBplus OPAC menu appears.

Limiting Searches

When a user selects Online Patron Access Catalog from the TECHLIBplus OPAC menu, the opening screen appears (Figure 39.3). From this screen a user can select functions such as **Libraries** to limit subsequent searching to selected libraries or **Materials** to limit subsequent searching to selected material types. Or the user can select the **Search** function to display the search screen. If the user has not limited libraries and/or material

types, he or she receives access to all libraries and material types.

The library selection screen (Figure 39.4) lets the user select which libraries to search. Using the **More** function, the user can see and select from more libraries than first appear on the screen. (Each site can define its own libraries.) The material selection screen (Figure 39.5) lets the user select which material types to search. (Each site can define its own material types.)

Searching

Online help for the search screen provides instructions for how to enter search values (Figure 39.6). Context-sensitive help describes each of the fields on the screen for which the user can provide search values or data. These fields are those followed by an underline. Field names followed by a > sign let users enter more search criteria than can fit on the line; the fields are scrollable.

Displayed as a pop-up window on the search screen is the context-sensitive help for the keywords field. To display this help, the user moved the screen cursor to the underline after Keywords> and pressed the context-sensitive Help key.

Searching by keywords lets a user enter one or more search values for searching author, subject, and title fields. Hence entering "king" as a keyword would retrieve items having King as their author or subject as well as items containing the word King in their title. If the library uses abstracts or tables of contents in its catalog, these fields may also be searched via the keywords field. Search terms can be entered in upper or lower case to find words containing characters of either case.

To search for all items about management, a user can type "management" as a search value for the subject field (Figure 39.7).

Displays and References

After a user has entered "management" as a search value for the subject field, results of the search are displayed (Figure 39.8). When thesaurus control has been added to the system, additional search terms are suggested, where appropriate. Here a user is advised to try searching later on "leadership," a synonym for "management."

The pop-up window disappears when the user presses the **Ok** function, and the search results screen displays information about the first six of a total of 27 items retrieved. The **More** and **Prev** functions let the user move the items of the result set forward and backward though the screen viewing area so he or she can view summary information about all 27 items.

Sorted Summary Displays

Each site can specify the default order for displaying multiple results. By selecting the **Command Mode** function and adding the appropriate sort clause to the displayed command, the user can display results in a different order—by call number, for example, as in Figure 39.9. For every search—whether by screen mode after a user has entered search values for fields on the Search screen or by command mode after a user has typed or revised a command on the command line—TECHLIBplus displays the system-constructed search command syntax in a scrollable area near the top of the screen.

Copy Availability

The user can display information about the availability of copies by typing "X" next to one or more of the titles. The copies display screen (Figure 39.10) displays information about the location and availability of copies of the cataloged item.

When the user enters an "R" next to an item, the patron information screen appears, where the user can supply his or her name and address (Figure 39.11). Using that information, a librarian can either send an available item to the user or place the user's name on a hold list for the item if it is currently out.

Multiple-Index Searching

When a user enters "Riggs" for author and "high tech*" for keywords on the search screen, TECHLIBplus searches for items authored by Riggs that have "high" and words beginning with "tech" as title, subject, or author. When a search retrieves only one item, information about its availability is immediately displayed (Figure 39.12). The **Search Again** function on screens lets the user return to the Search screen to perform another search.

Complete Display and Printing

After a user has selected the **Show Title** function from a screen, the first of three pages of catalog information about an item is displayed on the Title Display screen, Figure 39.13. Field names followed by a **>** sign contain more data than appears. The user can press a Scroll Box key to view additional information. The second page of the Title Display screen (Figure 39.14) displays the item's abstract. The third page of the title display screen (Figure 39.15) displays the item's table of contents. A site may define up to 99 pages for the title display screen. The user can print information about the item by selecting one of three formats (Figure 39.16).

Errors

Error messages such as the one displayed near the top of Figure 39.17 guide users. Each error message is identified by a number. Library database administrators can reword the messages if they wish. If TECHLIBplus finds no items matching the search value(s), a message states that no result set members were found.

Boolean Searching

The user can search for titles containing one or more specified words. The comma between words in a search value functions as a Boolean OR. An ampersand between words in a search value functions as a Boolean AND.

Access to full text

After a user enters a "U" by an item on the copies display screen, he or she receives access to the full text of that item if the item has been included in a BASISplus database (Figure 39.18). By using various scroll commands, the user can navigate through the text.

Browsing

Accessible from the TECHLIBplus OPAC menu, the Browse Subject Thesaurus selection lets a user browse subjects listed in the thesaurus. Browsing on subjects beginning with D displays several entries (Figure 39.19). A user can browse a portion of the shelf list by entering the beginning portion of a call number followed by an asterisk, which

serves a "wildcard" representing none, one, or more characters.

Set Review

The review sets (RS) command displays information about recently executed searches (Figure 39.20).

Current Contents

If the library has incorporated BASISplus/Current Contents Search into its TECHLIBplus menus, users can gain access to up-to-date information about recently published articles in journals. The Current Contents Article Search menu provides access to information about articles in recently issued journals.

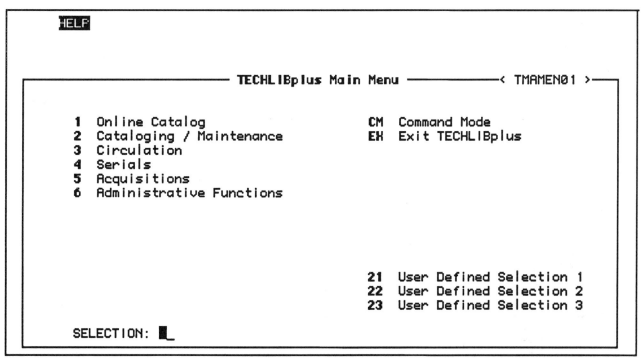

Figure 39.1: TECHLIBplus: Main menu

```
 HELP


                    ──── TECHLIBplus Main Menu ─────── < TMAMEN01 >──

        1  Online Catalog              CM  Command Mode
        2  Cataloging / Maintenance    EX  Exit TECHLIBplus
        3  Circulation
        4  Serials
        5  Acquisition│ KEYS  ▓
        6  Administrat│


                   │ This is the TECHLIBplus Main Menu screen which
                   │ gives you access to all of the components and
                   │ modules included in the system.

                   │ Select what you want by typing the menu number
                   │ in the selection box and pressing [ENTER].
                   │ (46764)

        SELECTION: __
```

Figure 39.2: TECHLIBplus: Help for main menu

```
 [ENTER] Search          F1 Help      F2 Libraries      F3 Materials
                         F7 Exit                         F9 Start Over
 ▉

                   ──── Online Patron Access Catalog ─────── < SCHOPA01 >──

        Welcome to the Information Dimensions Library Catalog
                  Library and Material Selection


   To search  ALL LIBRARIES

          for  ALL MATERIALS

   Press [ENTER]

    OR

   Press appropriate function key to limit search
```

Figure 39.3: TECHLIBplus: Catalog opening screen

```
 [ENTER] Show Lib/Materials  F1 Help      F2 More
         F4 Materials        F7 Exit                  F9 Start Over


                   ──── Library Selection ─────── < SCHOPA02 >──

   Press [ENTER] to select ALL libraries,
   OR type X next to selected libraries and press [ENTER].

   15 Libraries

    _  INFORMATION DIMENSIONS          ATLANTA
    _  INFORMATION DIMENSIONS          AUSTRALIA
    _  INFORMATION DIMENSIONS          CHICAGO
    _  INFORMATION DIMENSIONS          COLUMBUS
    _  INFORMATION DIMENSIONS          DALLAS
    _  INFORMATION DIMENSIONS          GENEVA
    _  INFORMATION DIMENSIONS          LONDON
    _  INFORMATION DIMENSIONS          LOS ANGELES
    _  INFORMATION DIMENSIONS          MILAN
    _  INFORMATION DIMENSIONS          NEW YORK
    _  INFORMATION DIMENSIONS          PARIS
    _  INFORMATION DIMENSIONS          ROME
```

Figure 39.4: TECHLIBplus: Library selection

```
[ENTER] Show Lib/Materials  F1 Help
    F4 Libraries            F7 Exit                      F9 Start Over


                    ———— Material Selection ————————< SCHOPA03 >——

   Press [ENTER] to select ALL materials,
   OR type X next to selected material(s) and press [ENTER].

   3   Material types


   █ BOOK
   _ SERIAL
   _ VIDEOTAPE
```

Figure 39.5: TECHLIBplus: Material selection

```
[ENTER] Search              F1 Help
                            F7 Exit        F8 Command Mode   F9 Start Over


                    ———————— Search ————————————< SCHINP01 >——
   Enter search terms
                        [ENTER] Ok      F2 Keys
   Searching ALL LIBRA  █
            for ALL MATER
                        This is the main search screen.  Use the TAB key
    Author> _____    to move the cursor to the field you want to
                        search.  Enter your search term in the field and
     Title> _____    press [ENTER] to execute the search.

   Subject> _____    To further narrow or qualify your search, you may
                        enter search terms in more than one field.  A
  Keywords> _____    Boolean AND is performed across the fields when
                        the search is executed.
   Call No: _____    (46753)
```

Figure 39.6: TECHLIBplus: Help for searching

```
[ENTER] Search           F1 Help
                         F7 Exit              F8 Command Mode   F9 Start Over


                 ─────────── Search ───────────────── < SCHINP01 >──
    Enter search terms and press [ENTER]

    Searching ALL LIBRARIES
          for ALL MATERIALS

      Author>  _____

       Title>  _____

     Subject>  MANAGEMENT_____

    Keywords>  _____

     Call No:  _____

```

Figure 39.7: TECHLIBplus: Subject search

```
[ENTER] Copies Display   F1 Help          F2 More
                         F7 Search Again  F8 Command Mode   F9 Start Over


                 ─────────── Search Results ────────── < SCHRSL01 >──
   To view copies, type X next to the item(s) and press [ENTER].
   OR to print, type P next to the item(s) and press [ENTER].
   Search Command>  SU PHRASE ALL WORDS 'MANAGEMENT'
   27      items found

   Item#
   _   1 100 best companies to work for in America         HF5549.2.U5L38
         Levering, Robert; Moskowitz, Milton Katz, Michael
   _   2 Developing tomorrow's managers today              HF5500.2.D55
         Dinsmore, Francis W.
   _                                               nt,     HD69.N4H55
       ┌──────────────────────────────────────────────┐
   _   │ [ENTER] Ok      F1 Help                        │   HD62.37.R53
       │                                                │
   _   │                                                │   HD62.4.M35
       │ MANAGEMENT                                     │
   _   │   SEE ALSO          LEADERSHIP                 │   HD58.8.B76
       └──────────────────────────────────────────────┘
   _     Brown, Arnold ;Weiner, Edith
```

Figure 39.8: TECHLIBplus: Reference in result

```
[ENTER] Copies Display      F1 Help          F2 More
                            F7 Search Again  F8 Command Mode   F9 Start Over


┌─────────────────────── Search Results ───────────────< SCHRSL01 >─┐
│ To view copies, type X next to the item(s) and press [ENTER].     │
│ OR to print, type P next to the item(s) and press [ENTER].        │
│ Search Command>  SU PHRASE ALL WORDS 'MANAGEMENT' SORT BY EVERY CA │
│ 27      items found                                               │
└───────────────────────────────────────────────────────────────────┘

   Item#
   _   1 The Coach : Creating partnerships for a competitive e
         Stowell, Steven J.
   _   2 Performing the operational audit
         Eifler, Thomas A.
   _   3 30 most common problems in management and how to solv  HD30.29.D44
         Delaney, William A.
   _   4 Managing creatively; a very practical guide in two vo  HD31.P59
         Pollock, Theodore Marvin
   _   5 Overcoming Murphy's law                                HD31.W235
         Waddell, William C.
   _   6 I Know it When I See It : A modern fable about qualit  HD38.G766
         Guaspari, John
```

Figure 39.9: TECHLIBplus: Multiple result, sorted

```
[ENTER] Search Results      F1 Help
               F6 Show Title  F7 Search Again  F8 Command Mode   F9 Start Over



┌─────────────────────── Copies Display ───────────────< SCHRSL02 >─┐
│ To print type P, to request type R next to an item and press [ENTER]. │
│ Search command> SU PHRASE ALL WORDS 'MANAGEMENT'                  │
│ 4        Copies for this Title                                    │
└───────────────────────────────────────────────── Title  1  of  1 ─┘
     Title> Competitive strategy : techniques for analyzing industries and
            competitors
    Author> Porter, Michael E.
    Call No: HD41.P67
    Subjects>      Competition

   Copy: Description: Date:  Avail.:  Libr/Location:  Date Due:  Item Id>
 ▌   1                        SHELF   IDI   COLS                 6761
 _   2                        SHELF   IDI   COLS                 4308
 _   1                        SHELF   IDI   DALLAS               6881
 _   1                        SHELF   IDI   ROME                 6510
```

Figure 39.10: TECHLIBplus: Copies display

```
[ENTER] OK     F1 Help     F3 Cancel


                        ———— Patron Information ————————< SCHPIN01 >——
         Please enter the following information to indicate where the item
         should be sent.
         Requesting>  Competitive strategy : techniques for a  IDI   COLS              1

            Last Name:  █_____
           First Name:  _____

            Patron Id:  _____

             Address:   _____
             Address:   _____

               Phone:   _____  Ext:  _____

         Pick-up Library:  IDI   COLS

         Notes>  _____
                 _____
```

Figure 39.11: TECHLIBplus: Patron information

```
[ENTER] Search                   F1 Help
             F6 Show Title    F7 Search Again   F8 Command Mode   F9 Start Over



                        ———— Copies Display ————————< SCHRSL02 >——
         To print type P, to request type R next to an item and press [ENTER].
         Search command>  AUTH PHRASE ALL WORDS 'RIGGS' AND KW PHRASE ALL WORDS 'HIG
         1      Copies for this Title
                                                   ———— Title  1  of  1  ——
            Title> Managing high-technology companies

            Author> Riggs, Henry E.
           Call No: HD62.37.R53
          Subjects> High technology industries -- Management.

         Copy:  Description:  Date:  Avail.:  Libr/Location:  Date Due:  Item Id>
          _       1                   SHELF    IDI   COLS                5451
```

Figure 39.12: TECHLIBplus: Multi-index result

```
[ENTER] Copies Display        F1 Help        F2 More  F3 Prev
                              F7 Search Again  F8 Command Mode    F9 Start Over
█

  ┌─ Title   1   of   1 ──── Title Display ───────────< SCHRSL03 >─┐
  │                                                     Page 1 of 3 │
  │                                                                 │
  │        Title> Managing high-technology companies                │
  │                                                                 │
  │                                                                 │
  │       Author> Riggs, Henry E.                                   │
  │                                                                 │
  │  Corp Author>                                                   │
  │                                                                 │
  │      Call No: HD62.37.R53                                       │
  │     Subjects> High technology industries -- Management.         │
  │    Collation> xvii, 333 p. : ill. 25 cm.                        │
  │    Publisher> Belmont, Calif. : Lifetime Learning Publications, │
  │      Edition>                                                   │
  │       Series>                                                   │
  │       Medium:                                                   │
  │        Notes> "Lifetime learning series in managing high technology"--Jacke │
  └─────────────────────────────────────────────────────────────────┘
```

Figure 39.13: TECHLIBplus: Title display (1 of 3)

```
[ENTER] Copies Display        F1 Help        F2 More  F3 Prev
                              F7 Search Again  F8 Command Mode    F9 Start Over



  ┌─ Title   1   of   1 ──── Title Display ───────────< SCHRSL03 >─┐
  │                                                     Page 2 of 3 │
  │  Abstract>                                                      │
  │  An in-depth analysis of the unique requirements for managing   │
  │  high-technology companies. Because of their sometimes rapid growth, │
  │  ever-changing markets, and a great dependence upon research and │
  │  development, high-technology companines experience many pressures that │
  │  other organizations may not. Case histories of both successful and │
  │  unsuccessful high-tech companies are presented, while offering practical │
  │  guidelines for managing in this dynamic and challenging environment. │
  │                                                                 │
  │                                                                 │
  │                                                                 │
  └─────────────────────────────────────────────────────────────────┘
```

Figure 39.14: TECHLIBplus: Title display (2 of 3)

```
[ENTER] Copies Display        F1 Help        F2 More  F3 Prev
                              F7 Search Again  F8 Command Mode    F9 Start Over


     ┌─ Title  1  of  1 ──── Title Display ─────────< SCHRSL03 >─┐
     │                                               Page 3 of 3  │
     │ Contents>                                                  │
     │ The Growth of High-Technology                              │
     │ The Special Pressures of High-Technology Industries        │
     │ Too Soon, Too Fast                                         │
     │ Learning How to Control Growth                             │
     │ Understanding the Marketplace                              │
     │ Tracking Finanacial Performance                            │
     │ Analyzing Financial Performance                            │
     │ How to Market High-tech Products                           │
     │ Quality and Service are Still Essential                    │
     │                                                            │
     │                                                            │
     │                                                            │
     └────────────────────────────────────────────────────────────┘
```

Figure 39.15: TECHLIBplus: Title display (3 of 3)

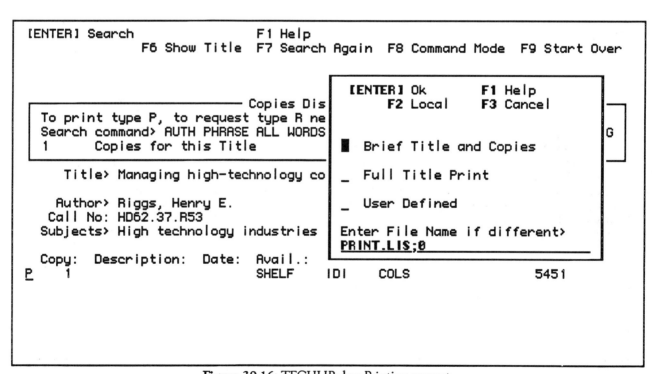

```
[ENTER] Search              F1 Help
          F6 Show Title  F7 Search Again  F8 Command Mode  F9 Start Over

                                    ┌─────────────────────────────┐
                                    │ [ENTER] Ok      F1 Help     │
                       ─ Copies Dis │     F2 Local    F3 Cancel   │
     To print type P, to request type R ne │                        │
     Search command> AUTH PHRASE ALL WORDS │  ■ Brief Title and Copies │ G
     1      Copies for this Title        │                         │
                                         │  _ Full Title Print      │
       Title> Managing high-technology co │                        │
                                         │  _ User Defined          │
      Author> Riggs, Henry E.            │                         │
      Call No: HD62.37.R53               │ Enter File Name if different> │
     Subjects> High technology industries │ PRINT.LIS;0             │
                                         └─────────────────────────────┘
      Copy: Description:  Date:  Avail.:
     P    1                      SHELF    IDI    COLS           5451
```

Figure 39.16: TECHLIBplus: Printing request

```
[ENTER] Copies Display      F1 Help         F2 More
                            F7 Search Again  F8 Command Mode   F9 Start Over
(46488) Please do not mix actions together, or request more than one item.


                    ———————— Search Results ——————————< SCHRSL01 >——
     To view copies, type X next to the item(s) and press [ENTER].
     OR to print, type P next to the item(s) and press [ENTER].
     Search Command>  SU PHRASE ALL WORDS 'INDUSTR*'
     19      items found


       Item#
     X    1 American disease                              JK467.L63
            Lodge, George C.
     P    2 Not of one mind                               HN59.N645
            Tarnowieski, Dale ;Graubard, Carla
     _    3 Managing high-technology companies            HD62.37.R53
            Riggs, Henry E.
     _    4 Competitive strategy : techniques for analyzing indus  HD41.P67
            Porter, Michael E.
     _    5 Quality assurance in research and development  TS156.R6
            Roberts, George W.
     _    6 Quality, productivity, and competitive position  TS156.D35
            Deming, W. Edwards
```

Figure 39.17: TECHLIBplus: Error message

```
Referencing the MINATECH Technical Documentation Database ...

       Result set 32 contains 1 members.
Author.............: C. H. Pike
Title..............: Wiring Circuits
Publisher..........: Drake Publishers, Ltd.
Date Published.....: 1971
Text:
 In the United Kingdom most consumers receive an electricity supply derived
from a high voltage 3-phase 50 Hz distribution system. Industrial consumers
with heavy load demands are given a supply at a high voltage that is either
used for a works distribution system with step-down transformer substations at
different points, or is stepped down in one main substation feeding a medium
voltage distribution system.


Text:
 For the largest industrial plants, the incoming supply may be derived from a
 Enter scroll command>
```

Figure 39.18: TECHLIBplus: Full-text result

```
Which Thesaurus do you wish to Browse?
  CO= Corporate Source
  SU= Subject Headings
  ME= Return to Menus

  Enter CO or SU or ME> SU
  Enter the term or stem you wish to Browse > D*
Thesaurus: SUBJECTS
Term id  Members  Ref(exact)  Level  Relation
-------  -------  ----------  -----  --------
   1        0         0              DAMPNESS IN BUILDINGS.
   2        0         0              DEFORMATION (MECHANICS) STRAINS
                                     AND STRESSES.
   3       11        23              DICTIONARIES
   4        0         0              DIRECTORIES -- RAILWAYS
   5        0         0              DOCUMENTARY -- UNITED STATES --
                                     STATES
   6        0         0              DOCUMENTS ON MICROFILM -- LAW
                                     AND LEGISLATION -- U
   7        0         0              DYES AND DYEING
   8        1         1                SEE ALSO    PIGMENTS
   9        0         0              DYES AND DYEING -- CHEMISTRY.
End of information was encountered.
TLP>
```

Figure 39.19: TECHLIBplus: Subject browse

```
[ENTER] Execute Command       F1 Help
                              F7 Search Again   F8 Screen Mode    F9 Start Over


     Command>  AUTH PHRASE ALL WORDS 'RIGGS' AND SU PHRASE ALL WORDS 'HIGH T
   ------------------------------ Review Sets ------------------< SCHCMD01 >------

 10  Active Sets

   Set    Members   Search command>
   ---    -------   --------------
   38        0      CA = 'Z678.'* ORDER BY CT
   39        2      CA = 'HD62.'* ORDER BY CT
   40        0      SU PHRASE ALL WORDS 'LIBRARY JOURNAL' ORDER BY CT
   41        0      SU PHRASE ALL WORDS 'LIBRARY' ORDER BY CT
   42        1      TITLES PHRASE ALL WORDS 'LIBRARY JOURNAL' ORDER BY CT
   45        1      TITLES PHRASE ALL WORDS 'OMNI' ORDER BY CT
   48        0      TITLES PHRASE ALL WORDS 'PC/COMPUTING' ORDER BY CT
   49        0      TITLES PHRASE ALL WORDS 'PC/COMPUTING' ORDER BY CT
   50       27      SU PHRASE ALL WORDS 'MANAGEMENT' ORDER BY CT
   55        1      AUTH PHRASE ALL WORDS 'RIGGS' AND SU PHRASE ALL WORDS 'HIGH
```

Figure 39.20: TECHLIBplus: Set review

40

TOMUS

Stephen R. Salmon

The designers of Carlyle's online catalog, TOMUS (The Online Multiple User System) set themselves a dual challenge: to provide the power of a command-driven interface in a system that was simple enough for people who had never used a computer, a terminal, or perhaps even a library before. The New York Public Library, with its diversity of users ranging from the completely untutored to the most sophisticated researcher, agreed to be the testbed.

To meet this challenge, the system assumes no knowledge of either computer or library jargon, and avoids the use of special symbols (such as the back slash or dollar sign). Function keys are also avoided, because users may dial into the system from their own terminals or personal computers, and in this case would not have their function keys programmed properly.

Help is provided at any point, and in the context of the search situation. Instructions provided by tutorial help messages are constructed in a "layered" fashion, so that the user sees them only when needed or desired.

No restrictions are placed on the search. Any number of terms and indexes may be combined with any number of Boolean operators, and search statements may be strung out indefinitely. A complex statement may be entered all at once, or step by step; in either case, the system reports intermediate results.

The language of the system is very similar to that later adopted for the Common Command Language standard, and now conforms fully to that standard.

In use, the New York Public Library and most subsequent installed sites have found that no training of users is necessary; use is intuitive, and users proceed on their own without the intervention of library staff.

Opening and Help for Searching

The opening screen (Figure 40.1) appears after a configurable time-out, or if the user types "start," "stop," or a synonym. The screen gives the system name assigned by the library and a brief message, composed by the library, defining the scope of the catalog. If the user already knows how to use the system from previous experience, a search may be entered immediately, and get immediate results, without the need to call up additional screens. If the user is new to the system, the Return key opens the first layer of instruction.

Most users find Figure 40.2 sufficient to begin simple searches. If more information is needed, the Return key brings it. Note in Figure 40.3 that the need to "press the key marked Return" after typing a search is reinforced. For further information, the system introduces the use of the **Help** (or H) command. In Figure 40.4, the user has reached a deeper layer, with more detailed instructions.

Asking for help on **Find** goes deeper (Figure 40.5). And asking for **Help Modify**, as suggested on the previous screen, begins the tutorial on Boolean searching (Figure 40.6). **Help OR** gets more information on that particular Boolean operator (Figure 40.7). Note that similar screens are available for AND and NOT.

Searches and Displays

For efficiency in typing a search (bottom of Figure 40.7), the user has shortened Find Title to "ft" and omitted the word "in" (the system would ignore it in any case if the library had configured "in" as a stopword).

The number of items found is reported and the user asks to display them in the brief format. At least 4 are sound recordings (Figure 40.8). The user asks to display number 4 in the normal format. The normal format is labeled (Figure 40.9), but omits notes and tracings. Now the user asks for number 5 in the full format (Figure 40.10). The user asks for number 1 in the MARC format (Figure 40.11). The MARC display includes all fields and subfields (including fixed fields) and all delimiters and indicators.

The user enters a search for "Subject Martin Luther King, Jr." The system ignores, or normalizes, the punctuation, so accuracy in punctuation is not necessary, and reports the normalized form actually searched. Pressing the Return key results in a display of the items found in the normal or default format (Figure 40.12). For each location, the system shows the name or symbol of the location chosen by the library, the call number, and the holdings (Figure 40.13).

User Errors

In Figure 40.14, the user asks for an item number greater than those found. Figure 40.15 shows the brief error message. If the brief error message is insufficient, **Help** brings more information (Figure 40.16).

The help message is tailored to the situation. Now the user makes a spelling error (bottom of Figure 40.16). The search retrieves no items, so the system suggests that the spelling be checked (Figure 40.17). The search is echoed, so that the spelling error can be spotted easily. A request for help suggests other techniques that might be tried.

Boolean and Multiple Index Searches

The next search (bottom of Figure 40.17) illustrates an explicit Boolean combination of a title search and an author search. There is also an implicit Boolean combination of the words "water" and "conservation" in the title part of the search, because all searches are keyword unless a phrase search is specifically requested.

Intermediate results are shown as the search proceeds (Figure 40.18). If the final results were nil, the user could thus determine at what point the search failed.

Exact Searching

To retrieve only *Vineland* and not titles containing the word "vineland" the user asks for the "Exact Title" and retrieves it (Figure 40.19).

Browsing

The **Browse** command retrieves all headings beginning with the characters entered (Figure 40.20). For subjects, the browse display is hierarchical (Figure 40.21).

Nonbook Materials and Special Indexes

In Figure 40.22, the user has used the machine index to find a DOS program. A Boolean search ending with the request to limit the search to Type Score retrieves the score of Bach's Mass in B Minor (Figure 40.23). A search may also be limited to other types of material, such as maps.

A search may include punctuation, such as the slash that appears in the names of some serials (e.g., *PC/Computing*). Normalization ensures its retrieval, even if the user omits the punctuation. Archival records may also be included.

Ending a Session

At the end of the session, a command of **End, Stop, Quit, Logout,** or a similar synonym returns the system to the opening screen. If the command is omitted, a configurable time-out accomplishes the same purpose. In either case, LAN connections are also disengaged automatically, so that the next user does not start in the midst of a previous session.

Special Features

The **At** command narrows a search to a particular library in a consortium (Figure 40.24). The **Set** command does the same thing for the session as a whole, changing the default universe searched. It may also be used to change the default display format (Figure 40.25).

Help is available on numerous topics, as well as in the context of a search or following an error (Figure 40.26). Additional help messages may be added by the library.

The standard indexes shown may be added to by the library (Figure 40.27). An index may be based on any field, subfield, or combination of fields and subfields. Finally, a variety of printing options is available.

```
                        Welcome
                          to
                  The Online Catalog
                       of the
             Princeton University Libraries


The Online Catalog includes books and other library materials cataloged
during the period January 1, 1980 through June 28, 1991.  The database
now contains records for 747,840 titles.

For access to the 1,750,000 other cataloged titles at Princeton, consult
the Card Catalog.

For information on how to use this catalog, press the key marked RETURN.

->
```

Figure 40.1: TOMUS: Opening Screen

```
    To look for a particular subject, type FIND SUBJECT (or just F S),
    then the subject; for example, FIND SUBJECT REFUGEES, or F S DANCE.

    To look for an author, type FIND AUTHOR (or just F A), then the
    author; for example, FIND AUTHOR BRUCE GRANT, or F A RICHARD KRAUS.

    To look for a title, type FIND TITLE (or just F T), then the title;
    for example, FIND TITLE BOAT PEOPLE, or F T HISTORY OF THE DANCE.

    To look for an item by author and title, type FIND AUTHOR, the author,
    AND TITLE, then the title; for example, FIND AUTHOR GRANT AND TITLE
    BOAT PEOPLE.

    After you have typed one of these commands, press the key marked RETURN.

    For information on how to DISPLAY the items you find or get HELP,
    press the RETURN key.

->
```

Figure 40.2: TOMUS: First layer of instruction

```
    Instructions to The Online Catalog are called commands.  Examples of
    commands are:

         FIND SUBJECT REFUGEES
         FIND AUTHOR BRUCE GRANT
         FIND TITLE BOAT PEOPLE

    After you have typed a command, press the key marked RETURN.  The Online
    Catalog will then search the catalog and report how many items it finds.

    To see these items, type DISPLAY (or just D) and press the RETURN
    key.  For full information, type DISPLAY FULL (or just DF).

    If you make a mistake in typing, press the key marked BACKSPACE to
    backspace over the mistake, then re-type.

    Always press the key marked RETURN when you finish typing.

    For more information, type HELP (or just H), then press RETURN.

-> h
```

Figure 40.3: TOMUS: Instruction for searches

```
To use The Online Catalog, type what you want it to do.  Use one of the words,
or "commands," that The Online Catalog understands.  Some of the more
frequent-ly used commands are explained below.  For a complete list of commands,
type HELP COMMAND.

To start a search, type the command FIND, then what you want The Online Catalog
to find; for example, FIND SUBJECT DANCE, or FIND AUTHOR KRAUS, or FIND TITLE
BOAT PEOPLE.  For more information on the command FIND, type HELP FIND.

If The Online Catalog tells you that some items were found as a result of your
search, you may press RETURN to see the items.  There are actually four differ-
ent types of display you may use.  For more information, type HELP DISPLAY.

At any time, if you are having trouble or want more information, you
may type HELP and receive an explanation.  For a list of available HELP
subjects, type HELP GLOSSARY.

To stop using The Online Catalog at any time, type STOP, END, QUIT or LOGOFF.

Always remember to press the RETURN key after you type a command.

To start over, or return to the first screen, type START, then press RETURN.
-> h find
```

Figure 40.4: TOMUS: More detailed instructions

```
The FIND command is used to search for library items.  Type FIND followed by
the kind of search you want to make- that is, whether you want to search by
author, title, or subject- followed by the keywords you want to search for.
   Examples:  FIND AUTHOR JOSEPH CONRAD
              FIND SUBJECT SOLAR ENERGY
              FIND TITLE TYPHOON

You may abbreviate FIND to F, AUTHOR to A, SUBJECT to S, and TITLE to T.
   Examples:  F A JOSEPH CONRAD                 F T TYPHOON
              F S SOLAR ENERGY

You may combine more than one type of search by continuing with a modifying
command, such as AND, OR or AND NOT.
   Examples:  AND TITLE TYPHOON                 OR SUBJECT POWER
              OR SUBJECT HEAT BUT NOT HEATING

You may also combine types of searches after the command FIND.
   Examples:  FIND AUTHOR JOSEPH CONRAD AND TITLE TYPHOON
              FIND SUBJECT SOLAR OR ATOMIC AND ENERGY

For more information on searching, type
   HELP AND        HELP OR        HELP DISPLAY      HELP KEYWORD
   HELP AND NOT    HELP TRUNCATE  HELP MODIFY       HELP STOPWORD
-> h modify
```

Figure 40.5: TOMUS: Help for FIND

```
After you have completed a search, and the results have been reported to you,
you may MODIFY the results by adding more search terms, or keywords.  Use a
modifying command (AND, OR, or AND NOT) followed by the type of search
(AUTHOR, TITLE, or SUBJECT), followed by the additional keywords.
For example,

     AND TITLE INFORMATION PROCESSING
     OR SUBJECT SOLAR
     AND NOT SUBJECT ENVIRONMENT

If you use the modifying command AND, it will limit the search so that you
see only those items that contain BOTH the keywords in your original search
and the keywords after the modifying command.  If you use the modifying
command OR, you will see those items that contain EITHER the keywords in
your original search OR the keywords after the modifying command.  If you use
AND NOT, you will see only those items with the keywords in the original
search AND NOT the keywords after the modifying command.

For related information, type
HELP AND         HELP DISPLAY      HELP KEYWORD     HELP SUBJECT    HELP OR
HELP AND NOT     HELP FIND         HELP AUTHOR      HELP TITLE      HELP BACKUP
-> h or
```

Figure 40.6: TOMUS: Help for MODIFY

```
OR is a modifying command that you may use to combine two different kinds of
searches, or to combine keywords in a search, usually to broaden a search.

When OR is used to combine two different kinds of searches, The Online Catalog
will find all items in EITHER the first kind or the second kind.  For example,
the search FIND AUTHOR JOSEPH CONRAD OR SUBJECT JOSEPH CONRAD will find all
items either by Joseph Conrad or about Joseph Conrad.

When OR is used to combine keywords in the same kind of search, The Online
Catalog will find all items that have ANY of the keywords used.  For example,
the search FIND SUBJECT SOLAR OR ENERGY OR HEATING will find all items that
contain any of the three words SOLAR, ENERGY or HEATING in a subject term.

For related information, type
   HELP MODIFY          HELP FIND            HELP KEYWORD

-> ft rhapsody blue
```

Figure 40.7: TOMUS: Help for OR; title search

```
Your search:  FIND TITLE RHAPSODY BLUE
Items found:  5 at PRINCETON LIBRARIES

1.   Gershwin, George, 1898-1937.  George Gershwin plays Rhapsody in blue
       [sound recording] ...
2.   Gershwin, George, 1898-1937.  Rhapsody in blue ; "I got rhythm"
       variations ; Concerto in F ; "Rialto Ripples" rag [sound recording
       ...
3.   Gershwin, George, 1898-1937.  Rhapsody in blue / ...
4.   Gershwin, George, 1898-1937.  Rhapsody in blue ; An American in Paris
       ; Piano concerto in F [sound recording] / ...
5.   Gershwin, George, 1898-1937.  Rhapsody in blue / [sound recording].
       ...

End of display.  Type a new command, or type HELP, then press RETURN.
-> dn4
```

Figure 40.8: TOMUS: Title search, multiple result

```
Your search:  FIND TITLE RHAPSODY BLUE
Items found:  5 at PRINCETON LIBRARIES

Item 4.

AUTHOR          Gershwin, George, 1898-1937.
TITLE           [Orchestra music. Selections]
                Rhapsody in blue ; An American in Paris ; Piano concerto in F
                  [sound recording] / George Gershwin.
PUBLICATION     Holland : Philips, p1985.

LOCATION        (MLis)
CALL NUMBER     CASS- 523

End of display.  Type a new command, or type HELP, then press RETURN.
-> df5
```

Figure 40.9: TOMUS: "Normal" display, recording

```
Your search:  FIND TITLE RHAPSODY BLUE
Items found:  5 at PRINCETON LIBRARIES

Item 5.

AUTHOR        Gershwin, George, 1898-1937.
TITLE         Rhapsody in blue / George Gershwin. Warsaw concerto / Richard
              Addinsell. Concerto symphonique. Scherzo / Henry Litolff.
              Fantasy on Polish airs : in A / Frederic Chopin. Polonaise
              brillante / Franz Liszt [sound recording].
PUBLICATION   Holland : Philips, p1984.
DESCRIPTION   1 sound cassette : analog, stereo., Dolby processed. 001531
              000804 000654 001349 000923
NOTES         The 1st work orchestrated by Ferde Grofe; the last, originally
              a piano work by Weber, arr. for piano and orchestra by Franz
              Liszt.
              Digital recording.
              Durations: 15:31; 8:04; 6:54; 13:49; 9:23.
              Issued also in LP (411 123-1) and compact disc (411 123-2).
              Misha Dichter, piano ; Philharmonia Orchestra ; Neville


Press RETURN to see next screen, or type HELP, then press RETURN.
-> dm1
```

Figure 40.10: TOMUS: Full display, recording

```
Your search:  FIND TITLE RHAPSODY BLUE
Items found:  5 at PRINCETON LIBRARIES

  260 = 0 $aMinneapolis, Minn. :$bIntersound,$cp1987.
  300 =   $a1 sound disc (61 min.) :$bdigital ;$c4 3/4 in
  306 =   $a010049
  500 =   $aCompact disc.
  505 = 0 $aStrike up the band : overture / arr. D. Rose (7:00) - American
          in Paris (18:24) - Rhapsody in blue (13:14) - Swanee / arr. N.
          Wayland - Piano solos (from Duo-Art piano rolls). Kicking the
          clouds away (3:01) ; Twee-oodle-um bum-bo (2:38) ; Drifting along
          with the tide (2:20) ; So am I (4:15) ; That certain feeling (2:42)
          ; Sweet and low down (3:08)
  511 = 0 $aGeorge Gershwin, piano (Duo-Art piano rolls) (3rd, 5th-10th
          works) ; Denver Symphony Orchestra ; Newton Wayland, conductor.
  518 =   $aRecorded at Boettcher Concert Hall, Denver, Colorado, Sept. 1987.
  650 = 0$aOvertures.
  650 = 0$aSymphonic poems.
  650 = 0$aPiano with orchestra.
  650 = 0$aMusicals$xExcerpts, Arranged.


Press RETURN to see next screen, or type HELP, then press RETURN.
->
```

Figure 40.11: TOMUS: MARC display, partial

```
Your search:  FIND SUBJECT MARTIN LUTHER KING JR
Items found:  22 at PRINCETON LIBRARIES

Item 2.

AUTHOR         Cone, James H.
TITLE          Martin & Malcolm & America : a dream or a nightmare / James H.
                  Cone.
PUBLICATION    Maryknoll, N.Y. : Orbis Books, c1991.

LOCATION       (AAS)
CALL NUMBER    E185.97.K5 C66 1991

End of display.  Type a new command, or type HELP, then press RETURN.
-> df2
```

Figure 40.12: TOMUS: Search for name as subject

```
Your search:  FIND TITLE AIR
Items found:  800 at PRINCETON LIBRARIES

Item 1.

AUTHOR         Douglas Aircraft Company.
TITLE          USAF stability and control datacom / McDonnell Douglas
                  Corporation, Douglas Aircraft Division ; A.F. project
                  engineer, D.E. Hoak ; principal investigator, R.D. Finck.
PUBLICATION    Rev. ed.  [Dayton, Ohio] : Flight Control Division, Air Force
                  Flight Dynamics Laboratory, Wright-Patterson Air Force Base ;
                  Springfield, VA : NTIS [distributor], 1975.

LOCATION       (ST)
CALL NUMBER    TL574.S7 D68 1975
LOCATION HAS   v.1-2,4-9

LOCATION       (TQ)
CALL NUMBER    TL574.S7 D68 1975
LOCATION HAS   v.1-9

End of display.  Type a new command, or type HELP, then press RETURN.
```

Figure 40.13: TOMUS: Multiple locations

```
Your search:  FIND SUBJECT UNITED STATES RACE RELATIONS
Items found:  360 at PRINCETON LIBRARIES

Item 1.

AUTHOR         Williams, Patricia J., 1951-
TITLE          The alchemy of race and rights / Patricia J. Williams.
PUBLICATION    Cambridge, Mass. : Harvard University Press, 1991.
DESCRIPTION    263 p. ; 24 cm.
NOTES          Includes bibliographical references and index.
SUBJECTS       1. Williams, Patricia J., 1951- 2. Afro-Americans- Civil
                  rights. 3. Law teachers- United States- Biography. 4.
                  Critical legal studies- United States. 5. Feminist
                  criticism- United States. 6. United States- Race relations.

LOCATION       (AAS)
CALL NUMBER    KF4757 .W53 1991

Press RETURN to see next item, or type HELP, then press RETURN.
-> dn361
```

Figure 40.14: TOMUS: Erroneous display attempt

```
Your search:  FIND SUBJECT UNITED STATES RACE RELATIONS
Items found:  360 at PRINCETON LIBRARIES


You have asked to DISPLAY item numbers that do not exist.

Type HELP for more information.

-> h
```

Figure 40.15: TOMUS: Result of range error

```
You have asked to DISPLAY an item number which is greater than
the 360 items found for your search.  TOMUS cannot display
an item number greater than 360 for this search.

For more information, type HELP DISPLAY.

-> fs matrin luther kign jr
```

Figure 40.16: TOMUS: Help for range error

```
Your search:  FIND SUBJECT MATRIN LUTHER KIGN JR
Items found:  0 at PRINCETON LIBRARIES

You may want to check the spelling of your search, or type HELP.

-> h

Your search,

     FIND SUBJECT MATRIN LUTHER KIGN JR

did not find any items.  First check the accuracy of the spelling or numbers
in your search request.  Then try the following:

    If you are searching for a subject, try other terms, fewer terms, or
    more general terms.  You may also look for TITLES with the terms in them
    by typing FIND TITLE and then your terms.  If you find some items this way:

        1. Type DISPLAY FULL.
        2. Look at the line marked SUBJECTS, to see what terms are used by the
           library to describe this subject.
        3. Then type FIND SUBJECT and these terms to find more items.

    If you are searching for an abbreviated title, try spelling it out.

    For additional help, consult a librarian.

You may now begin a new search with a FIND command, or end your search by
typing END or STOP.

-> ft water conservation and a perry
```

Figure 40.17: TOMUS: Help for spelling error

```
Your search:  FIND TITLE WATER CONSERVATION
Items found:  17 at PRINCETON LIBRARIES
Your search:  FIND TITLE WATER CONSERVATION AND AUTHOR PERRY
found one item at PRINCETON LIBRARIES

Press RETURN to see it, or type HELP, then press the key marked RETURN.

-> dn
```

Figure 40.18: TOMUS: Multiple-index search

```
Your search:  FIND EXACT TITLE VINELAND
found one item at PRINCETON LIBRARIES

Item 1.

AUTHOR        Pynchon, Thomas.
TITLE         Vineland / Thomas Pynchon.
PUBLICATION   1st ed.  Boston : Little, Brown, c1990.
DESCRIPTION   385 p. ; 24 cm.

LOCATION      (F)
CALL NUMBER   PS3566.Y55 V56 1990

End of display.  Type a new command, or type HELP, then press RETURN.
```

Figure 40.19: TOMUS: Exact title search

```
Your search:  BROWSE AUTHOR PYN
AUTHORS found:  22 at PRINCETON LIBRARIES

AUTHOR     ITEMS
NUMBER     FOUND     AUTHOR
_____

  1.         1      Pynacker, Adam, ca. 1620-1673.
  2.         2      Pynchon, Thomas.
  3.         3      Pynchon, Thomas.
  4.         1      Pyne, Jemima.
  5.         1      Pyne, John.
  6.         1      Pyne, Kathleen A., 1949-


  7.         1      Pyne, Peter.
  8.         2      Pyne, Stephen J., 1949-
  9.         4      Pyne, Stephen J., 1949-
 10.         1      Pyne, W. H. (William Henry), 1769-1843.

Press RETURN to see the next screen; or type SELECT and the number(s) of
the AUTHOR you want to search (for example, SELECT 1), then
press RETURN.
->
```

Figure 40.20: TOMUS: Author browse

```
Your search:  BROWSE SUBJECT DESKTOP
SUBJECTS found:  2 at PRINCETON LIBRARIES

SUBJECT    ITEMS
NUMBER     FOUND     SUBJECT
_____

  1.         6      Desktop publishing.
  2.         1      Desktop publishing- Bibliography.

There are no more items to display.  Type SELECT and the number(s) of the
SUBJECT you want to search (for example, SELECT 1), then press
RETURN; or type HELP, then press RETURN.
```

Figure 40.21: TOMUS: Subject browse

```
Your search:  FIND MACHINE DOS
Items found:  9 at PRINCETON LIBRARIES

Item 9.

TITLE           FONTASY [computer file] : on-screen fonts and drawing for IBM
                personal computers and other fully compatible MS-DOS
                micro-computers.
PUBLICATION     Version 2  Los Angeles : PROSOFT, 1986.
DESCRIPTION     2 computer disks ; 5 1/4 in. + manual (235 p., [10] p. of
                plates : ill. ; 21 cm.) + supplementary documentation.
NOTES           System requirements: IBM-PC or compatible; 512K-640K RAM; DOS
                2.0 or above; IBM-compatible graphics adaptor and monitor, or
                Hercules Monochrome Board, dot-matrix printer.
SUBJECTS        1. IBM Personal Computer- Programming. 2. FONTASY (Computer
                program) 3. Computer graphics- Computer programs.
OTHER HEADINGS  I. PROSOFT (Firm)

LOCATION        (ST)
CALL NUMBER     QA76 .8 .I2594 F65

End of display.  Type a new command, or type HELP, then press RETURN.
```

Figure 40.22: TOMUS: Special index, data file display

```
Your search:   FIND AUTHOR BACH AND TITLE MASS B MINOR LIMIT TYPE SCORE
Items found:   2 at PRINCETON LIBRARIES

Item 1.

AUTHOR         Bach, Johann Sebastian, 1685-1750.
TITLE          [ Masses, BWV 232, B minor. Latin]
               Mass in B minor : from the Bach-Gesellschaft edition / Johann
                 Sebastian Bach.
PUBLICATION    New York : Dover Publications, c1989.
DESCRIPTION    1 score ([x], 304 p.) ; 31 cm.
NOTES          Reprint, with original foreword omitted. Originally published:
                 Leipzig : Breitkopf & Hartel, 1856. Originally published in
                 the series: Johann Sebastian Bach's Werke ; v. 6.
               Words printed as text with English translation on p.
                 [viii]-[ix].
SUBJECTS       1. Masses- Scores.

LOCATION       (F)
CALL NUMBER    M2010.B2 M5 1989q

End of display.  Type a new command, or type HELP, then press RETURN.
```

Figure 40.23: TOMUS: Full display, score

```
The AT command may be used after a search is completed to see how many items
are at another library, or in all the libraries in this group.  For example,
if you are at Williams and you have completed a search, you may type

    AT OSWEGO

TOMUS will then tell you how many of the items you found are at the SUNY Oswego
library.  If you type a DISPLAY command, TOMUS will show you only the Oswego
library items.

If you want to see how many items matching your search are in all the libraries
type AT ALL.

You may type several AT commands after the same search, but you may only use
one library name with each AT command.

To limit all of your searches to a particular library, or to search all of the
libraries all of the time, use the SET LIBRARY command. Type HELP LIBRARY and
HELP SET for more information.

-> h set
```

Figure 40.24: TOMUS: Help for AT

```
The SET command is used to change the format that TOMUS normally uses for
displaying or printing items to another format.  The SET command is also used
to indicate the libraries to be searched by TOMUS.

Ordinarily, TOMUS will automatically display or print items in a fairly
short format that includes the basic bibliographic information, the call
numbers, and the locations of the items you have found.  If you want to
display or print the items automatically in a different format, type
SET DISPLAY followed by the name of the format; for example, SET DISPLAY
FULL.  To return to the normal format, type SET DISPLAY NORMAL or SET PRINT
NORMAL.  For more information on the different formats, type HELP BRIEF,
HELP NORMAL, HELP FULL or HELP MARC.

TOMUS will automatically search only for items in your library.  If you want
TOMUS to search for items in another library, type SET LIBRARY, followed by the
name of the library.  If you want TOMUS to search for items in all of the
libraries, type SET LIBRARIES ALL.  For more information on the different
libraries you can search, type HELP LIBRARIES.

Examples of the SET command are:
    SET DISPLAY BRIEF              SET PRINT FULL
    SET LIBRARY OSWEGO            SET LIBRARIES ALL

-> ft water
```

Figure 40.25: Help for SET

```
The GLOSSARY lists words and phrases used by The Online Catalog.  Type
HELP followed by the word or phrase you would like explained.  The following
words and phrases are now in the glossary:


AND                DIACRITICS      KEYWORD            NORMAL         SERIAL
AND NOT            DISPLAY         LANGUAGE           NOT            SET
ARCHIVES           END             LCCN               NUMBER         SHOW
AUTHOR             EXACT TITLE     LIMIT              OR             SPECIAL
BACKUP             FILM            LOCATION           PREVIOUS          CHARACTERS
BACKUP FIND        FIND            LOGOFF                SCREEN      START
BOOK               FORMAT          MACHINE            PUNCTUATION    STOP
BRIEF              FULL            MACHINE READABLE   QUIT           STOPWORD
BROWSE             GLOSSARY           DATA FILE       RECORDING      SUBJECT
BUT NOT            HELP            MANUSCRIPT         RETURN         TITLE
CALL NUMBER        INDEX           MAP                RLIN           TRUNCATE
CARLYLE            INDEX LIST      MARC               SCORE          TYPE
COMMAND            ISBN            MODIFY             SEARCH         VISUAL
DATE               ISSN            MUSIC NUMBER       SELECT            MATERIAL



-> help index list
```

Figure 40.26: TOMUS: Glossary for HELP

```
The indexes that may be used after the FIND, AND, AND NOT and OR commands are:

    Word Indexes:    Abbreviations:         Number Indexes:   Abbreviations:

    AUTHOR           A                      CALL              CAL
    TITLE            T                      ISBN              ISB
    EXACT TITLE      XT                     ISSN              ISN
    SUBJECT          S                      LCCN              LCC
    MACHINE          MAC                    MUSIC NUMBER      MUS NUM or MN
                                            RLIN              RLI

The indexes that may be used after the LIMIT TO command are as follows:

    Indexes:         Abbreviations:         Indexes:          Abbreviations:

    LANGUAGE         LAN                    DATE              DAT
    TYPE             TYP

    For information on any index listed above, type HELP, followed by the
index name.

-> h print
```

Figure 40.27: TOMUS: List of indexes, limits

41

Unicorn
at Portland State University

Gary Sampson

Sirsi Corporation's Unicorn Collection Management System is a complete library automation package. It includes modules for an online catalog, catalog control, circulation, reserve, acquisitions, serials, and downloading from bibliographic utilities. It also includes RIM, a module that allows Unicorn users to search other catalogs or commercial information banks with the Unicorn interface. Libraries may purchase the entire Unicorn system or pieces of it as needed.

The Portland State University Library used the Unicorn online catalog version 4.7 from June 1989 through August 1991. On September 1, 1991, a major upgrade, version 5.0, was installed. The PSU catalog runs on a Unisys model 5000-95 minicomputer with two coprocessors, 28 megabytes of RAM and four gigabytes of hard-disk storage. The operating system is Unix version 6.0. There are 13 hard-wired public terminals and 11 dedicated public LAN workstations providing access to the catalog. Another 14 terminals and workstations are used by the librarians. An additional 16 ports are reserved for dialing in from modems, the campus LAN, or the Internet. This configuration provides adequate response time for a catalog of 460,000 titles representing some 900,000 volumes. Approximately 85 percent of our holdings are in the online catalog. Sirsi/Unicorn software does not appear to be finicky about equipment. Unicorn catalogs run on a variety of Unix-based configurations around the country.

The PSU Unicorn catalog's Internet address is 131.252.129.52. Enter "dialin" at the **Login:** prompt and set terminal emulation for VT-100.

The distinguishing features of the Unicorn catalog are its "point-and-click" interface and hypertext approach to searching. Each Unicorn screen has two parts: a command area above the divider and a results area below the divider. The commands are single words written in capital letters across the screen. The active command is indicated by being shown in reverse video or having a blinking cursor at the first letter.[1] The user cycles through the commands by hitting the Tab key. The command is executed by hitting the Return key. "Point-and-click" means Tab and Return on Unicorn. Typing the first letter of a command selects and activates it at the same time. A **Help** button is on nearly every screen to give assistance in context.

Hypertext searching is invoked by the **Like** command, one of the choices available when a single record has been called up. The **Like** command generates a numbered list of authors, subject headings and other tracings. Choosing one of

---

1 This highlighting is represented by underlining in the screens in this chapter.

479

the numbers calls up other works by the selected author or other works on the same subject. When working with music records, for example, one can select by composer, conductor, orchestra, and other categories. It is possible to follow a research thread through an unlimited number of records in this way. Steps always can be retraced one at a time with the **Goback** command.

Starting Out

The initial screen (Figure 41.1) offers quick-start information about the commands (called "buttons" by Unicorn) and the use of Tab and Return. Executing the **Begin** command gives the user a list of public-access choices (Figure 41.2). Ignoring for a moment the library catalog, the user may go to the bulletin board screen (Figure 41.3) where he or she can find library hours and notices or leave suggestions and comments. The best comments will be answered here in a user-selectable file.

The public-access choices screen also allows a user to see what the library thinks he or she has checked out, to check for outstanding fines and to check on any holds he or she may have placed (Figures 41.4 through 41.6). These user records are accessed by having the patron type in the library bar code on his or her student identification card. The bar code is a random number assigned by the library, not the student's social security number. If the user wishes more security, the library can be asked to assign him or her a PIN (personal identification number) as well.

The **Reserve Desk** choice on the public-access choices screen lets students look up reserved items by course or instructor.

Finding Library Material

Choosing **Library Catalog** from the public-access choices screen gives the user the main catalog lookup screen (Figure 41.7).

The default choice, 1) **Word or phrase**, seeks words or phrases that appear in any single, searchable field. The term "phrase" is inaccurate here because the searching is really done by key-word. Entering "London Bridge" will call up any records containing the words "London" and "bridge" in a single field, not just records containing the phrase "London Bridge." The Sirsi/Unicorn system happens to use BRS/Search as part of its software, so it is possible to force true phrase searching by using BRS commands. For example, entering "London adj bridge" calls up appropriate records. These "advanced" BRS commands are not documented on the screen (yet), but are covered in library handouts and guides.

Choices two through five limit searches to the named fields. 5) **Author with title**, for example, is the quickest way to find *Vineland* by Thomas Pynchon. The same choice is valid for Bach's Mass in B Minor, although no score was turned up (Figures 41.8 and 41.9).

Boolean searching

Choice six, 6) **Other combinations**, brings up the Boolean screen. (Figure 41.10 shows the Help screen; Figure 41.11, the Boolean screen.) The **Other combinations** choice is a good one for finding *Rhapsody in Blue* on CD. "Rhapsody" and "blue" as keywords in the title field and "compact disc" as a phrase in any searchable field call up four records (Figure 41.12). After finding a list of records the active command button is **View** and the default record choice is **1**. The screen shows the title of each record, the author, the call number, the number of copies held by the library, the location of the copies, the type of material the record represents, and the publication year of the item. If the item is checked out, that information will appear in place of the location statement. The records are displayed in reverse chronological order. The items most recently added to the collection are displayed first. In most cases this means the newest books are at the top of the list, however, gifts and retrospective conversion items can sometimes confuse matters. There are no Sort options.

Single-Record Displays

To see a full display of an item, enter its number and hit "V" for View or hit the Return key. The full, labeled display of a CD, like the chosen version of *Rhapsody in Blue*, can take several screens to display (Figures 41.13). Once the user has selected a single item to view, he can use the **Option** command button to choose between full and brief displays (Figure 41.14).

The full display of a monograph is usually much simpler. The display for *"I Have a Dream"* : *the Quotations of Martin Luther King, Jr.* is typical (Figure 41.15).

If an item's location is shown as **CHECKEDOUT**, a user can place a hold on it by choosing the **Request** command button and entering his or her library barcode number and PIN (if he or she has one) (Figure 41.16).

Expert Searching

The draft Help screen for the **Other combinations** choice (Figure 41.10) is inadequate and will be changed very soon. It does not indicate that one can Tab to the default AND operators and type other Boolean operators over them. AND, OR, NOT, and XOR (if you can find a use for it) are possible. As a matter of fact, Unicorn supports full Boolean searching within and among fields and with nesting and keyword limitation to specific MARC fields. The fields are indicated by the MARC field number in brackets (Figures 41.17 and 41.18). Once again, this is documented in library handouts and guides to the OPAC, but not yet on the screen.

Searching for Related Works

As noted above, searching for related works is a Unicorn strong point. Choosing the **Like** command button from the selected version of *Rhapsody in Blue* gives 16 tracings to follow (Figure 41.19). If the user decided to find more symphonic poems, for example, he or she could have Unicorn Lookup number 5 on the tracings list. This would result in 56 recordings of such works (Figure 41.20). Executing the Goback command brings back the tracings list. The user could then Lookup number 1 and find other works by Gershwin.

Error Handling

Error handling is straightforward. If a word is not spelled correctly, a message will appear at the top of the screen saying, "Search word not in dictionary—XXXX." If the user selects a number outside the possible range, a similar message will appear saying, "You must select a number between X and Y."

Browsing

Unicorn allows browsing in any field. Go to the **Lookup** screen and select the desired field, enter the word or phrase, and select from the resulting list by number. The number of holdings under each entry is indicated on the right side of the screen (Figures 41.21 through 41.24).

Shelflist browsing is the one area that is not fully integrated into the user interface. The shelflist is accessed by pressing a labeled function key on the public catalog terminals called By Call Number. The command can be activated over the Internet or a modem by Control-N, but one couldn't know that from the screen alone. To return to the normal interface, one must press another labeled function key, Find. The control key equivalent for remote users is Control-F. Items in the shelflist display can only be viewed, not manipulated as in the rest of the catalog.

To find items in the area of Z678.9 one enters that call number and adds a space and the truncation symbol (a $ sign) (Figure 41.24). Entering the call number without the truncation will find nothing. Entering a complete call number will bring up the unique record. Use of the shelflist is also documented in library handouts and guides.

Impressions of Unicorn

The Unicorn online catalog was acquired after going through a stringent state agency bidding process. Of the six systems that answered our RFP, Sirsi's Unicorn system was deemed to offer the most value for the money. The version 4.7 that was in the library for two years was a solid, workmanlike catalog. Most comments in the catalog's suggestion box were positive. Negative comments (such as objecting to the fact that the call number was displayed at the end of a record instead of at the beginning) were saved and forwarded to the Sirsi Corporation. Sirsi corrected nearly all of the negative aspects in its version 5.0 upgrade and added many excellent new features. This catalog, with its clean screens, hypertext features, and complete Boolean capabilities, is undoubtedly one of the premier systems available today.

```
To select another button, press TAB.              (c) Sirsi Corporation
To begin using the library system, press RETURN now.

HELP
BEGIN        END
_____


                   UNICORN COLLECTION MANAGEMENT SYSTEM



          Above the line are buttons such as HELP and BEGIN.

        Simply select a button using the TAB key, then press RETURN.

              Or just type the first letter of a button.

        With some buttons you may also choose a number from a list
           using the up and down arrow keys or by typing the number.

      Every screen has helpful messages letting you know what the buttons can do.
```

Figure 41.1: Unicorn: Quick-Start Screen

```
To select another button, press TAB.              (c) Sirsi Corporation
Enter a number from below, then press RETURN.

HELP          GOBACK        STARTOVER
CHOOSE: 1
_____


                       PUBLIC ACCESS CHOICES:


                  1) LIBRARY CATALOG

                  2) BULLETIN BOARD

                  3) RESERVE DESK

                  4) USER STATUS
```

Figure 41.2: Unicorn: Public Access Choices

```
To select another button, press TAB.                    (c) Sirsi Corporation
Enter the number of a bulletin board item, then press RETURN.

HELP          GOBACK       STARTOVER
CHOOSE: 1
_____

                        BULLETIN BOARD CHOICES:

                              1) Suggestion Box

                    2) Library Hours

                    3) Notices
```

Figure 41.3: Unicorn: Bulletin Board choices

```
To select another button, press TAB.                    (c) Sirsi Corporation
Type in your user ID and PIN below, then press RETURN.

HELP          GOBACK       STARTOVER
TYPE
_____

                        INPUT YOUR ID FOR STATUS


     User ID ====>401100090085574

          PIN ====>
```

Figure 41.4: Unicorn: User status control

```
To select another button, press TAB.                    (c) Sirsi Corporation
To see your bills, checkouts, or holds, enter a number, then press RETURN.

HELP          GOBACK       STARTOVER
CHOOSE: 2
_____

                        USER STATUS CHOICES:


                        1) BILLS

                        2) CHECKOUTS

                        3) HOLDS
```

Figure 41.5: Unicorn: User status choices

```
To select another button, press TAB.                    (c) Sirsi Corporation
To see the previous page of information, press RETURN now.

HELP          GOBACK       STARTOVER
BACKWARD
_____

                              USER STATUS
Title\Author:Cadillac desert : the American West and it \ Reisner, Marc.
  call number:HD1739 .A17 R45 1986
     date due:6/8/92,0:59        charged:7/4/91,14:19


Title\Author:The solar system /                        \ Encrenaz, Therese,
  call number:QB601 .E5313 1990
     date due:6/8/92,0:59        charged:8/4/91,19:31

Title\Author:Arachne /                                 \ Mason, Lisa.
  call number:PS3563 .A7924 A89 1990
     date due:6/8/92,0:59        charged:7/23/91,13:12
```

Figure 41.6: Unicorn: Items checked out by user

```
To select another button, press TAB.                (c) Sirsi Corporation
Enter the number of the lookup you want to do, then press RETURN.

HELP        GOBACK      STARTOVER
CHOOSE:1
_____

                        LOOKUP IN CATALOG BY:

                     1)  WORD OR PHRASE

                     2)  AUTHOR

                     3)  TITLE

                     4)  SUBJECT

                     5)  AUTHOR WITH TITLE

                     6)  OTHER COMBINATIONS

                     7)  BROWSING
```

Figure 41.7: Unicorn: Catalog lookup

```
To select another button, press TAB.                (c) Sirsi Corporation
To get more detailed help, press RETURN now.

HELP        GOBACK      STARTOVER
TYPE        OPTIONS
_____

                  CATALOG LOOKUP BY AUTHOR WITH TITLE


     author:BACH

      title:B MINOR MASS
```

Figure 41.8: Unicorn: Author-title search

```
To select another button, press TAB.                (c) Sirsi Corporation
To see more about an item, enter its number, then press RETURN.

HELP        GOBACK      STARTOVER
VIEW:1
_____

                  YOU FOUND 4 ITEMS IN THE CATALOG

     1) Mass in B minor, BWV 232          copies: 1 (AV-SERVICE)
        Bach, Johann Sebastian,            type: PHONODISC
        PHONODSC ARC 3177-3179

     2) The high Mass, B minor.           copies: 1 (AV-SERVICE)
        Bach, Johann Sebastian,            type: BOOK
        M2010 .B2 S.232

     3) Mass in B minor [sound recording] /  copies: 1 (AV-SERVICE)
        Bach, Johann Sebastian,             type: COMDSC
        COMDSC NONE 79036                 pubyear: 1982

     4) Bach [sound recording].           copies: 1 (AV-SERVICE)
        Bach, Johann Sebastian,            type: PHONODISC
        PHONODSC STL 544
```

Figure 41.9: Unicorn: Author-title result

```
To select another button, press TAB.              (c) Sirsi Corporation
To go back to your current function, press RETURN now.

GOBACK
_____

Items in your library are described in many ways.  Make this selection to find
all library materials described using particular words or phrases in a
specific combination.  You may enter words or phrases in one, some or all of
the AUTHOR, TITLE, SUBJECT or GENERAL fields.  After typing in any one of
these fields, press RETURN to move to the next area. When you press SEND in
the last field, you will then see the location of every item in the library
that includes each word or phrase you entered in the specified position.

By selecting the OPTIONS button, you may limit the items found by author,
title, subject, or general combination to a particular publication year,
general or specific material type, library shelving location, language,
reading level or category.
```

Figure 41.10: Unicorn: Help for Boolean search

```
To select another button, press TAB.              (c) Sirsi Corporation
To get more detailed help, press RETURN now.

HELP        GOBACK        STARTOVER
TYPE        OPTIONS
_____

                    CATALOG LOOKUP BY OTHER COMBINATION
 author:
  AND

  title:RHAPSODY BLUE
  AND

subject:
  AND

 series:
  AND

general:COMPACT DISC
```

Figure 41.11: Unicorn: Multi-index search

```
To select another button, press TAB.              (c) Sirsi Corporation
To see more about an item, enter its number, then press RETURN.

HELP        GOBACK        STARTOVER
VIEW:1
_____

                    YOU FOUND 4 ITEMS IN THE CATALOG

     1) Rhapsody in blue;Preludes for piano ;    copies:1 (AV-SERVICE)
        Gershwin, George,                         type: COMDSC
        COMDSC MK 39699                           pubyear: 1985

     2) Rhapsody in blue = Rhapsodie en bleu : o  copies: 1 (AV-SERVICE)
        Gershwin, George,                         type: COMDSC
        COMDSC MK 42240                           pubyear: 1987

     3) Rhapsody in blue ; An American in Paris   copies: 1 (AV-SERVICE)
        Gershwin, George,                         type: COMDSC
        COMDSC CDC 747161                         pubyear: 1986

     4) The jazz album [sound recording] : a tri  copies: 1 (AV-SERVICE)
        Rattle, Simon,                            type: COMDSC
        COMDSC CDC 747991                         pubyear: 1987
```

Figure 41.12: Unicorn: Multi-index result

43

UTCAT
Applying Design Principles to an Online Catalog

John Kupersmith

Eliel Saarinen's maxim, "Always design a thing by considering it in its next larger context," is highly applicable to online catalogs and other public-access computer systems. The UTCAT online catalog at the University of Texas at Austin has been shaped by the context in which it is used.

More specifically, UTCAT was designed around a series of principles formulated in 1983, one year before the system went public in a prototype version. The first two principles stem from the fact that UT Austin has a campus population of more than 70,000, including some 15,000 potential new users each year—considerably more than we can instruct with a thinly spread public-services staff—as well as a significant number of long-term experienced users:

- Novice users should be able to operate the system without assistance.

- Experienced users should be able to operate the system with a minimum of interference from instructions, menus, etc., aimed at the novice.

To address this dilemma, we adopted what has been called a command-driven/ menu-augmented user interface. A search choices menu (Figure 43.1) is available from any point in the catalog. The user can invoke any of the ten possible searches simply with a one- or two-letter command (such as T for Title), calling up a search

input screen with instructions and examples (Figure 43.2). This menu mode works well for beginners, and is heavily used.

Experienced users who want shortcuts can bypass these input screens by entering their search command and search string together, e.g., "T Rhapsody in Blue." In order to move users along the learning curve, the menu screen gives search examples in this combined format. Also, it is not necessary to return to the menu to enter a new search; a full input line on all screens lets the user execute any search—or any other command—from virtually any point in the system.

Search and Display

The next two principles govern the search process and display of results and are based on the idea that for most users, finding materials takes priority over viewing detailed bibliographic information.

- The system should be programmed to eliminate or forgive common errors in operation (including alternative commands likely to be entered by users).

- All functions and displays should be designed primarily to lead to successful action by the user; technical accuracy of the information displayed is secondary.

507

Normalization and Synonyms

The UTCAT programs incorporate extensive normalization of search input. For example, all punctuation is stripped out and all letters are converted to upper case. Thus, an author or subject search on "king martin luther jr" gets the same result as "King, Martin Luther, Jr." Likewise, in some cases the system accepts alternative commands: for example, while the NISO-standard **Stop** is the officially advertised command, UTCAT will also accept Logoff, Off, Quit, End, Bye, etc. The design team came to recognize this principle of forgiveness with the motto "To err is human, to forgive is online."

Forgiveness Through Browsing

Most UTCAT searches operate in browse mode; that is, when the user enters a search, the system opens the file at that point, or the next possible point in alphanumeric order (Figure 43.3). The user can then page forward through successive entries, as far as he or she chooses (Figure 43.4). This arrangement, while it lacks Boolean precision, is more forgiving than a set-based search, since the user can examine additional entries occurring later in the file, often finding useful items through serendipity.

Display Options

Most searches default to the brief-display format, which, following the philosophy stated above, is designed primarily as a finding tool. It combines brief bibliographic information with the real-time circulation status of each item (e.g., entry 4 in Figure 43.3). To insure maximum retrieval, each item is listed under every relevant combination of author, co-author, editor, illustrator, performer (etc.) and title. For example, there is an entry for "Baskin, Leonard, 1922- / Auguries of Innocence," even though Baskin is the illustrator and William Blake the author of that book. In this case, technical accuracy (in librarians' terms) is traded off in order to bring the user into contact with as many relevant entries as possible.

Complete bibliographic information is given in the full-record display, available for any brief record by typing its entry number and pressing Enter. A vertically arranged, labeled format has proved to work very well (Figure 43.5, partial). Full records for maps (Figure 43.6) and computer software (Figure 43.7, partial) contain appropriate information in Description, Notes and other fields.

Cross References and Index Displays

The same philosophy of encouraging successful action by the user has guided the design of one of UTCAT's most distinctive features: built-in cross-reference displays. "Pointer" messages appear under the "see from" headings in brief displays (Figure 43.8); when the user selects one of these items, the system moves to the correct heading and opens the file there, displaying an explanatory message (Figure 43.9). We found that users did not take notice of this message when it was only two lines long, so it was expanded to a seven-line window.

Index-level displays are also available in UTCAT. In the case of the subject search, the index was made the default display, in order to expose users to the array of specific subdivisions (Figure 43.10). The author and title indexes can be called up by executing an author-index or title-index search. Also, users who are viewing brief record results for author, title, or subject searches can go directly to the corresponding indexes by giving the **index** command.

Boolean and Multi-Index Searches

At this time, the only Boolean search in UTCAT is the title-keyword search. The user specifies up to five keywords, and sees a set of matching records displayed in brief format (Figure 43.11). Special screens guide the user who has obtained a result of over 50 items (Figure 43.12) or a zero result (Figure 43.13). Stoplisted words input by a user are ignored in searching, and a special message informs the user that these words are not indexed. The title-keyword search is very popular, as it is often an excellent supplement to—or even a substitute for—the LCSH-based subject search.

The author-title search is a hybrid. It is not Boolean in nature, but instead guides the user through author input (Figure 43.14), the author index (Figure 43.15), and title input (Figure 43.16), arriving at author-search results beginning with the desired title (Figure 43.17). This multistep search is valuable mainly for combinations of prolific authors and common titles.

Reserve List

An interesting design problem arose when we wanted to add an online reserve list subsystem, for both staff processing of reserve materials and public display in UTCAT. Should this be presented to users as a completely separate section, accessible only by a special command? Eventually we decided to take the opposite course and integrate the instructor name and course number searches into the UTCAT menu and command structure, so that they can be invoked from any point in the system. After passing through an index screen (Figure 43.18), the user can browse through the reserve list for a particular class (Figure 43.19). A special message at the beginning of the reserve-list display calls attention to the fact that it includes only those copies on reserve for that class.

Clarity, Consistency, and Visibility

The next three design principles address the issues of visibility and wording of commands and other text:

- All instructions should be conveyed through the screen; external signage and other forms of instruction should be held to an absolute minimum.
- All text displayed should be in plain English, using unambiguous words and active verbs.
- Terminology, syntax, etc. should be consistent throughout the system and all related instructions and publicity.

So far, we have been able to have all available commands and options visible on all screens, by displaying two lines of command words and mnemonics at the bottom of the screen. This kind of display, visually patterned after the "bounce bar" found in Lotus 1-2-3 and some other text-based microcomputer programs, can be cryptic but is considerably better than hiding the commands on a separate screen. We have wrestled with the idea of Macintosh-style pull-down menus, but the limitations of the 3270 terminal environment and the lack of a pointing device for the user make that alternative unlikely.

UTCAT commands can be entered in three ways: with a whole word (HELP), a 3-letter abbreviation (HEL), or a function key (PF6). The commands are listed on the screen in a way that reminds users that they may abbreviate (HELp). Advertising the "plain English" commands on-screen, rather than the function keys, has been an important benefit to the more than 500 users per day who dial into UTCAT from remote terminals and microcomputers. For those who want to explore the options, PF-key and ESC-key equivalents are listed on a special KEYs screen.

Help and "Explain" Screens

Although both conventional wisdom and our own sampling indicate that help screens are little used, we feel it is important to provide them. Context-sensitive help screens are available at almost every point in the system (e.g., Figure 43.20). Perhaps more significant is the menu-driven explain system providing over 35 screens of general UTCAT information (e.g., Figures 43.21 and 43.22) and such useful data as current library hours. We are currently moving the help and explain information from individual screen maps to a new system that will display files created on the mainframe text editor.

However, UTCAT's function as a communications medium goes beyond these features. The news screen (Figure 43.23) carries announcements of current UTCAT developments, library programs, due dates for faculty reserve lists, etc. The welcome screen, seen by all users who dial in and by those who give the **Stop** command on library terminals, includes one or two banner lines calling attention to the news and explain screens.

Feedback

From the beginning, UTCAT's **comment** command has provided a means of two-way communication. We receive about 100 comments a week, ranging from the scatological to the profound and including considerable feedback about the catalog and suggestions for additional features. The comment function has recently been expanded to provide users with four explicit options, each of which leads to a specialized input screen (Figures 43.24 and 43.25). Using "welcome," News and Comment in combination, we have been able to conduct some unscientific but valuable user surveys.

Future Plans

Future plans for UTCAT include the capabilities to: display information on items on order or in process; search on a greater variety of Boolean combinations; search on author and subject keywords; limit searches by library location, language, date, and format; and easily download a set of records rather than a series of screen dumps. There are also ongoing plans for indexing improvements (particularly for music materials) and further enhancement of the database.

Background Information

UTCAT is being developed jointly by the University of Texas at Austin General Libraries and Data Processing Division, with the Academic Computation Center providing support for remote access. The catalog resides on an IBM ES/9000-720 mainframe and is based on Software AG's database management system, ADABAS. The "fourth generation" NATURAL programming language provides considerable flexibility, for example, in maintaining tables of variables and in changing screen maps. Locally written modules include the Interactive Circulation System and the UTCAT online public catalog; we are also using the INNOVACQ acquisitions system.

The UTCAT database now lists some 4,380,000 items (actually including over 16 million item, bibliographic, and authority records). A number of projects have expanded the UTCAT database beyond what is usually found in a traditional card catalog. Staff have created local records for more than 22,000 maps and 75,000 U.S., UN, Canadian, and Texas government documents; many other maps and documents have been cataloged using OCLC. Over 100,000 records list individual items in large microform sets. An innovative project has produced records for over 230 manuscript collections at the Barker Texas History Center (Figure 43.26) and the Benson Latin American Collection.

While most items listed in UTCAT are physically located on the UT Austin campus, we have loaded 223,000 records representing holdings of the Center for Research Libraries in Chicago. Moving away from the idea of physical holdings entirely, our Life Science Library has begun an Online Journals Project, in which dummy records for some 30 journals we do not hold have been placed in UTCAT, indicating that the user should ask about full-text online retrieval. Given sufficient staff time and funding, this experiment may be extended to other groups of journals, including some that are entirely electronic in format.

UTCAT is available for remote access via the Internet (telnet utcat.utexas.edu; when connection is made, press Enter or Return), or by direct dial-up (Even parity, 7 data bits, one stop bit; 1,200 baud: 512-471-9400; 2400 baud: 512-471-9420; at the CLASS= prompt, type utcat).

The UTCAT software is © 1988, The University of Texas at Austin. At this writing, the UTCAT system as described above is not available for sale; however, it has been licensed to Software AG for use in developing an integrated library system.

```
UT LIBRARY ONLINE CATALOG -- SEARCH CHOICES MENU
================================================================
CATALOG SEARCHES: Look up books and other items in the UT Austin libraries.
    COMMAND                    EXAMPLE
    A   = Author .............. a mowat, farley
    AI  = Author Index ........ ai mowat, farley
    T   = Title .............. t never cry wolf
    TI  = Title Index ........ ti never cry wolf
    TK  = Title Keyword ....... tk wolf cry
    AT  = Author-Title ........ at mowat, farley (you will be asked for title)
    S   = Subject ............. s wolves
    C   = Call Number ........ c ql 795 w8 m6

RESERVES SEARCHES: View this semester's reserve lists for UT Austin courses.
    IN  = INstructor Name ..... in clarke, s
    CO  = COurse Number ....... co his 389

================================================================
Type a command, a space, and the words you want to search, then press ENTER
OR For search instructions/examples, type only the command, then press ENTER
-> _____
Options:   EXPlain   HELp   NEWs   COMment   KEYs   STOp          C10023
```

Figure 43.1: UTCAT: Search choices menu

```
TITLE SEARCH
================================================================

   Omit any article at the beginning of a title.

        Example:  texan in england

        Example:  documentary history of the australian labor movement


================================================================

To find items for a title, type your search, then press ENTER

-> rhapsody in blue_____

Or type:   HELp   MENu   COMment   STOp   then press ENTER     C10023
```

Figure 43.2: UTCAT: Title search input screen

```
BRIEF RECORD RESULTS FOR TITLE SEARCH
================================================================
Your search: RHAPSODY IN BLUE
   1  Rhapsody in blue. / Classics and all that jazz the music of the 1920's.
       / Claremont, Sou* 1985(1927)
       PHNDISC MU 21,118  Fine Arts Library

   2  Rhapsody in blue. / Gershwin, George, 1898-1937. / New York 1942
       M 1010 G38 R4 1942B  Fine Arts Library

   3  Rhapsody in blue. / Gershwin, George, 1898-1937. / Netherlands 1983
       COMPACT DISC MU 584  Fine Arts Library

   4  Rhapsody in blue / Gershwin, George, 1898-1937. / Fiedler conducts
       Gershwin. / New York 1987
       COMPACT DISC MU 1595  Fine Arts Library  CHECKED OUT DUE 06/05/91

   5  Rhapsody in blue / Gershwin, George, 1898-1937. / Gershwin plays
================================================================
For full record, type entry number, press ENTER / For next screen, press ENTER
-> 4_____
Options:  INDex  REPeat  HELp  EXPlain  NEWs  COMment  KEYs  STOp
Search commands:  A  AI  T  TI  TK  AT  S  C  IN  CO  MENu     C00240
```

Figure 43.3: UTCAT: Browse from title search

```
BRIEF RECORD RESULTS FOR TITLE SEARCH
========================================================================
  5   Gershwin. / 1976(1924)
      PHNDISC 4052   UGL Audio Visual Collection

  6   Rhapsody in blue / Gershwin, George, 1898-1937. / Levant plays Gershwin.
      PHNDISC MU 8795   Fine Arts Library
      PHNDISC MU 8795   Fine Arts Library   COPY 2
      PHNDISC MU 8795   Fine Arts Library   COPY 3

  7   Rhapsody in blue / Gershwin, George, 1898-1937. / Piano roll
          discoveries. / New York 1959
      PHNDISC MU 18,626   Fine Arts Library

  8   Rhapsody in blue / Gershwin, George, 1898-1937. / Rhapsody in blue. /
          New York 1942
      M 1010 G38 R4 1942B   Fine Arts Library

========================================================================
For full record, type entry number, press ENTER / For next screen, press ENTER
-> _____
Options:   INDex  BACk  REPeat  HELp  EXPlain  NEWs  COMment  KEYs  STOp
Search commands:   A  AI  T  TI  TK  AT  S  C   IN  CO  MENu        C10023
```

Figure 43.4: UTCAT: Paging forward in browse

```
FULL RECORD                                                       Screen 1
========================================================================
AUTHOR:          Gershwin, George, 1898-1937.
UNIFORM TITLE:   Rhapsody in blue
TITLE:           Fiedler conducts Gershwin
PUBLISHED:       New York : RCA, 1987.
DESCRIPTION:     1 sound disc : digital, stereo. ; 4 3/4 in.
NOTES:           6519-2-RG RCA Papillon Collection
                 Boston Pops Orchestra; Earl Wild, pianist.
                 Compact disc.
SUBJECTS:        Orchestral music
                 Concertos (Piano)
                 Piano with orchestra
OTHER AUTHORS:   Wild, Earl.
                 Fiedler, Arthur, 1894-1979.
                 Gershwin, George, 1898-1937. / Concerto, piano, orchestra, F
                     major.
                 Gershwin, George, 1898-1937. / An American in Paris.
========================================================================
For next screen, press ENTER
-> _____
Options:   BACk   HELp   EXPlain   NEWs   COMment   KEYs   STOp
Search commands:   A  AI  T  TI  TK  AT  S  C   IN  CO  MENu        C00240
```

Figure 43.5: UTCAT: Full display, recording

```
FULL RECORD                                                       Screen 1
========================================================================
AUTHOR:      Australia. Division of National Mapping.
TITLE:       Australia 1:5,000,000 general reference map / produced by the
             Division of National Mapping, 1986.
MATH. DATA:  Scale 1:5,000,000 ; Simple conic proj. (E 1100--E 1600/S
             100--S 450).
PUBLISHED:   Canberra (A.C.T.) : The Division, (1986)
DESCRIPTION: 1 map : col. ; 79 x 94 cm.
NOTES:       Relief shown by shading, spot heights, and hypsometric tints.
             On verso: gazetteer.
             Title on map: Australia.
             "Natmap."
             "NMP/75/273."
SUBJECTS:    Australia--Maps.
SERIES:      Australia 1:5,000,000 map series.
OCLC NUMBER: 13801591

========================================================================
For next screen, press ENTER
-> _____
Options:   BACk   HELp   EXPlain   NEWs   COMment   KEYs   STOp
Search commands:   A  AI  T  TI  TK  AT  S  C   IN  CO  MENu        C10221
```

Figure 43.6: UTCAT: Full display, map

```
┌─────────────────────────────────────────────────────────────────────────────┐
│ FULL RECORD                                                         Screen 1  │
│ ============================================================================= │
│ TITLE:          Microsoft Word                                                │
│ EDITION:        Version 3.1.                                                   │
│ PUBLISHED:      Redmond, WA : Microsoft, c1986.                               │
│ DESCRIPTION:    6 computer disks, 2 tutorial disks : col. ; 5 1/4 in. + Using │
│                 Microsoft Word (xxi, 318 p. ; 24 cm.) + Reference to          │
│                 Microsoft Word (vii, 239 p. ; 24 cm.) + Printer information    │
│                 for Microsoft Word, Version 3.0 (viii, 97 p. ; 23 cm.) +      │
│                 Microsoft Word 3.1 additional information (iii, 53 p. ; 22     │
│                 cm.)                                                           │
│ NOTES:          System requirements: IBM PC or compatible; 256K; DOS 2.0 or   │
│                 higher; 2 disk drives or hard disk; color/graphics adapter;   │
│                 80-column monochrome or color monitor.                        │
│                 Summary: Word processor with a built in outlining capability. │
│                 Handles multiple documents in separate windows and can        │
│                 automatically generate form letters, indexes, tables of       │
│                 contents, and footnotes. Includes thesaurus and spelling      │
│ ============================================================================= │
│ For next screen, press ENTER                                                  │
│ -> ▌_____ │
│ Options:     BACk   HELp   EXPlain   NEWs   COMment   KEYs   STOp             │
│ Search commands:    A  AI   T  TI   TK  AT   S   C   IN  CO   MENu    CI0023  │
└─────────────────────────────────────────────────────────────────────────────┘
```

Figure 43.7: UTCAT: Full display, software

```
┌─────────────────────────────────────────────────────────────────────────────┐
│ LIBRARY CATALOG — AUTHOR SEARCH RESULTS   (BRIEF DISPLAY)                     │
│ ============================================================================= │
│ Your search: EL GRECO                                                         │
│   1  El Greco, 1541?-1614                                                      │
│      To see items by this author, type number and press ENTER                 │
│                                                                               │
│   2  El Grupo (Musical group) / Canciones y poesia de la lucha de los pueblos │
│      latinoamericanos. Songs and poetry of the Latin American struggle. /     │
│      1974                                                                      │
│      PHNDISC LA 77  Benson Latin American Collection                          │
│                                                                               │
│   3  El Grupo (Musical group) / Songs and poetry of the Latin American        │
│         struggle. / 1974                                                       │
│      PHNDISC LA 77  Benson Latin American Collection                          │
│                                                                               │
│   4  El Guindi, Fadwa. / The myth of ritual : a native's ethnography of       │
│         Zapotec life-crisis rituals. / Tucson 1986                            │
│      F 1221 Z3 E53 1986  Benson Latin American Collection   CHECKED OUT DUE   │
│ ============================================================================= │
│ For full display, type entry number, press ENTER / For next screen,press ENTER│
│ -> 1▌_____ │
│ Options:   INDex   REPeat   HELP   EXPlain   NEWs   COMment   KEYs   MENu      │
│ Search commands:    A  AI   T  TI   TK  AT   S   C   IN  CO       STOp=main menu│
└─────────────────────────────────────────────────────────────────────────────┘
```

Figure 43.8: UTCAT: Cross-reference

```
LIBRARY CATALOG — AUTHOR SEARCH RESULTS   (BRIEF DISPLAY)
==================================================================================
¦ The author you selected:                                                      ¦
¦   EL GRECO                                                                     ¦
¦                                                                               ¦
¦ is indexed as:                                                                ¦
¦   GRECO                                                                        ¦
¦                                                                               ¦
¦ Here are your search results, beginning with that name:                       ¦
+--------------------------------------------------------------------------------+
   1  Greco, 1541?-1614. / The complete paintings of El Greco, 1541-1614. /
         1983 ed.# New York 1983
      ND 813 T4 G7813 1983   Fine Arts Library

   2  Greco, 1541?-1614. / Domenikos Theotokopoulos called El Greco. / Paris
         1937
      ND 813 T4 L43   Fine Arts Library
      ND 813 T4 L43   Fine Arts Library      COPY 2
==================================================================================
For full display, type entry number, press ENTER / For next screen,press ENTER
-> █_____
Options:   INDex   REPeat   HELp   EXPlain   NEWs   COMment   KEYs   MENu
Search commands:    A  AI  T  TI  TK  AT  S  C   IN  CO          STOp=main menu
```

Figure 43.9: UTCAT: Explanation for redirection

```
SUBJECT INDEX                                                            ITEMS
==================================================================================
Your search: KING MARTIN LUTHER JR
    1  King, Martin Luther, Jr., 1929-1968.                                  94
    2  King, Martin Luther, Jr., 1929-1968.--Assassination.                  15
    3  King, Martin Luther, Jr., 1929-1968.--Assassination--Juvenile          2
         literature.
    4  King, Martin Luther, Jr., 1929-1968.--Bibliography.                    2
    5  King, Martin Luther, Jr., 1929-1968.--Homes and haunts.                1
    6  King, Martin Luther, Jr., 1929-1968.--Iconography.                     1
    7  King, Martin Luther, Jr., 1929-1968.--Juvenile literature.             6
    8  King, Martin Luther, Jr., 1929-1968.--Musical settings.                1
    9  King, Martin Luther, Jr., 1929-1968.--Poetry.                          1
   10  King, Martin Luther, Jr., 1929-1968.--Public opinion.                  1
   11  King, Martin Luther, Jr., 1929-1968.--Quotations.                      1
   12  King, Martin Luther, Jr., 1929-1968.--Religion.                        3
   13  King, Martin Luther, Jr., 1929-1968.--Songs and music.                 3
   14  King, Martin Luther, Jr., 1929-1968.--Views on community.              1
==================================================================================
To select, type entry number, press ENTER / For next screen, press ENTER
-> 1_____
Options:    REPeat    HELp    EXPlain    NEWs    COMment    KEYs    STOp
Search commands:    A  AI  T  TI  TK  AT  S  C   IN  CO   MENu        C00185
```

Figure 43.10: UTCAT: Subject browse

```
BRIEF RECORD RESULTS FOR TITLE KEYWORD SEARCH
================================================================================
Your search: FIRE MOON
matches 1 item
    1  Of a fire on the moon. / Mailer, Norman. / 1st ed. Boston 1970
       629.4 M2810  Undergraduate Library  COPY 1  CHECKED OUT DUE 04/23/91
       629.4 M2810  Undergraduate Library  COPY 2  CHECKED OUT DUE 04/16/91
       629.4 M2810  Undergraduate Library  COPY 3
       629.40973 M2810  PCL Stacks




================================================================================
For full record, type entry number, press ENTER / For next screen, press ENTER
-> _____
Options:    REPeat    HELp    EXPlain    NEWs    COMment    KEYs    STOp
Search commands:    A   AI   T   TI   TK   AT   S   C   IN   CO   MENu    C00209
```

Figure 43.11: UTCAT: Title keyword search

```
BRIEF RECORD RESULTS FOR TITLE KEYWORD SEARCH
================================================================================
Your search: TEXAS OIL
matches 294 items
with titles containing all the words you searched.


    Keyword:
       TEXAS                        matches    28402 items
       OIL                          matches     4975 items



================================================================================
To see all 294 items, press ENTER
OR To revise your keyword search, type TK and the new search, then press ENTER

-> _____
Options:    EXPlain    HELp    NEWs    COMment    KEYs    STOp
Search commands:    A   AI   T   TI   TK   AT   S   C   IN   CO   MENu    C10023
```

Figure 43.12: UTCAT: Boolean expansion

```
BRIEF RECORD RESULTS FOR TITLE KEYWORD SEARCH
================================================================================
Your search: RAPSODY BLUE
matches 0 items (KEYWORDS NOT INDEXED: IN )

The catalog has no items with titles containing all the words you searched.
    Keyword:
       RAPSODY                      matches        4 items
       BLUE                         matches     2227 items




You may revise your search by either:
       - including fewer words
       - using different words
================================================================================
To revise your keyword search, type TK and the new search, then press ENTER

-> █_____
Options:    EXPlain    HELp    NEWs    COMment    KEYs    STOp
Search commands:    A   AI   T   TI   TK   AT   S   C   IN   CO   MENu    C10023
```

Figure 43.13: UTCAT: Zero-result, Boolean

```
┌─────────────────────────────────────────────────────────────────────────┐
│ AUTHOR-TITLE SEARCH  (AUTHOR PORTION)                                     │
│ ========================================================================= │
│                                                                           │
│       Search the author first.                                            │
│                                                                           │
│       The Author Index will be displayed for you                          │
│          to select the author before you search the title.                │
│                                                                           │
│       For persons, type last name first                                   │
│                                                                           │
│         Example:  shakespeare, william                                    │
│                                                                           │
│       For other authors, use normal word order                            │
│                                                                           │
│         Example:  national council of teachers of english                 │
│                                                                           │
│ ========================================================================= │
│                                                                           │
│ Type your author search, then press ENTER                                 │
│                                                                           │
│ -> mozart_____ │
│                                                                           │
│ Or type:   HELp   MENu   COMment   STOp   then press ENTER       CI0023   │
└─────────────────────────────────────────────────────────────────────────┘
```

Figure 43.14: UTCAT: Author input for A-T search

```
┌─────────────────────────────────────────────────────────────────────────┐
│ AUTHOR INDEX                                                              │
│ ========================================================================= │
│ Your search: MOZART                                                       │
│     1  Mozart, 1756-1791                                                  │
│     2  Mozart, Amadeus, 1756-1791                                         │
│     3  Mozart, Constanze, 1763-1842.                                      │
│     4  Mozart, Constanze Weber, 1763-1842                                 │
│     5  Mozart Festival Orchestra                                          │
│     6  Mozart, Franz Xaver, 1791-1844.                                    │
│     7  Mozart, George, 1864?-1947.                                        │
│     8  Mozart, Johann Chrysostom Wolfgang Amadeus, 1756-1791              │
│     9  Mozart, Johann Chrysostom Wolfgang Amadeus, 1756-1791, supposed    │
│           author.                                                         │
│    10  Mozart, Johann Chrysostom Wolfgang Amadeus, 1756-1791.             │
│    11  Mozart, Johann Georg Leopold, 1719-1787                            │
│    12  Mozart-Klavierquartett.                                            │
│    13  Mozart, Leopold, 1719-1787.                                        │
│    14  Mozart, Leopold, 1719-1787.                                        │
│ ========================================================================= │
│ To select, type entry number, press ENTER / For next screen, press ENTER  │
│ -> 1_____ │
│ Options:     REPeat   HELp   EXPlain   NEWs   COMment   KEYs   STOp        │
│ Search commands:   A  AI  T  TI  TK  AT  S  C  IN  CO  MENu      C00209    │
└─────────────────────────────────────────────────────────────────────────┘
```

Figure 43.15: UTCAT: Author result for A-T search

```
┌─────────────────────────────────────────────────────────────────────────┐
│ AUTHOR-TITLE SEARCH  (TITLE PORTION)                                      │
│ ========================================================================= │
│                                                                           │
│ Author: MOZART WOLFGANG AMADEUS                                           │
│ matches your search: MOZART                                               │
│                                                                           │
│       Type the first word(s) of a title by this author.                   │
│                                                                           │
│       Omit any article at the beginning of a title.                       │
│                                                                           │
│                                                                           │
│ ========================================================================= │
│                                                                           │
│                                                                           │
│ Type your title search, then press ENTER                                  │
│                                                                           │
│ -> symphony█_____ │
│                                                                           │
│ Or type:   HELp   MENu   COMment   STOp   then press ENTER       CI0023   │
└─────────────────────────────────────────────────────────────────────────┘
```

Figure 43.16: UTCAT: Title input for A-T search

```
BRIEF RECORD RESULTS FOR AUTHOR SEARCH
===============================================================================
Your search: MOZART WOLFGANG AMADEUS  / SYMPHONY
has no exact match for the title searched. The next entry is:
    1  Mozart, Wolfgang Amadeus, 1756-1791. / Symphony : C major, "Linz", K. V.
          425. / London 19??
          M 1001 M92 K.425 B6   Fine Arts Library

    2  Mozart, Wolfgang Amadeus, 1756-1791. / Symphony, D major (Haffner)
          Kochel, no. 385. / Edited f* London 1900
          M 1001 M92 K.385 1900ZA  Fine Arts Library

    3  Mozart, Wolfgang Amadeus, 1756-1791. / Symphony, G minor : Kochel no.
          550. / London 1930
          M 1001 M92 K.550 K76  Fine Arts Library
          M 1001 M92 K.550 K76  Fine Arts Library   COPY 2

    4  Mozart, Wolfgang Amadeus, 1756-1791. / Symphony in A minor, K 16a
===============================================================================
For full record, type entry number, press ENTER / For next screen, press ENTER
-> ▮_____
Options:   INDex  REPeat  HELp  EXPlain  NEWs  COMment  KEYs  STOp
Search commands:    A  AI  T  TI  TK  AT  S  C   IN  CO   MENu        CI0023
```

Figure 43.17: UTCAT: End-result of A-T search

```
RESERVES SECTION -- INSTRUCTOR NAME INDEX
===============================================================================
Your search: CLARKE SALLY
has no exact match.  The next instructor name is:
ENTRY   INSTRUCTOR NAME       COURSE NO.  COURSE TITLE
    1  Clarke, Sally H        HIS  315L   United States Since 1865
    2  Clarke, Sally H        HIS  350L   Regulating American Business
    3  Clarke, Sally H.       HIS  389    Economics & Business History
    4  Cleaver, Harry M J     ECO  350K   Political Econ Of Intl Crisis
    5  Cleaves, Peter S.      GOV  384L   Comparative Politics: Latin Am
    6  Cleaves, Peter S.      LAS  384L   Comparative Politics: Latin Am
    7  Clinger, Charles K     CH   110L   Organic Chemistry Laboratory
    8  Clinger, Charles K     CH   610A   Organic Chemistry
    9  Clinger, Charles K     CH   610B   Organic Chemistry
   10  Clinger, Charles K     CH   618A   Organic Chemistry-Chem Engr
   11  Cloos, Mark P          GEO  428    Structural Geology
   12  Cogdell, John R        E E  325    Electromagnetic Engineering I
   13  Cogdell, John R        E E  335M   Electric Mach And Mag Devices
===============================================================================
To select, type entry number, press ENTER / For next screen, press ENTER
-> 2▮_____
Options:   REPeat    HELp   EXPlain   NEWs   COMment   KEYs   STOp
Search commands:    A  AI  T  TI  TK  AT  S  C   IN  CO   MENu        CI0202
```

Figure 43.18: UTCAT: Course reserve index

```
RESERVE LIST
================================================================================
|                                                                              |
|   INSTRUCTOR:    Clarke, Sally H            COURSE NO.:  HIS  350L           |
|   COURSE TITLE: Regulating American Business SEMESTER:    Spring 1991        |
|                                                                              |
|      This list contains only those copies now on reserve for this class.     |
|      To find all copies of an item, search it by Author or Title.            |
|                                                                              |
+------------------------------------------------------------------------------+

      1   Energy policy in America since 1945 : a study of business government
             relations. / Vietor, Richard H. K., 1945- / Cambridge 1984
          HD 9502 U52 V53 1984   PCL Reserves

      2   The fall of the Bell system : a study in prices and politics. / Temin,
             Peter. / Cambridge 1987
          HE 8846 A55 T44 1987   PCL Reserves

================================================================================
For full record, type entry number, press ENTER / For next screen, press ENTER
-> _____
Options:   INDex  REPeat  HELp  EXPlain  NEWs  COMment  KEYs STOp
Search commands:   A  AI  T  TI  TK  AT  S  C   IN  CO  MENu          CI0202
```

Figure 43.19: UTCAT: Course reserve list

```
HELP  --  BRIEF RECORD RESULTS FOR TITLE SEARCH            Screen 1 of 2
================================================================================
You have searched for a title and are viewing the results in Brief format.
Within the results, you can page forward by pressing ENTER, then page back to
review up to 10 screens you've already seen by typing BAC and pressing ENTER.


ENTRY NO.    TITLE                        AUTHOR                PUBLICATION DATA
   /           /                            /                         /
1     Adventures of Huckleberry Finn. / Twain, Mark, 1835-1910. / Boston, 1907
      817 C49 A7 1907  PCL Stacks  CHECKED OUT DUE 06/01/88
       /                   /                 /
    CALL NUMBER      LIBRARY LOCATION    STATUS (NONE SHOWN=ITEM AVAILABLE)


IMPORTANT: The Brief Record will help you find the book, but does not have
complete bibliographic information; for that, see the Full Record.
================================================================================
For next screen, press ENTER
-> _____
Options:   BACK  EXPlain  NEWs  COMment  KEYs  STOp
Search commands:   A  AI  T  TI  TK  AT  S  C   IN  CO  MENu          CI0023
```

Figure 43.20: UTCAT: Context-sensitive help

```
"EXPLAIN" MENU
================================================================================

            1  What's in the Online Catalog?
            2  Search commands
            3  Other commands
            4  Access for disabled users
            5  Access from outside the library
            6  Printed guides and telephone help
            7  Instruction in Online Catalog use
            8  Glossary of Online Catalog terms
            9  Technical information
           10  Future plans
           11  Library addresses and phone numbers
           12  Library hours
           13  PCL stack guide
     or    14  Return to your place in the catalog

================================================================================
Type the number of your choice and press ENTER
-> 4█
Options:     BACk    NEWs    COMment    KEYs    STOp
Search commands:    A  AI  T  TI  TK  AT  S  C   IN  CO   MENu        C10023
```

Figure 43.21: UTCAT: Menu for explain screens

```
"EXPLAIN"  --  ACCESS FOR DISABLED USERS
================================================================================

VISUALLY IMPAIRED USERS:  The Adaptive Technology Library Center in the
Undergraduate Library offers a magnified screen display, voice output,
Braille output, and floppy disk output.  For more information, call
Ann Neville, 471-5222.

WHEELCHAIR USERS:  Table-height terminals are located in:
      Perry-Castaneda Library (PCL) Reserve Room, level 2
      Undergraduate Library (UGL) Reference/Catalog area, level 1
      Life Science Library, near Circulation Desk
      Fine Arts Library, near Reference Desk
      Chemistry Library

Ask library staff for assistance in using the catalog,
getting books, making photocopies, etc.

================================================================================
To return to your place in the catalog, press ENTER
->
Options:     BACk   EXPlain   NEWs   COMment   KEYs   STOp
Search commands:    A  AI  T  TI  TK  AT  S  C   IN  CO   MENu        C10023
```

Figure 43.22: UTCAT: Explain screen

```
ONLINE CATALOG NEWS  --  March 12, 1991
================================================================================

COMMENT FUNCTION EXPANDED
The COMment command now leads to a menu with 4 options:

    Send a comment          Report a data error
    Ask a question          Suggest an item for purchase

Each option gives you a specialized screen for writing your message.
We've also taken steps to eliminate the problem of sending a message
prematurely.

The new system will also mean faster and more efficient processing
of your comments, since the messages generated by each of the four
options will go directly to the appropriate staff.  Based on expe-
rience with the new system, we may add more options in the future.

================================================================================
To return to your place in the catalog, press ENTER
->
Options:     BACk   EXPlain   COMment   KEYs   STOp
Search commands:    A  AI  T  TI  TK  AT  S  C   IN  CO   MENu        C10023
```

Figure 43.23: UTCAT: News screen

```
+------------------------------------------------------------------------------+
| WELCOME TO THE EXPANDED COMMENT FUNCTION                                      |
| ============================================================================ |
|                                                                              |
|         1   Send a comment                                                   |
|                                                                              |
|         2   Ask a question                                                   |
|                                                                              |
|         3   Report a data error                                             |
|                                                                              |
|         4   Suggest an item for purchase                                     |
|                                                                              |
|   or    5   Return to your place in the catalog                             |
|                                                                              |
|                                                                              |
| ============================================================================ |
| Type the number of your choice and press ENTER                               |
| -> 2█                                                                        |
| Options:    BACk    NEWs    COMment   KEYs    STOp                           |
| Search commands:    A   AI   T   TI   TK   AT   S   C   IN   CO   MENu   CI0023 |
+------------------------------------------------------------------------------+
```

Figure 43.24: UTCAT: Comment function options

```
+------------------------------------------------------------------------------+
|                              ASK A QUESTION                                   |
| To move to the next line, press the TAB or -->| key.                         |
| To send your question, press ENTER.                                          |
|                                                                              |
| Question:                                                                    |
|       _____        |
|       _____        |
|       _____        |
|       _____        |
|       _____        |
|       _____        |
|       _____        |
|       _____        |
|       _____        |
|       _____        |
|       _____        |
|       _____        |
|       _____        |
|                                                                              |
| Your name: _____                          |
| Mailing address: _____          |
| OR full E-mail address (ID @ node): _____          |
+------------------------------------------------------------------------------+
```

Figure 43.25: UTCAT: Comment entry screen

```
+------------------------------------------------------------------------------+
| FULL RECORD                                                        Screen 1  |
| ============================================================================ |
| AUTHOR:        Austin, Stephen F. (Stephen Fuller), 1793-1836.              |
| TITLE:         Austin papers, 1676-1889.                                     |
| DESCRIPTION:   9 ft., 6 in.                                                   |
| NOTES:         Correspondence, notes and lists, diaries, petitions,         |
|                certificates, maps, field notes and surveys, broadsides,      |
|                proclamations, inventories, financial and legal papers, land  |
|                grants and deeds, reports, and newspaper clippings arranged   |
|                in chronological order within series.                         |
|                References: Calendar and index Eugene C. Barker, ed., The     |
|                Austin Papers in 3 vols. (1924-1938)                          |
|                Cite as: Austin Papers, 1676-1889, Barker Texas History       |
|                Center, University of Texas at Austin.                        |
|                Published papers Eugene C. Barker, ed., The Austin Papers in 3 |
|                vols. (1924-1928)                                             |
|                Miscellaneous documents from other collections Transcripts and |
|                photocopies.                                                  |
| ============================================================================ |
| For next screen, press ENTER                                                 |
| ->                                                                           |
| Options:   BACk    HELp    EXPlain   NEWs    COMment   KEYs    STOp          |
| Search commands:   A   AI   T   TI   TK   AT   S   C   IN   CO   MENu   CI0221 |
+------------------------------------------------------------------------------+
```

Figure 43.26: UTCAT: Full disp., manuscript (part)

44

Winnebago CAT

Linda Eppelheimer

Winnebago CAT (Winnebago Software's online catalog program) is actually two catalogs in one. You can toggle between Regular CAT (where you can search for library materials by typing in all or part of a subject, a title, or an author name) and Key Word CAT (where you can search by typing in any combination of up to three key words or phrases).

To find materials, all you have to do is type in the word and press Enter. The program then displays a list of all the materials that match, including their call number, title, author, location, type, and status. The fill-in-the-blanks search screen makes it easy to use and keeps keystrokes to a minimum.

In Key Word CAT an approximate (incorrect) spelling brings up the option to browse the keyword list. You also can easily select the Boolean condition desired between each key element. And you can select the source(s) for your search (title, subject, author, and note fields as well as added entry fields). All the viable function keys are displayed in a list on the screen.

You can view each individual material found either in card format (as it would appear on a card from the card catalog) or in labeled format. You can also see the complete bibliographic (MARC) data available for any material you find.

After you have generated a list of materials, you can sort the results (display the records in call-number order), scratch materials from your list, and print your list in bibliographic form. You can even include the note field on the bibliographic report.

Both Key Word CAT and Regular CAT feature password protection and context-sensitive help screens.

Starting Out

Librarians reach the keyword search screen by selecting On-Line Catalog from the main menu of the CIRC/CAT program. They may have to enter one or two passwords (depending on how you have your passwords set up) before the keyword search screen appears (Figure 44.1).

Patrons turn on the computer and the batch file or network boot disk takes them directly to the keyword search screen.

Help

You can press the F1 function key to bring up a help screen that explains the general keyword search process (Figure 44.2). From this help screen, you can press the function key of the command you want more information on.

When you press the F2 function key (Change Boolean) while in the help mode (see previous screen), the program will display the first of two help screens that explain the concept of Boolean logic (Figures 44.3 and 44.4).

Searching

To find all works with Martin Luther King, Jr., as author or subject, type "martin" and "king" as keywords and use "King, Martin Luther" on the author line (Figure 44.5). The initial multiple-result list is not sorted (Figure 44.6). When you press the F9 function key, the list will be sorted in order by call number (see Figure 44.10).

You can type "civil" and "rights" to find other materials on a subject from a Martin Luther King search (Figure 44.7), but there is no direct related-works search. Use the F6 function key to change the source to only subjects.

Use the F8 function key to change an entry line from accepting a keyword to accepting a key phrase (Figure 44.8).

Displays

The briefest display of a record includes call number, title, author, location, material type, and status (Figures 44.9 and 44.10, unsorted and sorted by call number).

Winnebago's detailed material screen lets you see information about the material in a labeled manner (Figure 44.11).

At either the detailed material screen or the card image screen, you can press the letter M (for MARC) to see the material's complete bibliographic data (Figure 44.13, partial). You can use the arrow keys to scroll through the data if it doesn't all fit on one screen.

Cardlike Display

Winnebago gives you the option of viewing your records through the detailed material screen or a card image screen (Figure 44.12), depending on how a library sets up the system. You may view your records one way in the keyword catalog and the other way in the regular catalog.

Status Information

You can see information on the status of a material at the title list display. This also shows the number of copies and locations (Figure 44.14).

Errors

It is impossible to go past the end of a multirecord list, since cursor keys control the display. Any such attempt causes the cursor to wrap to the top of the screen.

As for spelling errors, the program will tell you when a word you typed in is not included on the keyword list (Figure 44.15). You have the choice of retyping the word or browsing the word list, starting at the closest match to the word you typed (Figure 44.16).

Approximate and Known-Item Searching

Type two keywords, "loadstone" and "magnetic," to find the material titled *On the Loadstone and Magnetic Bodies* (Figures 44.17 and 44.18).

For known items, the fastest route in the keyword catalog is to type in one or two keywords from the title and use the F6 function key to limit the source of keywords to title only (Figure 44.19).

Browsing

To browse through the author list, first press the F3 function key (Include Author or Other Index), which will present a window displaying the choice of indexes to search by. When selecting an index, the name of that index will appear below the keyword entry lines on the keyword search screen. You may enter any alphanumeric characters. To start browsing at a specific point, type in the author's last name (Figure 44.20). You can "arrow up" to see records before the first record in the list.

Use the F7 function key to switch to the regular catalog, where you can search only by subject (as well as only by author or title) (Figure 44.21).

Browse by call number by pressing F3 (Include Author or Other Index) and then selecting call number from the list of indexes. You can use the * as a wildcard to include all authors in the 686.2 range (Figures 44.22 and 44.23).

You can create a user-defined index by which you can search and browse. Your user-defined index can be of two parts (as illustrated) or of one part; for example, if you want to search only by fund, price, or the user-defined field. The example provided will give you a list of all the biographies, one of the material types, in this system (Figure 44.24 and 44.25).

Nonbook Displays

The nonbook information for all items is displayed in a card format. The call number or the physical description will tell what type of material it is.

Exiting

The online catalog can be set up to allow patrons to exit by pressing Escape (Figure 44.26). Or, it can give no information and the terminal will remain in the search mode all day. Exiting can also be password protected. A staff member can press Alt and F10 if they wish to use this workstation for another task. You can set up your catalog so that you can just press the Escape key to exit or so that patrons have no on-screen clue for exiting.

Printing

Press the F10 key to print a list, in bibliographic form, of the materials that you have found through a search. The program will first ask if you want to print bibliographies of your records (Figure 44.27). This option can be password protected. You can also include the note field in your printed report.

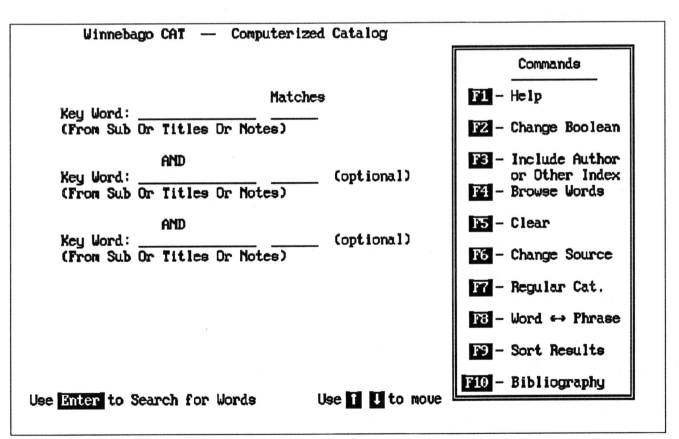

Figure 44.1: Winnebago: Key word search screen

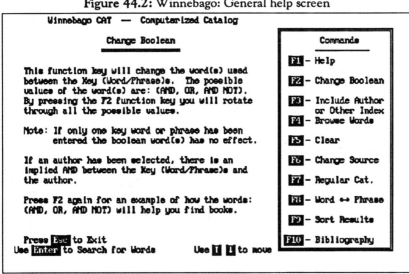

Figure 44.2: Winnebago: General help screen

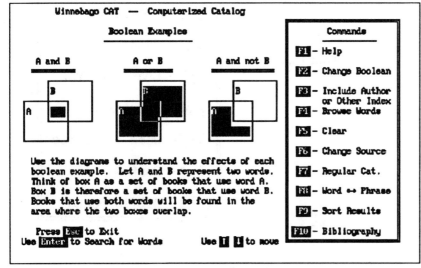

Figure 44.3: Winnebago: Boolean help (1)

Figure 44.4: Winnebago: Boolean help (2)

```
        Winnebago CAT  —  Computerized Catalog
                                                    ┌─────────────────┐
                                                    │     Commands    │
                                                    │     ─────────   │
                            Matches                 │ F1 - Help       │
        Key Word: king_____  40____              │                 │
        (From Sub Or Titles Or Notes)               │ F2 - Change Boolean │
                                                    │                 │
                      AND                           │ F3 - Remove Author  │
        Key Word: martin_____  18____ (optional)  │                 │
        (From Sub Or Titles Or Notes)               │ F4 - Browse Authors │
                                                    │                 │
                      AND                           │ F5 - Clear      │
        Key Word: _____  _____ (optional)    │                 │
        (From Sub Or Titles Or Notes)               │ F6 - Not in Use │
                                                    │                 │
        Author: KING, MARTIN LUTHER_____       │ F7 - Regular Cat.   │
                                                    │                 │
                                                    │ F8 - Not in Use │
                                                    │                 │
                                                    │ F9 - Sort Results   │
                                                    │                 │
        Use Enter to Search for Words   Use ↑ ↓ to move │ F10 - Bibliography │
                                                    └─────────────────┘
```

Figure 44.5: Winnebago: Martin Luther (keyword)

```
        Winnebago CAT — Computerized Catalog        10 Materials found
                                                     (Search Complete)

Call #     Material Title          Author    Location  Mat. Type   Status

812.54 BE  Martin Luther King, Jr. :   Behrens,  HS Libra  800 - 899   In
BIO KING,  My first Martin Luther King Lillegard HS Libra  Biography   In
323.4092   Martin Luther King.                           300 - 399   In
           New morning for the world : Schwantne         music sco   In
323.4092   Martin Luther King, Jr.—th                    300 - 399   In
323.4092_  Martin Luther King, Jr.                       300 - 399   In
Y 1.1/8:9  Martin Luther King, Jr. Fed                   document    In
323.4092_  Martin Luther King, Jr., Da                   300 - 999   In
323.1092   Martin Luther King, Jr.—th                    300 - 399   In
           Martin Luther King, Jr., a                    cassettes   In

Use ↑ ↓ PgUp PgDn Home End to Move   F9 to Sort Results  Enter to Select
Use Esc to Backup                    F10 Bibliography     Del to Delete
```

Figure 44.6: Winnebago: Multiple result list

```
        Winnebago CAT  —  Computerized Catalog
                                                    ┌─────────────────┐
                                                    │     Commands    │
                                                    │     ─────────   │
                            Matches                 │ F1 - Help       │
        Key Word: civil_____  27____             │                 │
        (From Subjects)                             │ F2 - Change Boolean │
                                                    │                 │
                      AND                           │ F3 - Include Author │
        Key Word: rights_____  26____ (optional)  │      or Other Index │
        (From Subjects)                             │ F4 - Browse Words   │
                                                    │                 │
                      AND                           │ F5 - Clear      │
        Key Word: _____  _____ (optional)    │                 │
        (From Sub Or Titles Or Notes)               │ F6 - Change Source  │
                                                    │                 │
                                                    │ F7 - Regular Cat.   │
                                                    │                 │
                13 Materials Found                  │ F8 - Word ↔ Phrase  │
                (Search Complete)                   │                 │
                                                    │ F9 - Sort Results   │
                                                    │                 │
        Use Enter to Search for Words   Use ↑ ↓ to move │ F10 - Bibliography │
                                                    └─────────────────┘
```

Figure 44.7: Winnebago: Key word search screen

```
 Winnebago CAT — Computerized Catalog

                                    Matches               Commands
Key Phrase: north star_____          F1 — Help
(From Sub Or Titles Or Notes)                       F2 — Change Boolean
                    AND                             F3 — Include Author
Key Word: _____ _____ (optional)               or Other Index
(From Sub Or Titles Or Notes)                       F4 — Not In Use
                    AND                             F5 — Clear
Key Word: _____ _____ (optional)          F6 — Change Source
(From Sub Or Titles Or Notes)
                                                    F7 — Regular Cat.

              2 Materials Found                     F8 — Word ↔ Phrase
              (Search Complete)
                                                    F9 — Sort Results

Use Enter to Search for Words    Use ↑ ↓ to move    F10 — Bibliography
```

Figure 44.8: Winnebago: Phrase search

```
    Winnebago CAT — Computerized Catalog        13 Materials found
                                                (Search Complete)

Call #     Material Title        Author   Location  Mat. Type  Status

976.147 S  The story of the Montgomery  Stein, R.  HS Libra  900 - 999  In
342.73 CO  The Bill of Rights /  Colman, W  HS Libra  300 - 399  In
323.4092   Martin Luther King.                       300 - 399  In
323.4 MAN  Equality /            Mannetti,  Elementa  300 - 399  In
           Dr. Martin Luther King, Jr.  King, Mar            cassettes  In
323.4092   Martin Luther King, Jr.—th              300 - 399  In
329.4092_  Martin Luther King, Jr.                 300 - 399  In
329.4092_  Martin Luther King, Jr., Da             300 - 999  In
323.1092   Martin Luther King, Jr.—th              300 - 399  In
           Martin Luther King, Jr., a              cassettes  In
J B 973.9  Jesse Jackson :       Martin, P  Elementa  Juvenile  In
301.45196  Racism;               Lapides,  Public L  300 - 399  In
329.4 K53  Why we can't wait.    King, Mar            300 - 999  In


Use ↑ ↓ PgUp PgDn Home End to Move    F9 to Sort Results  Enter to Select
Use Esc to Backup                     F10 Bibliography     Del to Delete
```

Figure 44.9: Winnebago: Subject result, unsorted

```
    Winnebago CAT — Computerized Catalog        13 Materials found
                                                (Search Complete)

Call #     Material Title        Author   Location  Mat. Type  Status

           Martin Luther King, Jr., a                       cassettes  In
           Dr. Martin Luther King, Jr.  King, Mar            cassettes  In
301.45196  Racism;               Lapides,  Public L  300 - 399  In
323.1092   Martin Luther King, Jr.—th              300 - 399  In
323.4 MAN  Equality /            Mannetti,  Elementa  300 - 399  In
323.4092   Martin Luther King, Jr.—th              300 - 399  In
329.4092   Martin Luther King.                     300 - 399  In
329.4092_  Martin Luther King, Jr.                 300 - 999  In
323.4092_  Martin Luther King, Jr., Da             300 - 399  In
342.73 CO  The Bill of Rights /  Colman, W  HS Libra  300 - 399  In
975.147 S  The story of the Montgomery  Stein, R.  HS Libra  900 - 999  In
J B 973.9  Jesse Jackson :       Martin, P  Elementa  Juvenile  In
329.4 K53  Why we can't wait.    King, Mar            300 - 999  In


Use ↑ ↓ PgUp PgDn Home End to Move    F9 to Sort Results  Enter to Select
Use Esc to Backup                     F10 Bibliography     Del to Delete
```

Figure 44.10: Winnebago: Subject result, sorted

```
                    Detailed Material Screen

Mat Barcode      13192___
Title            Martin Luther King, Jr., Day_____
Author           _____
Call Number      323.4092_219____       Copyright     1983.
ISBN / LCN       _____           Fund          _____
Material Type    300 - 399              Location      _____
Publisher        The Corporation,____   User Defined  _____


   1 filmstrip (62 fr.) : col. ; 35 mm. +
       Traces Dr. King's early life as a clergyman in Atlanta to
   leadership in the national civil rights movement. Includes scenes
   from the bus boycott in Montgomery, Ala., and the march on Washington,
   D.C.

   Subjects:     King, Martin Luther, — Jr., (1929-1968) — Juvenl
     (6)         King, Martin Luther, — Jr., (1929-1968)._____
                 Afro-Americans — Civil rights — Juvenile films._
                 Afro-Americans — Biography — Juvenile films.____



   Use ▮Esc▮ to Back Up      Press ▮M▮ for MARC      Use ▮↑▮ ▮↓▮ to scroll subjects
```

Figure 44.11: Winnebago: Detailed Material screen

```
323.4092 Martin Luther King, Jr., Day : Encyclopaedia Britannica
219         Educational Corporation ; producer, Bob Clark. Chicago,
       Ill. :   The Corporation, 1983.
           1 filmstrip (62 fr.) : col. ; 35 mm. +
           Traces Dr. King's early life as a clergyman in Atlanta
       to leadership in the national civil rights movement.
       Includes scenes from the bus boycott in Montgomery, Ala.,
       and the march on Washington, D.C.

           1. King, Martin Luther, — Jr., (1929-1968) —
       Juvenlms. 2. King, Martin Luther, — Jr., (1929-1968). 3.
       Afro-Americans — Civil rights — Juvenile films. 4.
       Afro-Americans — Biography — Juvenile films. 5. Civil
       rights workers. 6. Afro-Americans — Biography.




                            ○_)
```

```
▮Esc▮ for Previous Screen   ▮PgUp▮ Previous Card   ▮PgDn▮ Next Card   ▮M▮ for Marc
```

Figure 44.12: Winnebago: Card image for 44.11

```
              LDR 01165cgm 22    1a 4500^
Control #     001     84730148 /F/r87^
              005 19880411073651.3^
Phys Desc     007 goucnbff^
Fixed Data    008 841022s1983    xxu062 c       6fneng c^
ISBN          020   _cFor sale ($31.00)^
Catalog Src   040   _aEBEC^
Geog Area     043   _an-us——^
LC Call #     050 10_aE185.97^
Dewey dec #   082 10_a^
Title Stmt    245 00_aMartin Luther King, Jr., Day _h[filmstrip] /_cEncyclopaedi
                  a Britannica Educational Corporation ; producer, Bob Clark.^
Imprint stmt  260   _aChicago, Ill. :_bThe Corporation,_c1983.^
Phys Descrip  300   _a1 filmstrip (62 fr.) :_bcol. ;_c35 mm. +_e1 sound cassette
                  (11 min.)+ 1 teacher's guide.^
General Note  500   _aTitle from data sheet.^
General Note  500   _aIntended audience: Primary grades through junior high scho
                  ol.^
Summary note  520   _aTraces Dr. King's early life as a clergyman in Atlanta to
                  leadership in the national civil rights movement. Includes sce
                  nce from the bus boycott in Montgomery, Ala., and the march on
                  Washington, D.C.^
Subj: Name    600 10_aKing, Martin Luther, _c Jr., _d 1929-1968 _x Juveniles.^
```

Use `Esc` To Exit   Use `↑` `↓` To Move

Figure 44.13: Winnebago: MARC screen

```
     Winnebago CAT — Computerized Catalog           4 Materials found
                                                     (Search Complete)

Call #     Material Title          Author    Location  Mat. Type  Status

780.92 GE  George Gershwin—rhapsody i          Middle S  700 - 799  Res
780.52 GE  George Gershwin—rhapsody i          High Sch  700 - 799  Out
RHA        Rhapsody in blue /       Gershwin,  Public L  records    In
RHA        Rhapsody in blue /       Gershwin,  Public L  records    Out
```

Use `↑` `↓` `PgUp` `PgDn` `Home` `End` to Move   `F9` to Sort Results `Enter` to Select

Use `Esc` to Backup   `F10` Bibliography   `Del` to Delete

Figure 44.14: Winnebago: Status information

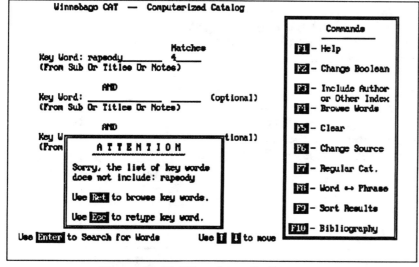

Figure 44.15: Winnebago: Spelling error

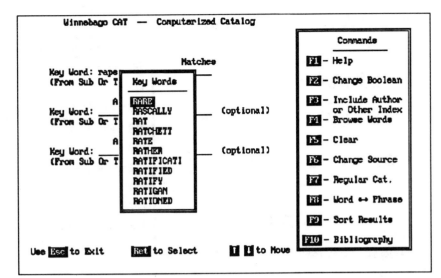

Figure 44.16: Winnebago: Key word browse

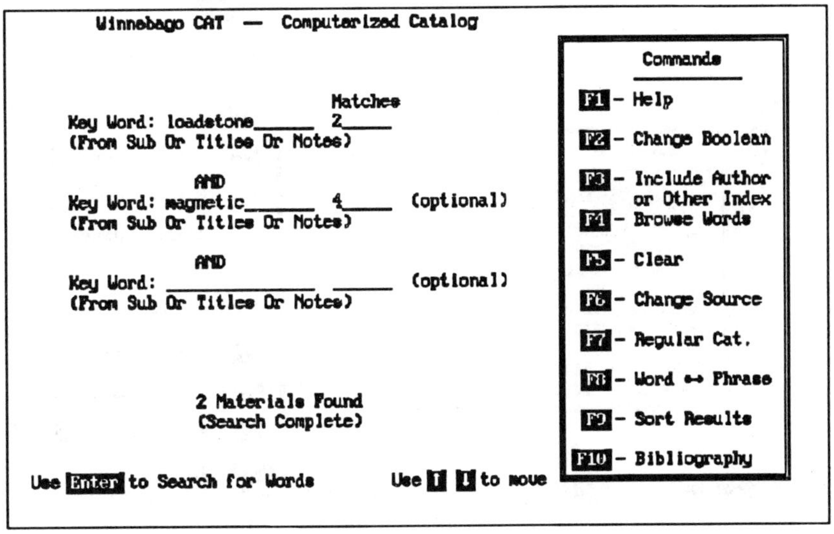

Figure 44.17: Winnebago: Partially-known title

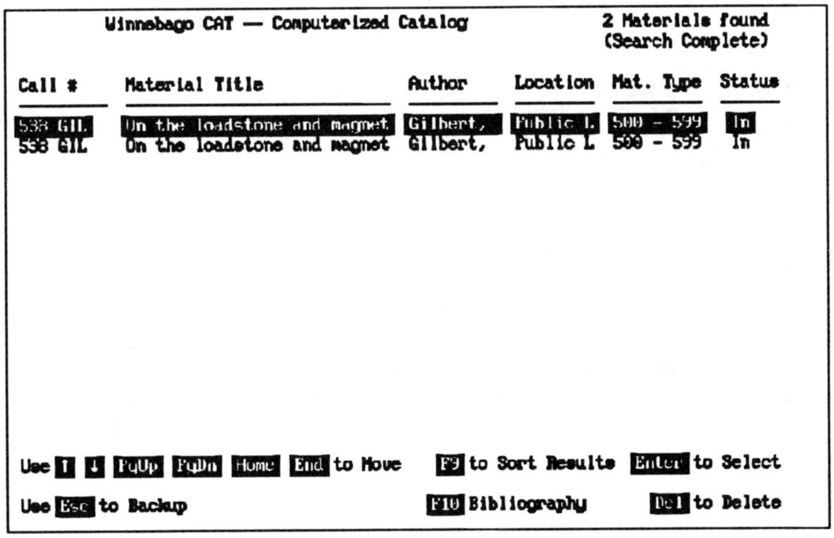

Figure 44.18: Winnebago: Partially-known, result

Winnebago CAT — Computerized Catalog

Key Word: anna_____ Matches: 8____
    (From Titles)

AND
Key Word: karenina_____ 6____ (optional)
    (From Titles)

AND
Key Word: _____ ____ (optional)
    (From Sub Or Titles Or Notes)

6 Materials Found
(Search Complete)

Commands

F1 – Help
F2 – Change Boolean
F3 – Include Author
      or Other Index
F4 – Browse Words
F5 – Clear
F6 – Change Source
F7 – Regular Cat.
F8 – Word ↔ Phrase
F9 – Sort Results
F10 – Bibliography

Use Enter to Search for Words   Use ↑ ↓ to move

Figure 44.19: Winnebago: Known-item search

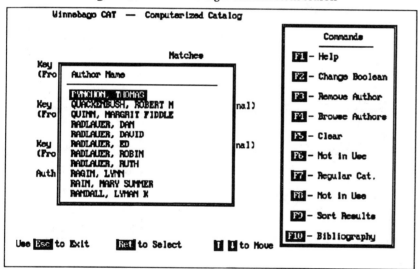

Figure 44.20: Winnebago: Author browse

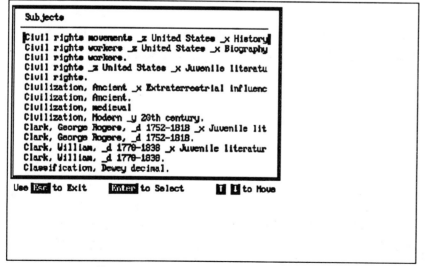

Figure 44.21: Winnebago: Subject browse

```
        Winnebago CAT  —  Computerized Catalog

                                                      ┌──────────────────────┐
                                                      │        Commands       │
                                                      │        ─────────      │
                              Matches                 │  F1 - Help            │
        Key Word: _____  _____              │                       │
        (From Sub Or Titles Or Notes)                 │  F2 - Change Boolean  │
                                                       │                       │
                   AND                                 │  F3 - Remove Call #   │
        Key Word: _____  _____  (optional)   │                       │
        (From Sub Or Titles Or Notes)                  │  F4 - Browse Call #   │
                                                       │                       │
                   AND                                 │  F5 - Clear           │
        Key Word: _____  _____  (optional)   │                       │
        (From Sub Or Titles Or Notes)                  │  F6 - Not in Use      │
                                                       │                       │
        Call Number: 686.2*_____                  │  F7 - Regular Cat.    │
                                                       │                       │
                                                       │  F8 - Not in Use      │
                                                       │                       │
                                                       │  F9 - Sort Results    │
                                                       │                       │
                                                       │  F10 - Bibliography   │
        Use Enter to Search for Words   Use ↑ ↓ to move└──────────────────────┘
```

Figure 44.22: Winnebago: Call number browse (1)

```
        Winnebago CAT — Computerized Catalog        6 Materials found
                                                     (Search Complete)

     Call #    Material Title         Author   Location  Mat. Type  Status

    686.2 AHL  Books /                Ahlstrom, Elementa 600 - 699  In
    686.2 B47  The official print shop han  Benton, R       600 - 699  In
    686.2 BAK  I want to be a printer /  Baker, Eu  HS Libra 600 - 699  In
    686.2 L74  ABC of lettering and printi  Lindegren       600 - 699  In
    686.2 P73  Pocket pal :                               600 - 699  In
    686.2/823  VIP who print and publish,  Freeman,  HS Libra 600 - 699  In




    Use ↑ ↓ PgUp PgDn Home End to Move   F9 to Sort Results  Enter to Select

    Use Esc to Backup                    F10 Bibliography    Del to Delete
```

Figure 44.23: Winnebago: Call-number browse (2)

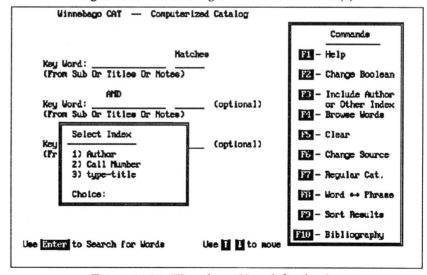

Figure 44.24: Winnebago: User-defined index

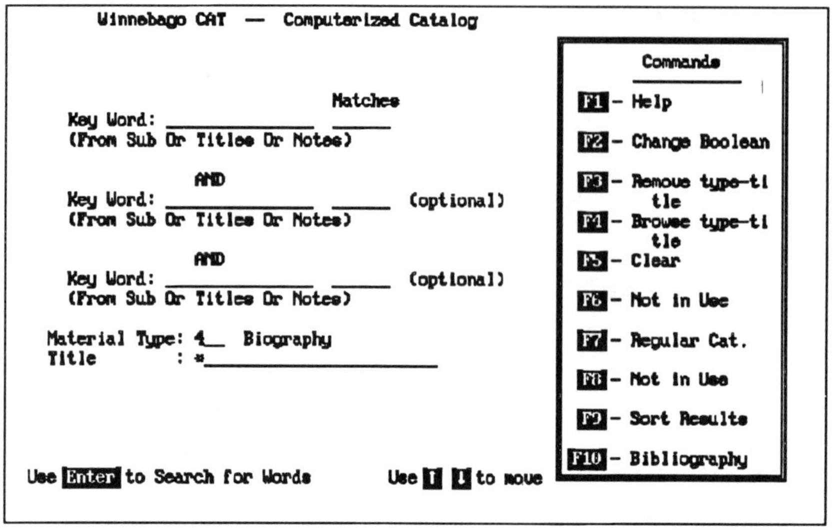

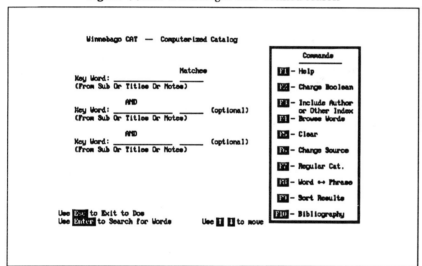

Figure 44.25: Winnebago: User-defined search

Figure 44.26: Winnebago: Exit prompt

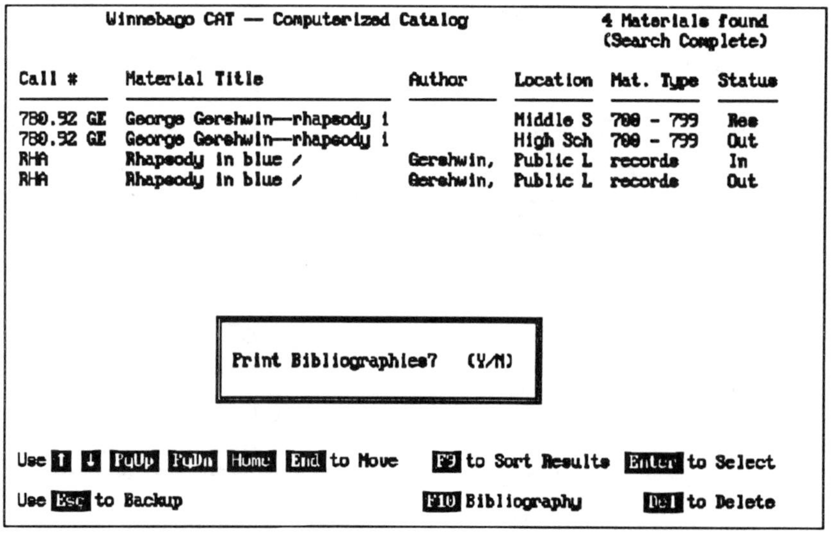

Figure 44.27: Winnebago: Bibliography prompt

About the Author

Walt Crawford is a senior analyst in the Development Division of The Research Libraries Group, Inc. (RLG), working extensively in the area of user-interface design. He is active in the Library and Information Technology Association (LITA) of the American Library Association (ALA), serving as editor of the *LITA Newsletter* since 1985 and as vice-president of LITA in 1991–1992 (president 1992–1993). Crawford was the founding editor of *Information Standards Quarterly* (1989–1991) and is a writer and speaker in the field of library automation. This is his ninth book in the Professional Librarian Series.

About the Contributors

Judith Aldus is head of Technical Services, UNB Libraries, University of New Brunswick.

Alan Alexander-Manifold is Systems Implementation Manager in the Purdue University Libraries' Information Technology Department. He has been at Purdue since 1980. In his tenure at Purdue, Alan has worked on six different online catalogs. He served as manager of the *plus* project and was largely responsible for both the technical and functional design of that system. He currently manages implementation of Purdue's NOTIS-based system, THOR. Alan has a degree in English literature from Earlham College in Richmond, Indiana, where he worked for bibliographic instruction greats Evan Farber and Tom Kirk

Dr. Ann Coder is the head of the General and Humanities/Social Sciences Reference Department, Hamilton Library, University of Hawaii, Manoa. She served on the task force that developed instructional materials and trained library staff on the newly installed CARL online catalog. She was formerly the library director at Golden Gate University in San Francisco. Her degrees include M.L.S., University of California,

Berkeley; M.A. in English, San Francisco State University; Ed.D., University of San Francisco.

Selden S. Deemer has been Library Systems Manager at Emory since 1985. He is a Macintosh enthusiast and has been a DOBIS user since 1979.

Genevieve Engel is in the MELVYL system user services group of the Division of Library Automation, University of California. She can be reached via electronic mail at genol@uccmvsa. bitnet.

Linda Eppelheimer has worked at Winnebago for seven years as a programmer, customer support manager, and (as of summer 1991) director of education. She has seen the company double in size (both sales and number of employees) each year for three years. Their software has grown and matured, and she has been intimately involved in the development and improvements. She has presented many workshops nationwide to train Winnebago's customers and improve their skills in working with the systems.

Polly-Alida Farrington, Marilyn Moody, Irving E. Stephens, and **Joseph Thornton** are all on the staff of the Richard G. Folsom Library, Rensselaer Polytechnic Institute.

Joni Gomez received her M.L.S. from the University of Arizona. She is currently special collections cataloger at Texas A&M University. Her research interests include cataloging, workstations and CD-ROM technology. She has published articles in *CD-ROM Professional*, *RQ* and *Cataloging & Classification Quarterly*.

Carl Grant is vice president of Marketing at Data Research Associates. He began at Data Research in 1984 as a consultant and has held a variety of management positions within the company. Previous to working for Data Research he spent 13 years in libraries where he implemented and managed library automation systems. Grant has an M.L.S. from the University of Missouri and is a participant in ALA, LITA, NISO, AVIAC, and CNI activities.

Timothy N. Holthoff became assistant librarian, Arkansas Supreme Court Library, in 1991, after serving as a library technical assistant earlier on (at which time he helped to select The Assistant). From 1988 to 1991, he was the automated systems librarian, W.B. Roberts Library, Delta State University, where he managed a CLSI online system. He has a B.S. in computer science and an M.L.S. from Vanderbilt University.

Ron Johnson is the Online Systems Coordinator and head of Circulation at the William Madison Randall Library, University of North Carolina at Wilmington.

Katharina Klemperer is director of Library Automation for the Dartmouth College Library

John Kupersmith is assistant for Computer-based Information Services at the University of Texas at Austin General Libraries. He has been involved in the UTCAT development effort since 1983 and has also worked in the areas of online searching, reference, bibliographic instruction, and library graphics and sign systems. Special thanks to Susan K. Phillips, Curtis Ohlendorf, and Robert C. Stewart for help in preparing the chapter on UTCAT.

Myoung-ja Lee Kwon is associate university librarian for Systems and Budget, University of Nevada, Las Vegas. She has published and presented papers on various aspects of library automation.

Joel M. Lee is marketing manager, Auto-Graphics, Inc. Before joining Auto-Graphics in October 1988 he was senior manager, Information Technology Publishing at the American Library Association (1986–88) and ALA's Headquarters Librarian (1977–86).

Stephen C. Lucchetti is currently head, Systems and Database Development, Technical Information Section, Ford Motor Company. He was awarded the 1989 Ford Motor Company Research Staff Operational Excellence award for BiblioTech development. Lucchetti is a member of the Special Libraries Association and Ford North American Image Council. Within SLA, he has served as Chemistry Division Chair, 1990; Michigan Chapter President, 1985. Lucchetti has an A.M.L.S. from the University of Michigan and an M.S. in astronomy from Pennsylvania State University.

Stuart W. Miller is currently Product and Communications Manager at NOTIS Systems. Since starting with NOTIS in 1987, he has worked in both Documentation Services and Marketing and Sales. Prior to NOTIS, he worked for eleven years as librarian in a nonprofit association located in Chicago. Miller has a B.A. from Wabash College and an M.A.T. and M.A. in library science from the University of Chicago. He is a member of Beta Phi Mu and currently reviews mysteries for *Booklist*. Miller was chair of the *Reference Books Bulletin* Editorial Board from 1983–1985 and is the author of *The Concise Dictionary of Acronyms and Initialisms* (Facts on File) and a contributor to the *Encyclopedia of Reference Landmarks* (Oryx).

Pat Nicholls is associate director of Automated Systems and Services for the University of Manitoba Libraries with responsibility for the implementation of PALS in the University Library and the St. Boniface General Hospital Libraries.

Carol A. Parkhurst is assistant university librarian for Systems and Technical Services, University of Nevada, Reno. She served as president of the Library and Information Technology Association (LITA) in 1989/90 and as chair of LITA's Second National Conference in 1988. She edited *Library Perspectives on NREN: The National Research and Education Network* (1990).

Judy Parr, senior technical writer at Information Dimensions, writes TECHLIBplus reference manuals and edits TECHLIBplus training materials. The TECHLIBplus Online Access Catalog was designed and built by a team of professional librarians, programmers, and systems analysts.

Howard Pasternack is Library Systems/Planning Officer at Brown University and is responsible for managing Josiah, the Brown University Library Online Catalog. He has an M.A. in Library Science from the University of Chicago and an M.B.A. in Management Science, also from Chicago.

Deanna Petersson is the vice president of Marketing for Accuware Business Solutions. She has a bachelor of commerce degree in Marketing and Management Information Systems. She has four years of experience in systems development, end-user support, and systems and software support. Much of this experience was on the Macintosh and IBM PC platforms. Deanna also has some seven years experience in various types of marketing, sales, and employee management. At her last assignment at Esso Resources Canada Limited, she was very involved in developing a plan for automating and influential in convincing management to automate the Natural Gas Marketing Resource Center.

J. Howard Pringle is the Library Computer Systems Manager at the Waukesha Public Library, Waukesha, Wisconsin. Pringle attended the University of Wisconsin and has served the library over the years in a variety of positions ranging from page to acting codirector. During his tenure as head of Interlibrary Loan, he was codesigner and implementer of the first microcomputer-based interlibrary loan borrowing network in Wisconsin. After being appointed systems manager he was responsible for the specification, implementation, and support of all phases of the library's automation project together with office automation and network implementation projects. He has served a term as president of the national INLEX User Group and currently serves as its membership chair. In 1989 Pringle received the Hewlett-Packard Company's State and Local Government High Technology Award for the Waukesha library automation project.

Melinda Ann Reagor is head, Copy Cataloging Department, and recon coordinator for the Rutgers University Libraries.

Ilene F. Rockman is currently the interim associate dean of Library Services at California Polytechnic State University, San Luis Obispo. She previously served as coordinator of Reference Services and chair of the library's Polycat Education Committee, which designed instructional materials, conducted training sessions, and wrote help screens. Her research interests include electronic reference services, and in her spare time she edits *Reference Services Review*.

Stephen R. Salmon is the founder and chairman of Carlyle Systems, Inc. He was formerly assistant vice president for Library Plans and Policies for the nine-campus University of California system, with responsibility for the university's Division of Library Automation as well as university-wide library policy. Previously he was director or assistant director of the libraries at the University of Houston, Washington University (St. Louis), and George Mason University, and also held a number of positions at the Library of Congress, most recently as assistant director for Processing Services. He was the founder and first president of the Library and Information Technology Association (LITA, a division of ALA) and is the author of *Library Automation Systems*, several other books, and numerous journal articles.

Gary Sampson has an M.L.S. from the University of California at Berkeley (1972) and has spent two years in administration, four in acquisitions, ten in business reference and online searching, and three in systems administration, all at Portland State University. Before library school, Gary worked in the Systems and Procedures department of a large bank, on several newspapers as a reporter, and as a soldier in the U.S. Army.

Stephen Sloan has been a librarian at the UNB Engineering Library since 1988. He has a charming wife, three children, and a hobgoblin living in his sock drawer. In 1985 he demonstrated his financial acumen by selling off his extensive baseball card collection. In recent years he has become obsessed with his own death, which occurred in 1981.

Russ Stephens was a summer intern at the Apple Corporation Library, working in Technical Services, when he prepared the chapter on MacLAP. He was finishing his M.L.S. at San Jose State University. Before coming to Apple, he completed an M.A. in Near Eastern Languages and Cultures (specializing in Egyptology) at UCLA. Part of his studies at UCLA included enrollment at the American University in Cairo, during which time he was able to travel extensively throughout Egypt. He hopes to be able to combine the two degrees in an academic setting after completing studies at San Jose State and the internship at Apple.

Leslie Troutman is Music User-Services Coordinator and assistant professor of Library Administration at the University of Illinois at Urbana-Champaign. She holds degrees from Bowling Green State University, University of North Carolina at Chapel Hill, and the University of Illinois at Urbana-Champaign. She is currently working toward her Ph.D. in musicology. Leslie's research interests include user-interface development, music materials in the online environment, and the music of the second Viennese School.

Paul E. Venancio is director of Media Services for the Middletown, Rhode Island, Public Schools and has been a Circulation Plus and Catalog Plus user at his district's high school since 1988. An outspoken advocate for library automation, Paul is a frequent presenter at regional conferences and has written several articles about school library automation and about evaluating the quality of electronic data. He serves as an area Follett trainer and is a member of the board of directors of the Rhode Island Educational Media Association, where he chairs the committee on electronic networking.

John Waiblinger is the assistant university librarian for Academic Information Services and associate director of the Center for Scholarly Technology at the University of Southern California, and has primary overall responsibility for management of USCInfo development and operations. Other key USCInfo developers are Mark

Brown, Karl Geiger, Karen Howell, Royd Muraoka, Bill Scheding, Chris Sterback, and Lucy Wegner. Special thanks to Mike McHugh for all his help in preparing the chapter on USCInfo.

Mary Ann Walker is the coordinator of Library Systems and Automation for the University of Dayton. She holds an M.L.S. from Kent State University and an M.B.A. from the University of Dayton. She has served on several committees for the OhioLINK project (Ohio's statewide library and information network). She is currently chair of the OhioLINK OPAC Committee. She is also a member of the CODI (Customers of Dynix, Inc.) Executive Board.

Bob Warwick is Bibliographic Database Manager and head of the Catalog Services Department for the Rutgers University Libraries.

Crickett Goodsell Willardsen received her B.A. and M.A. in English. At Dynix Marquis, she creates documentation manuals and other training materials for Marquis system use. She has also edited manuscripts of and coauthored several nonfiction books.

Brian Williams was the coordinator for telecommunications and microcomputers at Cal Poly's Kennedy Library when the chapter on CL-CAT was prepared, and has since become automated system manager at Multnomah County Library in Portland, Oregon.

Jacqueline S. Wright is a lawyer and a librarian. She received her law degree from the University of Oklahoma in 1973 and her library degree from the University of Arkansas at Little Rock in 1985. She has been the librarian at the Arkansas Supreme Court since 1979. Jackie wrote the *Manual on Appellate Procedure in the Arkansas Supreme Court and Court of Appeals*, which was published in 1980 and supplemented in 1984. She contributed the chapter on "Appellate Procedure" for the *Arkansas Form Book*, published in 1988. She is an active member of the Arkansas Bar Association, the Pulaski County Bar Association, the Arkansas Association of Women Lawyers, the Arkansas Library Association, the American Association of Law Libraries, the SouthWest Association of Law Libraries, and several special-interest sections of those organizations.

Index